I0824124

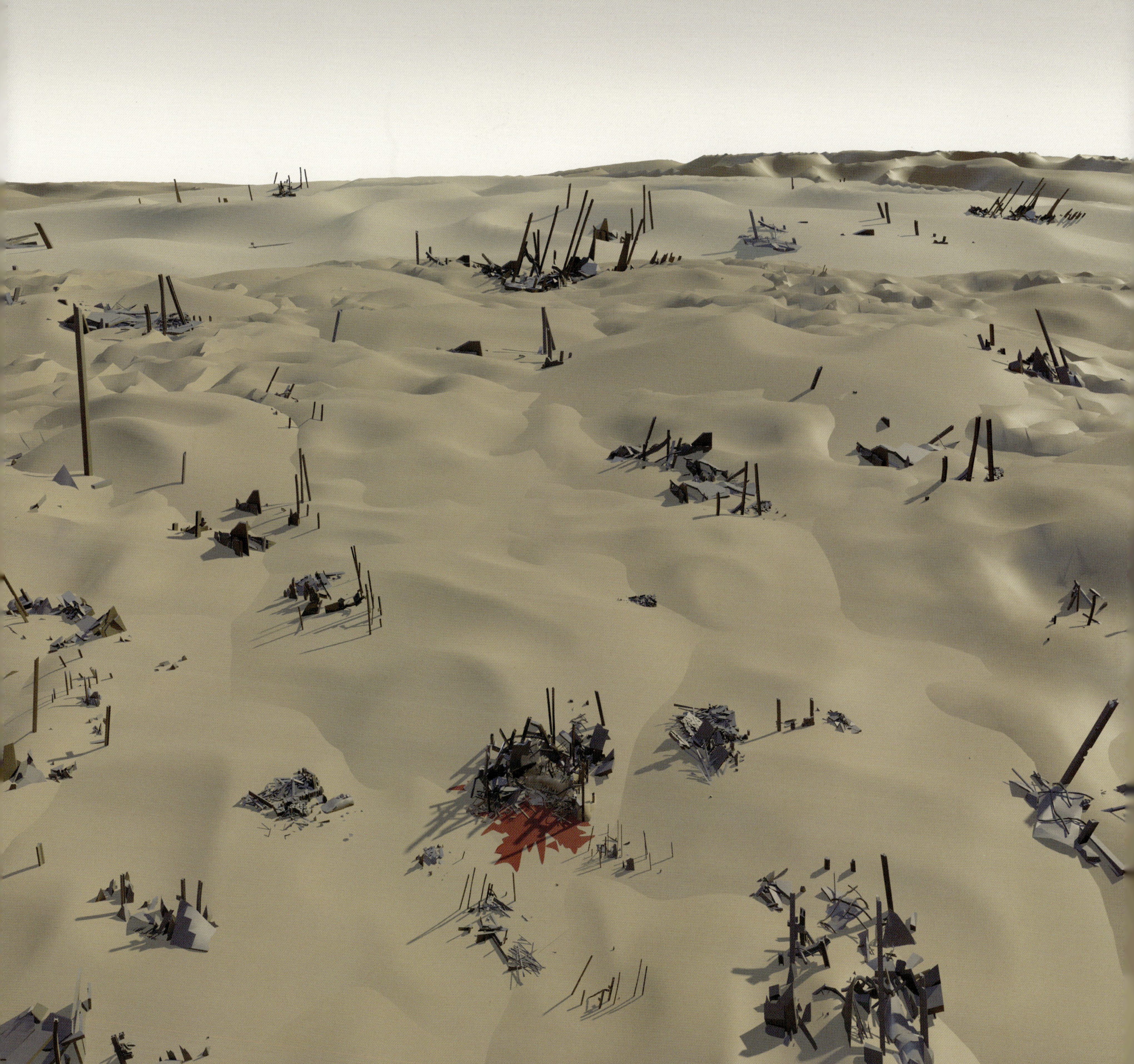

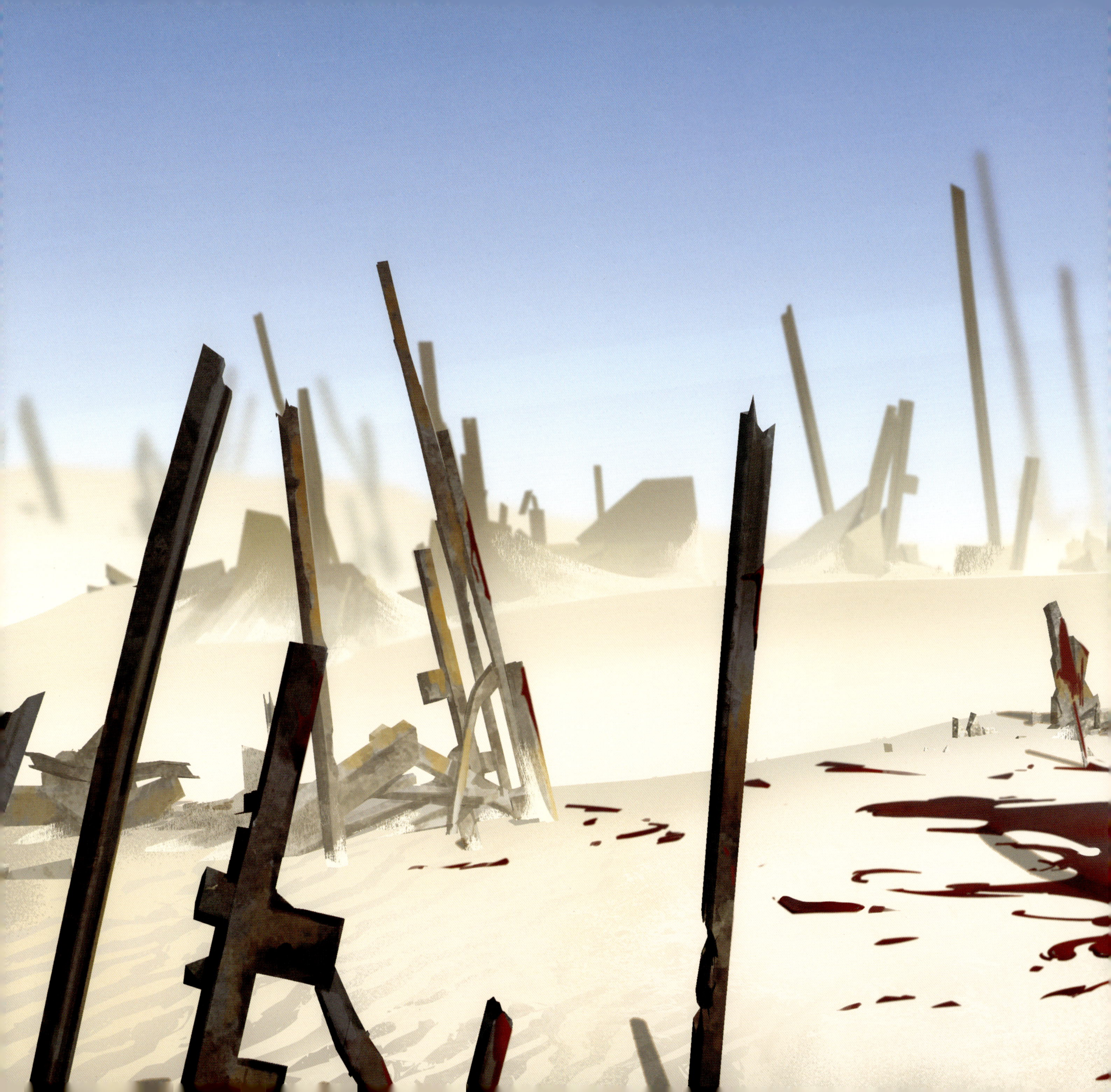

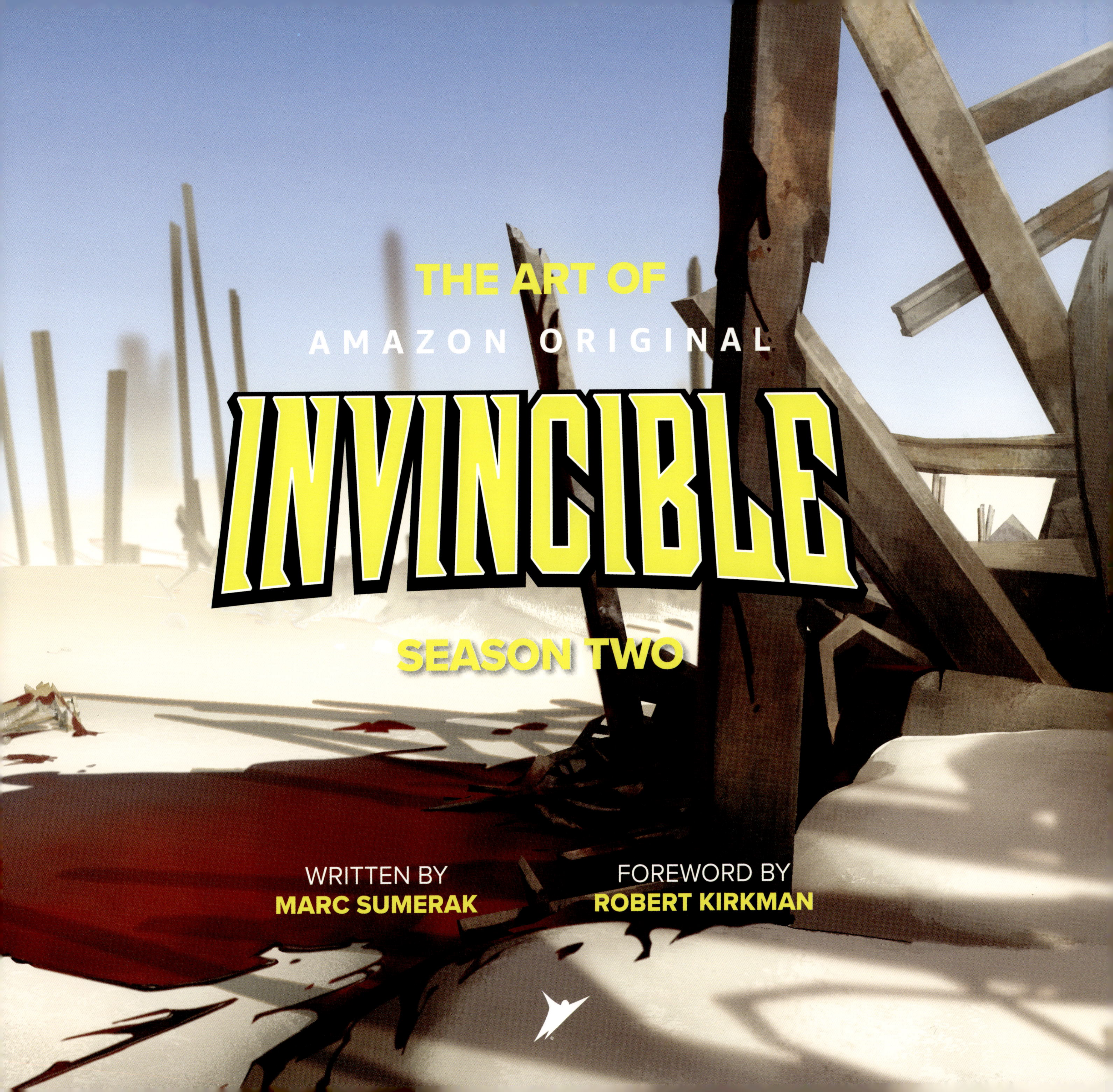

THE ART OF

AMAZON ORIGINAL

INVINCIBLE

SEASON TWO

WRITTEN BY
MARC SUMERAK

FOREWORD BY
ROBERT KIRKMAN

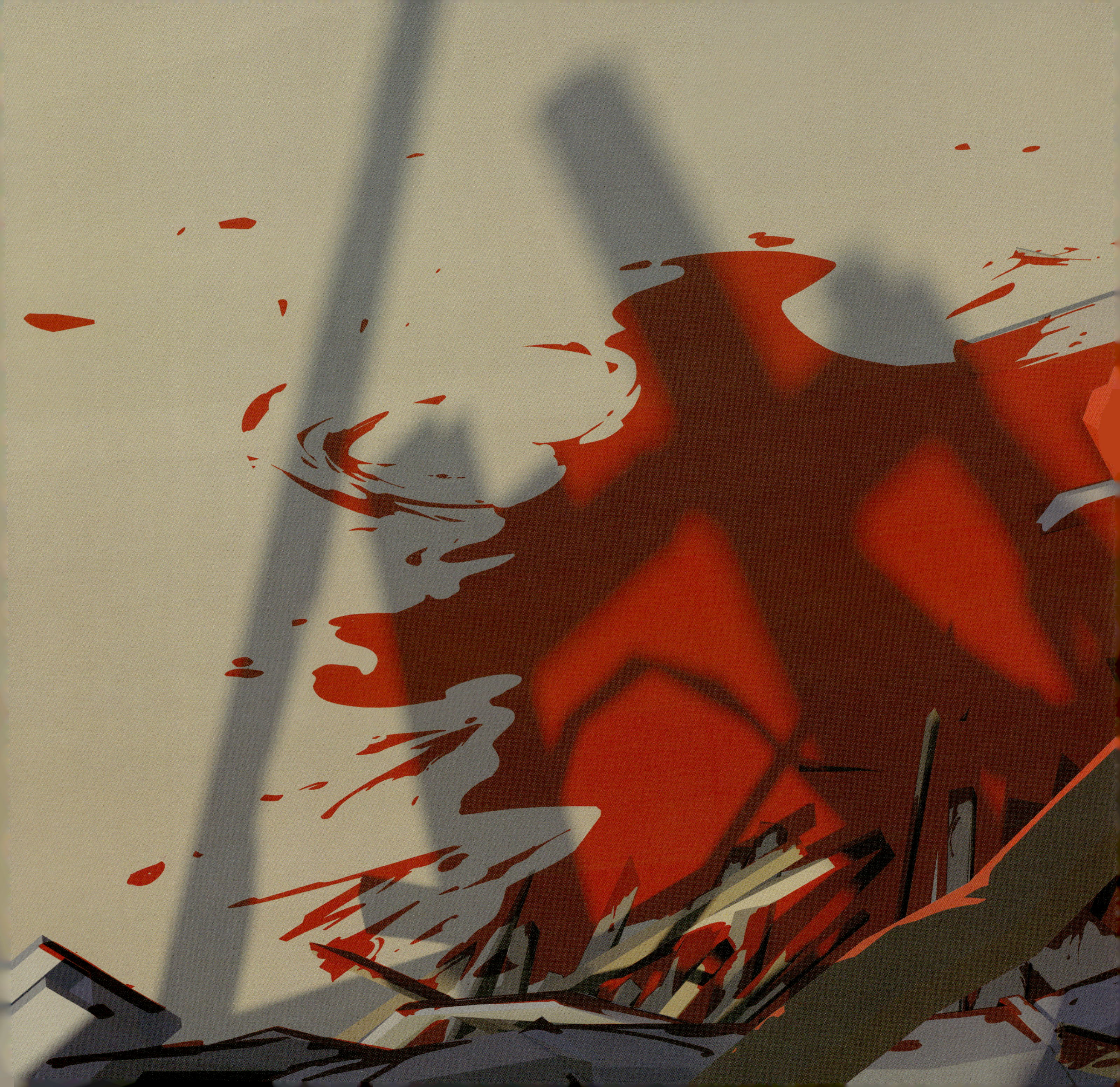

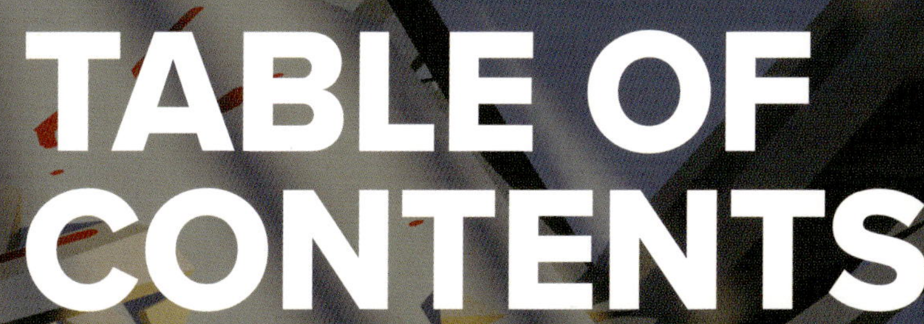

TABLE OF CONTENTS

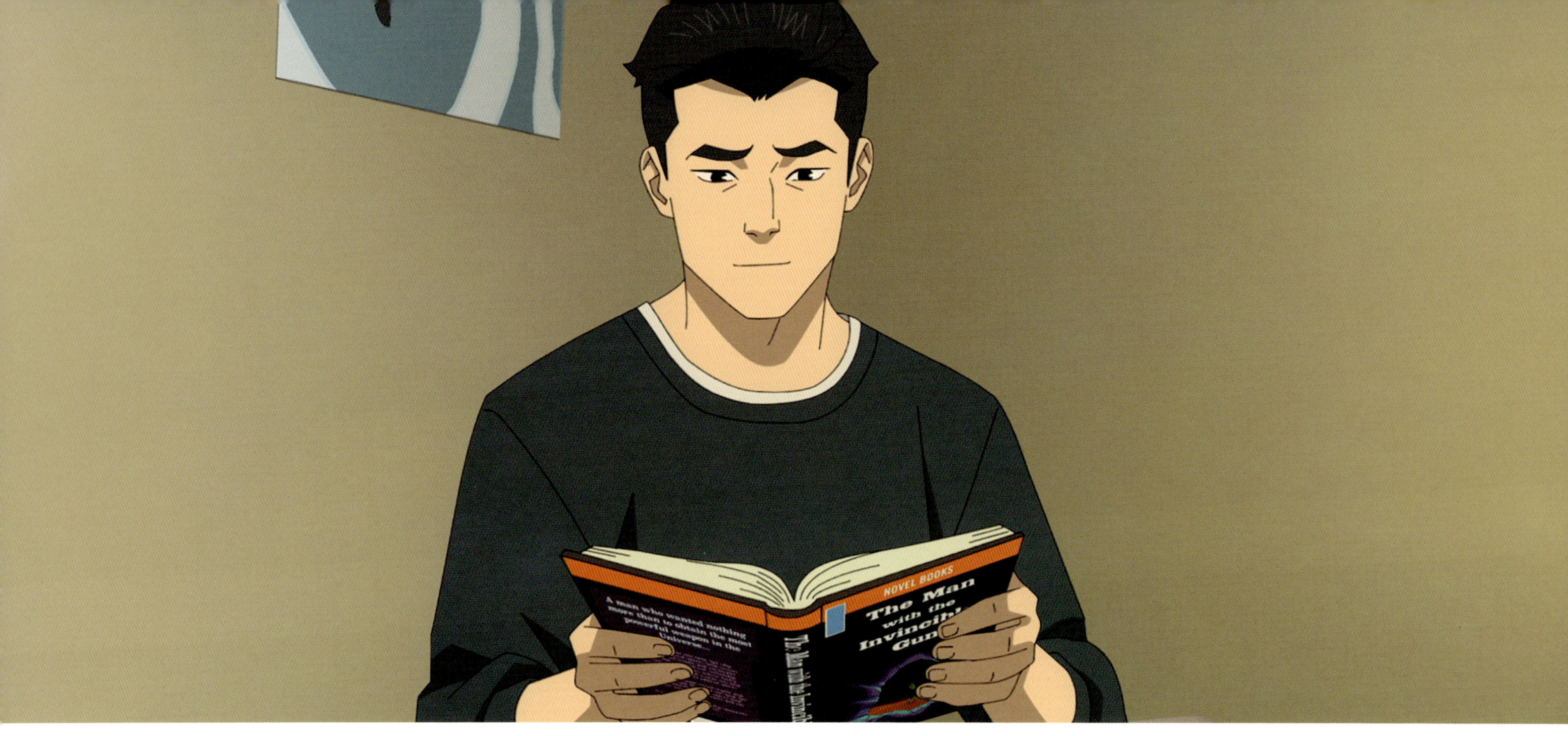

FOREWORD

BY **ROBERT KIRKMAN**

Shaun Goddamn O'Neil.

Not Shawn, or Sean, or Schon... it's SHAUN. Get it right.

I met Shaun, I'm going to guess around 2005 or so. Maybe 2006. Shaun was an aspiring comic book artist. I was very taken with his clean, precise, structured work that was very reminiscent of one Cory J. Walker. He was at the Heroes Convention in Charlotte, North Carolina. I vaguely recall he had a sketchbook of his work he was selling. It was awesome, and I saw him as someone I could eventually work with on future projects.

One thing I definitely recall is Shaun distinctly being what I affectionately refer to as "a delightful curmudgeon". He's very open with his opinions, and he doesn't spare feelings. Some people may find this abrasive, but I think those people are weak simpletons who need to toughen up. You always know where you stand with Shaun, people like him are worth their weight in gold.

Shortly after that convention, I was asked to write a short story for a western anthology. I thought this was the perfect time to try out this new artist I'd met. I asked Shaun if he was interested, he said he was, and we produced a pretty cool little tale about two young kids growing up in the wild west. I'd always intended to do more stories about those kids with Shaun. Do I think the world needs more stories about adolescents accidentally killing people, hiding the body, only to find out they're wanted criminals and digging them up to get the reward? Yeah, I do. Maybe someday.

Around this time, Shaun also did some pin-ups for my

books. So, if you look back at the old issues of INVINCIBLE, you'll find a pretty awesome pin-up by Shaun. I believe it was in the 40s or maybe the 50s, somewhere around there? Maybe some kind editor proofing this will find the issue number and add it in here ***(INVINCIBLE #54 --Some Kind Editor)***. He also did a pin-up for another series I was doing at the time, THE ASTOUNDING WOLF-MAN. That pin-up is also awesome. Additionally awesome is that when Shaun posted the pin-up to his DeviantArt account, he talked about how much he hated doing the pin-up because he thinks The Astounding Wolf-Man is a "stupid looking character". This is also something Shaun said directly to my face when the character was showing up briefly in Season Three.

It may seem like I'm complaining, or doing this to simply poke fun or antagonize Shaun in print. I AM NOT. When Shaun says, "I like this," when Shaun says, "This is cool," it has a tremendous amount of weight, because you know he means it.

If I had a dollar for every time Cory Walker told me he didn't like something I did, or he wasn't going to read something of mine because it doesn't interest him... I'd have a sizable stack of dollars. I try to surround myself with people who hate me.

Anyway... Shaun and *Invincible* the show.

Shaun was a director on Season One of the show, he worked on episodes three and five that season. He storyboarded most of the Guardians tryouts from episode three, and he worked very closely with Cory Walker.

During Season One, Shaun was meticulously dedicated to the quality of the show. He was very vocal about processes and how he thought they could be streamlined and made more efficient, and he showed a level of dedication and care that exceeded that of many other people on the team. He was very impressive.

During the long production gap between Seasons One and Two, Cory and I were talking about who we wanted to try to bring back. Most people had gone on to find other jobs, so we really were rebuilding the team from scratch. Additionally, Cory wanted to step down as Lead Character Designer. At the same time, both of us knew that role had to be filled by someone we trusted. Someone who had a vast understanding of the characters and understood what Cory was trying to accomplish with Season One.

I remember Cory said, "The only guy I know I can trust in that role is Shaun O'Neil."

Shaun had been a Character Designer in the past, but he'd mostly done storyboarding and was making the move into directing. We didn't know if he'd even be interested. At the same time, we were looking at the esteemed Daniel Bartholomew Duncan III to take over as Supervising Director. Most people know him as Dan Duncan. Dan and Shaun had been working closely for years and actually attended the Kubert School of Cartoon and Graphic Art together. To make a long story short, Dan came on board and Shaun took on the role of not only Lead Character Designer, but also Art Director.

So, starting with Season Two, Shaun was chiefly in control of the whole look and feel of the show. Pretty much everything you see in this book was his purview. He assembled the greatest team of artists and worked alongside them to create the masterpieces you'll see in this volume. Over the course of it, you'll come to understand as much as I do how much Shaun cares about his work and the time spent making sure everything is just right. He's one of the few elements to this show that has been present for every season, and in a lot of ways I consider Shaun to be the backbone of the show. Spoiler alert, he only acted as Art Director for Season Two and Three, and then graduated to Co-Supervising Director with the aforementioned Dandronius Euclid Archibald Duncan Esquire starting with Season Four. So now he's working with Dan to oversee the entire show and honestly, the show couldn't be in better hands.

But really, stop reading this intro, turn the page and go see for yourself.

—**Robert Kirkman**
Backwoods, CA
2025

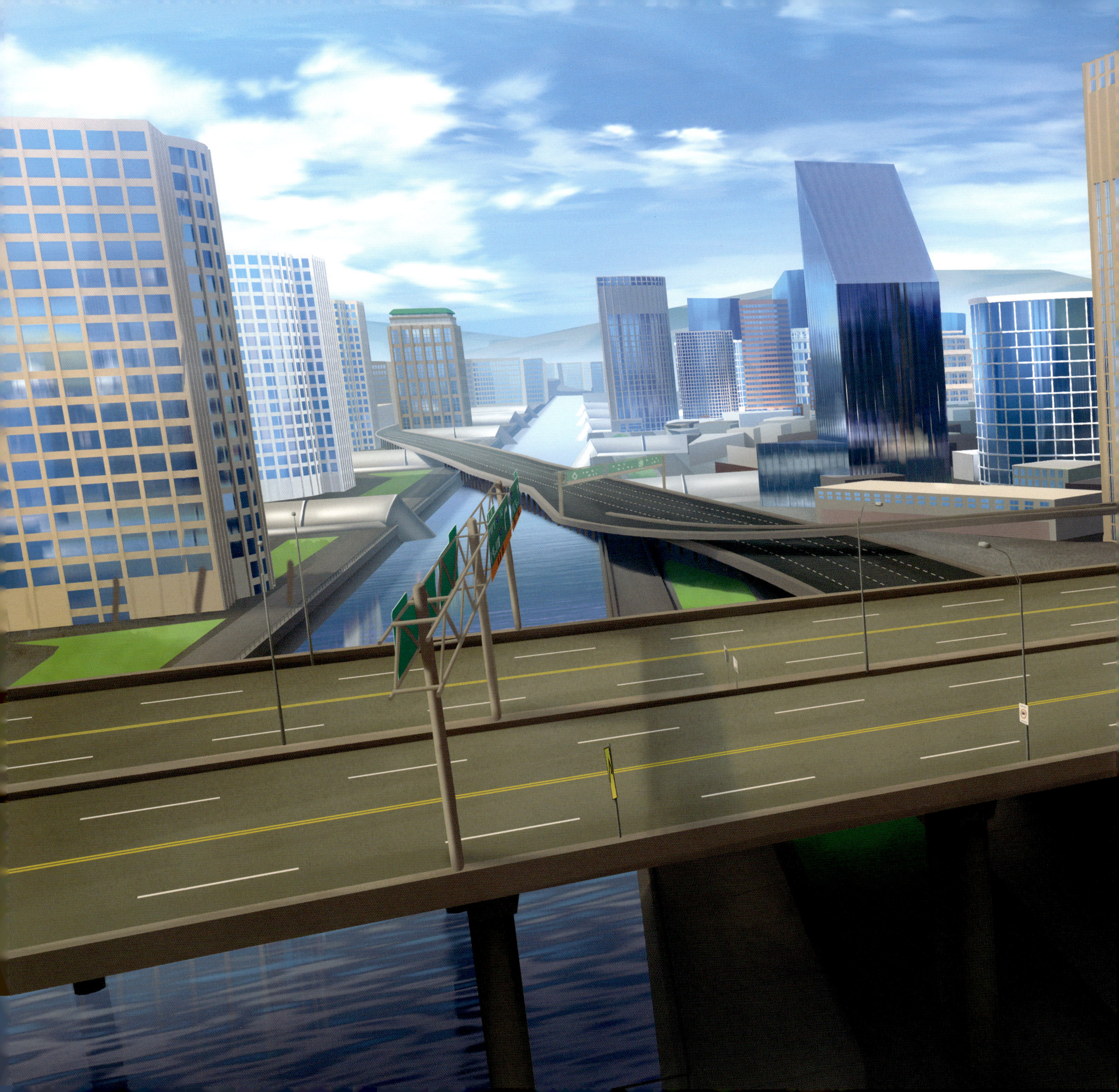

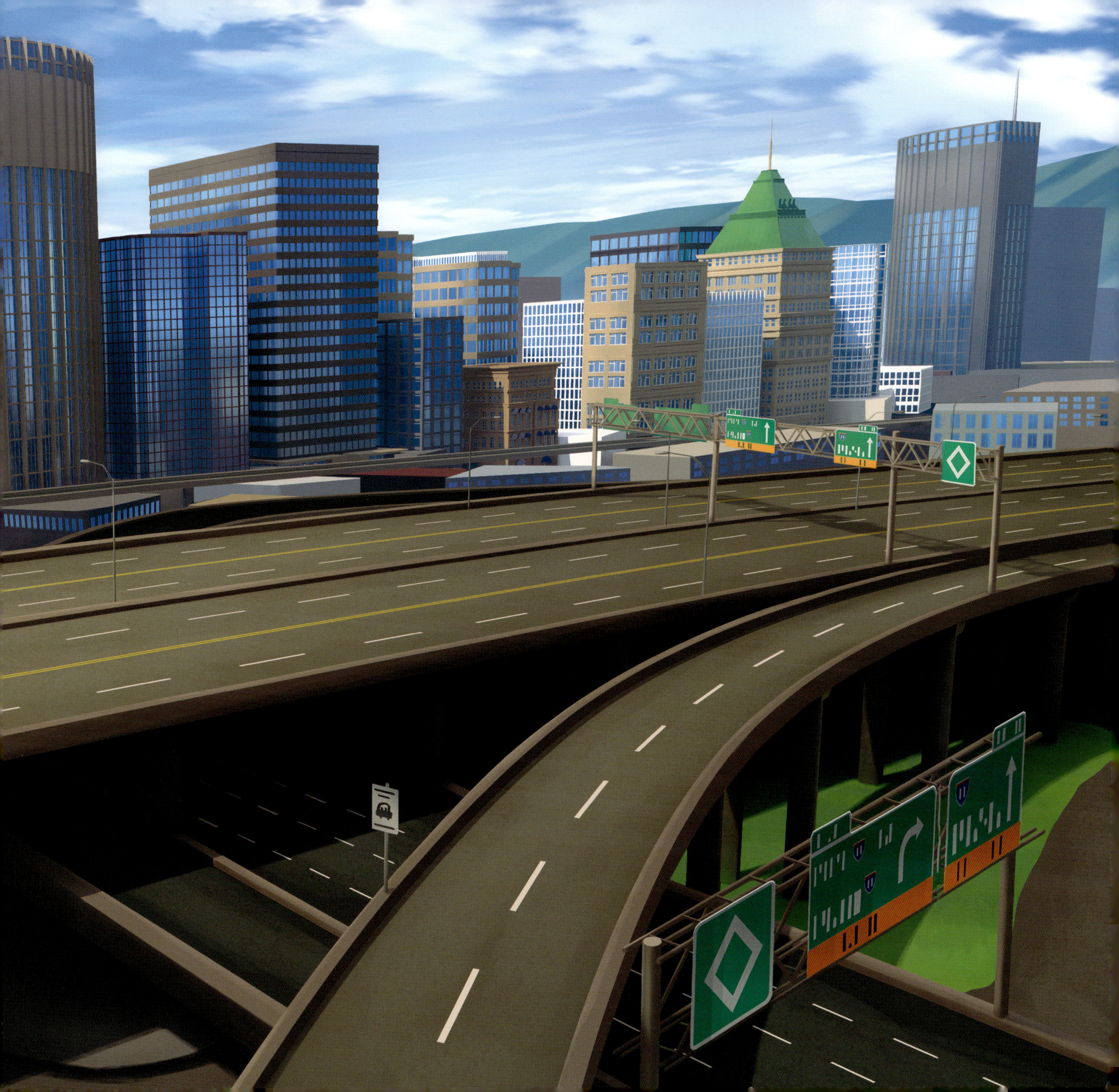

INTRODUCTION

When the first season of the *Invincible* animated series premiered on Amazon Prime Video March 25th, 2021, it became an instant sensation. The fan-favorite comic book created by Robert Kirkman and Cory Walker quickly became a critical darling, and one of Amazon's most viewed shows.

Invincible Season One introduced viewers to teenage superhero Mark Grayson — a.k.a. Invincible — and followed him as he learned to use his new powers in an attempt to live up to the grand legacy of his father, Nolan — a.k.a. Omni-Man. When the truth came out that Omni-Man was not actually the great hero that the world believed him to be, but rather an advance scout preparing the planet for invasion by a race of aliens known as Viltrumites, Mark was forced to choose a side. He decided to stand against his father, leading to a brutal brawl in the season finale that left Mark on the brink of death as Nolan abandoned the planet and his family.

The show's creative team was tasked with an epic mission: putting together a second season worthy of following *Invincible*'s acclaimed debut run.

Just as Mark had found himself constantly evolving as he learned more about himself, his powers, and his family, the talented team behind *Invincible* would need to evolve to face the new challenges ahead.

"There were a lot of changes between Season One and Season Two," says Executive Producer and Co-Creator Robert Kirkman. "I was kind of doing the job already, but I guess I became Co-Showrunner in an official capacity in Season Two. So, I took a more hands-on role, and I'm a little bit more plugged into a lot of different aspects of the making of the show, which is kind of fun."

While Kirkman's responsibilities on the animated series increased as the new season began production, *Invincible* Co-Creator Cory Walker decided to take a step back from his demanding Season One role as the show's Lead Character Designer.

"As a first timer on Season One, it was a lot of work for me," says Walker, who shifted to the role of Co-Executive Producer on Season Two. "I learned a lot, obviously, but I found myself wanting to be able to pass the bulk of that responsibility off to someone else. Ideally, someone more experienced. So that's where Shaun O'Neil comes in. Shaun and I are friends, so I was very hopeful that he would be willing to do it."

O'Neil had previously served as a part of the *Invincible* creative team, working as an Episode Director on two of the first season's installments. Even after he exited that role to pursue other opportunities in animation, his admiration for the material and its creators continued.

"I love this comic book," says O'Neil. "I love Cory in particular. Talking to Robert and Cory over the years, I tried to maintain a friendship, because I very much like them. I very much appreciated what they were doing."

While O'Neil recalled that his role on the first season of *Invincible* wasn't the best fit for him at the time, the stars seemed to be aligning for a renewed partnership. As Season Two approached, O'Neil and his longtime friend and collaborator Dan Duncan happened to be looking for work.

"Dan and I were rolling off our previous gig at Rooster Teeth, trying to figure out where to go next," says O'Neil. "And it looked like we were going to go our separate ways until I talked to Cory about coming on for a Character Lead position to take over for him."

O'Neil had plenty of experience when it came to character design, dating back to his time as a Storyboard Artist on the *Ultimate Spider-Man* animated series in the early 2010s, a job where he worked closely with Duncan.

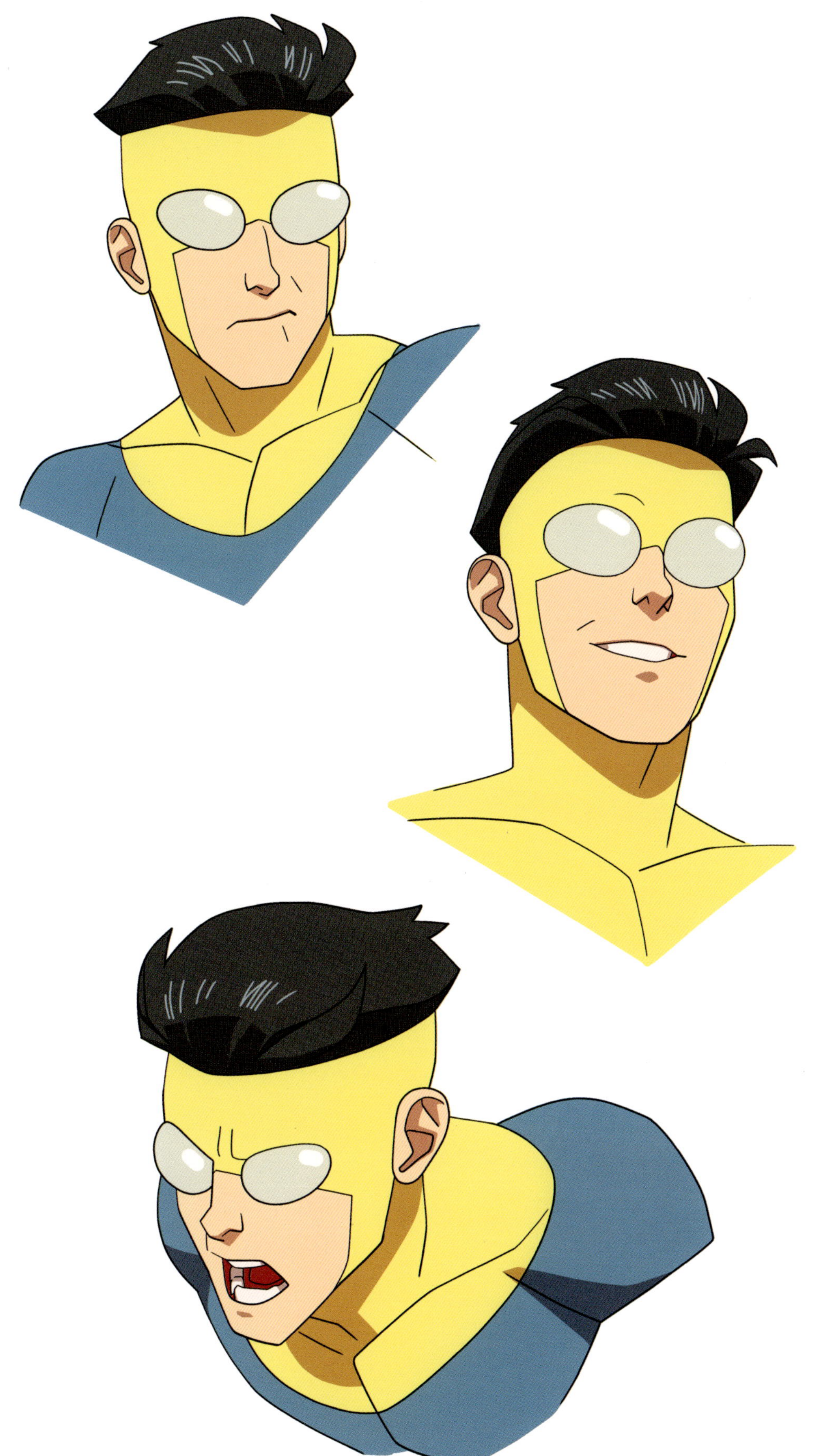

When it came to his artistic abilities and experience, O'Neil had already made quite an impression on the Invincible team.

"Shaun has incredible experience," says Executive Producer and Co-Showrunner Simon Racioppa. "He's an incredible artist. Shaun did design work for me on [*The Boys Present: Diabolical*], and it was great. We did an episode that was all based on the Garth Ennis (and Darick Robertson) comic book series of *The Boys*. And Shaun came in and did Butcher, did all the character designs, and did such a great job on that. He's super talented."

But while O'Neil had an unquestionable track record as a Character Designer, a Storyboard Artist, and an Episode Director, he had never served as an Art Director on a series. So, when discussions about his role with the *Invincible* team expanded to include that position, O'Neil had to decide if coming back would be the right fit after all.

"I got to do some black-and-white lead for *The Boys* anthology shorts," says O'Neil, "which was a really great crash course in all things art direction, working with some of the folks over at Titmouse. But when the opportunity came around to do Art Direction for [*Invincible*], my brain was like, 'Probably not ready for that.' My mouth was like, 'Yes.'"

O'Neil may not have been fully convinced that he was prepared to step up and take the reins of *Invincible*'s art team, but Kirkman and Walker knew they had found the right man for the job and made the call to bring him aboard. O'Neil's new role took some of the responsibility off Walker's shoulders as planned, and Walker would still remain an active force guiding the show's artistic vision.

"Shaun O'Neil came back as Art Director," says Kirkman, "so he was overseeing everything on the art side. He was also functioning as Lead Character Designer, taking Cory's role. But Cory was very much involved in approving things, and still coming in and doing drawovers and getting things on model and all that kind of stuff."

"It was amazing having an artist whose work I enjoy come in and add to whatever good and bad stuff I had done in the first season," says Walker. "From that point on for Season Two, after Shaun came on, I was — fortunately for me — less hands on. Less in the trenches day-to-day, and more just making sure that, aesthetically and in a design sense, things stayed on track. Just trying to make sure everything felt authentic to *Invincible* and what was established. It's been asset review and giving notes, that type of thing. I have helped a little bit from time-to-time when they needed it. I've done a couple turns and designs myself, but I am not doing the bulk of the work like I was in the first season."

"When I agreed to take on the role, I was terrified," says O'Neil. "I've got a lot of friends who are very good at this, and the last thing I wanted to do was embarrass myself. You want to try and measure up, right? So I spent a ton of time doing homework. 'What does the pipeline look like fully from a design standpoint? What is my role as an Art Director?' And it was a really hard thing to pin down, because in the back of your head, you're like, 'Yeah, I'm going to do the design side of things,' but what does that mean? And how do you describe it? [French animation studio] Everybody On Deck had an Art Director who put it really well, and I wrote it down to keep reminding myself what the purpose was. 'The job as Art Director is to be present from the beginning to the end of a production, to maintain a strong graphic identity, and provide design reference to the very end.' And so that was it. Trying to staff a team with really strong artists, first and foremost. Trying to get them to understand the brief."

With a better understanding of his role came the realization that O'Neil had a big job ahead of him. Fortunately, in Dan Duncan, he would have one of his most trusted collaborators at his side.

"Cory was talking about looking for a Director to come on and take on the Atom Eve special, who would inevitably wind up being the show's Supervising Director," says O'Neil. "And so when Dan hit me up and was like, 'I got a call from [Head of Skybound Animation Studio] Marge [Dean],' I was like, 'I know exactly what that's about. You should call them back and say yes, and then we can go and make *Invincible* together.' And here we are, doing the

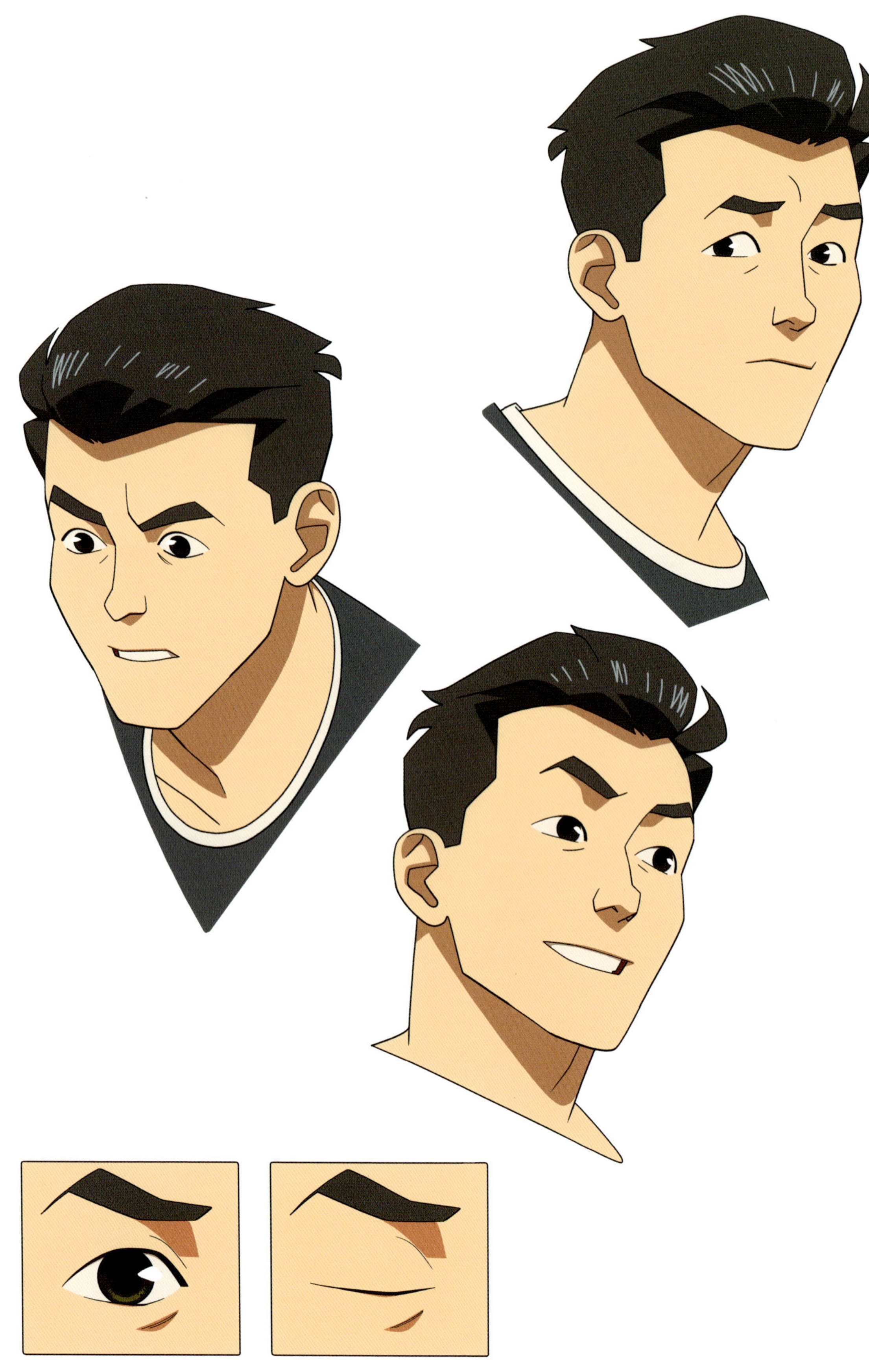

thing. So it's nice. I can't think of a better partner in crime."

"I was the Supervising Director on Season Two," says Duncan. "I would work with Shaun and the Art Department. But a lot of my time went to working with the story team, the Episode Directors that we had, the Storyboard Artists and Revisionists that we had, putting together the animatics and translating the script into that first pass. Working with Shaun, we had a lot of back and forth on getting the assets ready to ship overseas to make sure that they were in-line with the scripts and the boards. And then, just communicating with the overseas team. Then post-production — putting stuff together, editing it down, working with [Composer] John Paesano and doing the score, and the people at Boom Box Post getting sound effects, and any VFX stuff that we did with The Product Factory. So, I get to work with everybody. It was really fun job."

Duncan brought along with him a wealth of animation experience that would help the *Invincible* team to launch into production for the new season without repeating mistakes from the first one.

"Season One, part of it was figuring things out," says Racioppa. "So it was a lot of putting out fires, just keeping the show going. We had some personnel changes in Season One that weren't ideal. So bringing Dan Duncan on board, he was a great Supervising Director who was able to come in with lots of experience and clear ideas about how to keep the show going forwards consistently with great designs, great action, and great storyboards, and bring his own voice to the show while still helping to execute on what we'd already done in Season One. So we weren't reinventing the show so much as tweaking, improving. A lot of the best changes are sort of underneath the hood. They're on the pipeline of the show. A big choke point for us is design, just because our scope for the show is so big. There's so many locations, so many characters, so many actors, so many props. That's something Robert and I don't really want to compromise on usually, because that's what makes the book so great. So it's about finding the most efficient pipeline way to get all those designs done and get them approved through Shaun, and just making sure that it's all consistent, it's all great, and it comes through to the show and into the machine in a timely manner so that it can enter the episodes."

The show's creators were confident that Duncan and O'Neil would be fully capable of pushing *Invincible* to new heights in Season Two while still maintaining what had already been put in place during the show's first season.

"Cory had established a really unique look for the show in Season One," says Kirkman, "and Shaun O'Neil was one of the guys that really gravitated to that style and was really well acclimated to that style when he was boarding and directing on Season One. His boards were always very on model, and you could see that he grasped Cory's style in a way that a lot of people just can't. And Dan is somebody that definitely has a keen eye for that stuff. But there's a lot of nuance to Cory's style that is somewhat difficult to replicate. It's not a typical animation style. A lot of shows have kind of fallen into the school of — whether it's Bruce Timm or Phil Bourassa — there's a house style at certain places that people are accustomed to because they've been working with these Lead Designers for decades. And so it becomes second nature for them. And so for Cory's style to be so unique and new, it's difficult to find somebody who can replicate that. But we knew that Shaun and Dan would be committed to not only continuing what it was that Cory did, but also streamlining it in some really efficient and cool ways. And enhancing it."

"The nice thing is," says Duncan, "we're both such big fans of Cory's work that the art direction was like, 'This is already in a good spot. We don't need to fix it. We just want to finesse it and put our spin on it.' And it was the same with the directing and the boarding. I loved Season One. I really liked it. So, being respectful of that is not that hard if you like what you're coming into."

One of Duncan and O'Neil's first tasks would be to bring on a crew of seasoned designers that could help them maintain the aesthetic style and the level of visual quality seen in *Invincible* Season One.

"The whole team for Season Two had to be rebuilt

because of the gap in time between Season One and Season Two," says Kirkman. "So many of the artists on Season One got other jobs and weren't available. And so we kind of had to build a new team from the ground up. But because we had Season Two and Three picked up, we were able to plan for a more long term thing and put together a bigger group of people that theoretically would be able to stay on for the long haul."

It wasn't long before the *Invincible* art team's vacant design roles were filled with a number of extremely talented artists.

"I had some very excellent lead staff in Ashley Stoddard, our Color Supervisor, Edwin Fong, our Environments Supervisor, and then I handled most of the black-and-white stuff directly for a long time," says O'Neil. "And so it's all about being able to communicate with them. Being able to communicate with Tracy Nicoletti, our Assistant Production Manager, so that we were all on the same page. After a while, when stuff got busier and we started getting into post-production and you can't be everywhere that you need to be, they were very good at picking up the ball and running with it."

The new members of *Invincible*'s art team not only eased the pressure on O'Neil, they also applied their own unique talents in ways that brought new life to the show's signature style.

"Shaun was able to assemble a team of designers that can stay true to what Cory established," says Kirkman, "but also refine it to make it a little bit more animation friendly in places and smooth out some of the bumps in the road that we experienced on Season One."

"They have different tools in their toolbox," says Walker. "You look at my stuff, I think I tend to go to a lot of the same shapes over and over. Everybody brings a little bit of something from somewhere else instead of having everything basically cooked by one guy. Getting some fresh flavors in the pot has been a big thing... I don't want the show to not be recognizable as what it is, but I hope that people can add a little bit of themselves to what I started, more than anything, so that it can look less like my drawings."

Recognizing and relying on the unique abilities of his fellow artists was a fundamental part of O'Neil's approach as the show's Art Director.

"I don't have to be the best person in the room," says O'Neil. "I just have to know who is. You have to know your team's strengths. You have to know what they can and can't do so you can break down and assign the work. And you have to know the vocabulary. I think that was the biggest part, going from a mostly black-and-white

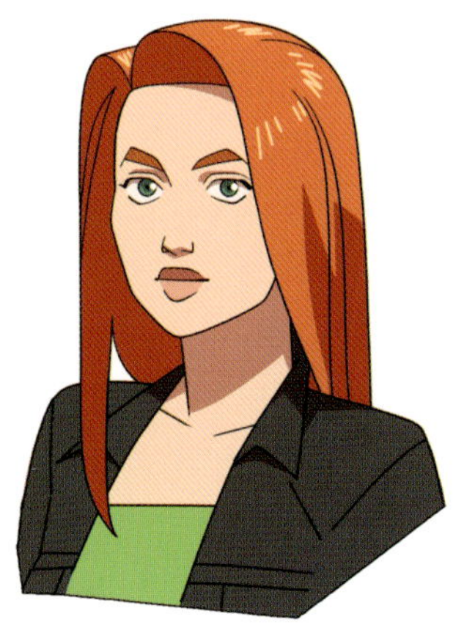

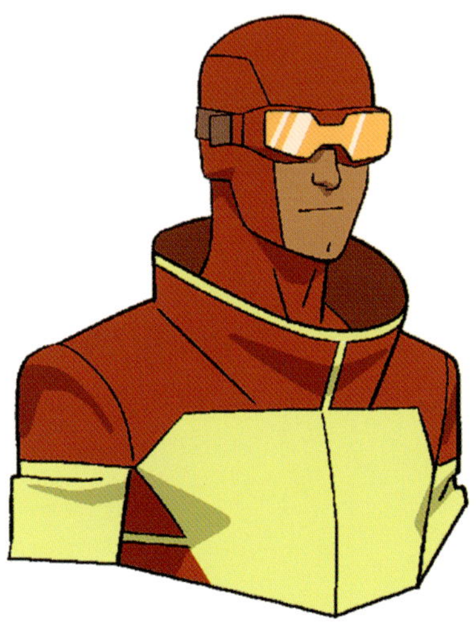

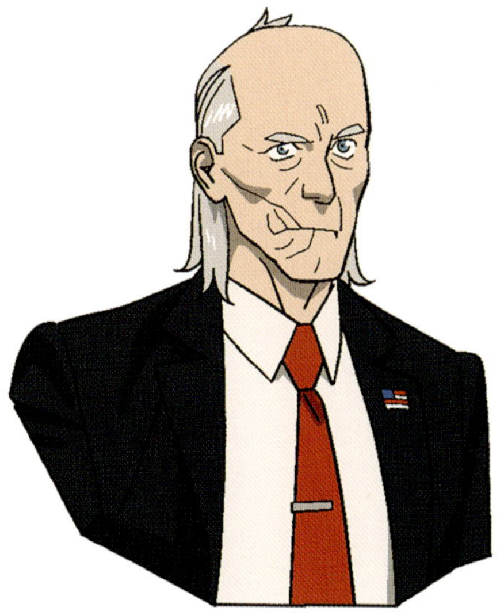

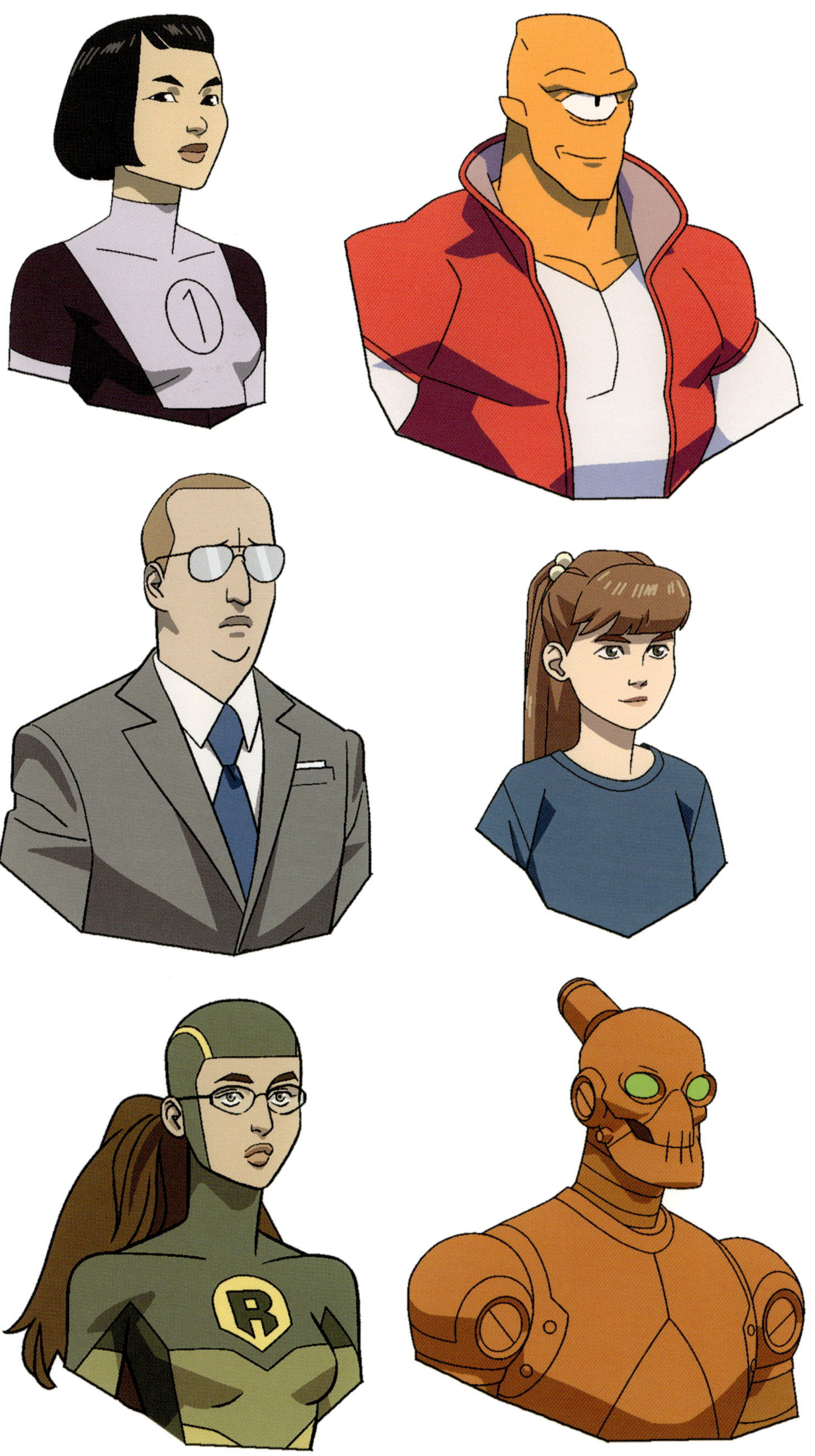

background to now having oversight over everything required a lot of constant checking. Just like, 'Hey, team, if you hear me say something crazy, say something. You're never gonna hurt my feelings. We've just got to get to the bottom of this. We have to reach some kind of even level.' If I can take credit for any one thing, it's that I hired well. We had a really great staff on the design team. And I think taking the time to really make sure that we were hiring people who were talented, but also hiring people who could work in the environment that I was requesting them to work in, made my job easier."

It wasn't just the design team that underwent changes between seasons. Nearly all of the *Invincible* creative team had to be rebuilt from the ground up.

"One of the cool things about Season Two and Three was that we got the pick-up for two seasons," says Kirkman. "So whereas there were a lot of unknowns with the first season story-wise, I was able to work with Simon Racioppa and Helen Leigh and Ross Stracke. And then we got to bring in some really great directors, like Tanner Johnson and Sol Choi and Ian Abando. And then Haylee Herrick, who came in and directed our Atom Eve special and stayed on as a series director on Season Two and Season Three. So it was really great group. And Marge Dean came in to run Skybound Animation and helped us build the apparatuses needed to make Season Two and Three. It was great to have everything in-house at Skybound. This is a show that Amazon Prime contracts from us, but we get to produce it completely in-house. So that means that all the nuts and bolts of making the show, I get to kind of be the final word, for better or for worse."

While the entire *Invincible* crew may have gone through a massive overhaul between seasons, it was important that the show itself was able to maintain a level of consistency and continuity.

"We had a job to do in terms of visual identity," says O'Neil. "We were tied to Season One. Whatever we did, we had to start there because the show had to have parity. You don't want a [series] where [season] one is a huge departure, and then the rest of it looks like something else completely. So the goal was, 'How fast can we move from Season One into our own thing?'"

One way to do that was to make minor adjustments to familiar character designs, something that Walker himself championed.

"It was pretty important to me, at least for the main cast, that we do costume changes," says Walker. "Because I think that probably everyone would have just been wearing the same clothes again, and I think that's bad. In the first season, you don't really get a sense of how much time has passed over the course of the season. And I wish we would have been able to do more civilian clothing changes so that you could get a sense of time passing. So at least every season, I want the core cast to change clothes in any way that we can. Some of the lesser characters, just palette swap them. Just color their clothes new colors. That's not that hard. But more important characters, let them change those dirty old clothes, get some spiffy new duds. As far as I'm concerned, it's a small thing that goes a long way. So they're looking a little different, for the better."

"I think there are very few characters that we use exactly the same design from Season One to Season Two," says Racioppa. "I think almost everybody was tweaked and updated. Mark's wardrobe changes. Eve's wardrobe changes. It's a cartoon thing. Bart Simpson wears the same shirt and pants every single year, right? Most cartoon series do. *Scooby-Doo*, they all wore the same clothes. We want to make sure our outfits change at least on a season-by-season basis, if not more often than that. They have more than one set of clothes in their closet."

"I think it's cool to see characters changing and evolving from season to season," says Kirkman. "New costumes are always a great thing in comics, and we want to carry that over here. So anytime we can give a character a new season-specific look, we're going to try to do that."

But in animation, changing the look of a character takes a significant amount of time and effort, so careful consideration had to be taken as to just how often those types of adjustments could be made.

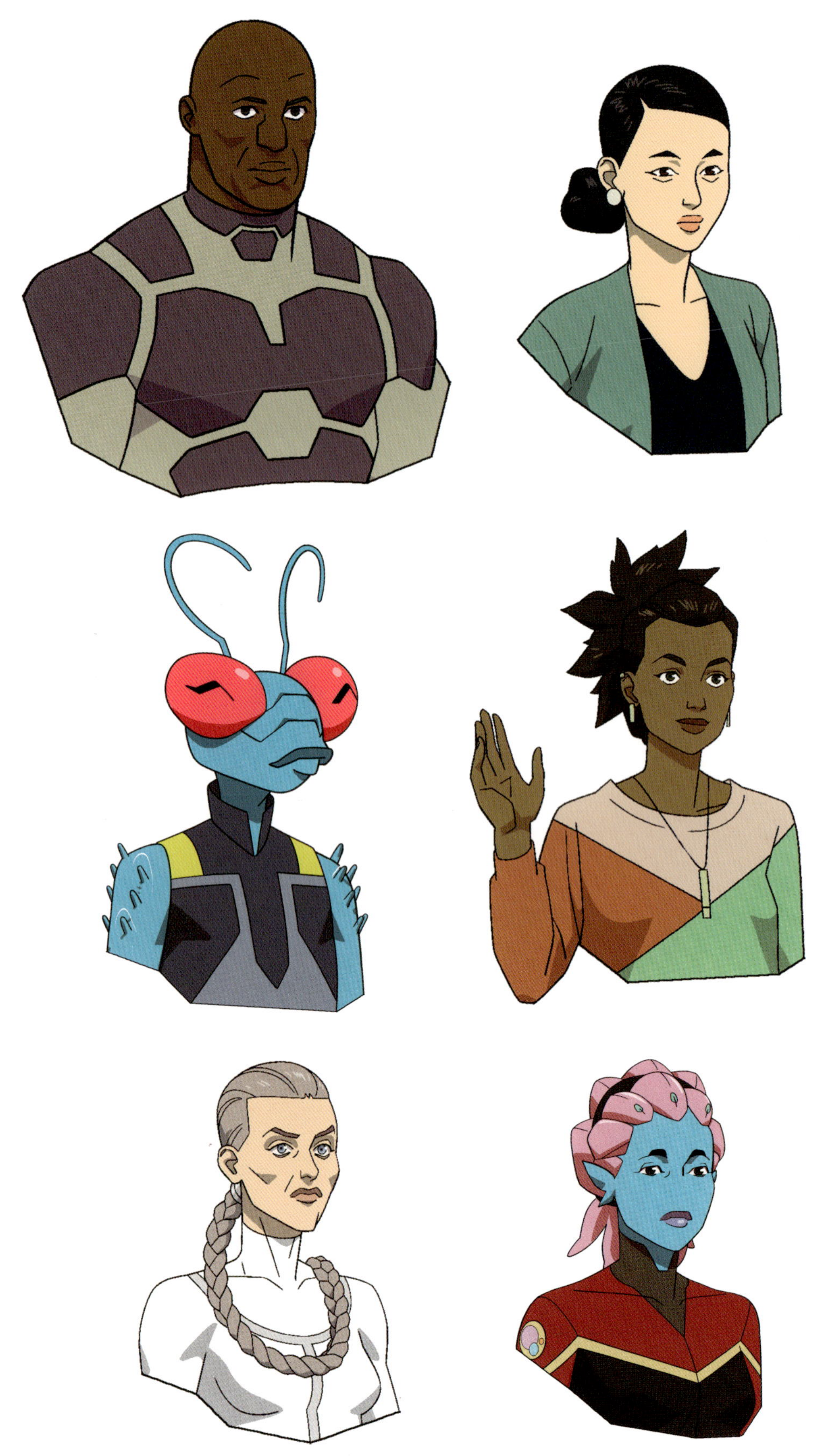

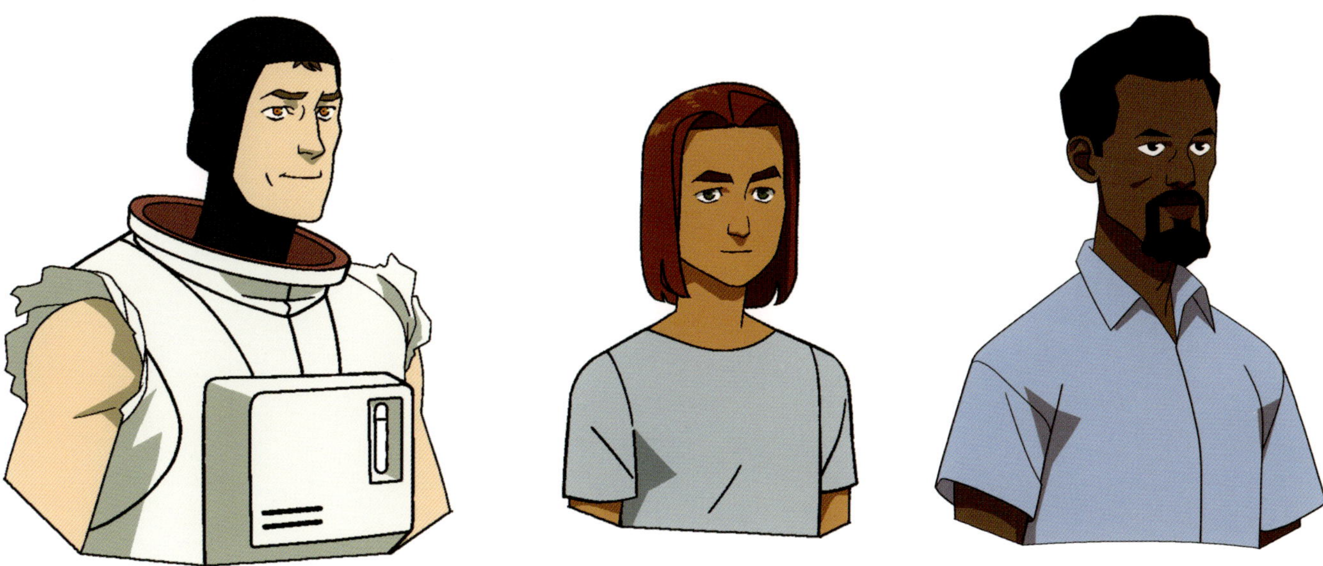

"I think we're getting smarter about some of that stuff," says O'Neil. "You want something high production value. You want something that feels like the attention to detail is there. But it's a time conversation. It's resources, personnel and otherwise. Cory had a pitch to put appropriate costume changes as you would in real life. You come home from a fight, you change your clothes. You go outside to do some stuff, go to sleep, you wake up the next day, you change your clothes. It's great in concept. And I think if we had been able to identify some other places to compromise, we might have gotten a little closer to that. But, even still, we settled on a process where now, season over season, we do seasonal overhauls to a character's civilian outfits. So every time we get to a new chapter in the story, we go back and we reevaluate costume. What did we do last time? What can we do now? Thematically, one of the things that I try to keep an eye on is what's happening to these characters. Design tells a story in and of itself. And if you're doing it right, then what you see, without the context, should tell you what kind of a day somebody is having. Are they in a good mood? Are they in a bad mood? But I think the other part of it, too, was that, after the success of Season One, there was an opportunity, with this sort of restart that we had as a studio to figure out what we really like — What worked and what didn't? What do we want to do as a studio? What do we want to do as artists? What do Robert and Cory want to do as creators? — to make some meaningful changes that we could adhere to now that we had all that experience from Season One."

New costumes and updated clothing weren't the only adjustments being made to the character designs for Season Two.

"There were a few design elements here and there that Cory had at the beginning of Season One that he had kind of gotten rid of by the end of Season One," says Kirkman. "And there were a few things that he wanted to change. Cory came into Season Two with a checklist, if you will, of things that he wanted to update and get rid of. You know, 'I want Atom Eve's eyes to be like this now instead of like this.' And he wanted to refine Mark's face in a certain way. And so while we were putting together new characters and new environments and all kinds of different stuff for Season Two, he was cooperating with Shaun's team to come in and kind of improve and alter the main character models for the main cast in some very subtle ways that people may not have necessarily noticed. But it did improve things quite a bit."

"Mark was the biggest example of that," says O'Neil. "I have posted some turnaround material from Mark, and the number one question I get is, 'Why does he look like that?' And it's just like, 'Because that's what we want.' First and foremost, Mark is an Asian-American-Viltrumite alien. He didn't really feel like that in Season One. Full stop. He kind of felt like another white kid. So what can we do to represent a little bit more of his background? A little bit more of [his mother] Debbie and that side of the family? And so it was a very particular game of ping pong between me and Cory. I think he came through with most of the core changes, and a lot of what I was doing was just like, 'Hey, is there something that's not working for movement?' Mark has a very particular eye treatment that no other character on the show has. Even Dupli-Kate and Multi-Paul have a different treatment from Mark. We have this setup of features that only works for him, that requires spelling it out a little bit more, making sure that overseas understands what it is that you're looking at, how that stuff should be handled frame-to-frame, pose-to-pose. So it was a lot of work to go back through and figure out how we wanted to represent him and not completely put off an audience who's had eight episodes of something different. And I think we were successful in that. I like this Mark, and I'll fight motherfuckers who don't."

Though a number of character designs went through positive adjustments for Season Two, they still had to remain fairly close to what had come before for the sake of continuity. However, the art team found other areas where they could push in the show's visuals in exciting new directions.

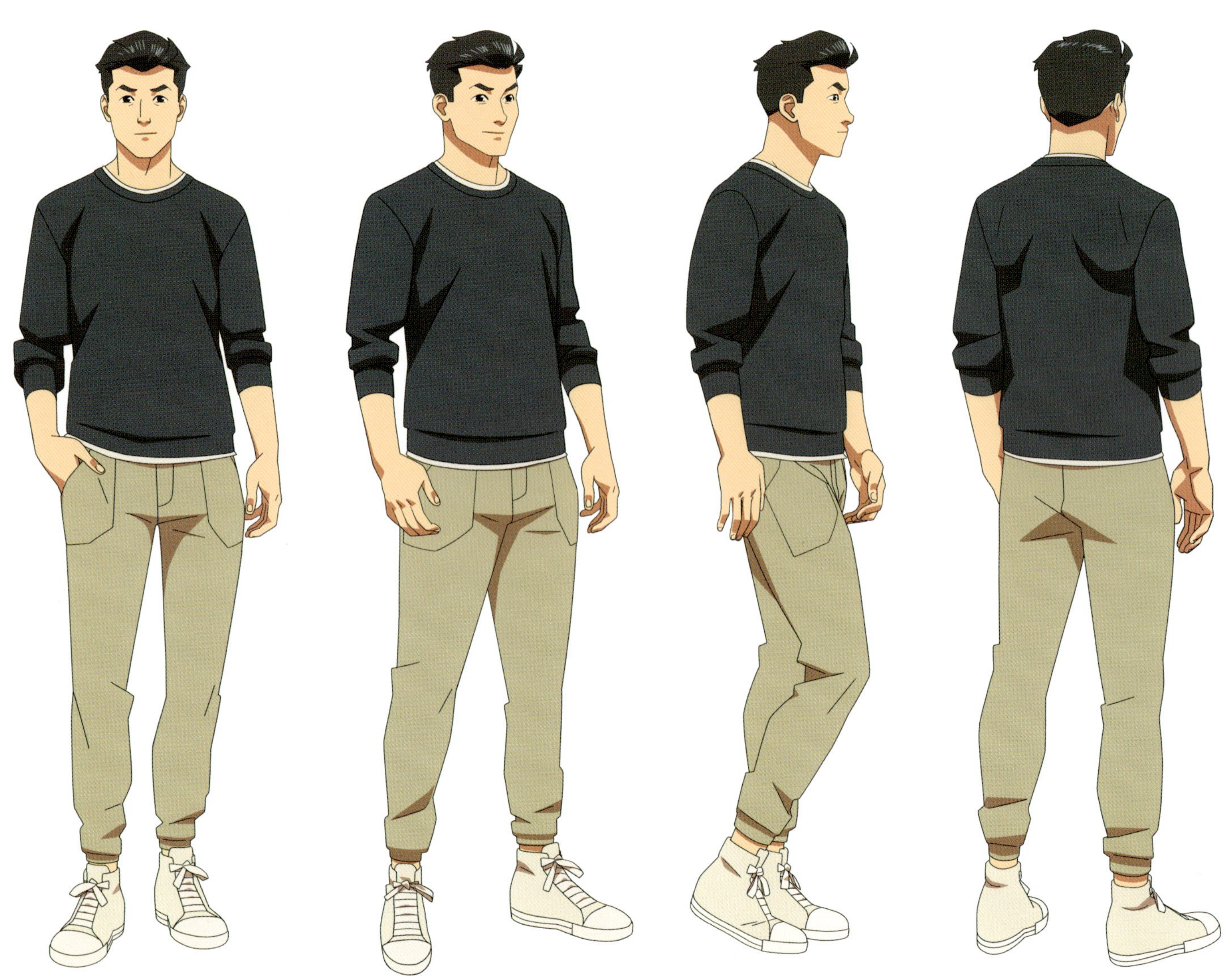

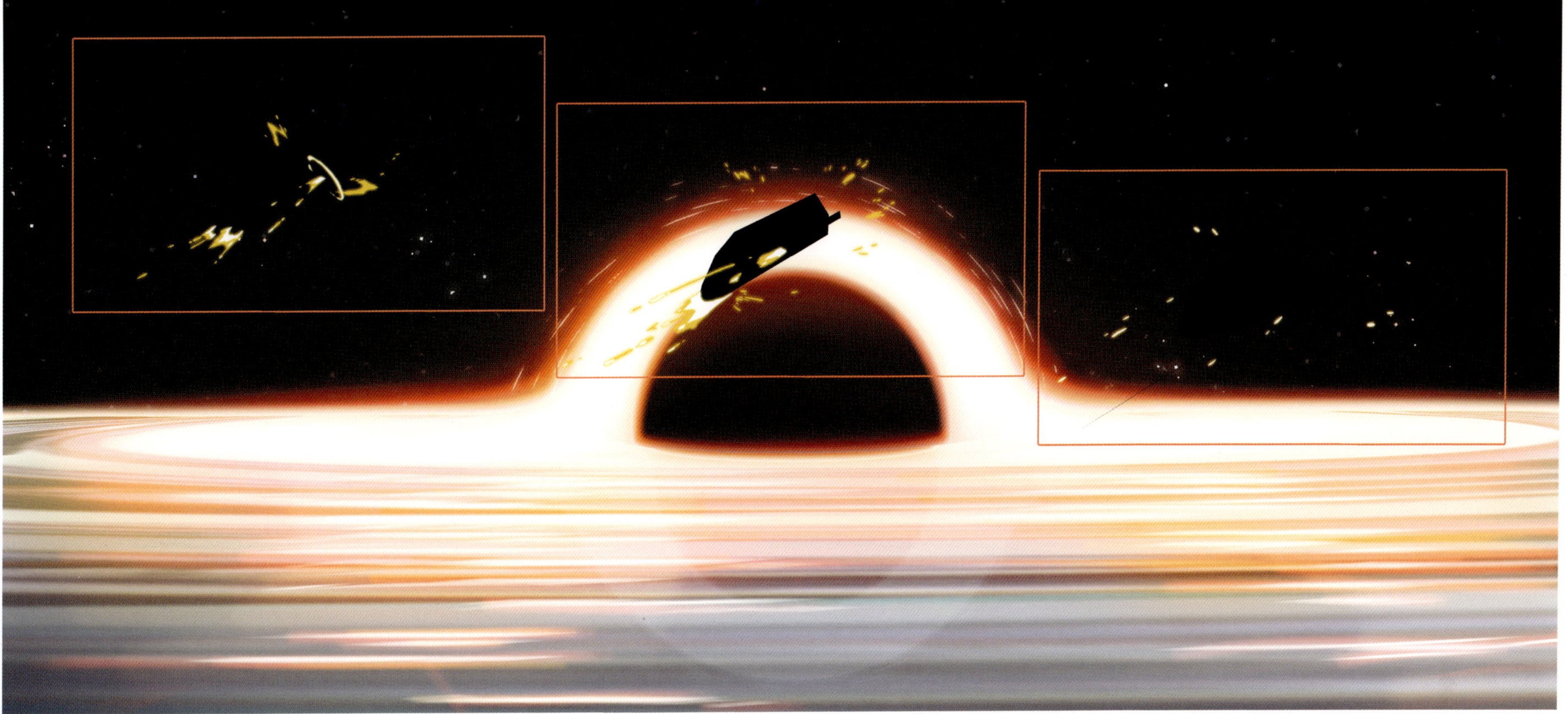

"I think environments gave us like the biggest leeway," says O'Neil. "Specifically, how this comic goes from Earth, which is kind of mundane superhero stuff on the surface, but then you graduate to space and you go to crazy worlds, and you meet crazy people, and you get a best friend with one eye and shit like that. So it's like, 'How can we start to bridge that gap so it feels like there's a comfortable ramp, and then — for this season and for future seasons — prep ourselves to be able to move into spaces that really feel like they're our own?' So you might not feel it at the start, but at the end you're like, 'Holy shit, that's a departure. That's different.' You know, just evolve, like a show should. Also, with that in mind, the goal is to set up your black-and-white teams, to set up your color teams."

"Color design starting in Season Two is a completely different animal than it was in Season One," says Walker. "That's not to disparage the color designer from Season One at all. It's just the approach now is a lot heavier on matching the scene. Everything fits together in a really nice way. One of the things I think we can even still try to lean into is a little more unique places color-wise. But I think we're on the right track."

"We're trying to iterate and get better every season," says Racioppa. "So I would say Season Three looks better than Season Two, and hopefully Season Four will look better than Three. And finally when we're in the last season, the show is going to look absolutely perfect. No, I'm kidding. Ultimately, we're still on a TV schedule and on a TV budget, and there are things that sometimes, for various reasons, you're like, 'That is good. That can go,' rather than, 'We have four more days. Maybe we could polish it up a bit more.' Every time I talk to Dan, he's just like, 'If we had a little more time, we could really push this.' But sometimes you have the time and sometimes you don't."

These advancements in character, environment, and color design all added up to a second season that made huge visual strides beyond what had been established in *Invincible*'s initial outing and created room for continued growth in future seasons. The plans around kicking off Season Two would also provide an opportunity to do something the show had never done before, in an ambitious special episode.

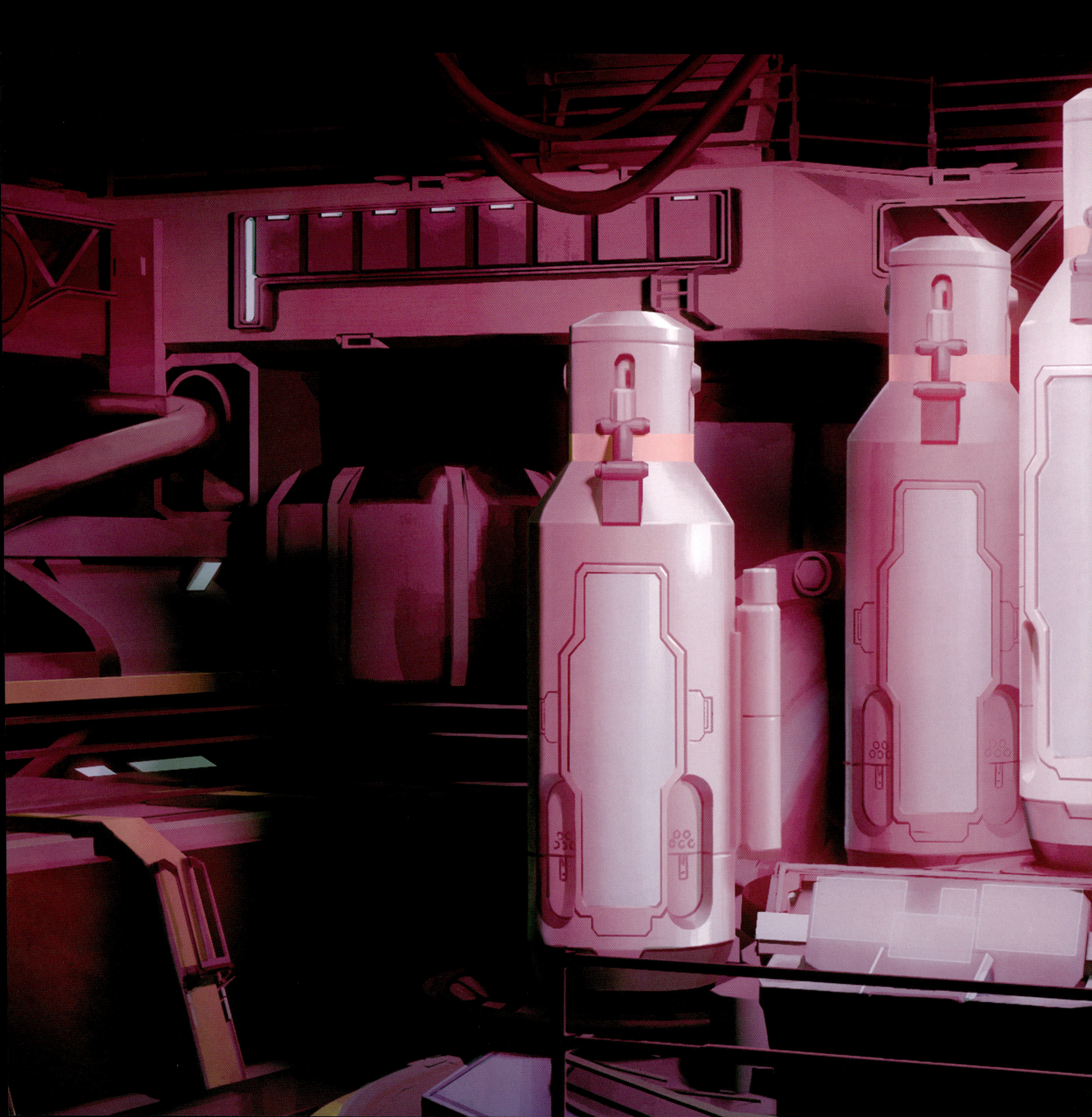

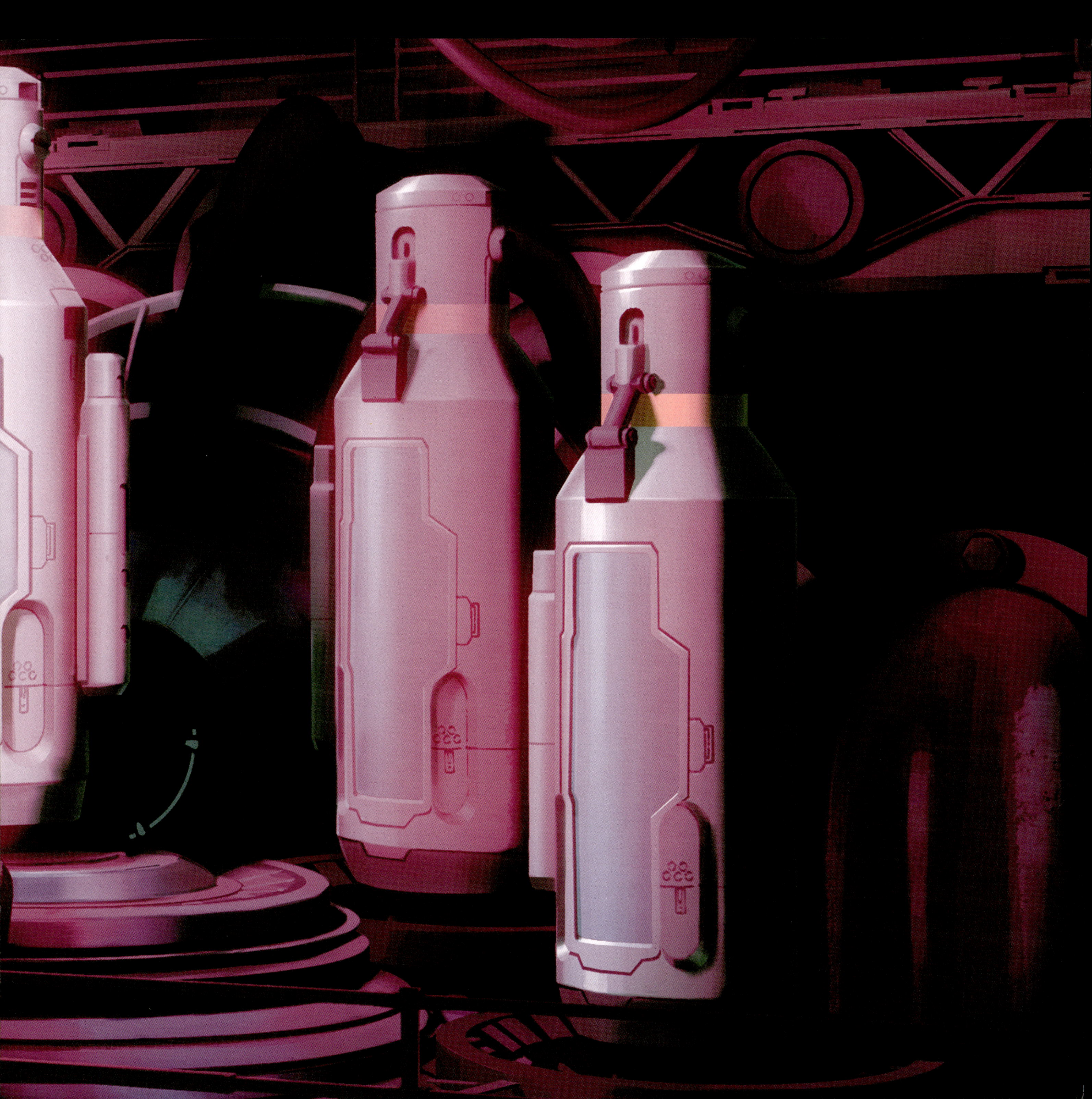

ATOM EVE SPECIAL

From the moment that the *Invincible* Season One finale aired, fans were left clamoring for more. But they would have to wait longer than expected for the stories of Mark Grayson and his fellow heroes to continue.

"When we got picked up for Seasons Two and Three, there was this massive delay," says Executive Producer, Co-Showrunner, and Co-Creator Robert Kirkman, "because we had to wait until Season One came out before we got the pick-up, to see how successful the show was going to be. And so we came up with this idea of doing this special to fill in the gap a little bit, to give fans something before the much delayed Season Two premiere. And so as we got the greenlight, we had to hit the ground running on this Atom Eve special from the get-go and put that first in the pipeline, so that it would get done in time to come out any number of months before Season Two was actually ready to debut."

In the comics, Kirkman with writer Benito Cereno and artist Nate Bellegarde had previously detailed the origins of *Invincible*'s fellow superhero Atom Eve in a special two-issue series. That storyline seemed the perfect choice to adapt into a standalone episode for the show.

"We had a great script written by Helen Leigh with Robert," says Executive Producer and Co-Showrunner Simon Racioppa. "The two of them wrote the script, and then I came in and helped edit it and produce it. It was just a fun way to jump back into Eve's past, give you a little taste of how she got her powers, what drives her, and what gives her the values of her character in the present day."

For Art Director Shaun O'Neil and Supervising Director Dan Duncan, this would be their first crack at helming an episode of the series.

"Atom Eve was what kicked us off," says O'Neil. "I mean, that episode was a guinea pig and a half. It was huge. There

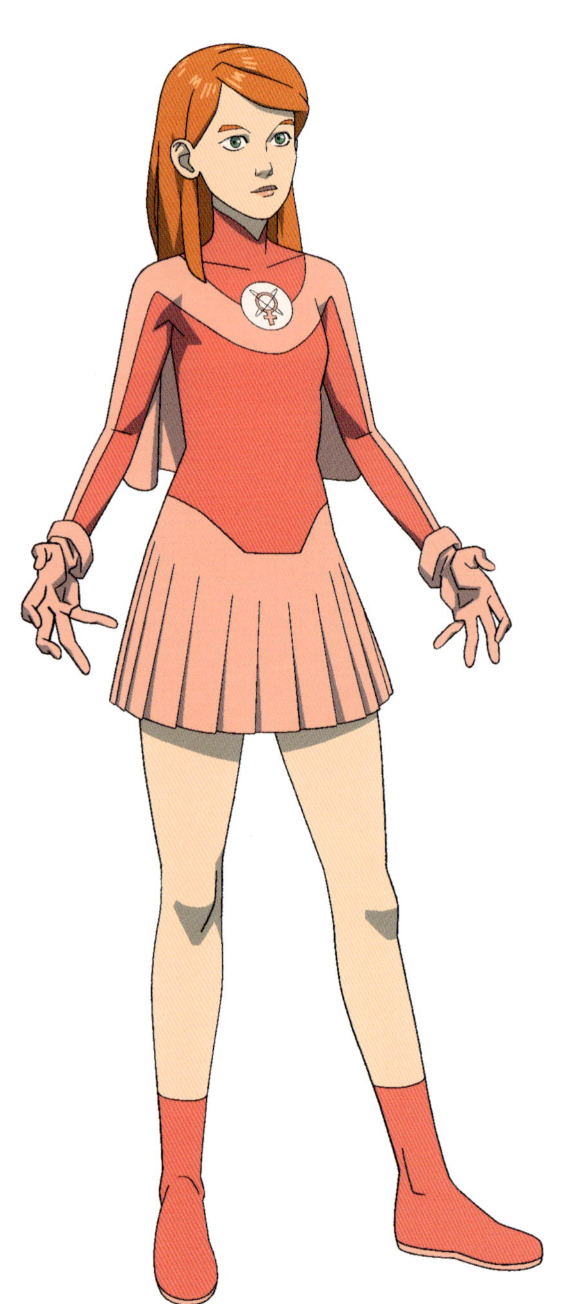

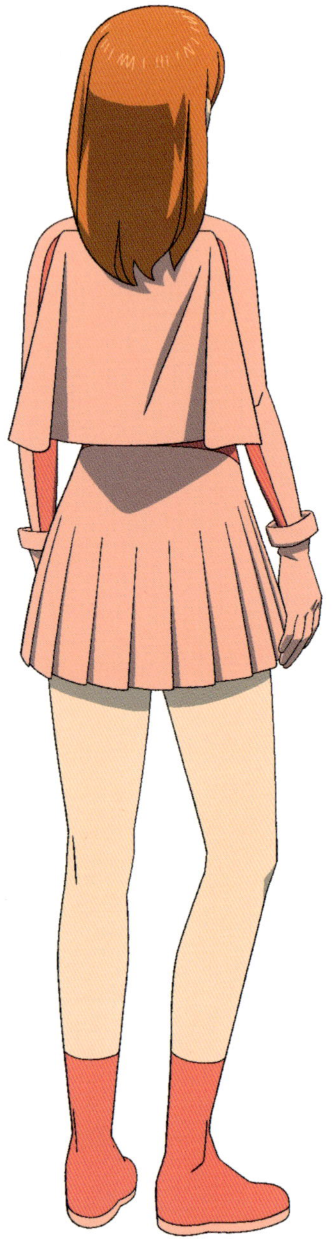

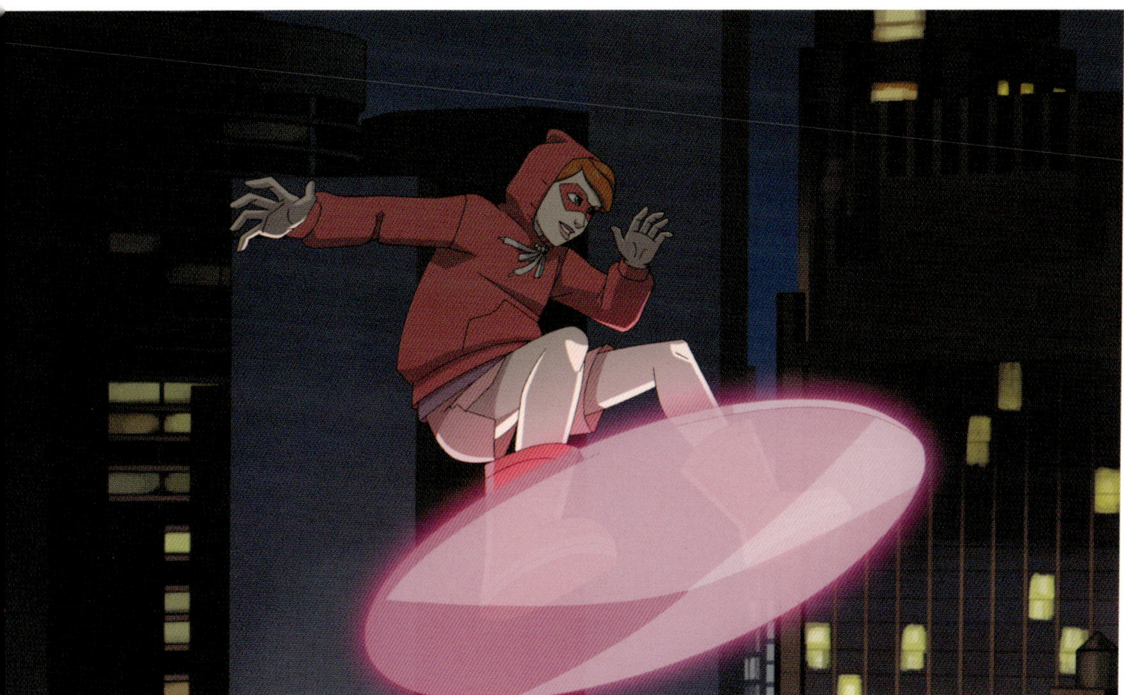

was just a ton of work to do. And it was a good stress test. I know it sounds cliché to call it the proving ground, but it really was."

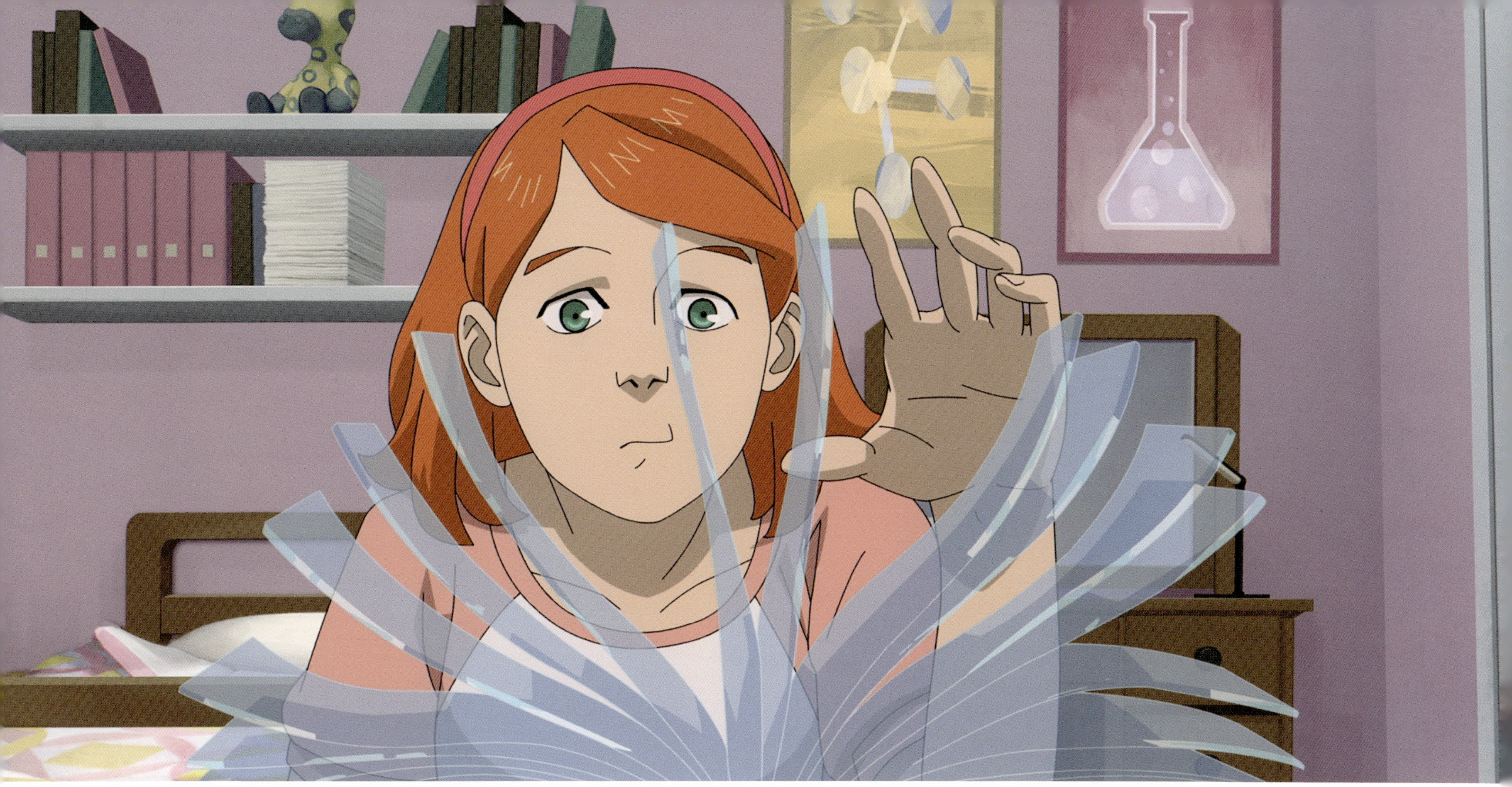

"We all love Eve a lot," says Duncan. "For a lot of people, she's a favorite character. She was also portrayed really well in Season One. That's the nice thing about having a comic that's been written to completion with twenty years of history and space between it. Robert knows who all of these characters are, what they are comprised of, what makes them tick. So if you ever have any questions, you can ask somebody. But also, it came through really, really clear in Season One. Haylee [Herrick], the Director for [the Atom Eve special] really understood Eve well and really brought a lot to this."

The episode followed Eve from her birth to her earliest days as a young teen superhero, shedding some light on how her difficult past impacted who she is today. But

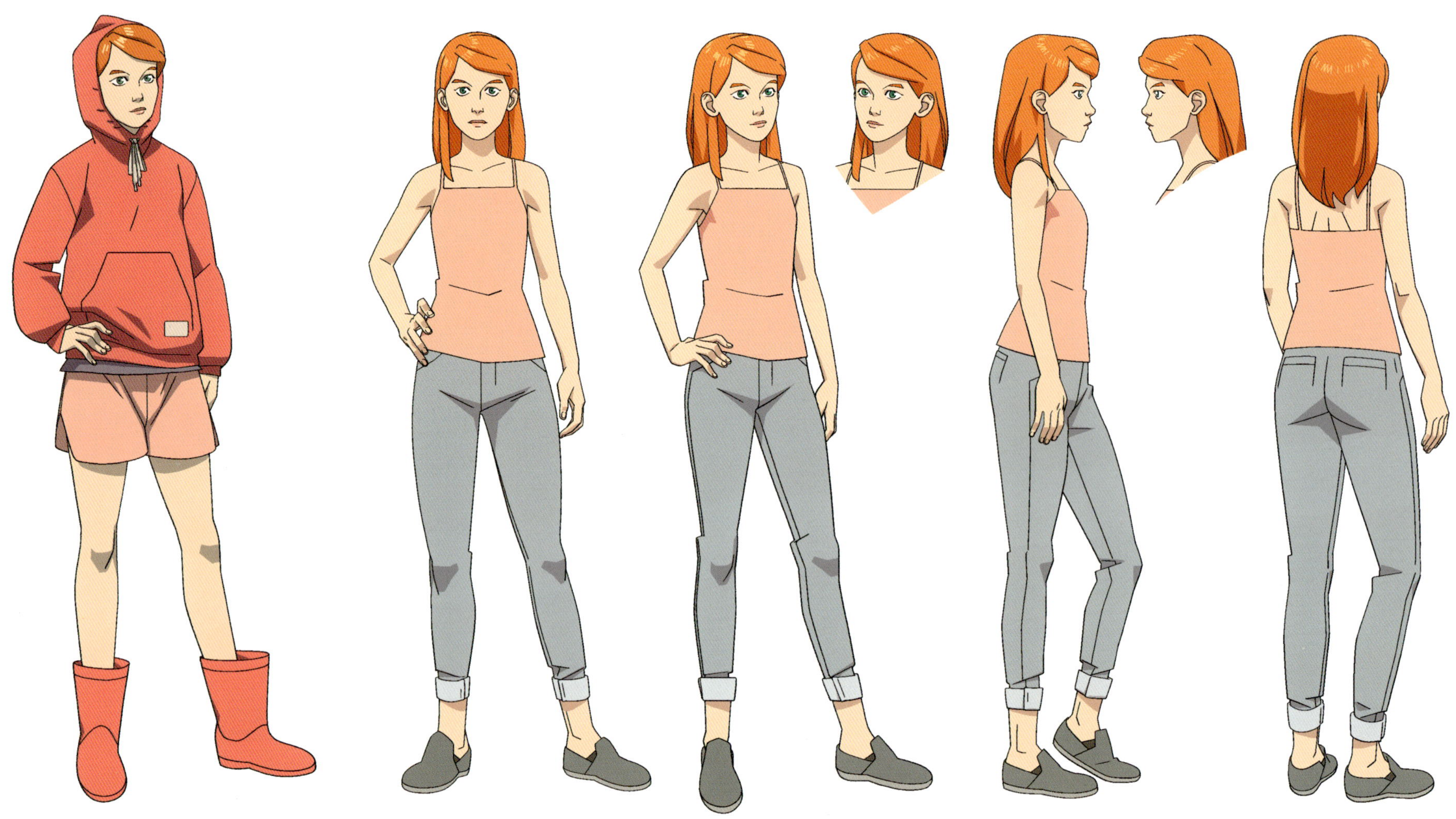

exploring such a large portion of Eve's life was no easy task for the show's designers.

"There was a lot of work done to show the passage of time," says Kirkman. "So Eve got like a dozen different looks in that episode, and she has a few different age periods, from a baby to a pre-teen to early teens. There's a lot of effort that goes into making sure a character that's being shown at that many different stages looks like the same character."

"I was real happy with how she turned out," says Co-Executive Producer and Co-Creator Cory Walker. "The choices made on the design. I think it's really great. And I liked her little proto-costume. Her hoodie and her big galoshes or whatever. Very good."

The amount of new design assets required for the episode pushed the series' new creative team to its limits right out of the gate.

"It was a ton," says O'Neil. "Just looking at the episode breakdown, we had like fifty different environments, not including whatever reuse we could pull from Season One, which admittedly wasn't a lot. We had a ton of assets that we had prepped to grab that we cut. Eve herself, I took that on almost exclusively and, not counting special poses and expression sheets, there's like twenty-seven different model sheets for her throughout that episode. That's insane. That's some other shows' whole episodes. It was a ton of work. You have some ideas and you plan, but you get in and you start interacting with what material is there, and you're just like, 'Holy shit, how are we going to get to the other end of this?' Stuff like that, I always go back to in my mind. Just the sheer scale, the sheer amount of assets that we bumped through for this. It was like hundreds of items. I pray we never have to do it again."

Fortunately, there were a few characters in the special who had appeared in the previous season. Since the episode is set in the show's past, it was able to begin with a scene that featured the original Guardians of the Globe — a group of heroes that were brutally murdered by Mark's own father, Omni-Man, at the end of the Season One premiere.

"I had a lot of fun with that intro sequence," says Kirkman, "because it was nice to see the Guardians of the Globe again. To have all those fun little bits of dialogue about Nolan getting his costume and Darkwing being injured in a fight with Chronodile. Will we ever see that fight? I don't know. But that's kind of fun backstory and lore to hide in there. It was neat seeing the original Black Samson costume

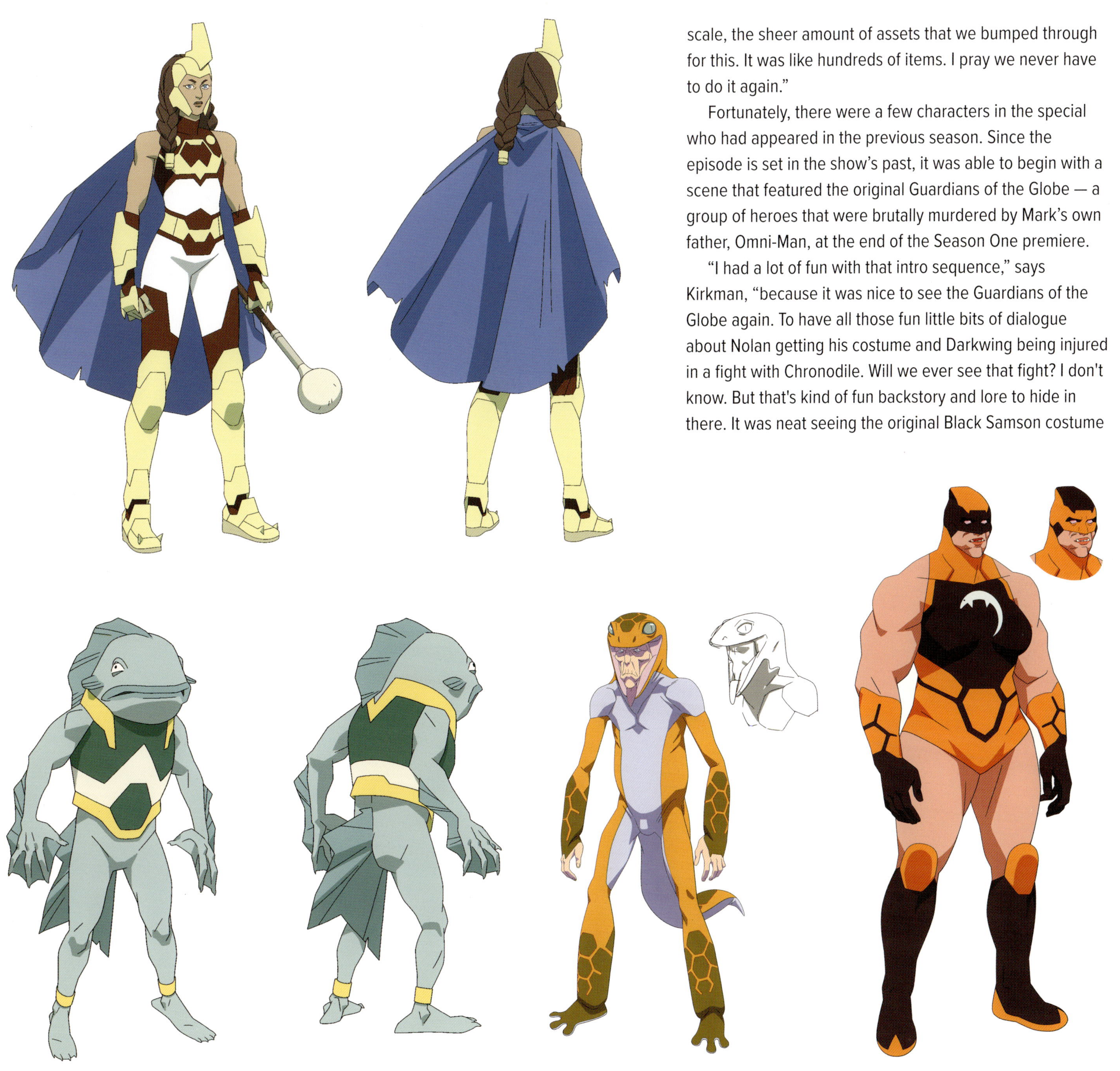

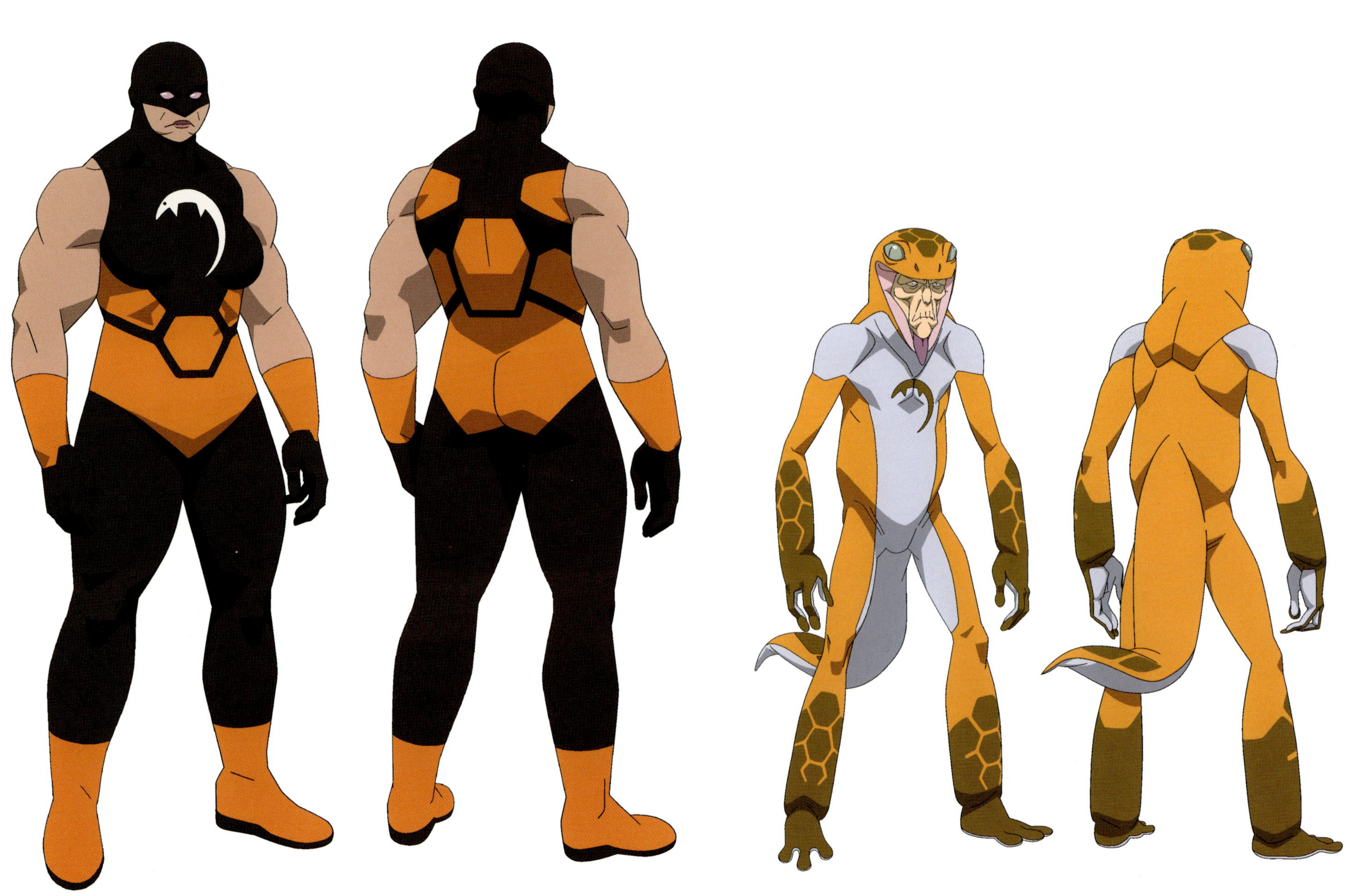

and some slight tweaks on those characters, just because they're a little bit younger."

The sequence showcased the Guardians in battle against a group of villains known as the Lizard League, who were briefly seen in the Season One finale. And while they may have looked silly in their reptilian-themed costumes, they would eventually go on to become one of Season Two's most dangerous threats.

"Can I request that you add in somewhere in my copy that I said explicitly that, 'The Lizard League is no laughing matter'?" asks O'Neil. "That was the through line with them, that they are joke characters. They are a throwaway set of goons. They don't match. They have no unified look to them. Their only through line is that they are named after, and maybe vaguely resemble, something reptilian. And so I think for a lot of us, we wanted to treat them like a goof, because they are. And the feedback from Robert was that these guys are serious business. They're not a joke. And you're like, 'What the fuck are you talking about, dude? Just look at them!'"

The fact that the Lizard League didn't appear to be as dangerous as they actually were was by design.

"I think that even the joke characters in *Invincible* need to be taken seriously," says Kirkman. "It's kind of the mode of action I've tried to live by."

As with any job, whether it's making an animated series or taking over the world, sometimes being successful comes down to having the right people in charge.

"It depends on their leadership," says Racioppa. "With the proper leadership, they can get stuff done. With poor leadership, they're less effective. Seeing Prince Lizard before he becomes King Lizard is super fun. It's just fun, pulpy comic book stuff, even maybe more so in the special than we do in the regular show."

In this flashback sequence, the Lizard League hadn't quite reached the full potential that they would achieve later in Season Two. The Guardians swiftly defeated the group of reptilian rogues, including two new — or, rather, old — members, Gecko and Gila Monster.

"Gecko was a new Lizard that was added," says Kirkman, "and that design came in and it was kind of funny. But it was so cool and unique and interesting looking that I was like, 'You know what? I'll allow this one to be kind of funny.' There's a cool bit where he seems to have a heart attack just before you see him for the last time. And that came from the design, making him look like this old man, which wasn't necessarily what was planned. And I like that. There's that little bit of a hint of, like, 'This guy's not so healthy.' So that's why you don't see him in modern times. This guy is totally dead."

"I really like the handful of new Lizard Leaguers that we hadn't seen before," says Walker. "Gila Monster took a little bit of trying to figure out, just because of what those things look like. How do you design that character without just making it look like the salamander guy? But I think we landed in a pretty cool spot."

"When I was writing that sequence, I just wanted to throw some characters in that weren't present in modern times," says Kirkman, "because I actually have a lot of pet peeves when it comes to prequels. I don't like it when things are buttoned up completely. Even though there might be a large gap of time between the prequel and the thing that comes after it, you have a checklist of everything that is done. I've always said that the opening sequence to [*Indiana Jones and*] *The Last Crusade* was the thing that set the tone for prequels that makes me dislike them so much. Because it's this really cool sequence with River Phoenix, but in that one sequence you're like, here's how Indiana Jones got his hat, his whip, his scar, and his passion for being an archeologist, and his fear of snakes. It's all in this one [short period] of his life, and that drives me nuts. So I like that Gila Monster is this character that's introduced in the past, and we have no idea where she went. There's a large gap of time between when we saw her and when we see the Lizard League again. And she is no longer part of the Lizard League, and we don't know why. It's a mystery. I like that you're not dotting those 'i's and crossing the 't's as much."

Other characters that wouldn't survive beyond this special included Eve's newly-discovered extended family, the batch of superhuman experiments known as the

Phases. When it came to translating them from the comic to the screen, the team went to the source — artist Nate Bellegarde, who had also served as a Character Designer on Season One of the show.

"Nate Bellegarde drew the original [*Invincible Presents:*] *Atom Eve* miniseries," says Kirkman, "so it was kind of cool to have him come in and design updated versions of the characters that he had designed for the actual comic book series. Trying to make them a little bit more animation friendly, we cut the [number of] Phases down from five to four. So there's actually an extra guy in the comics. I think some of their details were kind of smoothed out, but they have a really cool look to them, and they're really unique and creepy and scary."

Bellegarde worked in conjunction with O'Neil and his team to adapt the Phases' unique malleable physiology in a way that would work in animated form.

"I did the initial concepts for Phase Two and some of the rougher concepts for the other Phases," says O'Neil, "but most of that stuff was helmed by Nick Lombardo, one of our character artists, who did a dynamite job turning all those characters and making sense of them. Nate helped me on the 'What does it look like in terms of movement?' side of things. We had a couple of beats in the laboratory where Phase Two's skin is moving. The script was just like, 'The surface is constantly crawling,' and you're like, 'My God, what does that look like?' But we found some nice compromises that gave us little burps of movement over the course of the character. And so it was stuff where we get POV shots of the hand, and some of that stuff crawls across and we reveal some of the underlying tissues. And same with across his face, revealing his skeleton. Nate did this nasty, absolutely nightmare fuel drawing of what a child's skull looks like when it still has all of its adult teeth that are there from birth. And I was like, 'It's too much, dog. It's too fucking much. Dial it back. I gotta sleep at night.' When we were done, I did a lot of the action posing for them, then Nick helped me out with some of the state change stuff that we did. They came out really good. Some of the end stuff,

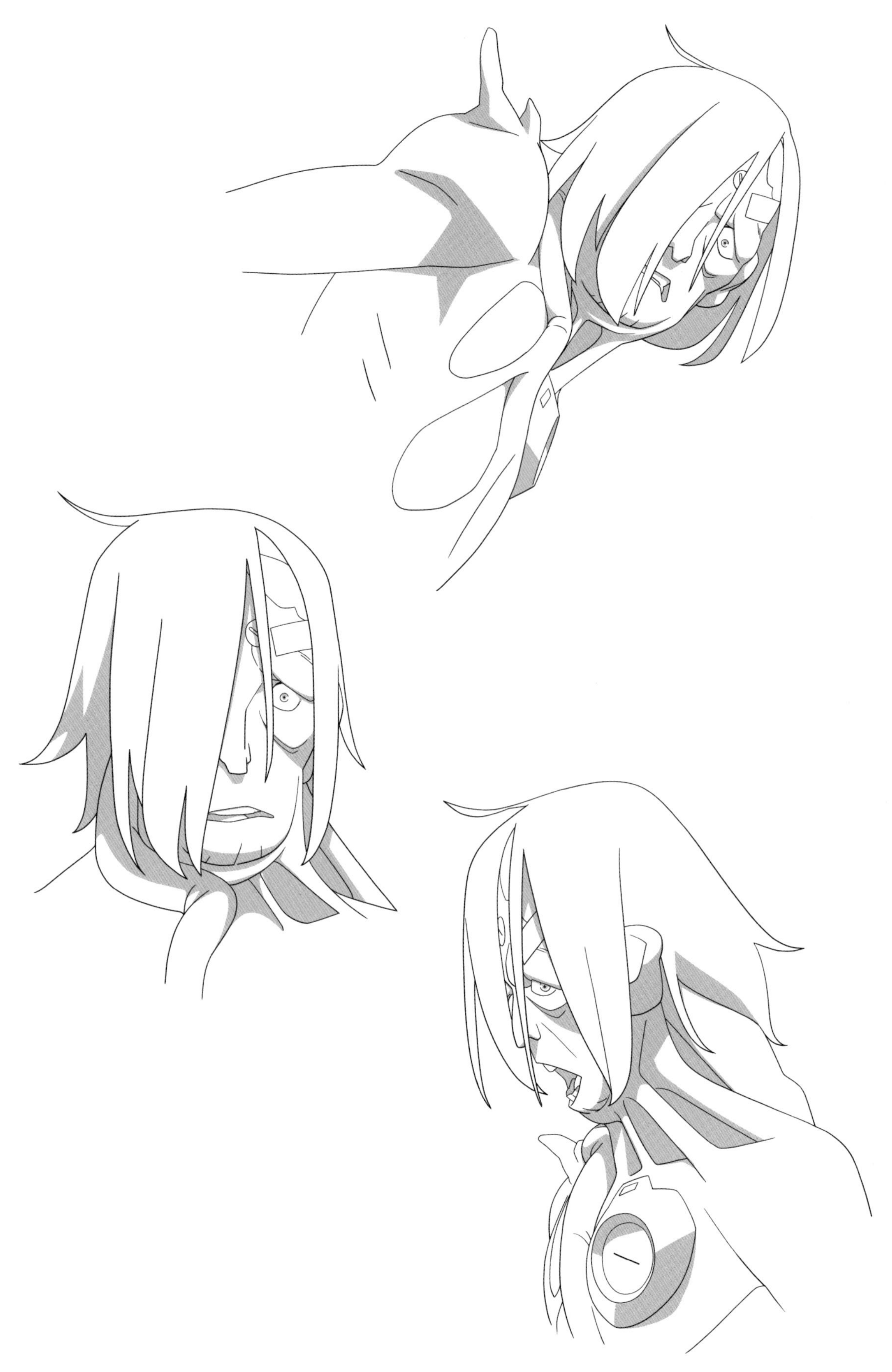

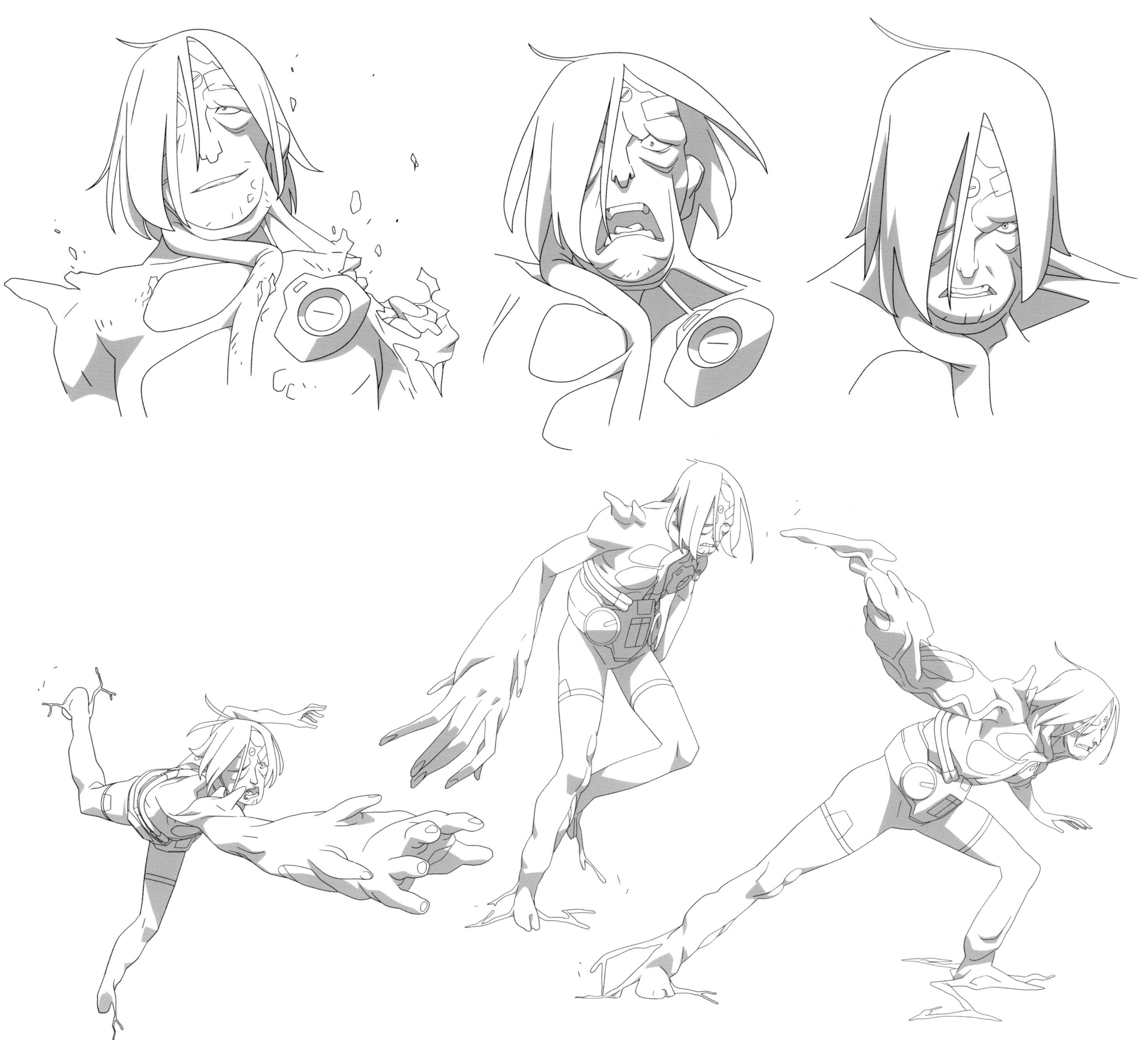

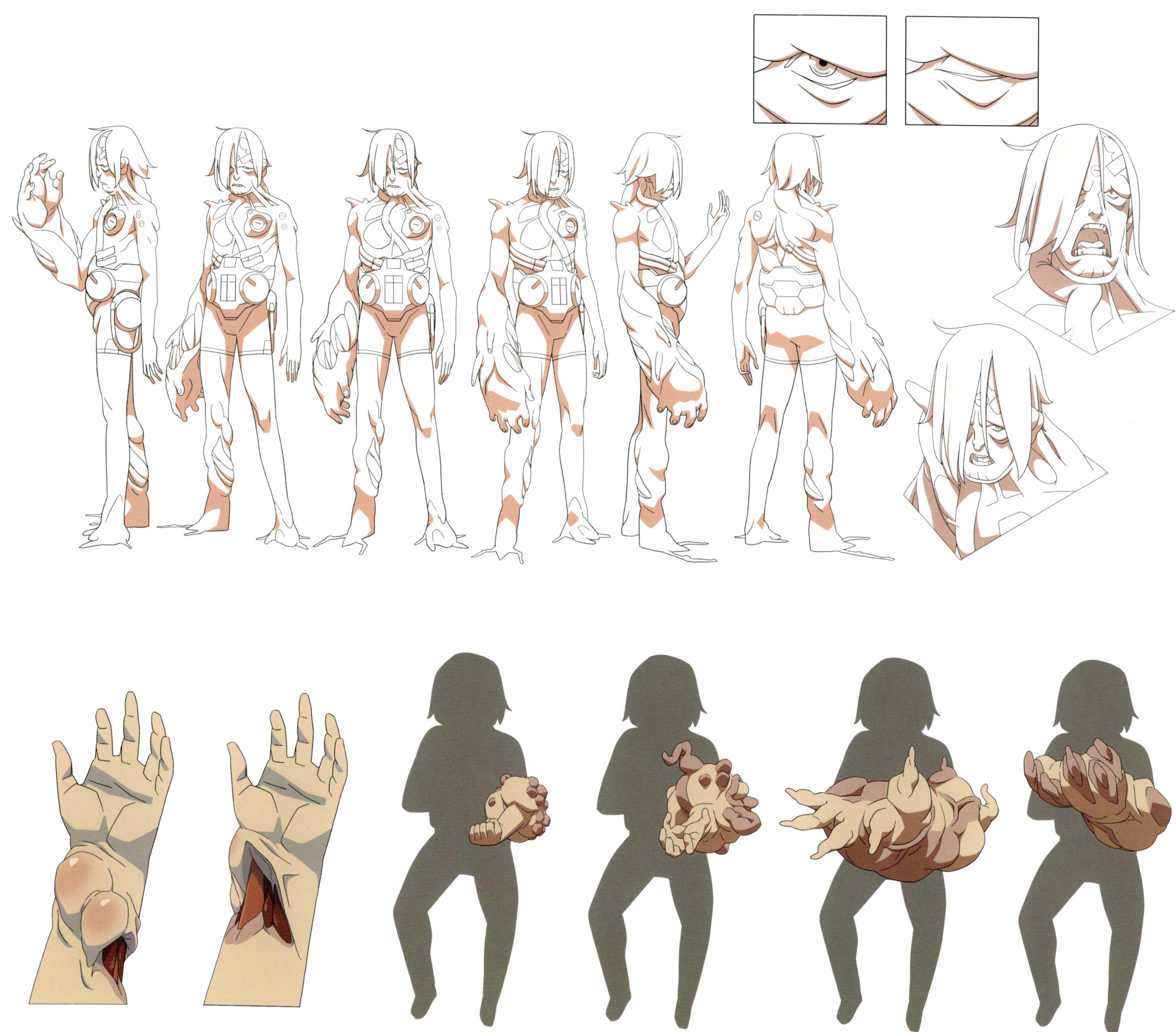

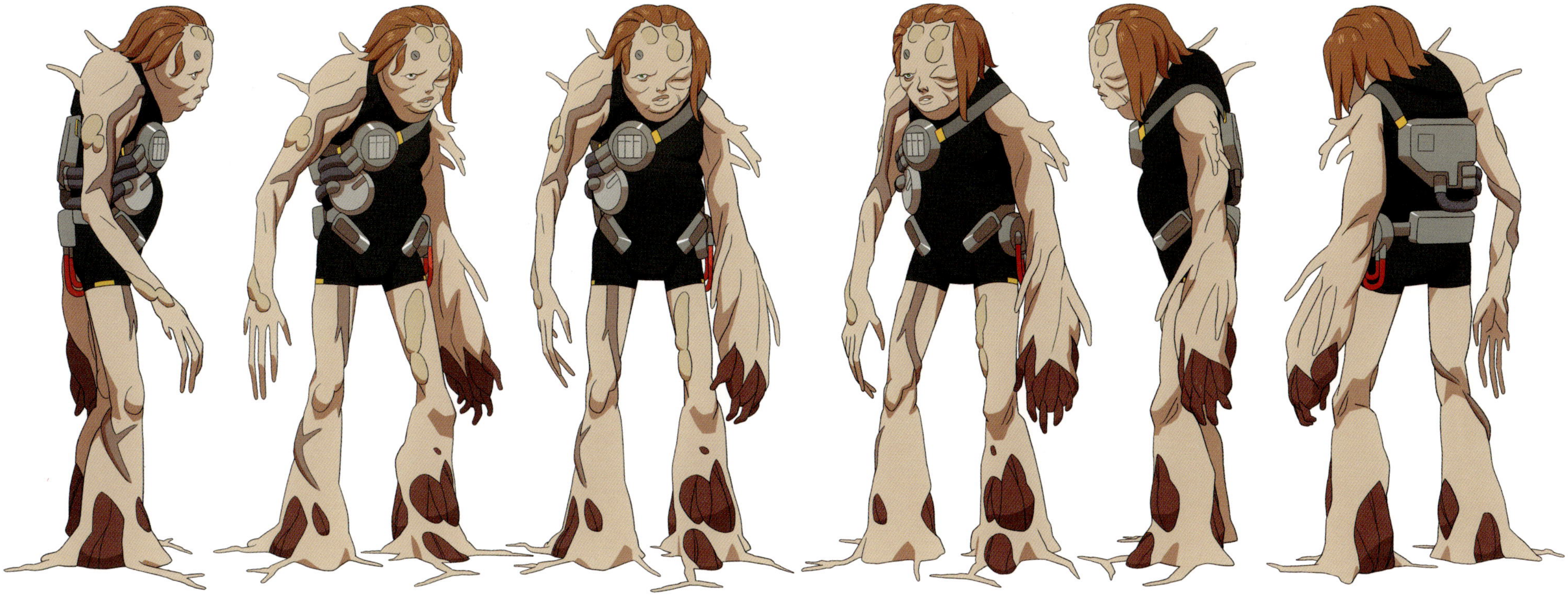

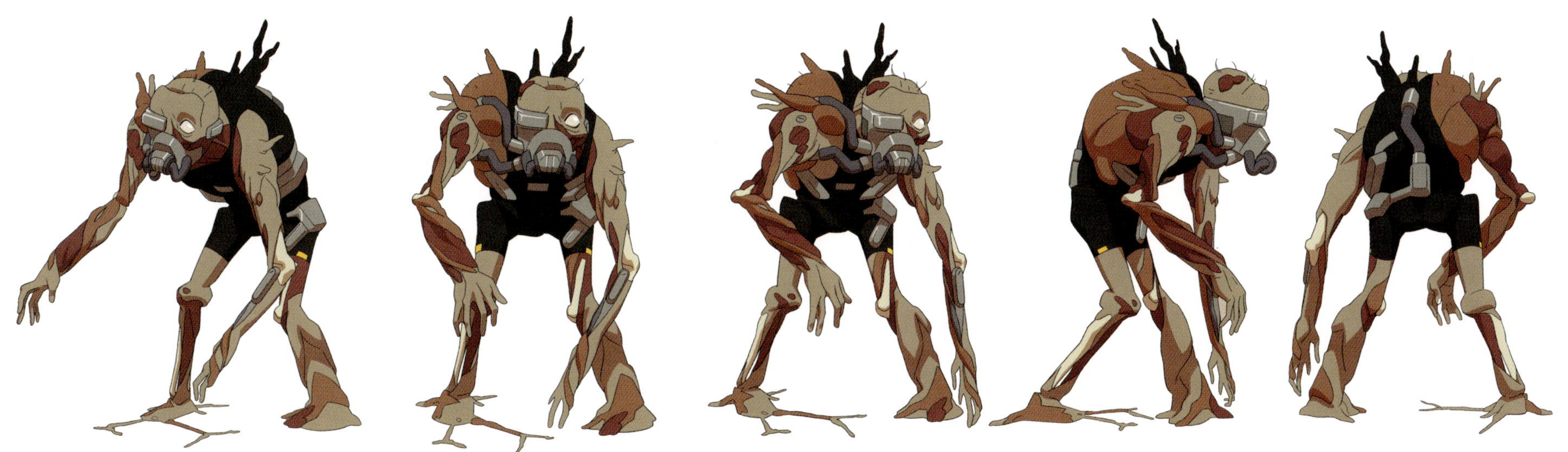

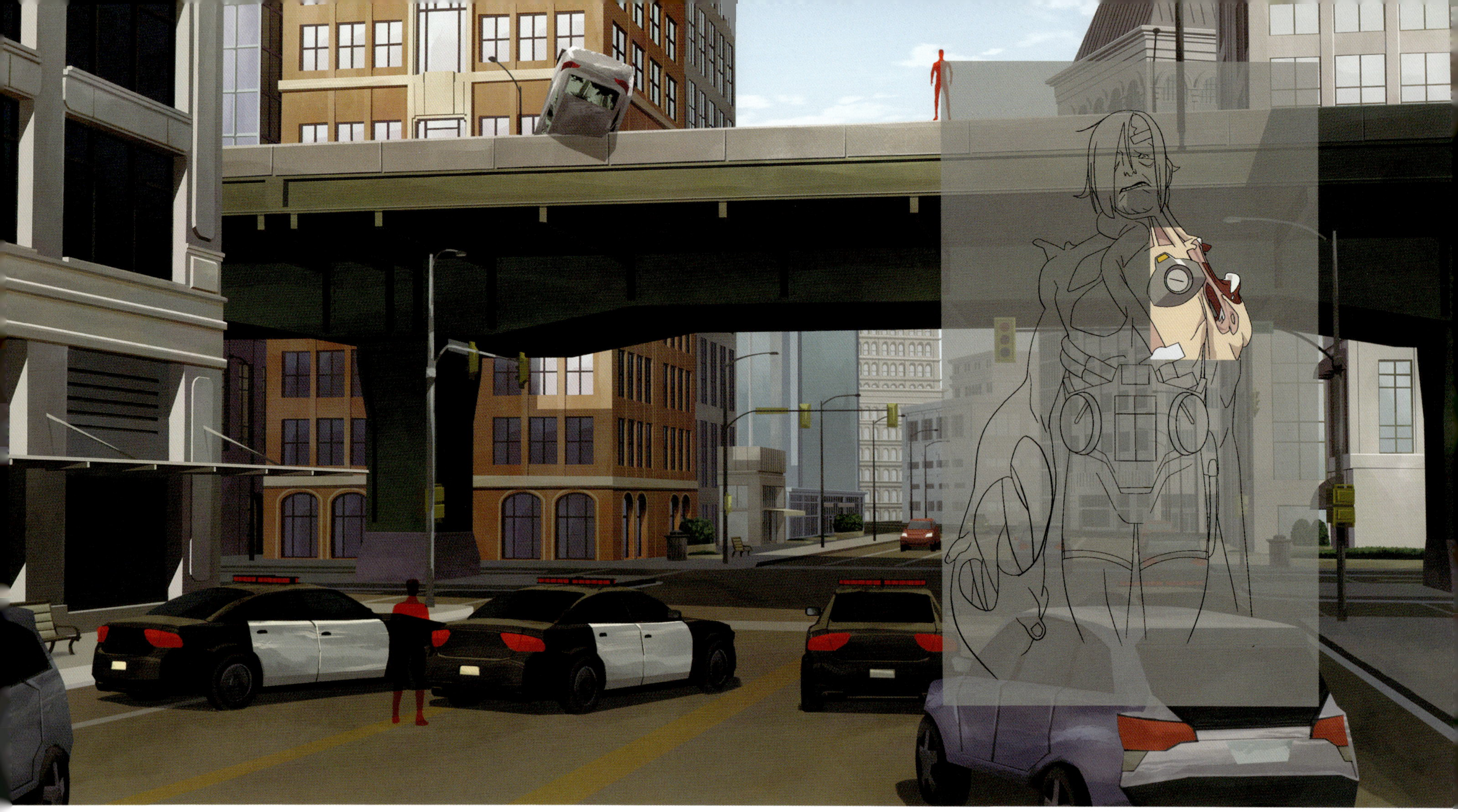

Dan and I went back in to do some considerable character layout overhauls for Phase Two dying. I'm proud of that."

The team effort resulted in a handful of characters that transcended the horror of their physical forms to bring real emotion to the episode and left a long-lasting impact on its lead character.

"I will admit, I'm a big fan of the comic book," says Walker, "and the art in particular, which was done by Nate Bellegarde. I just loved that stuff. I really loved his take on the Phases in the comic, and I was not super into the idea of not just replicating those for the show. But I think what they came up with is really cool. So I'll eat crow in that regard."

Though the young Eve eventually came to see the Phases as her family, it was only after she found herself at odds with them, confronting them on a highway overpass in an epic

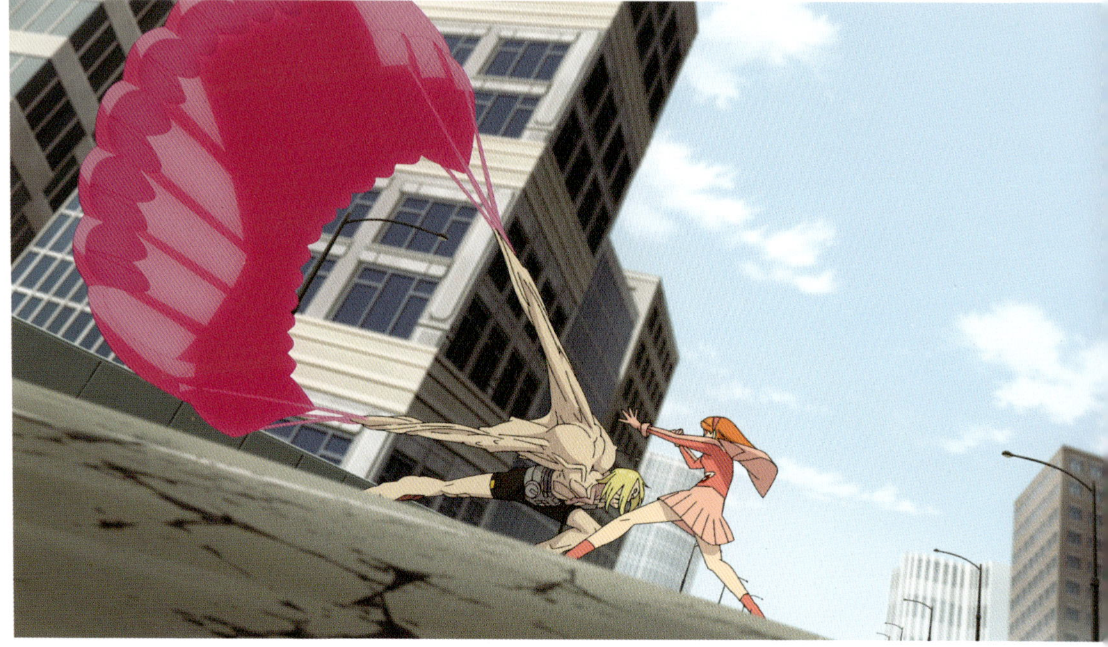

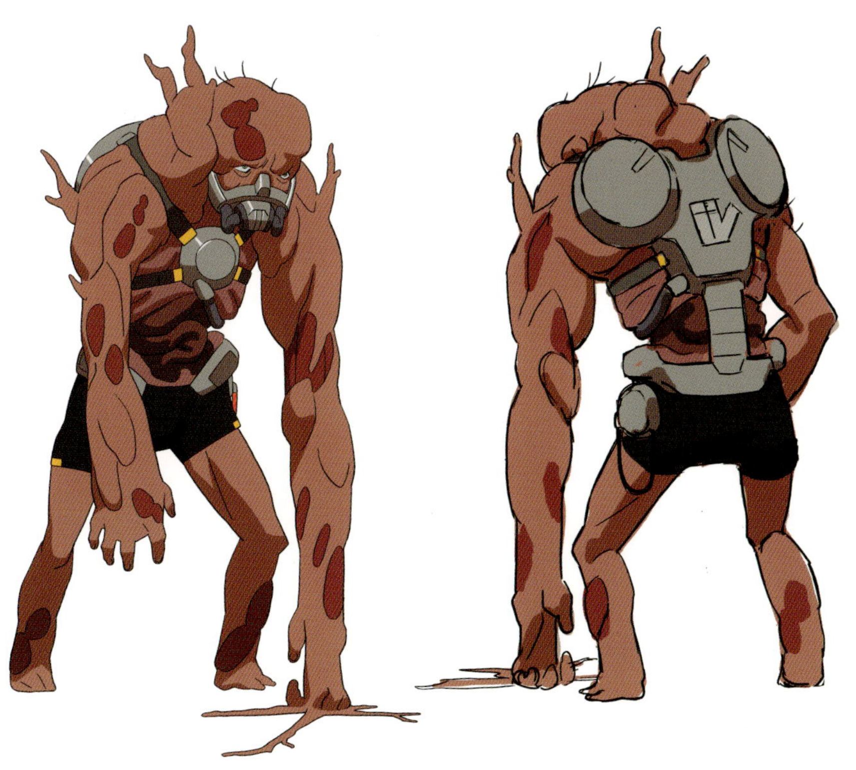

action sequence that was arguably one of the new season's best.

"The highway fight for me was one of those moments that I was like, 'Yes. We hit the bar there,'" says Racioppa. "The team — Dan and Shaun, Haylee — just hit it out of the park with that sequence. Just like a great, awesome visual highway fight that also had some heart, had some emotion. Certainly at the end as the Phases are breaking down. I thought that was spectacular."

The sequence forced the newer members of the show's creative team to consider how they would be approaching *Invincible*'s trademark violence both in this special and in the rest of the season ahead.

"How violent do you go? When do you stop?" asks Duncan. "We all walked into this where we liked how violent it could get. We liked the action stuff, but really, it's a character drama. It's a soap opera. One of the things

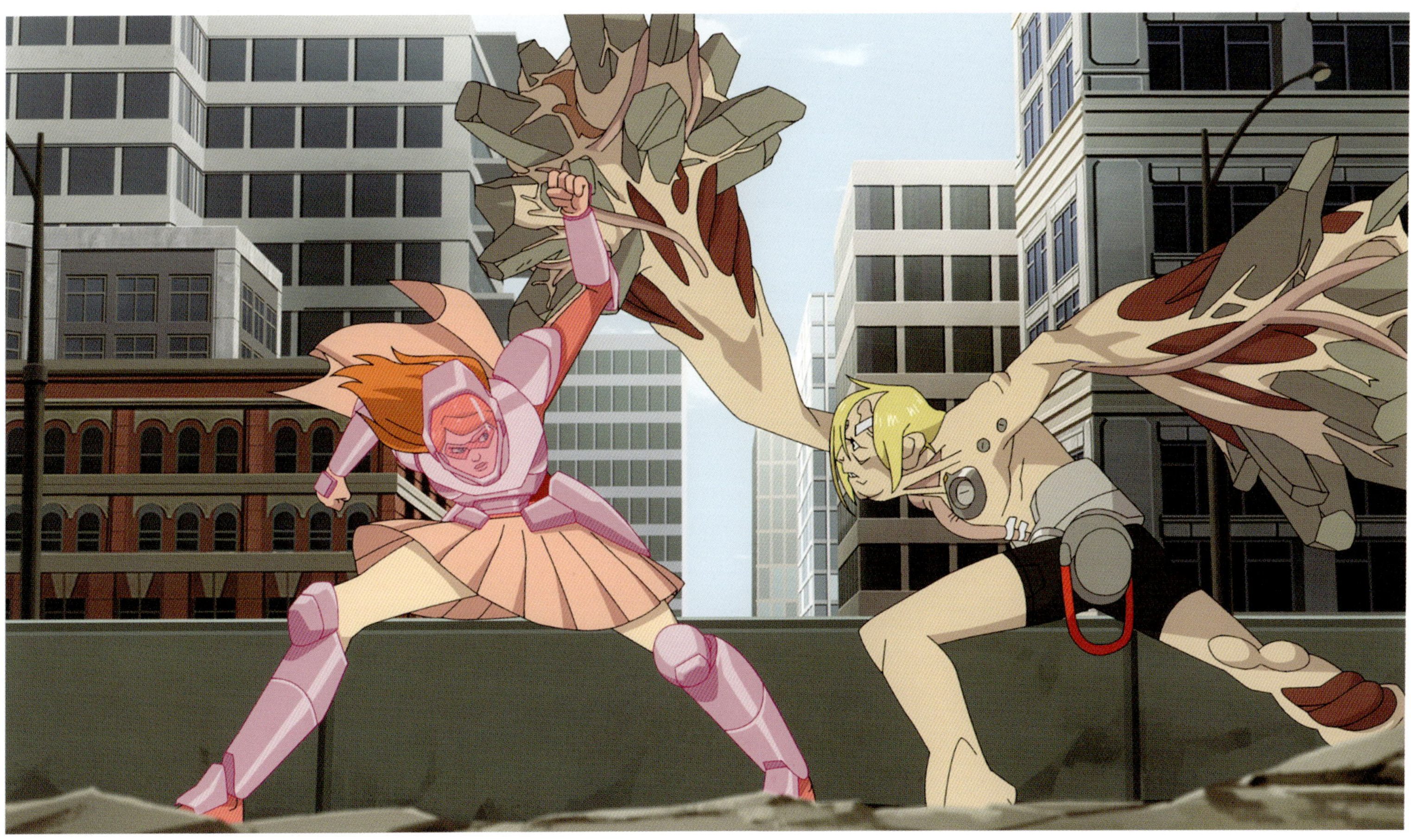

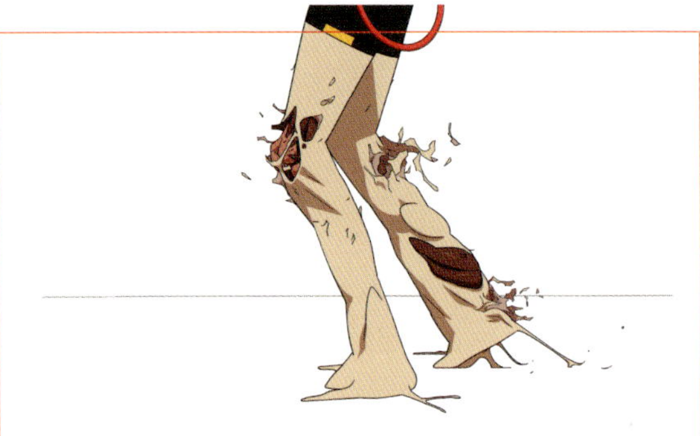

200_010_2740

- Left knee starts to shear forward at the joint, tearing the surface material as it breaks
- Femur/Patella slide forward over the Tibia/Fibula
- Right calf/heel begin to peel and flake

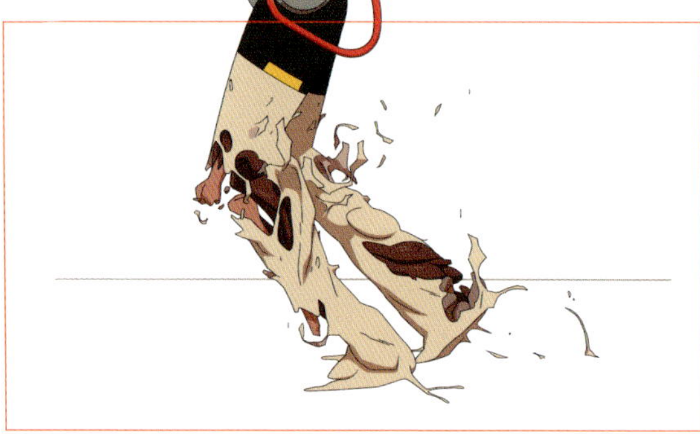

- Left knee action continues. Phase2 begins to buckle as the left leg structure breaks down
- Tibia/Fibula and the surrounding material unravels
- Right calf/heel action continues, heel begins to separate from the ankle

- Left leg action continues, Phase2 antics fwd into fall
- Right calf/heel completely dissintigrate

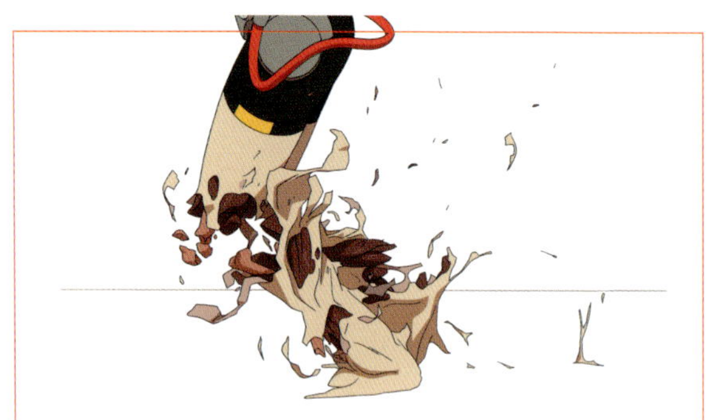

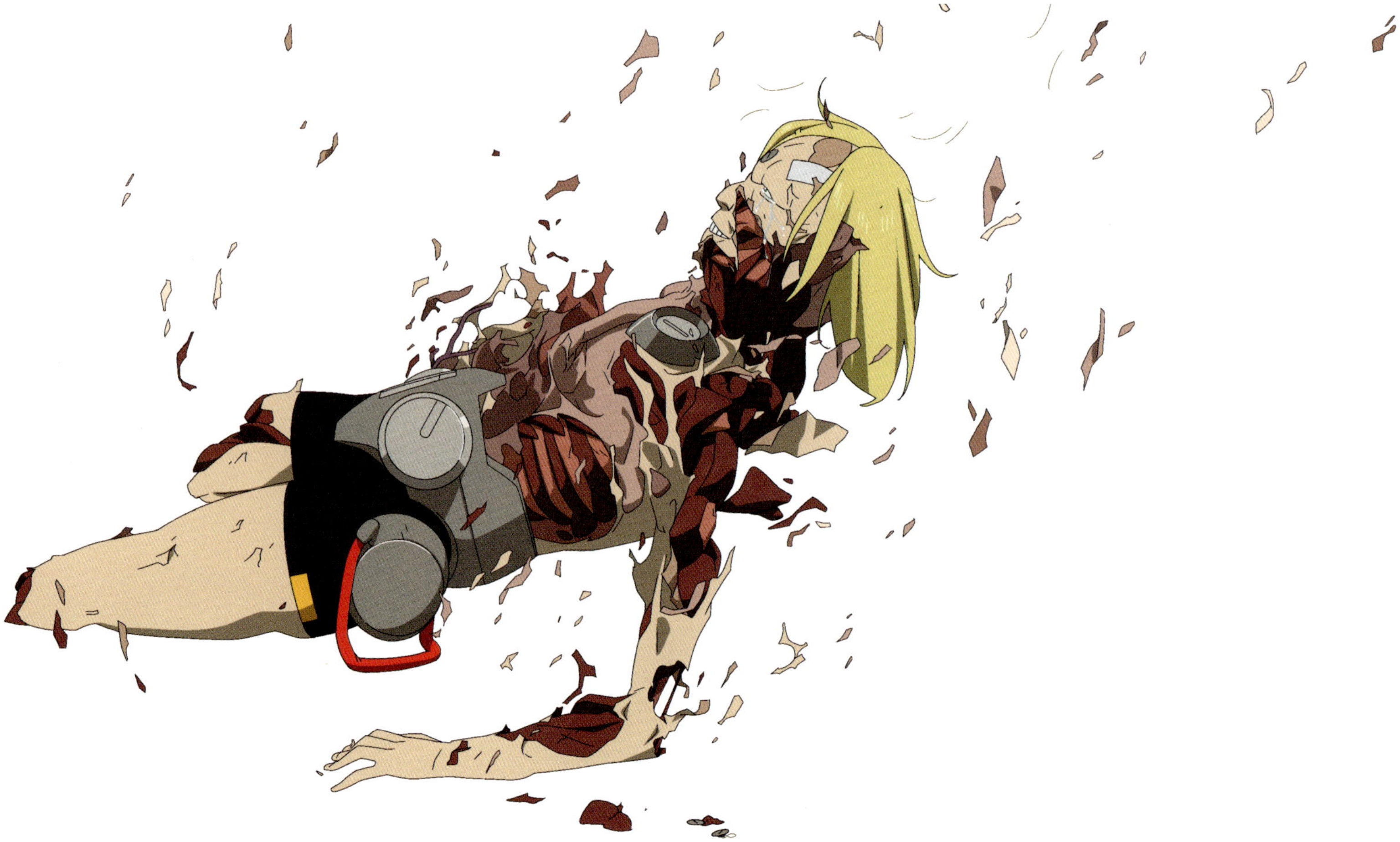

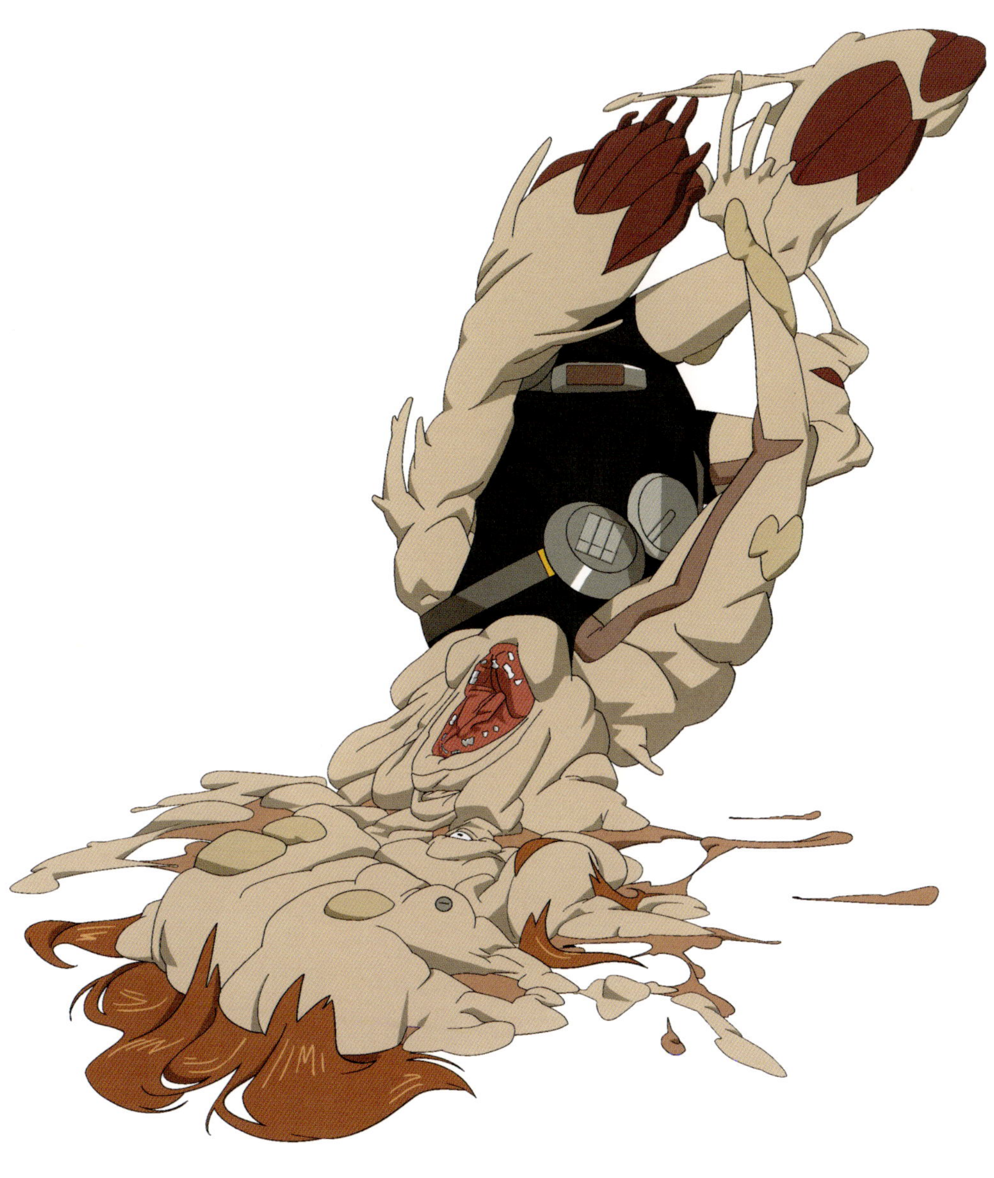

that makes it so compelling to me are the stakes and the consequences. So that's why the violence is cool. It's because it means something. It matters. Somebody is getting hurt and those consequences are going to be felt. So when we did that with Eve, it was trying to understand how Robert felt about that stuff, where we could go big, where we needed to shy away from it. So the highway fight at the end of the episode was tonally changed a lot from what we got in the initial boards to what we aired on Amazon, and it was a big proving ground for that. Trying to understand what Robert is looking for is something we're still pursuing. I don't think that we'll ever quite get there. But it's a fun game to play most of the time."

The deft balance of brutal violence and heart-wrenching loss helped show viewers how Eve became the hero she is today. And as with most things in life, even though she won the day, she didn't come out unscathed.

"Things don't always work out," says Racioppa. "She doesn't make up with her friend Val. She gets rejected for having powers and for being weird. Her parents are still terrible, even at the end of the episode. Sometimes life isn't great. It's not an up episode for Eve, even though she finds out about her past and she finds out about this family she never had. It's not a positive ending for her, even though she's able to move on."

Just as Eve found the strength to forge ahead after her harrowing experience with the Phases, the *Invincible* team carried what they learned from the challenges of producing this special episode with them into the rest of Season Two.

"Out of all of the Season Two stuff, I think I'm probably most proud of the Atom Eve special," says Duncan, "because it was our first thing. We went as hard as we possibly could on that. Sometimes to our detriment. Like, if we had maybe just cooled it a little bit, we would have had more time to work on the rest of Season Two. But, you know, you learn lessons, and you can't really stress test something if you don't actually put it in through its paces. And I think we still came out with something that I'm insanely proud of."

"Again, this was put first in the pipeline," says Kirkman. "So this was the team kind of coming together and having

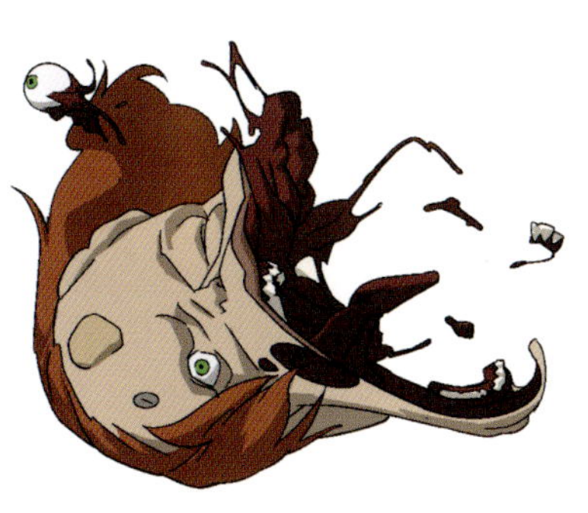

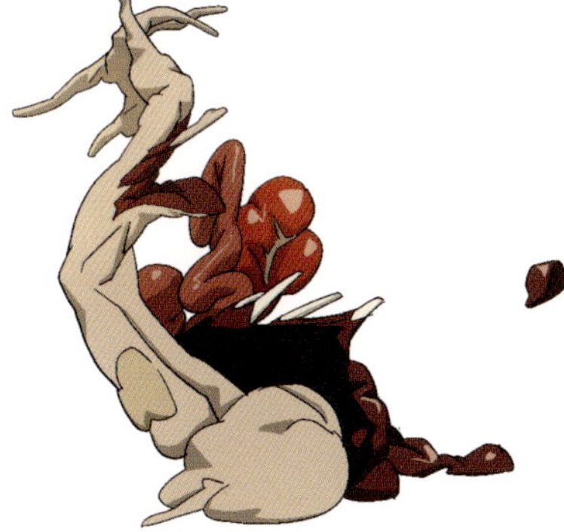

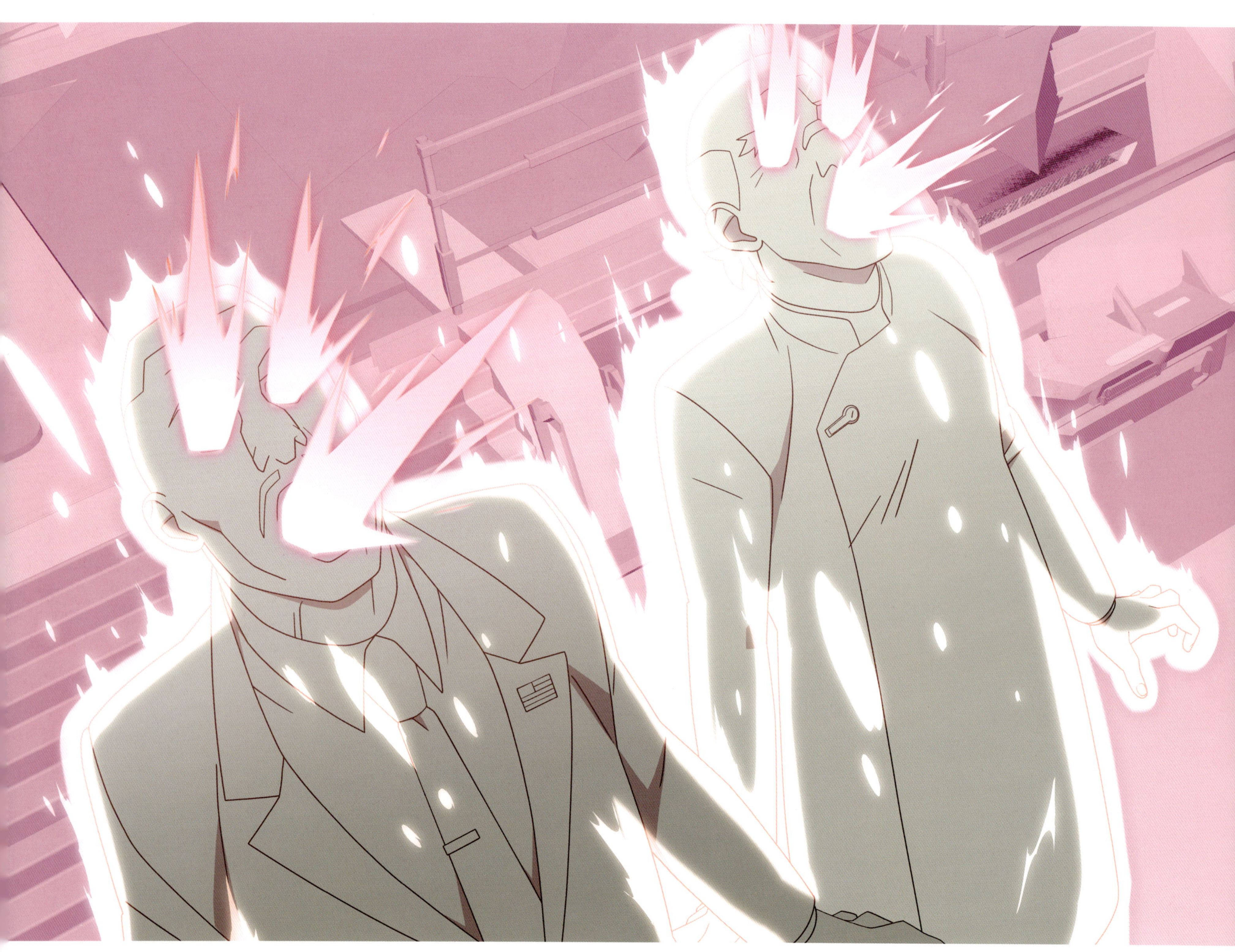

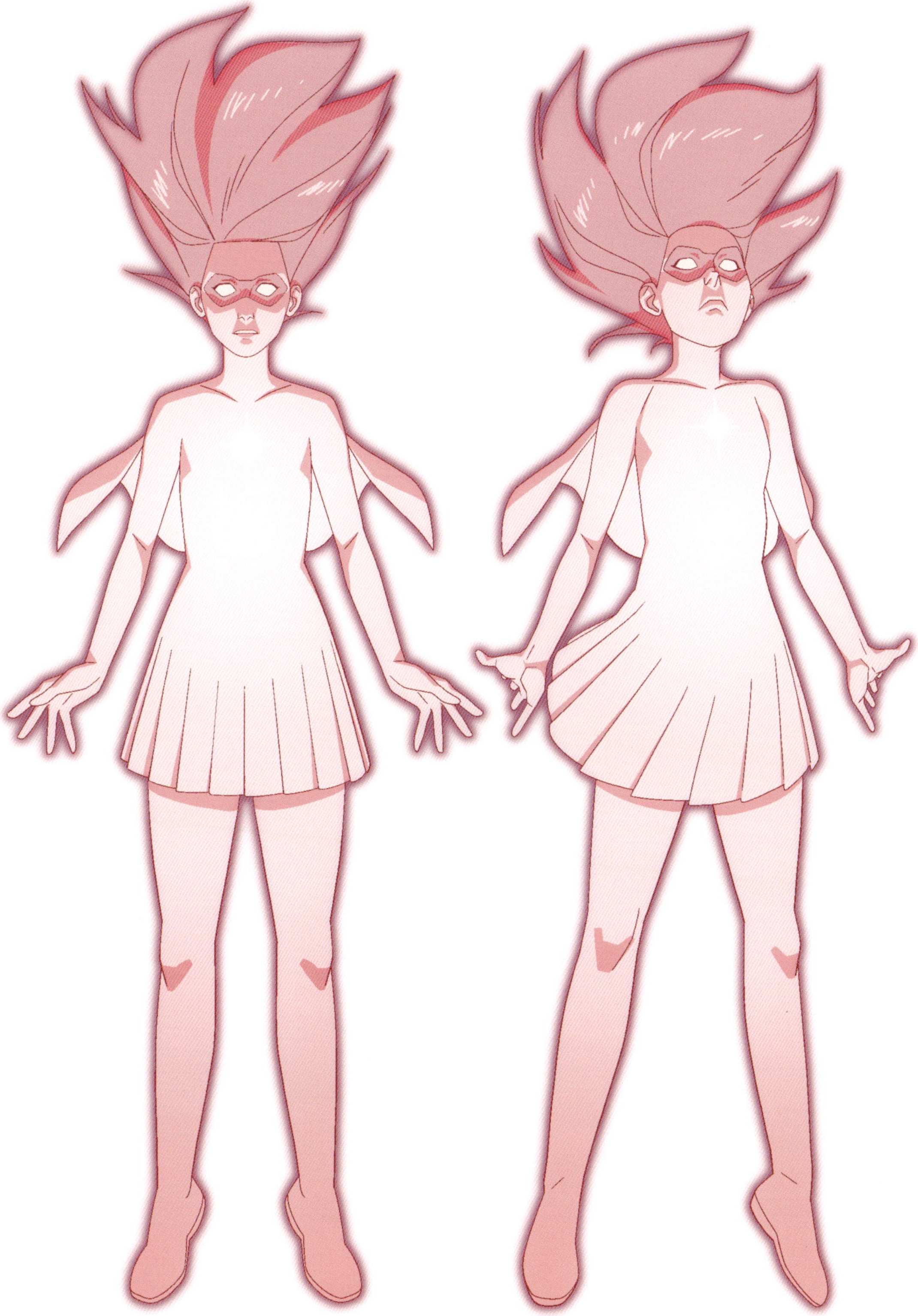

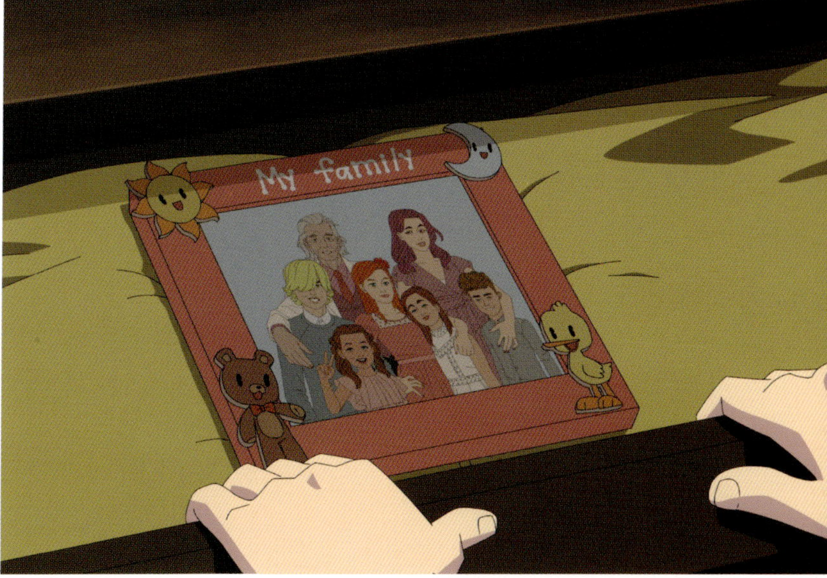

to hit the ground running with this episode at the exact same time. So it's crazy how great all of this stuff is under the conditions that everything was done in, just because we were very much under the gun trying to get this special produced as quickly as possible without sacrificing any quality."

"I think the first time that I really got to see that episode in total was when we went to color correction," says O'Neil, "and it was picture, sound, score, all of the dialogue. And you're watching it on a perfect monitor, and you're like, 'Oh my God. Single tear. We fucking did it.' It was a little emotional because, for all the things that I had been a part of before, where you're on a board team and you do a couple episodes, or you're on a design team and you're a character artist, it's like, 'There's your part.' But I think this was the first time where, after boarding, designing, directing, coming on to this, you are really on something from the start to that very end. And to watch it be complete after going through that entire side of the process was like, 'Holy shit. All right. Let's do the rest of it.'"

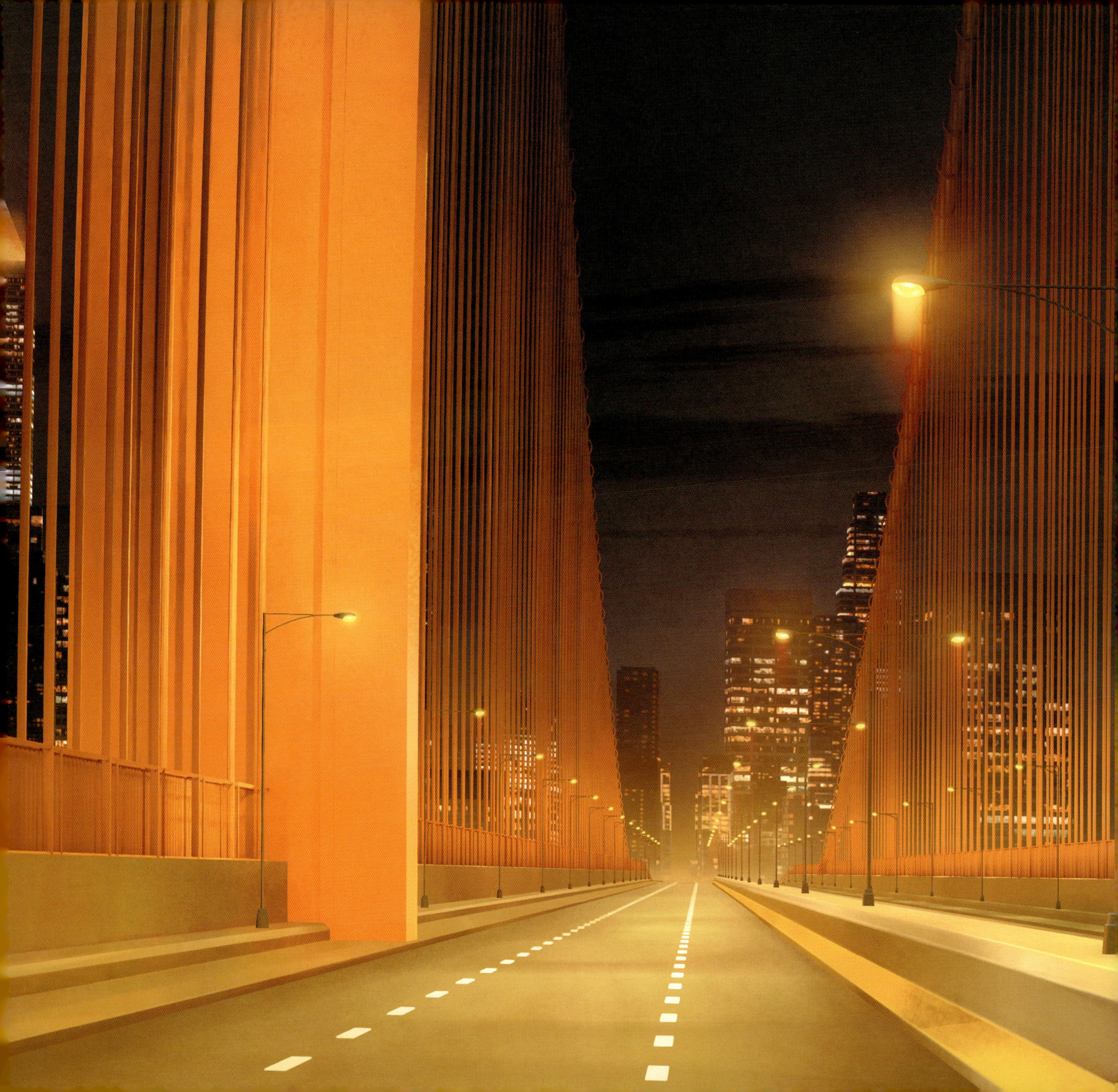

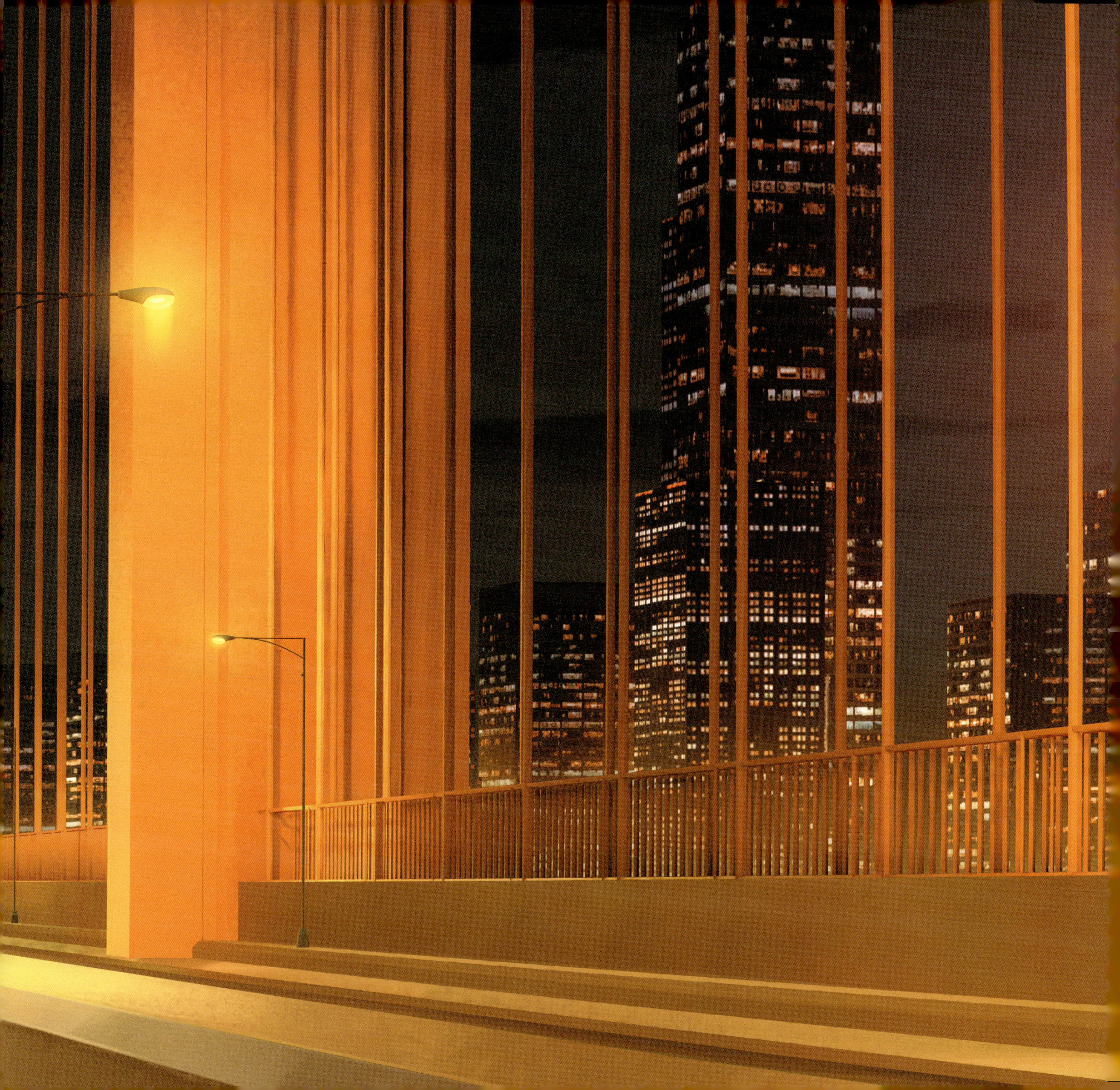

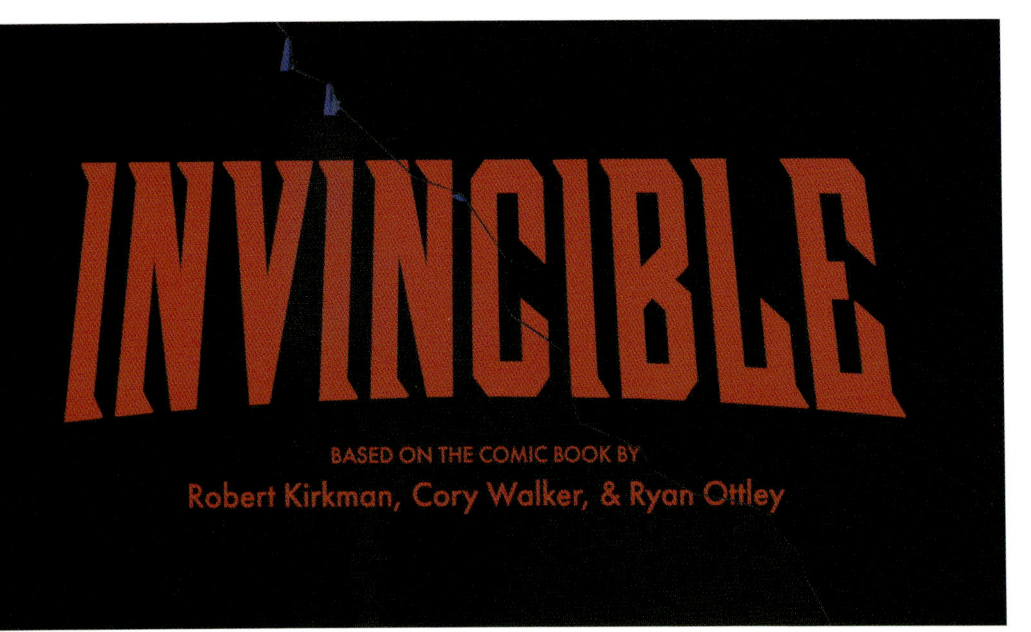
INVINCIBLE
BASED ON THE COMIC BOOK BY
Robert Kirkman, Cory Walker, & Ryan Ottley

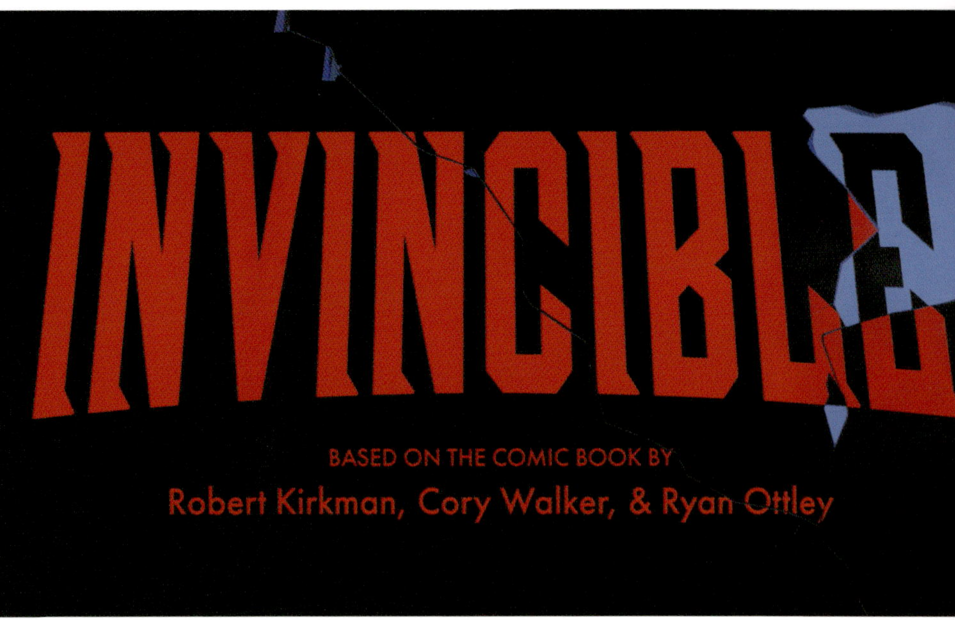
INVINCIBLE
BASED ON THE COMIC BOOK BY
Robert Kirkman, Cory Walker, & Ryan Ottley

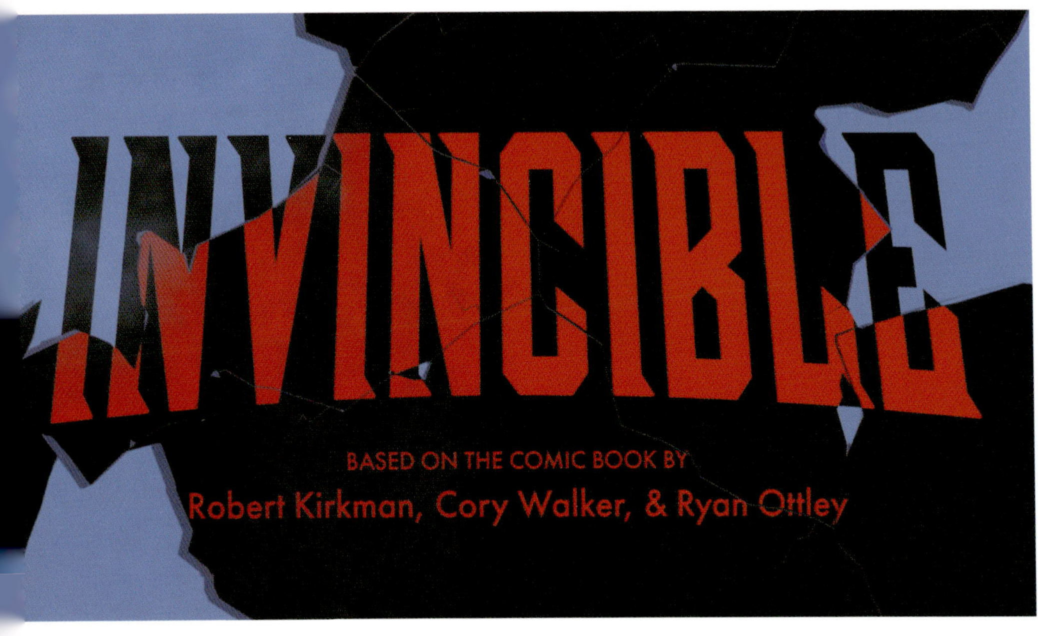
INVINCIBLE
BASED ON THE COMIC BOOK BY
Robert Kirkman, Cory Walker, & Ryan Ottley

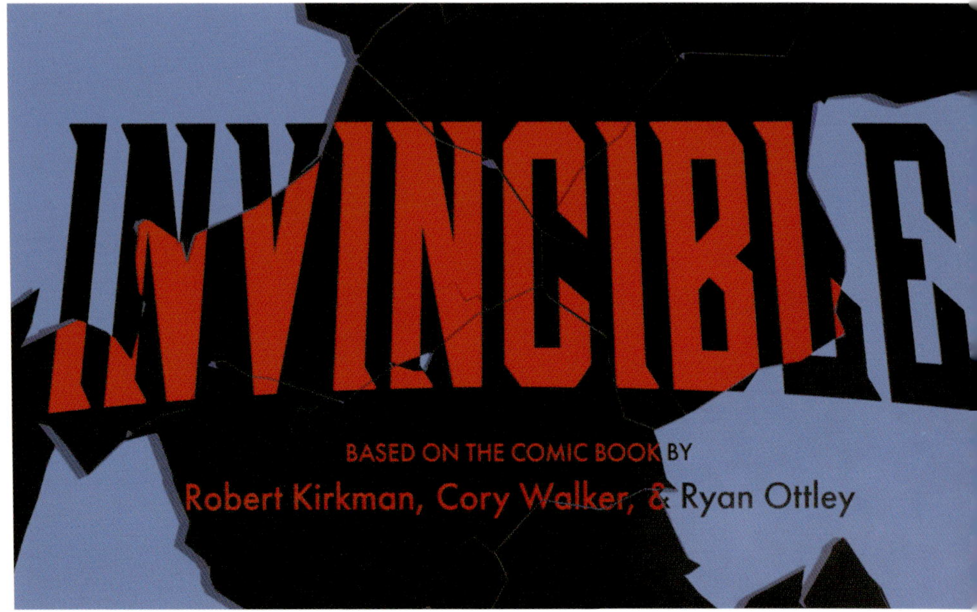
INVINCIBLE
BASED ON THE COMIC BOOK BY
Robert Kirkman, Cory Walker, & Ryan Ottley

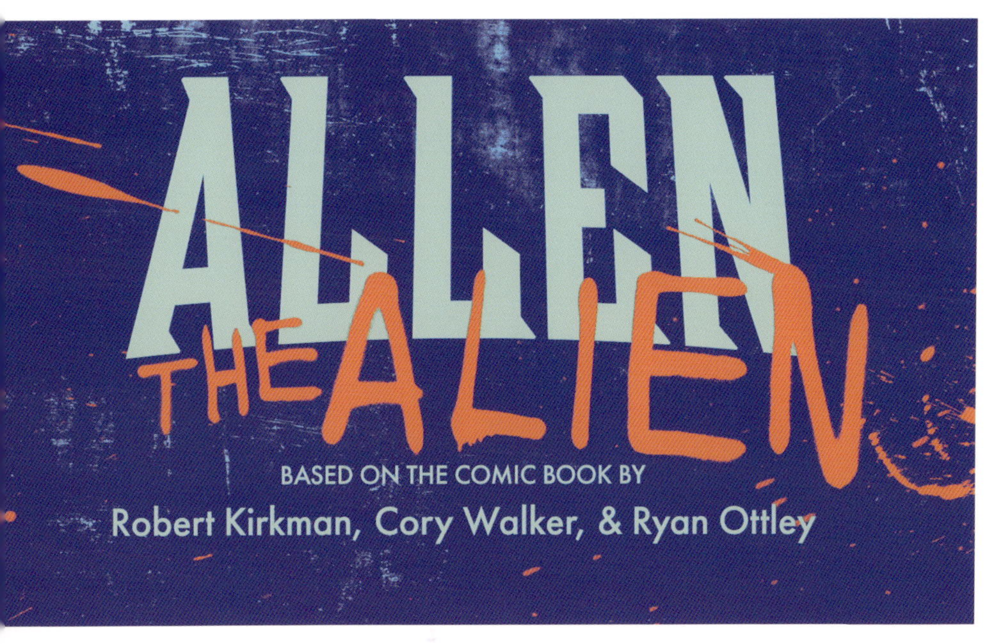
ALLEN
THE ALIEN
BASED ON THE COMIC BOOK BY
Robert Kirkman, Cory Walker, & Ryan Ottley

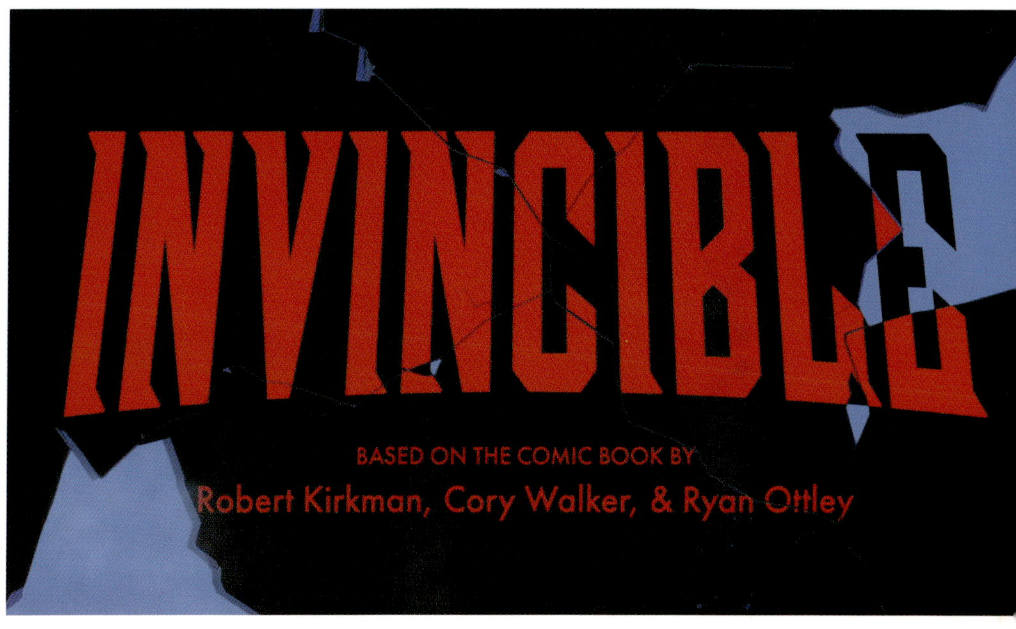
INVINCIBLE
BASED ON THE COMIC BOOK BY
Robert Kirkman, Cory Walker, & Ryan Ottley

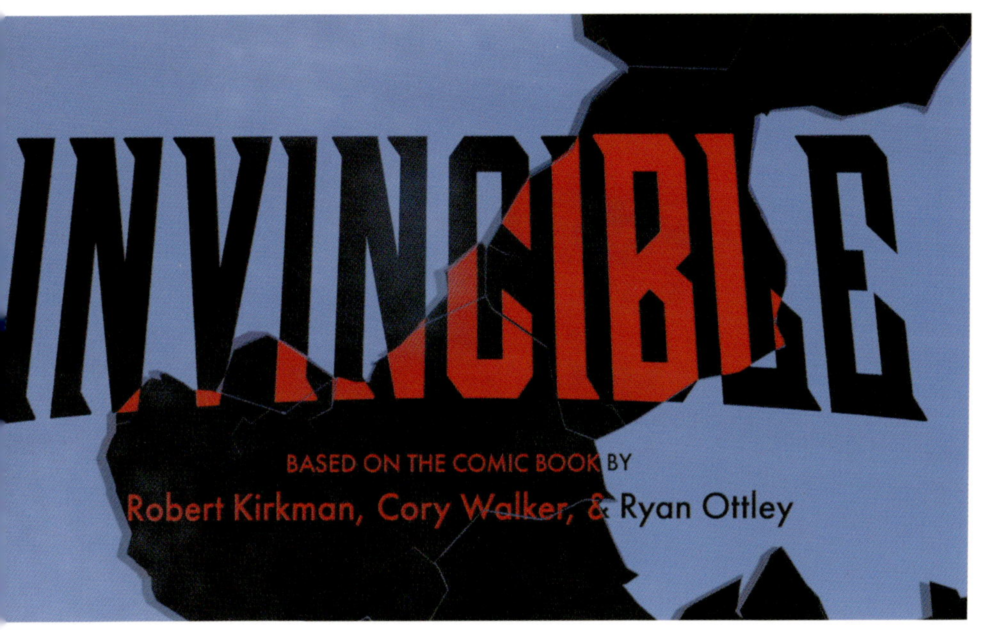
INVINCIBLE
BASED ON THE COMIC BOOK BY
Robert Kirkman, Cory Walker, & Ryan Ottley

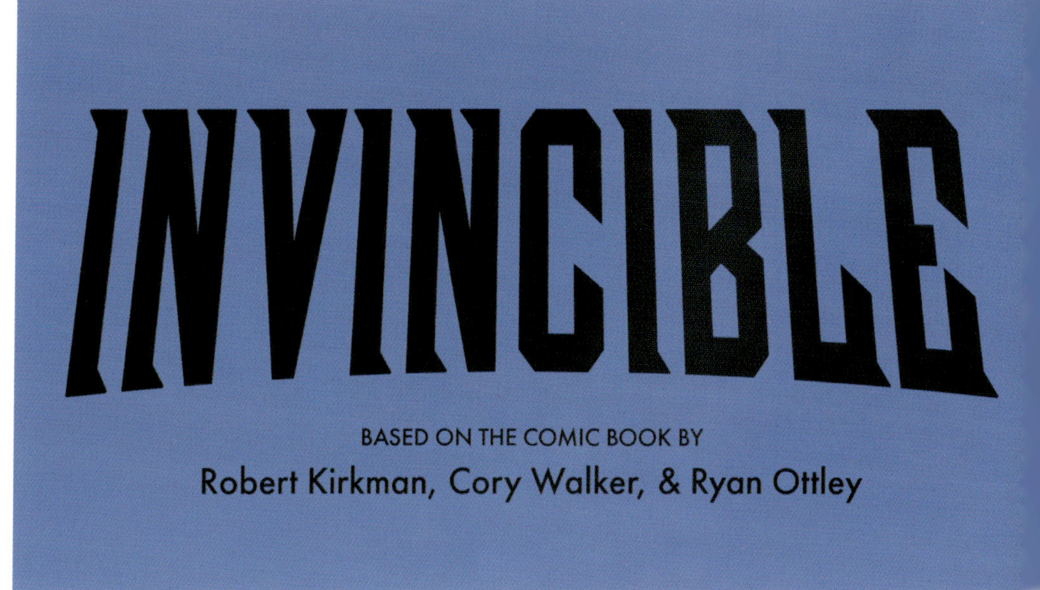
INVINCIBLE
BASED ON THE COMIC BOOK BY
Robert Kirkman, Cory Walker, & Ryan Ottley

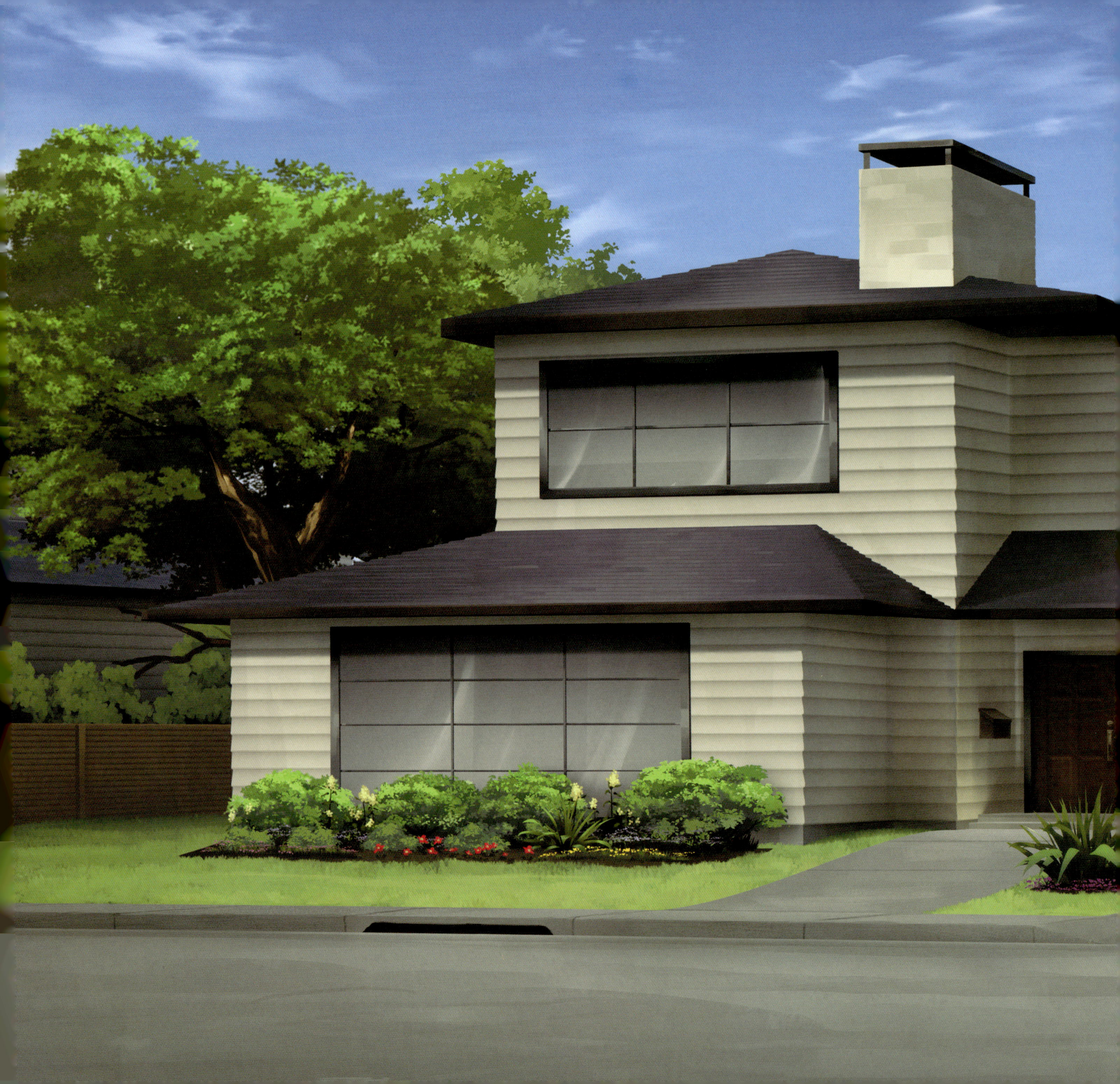

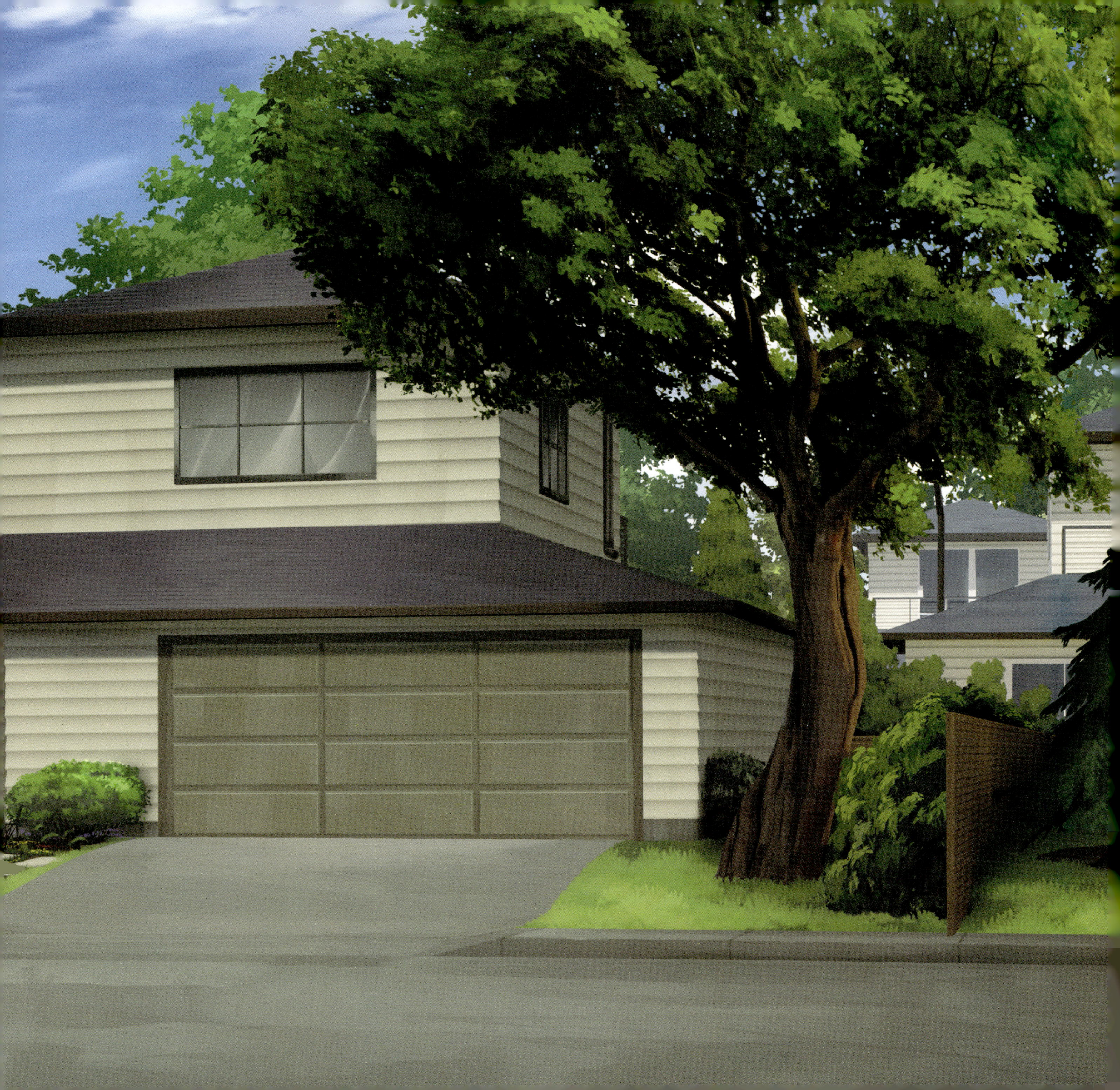

EPISODE 1:

A LESSON FOR YOUR NEXT LIFE

By the time the first official episode of *Invincible* Season Two dropped on Prime Video November 3, 2023, over two-and-a-half years had passed since the release of the Season One finale. As such, it was important to bring viewers back into the fold in an exciting and original way.

"That opening sequence for Season Two was cool because we knew that there would be this gap," says Executive Producer, Co-Showrunner, and Co-Creator Robert Kirkman, "and we knew that fans would be coming into Season Two like, 'Okay, impress me. We've had to wait a long time.' We very much felt like we were going to have to hook the audience again. Or at least we prepared for that. It turns out that the audience was very excited for Season Two and was 100% there. And that really shocked us. But we kind of came in feeling like we had to prove ourselves again and we had to entice people into loving the show again. And so that's why we started with this bizarre sequence where you're kind of reintroduced to the characters, but they're not the same characters. I loved the idea of people coming in going, 'Did I miss an episode? What's going on? I don't understand this at all!'"

The opening of the season premiere, set in a dystopian world where Invincible and Omni-Man had conquered Earth, was designed to leave viewers wondering what could have happened between episodes. However, the length of time between seasons meant that the creators had to be cautious

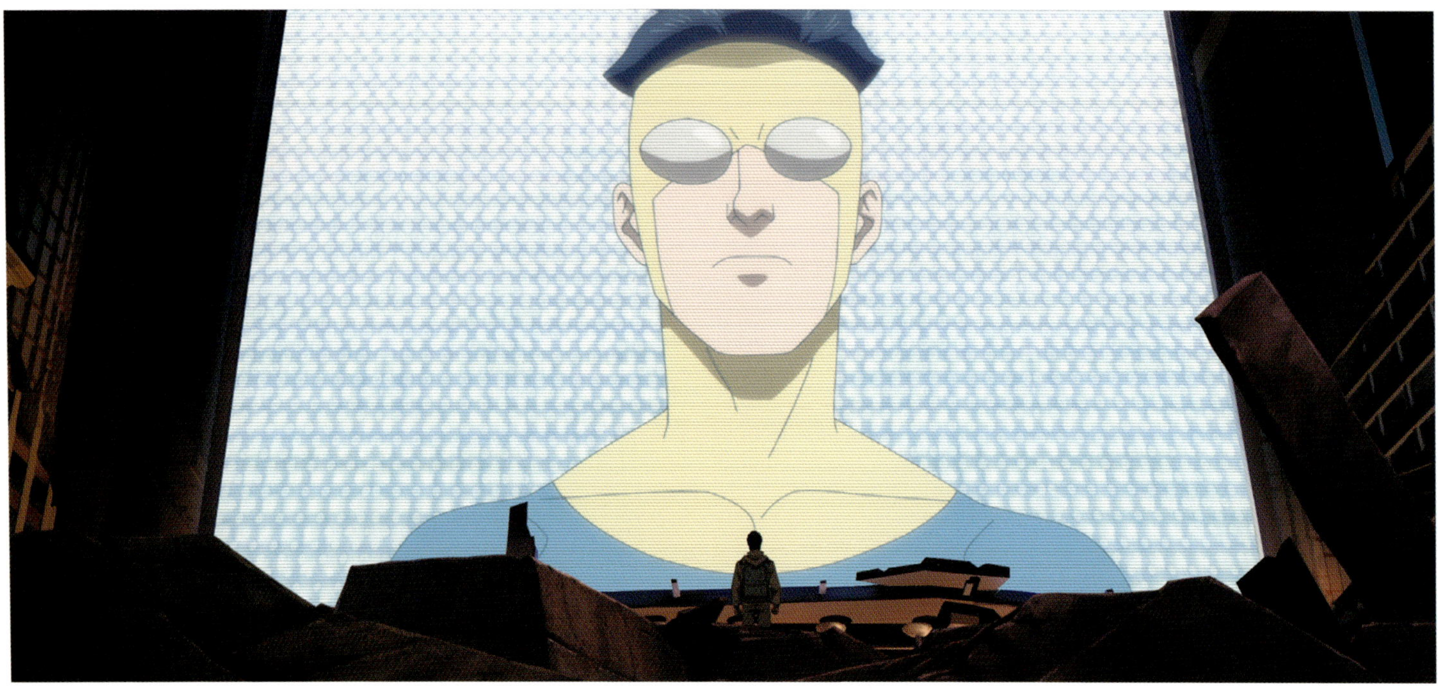

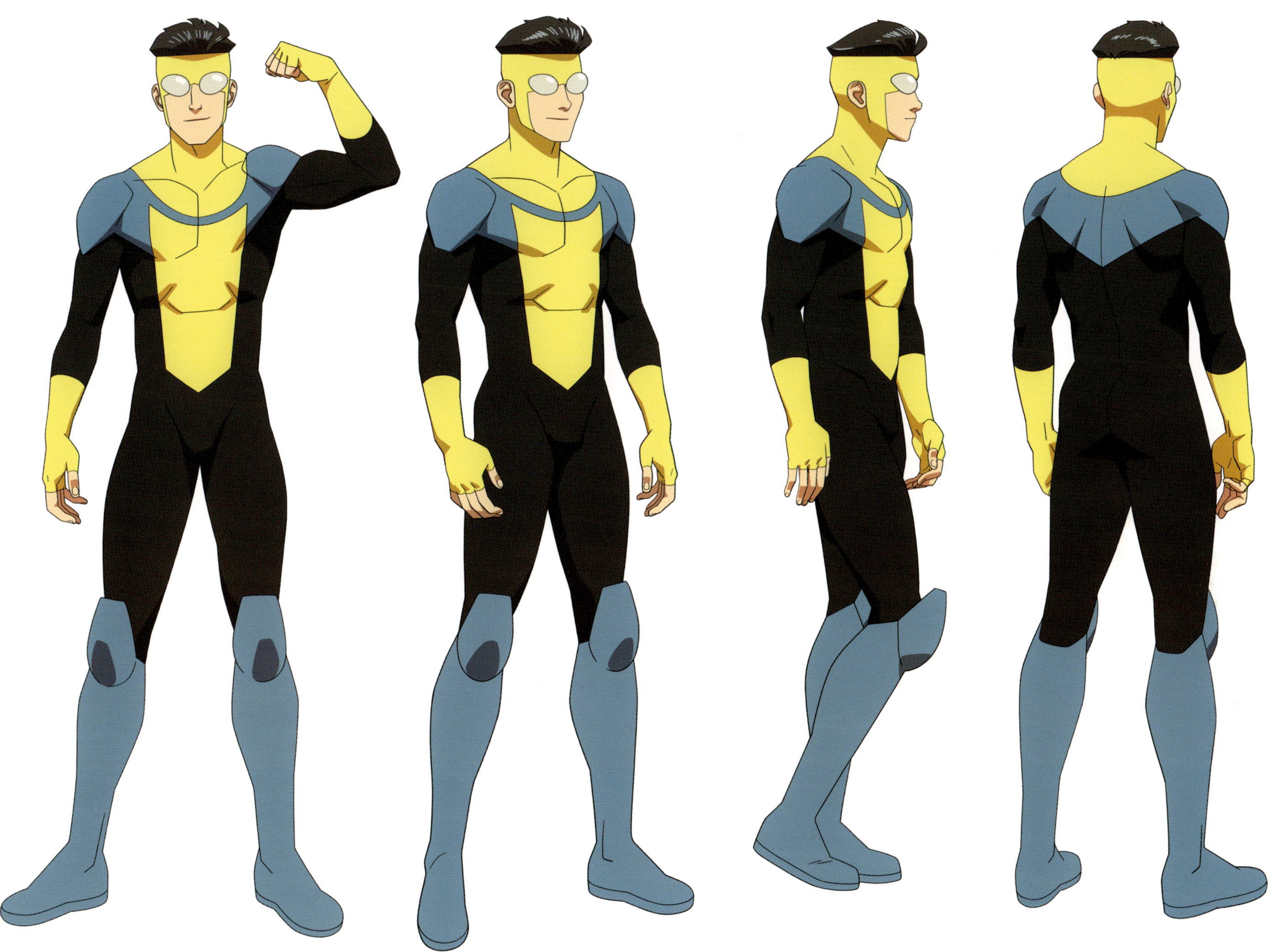

about just how disorienting the sequence ended up being.

"Originally, we had a much longer opening set in the alternate dimension," says Executive Producer and Co-Showrunner Simon Racioppa, "because we didn't think our gap was going to be that long. So, we had this much longer sequence set in the other world, following Angstrom [Levy] and some of the resistance members as they were trying to free the Immortal, who was being held as bait to lure them out by an evil Mark and an evil Omni-Man. And what we decided when it looked like our gap was going to be longer than we thought, we wanted to make that a little shorter to get the audience back to our Mark sooner. So that sequence got a little truncated. I think it still works well, maybe it's even better. Usually with television and film, if you can make something a little more distilled, if you can make it a little shorter, it's usually better to begin with. So

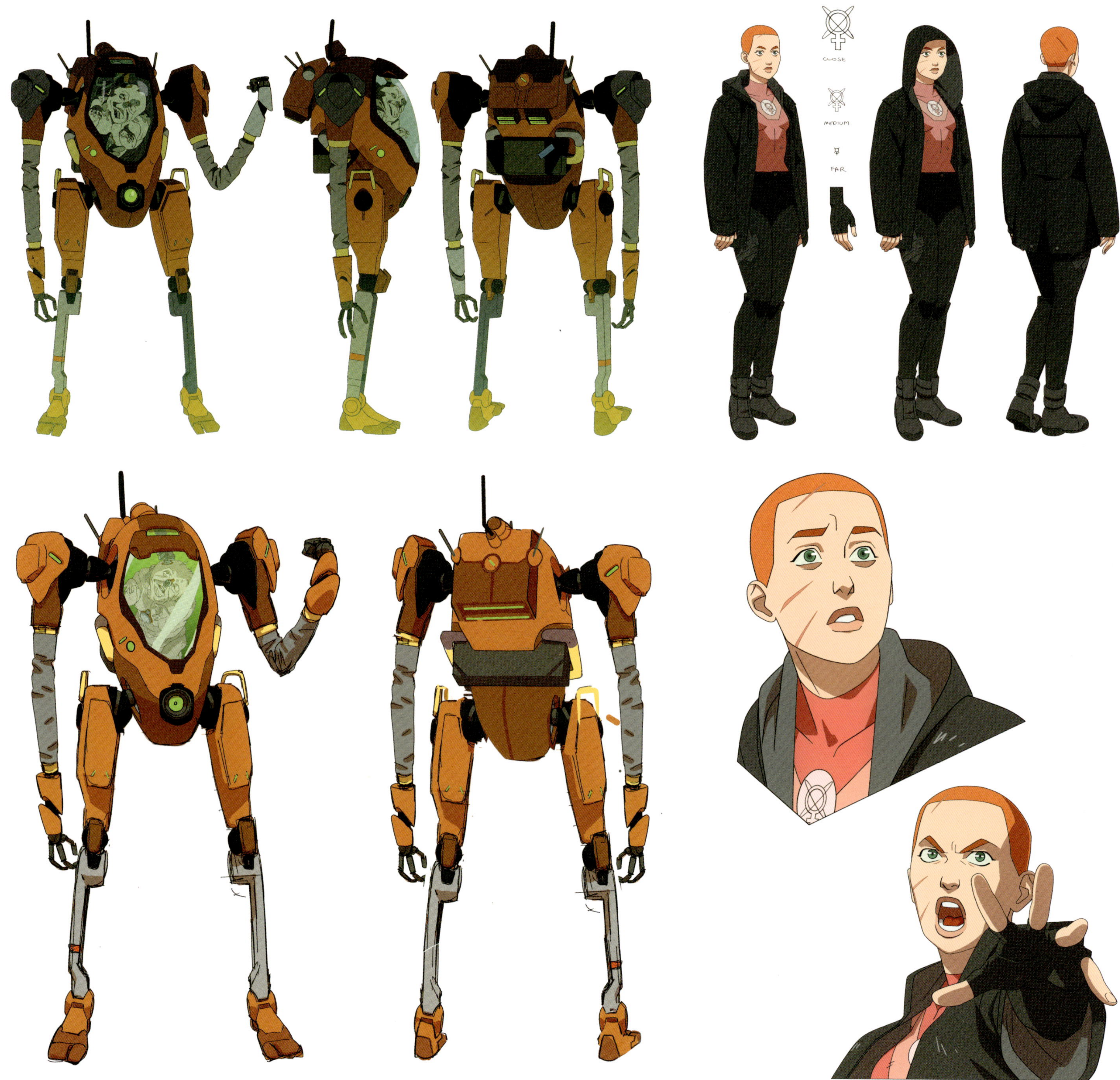
CLOSE
MEDIUM
FAR

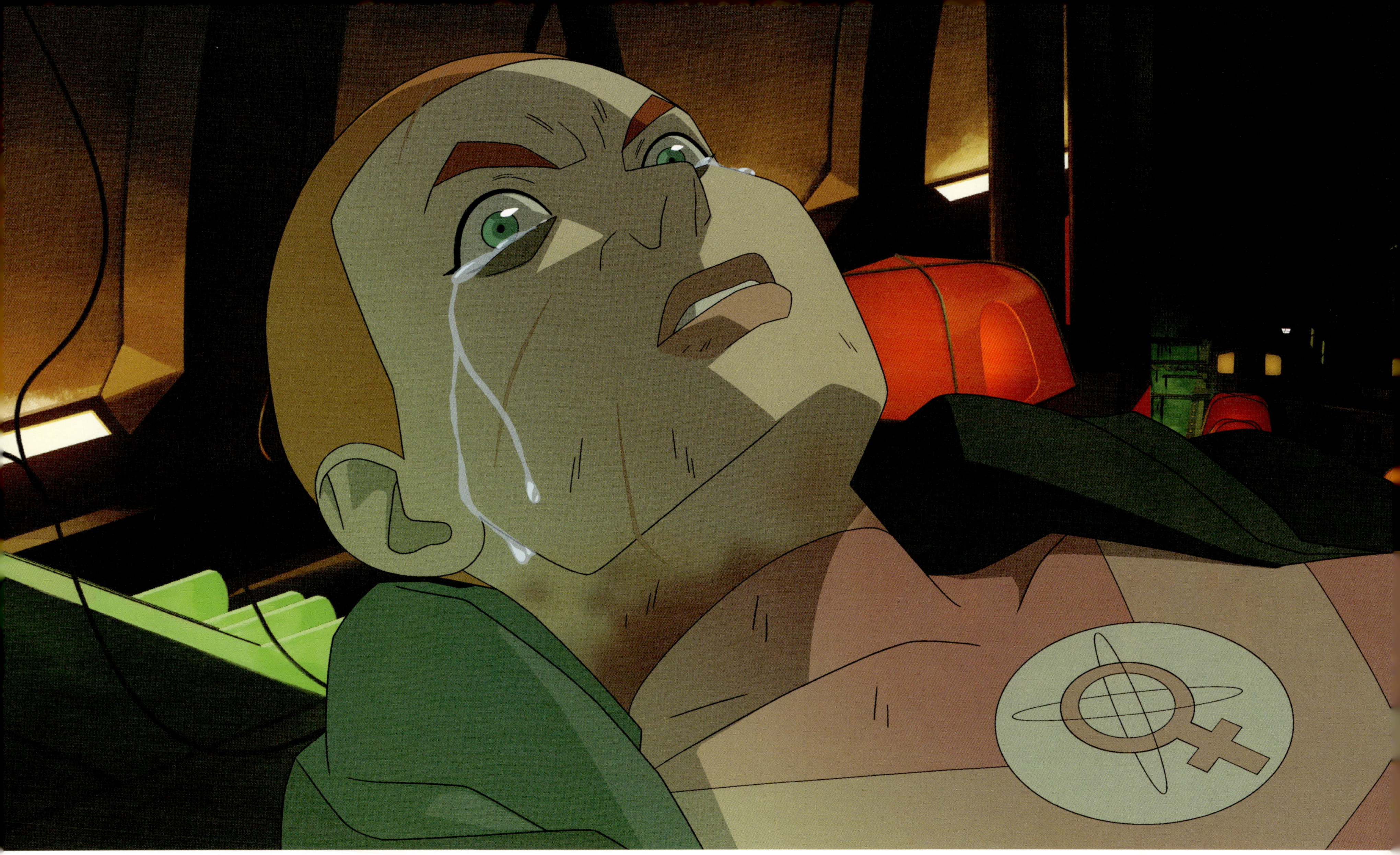

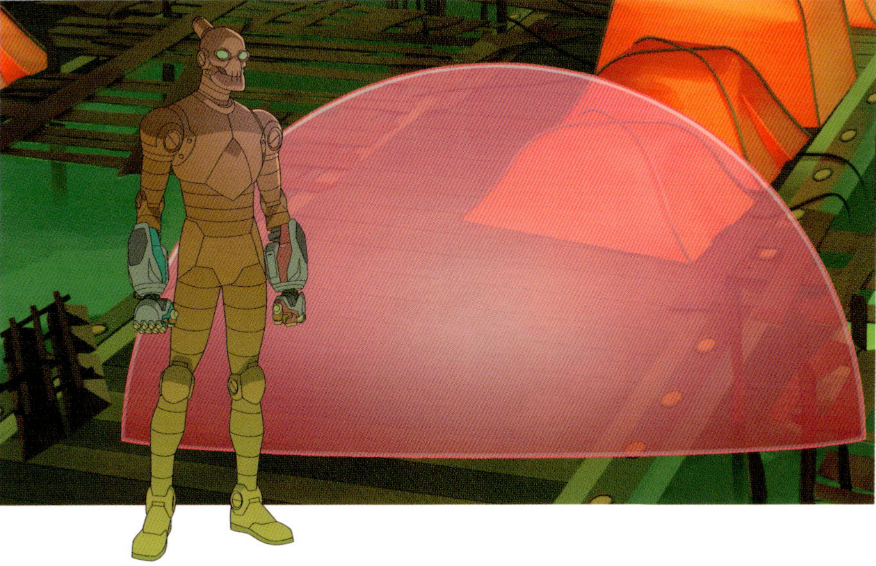

this was potentially the better version that we made and the audience has seen. It's a fun start."

Even though the sequence may have been trimmed down, it still introduced a number of exciting design elements right off the bat, including some interdimensional variants of popular characters.

"It gave us a cool, altered Robot," says Kirkman. "And we got to bring back the Rudy in the tank from Season One, in a way, with his cool mechanized body that was a little bit more mobile than when we saw him last time. And our dystopian future Eve, with her shaved head and her tough jacket and everything — the no-nonsense, scarred-up Eve — was pretty cool."

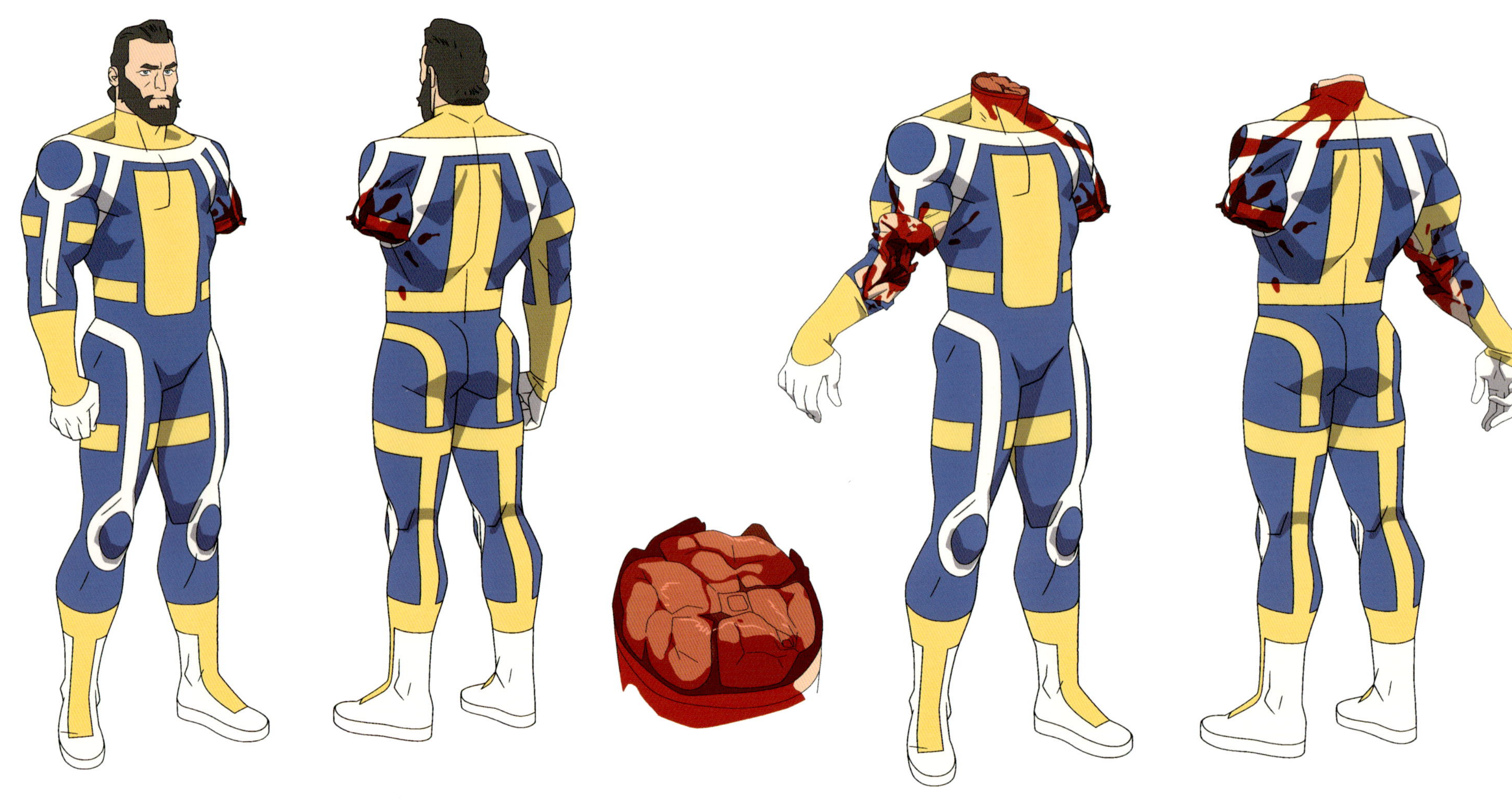

"It feels kind of gross and basic to say it," says Co-Executive Producer and Co-Creator Cory Walker, "but I am a bit of a sucker for alternate takes on characters I know and love. Especially our own characters. I really liked all this stuff we were able to do in that alternate dimension."

The opening sequence's alternate reality setting also allowed for the return of a character who had been taken off the board at the end of Season One, as well as the introduction of a brand new threat who would carry through the rest of Season Two.

"It was a cool way to get Omni-Man back in the show from the get-go," says Kirkman, "because Omni-Man's not the core of the show, but a very, very important and very popular element of the show. And so by starting in the alternate dimension and introducing Angstrom Levy, our season villain, through that sequence, it gave us that added bonus of being able to have Omni-Man present."

With the bait-and-switch of the episode's opening, the creative team hoped to set the tone for the rest of the season, alerting both returning fans and new viewers alike that they should expect the unexpected.

"I'd love to know," says Racioppa, "if someone was watching the show without reading the comic books, how long were they fooled before they realized it was another dimension? Was that satisfying or did they feel like they were ripped off? I don't know."

As the episode transitioned back to the reality — and the Invincible — that viewers know and love, Mark was struggling to deal with the aftermath of his clash with his father.

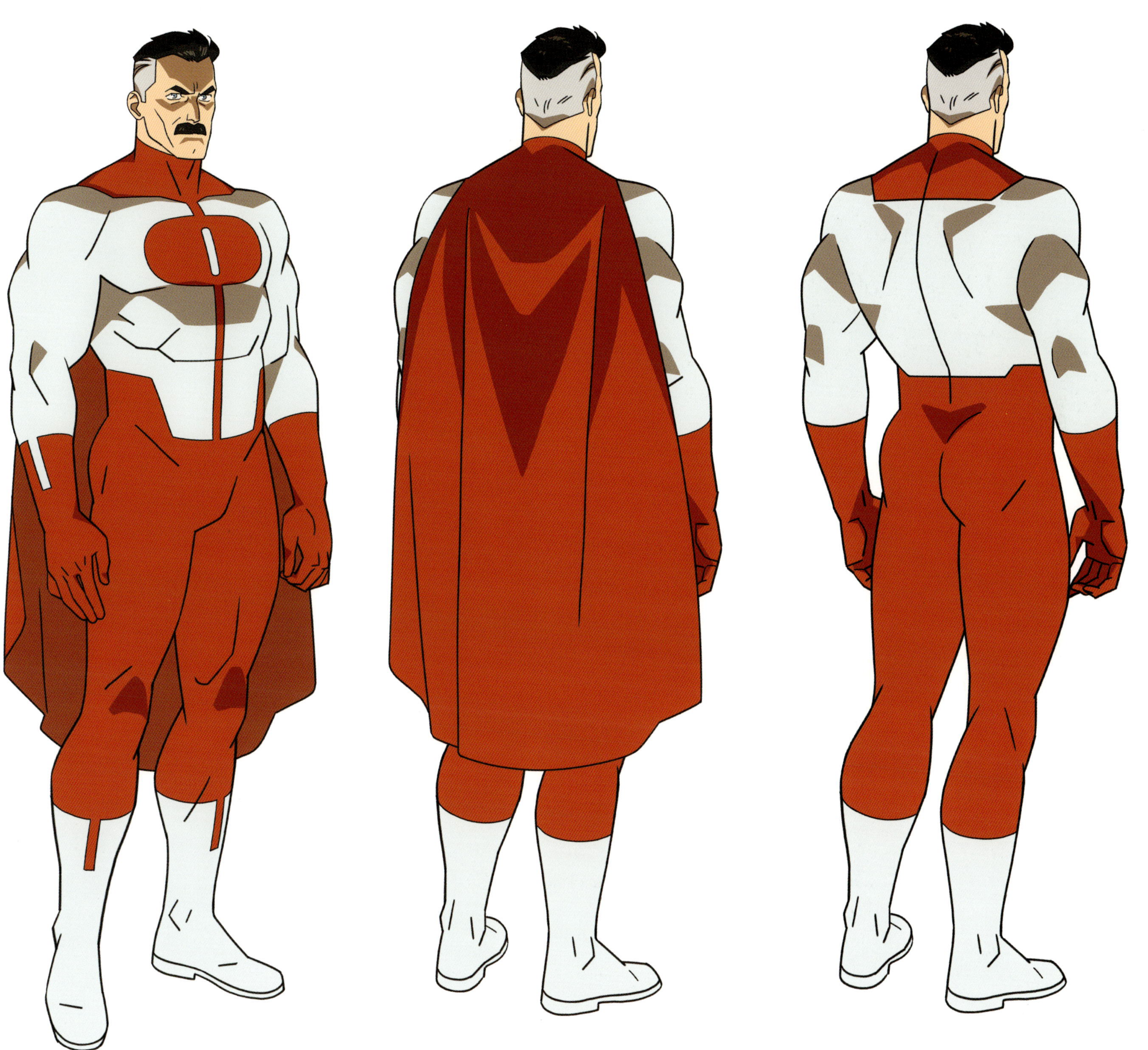

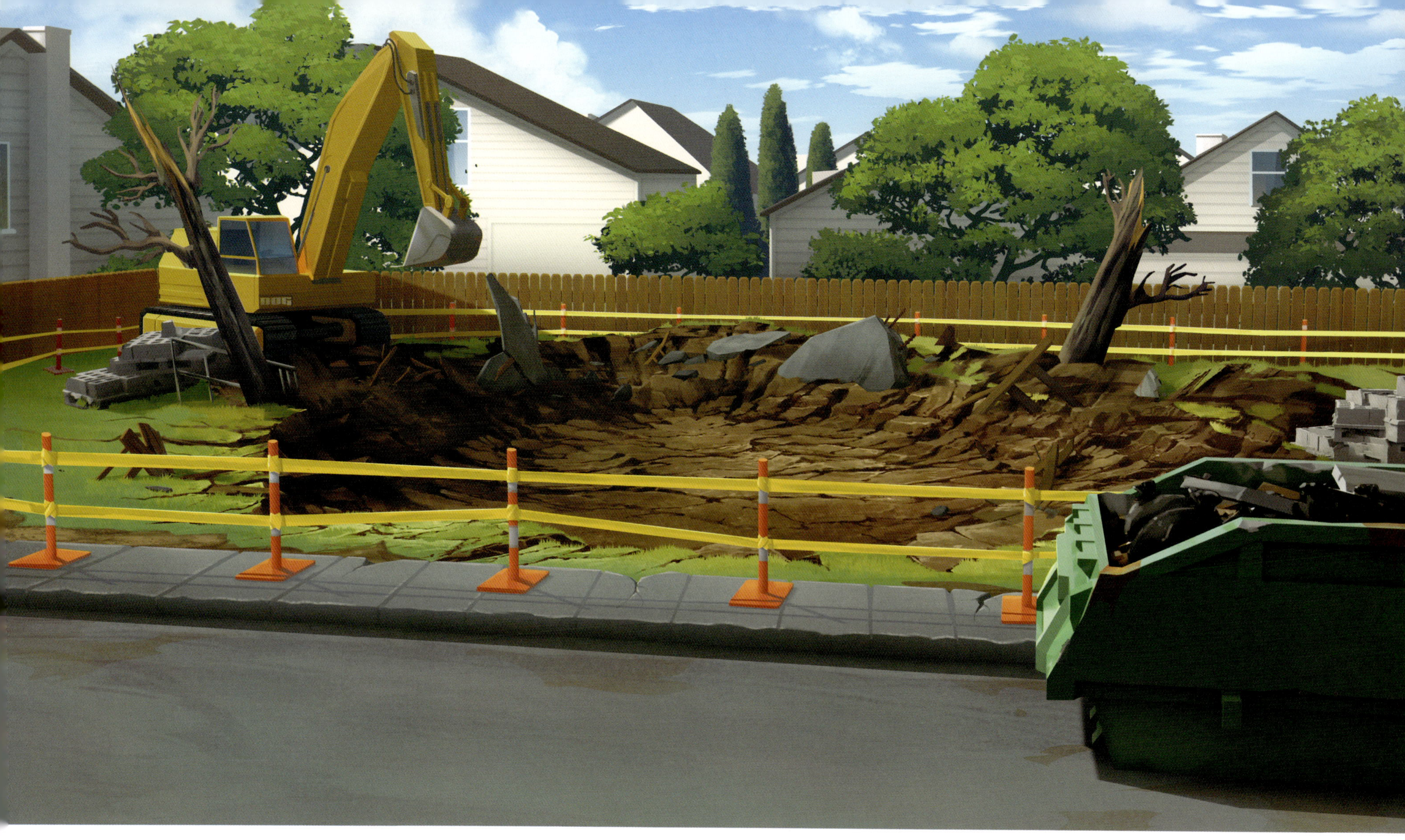

"The big thing for me was that, when we loop back and start with our Mark again, Mark had to be in a similar headspace to where he was at the end of [Episode] 108," says Racioppa. "The big thing about *Invincible*, and I think the promise of the show, is that we don't reset things. We never reset our characters, we never reset the world. Obviously, Spider-Man's been running for years, but there's sequences where you can jump in where he doesn't seem to remember the stuff that happened to him two years ago. And with Mark, the end of Season One was very fresh in his mind. He's not in a good space in Season Two. So that was really important for me, that we capture that in terms of the look of the show — even some of the lighting stuff on that day, when he's still sort of trying to fight crime but not really feeling it — and in his body language, too. He comes and lands on the roof and takes off his mask and just sits there with his head in his hands. I think that proves to the audience, hopefully, that we're not a standard superhero show. We're not resetting things. This is one story, and we're picking up literally weeks after [Season One]."

While it was essential to get across Mark's state of mind, it was equally important to get viewers back up to speed on the state of the world after Omni-Man's attack.

"You have to hit the new status quo," says Supervising Director Dan Duncan. "Omni-Man has beaten Mark half-to-death, and then left the planet — and his wife. The world is a

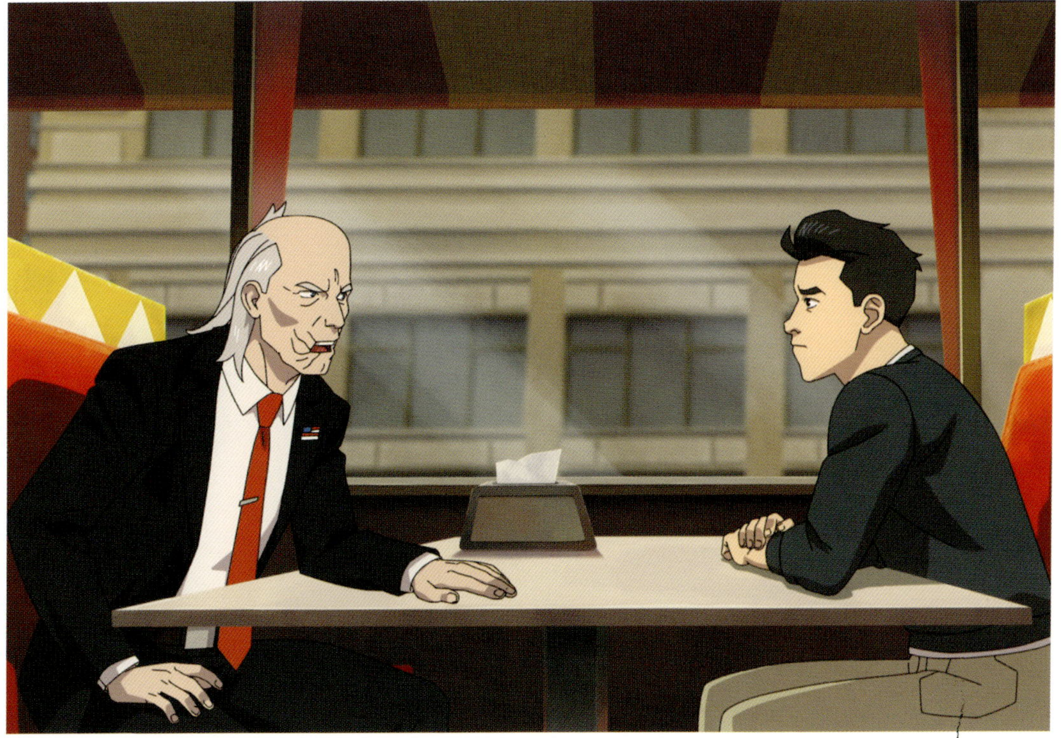

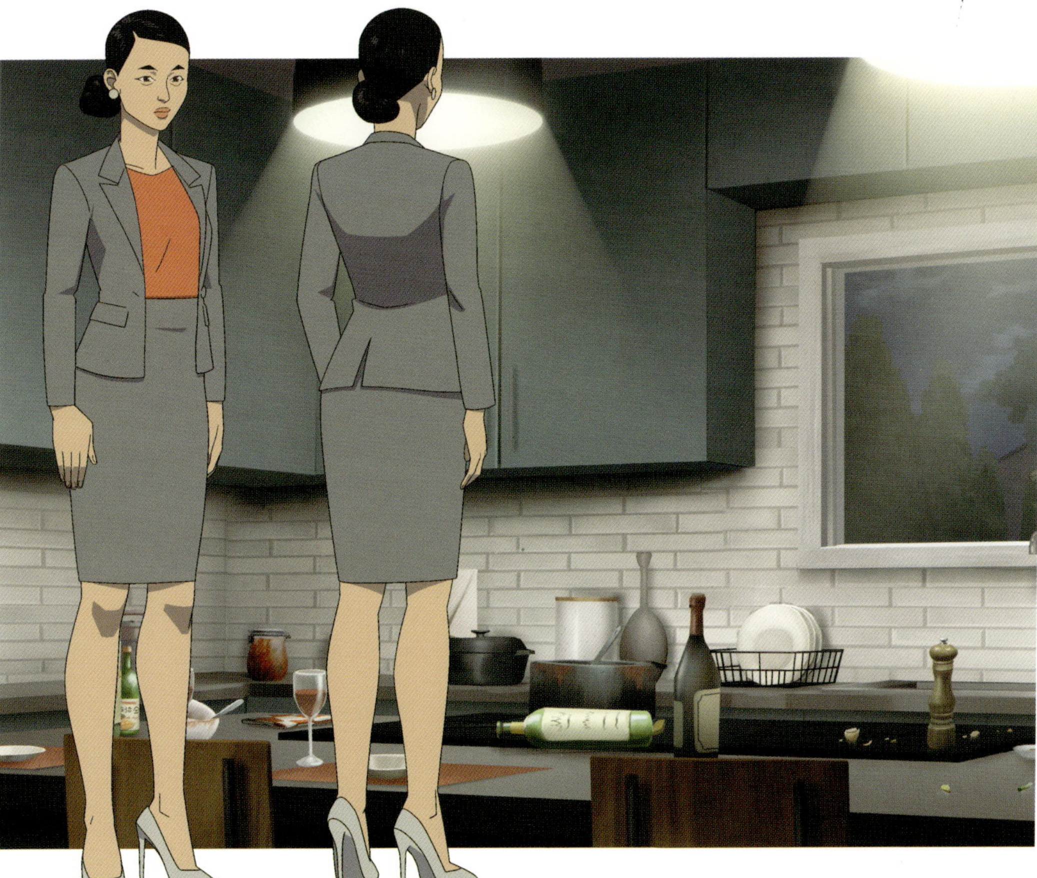

very different place. The story is in a very different place."

Returning to a more familiar world also gave the team a chance to draw on some existing design assets, lightening the load a bit in comparison to the *Atom Eve* special.

"With *Atom Eve*, we had a lot of characters who were brand new," says Art Director Shaun O'Neil. "And so, character-wise, you're building facial structures that have to fit inside the show, but are completely new and fresh. They have to feel like individuals, apart from any sort template reuse stuff that you would do in a season. Same with environments. It's a lot of places that you don't see. So the nice part [about episode 201] was getting to kind of dive into some stuff what was familiar, that did have some background to it."

The team also got to benefit from some exploratory work that had been done in advance of Season Two being greenlit.

"We got to use some of the material that had been left over from the Season One team," says O'Neil, "when they had started Season Two and then got put on pause. We got midway through our pre-production phase and found a wealth of unfinished projects. And it was just like, 'Oh, hey, we have a lot of stuff here we can work with.' So taking it all, retrofitting it, stuffing some of the ideas we had in progress into it, and get rid of what we needed to get rid of was super helpful."

One location that remained in the same dire state that it had last appeared in during Season One was the decimated Global Defense Agency monitoring station located across the street from the Grayson family home.

"It's a nice visual reminder that we're not resetting the world," says Racioppa. "That this still happened. This is still weighing on them. Every time they step out their door, across the street there's a reminder of what they just went through. And we reference that very directly in Episode One where [Mark and Debbie] come out and they look at it, and then they're like, 'Are you ready to go back to work? Are you ready to go back to school? Okay, let's do this.' And then they sort of go off. But again, they still carry the trauma that they both have from Season One through the rest of this season."

While the GDA's secret base may have remained obliterated, a fan-favorite character who was caught in that destruction — GDA Agent Donald Ferguson — made an unexpected return.

"Everybody loves Donald," says Racioppa. "We wanted to bring Donald back. But also, like, 'Wait a second. Didn't something happen to Donald?' That was actually really fun, because we didn't say anything off the bat. We just wanted to have Donald back in the show and have people be like, 'Did they screw up? Did they forget that they killed Donald?' Because we put him on the poster, and people were like, 'Didn't that guy explode in Season One?' Which is exactly the response we wanted. We wanted to start a conversation about that, and then just slowly introduce you and then give you his story — show you why he's back, how he's back, and what the effect is on him. So that was a fun story to give him. Everybody seemed to like him from Season One. Chris Diamantopoulos plays him so well. So we're like, 'Let's give Donald some more screen time. Let's get into his story a bit more.'"

As one character made his mysterious return, another made his animated debut looking almost identical to how he appeared in the comics that inspired the series.

"Our approach was, 'If it ain't broke, don't fix it,'" says Kirkman. "This show is so massive and so sprawling, and there are so many new characters being introduced. If there was anything from the comics that seemed like it could be adapted more-or-less directly, our efforts are to try and do that. And so Bulletproof is kind of a seamless introduction that very much follows the way he looks in the comics."

As the episode progressed, it became clear that the opening sequence in the alternate dimension was more than just a throwaway scene. One of the characters that appeared there, Angstrom Levy, would soon go on to become Mark's nemesis.

"Angstrom is the big new character in Season Two," says Racioppa. "And he's also the first villain that is all Mark's. He's not an Omni-Man villain. He doesn't come from the GDA. He didn't pre-exist Mark. He comes from Mark's experience. Mark was there when he was created. So that

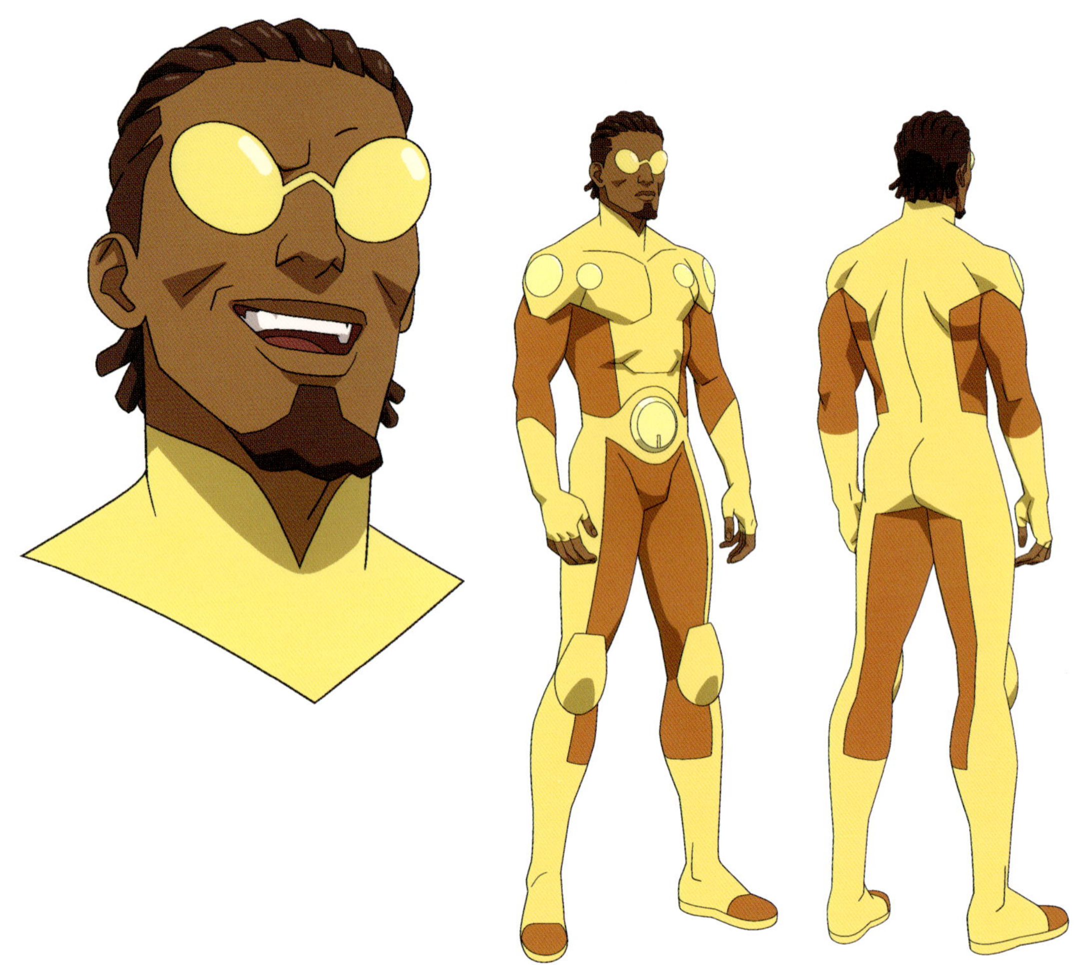

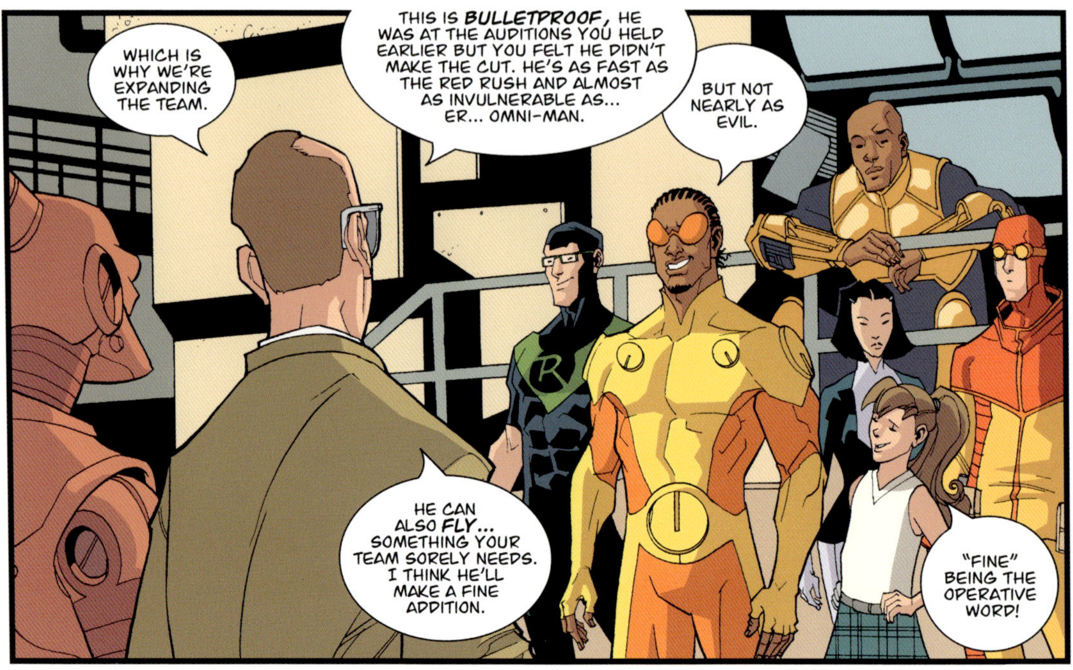

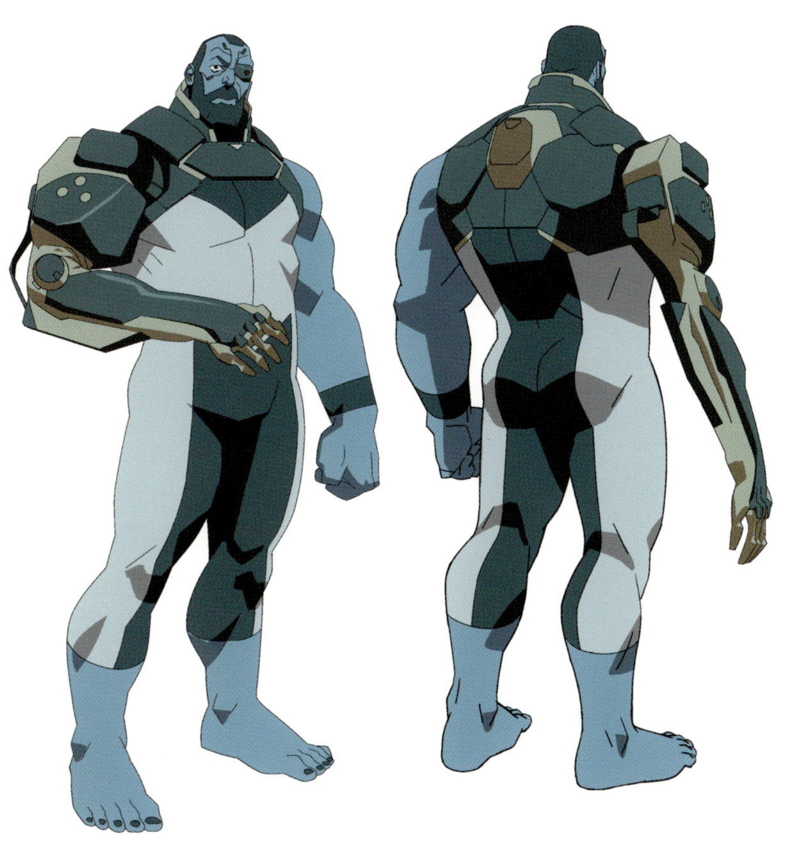

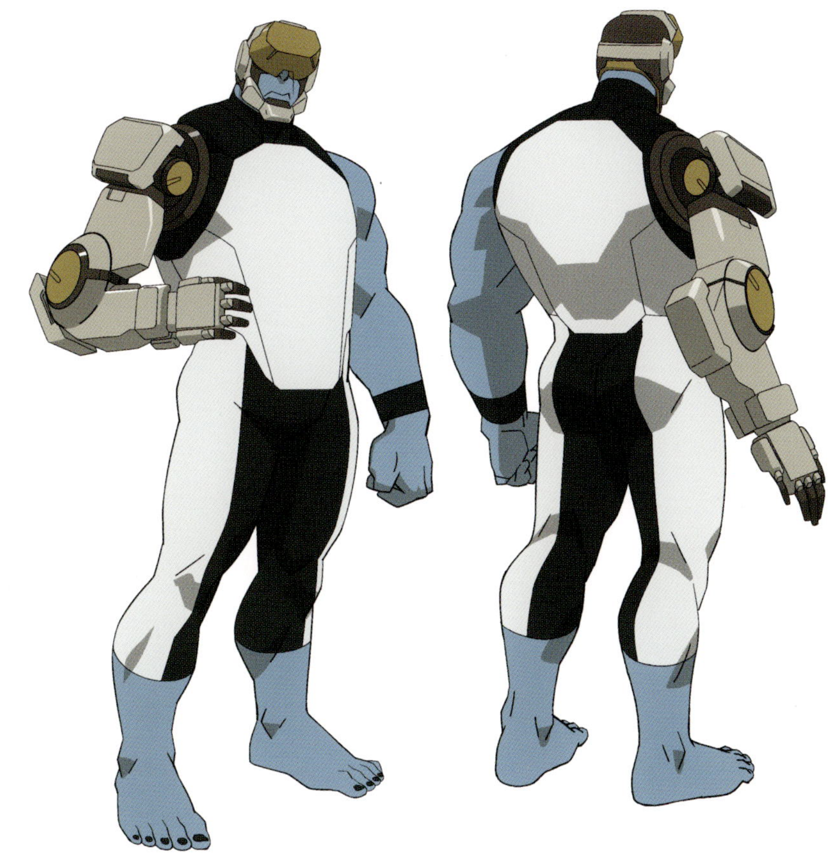

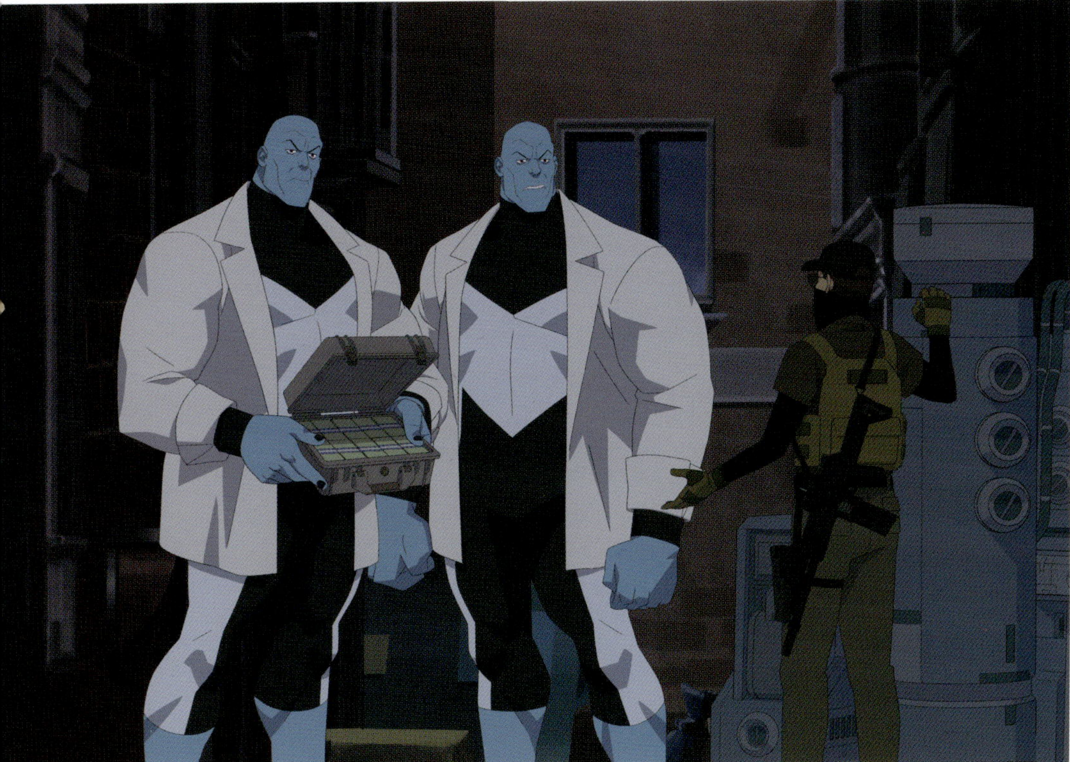

sort of ties him to Mark and gives them a relationship that will stretch across the whole season and potentially future seasons."

Levy's ability to open interdimensional portals created a scenario where the team's character designers had to create dozens of alternate looks for Levy and his associates, the blue-skinned scientists known as the Maulers.

"This was a difficult season as a whole design-wise because of Angstrom Levy," says Kirkman. "Just in this episode, you can see there's a tremendous amount of assets, because Angstrom brings in this multiverse element where it's like, 'Okay, now you have to design thirty different Maulers.' But the design team really had a good time with that. And there's some that we were like, 'These are the coolest things ever, but maybe this is a little too far.' There's definitely some things, here and there, where some amazing designs were left on the cutting room floor just because they were a little bit too unique or a little bit too cool and didn't necessarily fit the scene."

"I fortunately didn't have to be in the dirt for that," says Walker. "I hope that it was mostly fun for the team. Because you have a few that are important to the story and have to feel and look a certain way. But I'm sure you can tell looking through the material or watching the episode, there are a couple of them that they just went to town on and had a lot of fun. I imagine, especially with Angstrom, trying to keep him recognizable is a bit of a challenge, because he's just a guy, right? Maulers, you can kind of go wild as long as they're big and blue-skinned. Like, there's a lady Mauler, and you don't wonder for a second, 'Is that a Mauler?' You just know. There are some fun and funny ones in the mix. There are a lot of Maulers that are really cool."

"That was the biggest challenge," says O'Neil, "just the character count between those two. The Maulers had a bunch of alternate versions and Angstrom had a bunch of alternate versions."

It wasn't just the number of different takes on the characters themselves that was an issue in terms of design. It was also the technology that those characters created. Bringing to life the enormous mind-transfer device that Levy used to siphon the memories from his dimensional duplicates — known as a Somatic Encoder — posed a unique challenge for the art team.

"I think we call that the Christmas tree," says Kirkman, "but maybe that was just Cory and I. In the comics, I think it seated four or five on each arm. And there was some discussion about simplifying things, and we eventually fell on there being three Angstroms on each side of each arm. That's the kind of stuff that makes animation a little bit more doable. But it's funny to see this crazy, complicated, weird thing that [*Invincible* artist and contributing creator] Ryan [Ottley] designed for the comics get translated into the show, and all of a sudden you've got people going, 'How does this work in 3D? How can we show this from different angles and make sure that it's consistent?' These are all the considerations we don't have to think about in comics."

"Sometimes you'd think taking something from one place

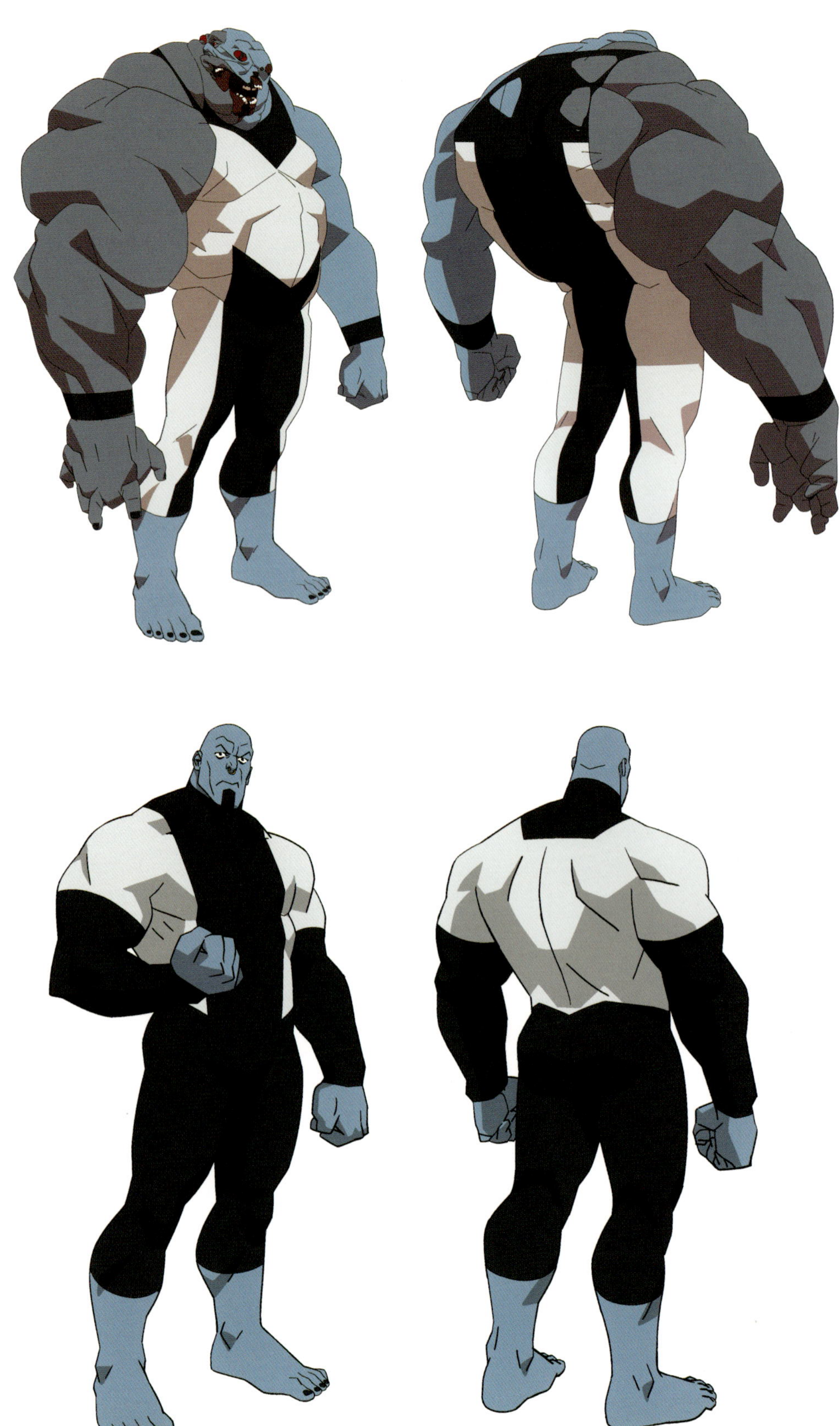

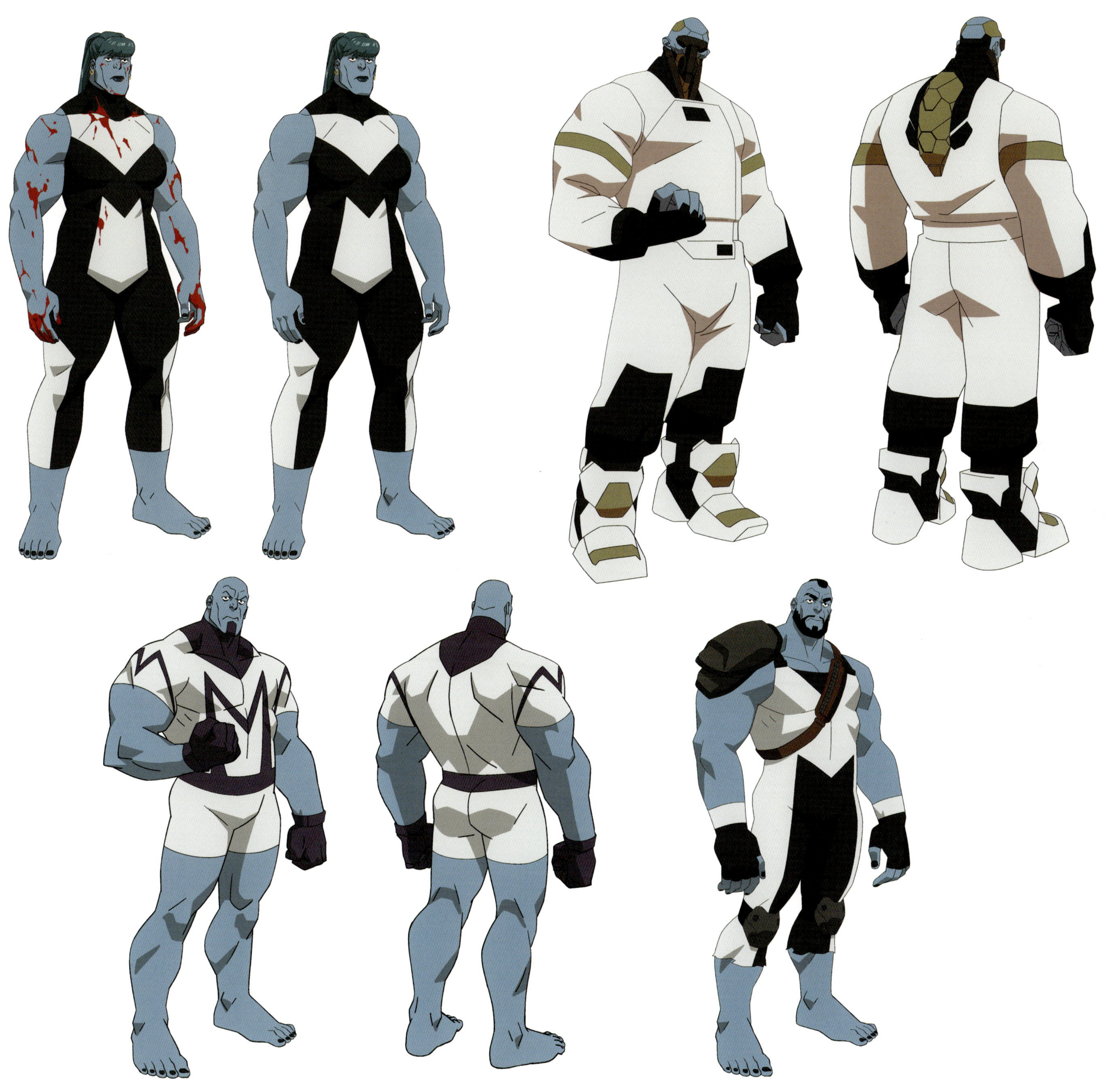

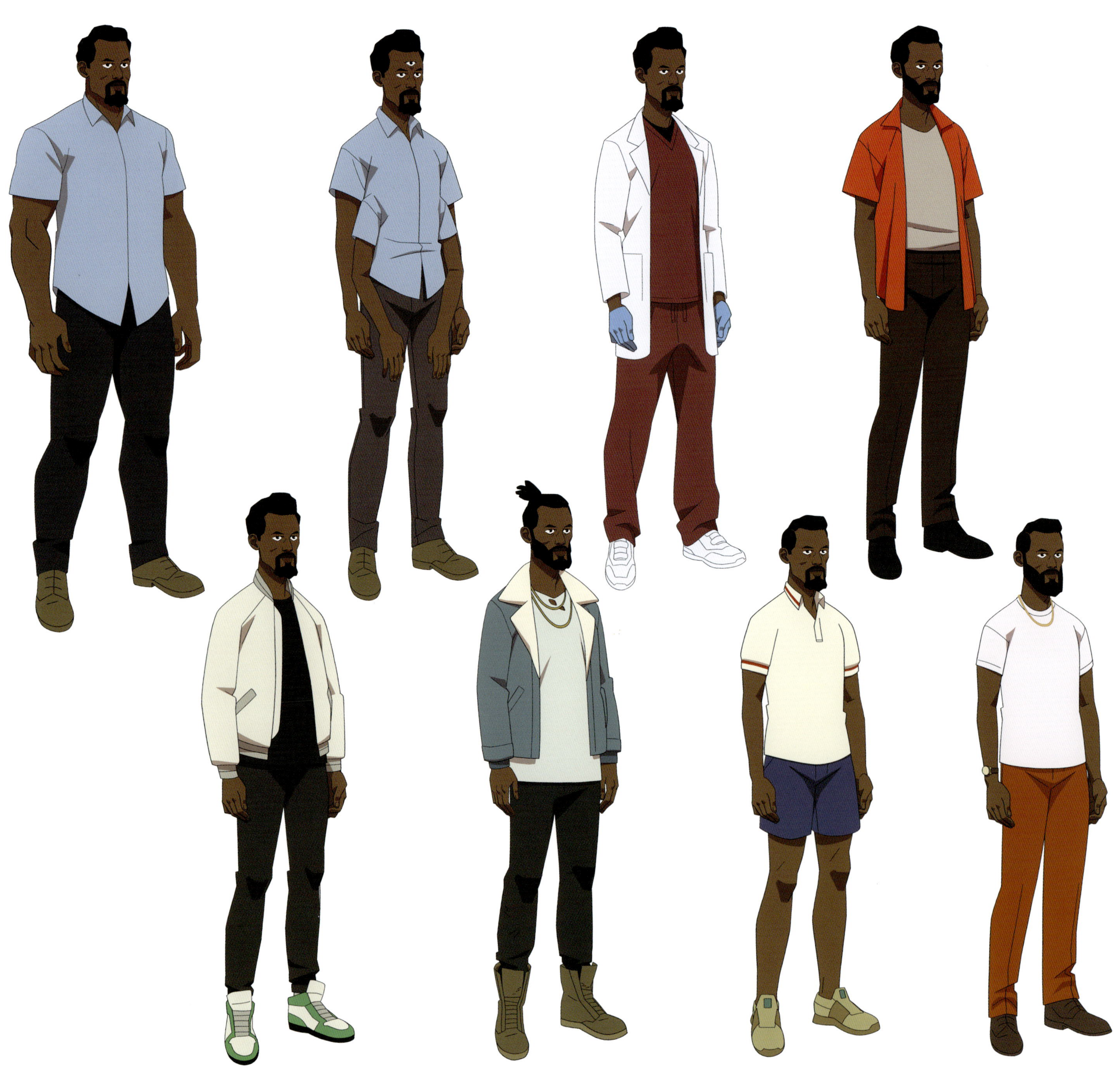

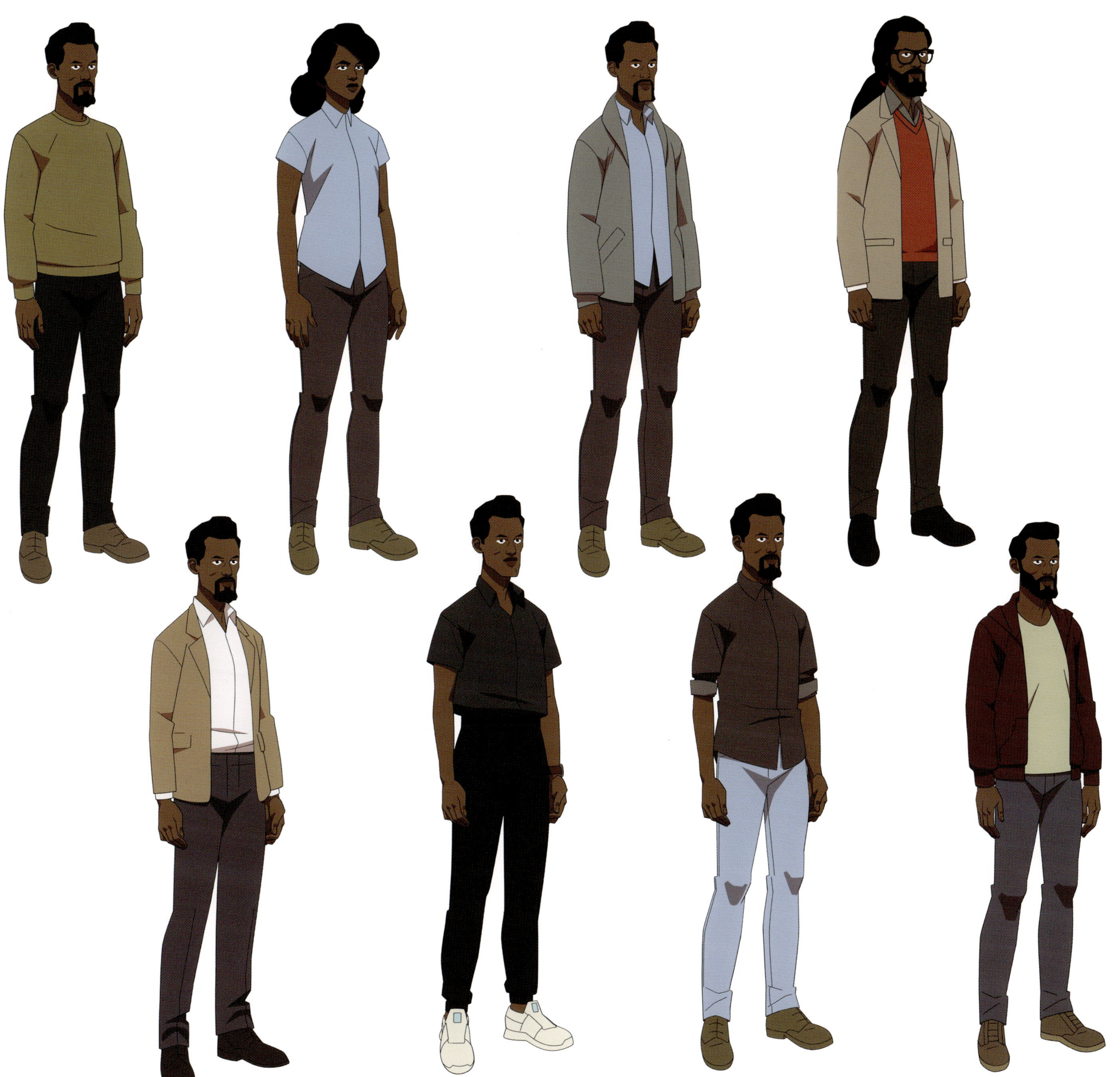

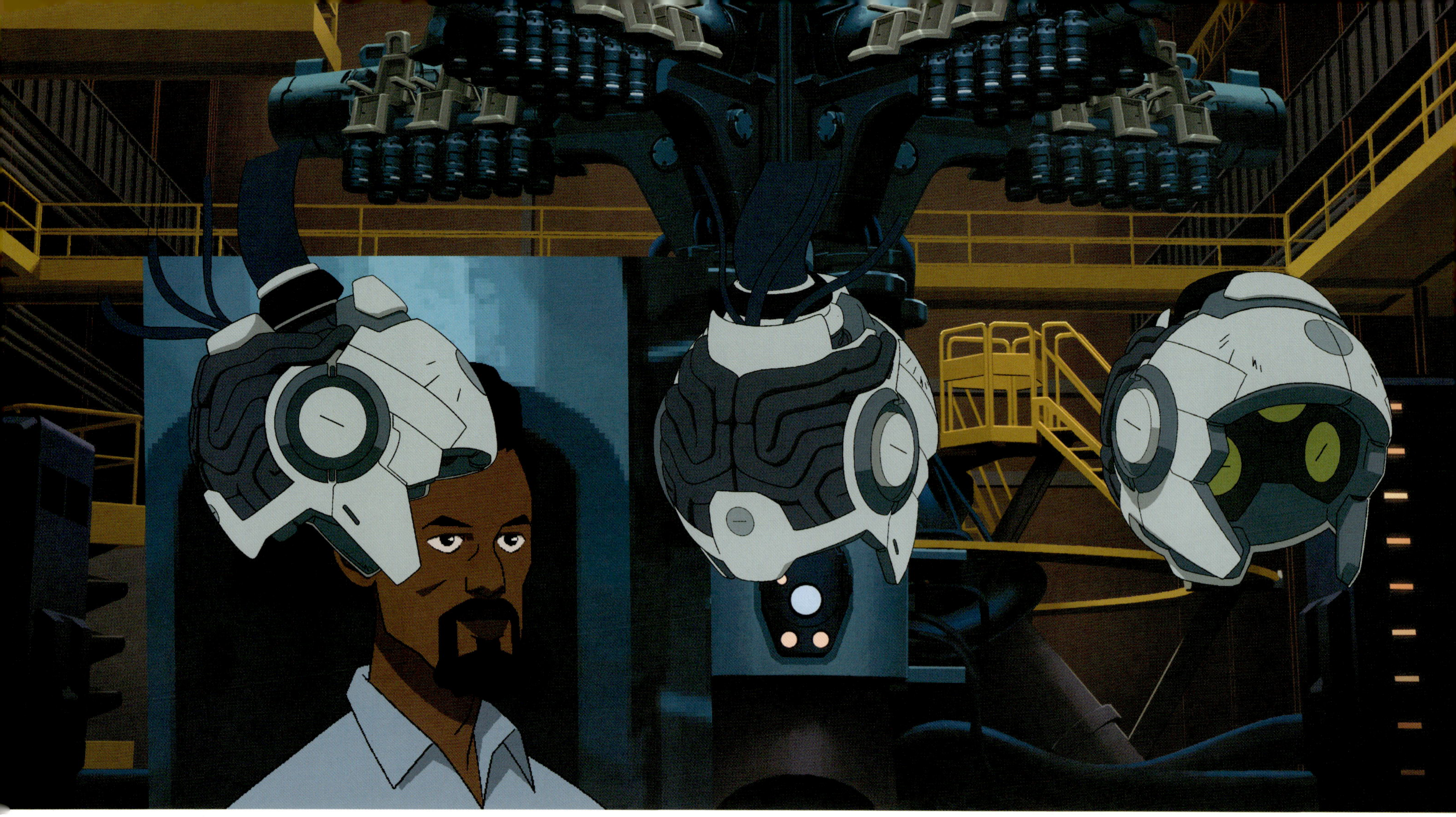

and putting it somewhere else would be easy," says Walker. "But that was always a bit of a challenge. Not only in terms of translating it, but maintaining the scale and trying to find solutions for that. I remember at one point the ground level [of the warehouse] was actually like the mid-point of it, so there was a pit that half of the thing was in, and then it was going all the way to the roof and stuff. Just working that out, working out how the cables connect in the other dimensions, stuff that you don't really think about in comics because you can just say something happened. You take it for granted. But you actually have to spell things out and make them make sense when they're happening in moving pictures. I imagine that thing was a monster to actually put together. I can't believe Ryan drew it in the first place. And then to do a good job of replicating it... That was a really cool thing, just because it's an iconic thing to see translated from the comic."

As intricate as some of the set pieces were to build for the show, equal effort had to be put into destroying them.

"I think one of my favorite things from that episode is the warehouse that Angstrom is set up in," says O'Neil. "Two folks that worked really hard on that space, interior and exterior, were Yoshi Vu, one of our background layout artists, and Patrick Bryson, one of our painters, because I think the two of them almost single-handedly managed that space through all of its lighting conditions, designing the tree — the Somatic Encoder— that Angstrom uses. It was an awesome design. I think we went through a couple iterations before we landed on what we landed on. The warehouse that it was in was also really cool. Yoshi was a 3D generalist

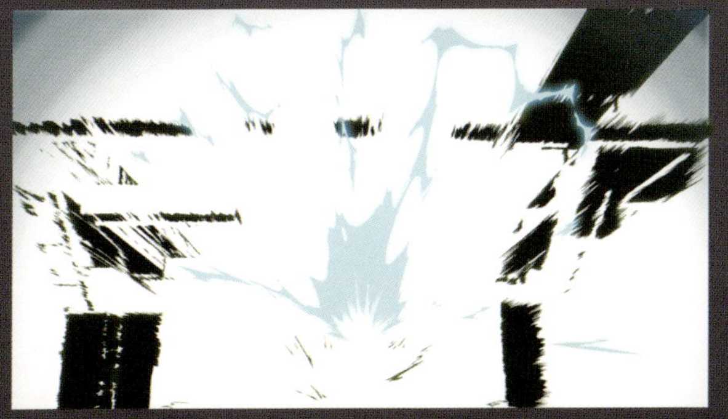

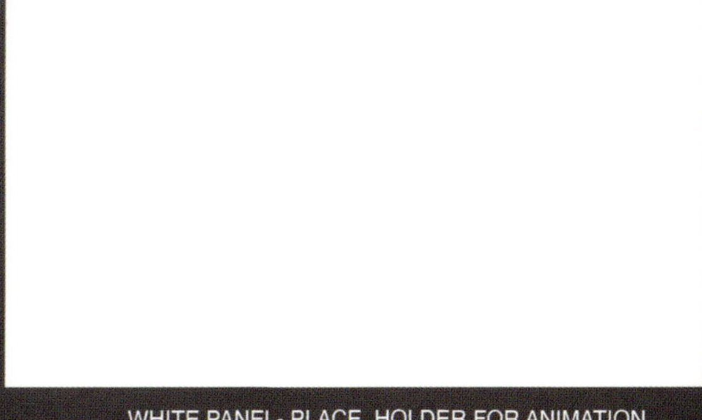

WHITE PANEL- PLACE_HOLDER FOR ANIMATION

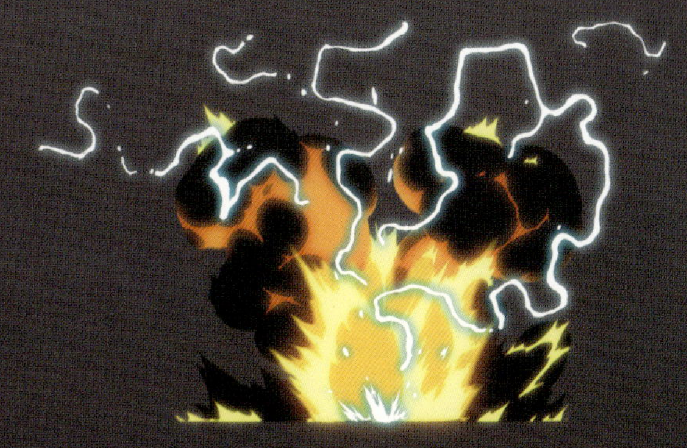

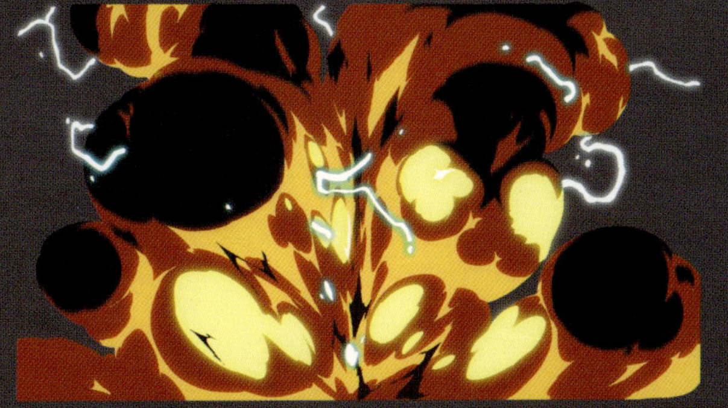

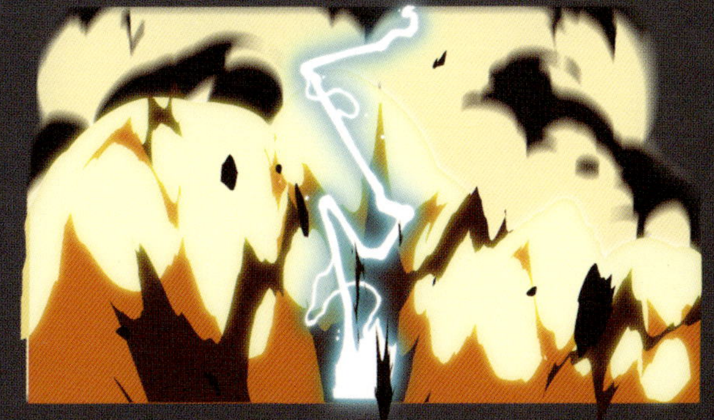

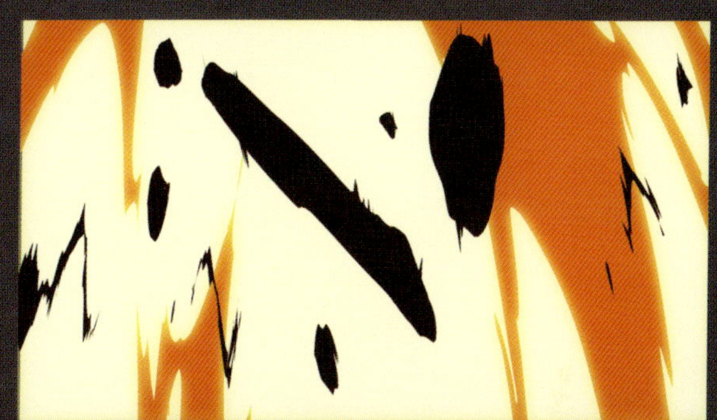

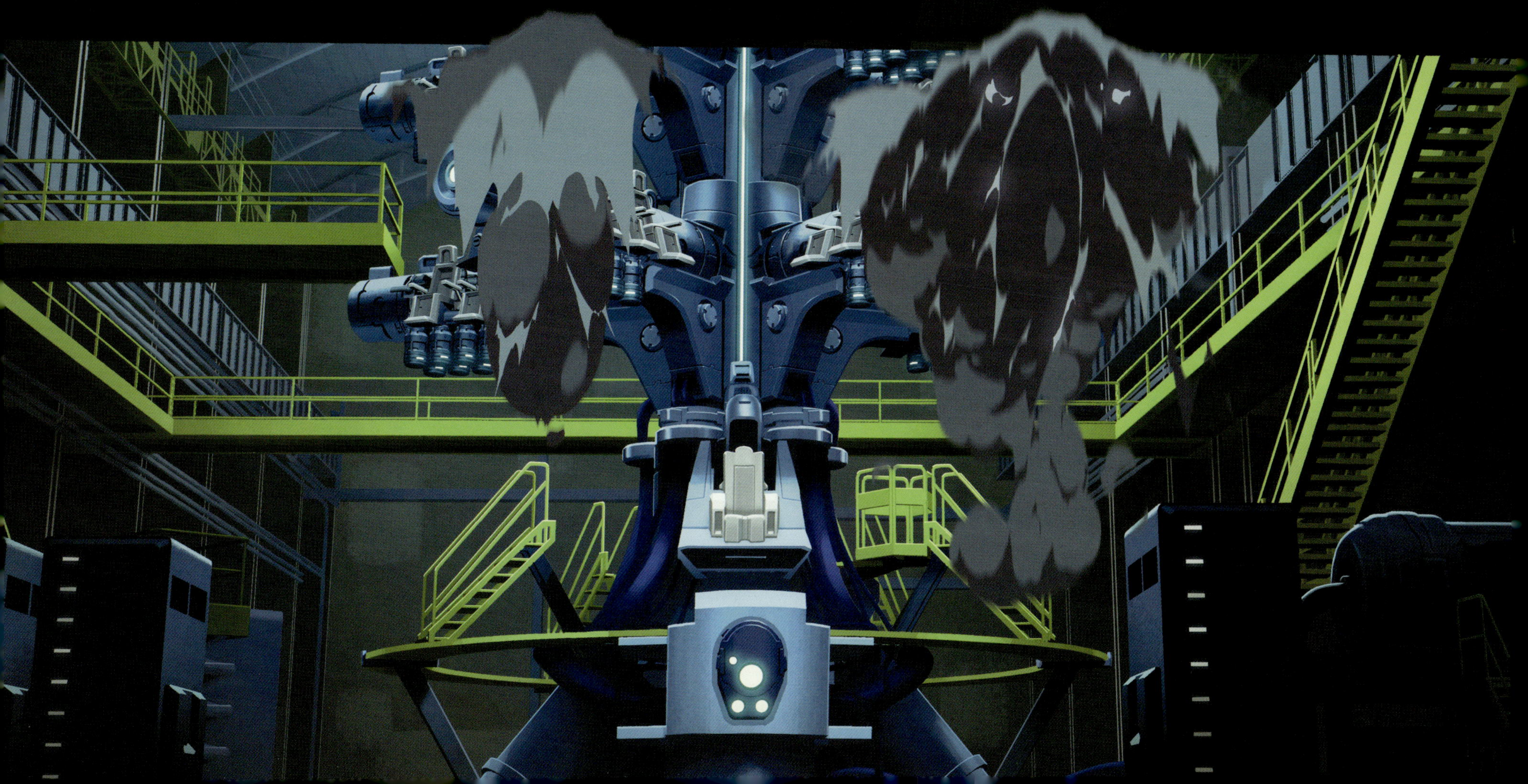

at Lucasfilm before he came to us. And he did this physics sim where the warehouse explodes, just shatters into pieces. He did some Houdini stuff where it breaks apart, it all gets blown back, and then pieces settle. And that was the basis for what we had done with the exploded warehouse. We wound up taking that, where all the pieces landed, and punched it up with added detail and noise, fine detail stuff. And then the paint job that Patrick put over top of that set, the nighttime, and there's still some glowing embers in the debris kind of stuff. It's spooky. It's really good."

When the final battle was over and the dust cleared, Mark left the destroyed warehouse behind, unaware that his encounter with Angstrom Levy would soon come back to haunt him. When Levy emerged from the debris, he was quite literally a changed man — the absorbed memories of his multiversal counterparts caused his brain to mutate and grow exponentially.

"Angstrom came with a really great rough design from Cory," says O'Neil. "And a lot of my job for him was trying to tie that down and do it justice, to make sure that we kept a lot of what was in the rough consistent throughout a full turn and expressions. The biggest challenge, which at some point turned into an all-hands assignment, was 'Angstrom proper'. We see Angstrom as a human being who has powers and does the portals thing, but I think Angstrom really is a big-brained, deformed villain. That's who I think about when I go there. And that was a complex design from the comics, something that has a ton of line mileage and we have to keep moving."

"Working out the brainy Angstrom, it was a bit of a job," says Walker. "A little bit of back and forth just trying to wrap our heads around it, especially with a mind towards getting the guy dressed later in the season. I don't know that there aren't things I wouldn't change now, but I think that where we landed was pretty successful."

The difficulties that designing Angstrom Levy's physical form caused for the design team were significant, but they would pale in comparison to the difficulties that Levy himself would cause for Mark as the season progressed.

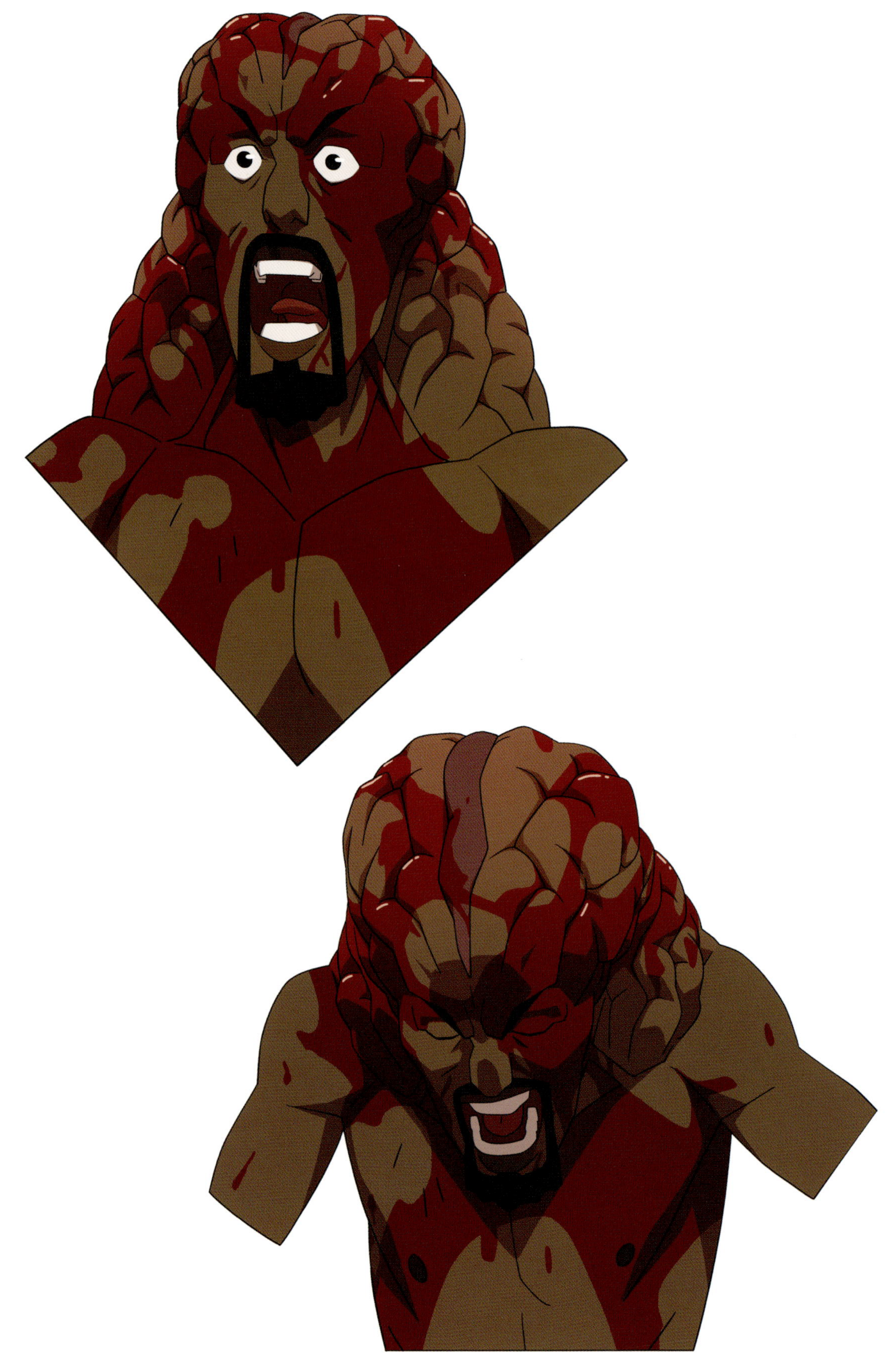

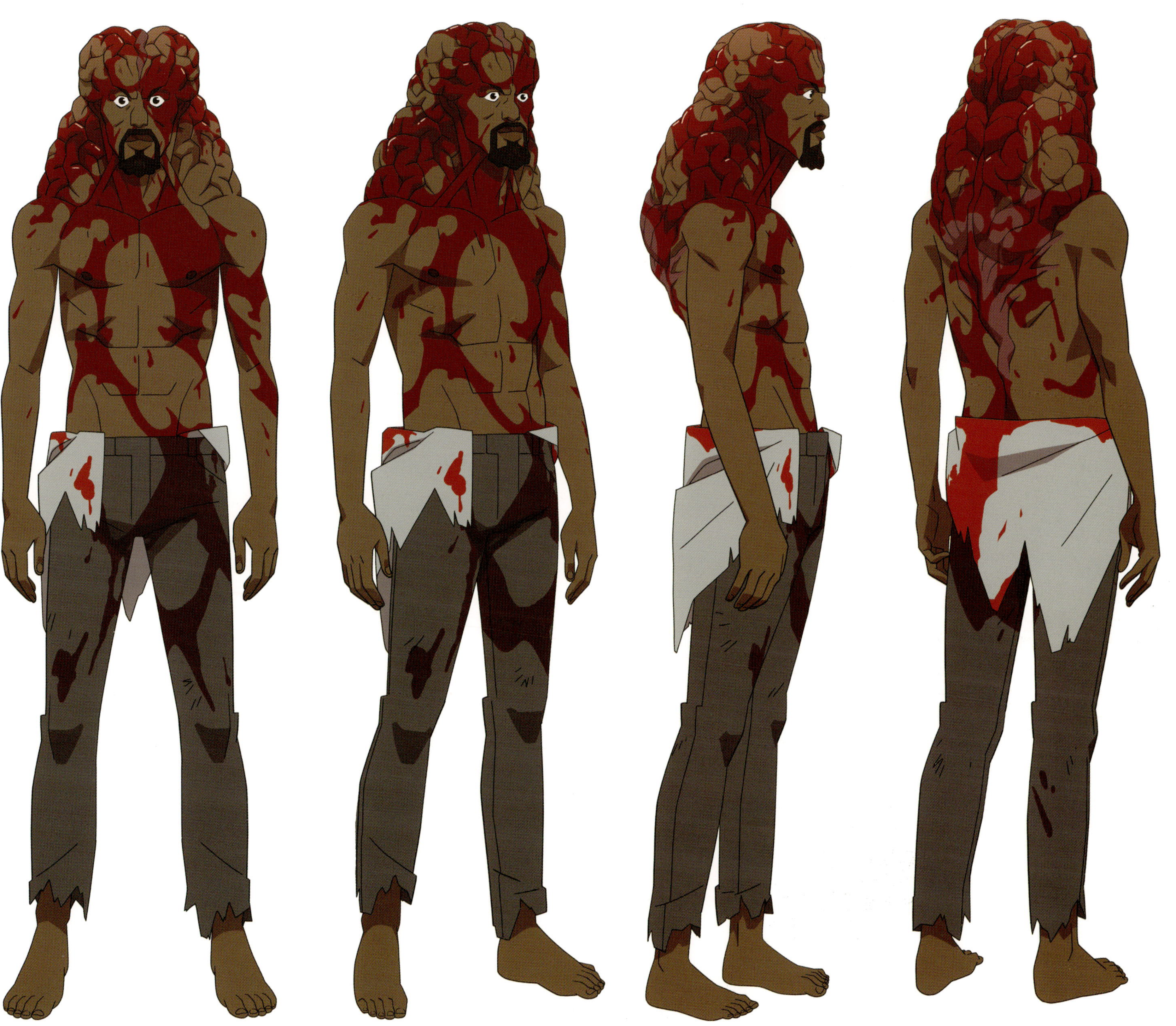

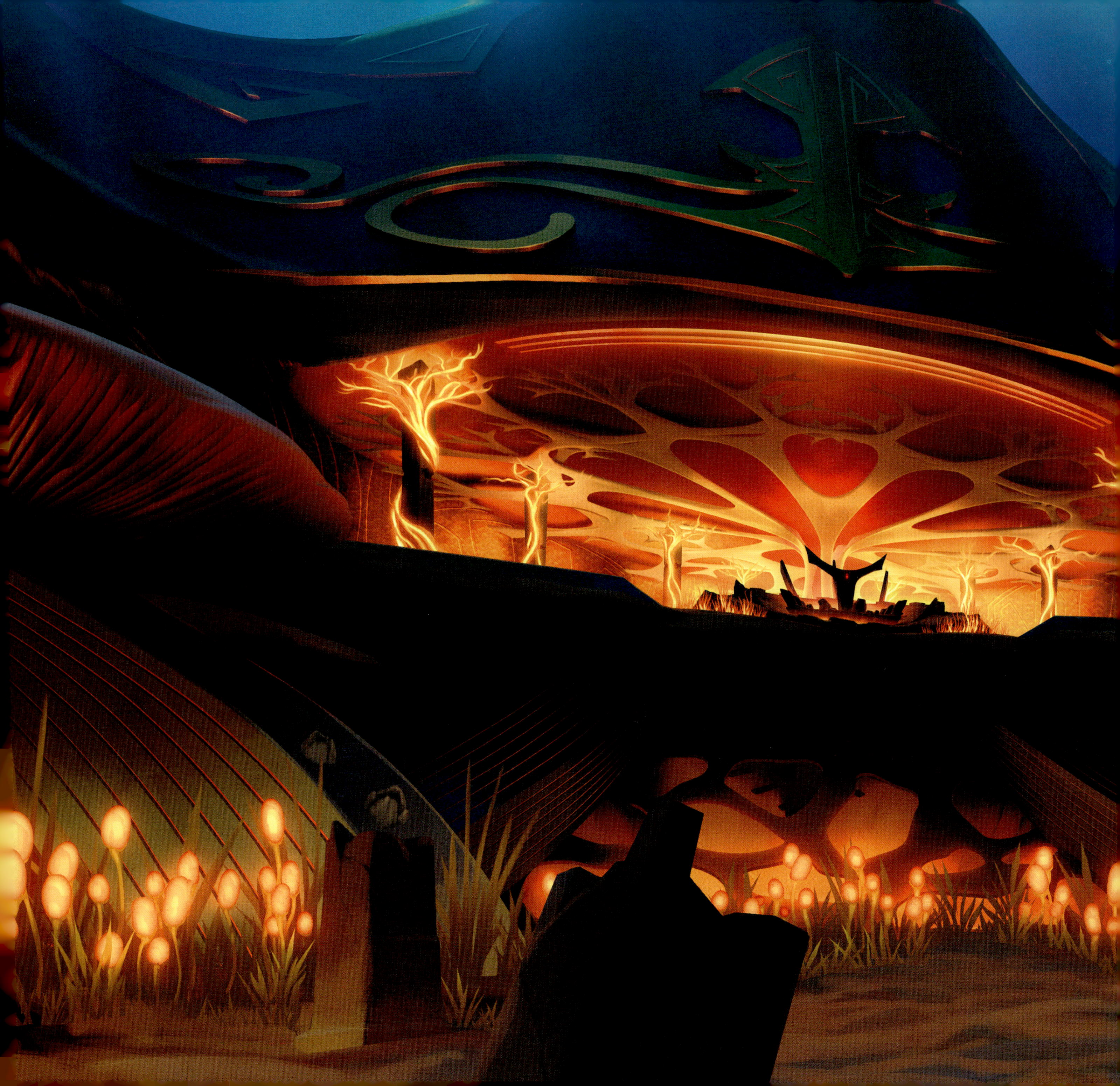

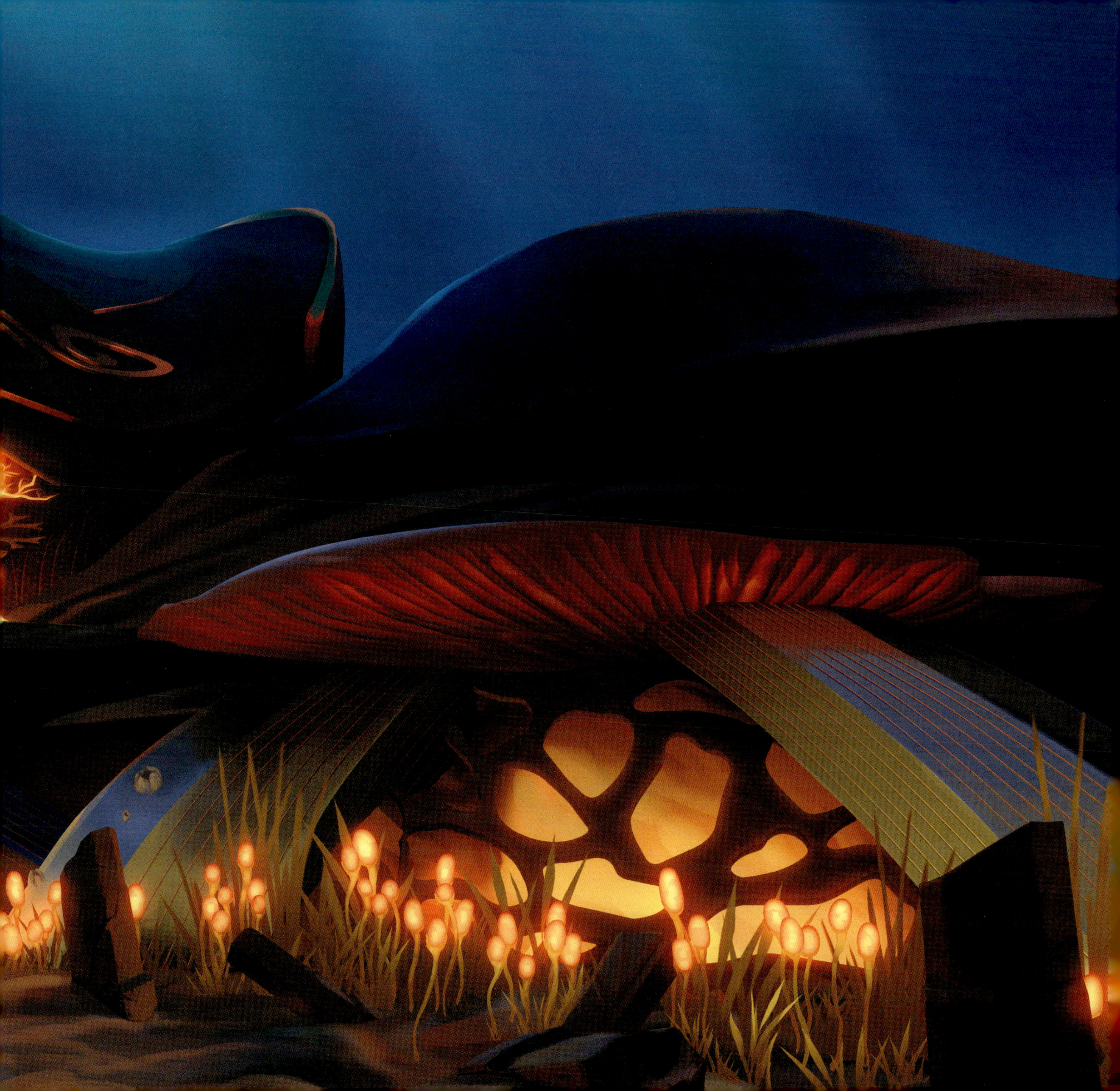

EPISODE 2:

IN ABOUT SIX HOURS, I LOSE MY VIRGINITY TO A FISH

If you thought that Mark Grayson would have a chance to rest after his encounter with Angstrom Levy and the Maulers in the season premiere, then you obviously hadn't been watching enough *Invincible*. The season's second episode only ratcheted up the action further, introducing an avalanche of formidable foes and exotic locations.

"Episode Two is busy," says Executive Producer and Co-Showrunner Simon Racioppa. "We really go a lot of places. It's setting a lot of things up. It's probably one of our busiest episodes, because we go to Atlantis, we go to Midnight City, we have a graduation. Matt Lambert wrote it. He came in and was like, 'Let's just have fun with this. It feels really comic book-y. Let's see how much fun stuff we can cram into this episode.'"

The fun began in Washington, D.C. as Mark faced off against a villain that he and Atom Eve had previously defeated together — the earthquake-inducing Doc Seismic, who was last seen plotting his revenge in the Season One finale.

"I think that was the first of the many teases at the end of Season One that we paid off," says Executive Producer, Co-Showrunner, and Co-Creator Robert Kirkman, "because we had shown some of the Magmanites bowing to Doc Seismic. There were a couple of those teases that we don't pay off until Season Three, but we were trying to check those boxes as we went."

Though Doc Seismic was a returning character, he had

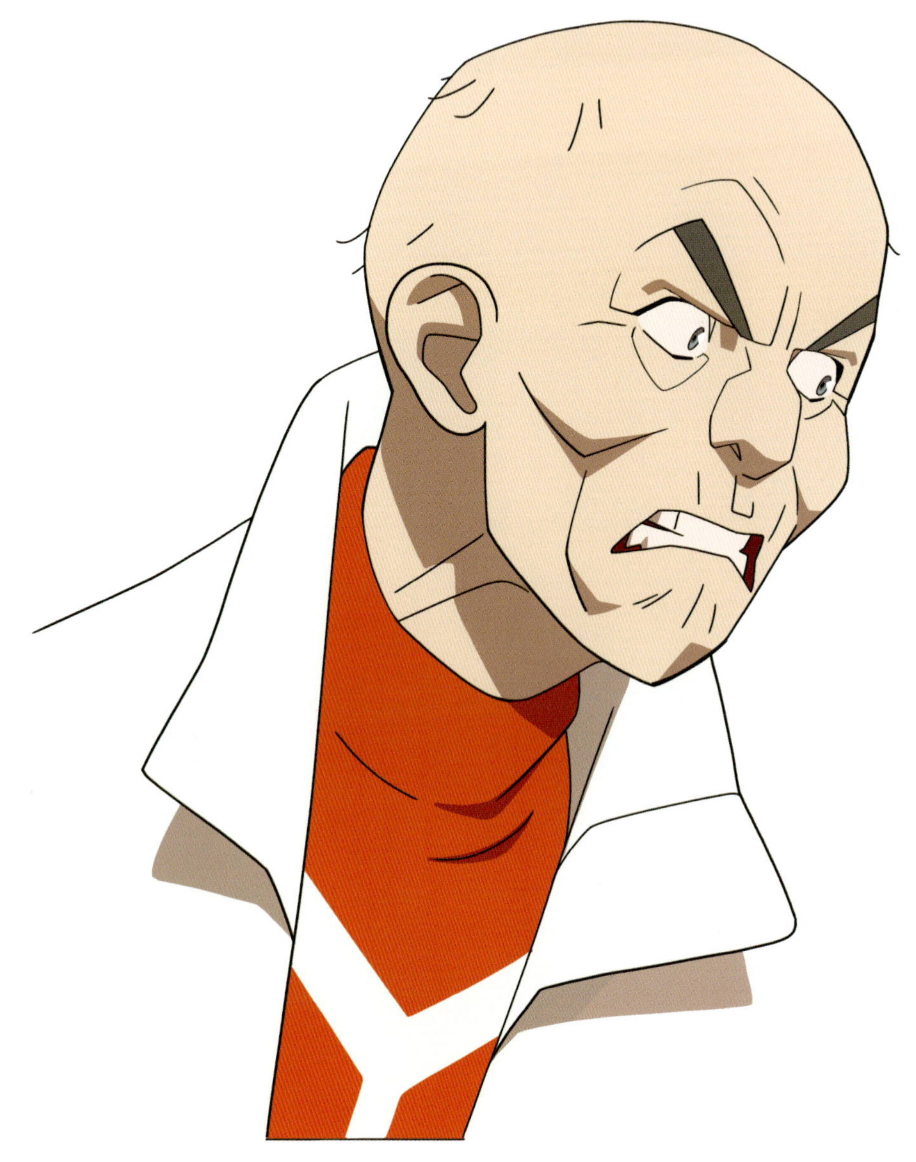

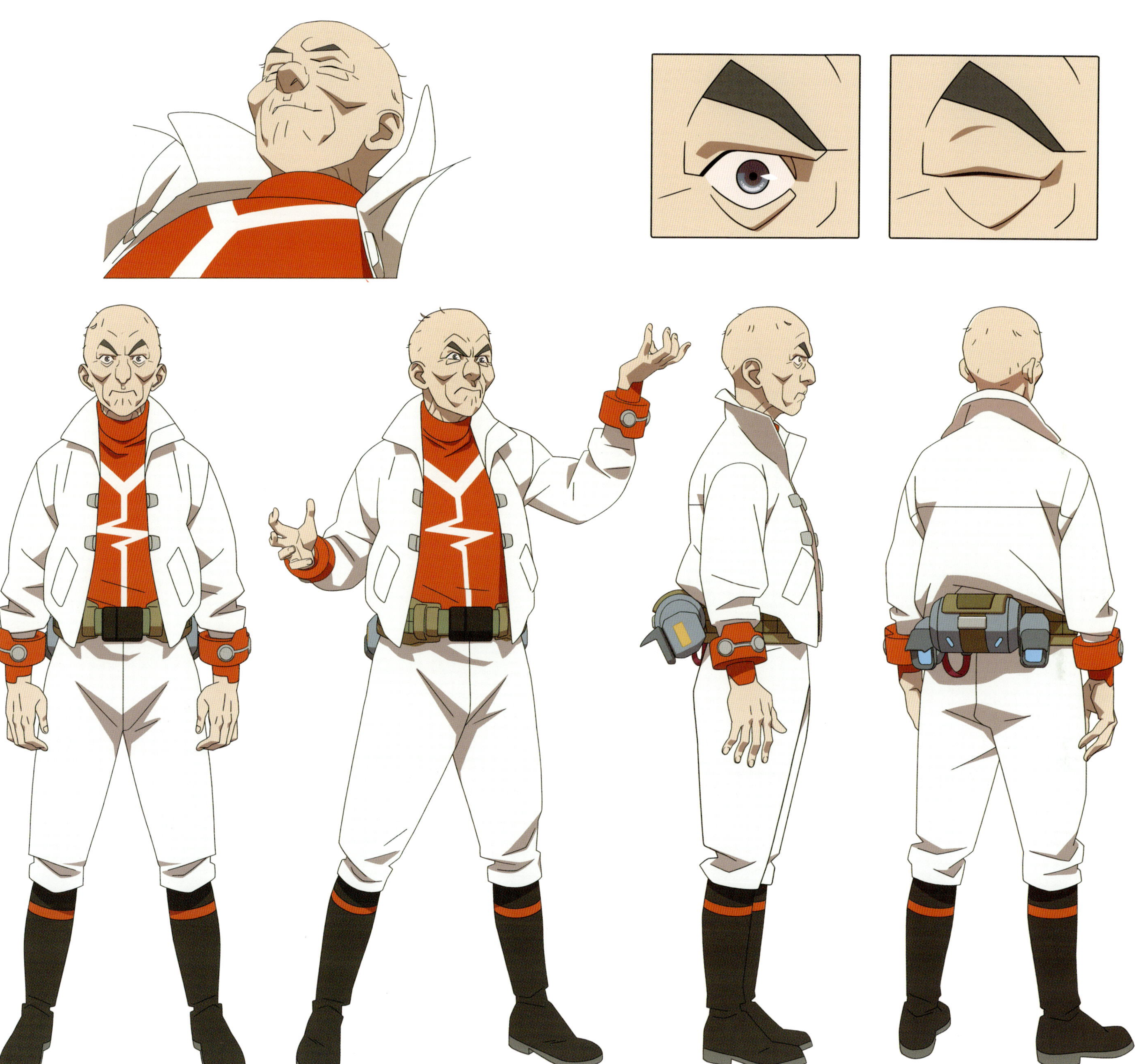

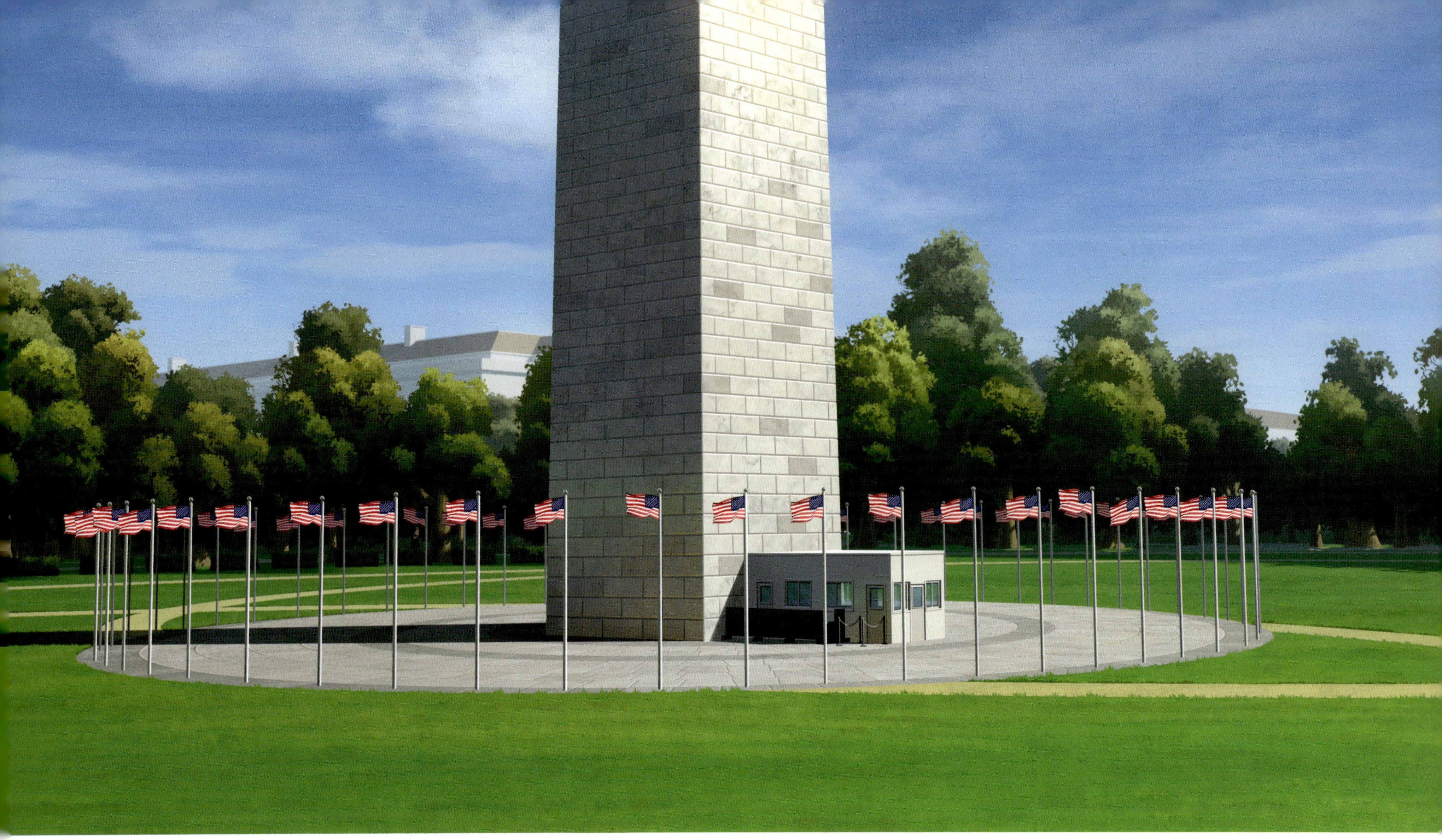

gotten some new gear since his last appearance — and upgraded equipment required updated designs.

"We had the line of dialogue where he says he should have built a jetpack at the end of the sequence in Season One," says Kirkman, "and so we were able to introduce the jetpack — which Cory had relegated to a jet belt, just because he thought that would look cooler and he didn't want to have a bulky jetpack cluttering the design. There was a lot of talk about the gauntlets. We updated the gauntlets so that they weren't earthquake bracelets anymore, because he had felt self-conscious about that ridicule that came from Invincible."

Co-Executive Producer and Co-Creator Cory Walker worked with Art Director Shaun O'Neil on Doc Seismic's new

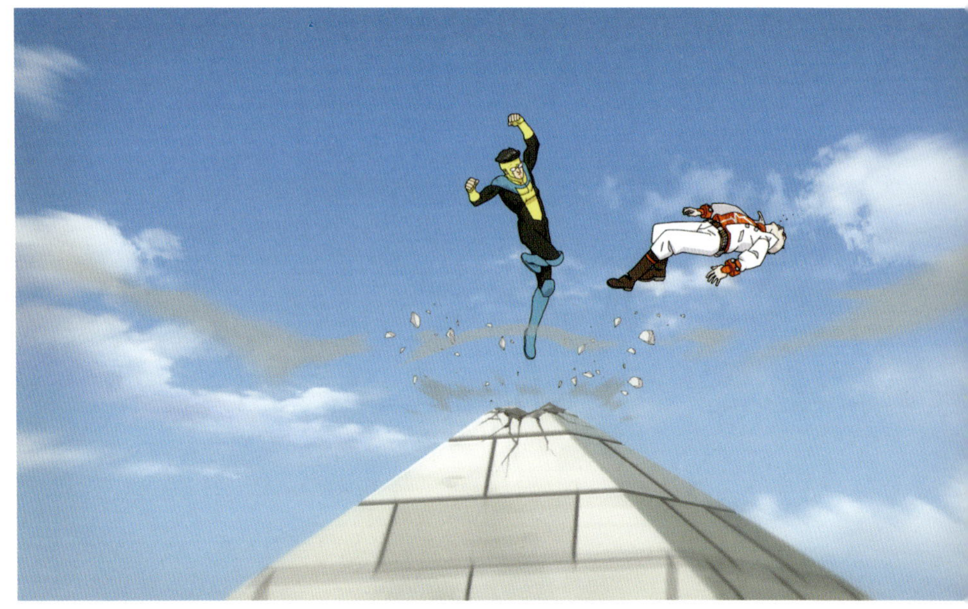

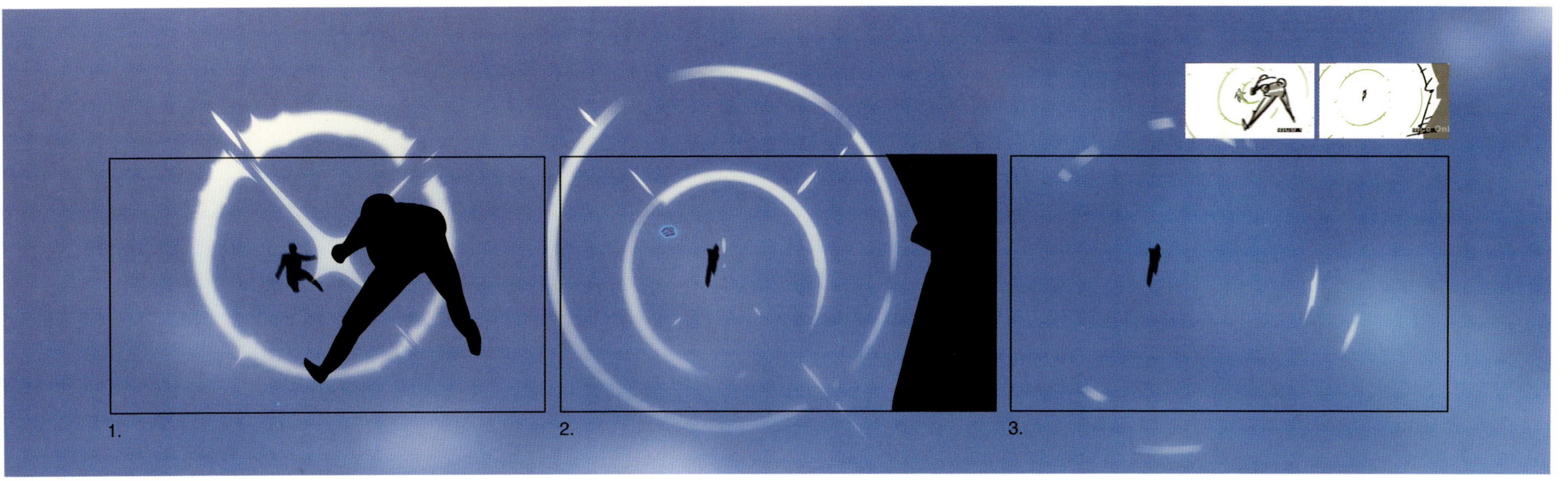

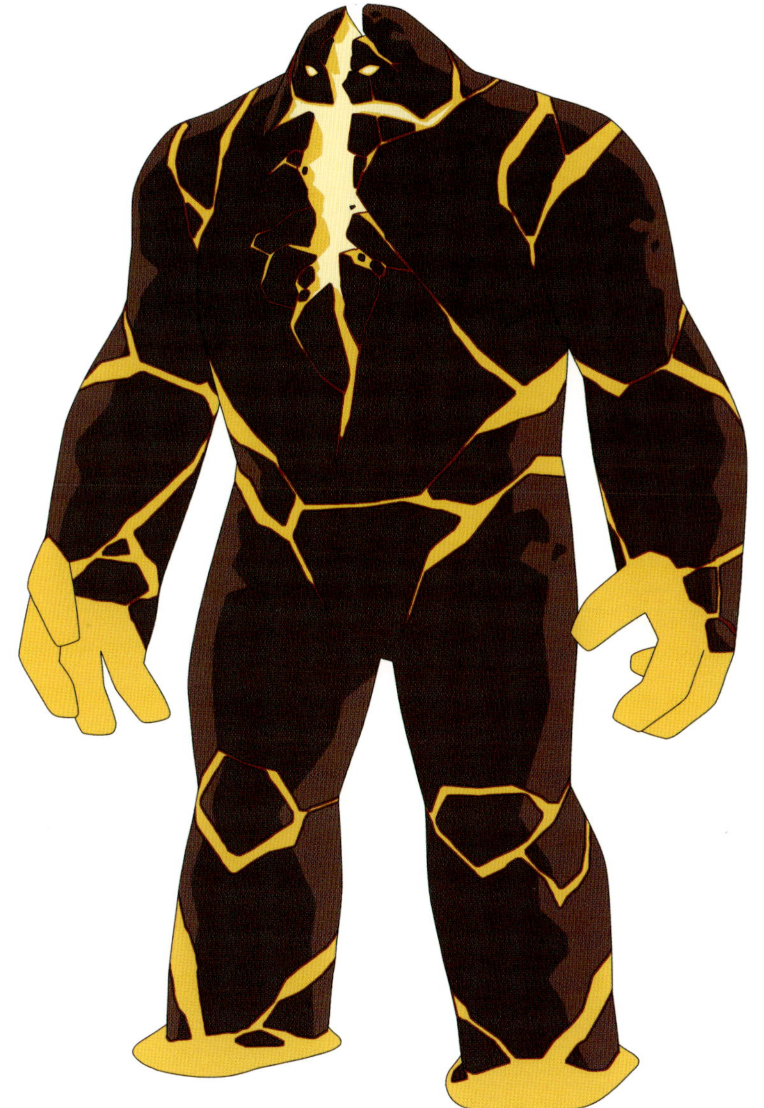

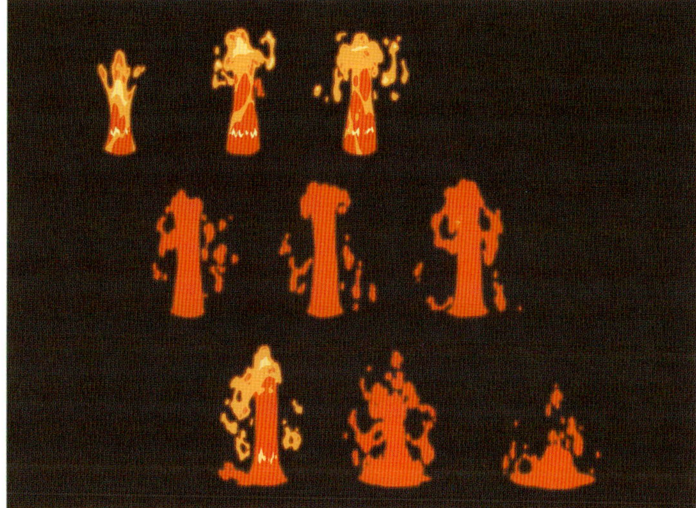

look.

"I gave Shaun just a notion of what I was picturing for the jetpack," says Walker, "and then he came back with something super cool. Obviously, Seismic needed a shorter jacket for that. I love that. The set piece, the Washington Monument, was really cool, too. The destruction that we did to it was pretty impressive."

This over-the-top, down-on-his-luck villain had plenty of fans within the *Invincible* creative team.

"It feels like we need Doc Seismic at the start of every season," says Racioppa. "We wanted to move him on a little bit. He's adjusted his policies a little bit. Now he's taking every building built of stone back into the earth, because he's a little crazy. But he's got a jetpack, because he learned that from Season One. Stuff like that is fun. You just want to keep the characters updated. We don't want to have them do the same thing over and over again, obviously. So he's learned. He's not moved on, but he's adjusted his goals. And if you see him again, I think you'll see the same thing. He'll change, too."

"I think the Doc Seismic stuff is always great," says O'Neil. "He was a lot of fun in [Episode] 103. It was probably one of my favorite parts of that episode. I think it's always fun, just in general, when he comes back. Mostly because he's right. A lot of times he's just right, and we go out of our way to beat him down into the dirt when he's just kind of trying to help us. And I think that that's funny."

Doc Seismic's minions, the Magmanites, made their full debut in this episode, but these lava monsters had a long history of appearances in the *Invincible* comic.

"Those are stalwart additions from the comic book series that were ever-present and would show up anytime I needed some kind of sequence to break things up," says Kirkman. "I'd be like, 'The Magmanites attack again. Whatever.' So it's cool seeing them on the show."

After defeating Doc Seismic once again, Mark had time to attend his own high school graduation ceremony. But it wasn't long before Mark found himself following GDA orders and traveling to Midnight City — an urban metropolis trapped under a dome of perpetual darkness. Its design drew inspiration from another famous animated superhero city.

"Obviously, it's supposed to be an homage to the Gotham of *Batman: The Animated Series* with the red sky," says Walker. "We did have to kind of figure out the best way to visualize that from the outside with the dome. But again, I think we ended up with a pretty good solution for that. Otherwise, it's a pretty straightforward city."

"We had fortunately seen some of [Midnight City] in Season One," says O'Neil, "but personally, not a huge fan of the direction. I felt like it was a little flat. It was a brief place that we went to in [Season One,] Episode One. We

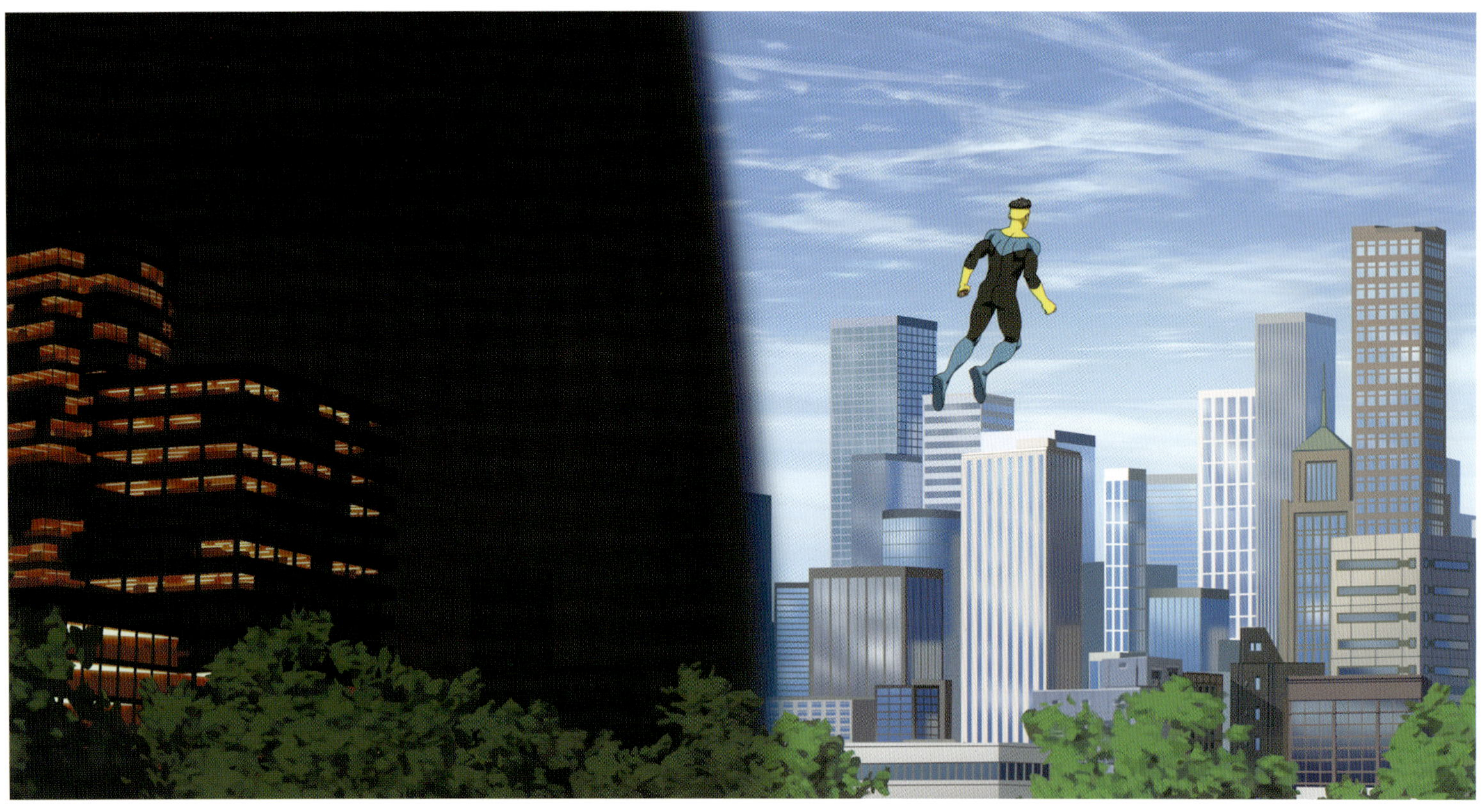

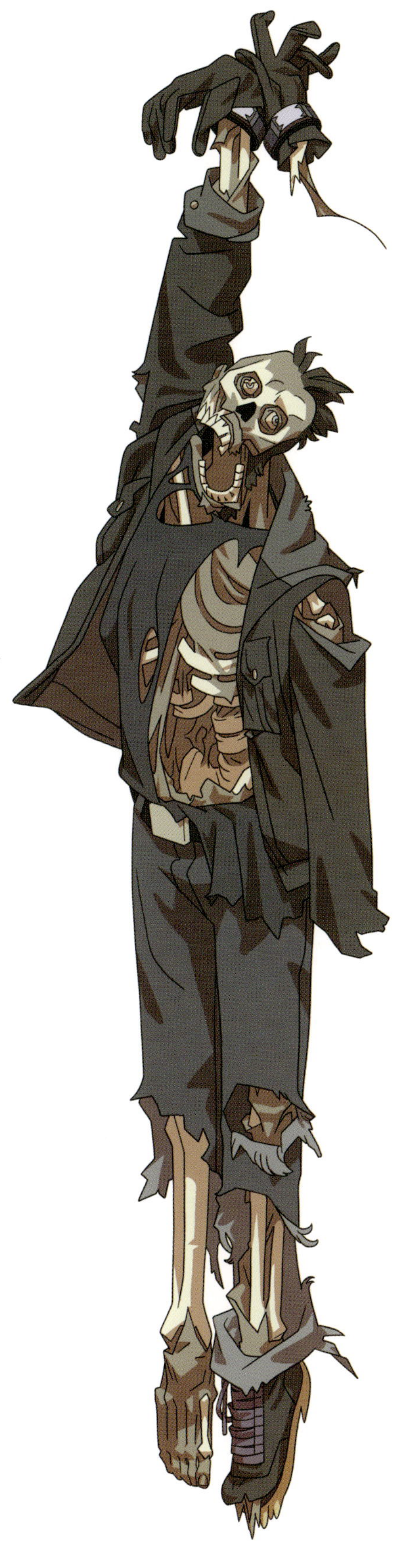

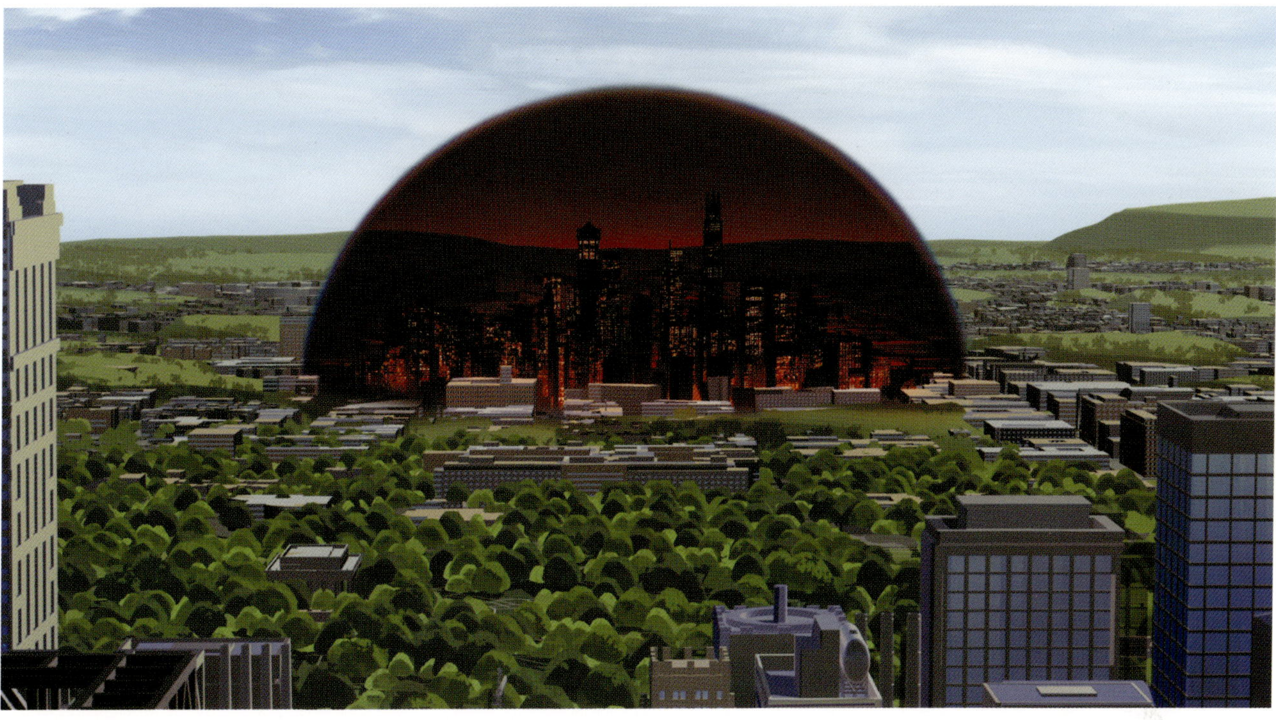

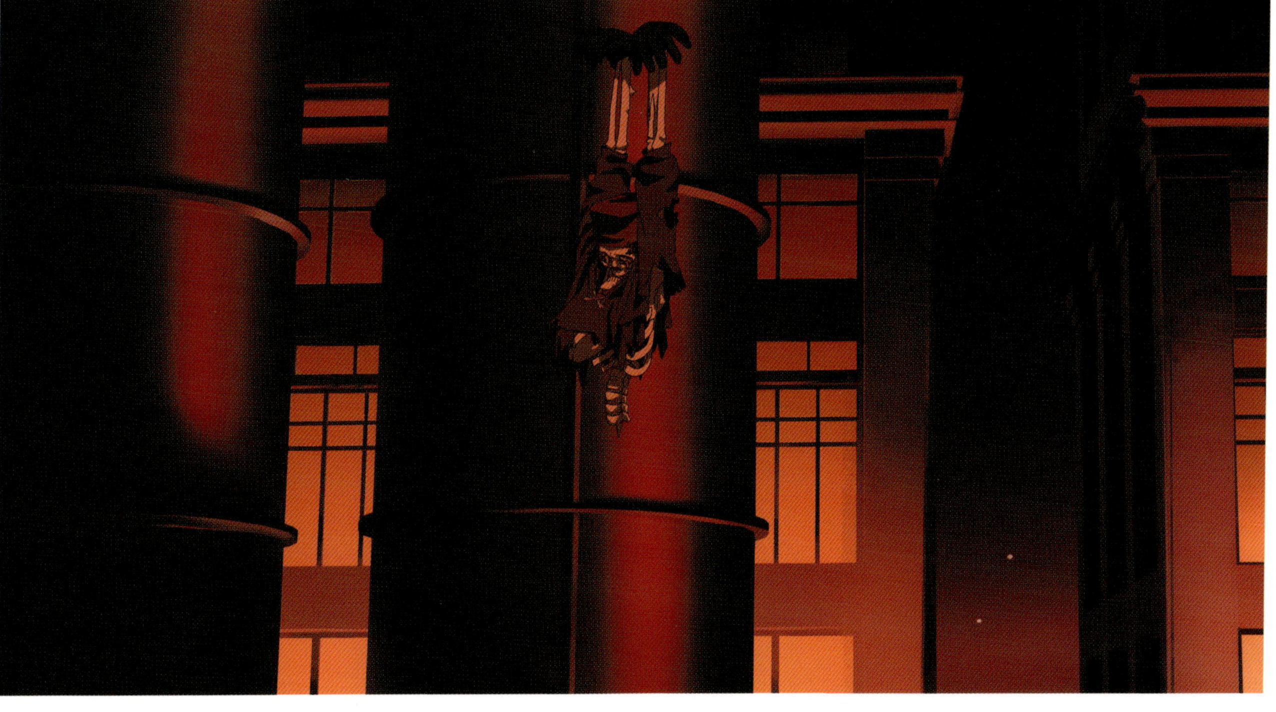

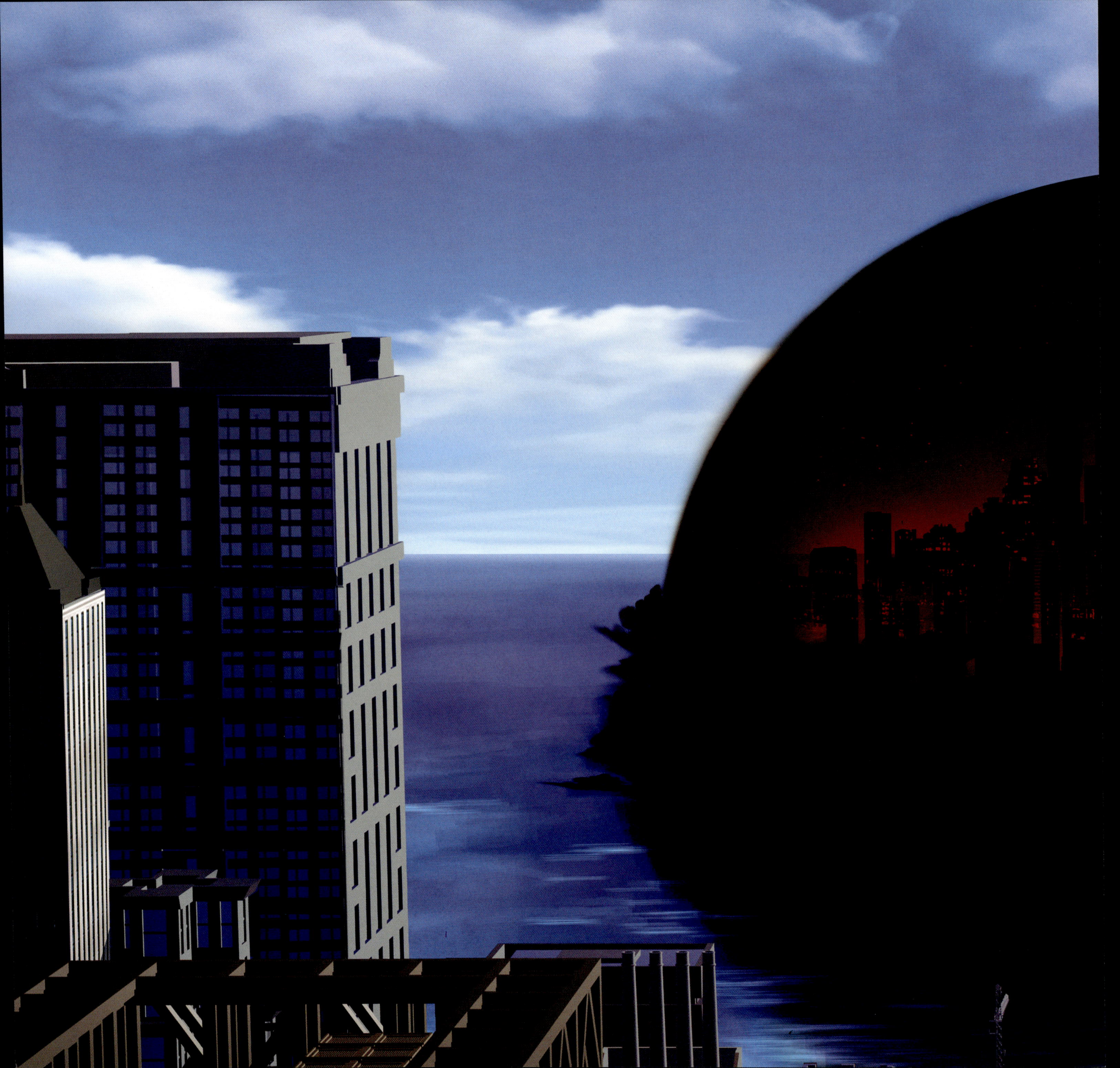

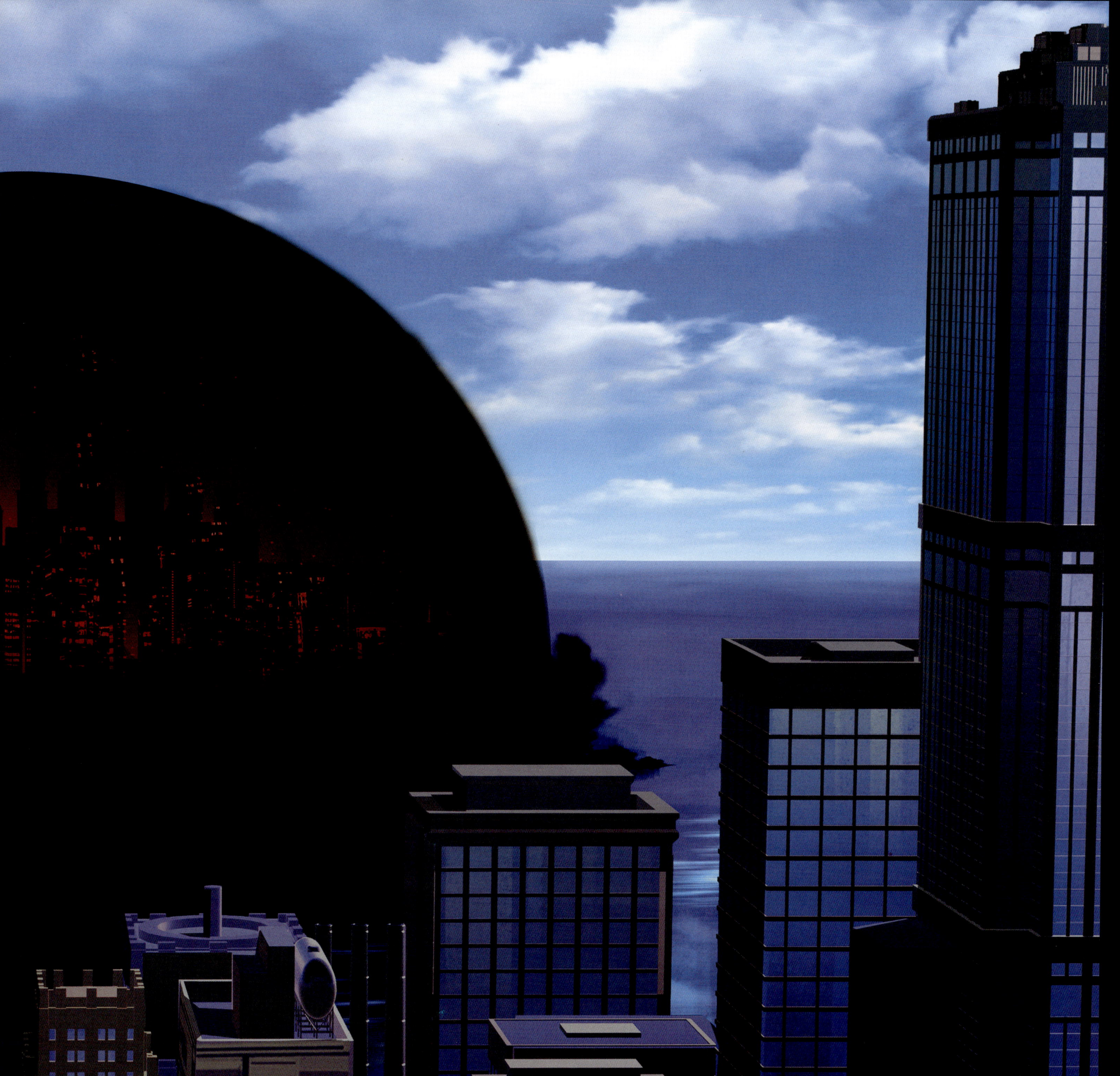

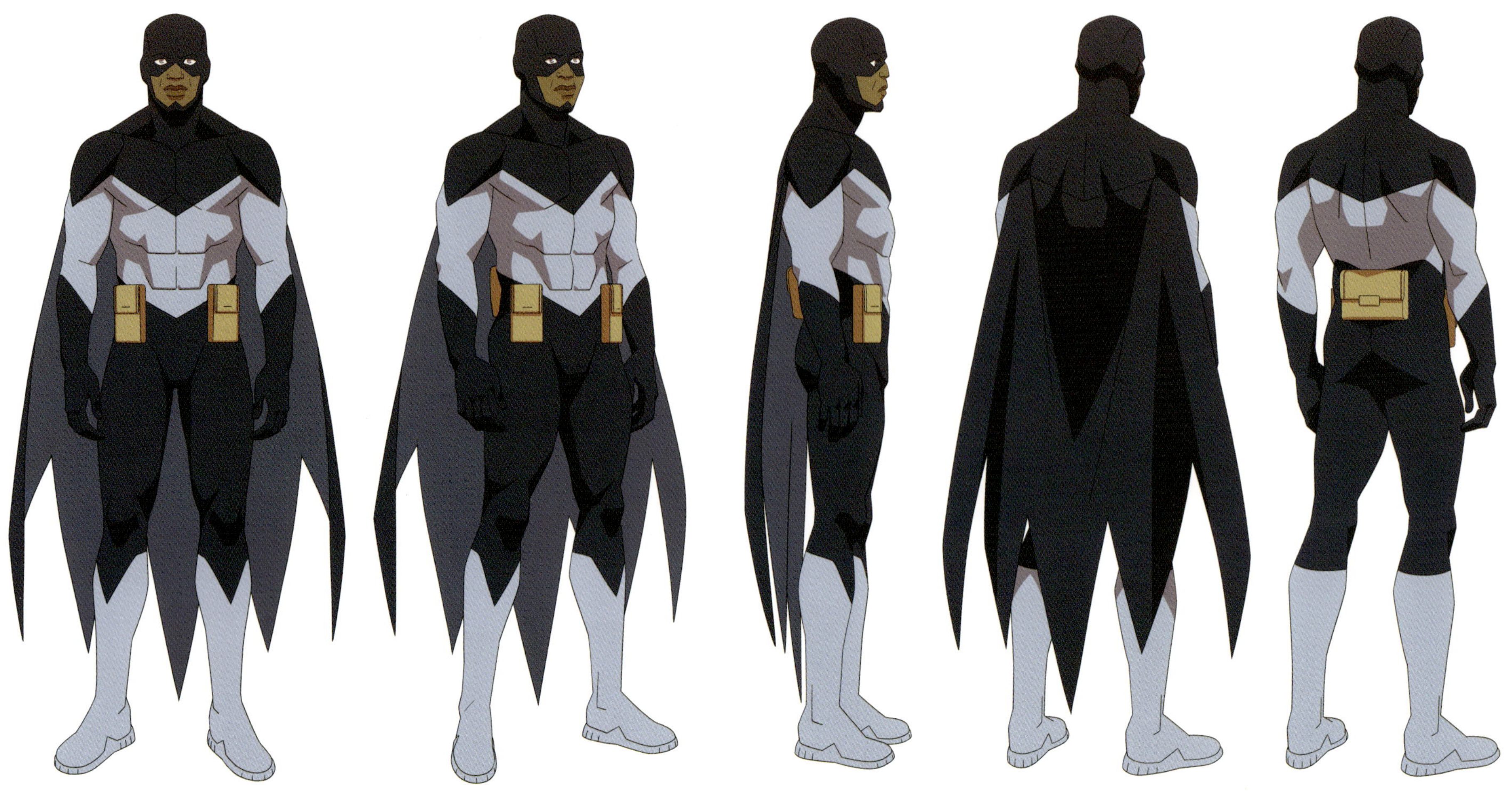

went there for less than a minute, and I don't think it got the attention that it deserved. I was like, 'What can we do? All I want is for this place to feel like a fucking *Batman: The Animated Series* background' — just like deep, dark blacks, heavy shadows, and that sort of impossible red that they get with some of their night sky stuff, trying to do that super-lit city against an overcast cloud cover kind of thing. The whole brief was just, 'Get us there.' So I think it was Jon [Finch] and Kelly [Mai] on that space. And then one of our painters, Hiro Shen, did a bang-up job of bringing that whole Batman thing to life. Just trying to keep that motif associated with the archetype of that character alive, it was awesome. I love that set. Those paints are great."

Once Mark entered Midnight City, he encountered its protector, Darkwing… or, as it turned out, the former sidekick of Darkwing who had taken up the mantle after his mentor was killed by Omni-Man.

"The designs for the new Darkwing were pretty cool," says Kirkman. "Again, kind of playing off what Ryan Ottley did in the comics, but updating it a little bit more. A lot of work was put into figuring out how the Shadowverse looked and how the shadow powers that Darkwing has, where he can kind of jump into shadows and jump out of them, how that was going to work."

While Kirkman was pleased with Darkwing's new look, Walker believed he could have done better.

"Darkwing II was probably my fault," says Walker. "I think it was based on something early I did. I probably could've done a more interesting design for that, especially given the remark about it being an exoskeleton that makes him stronger or whatever. We could have incorporated some bulk in that. But again, that's Cory's fault."

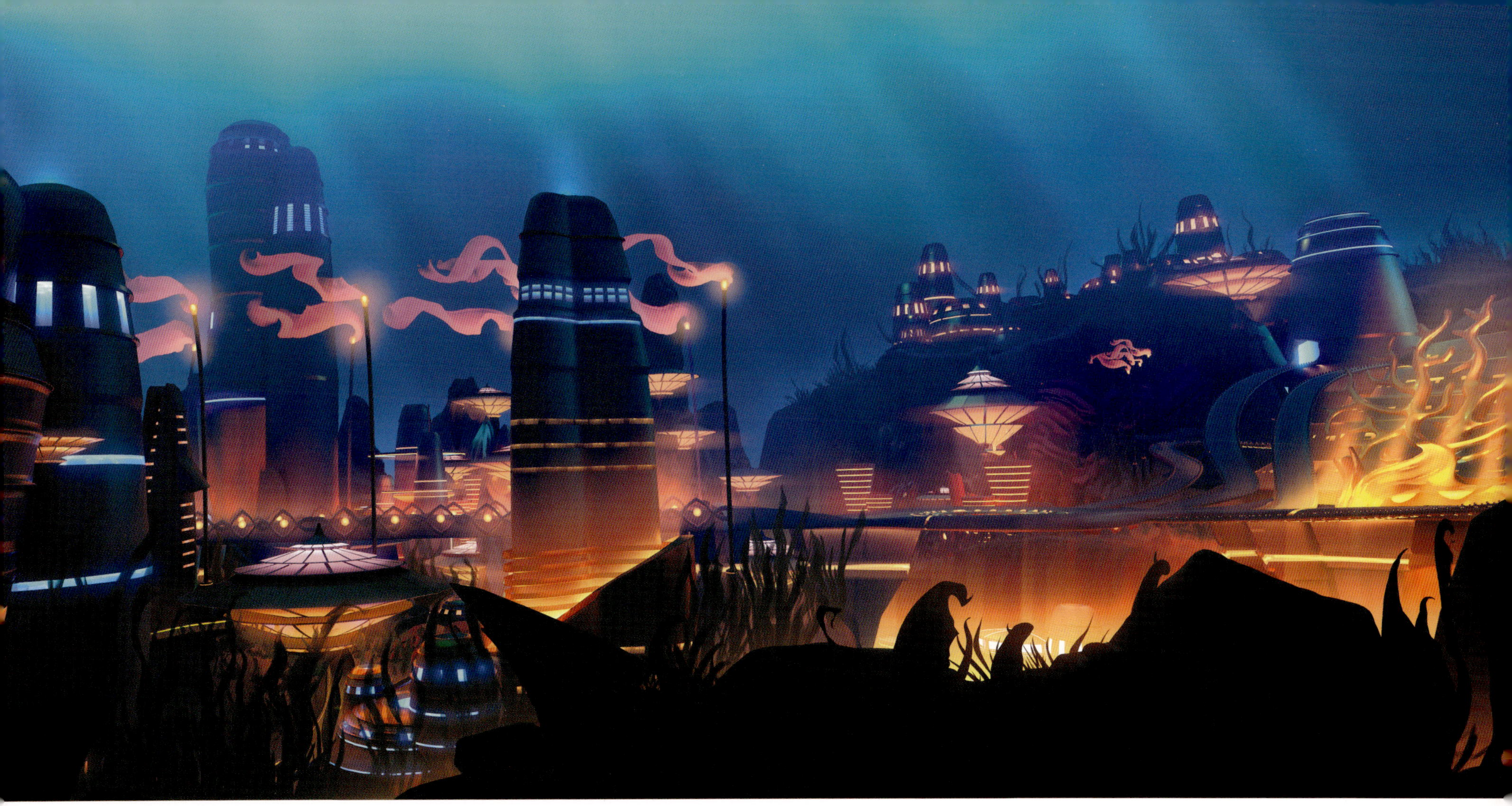

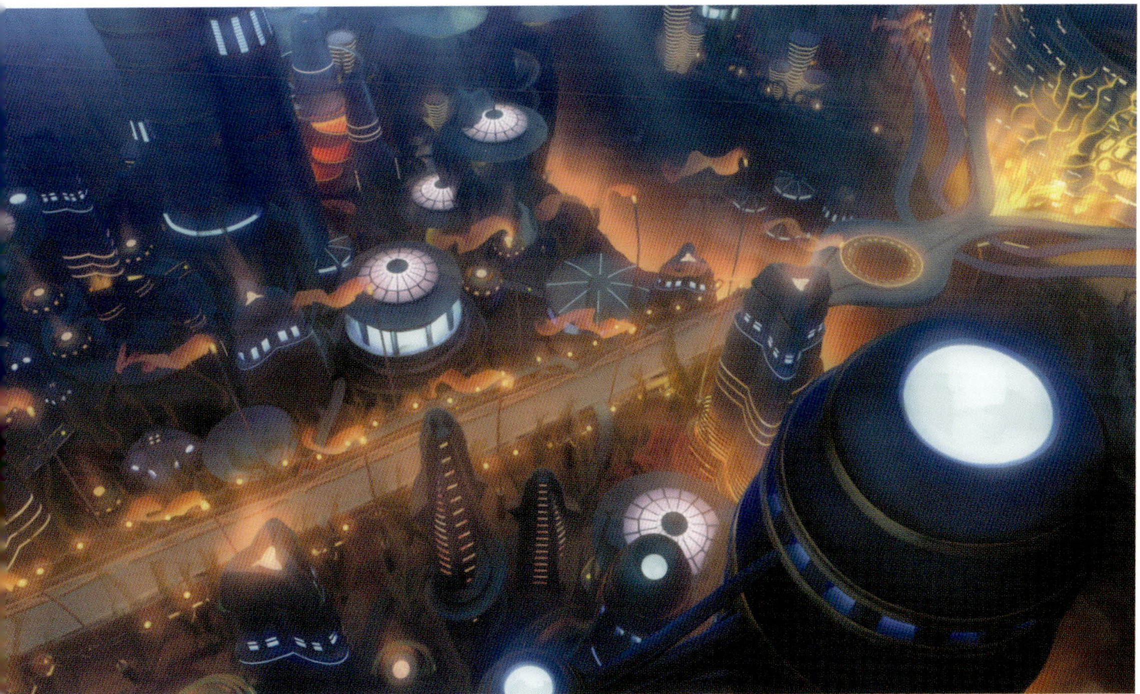

Whether or not the new Darkwing lived up to his full potential as a design or as a hero, there was still evidence of his mentor's work on display in Midnight City for those with a keen eye and a good memory.

"Obviously, [there was] a quick throwback reference to Episode One of Season One," says Racioppa. "The criminals that Darkwing catches there and says he'll come back to, and then he's obviously unable to get back to them. They're still there. And they're dead. So dead."

"It was very important to me that we paid off the little gag of Darkwing leaving the two guys chained up," says Kirkman. "Hopefully people noticed when they watched the episode. I just love little Easter eggs like that, and that felt like a really great opportunity."

Midnight City wasn't the only location dealing with the loss of its champion. The home of another Guardians of

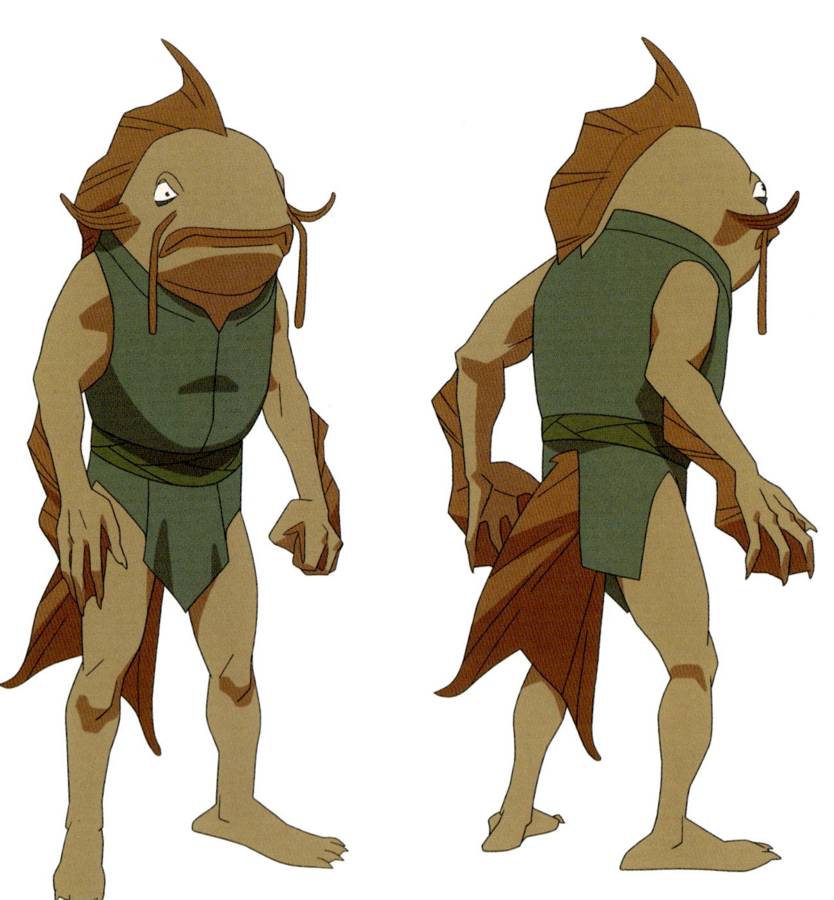

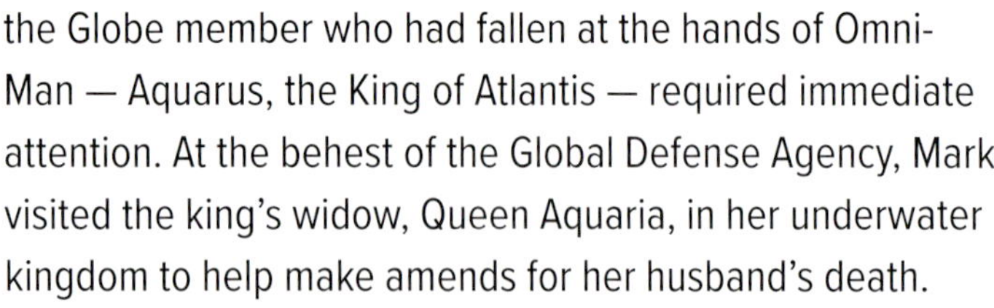

the Globe member who had fallen at the hands of Omni-Man — Aquarus, the King of Atlantis — required immediate attention. At the behest of the Global Defense Agency, Mark visited the king's widow, Queen Aquaria, in her underwater kingdom to help make amends for her husband's death.

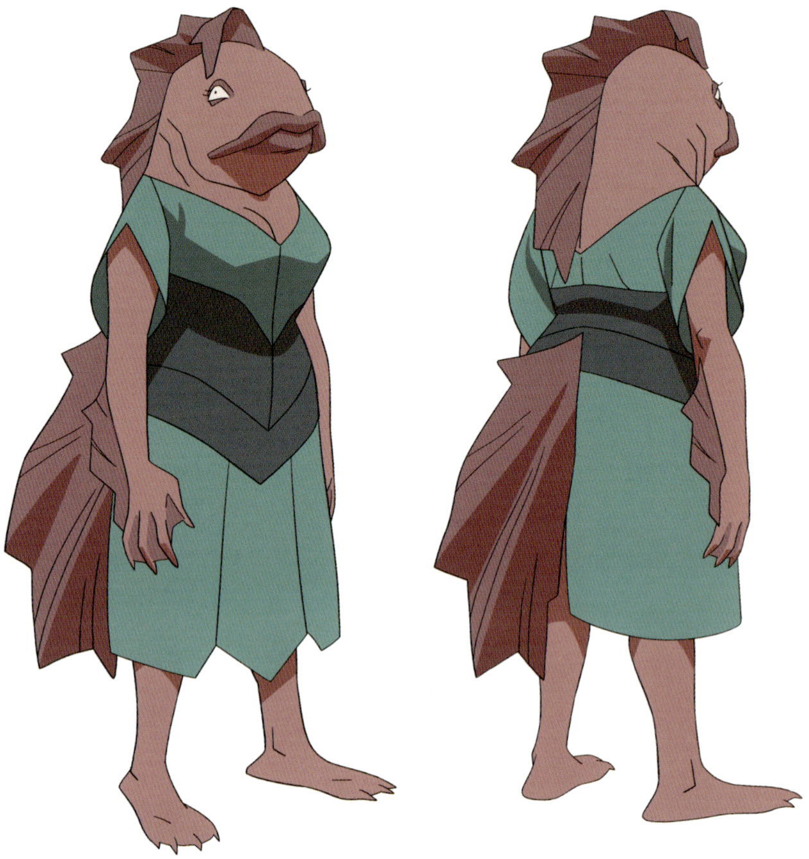

"Atlantis was great," says Racioppa. "Atlantis was a story that was from the comic books that was a little smaller, that we managed to expand a little bit and tried to weave a little bit more into Mark's story about where he is right now."

Atlantis had appeared in early issues of the *Invincible* comic, but when it came to bringing the kingdom's design into the show, the design team chose to go a new direction.

"Dave Johnson actually drew one page of the Aquarus sequence [in the comics] based on my initial design for Aquarus," says Kirkman, "which was a boxy guy with a fish head. He drew an Atlantis on that page that we used for the comics. Everything about Atlantis was kind of extrapolated

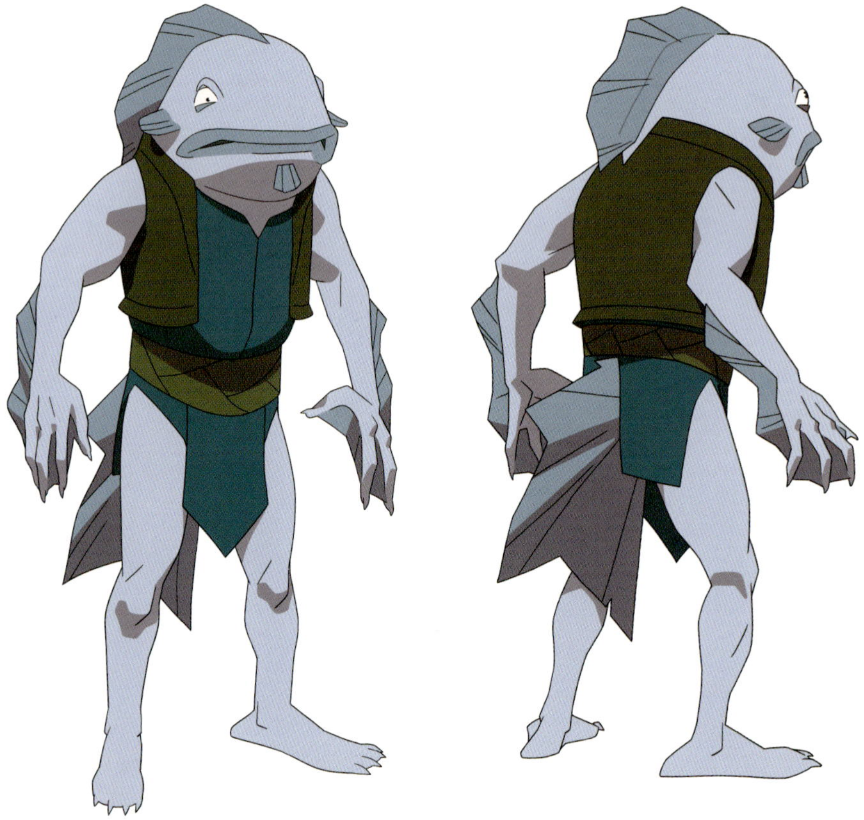

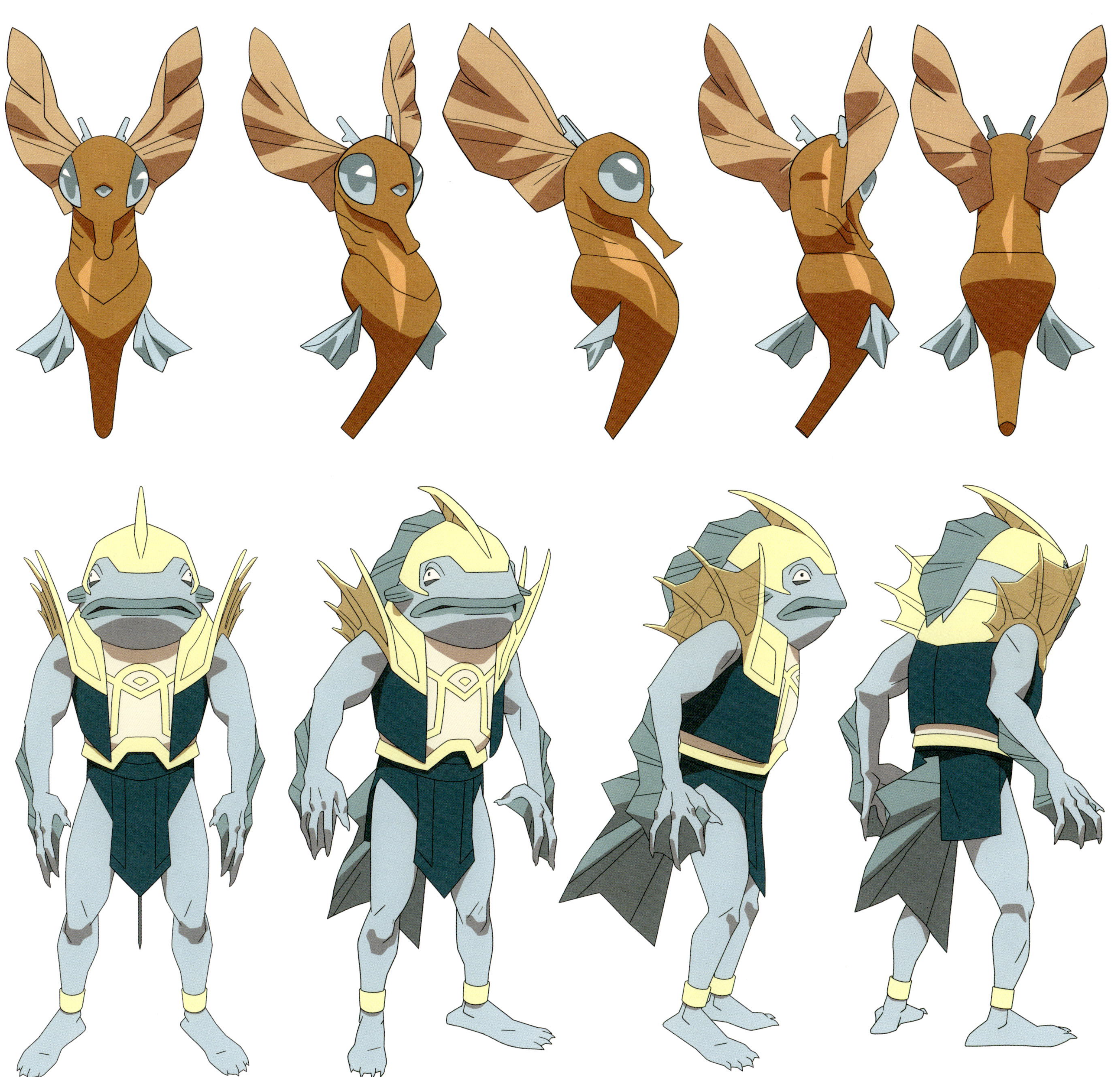

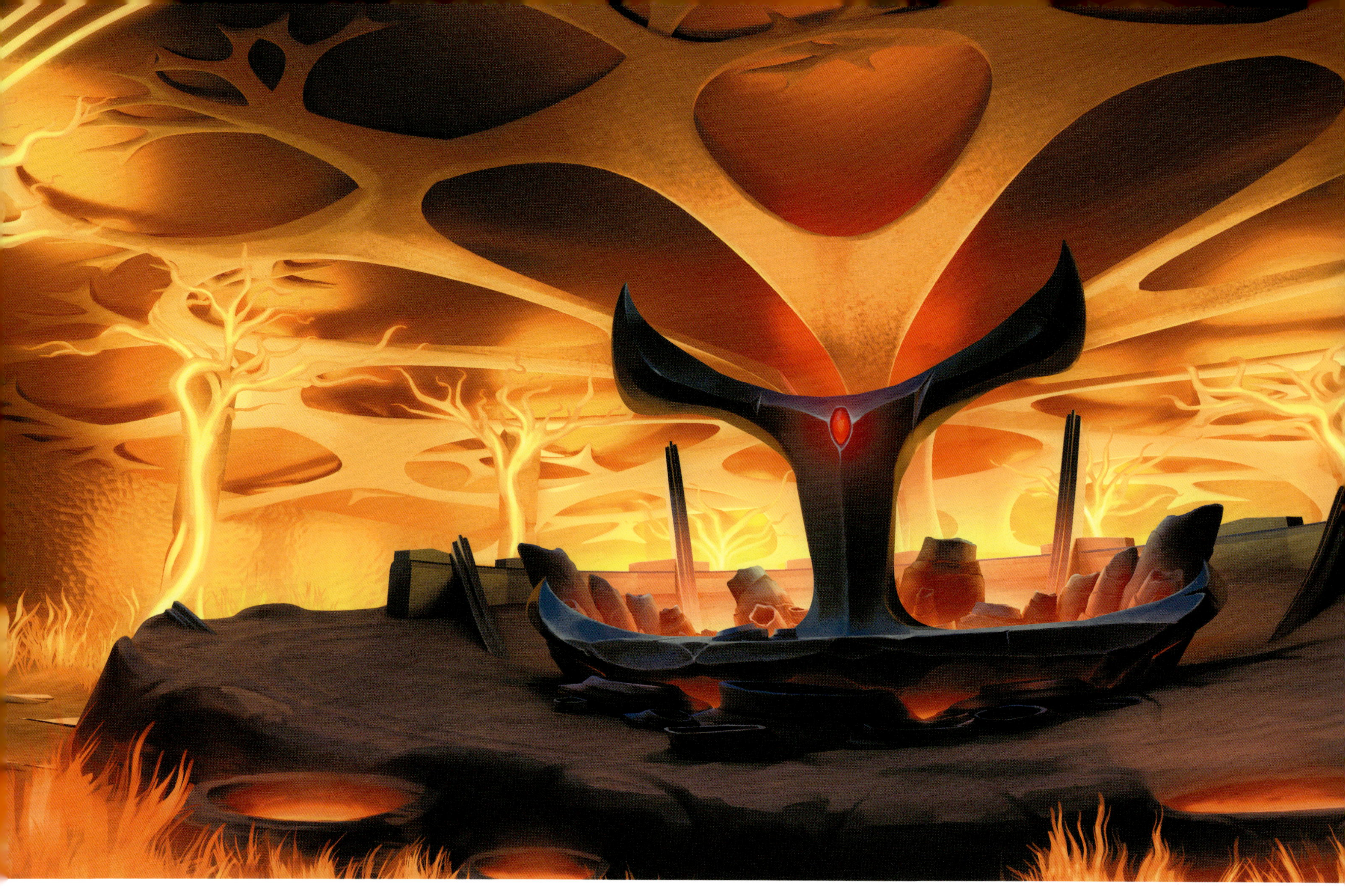

from that one page, up to the point where Cory did a cover for issue #15 that Dave joked, 'Am I getting a credit on this cover?' Most of it was the throne room that he drew in one panel redrawn for the cover. But I don't think a lot of that was used in the show. In the show, we kind of went with a different looking Atlantis to update it a little bit, but also to play to our strengths in animation and do some different things and make things a little bit more story specific to the way things went in the script. So there are some vehicles and things that didn't appear in the comics. The whole sequence is actually laid out vastly different than how it went in the comics. It's difficult to do an Atlantis that isn't similar to any of the myriad of times we've seen it in other media, so it's pretty amazing that the team was able to come up with some unique aspects for it for the show."

"The Atlantis stuff was wild," says O'Neil. "We didn't see a lot of it in the comic. So it was a lot of exploratory stuff. It was a lot of, 'What do we need from the script? How can we move through this space, give ourselves enough coverage, and then get into the meat and potatoes of the arena?' And

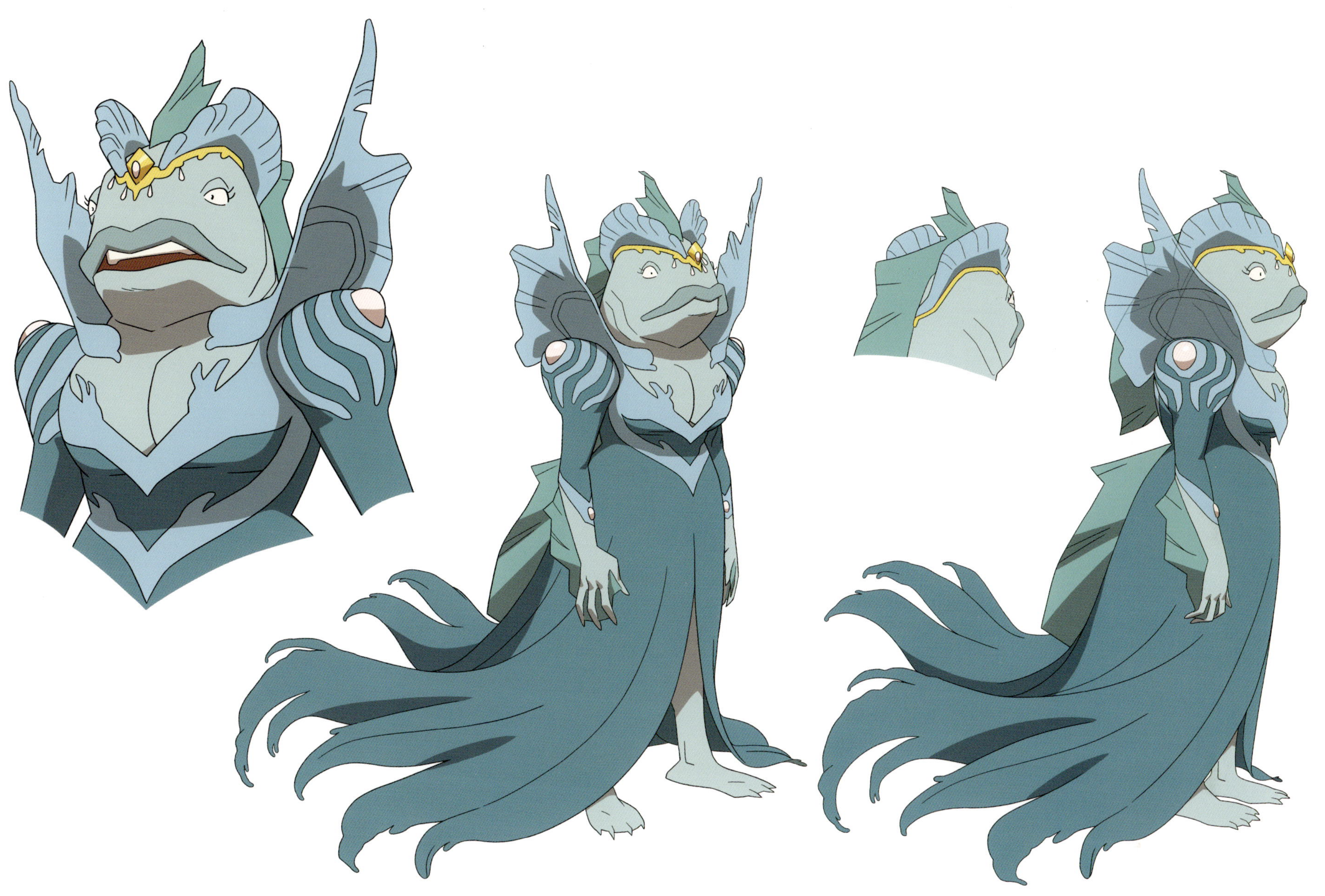

so, a lot of it was motif, a lot of it was just like working with [Environments Supervisor] Edwin [Fong] and Kelly [Mai] to really kind of pin down scale, first and foremost, and motif. How far can we push a *Little Mermaid* aesthetic without it breaking? And then what does the space outside of it look like, so that we can move through it in the establishing shots? Because we tried to cut around a ton of it. We tried to go from surface to arena and keep it real truncated. But Robert very much was like, 'No, I want to see the space. We kind of have to walk through this,' and you're just like, 'All right, cool. So what is that?' So then it's extrapolating shapes out of the arena, populating with stuff so you feel like you have a city, you have a space that's civilized and purpose-built. I think Addison [Bell] did most of the paints for that space, and it was just like, 'Go full tilt blorange' — cool sea colors, warm points to make stuff pop. And we wound up with some very, very awesome shit. It was a true team effort."

"Atlantis being in the recent *Aquaman* movies, we wanted to make sure it didn't feel like it does there," says Walker.

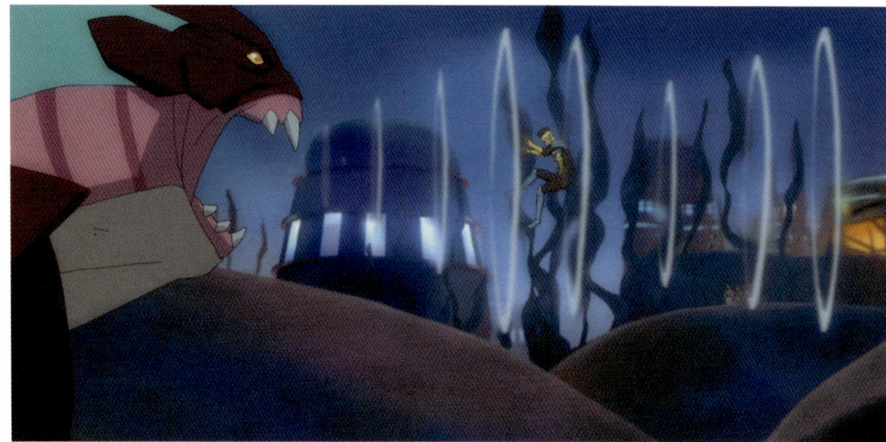

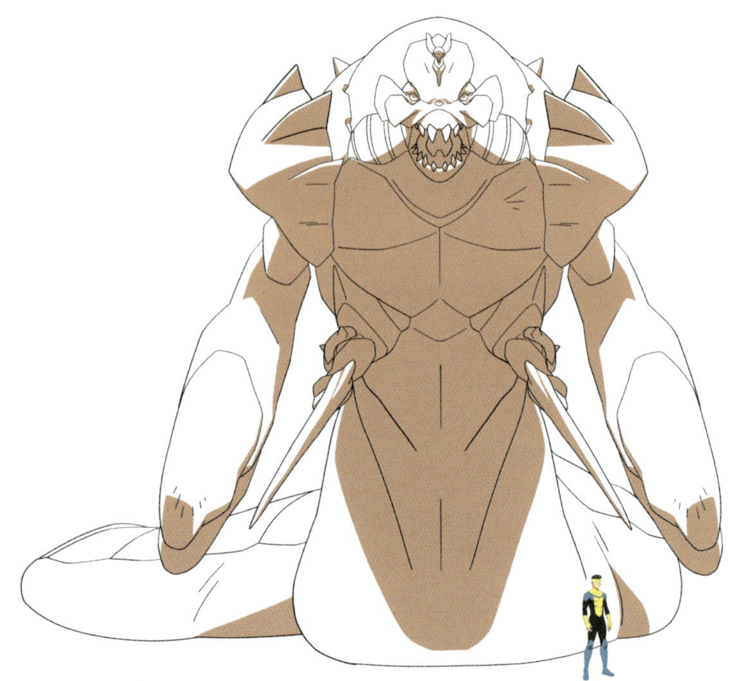

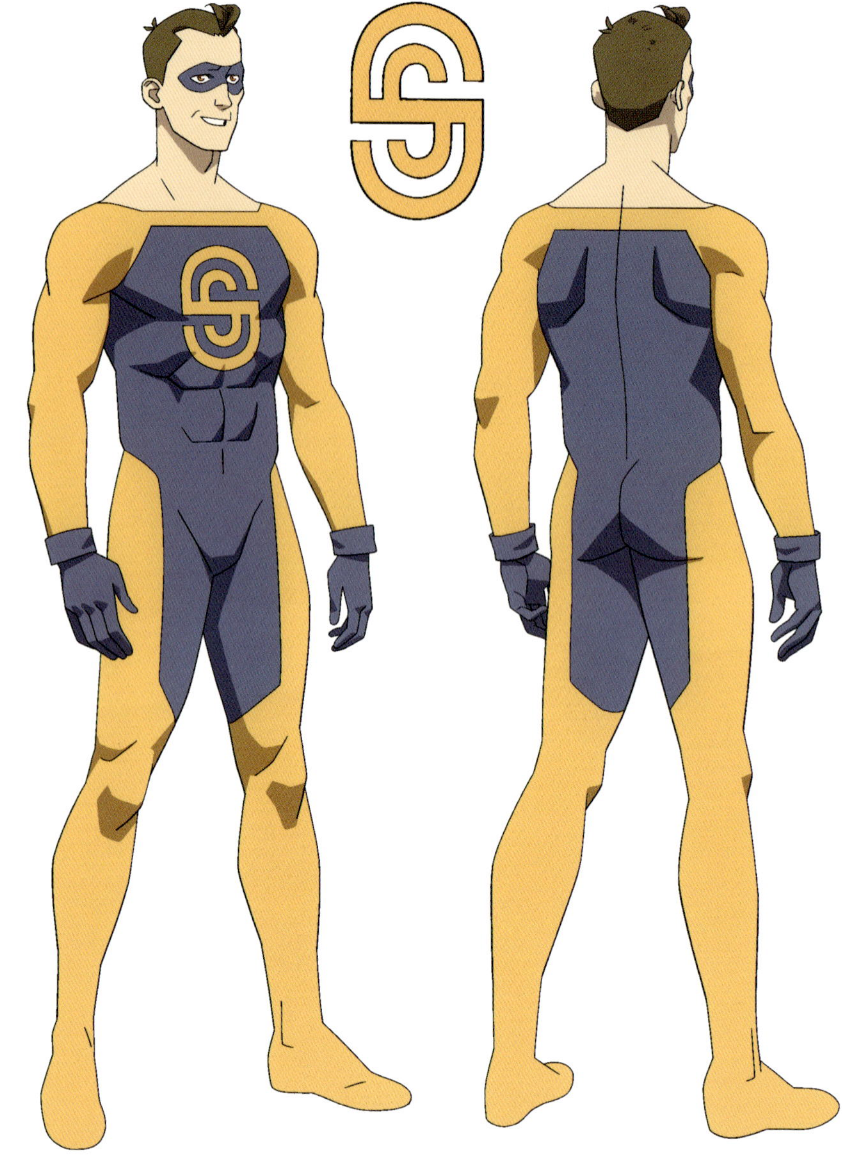

"Did we do that? I hope so."

When Mark arrived in Atlantis, he believed he'd have to marry Queen Aquaria in order to make peace. But instead, he found himself in an undersea arena facing off against a monster called the Depth Dweller in trial by combat.

"We had we had our own ideas of how the colosseum should be," says Walker. "Fish people kind of floating in their seats. I wish there'd been more floating, but we got some floating in there. I think it was unique enough and very much *Invincible*. If we had replicated [the Atlantis from the comic] for the show, it maybe would have come across too similar to Viltrum or other advanced places we've seen."

And it wasn't just Atlantis itself that had received a significant visual overhaul for the animated series.

"[The Depth Dweller was] a lot different from the comic, if I'm remembering correctly," says Walker. "It's a treat when we can depart from the comic. Sometimes we can't, but sometimes it makes sense to. So that was fun."

Mark managed to defeat the beast and make his exit from Atlantis alive and unmarried, but the GDA learned an interesting fact during the battle that may prove useful in the future.

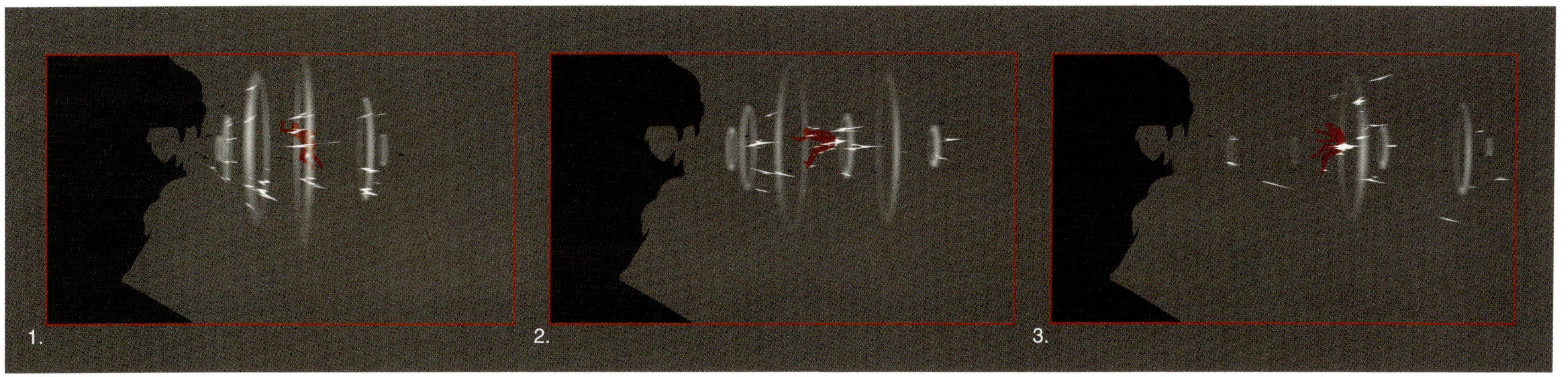
1.
2.
3.

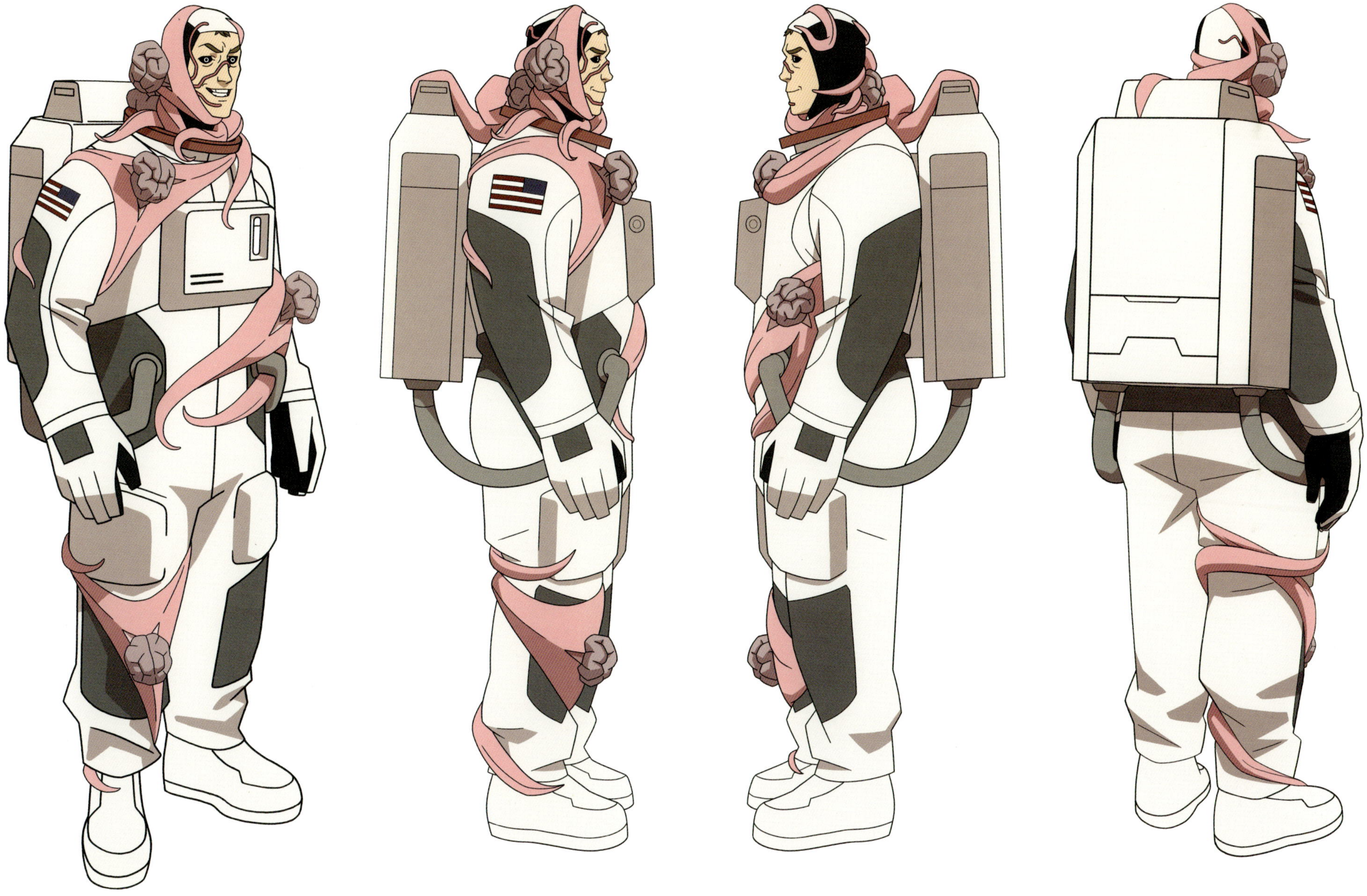

"The money shot from the episode is the fight with the Depth Dweller," says Racioppa. "Also, there's a hint of a weakness that Mark might have, with the sound it makes."

During the course of the episode, viewers are also reintroduced to a Martian who had disguised himself as a human astronaut named Rus Livingston and stowed away to Earth during Season One. In this episode, the character decided to put his natural shape-shifting abilities to good use as a new member of the Guardians of the Globe, Shapesmith.

"In the comics, Ryan Ottley just drew Shapesmith's costume based on what the Martians wore on Mars," says Kirkman, "and it's slightly altered into a superhero costume. Even Ryan wasn't really happy with that. So that's why we eventually gave him the blue and yellow pajama costume that he has in the comics. So we decided just to jump to that and have him wearing that, much the same way we did with Shrinking Rae. [The male] Shrinking Ray had a really crappy costume that I designed originally in the comics, and then eventually Ryan designed a new costume for him that was a lot better. And the female version of Shrinking Rae has a completely different costume that's a little bit more like the one that Ryan designed. So in the show, we've just kind of been jumping to the better costume that we eventually gave characters in a lot of cases, and Shapesmith is one of those."

Kirkman himself was able to take credit for one aspect of Shapesmith's costume.

"I actually designed that double 'S' pattern that's Shapesmith's chest logo," says Kirkman. "So I'll put that feather in my own cap. The inspiration being from a pizza box, I don't know exactly where that came from, but I know Cory did the little pizza mascot himself. So that's a Cory Walker original that was pasted into the show that inspired Shapesmith's costume."

Shapesmith's updated look was only enhanced further by superb voice acting by Ben Schwartz.

"He's so perfect and brings so much fun," says Racioppa. "He adlibs a lot of the time, which is great. We use that stuff. The character, he's the cause of some terrible, terrible stuff. So having him be kind of a lovable doofus who's kind

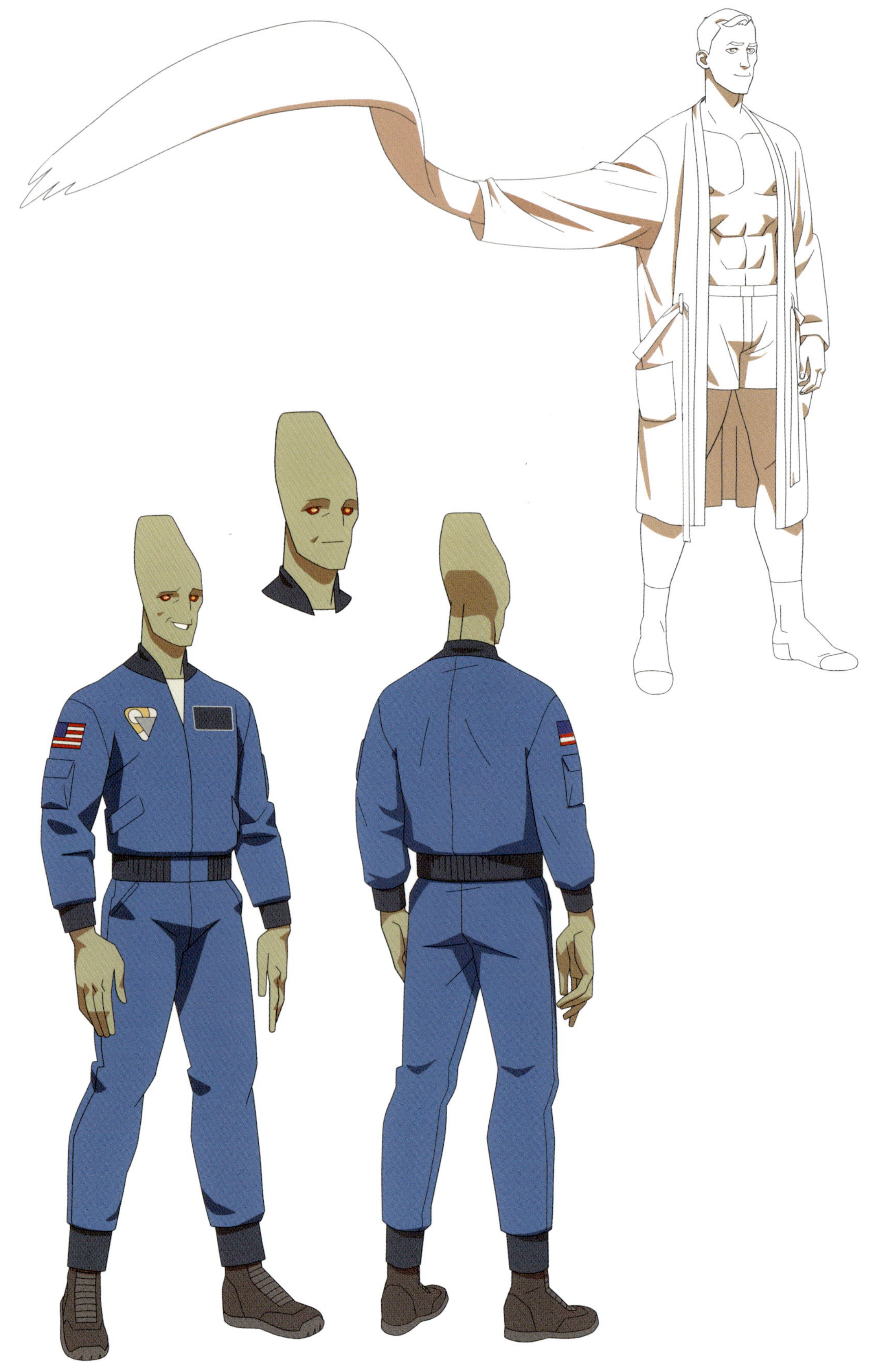

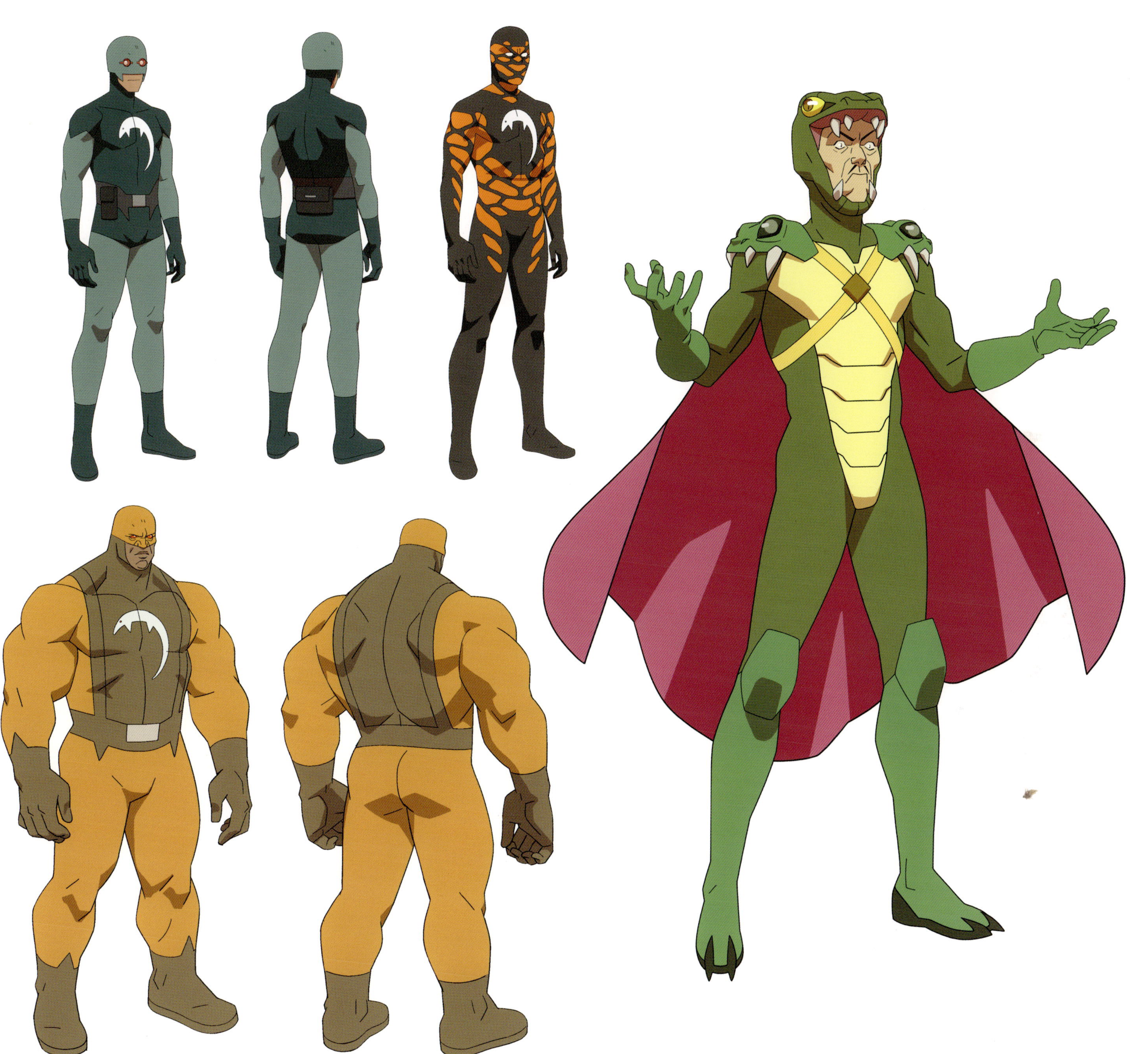

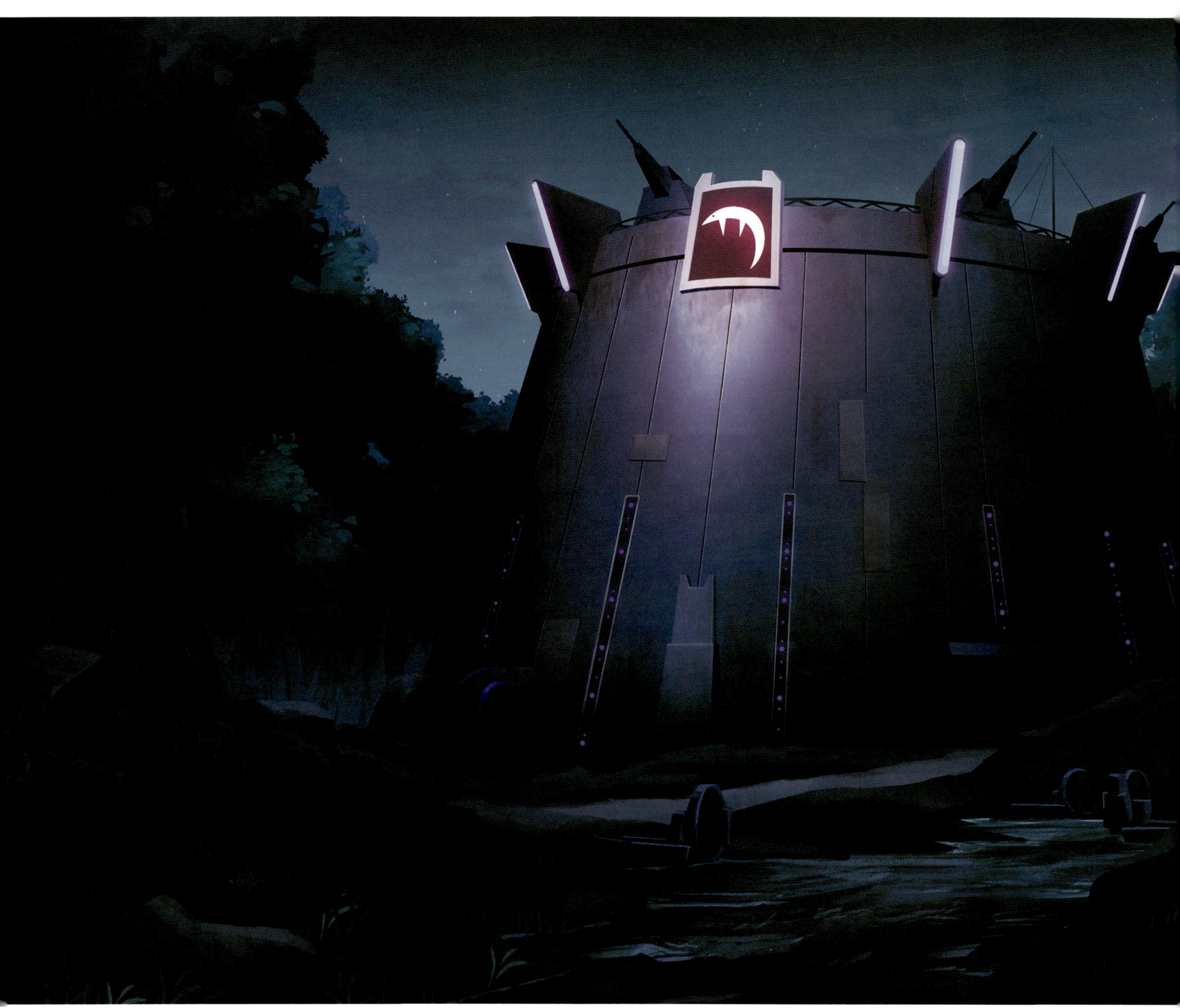

of sorry about all the stuff he did is helpful. It's fun for the character, because you're like, 'Oh, I should hate you, but I can't.'"

Meanwhile, in another dimension, Angstrom Levy had begun his quest for vengeance against Invincible, only to encounter two almost familiar faces: the gender-swapped interdimensional counterparts of the GDA's own Cecil Steadman and Donald Ferguson.

"Angstrom is jumping around looking for weaknesses, ways to beat Mark, because he knows he can't go hand-to-hand against him," say Racioppa. "He also wants to prolong it. Doesn't want to just kill Mark, he wants to make him suffer, because obviously he's a little crazy and he has all these memories of Mark doing terrible things in other dimensions. So we were joking about how he would go to dimensions where somebody beat Mark, somebody defeated Omni-Man, and find those places. And we were like, 'Wouldn't it be funny if it was the place where women were in charge of the GDA and they were like, 'Oh, we know how to do it.' And they're the ones effective enough to take down Mark and Nolan.' So that's where the idea came from for Caitlin and Denise."

As the jam-packed episode drew to a close, the Lizard League made their modern day return and went through a sudden and surprising change in leadership.

"That coda at the end of the episode is awesome ," says O'Neil, "where we get to see the Lizard League and [Supreme Lizard] is like, 'We're not a joke. I don't care what social media says.' And then he gets shot in the head [by King Lizard]."

"Again, Lizard League, with proper leadership they can be effective," says Racioppa. "He knows how to run them, versus his predecessor."

Though the Lizard League was about to benefit from unexpected change, the *Invincible* team had discovered the value of consistency, particularly in regards to the quality of the show's scripts.

"The scripts are always there for us," says Supervising Director Dan Duncan. "Robert, Simon, Helen, and the various writers that we've had on all of the seasons are great. Even before I worked on the show, I would hear, 'These are the best writers! These scripts!' If there's anything wrong with the show, it's not the scripts. The story team has been very versatile and [Director] Ian Abando and his team — they did [Episode] 202 — they're great. They've got a great sense of humor, and they came in and wanted to learn the show and really wanted to impress everybody. So they really got it. They were able to do the fun stuff. That was the stuff that really vibed for them and the stuff that came most naturally. And so then it was just, 'Okay, well, push this darker, push this darker.' Whereas most of the other episodes, you get people who really have some shit they gotta get out of their system and they want to just do people ripping other people in half. And so, to try and get those people to lighten up is very difficult. But when we have a lighter crew that's just kind of here to have a good time, to get them to make it a little bit darker is easier. Even when Mark beats the Depth Dweller and crawls out and he's throwing up all over, it's hilarious. And so, that was the vibe that team brought. They were able to keep the serious stuff... they were able to hit those beats and do those things and they latched on to that. They're very story minded. When you get the story, you just kind of know what it needs."

The story team also knew what Mark needed after this action-packed episode, and that was a bit of a break. Fortunately, he was about to get one, as the focus of the following episode was about to shift beyond Earth to bold new worlds.

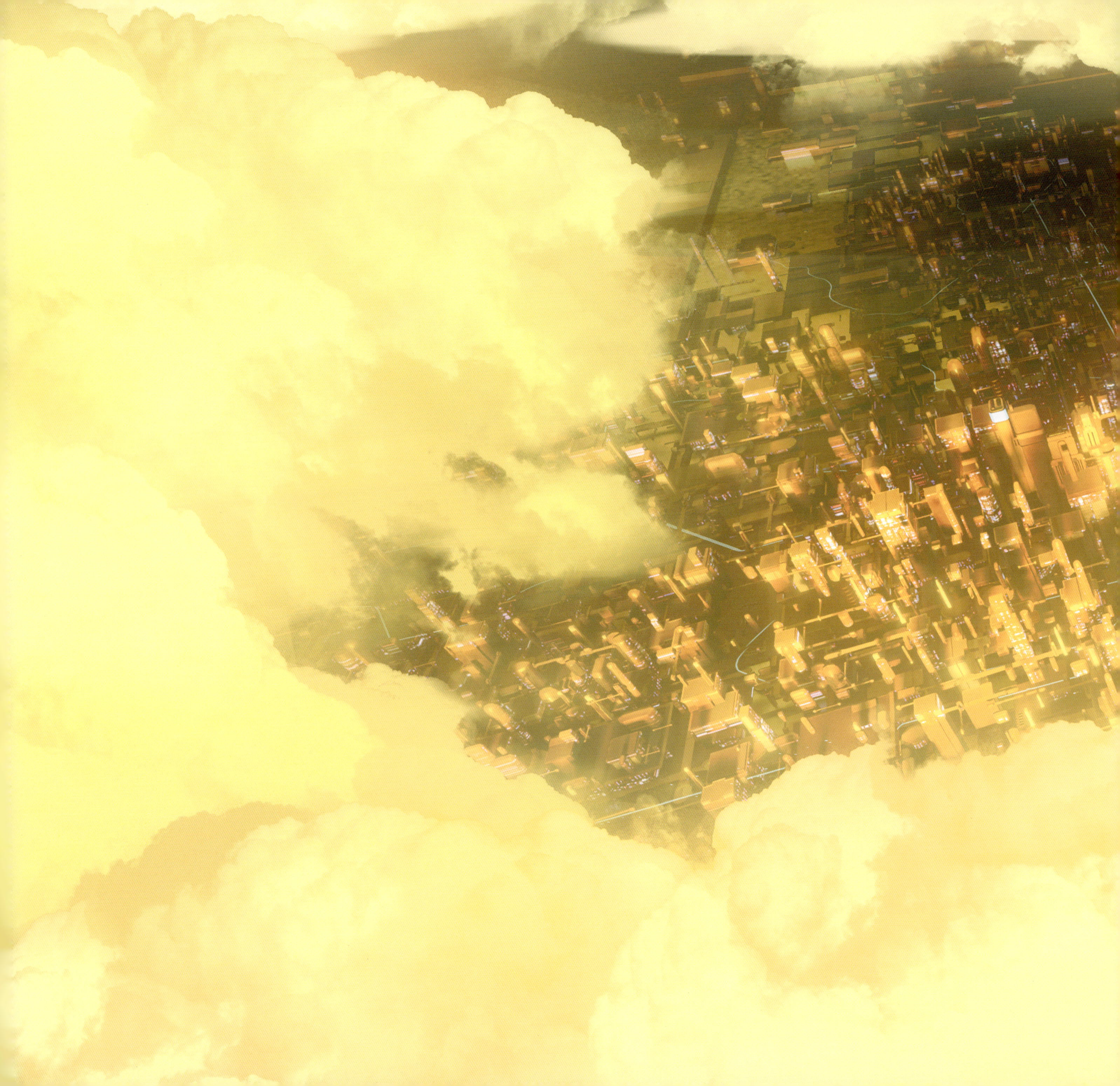

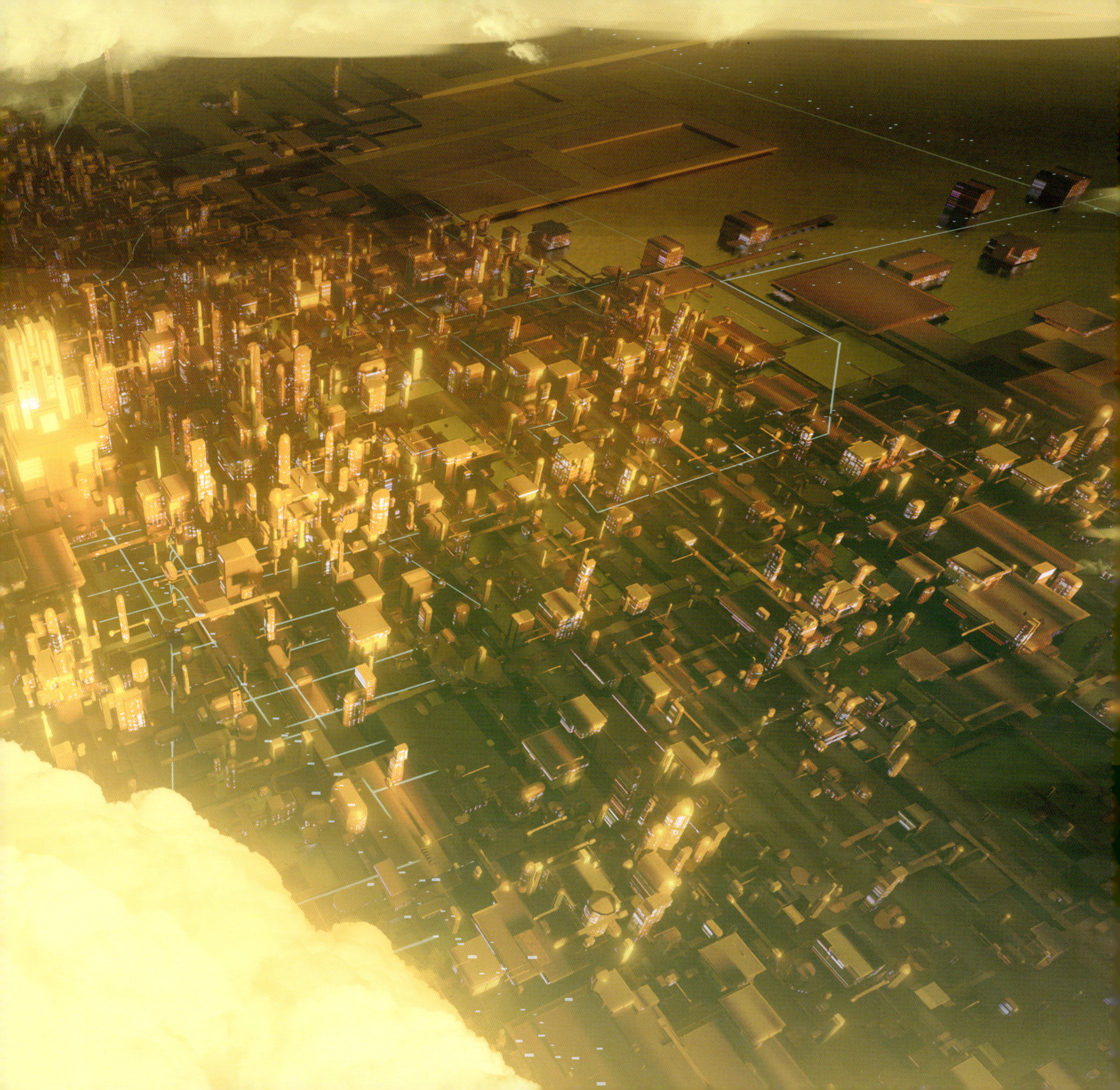

EPISODE 3:

THIS MISSIVE, THIS MACHINATION!

After the whirlwind second episode of *Invincible* Season Two, this episode began with Mark Grayson getting some much needed respite from his superhero life as he began classes at Upstate University, alongside his girlfriend, Amber and his best friend, William. However, while Invincible himself may have finally had a moment to breathe, the creative team behind his show most certainly did not.

The episode almost immediately shifted its focus to Allen the Alien, an ally of Invincible from Season One, and his adventures deep in space.

"If you read the comics, a lot of *Invincible* in the back half takes place in space, on other planets," says Executive Producer and Co-Showrunner Simon Racioppa. "So this is a nice episode to just kind of introduce people to it without slamming them with a whole bunch of made-up words, which can turn people off. If you're like, 'Oh, they're Talescrians and they're Flub-Flobs and they're Glib-Globs,' and all that kind of stuff, people are like, 'Whoa, wait a sec.' So it was a nice way to just sort of bring us in. We get Allen's backstory first, so we get to know a little bit about him — what motivates him, where he comes from, why he is the way he is. Then we see him return to Talescria. So it's kind of a nice way to ease people into the bigger scale of *Invincible*, because Season One was really, in a way, grounded. It's just superheroes. We don't go to a ton of crazy places. So Season Two is kind of opening up the door and being like, 'Okay, you liked Season One, a family drama. Well, it's still a family drama, but now we're going to open up the doors and take you to a few crazier places, a few more interesting things, and show you the scale of the story is much bigger than it was in Season One.' And, hopefully, we do that in a way that keeps you interested and along and understanding what's going on."

Introducing entirely new alien civilizations into an animated series can be a daunting task for any art team. Fortunately, the unique new settings introduced in this episode allowed the designers to push in bold new directions.

"It was a lot to get into because, especially for the Allen stuff, it was almost like it was a completely different show," says Co-Executive Producer and Co-Creator Cory Walker. "Like we were designing a new show with all new assets.

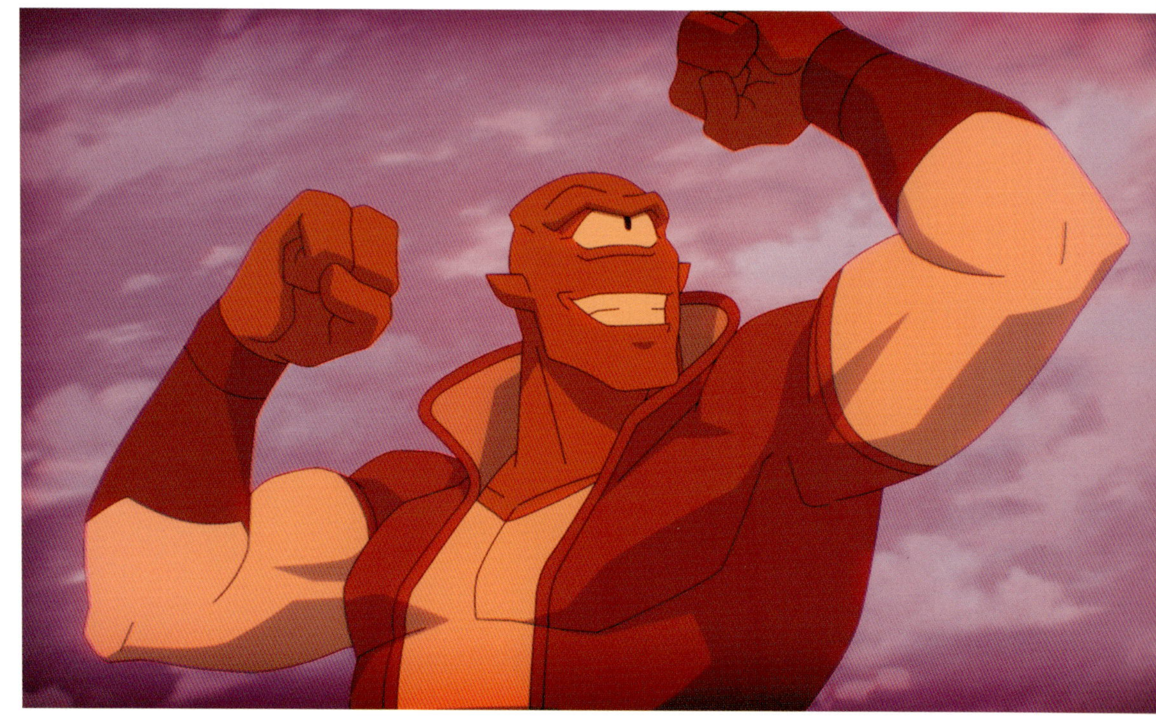

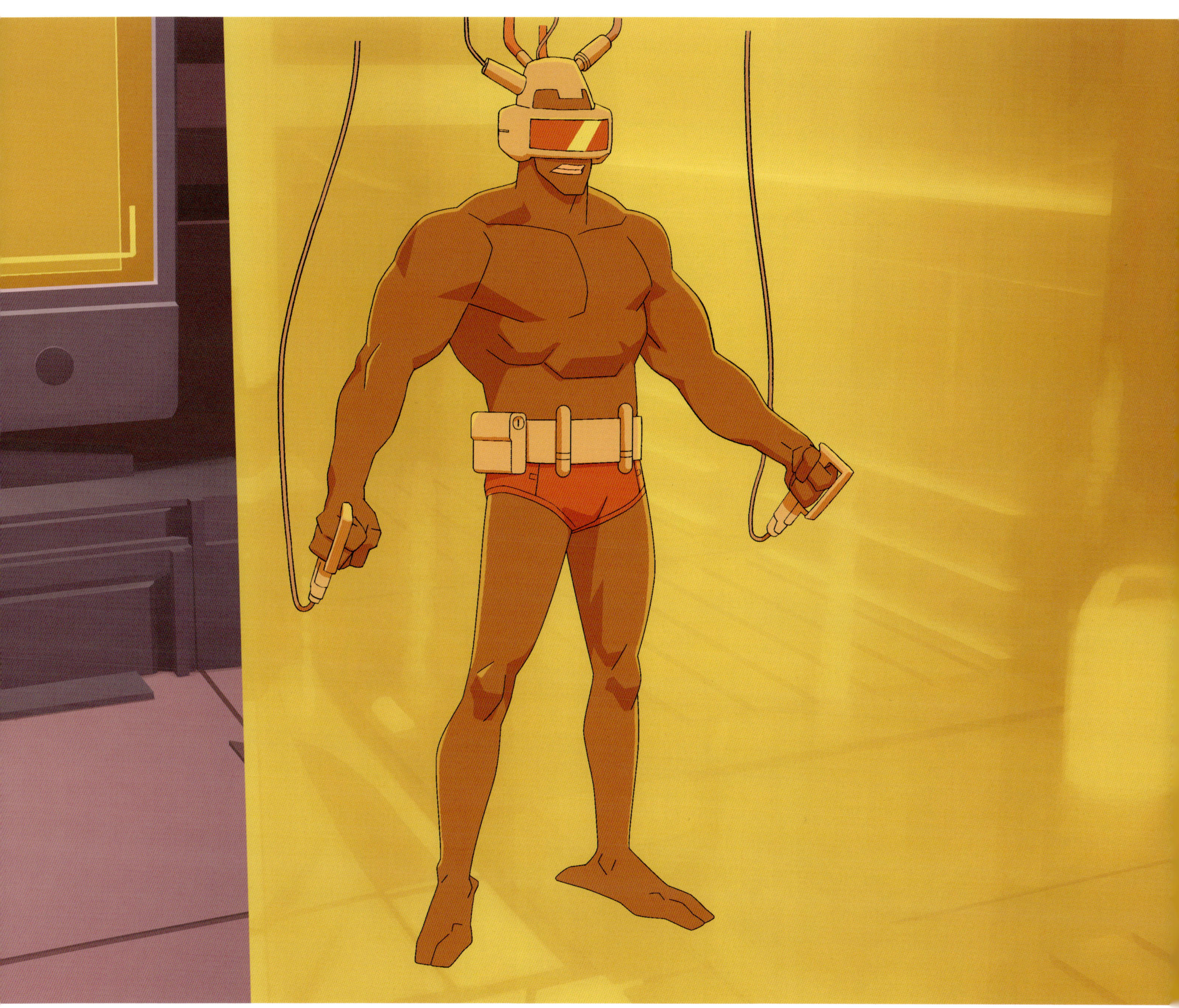

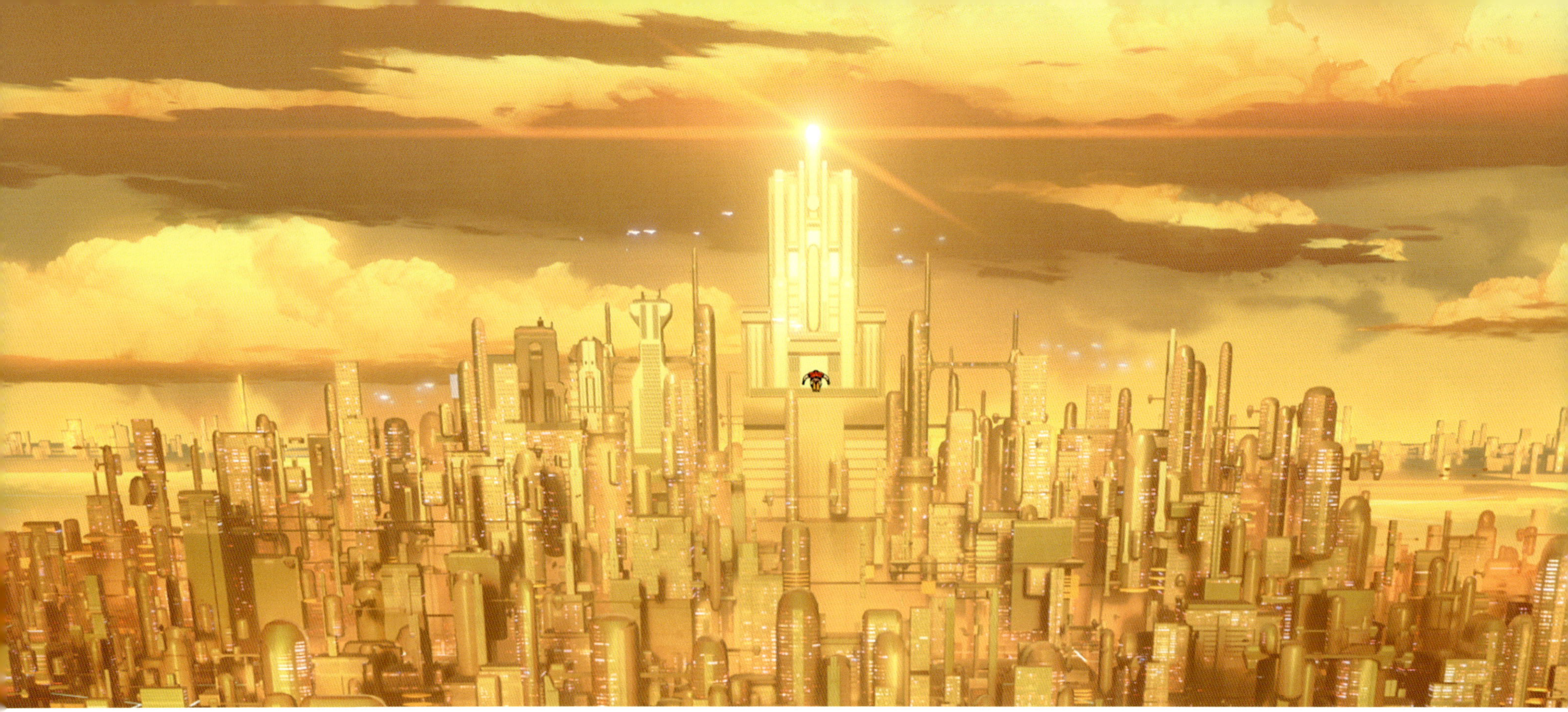

So, that's a job."

"We had a lot to adhere to from Season One," says Art Director Shaun O'Neil, "but the thing that gave us a lot of wiggle room was that we were traveling to space. And so the further away we go from Earth, the more the rules just didn't apply. For this one in particular, Talescria was our first location in the season away from Earth. And I was like, 'Let's just go as hard as we can. Let's really try and make this feel like a place that's different.' I think the rule was, the further out we go, the more fantastic things can get. So it's like Earth and Earth orbit is very boring, very generic. General space is black, maybe a little dusty. But once you start getting towards alternate locations, we start bringing in a rainbow to the cosmic space dust of it all. And so, for the introduction of Talescria, it was a lot of that. It's like, 'Let's just go full Technicolor. And when we go down to the surface of the planet, it's just like golden sunset. Let's get a lighting that's beautiful, but is not something that we could have.' And I think the team did a really good job with it. I think that space in the comics was always something that was very, very cool to me because, especially when we got the early introductions to it, it was a lot of Cory stuff. And so you get a lot of those simple geometry shapes that are stacked in really great ways that are really appealing. So it was trying to make sure that we could represent some of that, trying to make sure that we could keep that appeal and that interest."

But it was also important to Walker that the team not feel too beholden to what had come before in the comic when translating these new worlds to the screen.

"Sometimes we do have enough that we can pull from the book," says Walker. "But again, at the same time, it was two guys that drew the book. So I think one of the major benefits we have is, again, some unique voices to bring their spin on things. It adds a lot to it. I like to say, 'It's a bit of a cosmic gumbo.' I think that it is tricky. But the best weapon we have toward making sure we have some unique visuals is the number of talented artists that we can go to."

Talescria served as the gathering place for the Coalition of Planets, a group of aliens from various worlds who banded together to fight back against Viltrumite domination.

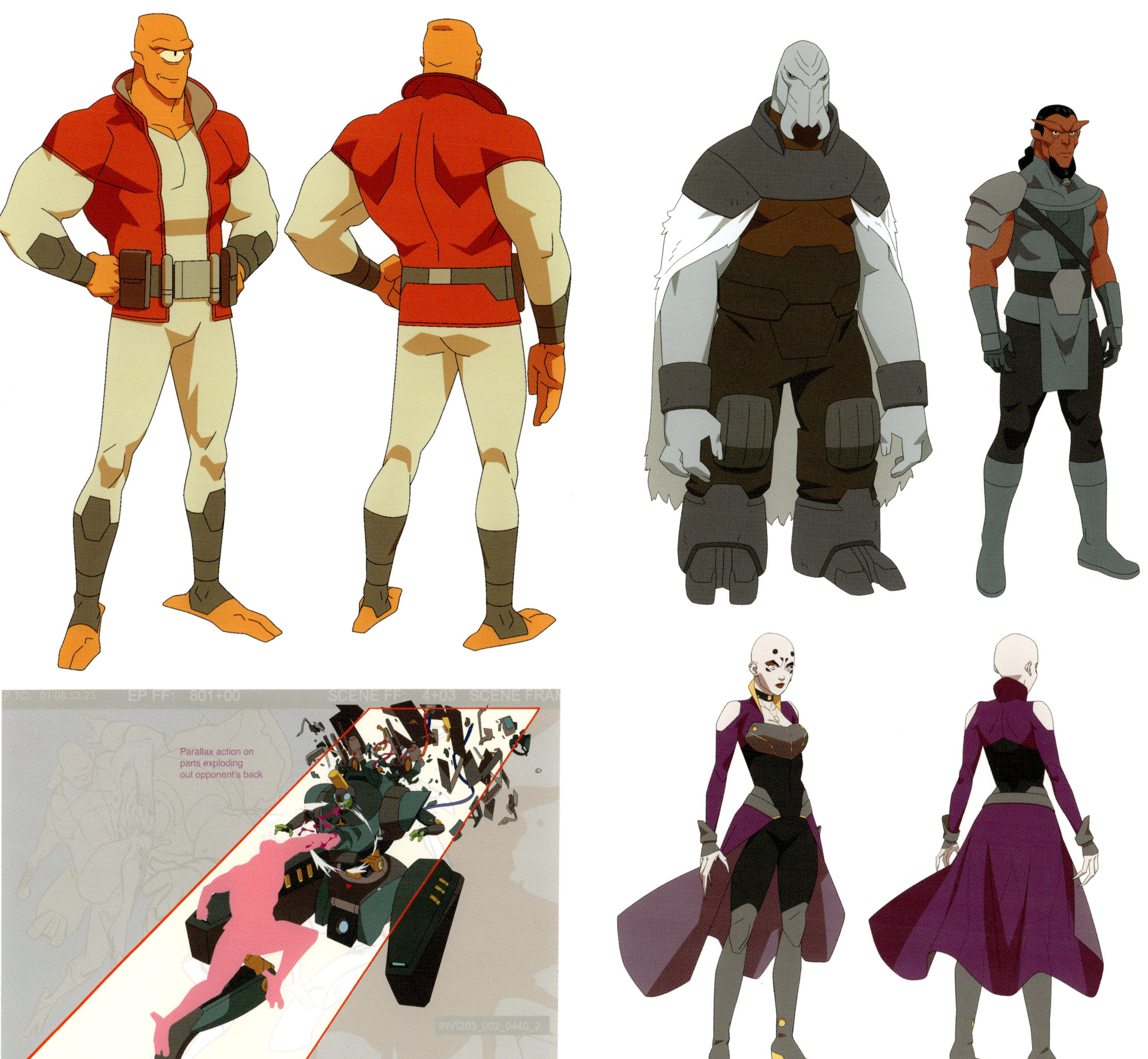
EP FF: 801+00
SCENE FF: 4+03
Parallax action on parts exploding out opponent's back
SEQUENCE 02
SCENE 0440

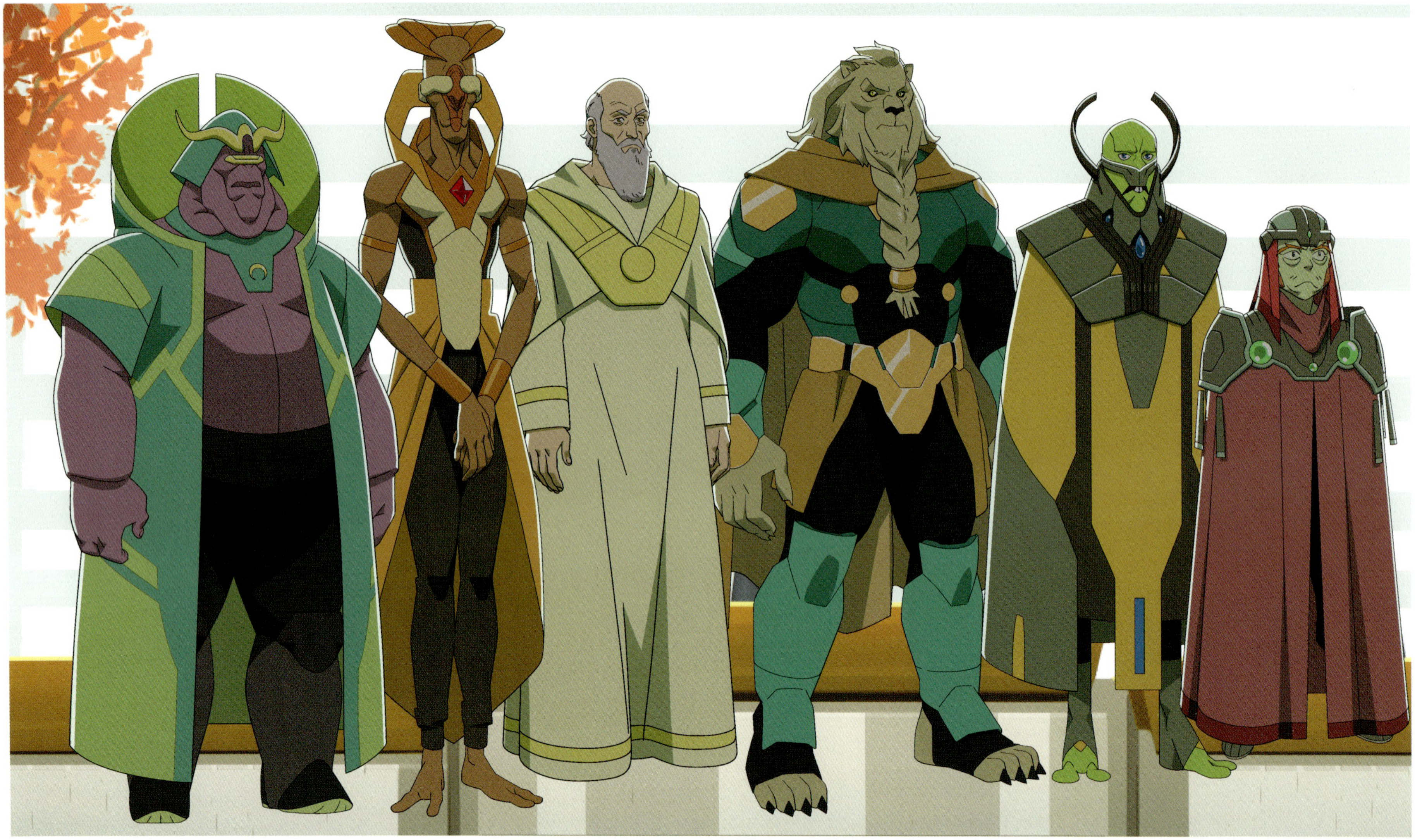

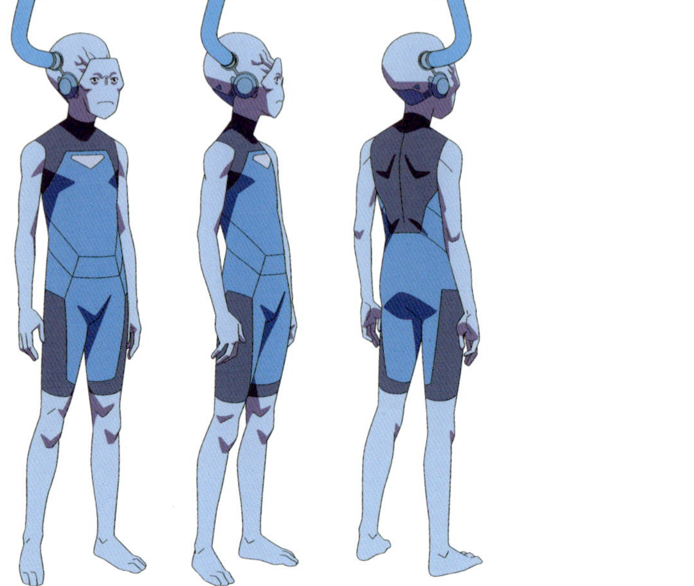

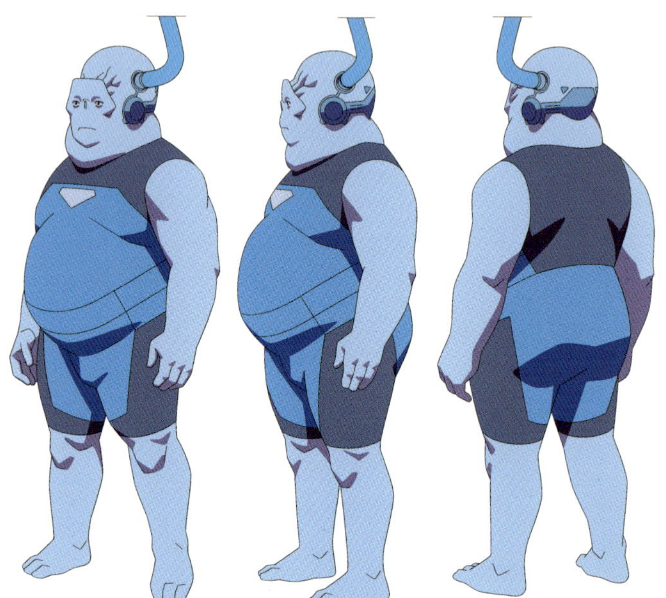

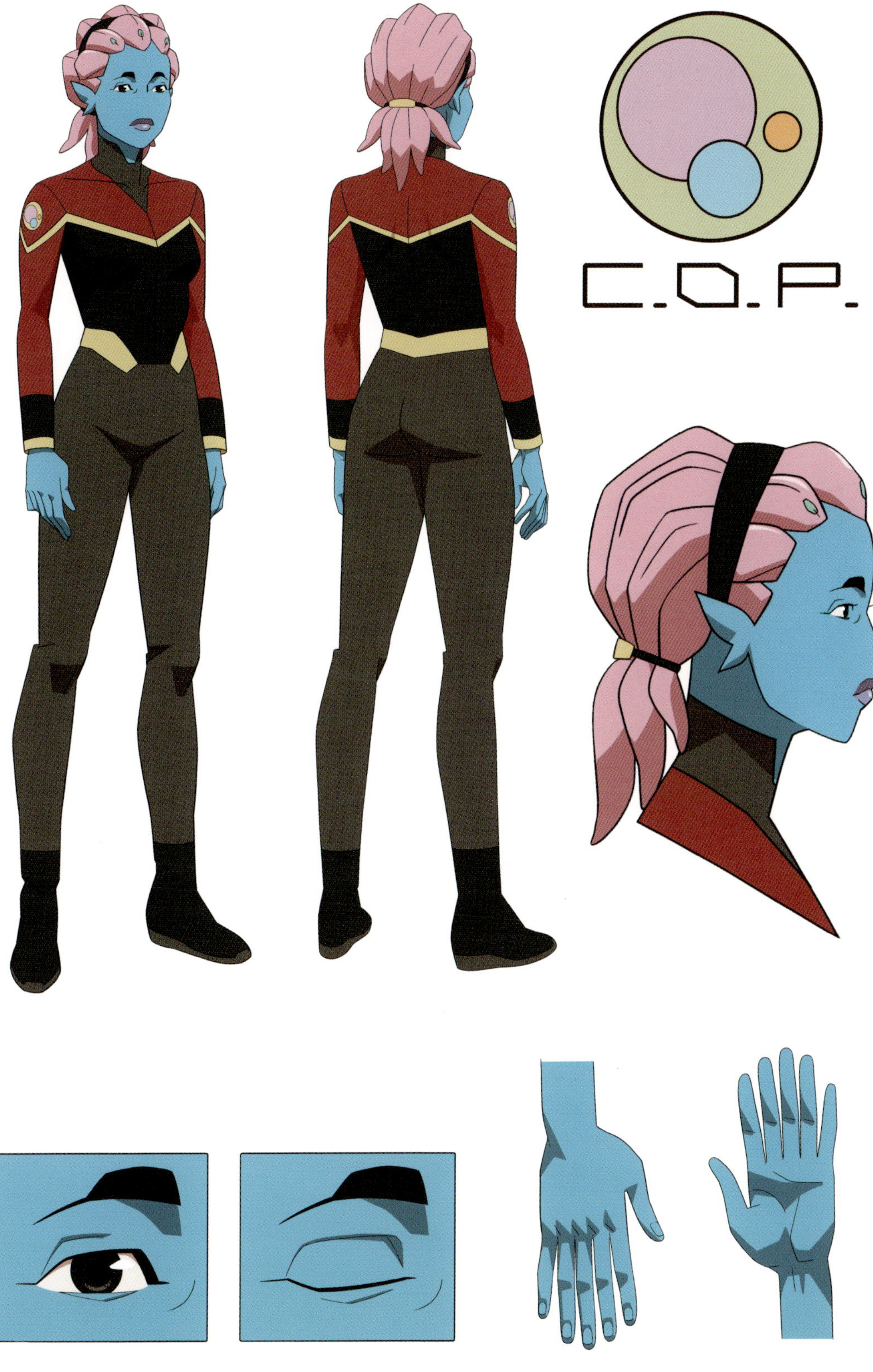

"We get a little bit of intro about the bigger scope of the Viltrumites," says Racioppa, "because in Season One, we just know they're out there. Nolan tells his story, but we don't know if that's true necessarily. The scope of his story is pretty small. He's like, 'Oh, we're this interplanetary race,' and stuff. Now, we're like, 'Oh, there's other aliens out here. They're all in league against the Viltrumites. Viltrumites have captured some planets. They have slaves.' We get a bigger picture of what's happening off Earth without spending the entire episode there."

Talescria becomes a major part of *Invincible*'s story moving forward, which made the time spent designing the world for this episode all the more important.

"With Episode 203, we knew that we were going to be doing Talescria stuff and that it was going to be a huge undertaking," says Executive Producer, Co-Showrunner, and Co-Creator Robert Kirkman. "But in animation, it's all about, 'How much are you going to reuse?' And we spend a lot of time on Talescria as time goes on, so all the work that goes into this episode is work that doesn't have to go into future episodes. So that's the way we try to look at it."

While on Talescria, Allen went about his daily life and interacted with a number of new characters who will go on to play significant roles in the future, including Thaedus, the leader of the Coalition, and Telia, a Coalition general who is also Allen's romantic partner.

"We got to do Thaedus, which was really cool," says Kirkman. "I cannot believe that we were able to get Peter Cullen (legendary voice actor of Optimus Prime from *The Transformers*) to play Thaedus. It's the greatest moment of my life [recording] with that guy. And again, Thaedus is another character design that was adapted pretty closely from the comics."

"Getting to introduce Telia finally was really cool," says Walker. "And her having a different role than she had in the comic, a little bit more important, is cool."

"She wears more clothes," says Kirkman. "As she should."

After a romantic interlude, Allen and Telia went to a space diner to enjoy a nice, squirming bowl of *Invincible*'s signature alien snack, kanslok.

"This is not the first appearance of kanslok [in the show]," says Kirkman, "but it's our first real appearance of kanslok. As opposed to it just appearing in Nolan's flashback tale at the beginning of Episode 108, floating in the air like a cigar."

What started as a relatively quiet episode in terms of action quickly escalated when a trio of Viltrumites ambushed Allen. The group included a face familiar to comic readers — and to viewers who paid attention to the Viltrum flashback sequence in the Season One finale.

"Thula actually appeared in that sequence," says Kirkman. "So this is her first speaking appearance. Thula was a Viltrumite who appears for the first time much later in the comic book series. I don't think she appears until the 'Viltrumite War' in the comic series. And we thought it'd be good to introduce her a little bit earlier here."

Another of the Viltrumites looked very familiar as well, but mostly to the members of the *Invincible* creative team.

"Vidor is based on [writer] Ross Stracke," says Kirkman. "Because Ross Stracke always has a mustache. And so anybody [working] on the show that has a mustache gets turned into a Viltrumite extra. That's not a rule, but it worked for Ross Stracke."

And the third Viltrumite warrior...?

"I think the other Viltrumite is just a random guy," says Kirkman. "So who cares about him?"

Allen was clearly outmatched against the three alien attackers, each one as powerful as Omni-Man. While he did everything in his power to fight back and protect other innocent aliens, Allen took severe battle damage in the process.

"Battle damage is a nice way to put it," says Racioppa. "I mean, he basically gets brutally murdered and, almost, left for dead. Don't cross a Viltrumite. That sequence, in my head, was kind of the opposite of Nolan killing the Guardians in Season One. So, Nolan killing the Guardians at the end of Season One, we did with just sound effects. We killed all the score. After a certain point, it's just the sound effects. We thought that would be the most visceral way to do it. So really, it's just everyone breathing. We spent a lot of time doing ADR, bringing the actors back in to really try and get the best sound work for that sequence. The weapons, the splat of brains scattering everywhere. This one, we were in space. We don't have those sounds. There's nothing. He wasn't being smushed up against an asteroid. And even if he was, we sort of mute the sounds in space, because obviously there's not really any sound in space. Although, if you got crushed into something, you would hear it internally. You'd hear it still within your own head, just through bone

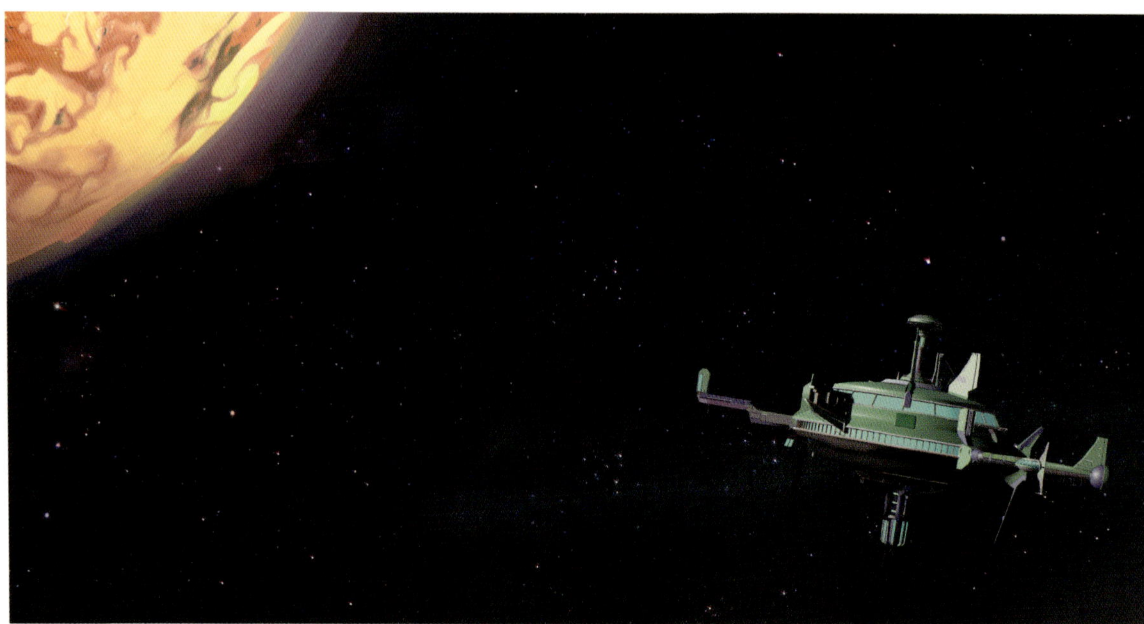

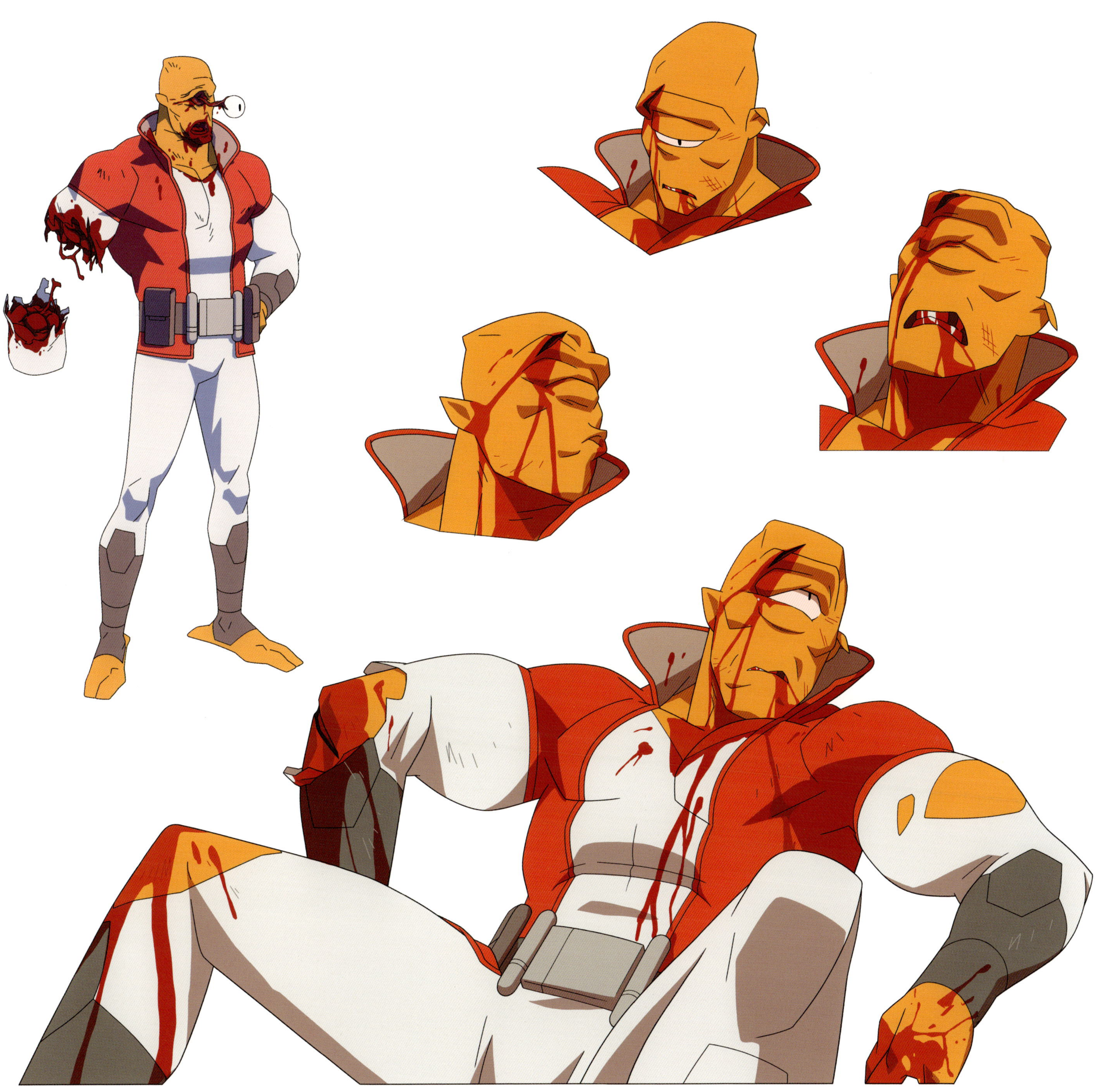

conduction and stuff like that. So we're like, 'Let's do it with music. Let's try and make this beautiful sequence, and make it the opposite of what we already saw.' So another terrible, brutal murder sequence. A brutality sequence. But let's make it kind of kind of gorgeous and kind of beautiful. That's what the music helped us achieve."

While sound certainly helped enhance the mood of the scene, it was the shocking depictions of the injuries inflicted upon Allen that pushed the show's art team to their limits.

"Shout out to the whole team, because not everybody is comfortable with it," says O'Neil. "I've worked on some shows and projects that have leaned into some gratuitous material. This show in particular goes so hard on the violence part of it that it's hard to explain to people coming in what they're going to be dealing with. You can tell them, but you have to see it with your own eyes. You have to get an assignment. I think, for me, biggest props to the character team because, I think the term they made up for themselves was 'Gore Kings'. On the money. It's super appropriate. When you have an assignment where you're like, 'You have to punch a hole in this guy.' And when that assignment comes through, and I'm like, 'No. Not a fake hole. Not a cartoon hole. Like a real hole. Like we have to reference this. We have to dig into the viscera.' And you start blocking out shapes for them, and you start having the conversations about body parts and what you have to look for. We have a couple people — I always think of poor Charles [Tan] — who very much did not enjoy that work, but did such a good job with it. It was hard. You've got to pace people out. You got to kind of break it up. You get a little bit of it this episode. The next guy gets it the next episode. And when you absolutely have to, we're all in it together. Some of the episodes, like 204, like 208, it's just like, 'We're going to be here until it's done. So we might as well put our best foot forward and get through it, and then take breathers where we can, because it's tough.'"

To make sure the gore was depicted on screen exactly as intended, the designers would often create Character Special Poses — images that were extremely detailed and rendered, which were then inserted directly into the

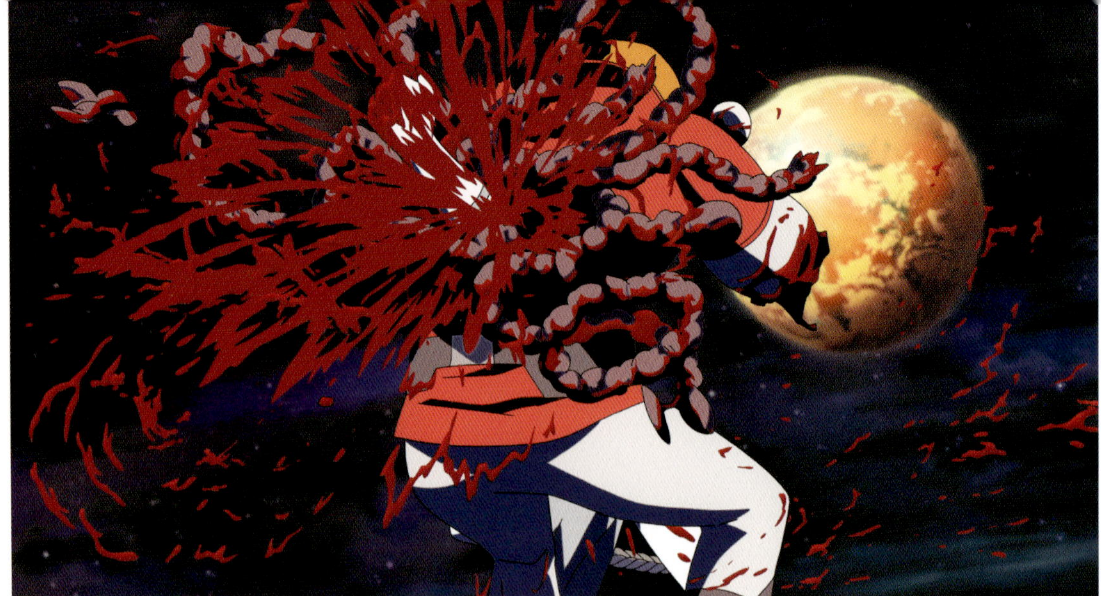

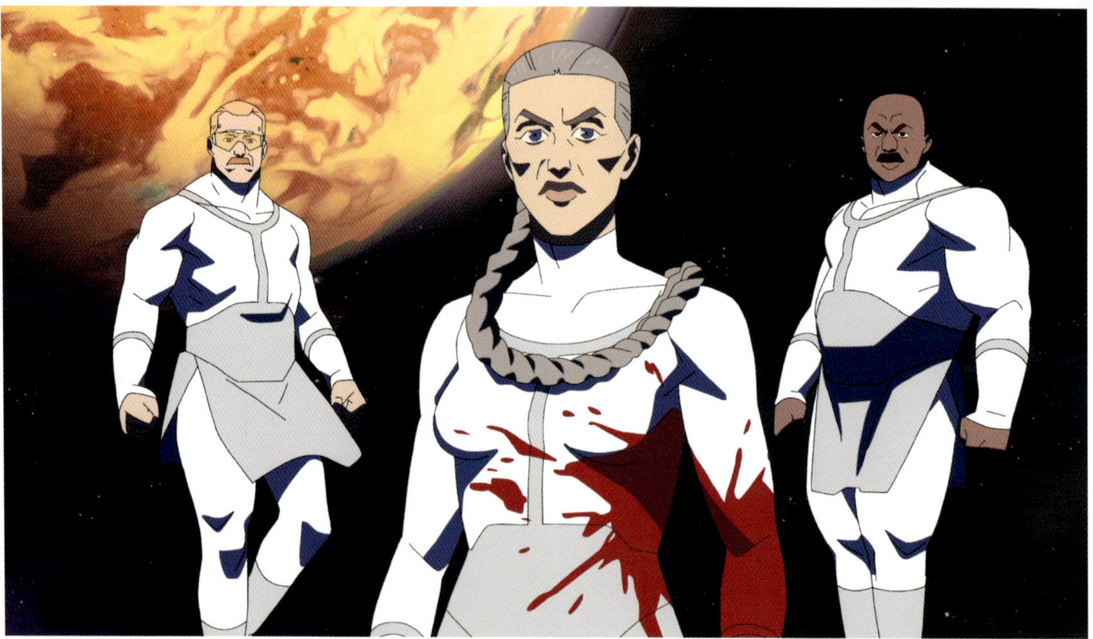

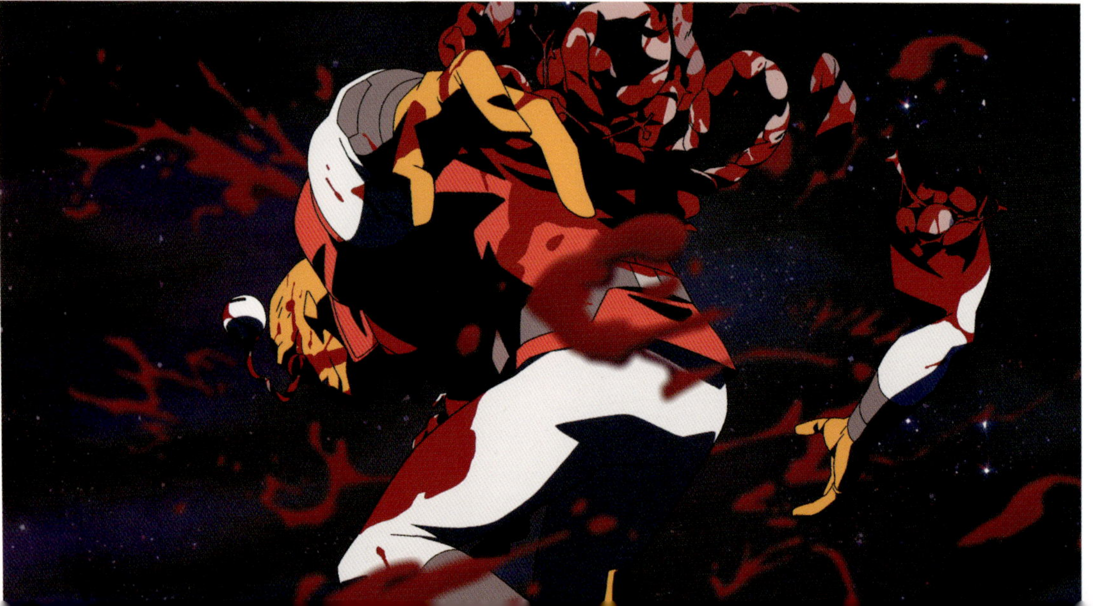

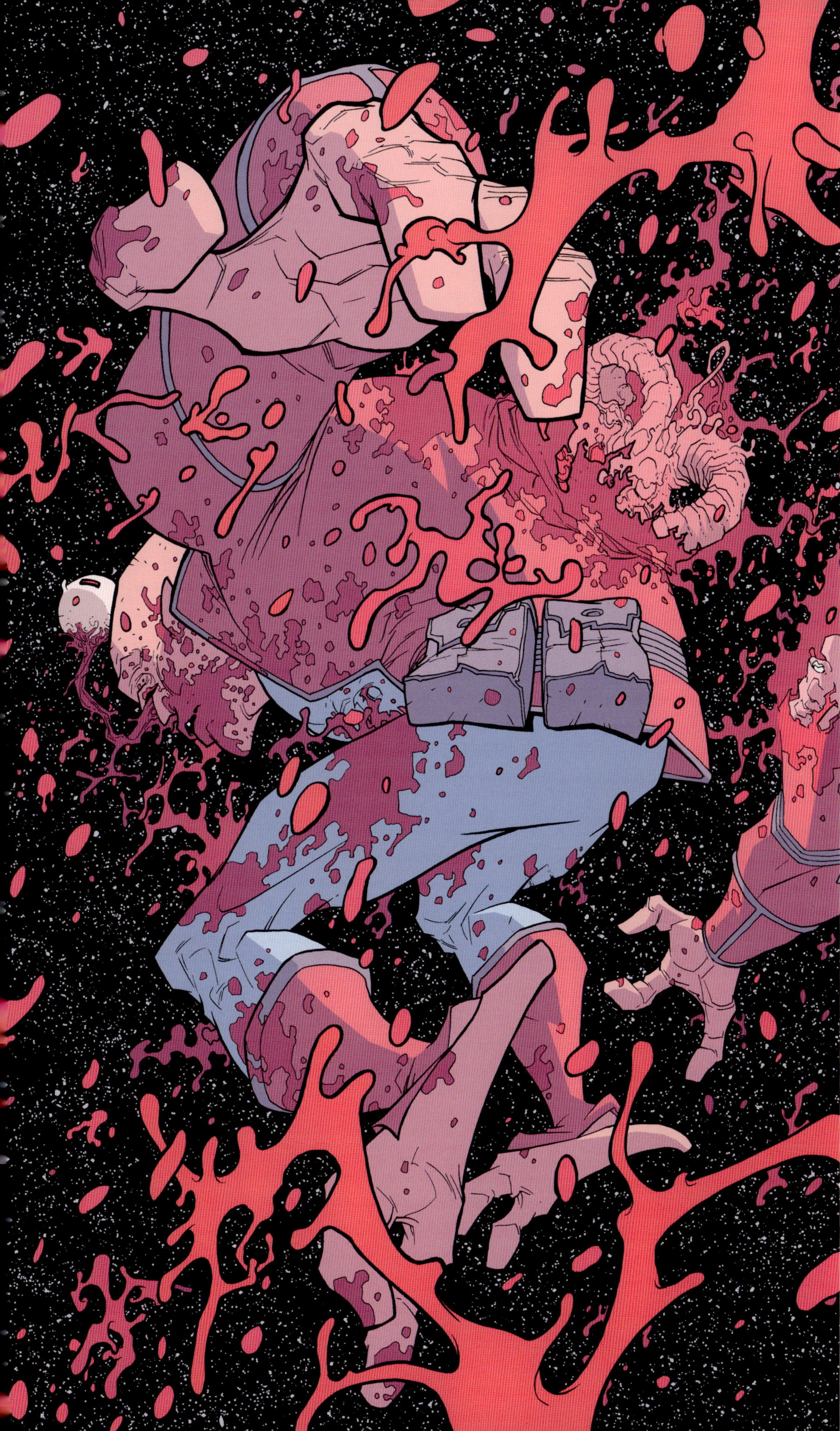

animation with minimal changes.

"I loved doing the one in [Episode] 203 for Allen, that final shot that we end on," says O'Neil. "It was such a great beat from the comics. [Director] Tanner [Johnson] did a really great job, with his team kind of beating it out on the boards and getting us there. I think we had given it to overseas first, and what we got back, we were just like, 'This is okay, but this is not it.' And so it was like, 'Let's just take it. We'll break it down into pieces. We'll do a very limited animation thing with it, and we'll just tie it all down.' And I went full tilt, and it's one of the things I'm proudest of in terms of character in the show. I'm not going to be shy about it."

While Allen's battle against the Viltrumites ended on a truly horrific note, things back on Earth weren't going all that well either, at least emotionally. Mark's mother, Debbie, had gone to an anonymous support group for the spouses of fallen superheroes in an attempt to work through the trauma caused by her husband's role in the deaths of the Guardians of the Globe and countless others. The simple, straightforward meeting place was a huge shift from the wild outer space environments seen in the first half of the episode.

"I remember as a kid, community centers always seemed to be in church basements," says Racioppa, "with the old coffee that came in the big stainless steel heaters and percolators, and it was always Styrofoam cups and stuff like that. So I wanted to try to bring that into this, because that's how I picture these kind of places. The chairs all stack and are against one wall and people pull them out. So that's kind of the idea there."

At the meeting, Debbie encountered Theo, the husband of the now-deceased Green Ghost — another hero murdered by Debbie's own husband Nolan. When Theo learned who Debbie really was, the initial connection that the two shared was immediately shattered.

"His rejection of her came out of real research about how, in some cases, the partners of someone who's done something terrible are also blamed," says Racioppa. "That's a real thing that happens. We did some research, and we found there would be cases where someone would be partnered with someone who turned out to be a murderer — didn't know, had no idea, and were also traumatized or also a victim — but then were blamed by the outside community. Like, 'You should have known. How could you not have known? You're just as much a part of this as he was or she was,' even when that person was completely innocent. And we sort of wanted to play that storyline here, because it's a real thing that happens. So that's where that idea came from."

It was an emotional scene that was a big departure from *Invincible*'s trademark superhero action.

"I think that's a good idea of how the series has matured," says Racioppa. "There's a long sequence just following Debbie, her own feelings, going to this community center. Just conversational. No superheroes, no big action, no murder, no violence, no blood. Just Debbie talking through her feelings with someone who she thinks is an ally, and then turns out to be difficult for her. It seems to work successfully. Our fans seemed to like it. I think it works on

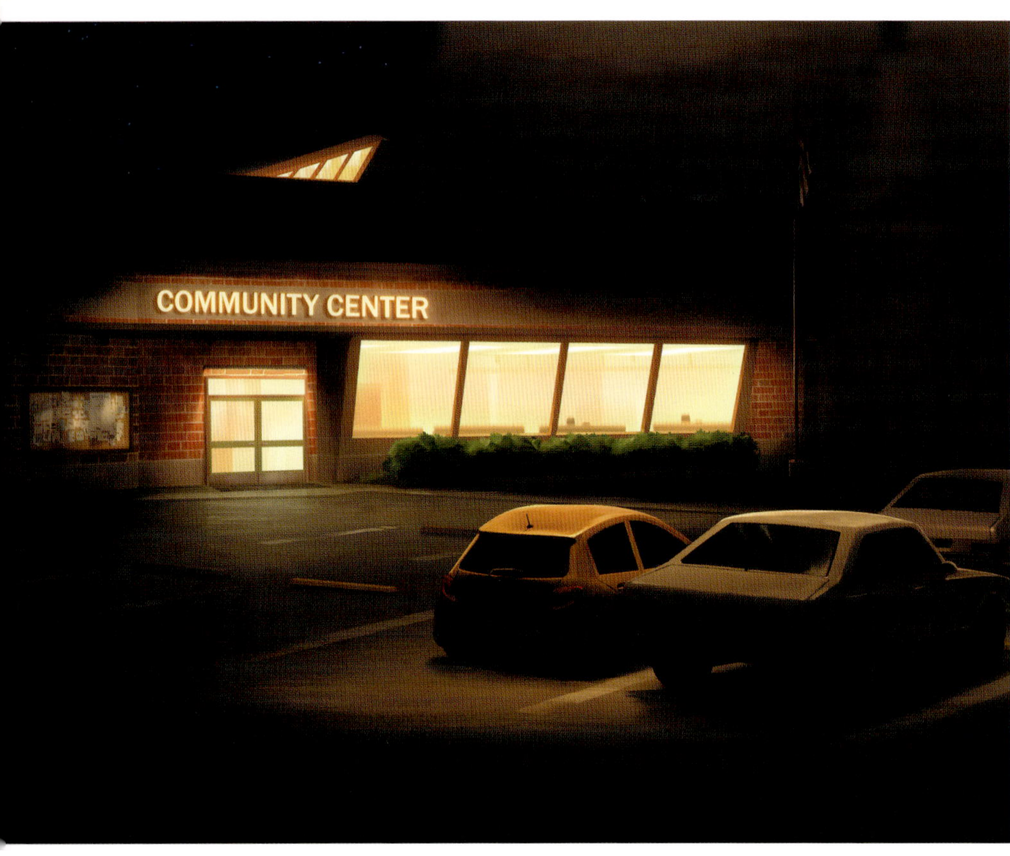

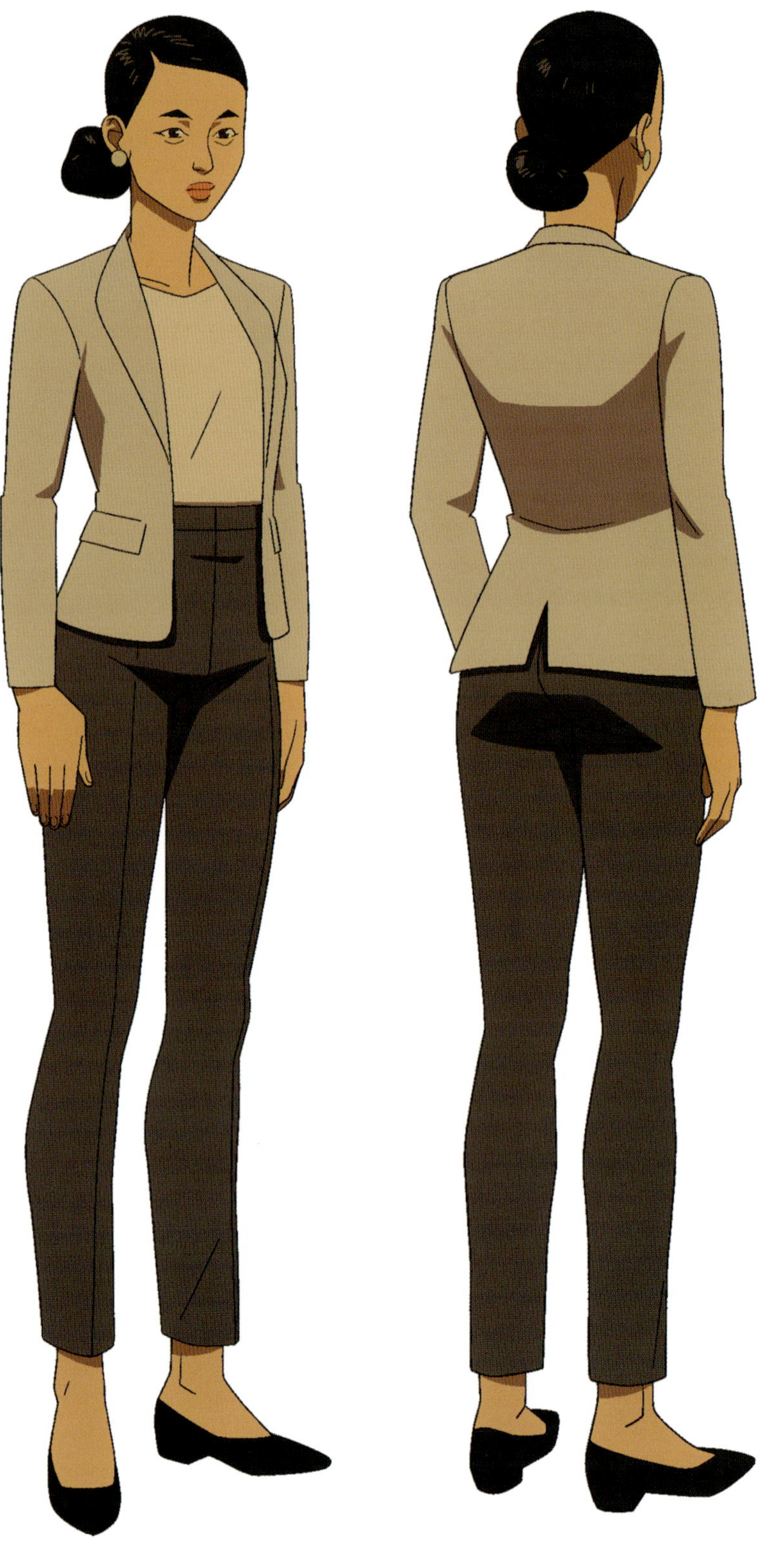

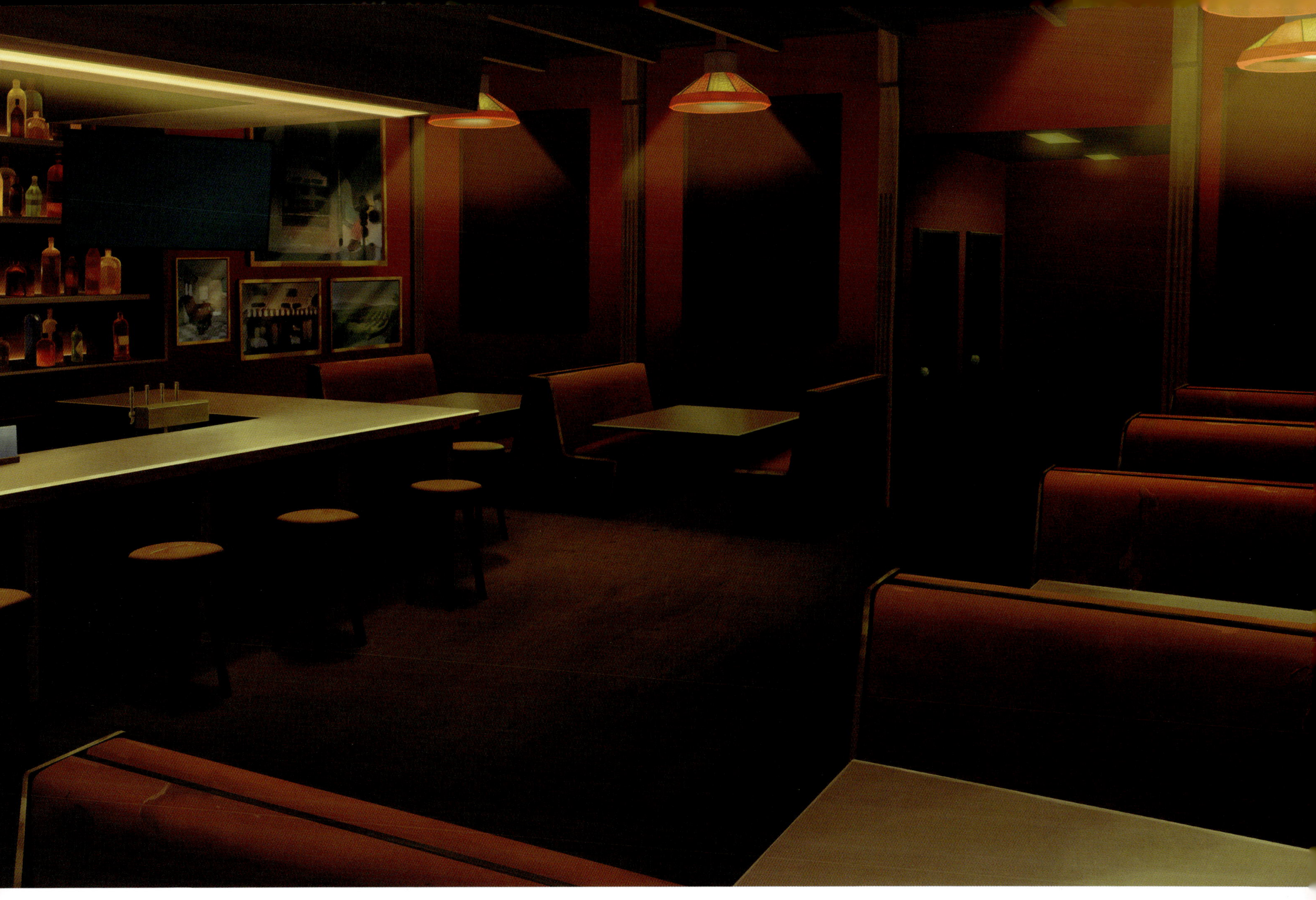

screen. So it's a nice show of maturity of the show, that we can do those kind of things, even in a colorful superhero world."

While Debbie struggled to deal with the shocking revelations about her husband, Mark got a shock of his own when his favorite fictional superhero, Séance Dog, showed up at his dorm room asking for help. Up until then, the character had only graced the show in the form of posters, comics, and an action figure, so it was fun for the team to finally bring this unusual hero to life.

"All the Séance Dog stuff is absurd," says O'Neil. "I think, as an episode, it's my favorite one of the season just because it does that Kansas City Shuffle. It's like, 'Hey, this is normal stuff, right?' And then, nope. We're going someplace else. And then we have that big pivot... and it's great because of it."

"That whole sequence plays out great," says Racioppa. "It's some nice comedy, some levity, too. And the [other] sequence has Debbie going through some really terrible things. We don't want to be a downner the entire time.

We want to treat emotions realistically. We want to keep the show grounded, but at the same time, we don't want everyone to be like, 'Oh my God, that was awful the whole time.' We also want to have moments of fun and superheroes, so it's trying to find a balance of that. So that was an example of a fun sequence. He's out doing pretend magic, and Mark has this great little dialogue scene with him where Séance Dog is trying to convince him that dogs are magical and you should believe in them. And Mark's like, 'I do believe in dogs. We have dogs. I just don't believe in you.'"

Séance Dog was a brand new character for the *Invincible* animated series, inspired by one of Kirkman and Walker's early comic book creations, Science Dog.

"It was cool to come up with something fresh for the show," says Walker. "I see a lot of people talk often about Science Dog being part of the Invincible Universe, and it's really not. It's a completely separate thing that just happens to also be a comic book that exists in the Invincible Universe. Mark reads it. So we had to come up with something new, because we weren't just going to give Science Dog away and fold it into basically a gag or whatever. Robert had a couple ideas of how we could change the name with it still being recognizably a nod to Science Dog. We could have done Chemistry Beaver or something, but it doesn't sound like Science Dog. So Séance Dog was the best option. And so obviously, I think that just lends itself to the Doctor Strange-type. So that's where we went. I was fortunate enough to get to work a little bit on the Séance Dog model. So I get to take a little bit of credit for that, based on a poster I had done for the first season anyway."

Mark quickly realized that something is amiss, and Séance Dog soon revealed his true identity. He was actually an alien named Nuolzot from the planet Thraxa, sent to Earth to ask Invincible to save his homeworld.

"It's this fun, kind of semi-ridiculous sequence where we have an alien who comes there pretending to be Mark's childhood favorite character, and then reveals himself, asking for Mark's help," says Racioppa. "And even if you're watching it, you should be like, 'This story is a little... Really?'

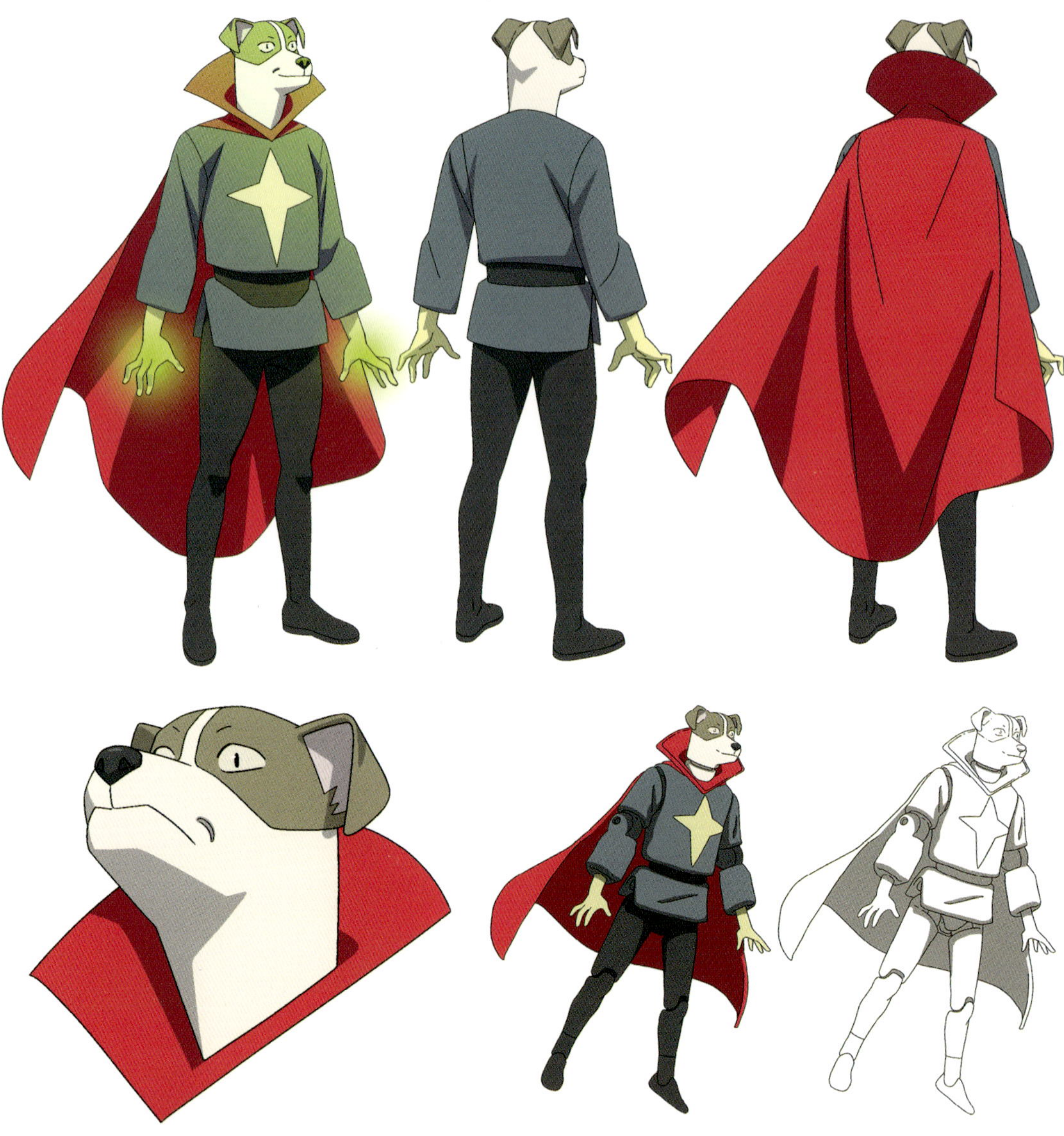

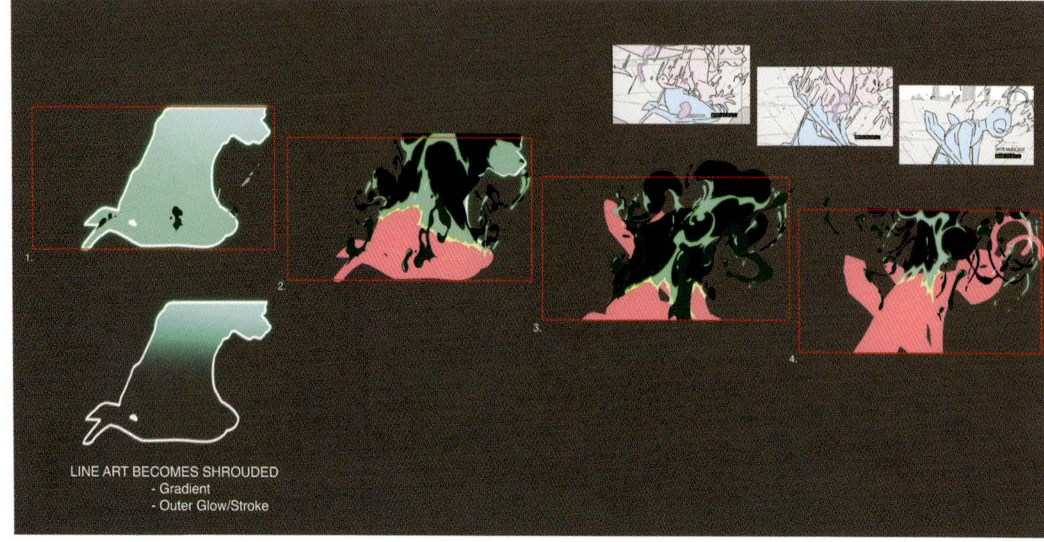

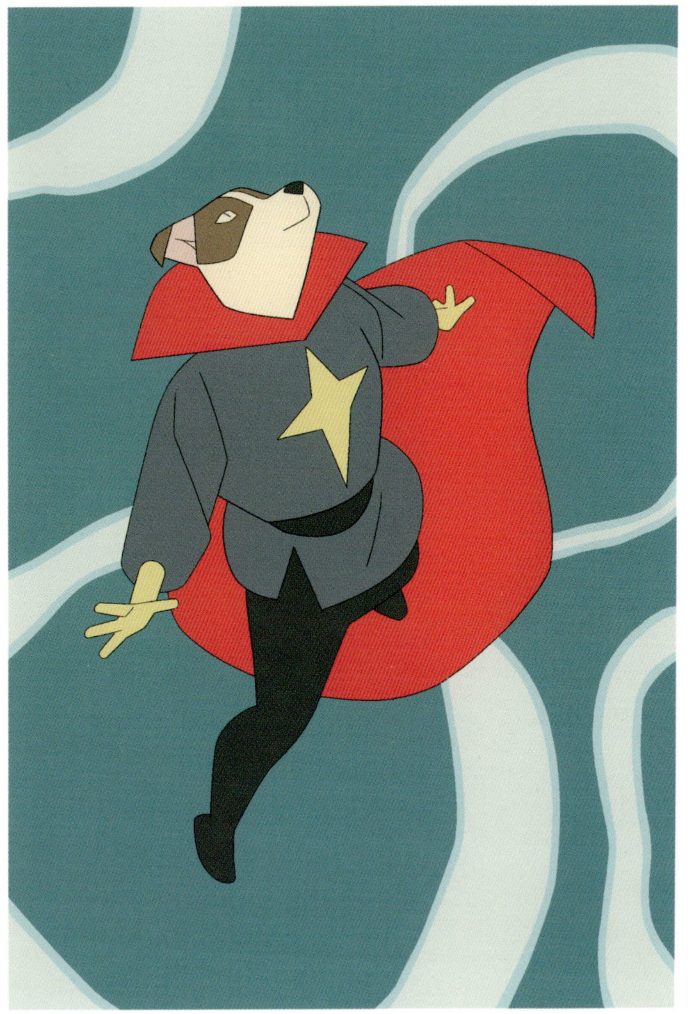

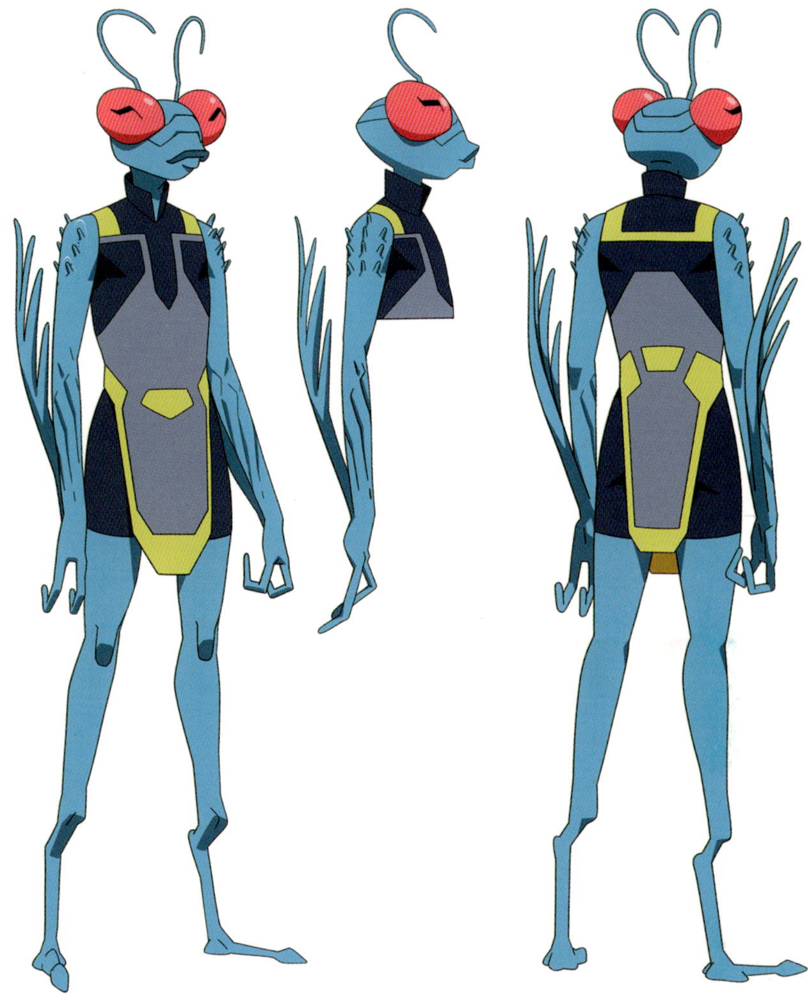

Because it's not true."

When Mark arrived on Thraxa, he learned that the truth was even more alarming than meeting his childhood comic book hero. Omni-Man was there waiting for him.

"[Nuolzot] was sent there by Nolan to bring Mark to Thraxa," says Racioppa. "Because Nolan knows if he asked directly, Mark probably wouldn't come. Obviously, Mark still has strong feelings towards the father who just tried to kill him a few months ago."

It was uncertain at first what Nolan's intentions were, but it was immediately clear that he had gone through some changes since we last saw him on Earth. Omni-Man was sporting a new costume that included Thraxan armor.

"Omni-Man's Thraxan look is fairly ornate and complicated in the comics," says Kirkman. "So streamlining that and making it animation friendly was no easy task."

The Thraxans themselves were also complicated designs, but the art team tried to keep them as close as possible to their comic book counterparts.

"It was a challenge to interpret the Thraxans," says O'Neil, "because the comics had a lot of freedom in terms of the level of detail, and they've got weird praying mantis hands and shit like that. And it's cool when it's a panel-by-panel scenario. But again, once it starts moving, it presents a ton of challenge. They only have two fingers. So how do they interact with stuff? How do we do that so if we have to have a normal hand motion or movement or gesture?"

"There was a plan at a certain point to do a bunch of different color Thraxans to give some variety," says Kirkman. "There were pink ones and green ones and things like that.

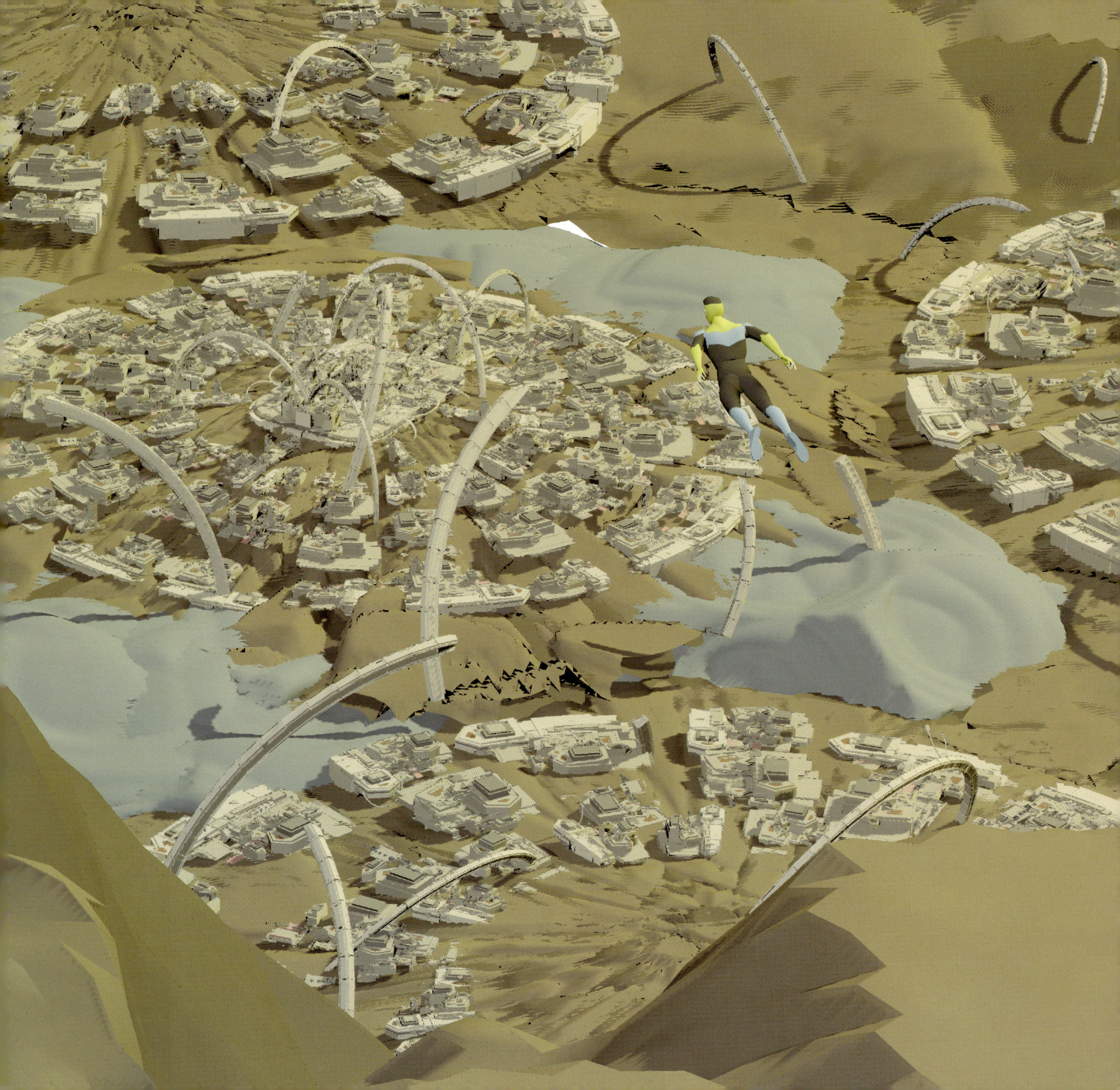

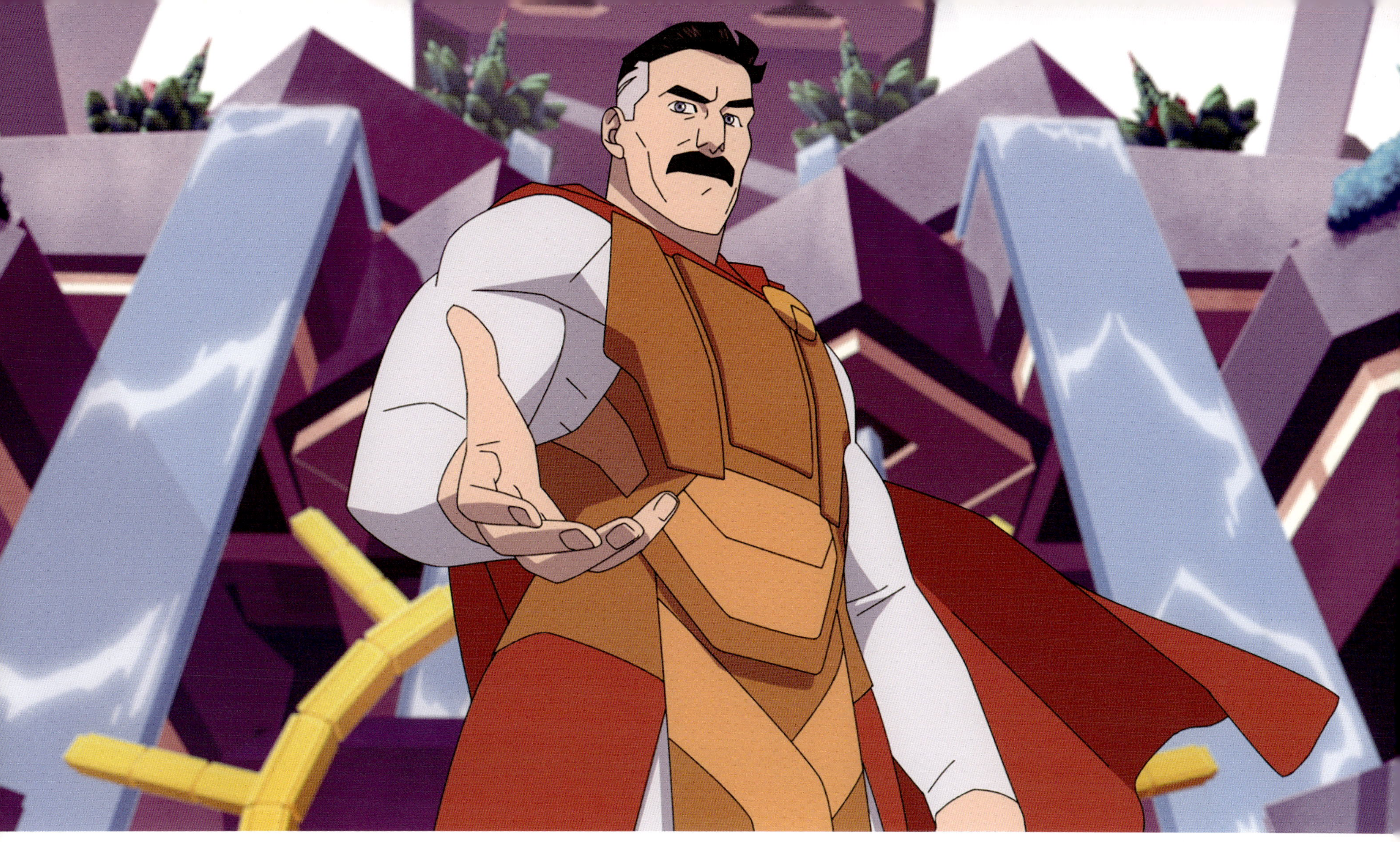

And I think it was decided, 'Let's just keep it like the comics.' They start to look like they're different aliens when they're such different colors."

Another challenge was designing the planet Thraxa itself, the second unique alien civilization to appear in this episode alone. But the team was happy with what they came up with.

"The button on the end is perfect," says O'Neil. "The introduction to Thraxa. I think we got all of the most beautiful wide shots so you could see how the place was set up."

"Thraxa was awesome," says Supervising Director Dan Duncan. "Getting to tease that in [episode] 203, those are some of my favorite paintings from that location."

But Mark had precious little time to enjoy the planet's splendor. Instead, the episode wrapped with a tense sequence as Nolan asked for Mark's help, and viewers were left wondering how Mark would react to seeing the father who had left him behind, beaten him nearly to death, after their last encounter.

"I had a lot of fun really trying to push that final shot of [Omni-Man] with a hand out," says O'Neil. "We spent a little bit of time going back and forth on just trying to make sure that hit and looked great. If you're going to go out, you want to go out on something that looks just 100% visually."

It was a harrowing ending to an absolute rollercoaster of an episode.

"We got to do some really big tone swings in this one,"

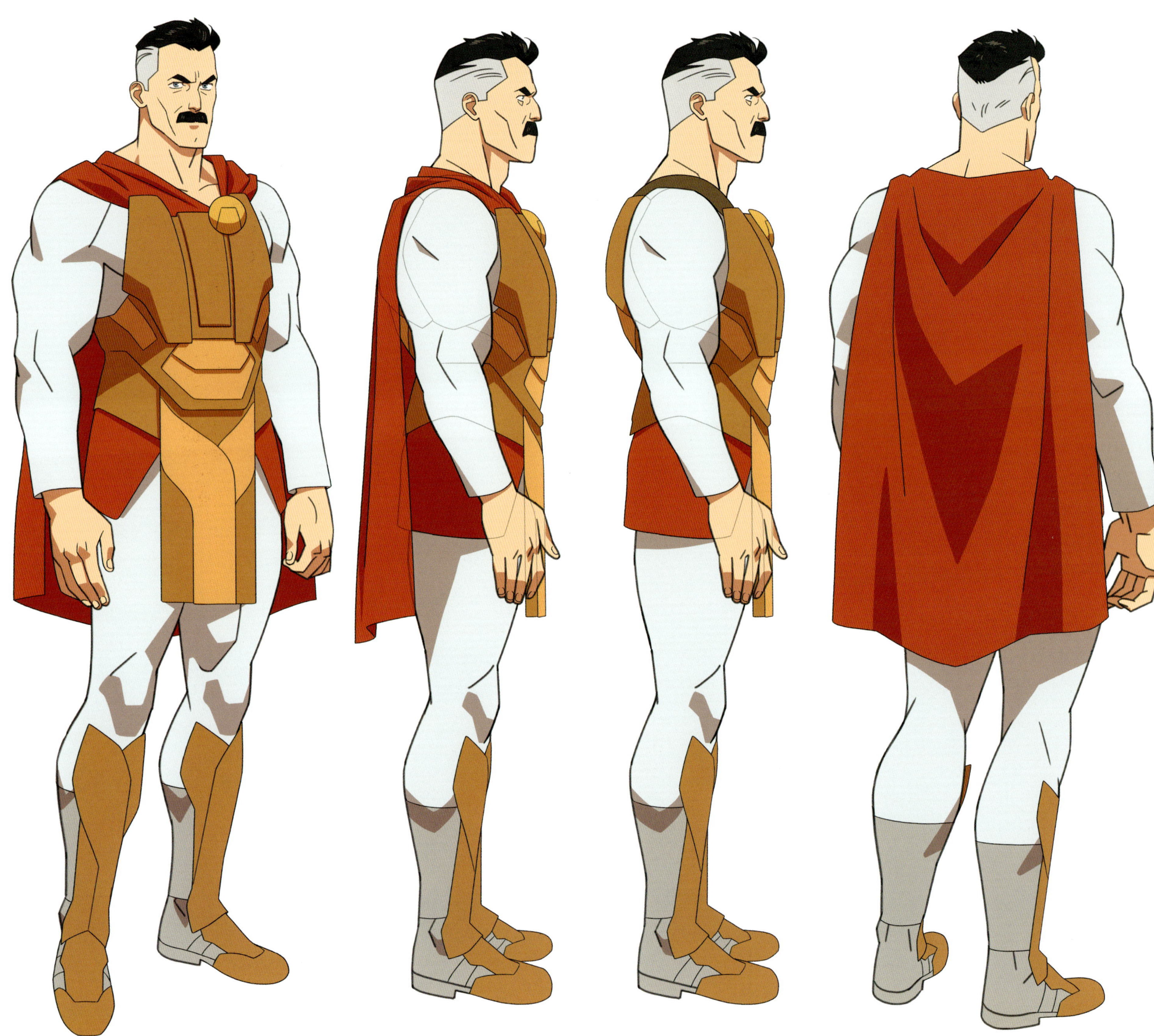

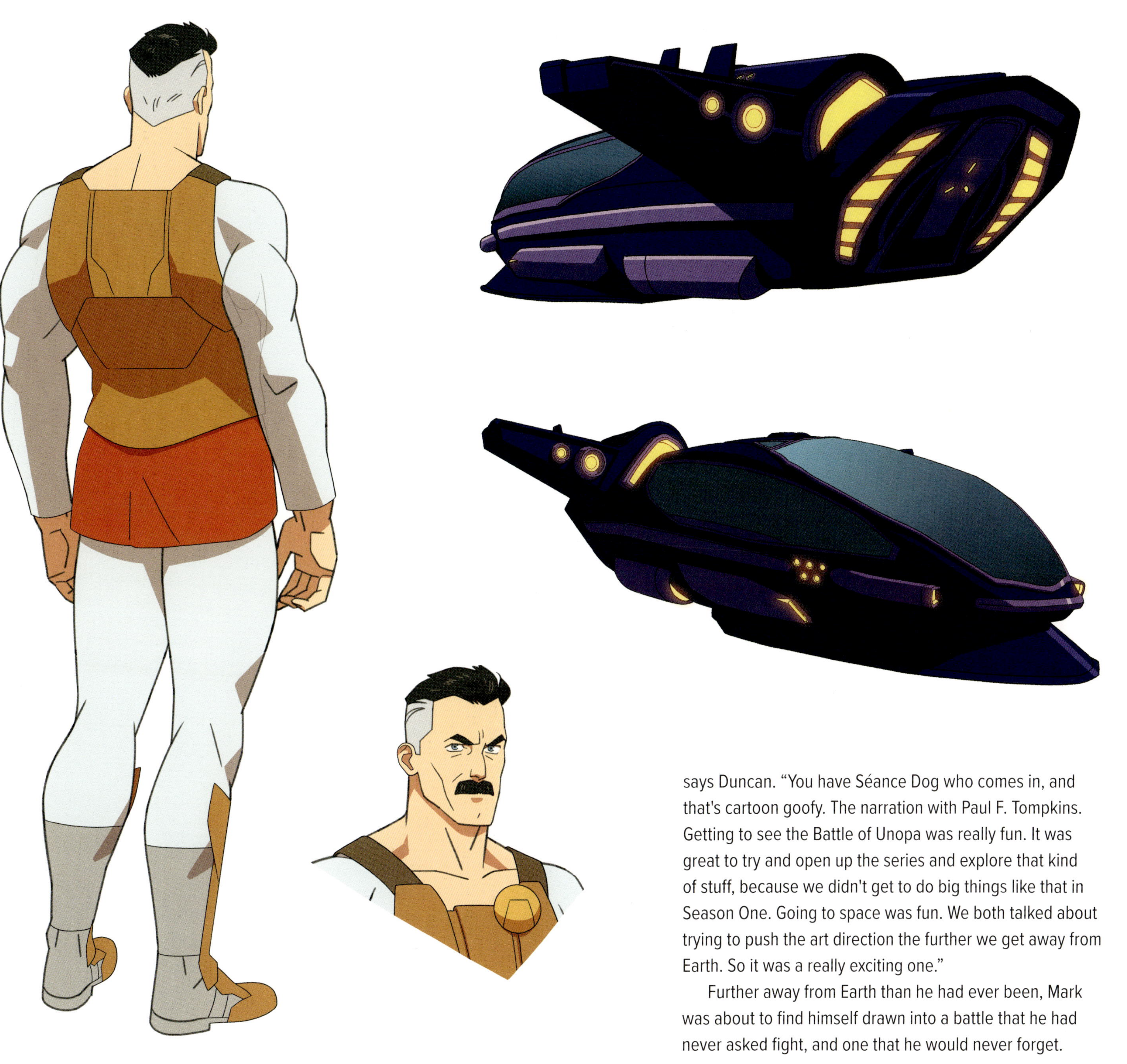

says Duncan. “You have Séance Dog who comes in, and that's cartoon goofy. The narration with Paul F. Tompkins. Getting to see the Battle of Unopa was really fun. It was great to try and open up the series and explore that kind of stuff, because we didn't get to do big things like that in Season One. Going to space was fun. We both talked about trying to push the art direction the further we get away from Earth. So it was a really exciting one.”

Further away from Earth than he had ever been, Mark was about to find himself drawn into a battle that he had never asked fight, and one that he would never forget.

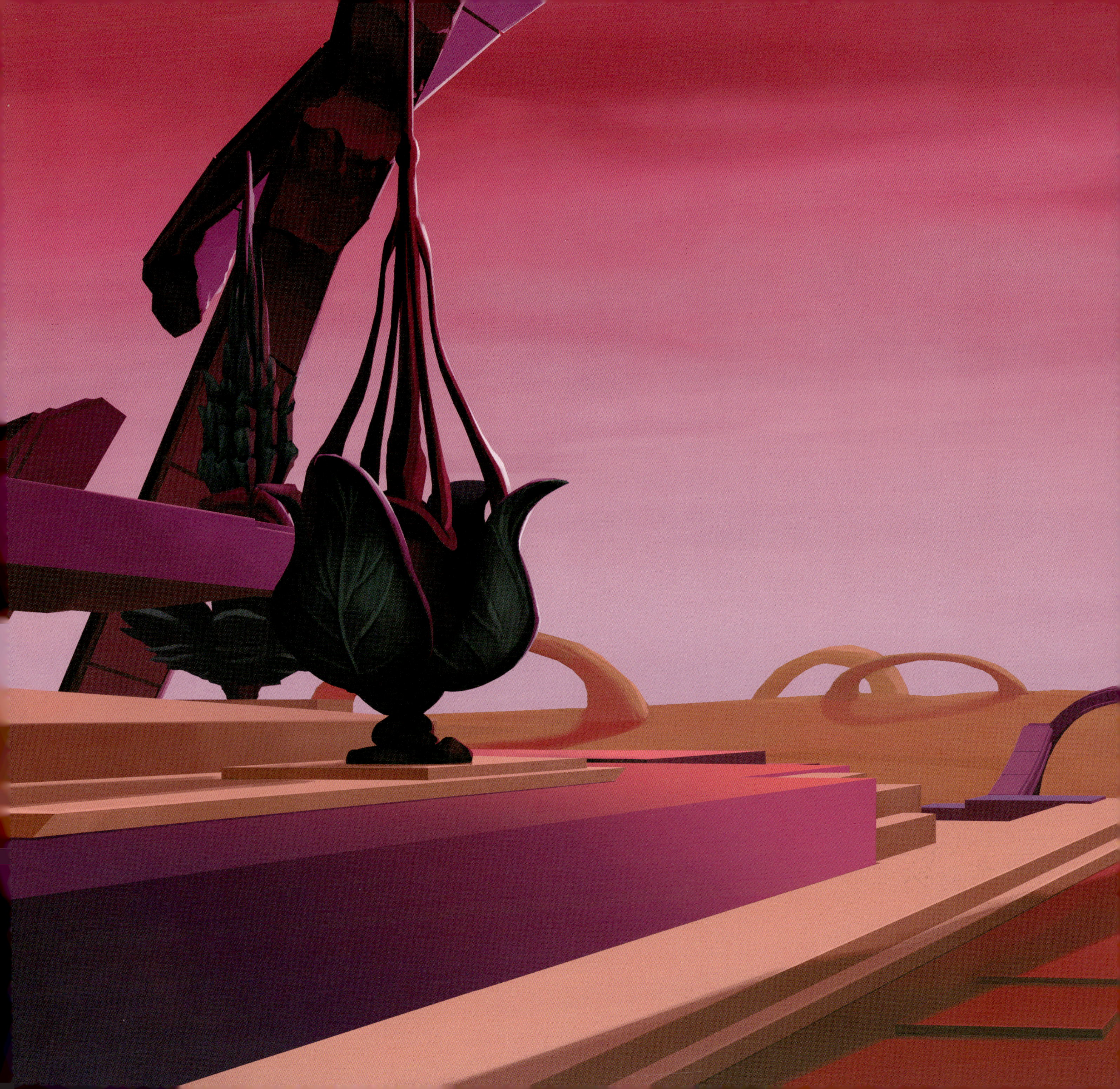

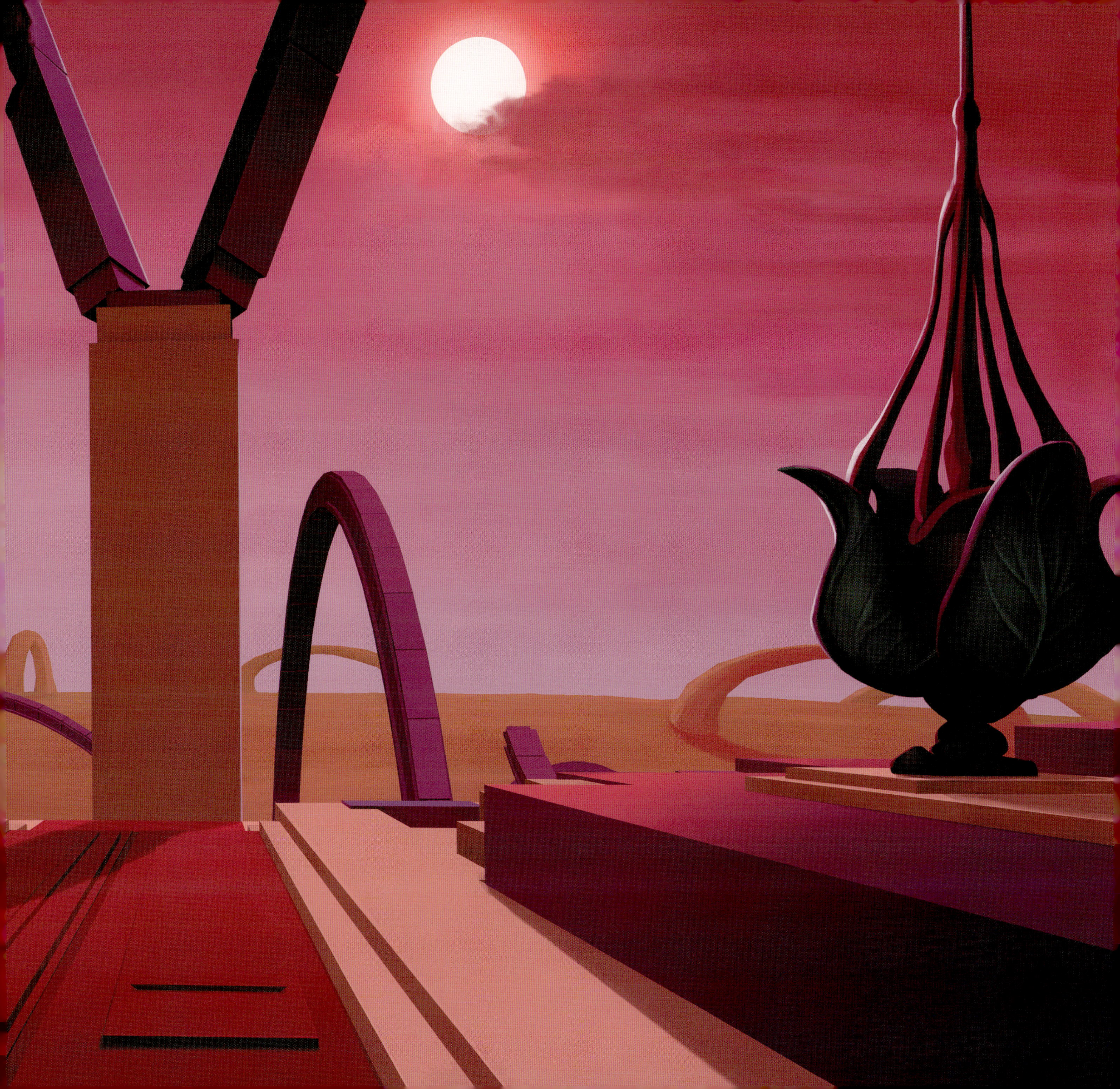

EPISODE 4:

IT'S BEEN A WHILE

When viewers last saw Invincible, he had just arrived on the planet Thraxa, only to learn that his father, Omni-Man, was the one who had summoned him there. Fans waited with eager anticipation to see what Mark's reaction would be upon encountering the man who had recently betrayed his trust and his planet – and nearly killed his son.

"We pick up the episode from 203, and there's a moment where there's just tension between Mark and Nolan," says Art Director Shaun O'Neil. "And you don't know where it's going to go. And then, Mark rushes in for the hug, and we managed to sneak in a little thing where Nolan doesn't know where it's going to go as much as Mark doesn't know where it's going to go. And so Mark decides that he's just going to kind of let it go for a moment. But as he rushes in, Nolan kind of pulls one [fist] back because he's not sure where this is going to go. Mark doesn't see it. It's just a short thing. And then he's just like, 'Okay, we're gonna hug. We'll put it away.' But none of that was in any of the stuff that we did previously. And I feel like this is one of those things where you just you put a little bit more character into something. We don't really know Nolan. Nolan doesn't really know what he's doing because this is such new territory. And that defensiveness was super fun to me. I was super glad that that came through."

"Doing that story beat in 204 was awesome," says Supervising Director Dan Duncan. "We had two directors on that. We had Mari Yang who came in at the start, and she worked on that episode for a long time. She got another gig and left, and then Jason Zurek came in and got it over the finish line. This one was fun to really push the limits of the runtime that we have. Everybody's so used to doing smaller episodes with tighter runtimes. And so when you want to give a scene time to breathe, it's a very limited concept, but here we could really stretch it out. So when Mark and Nolan first meet, we try to give that as much time as we possibly could without breaking the scene and breaking the tension there."

"Every once in a while, you get these opportunities," says O'Neil, "You only do it if it really feels true to the character. But sometimes you find moments that you didn't find before. And that's the beauty of this."

While Mark unexpectedly reconciled with his father, all was not forgiven. Mark still held a great deal of resentment towards Nolan, which was only amplified when he met Nolan's new son, a half-Viltrumite/half-Thraxan baby.

"He looks like an Italian mobster," says Co-Executive Producer and Co-Creator Cory Walker. "Little fat baby Oliver,

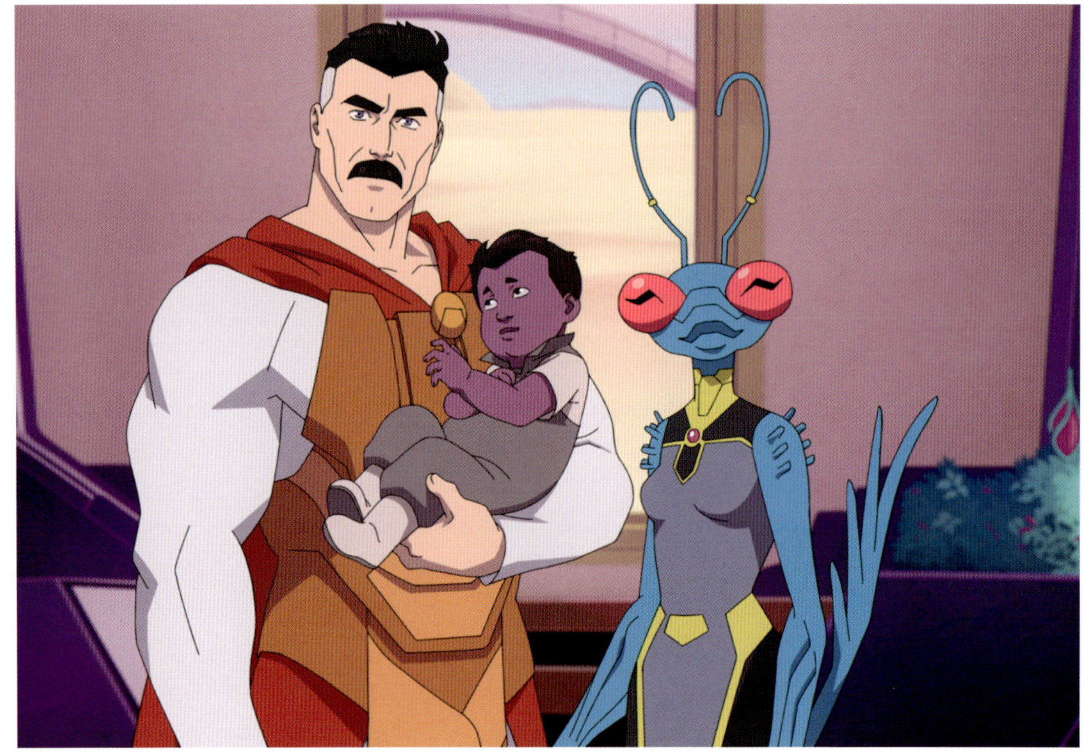

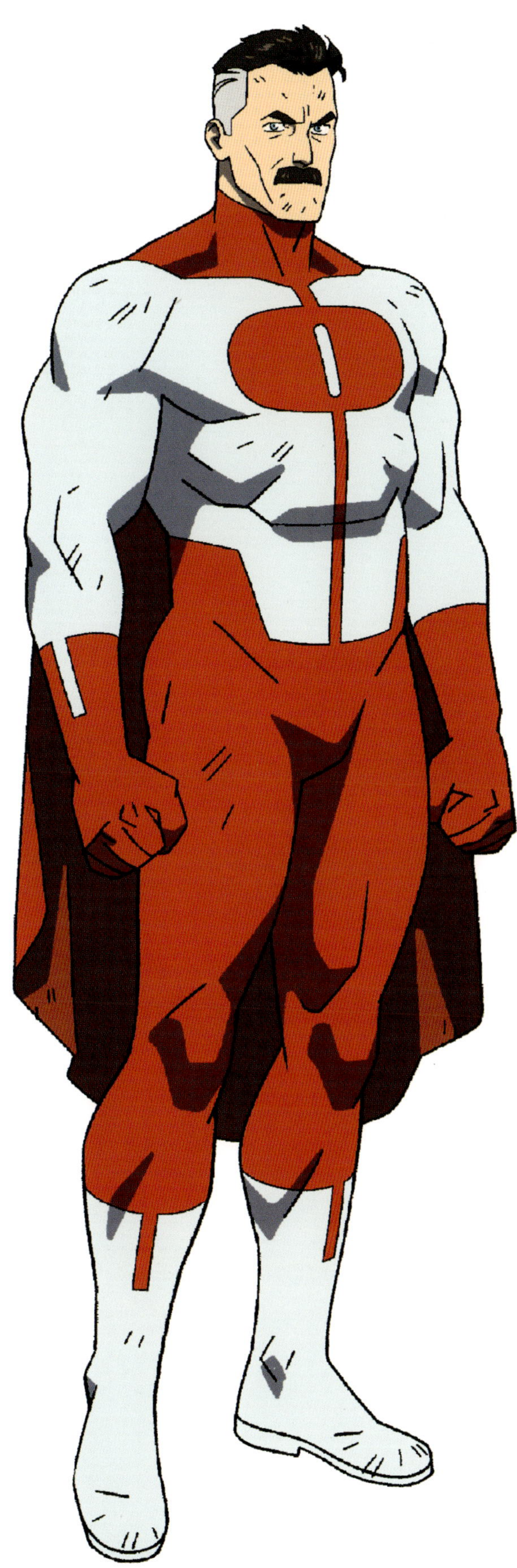

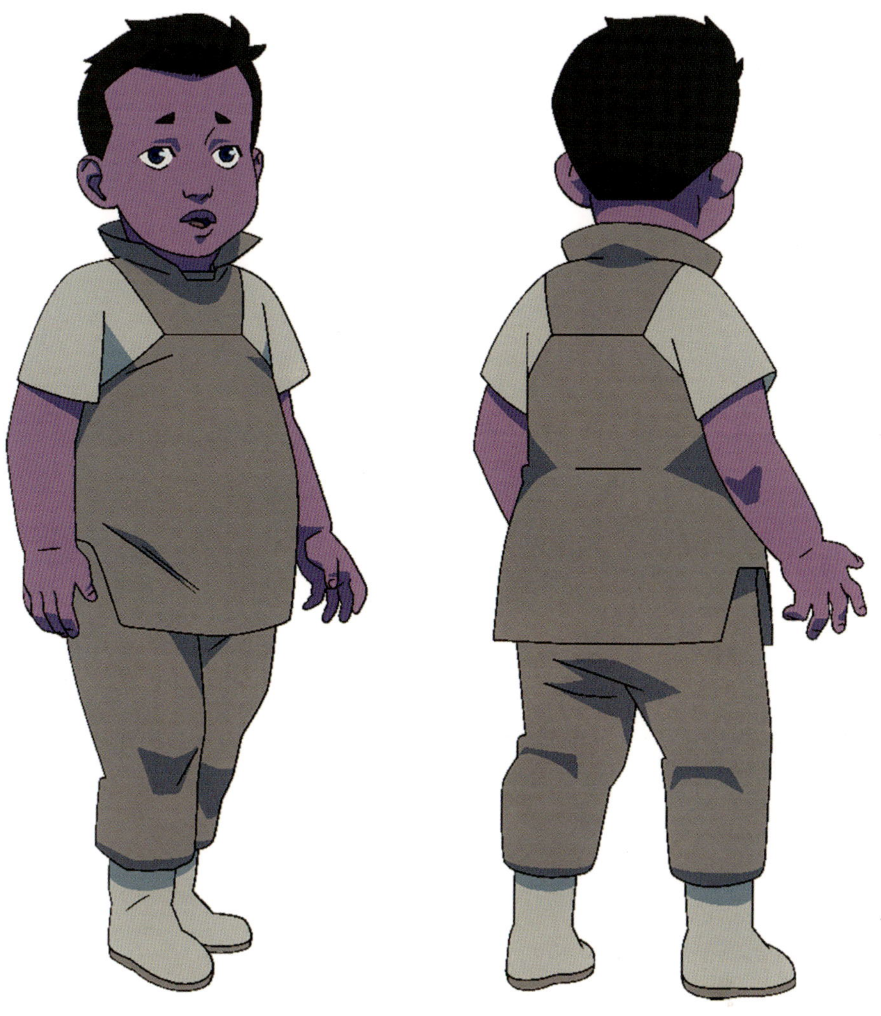

with the thickest head of hair you ever did see. He's great. I love him."

Viewers then got a glimpse of Nolan's emotional journey from Earth to Thraxa, as told through a beautiful dialogue-free sequence set to a haunting cover of Leonard Cohen's "Avalanche".

"A lot of the initial direction, where we see Nolan going through space, that was all Mari and the board team," says Duncan. "It's really, really cool stuff."

As Omni-Man traveled through space, clearly struggling with his feelings and his place as a Viltrumite, he paused at a black hole and almost let its gravity take him in. It was

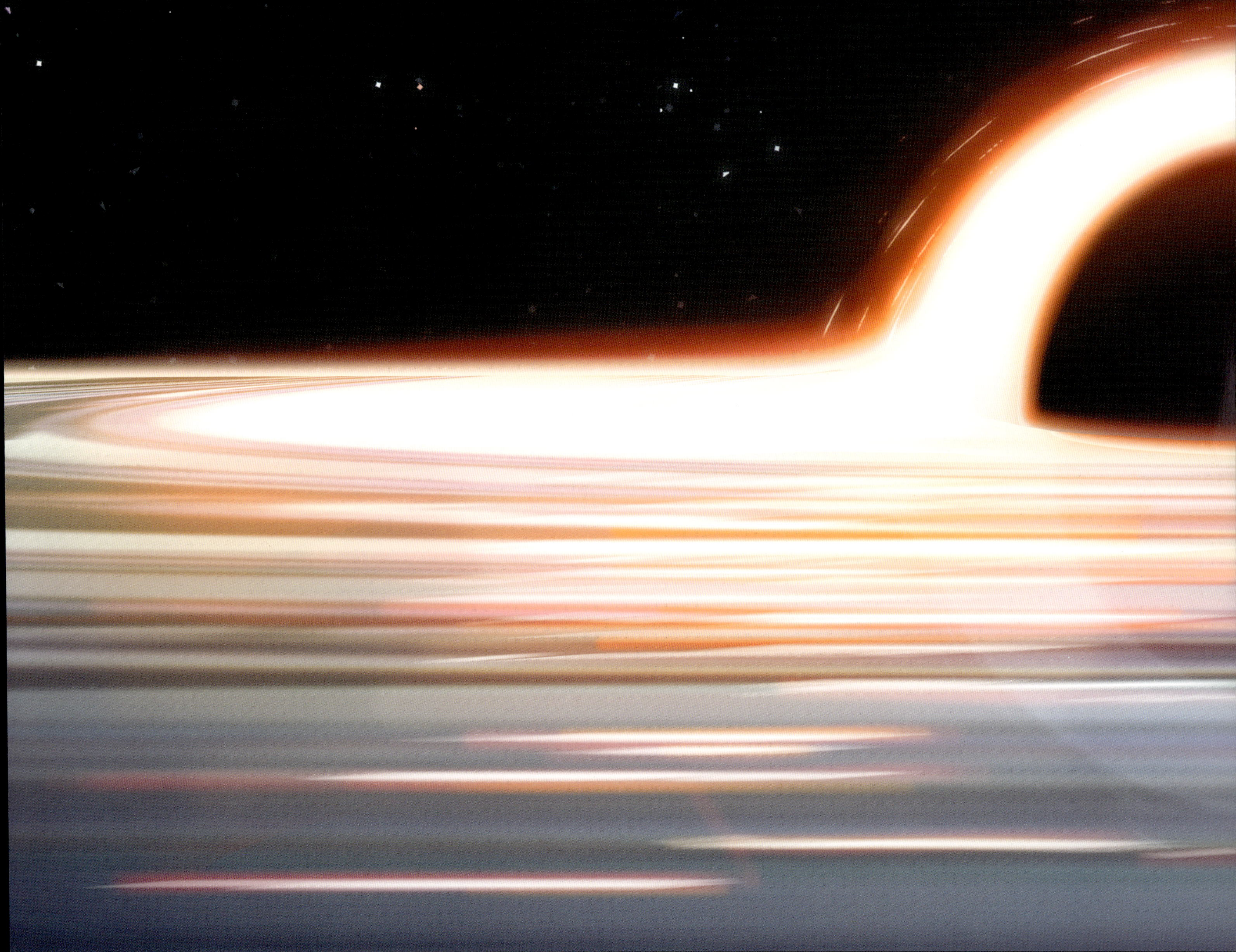

a sad but lovely moment in a sequence filled with stunning imagery.

"He's at the black hole and he's going to let himself go in," says Walker. "That obviously tells a story. But even the quieter [moments], where he's just drifting through space really get it across. It's all down to the way the artists handled it. I love that stuff."

Before he could end his own life, Omni-Man encountered some Thraxans in peril and found renewed purpose when he brought them back to their homeworld. Omni-Man became

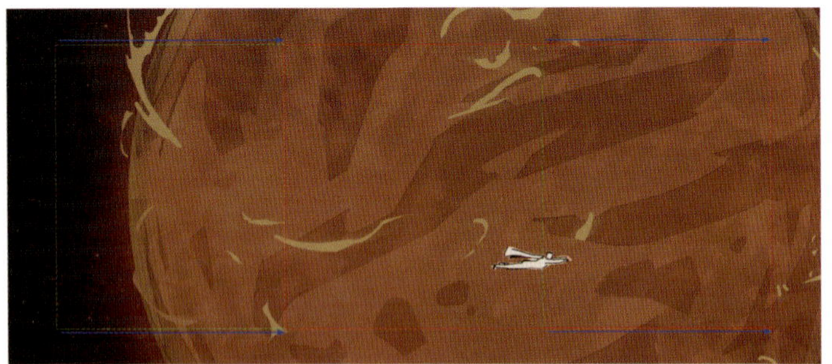

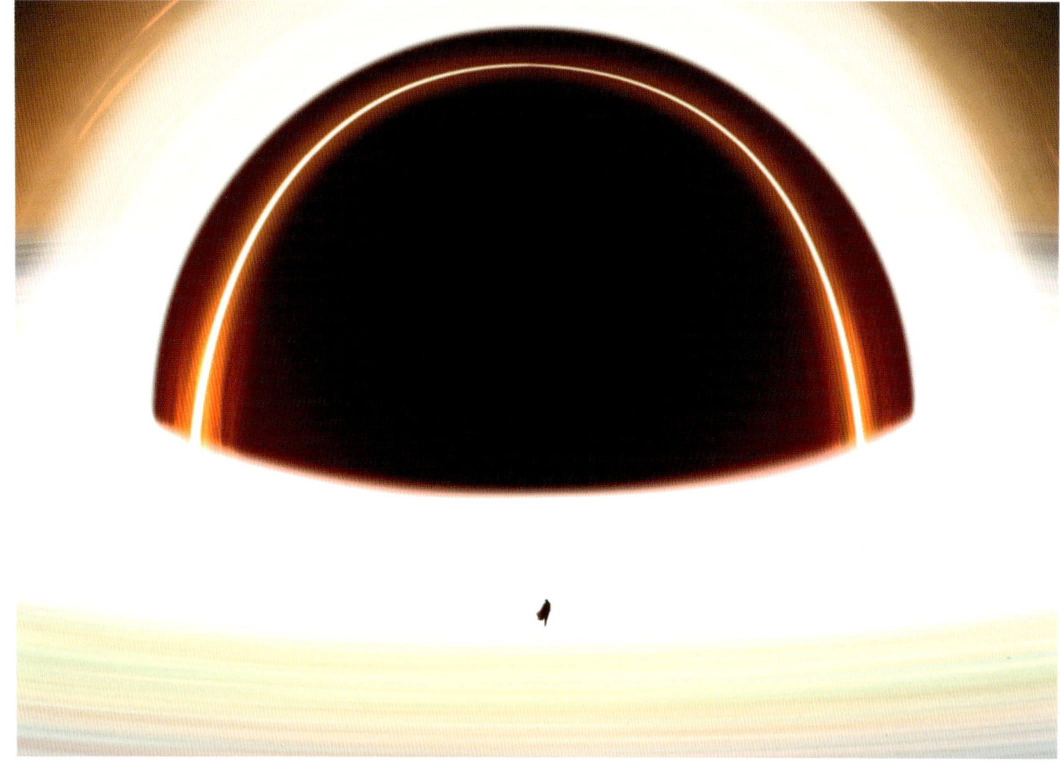

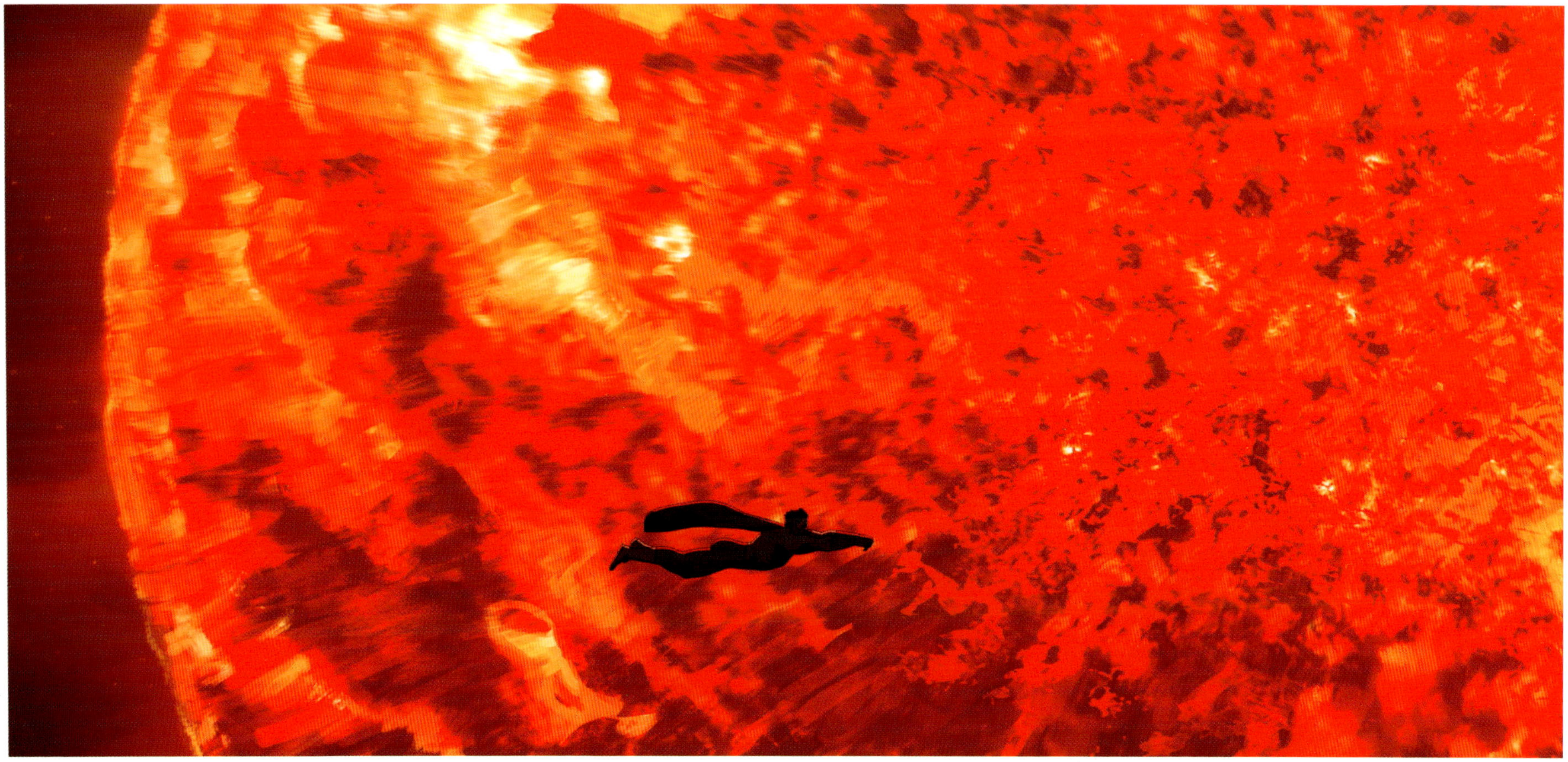

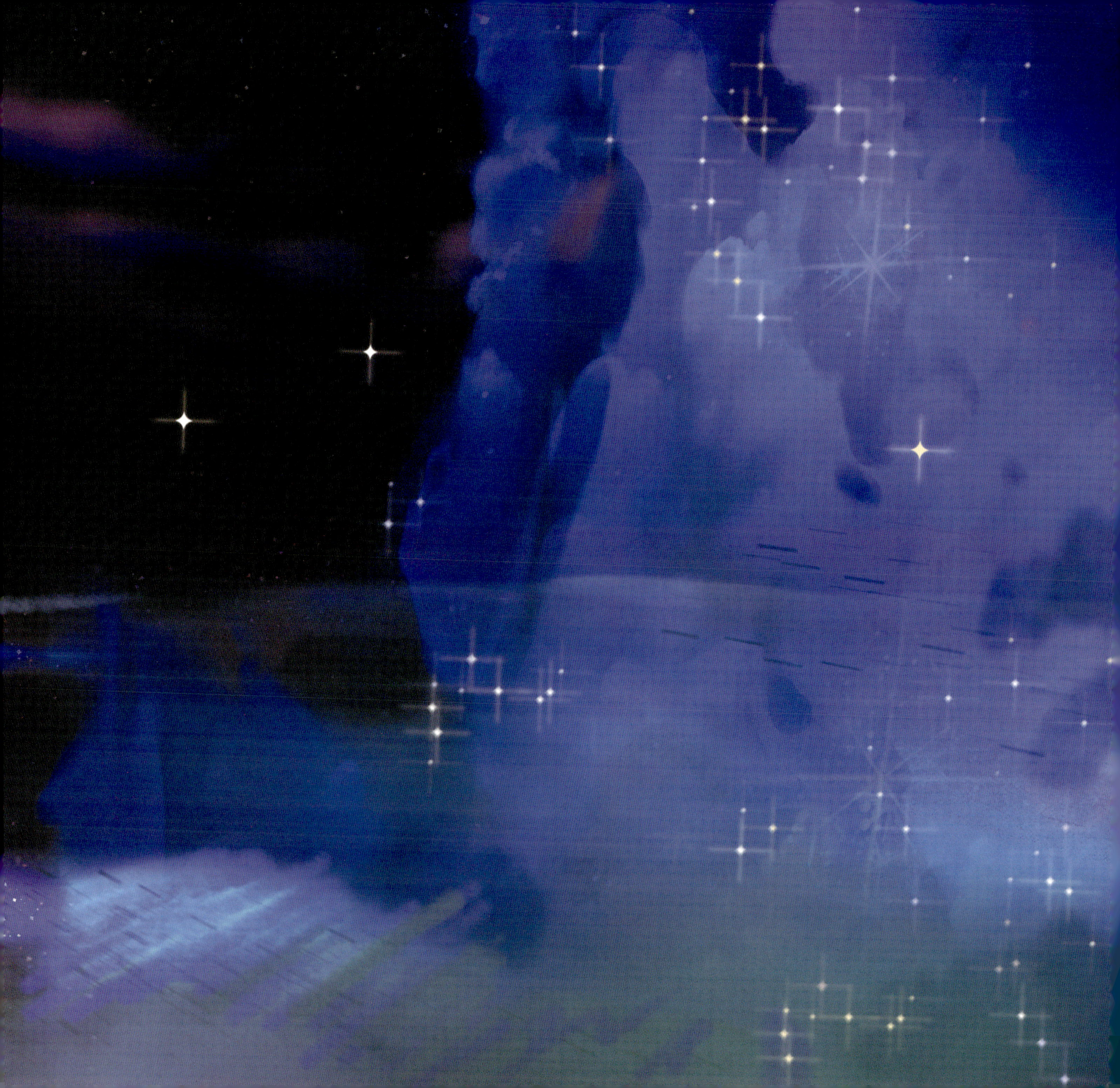

their new leader and champion, devoted to protecting them from any oncoming threats.

But some threats even Omni-Man couldn't handle alone, which is why he summoned Mark to Thraxa. Nolan warned his son that his fellow Viltrumites were coming, and not long after, three alien warriors plummeted to Thraxa's surface like living bombs.

"We've seen [two of] those Viltrumites before," says Executive Produce and Co-Showrunner Simon Racioppa. "We saw them back in the Allen episode. And that was important to set them up a little bit. We've seen Nolan, obviously, and what Nolan can do, in Season One. But we hadn't really seen what other Viltrumites could do. Are they the same level was Nolan? Was he exceptionally strong? And here we're saying, 'Oh no, they're all Nolan-like or close to Nolan levels.' And we wanted to show that with Allen. So now, when you see them dropping [onto Thraxa], you're like, 'Oh, there's three of them?'"

The three Viltrumites included Thula and Vidor, who were seen in episode 203, and a new addition to their ranks, Lucan.

"Cory had a hand in [Lucan's] design," says Executive Producer, Co-Showrunner, and Co-Creator Robert Kirkman. "I don't think he outright did it himself, but Cory wants to make sure that there's unique body types to these characters and that they're not just all completely similar. And so that's why you get that big barrel chest and body on Lucan. He's got a fairly unique build. Definitely a lot of strength to that image. He looks like a tank of a man, which is really cool."

The battle against the Viltrumites on Thraxa quickly escalated, but Invincible and Omni-Man weren't the only ones who found themselves in a difficult situation. While Thraxa may have looked beautiful in the designs, it was not a terribly practical set for the fight scene that needed to be staged there.

"What a nightmare," says O'Neil. "For me at least. It's a whole new space, and I think my lack of experience made that space as difficult as it could possibly get. The first time interacting with something of that scope — just the set alone, just the scale of it. We tried to build it all out, and

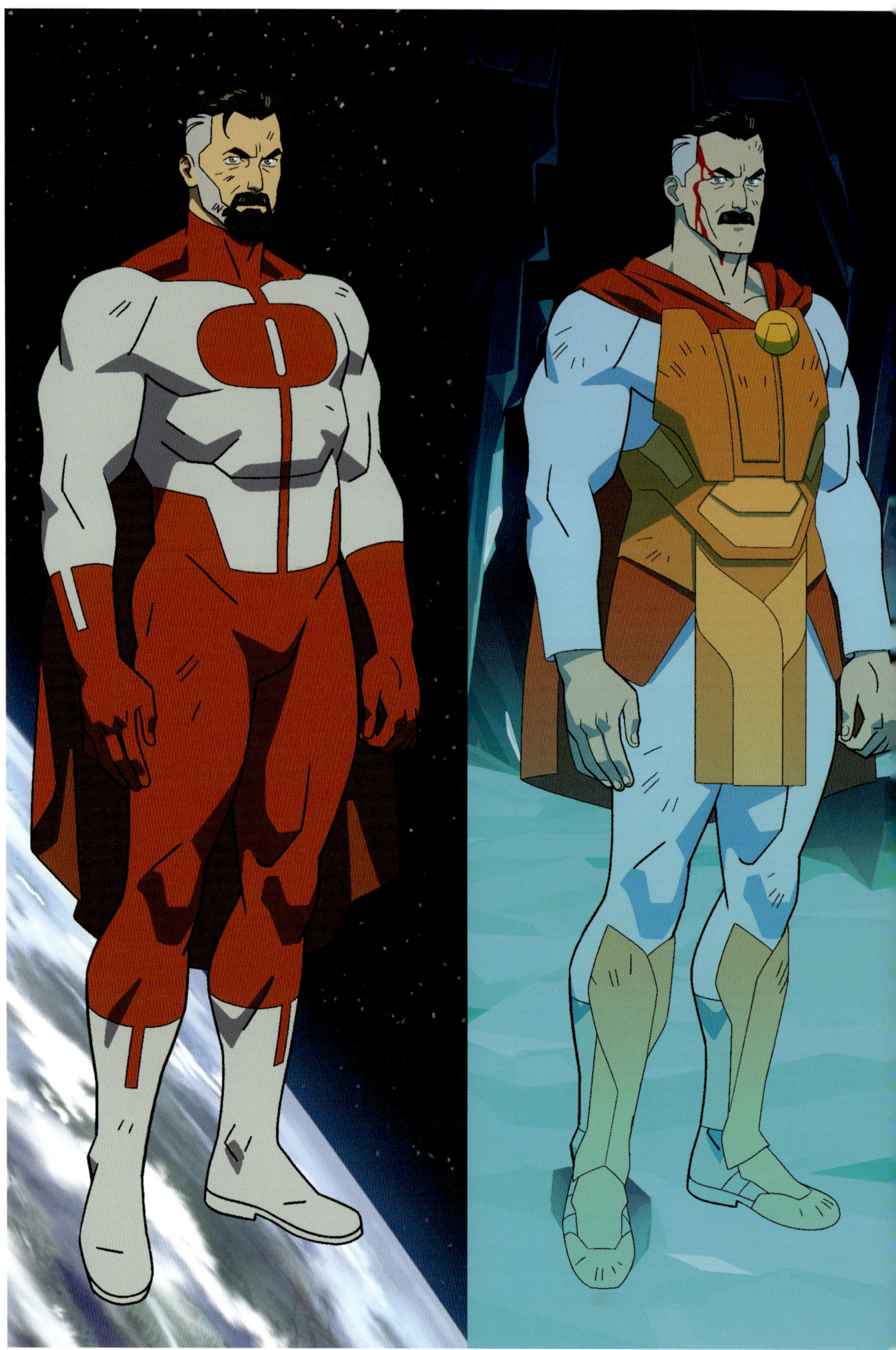

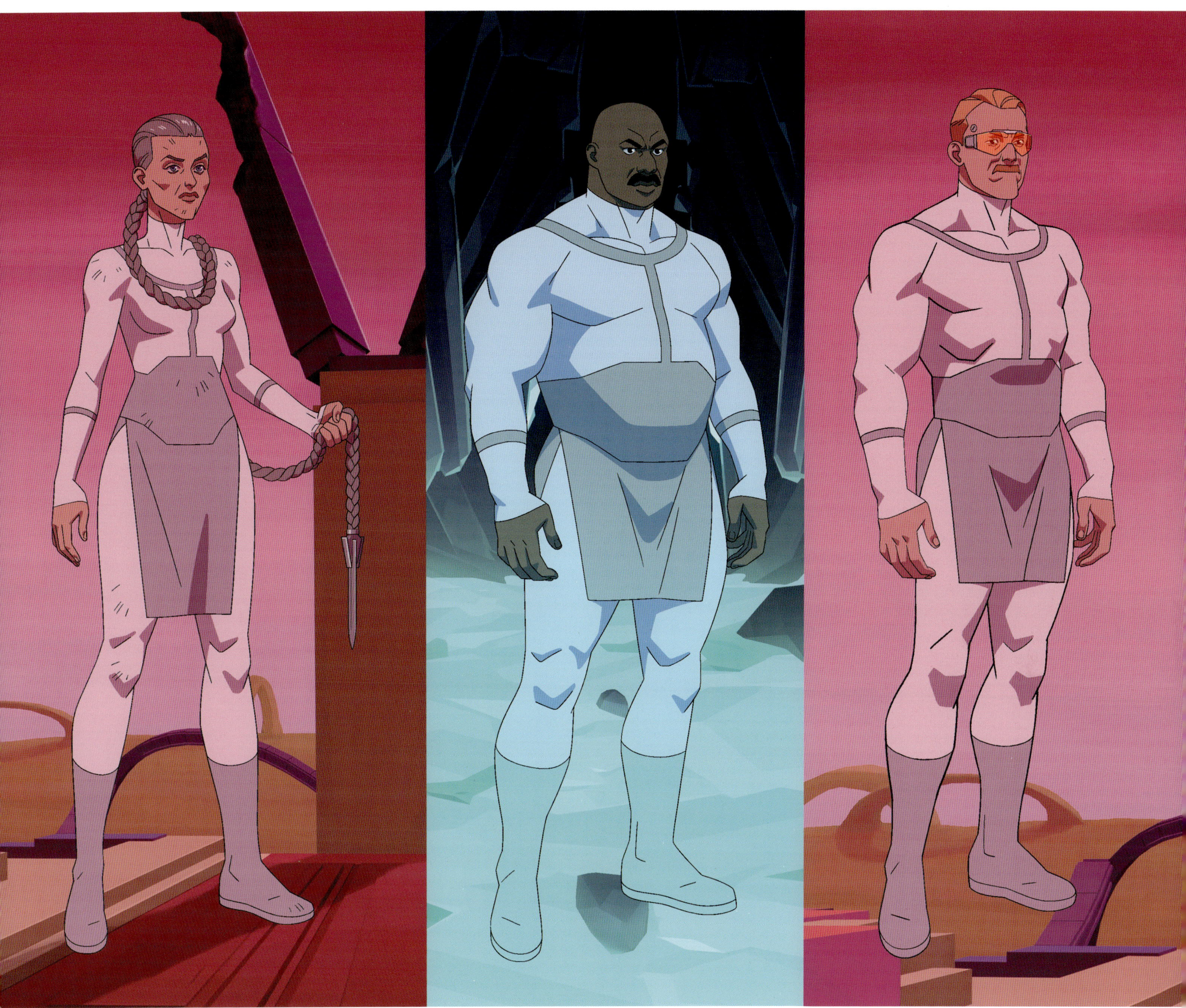

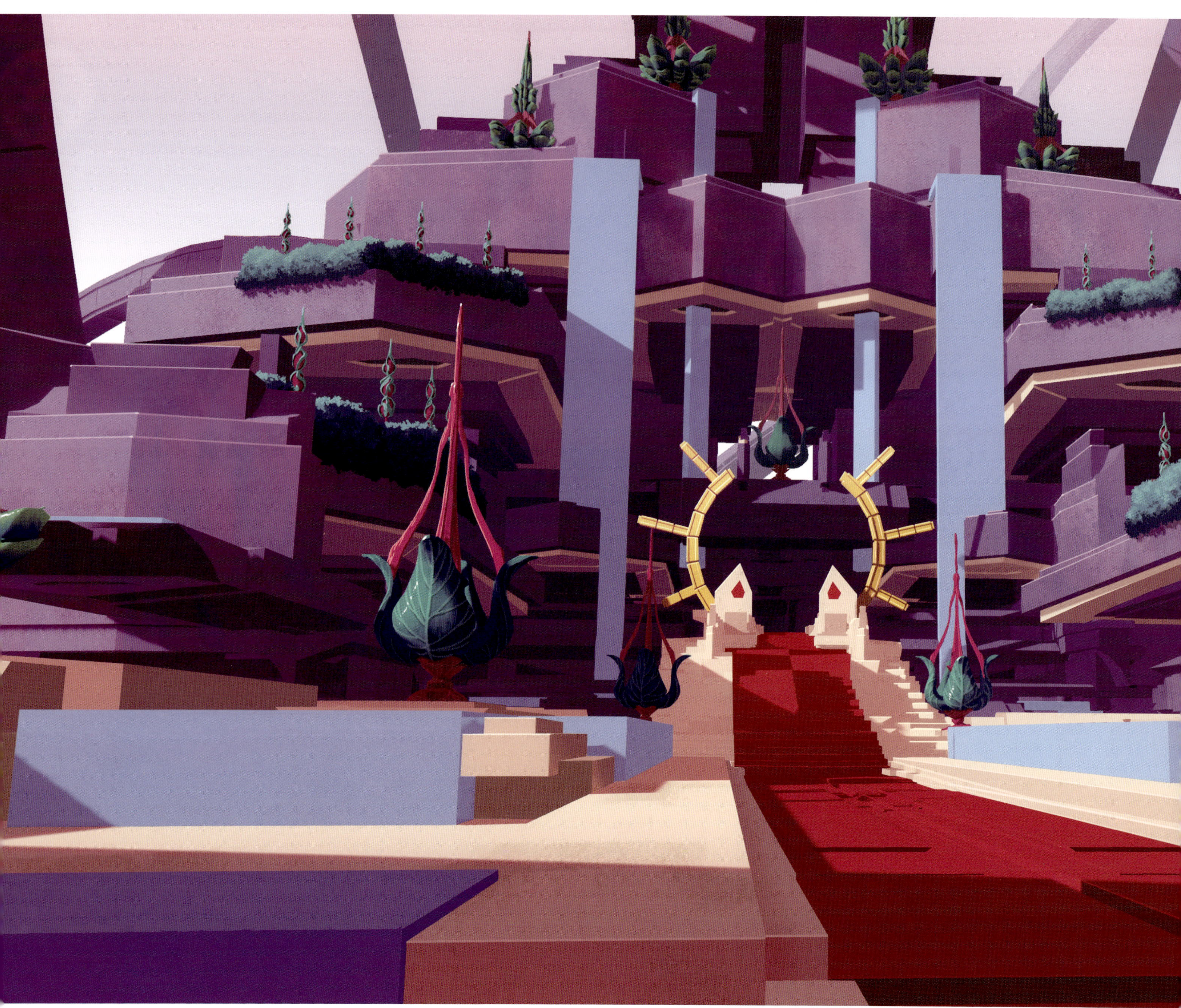

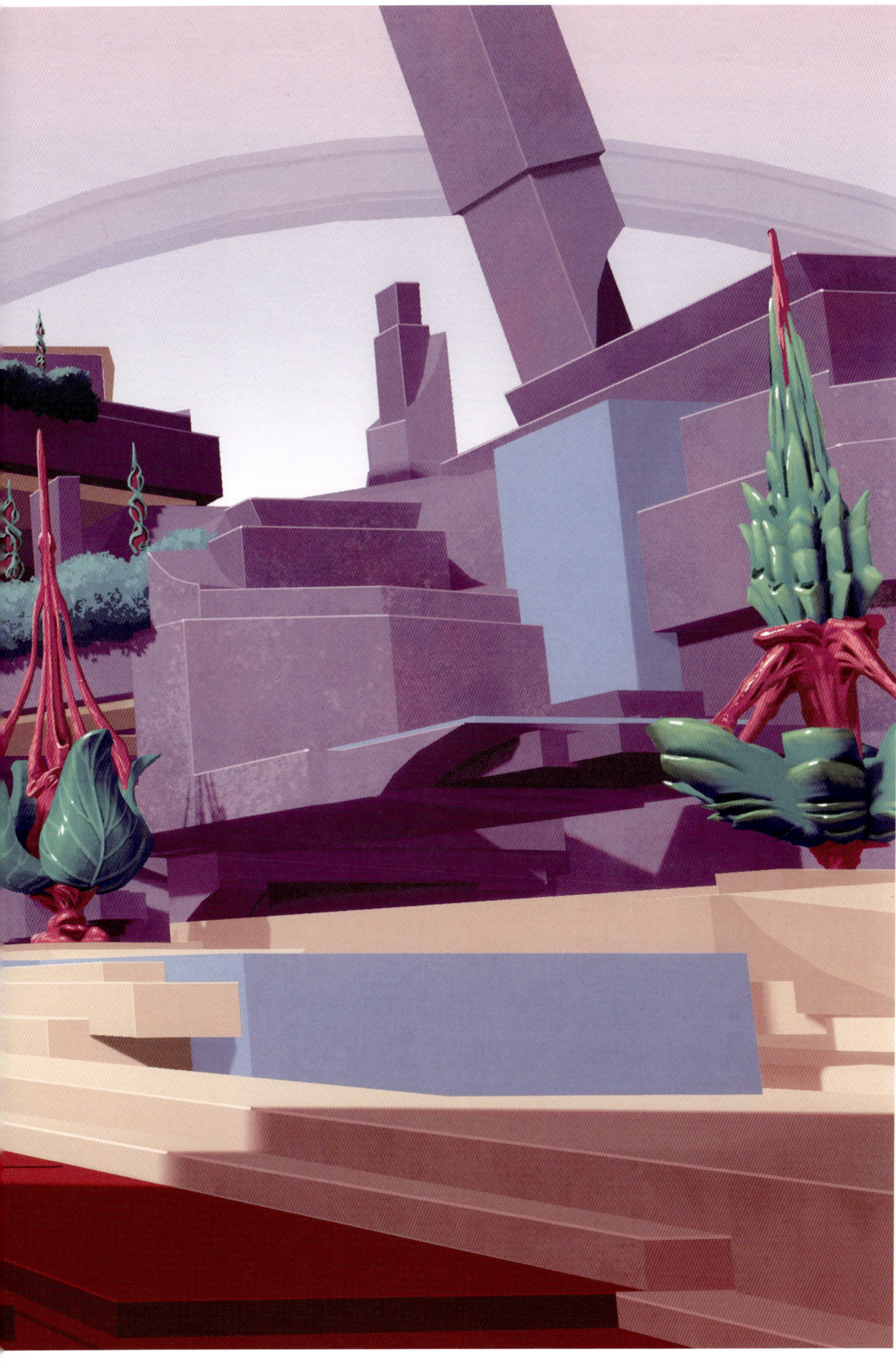

Edwin [Fong] and the environment guys, they did a great job of giving us interesting shapes. But I think in terms of purpose, it was a true trial by fire in terms of making something that was functional. Lessons in 'less is more'. It was super busy. And so we got into post and we were trying to control a lot of what didn't come back great. There was just so much noise to contend with that it was just like, 'Oh, if I could do stuff different, this would be where I would spend all my time.'"

Big steps had to be taken to create a final space that would be more suitable for the battle.

"[The plan] started as, we'd build that space out and then break it all down," says O'Neil, "then find spaces to build up, arenas to do the action set pieces. And it was just impossible. It was too busy, and we hadn't planned — or I hadn't planned — far enough ahead for what we were going to see on boards. And so when we finally got back the animatic and went back into our shipping phase and tried to finalize stuff that still needed some love, we wound up building a whole separate Thraxa set for a lot of our action. We had a couple of opportunities on the board to really get them out to a wasteland, and so that's where we're going to go, because we can't get away from all of this stuff that we did wrong, and we can kind of reset before we go back for [Episode] 205. I think somewhere along there, it was just like, 'Yeah, okay. We're here now. The only way out is through. And we just gotta figure it out as we go.' It was just a challenging episode all around. And I think I'm proud of how much we pulled together in post, to make that episode compete with the rest of the season. But I think that was the largest hurdle in Season Two."

"I think it underscores how the process works," says Duncan. "It's not over 'til it's over. You're not done until it's done. We're always reevaluating what we have until we finally just have to turn it in. We work with Robert and Simon on the scripts. We work with Robert and Simon on the animatics. We push things in the design phase before it ships, and then all through animation, VFX, we're always pushing stuff."

And just as the art team was pushing their limits

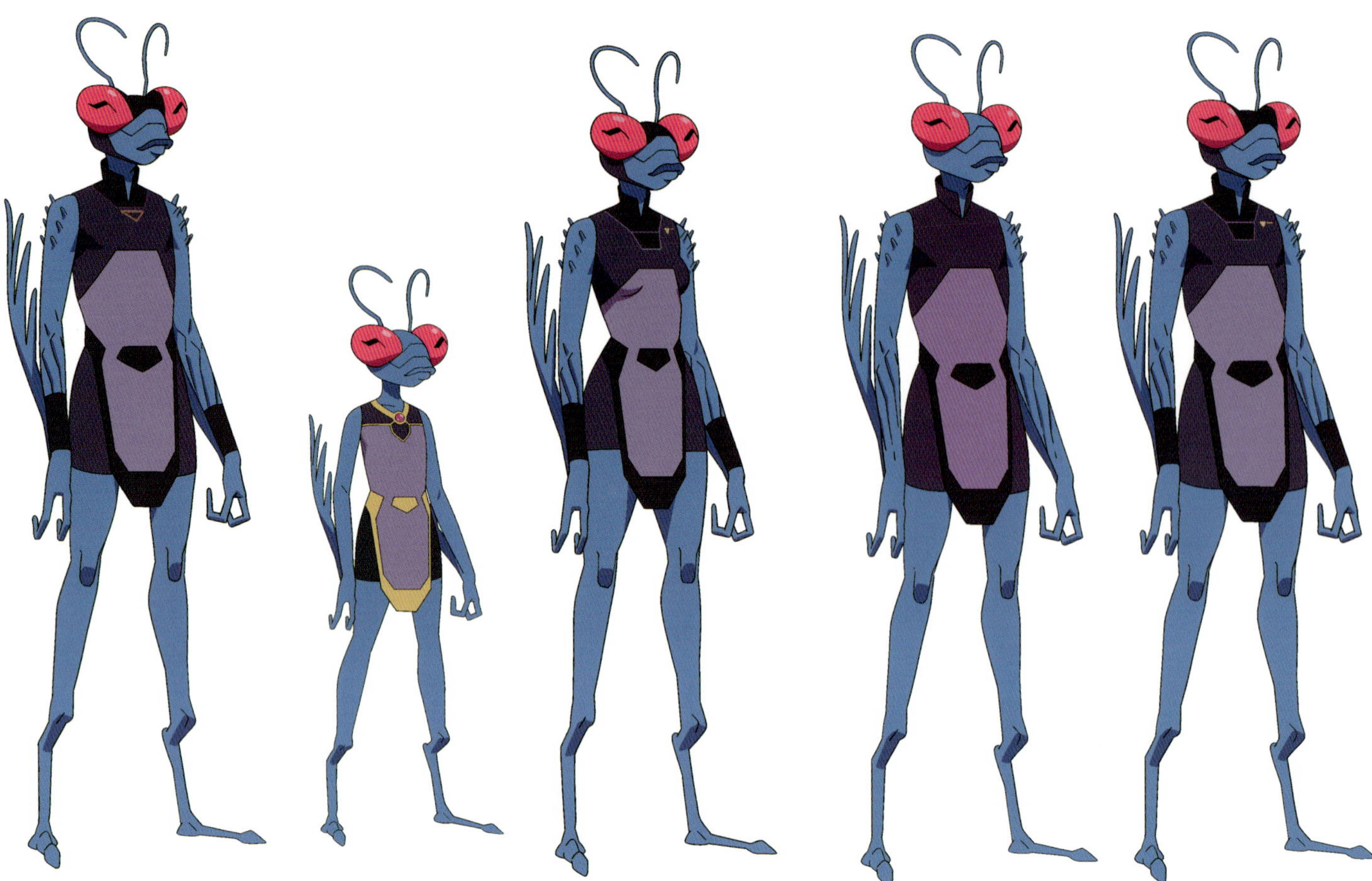

creatively, Omni-Man was pushing his son to be the best hero — and Viltrumite — that he could be.

"Mark is still kind of learning his powers and still fights like a person," says Racioppa. "I think we looked at stats of war, and most soldiers don't fire their gun. It's a hard thing to actually try to kill somebody. Most of us raised human obviously don't want to do that generally, and you would find a hard time following through on that. You might beat someone up, but to do a killing blow... That's what that sequence is about. Nolan's like, 'You're fighting like a person. You've gotta fight like a Viltrumite. If we want to win this, you have to be savage. You have to be decisive. You have to kill.' And Mark is like, 'I don't want to do that. I don't want to be you. I don't want to be a Viltrumite at all.' So that's part of the problem. And he manages to open that door a little bit through desperation."

The level of violence intensified as the battle went on.

"Damage states are one of the most difficult things to accomplish in animation," says Kirkman. "And we have so many damage states for so many characters. The team is always pushing the envelope to make sure that you get to see those differences and how things progress during a fight. A lot of times, if you really pay attention, there will be a limit to like one or two damage states in a fight. And I feel really fortunate to have a team that's willing to go that extra mile and have like five or six different damage states, especially when we have these massive fight sequences."

"Everybody touched a little bit of 204," says O'Neil. "The tough part is, you have to pace yourself, not just in terms of the work, but in terms of where you go extreme with the gore. Because if it's all extreme, none of it matters and people get desensitized. So it's trying to pick your battles."

In this episode, those battles had been picked, and they were as gruesome as any that had come before on the show. When Lucan set his sights on both of Nolan's sons, Omni-Man ruthlessly disemboweled the massive Viltrumite with a swift strike to his gut.

"There's a lot more material in there for him to lose," says

Kirkman.

As the battle raged on, Omni-Man smashed Vidor's head between his powerful fists.

"On the storyboard side up front, we had a lot of people who were maybe a little too excited to do some of [the violence]," says Duncan, "and it was not the appropriate time or place. And so we got a bunch of notes. And then on this episode, I think people were a little bit more restrained. And so then it was working with Robert and it's like, 'No, this needs to be big. This is where we need to really go.' And so from that point on, everybody just kept pushing it harder and harder, like crushing Vidor's head in half."

Vidor's grisly death was made slightly more awkward by the fact that the character's design was based on a member

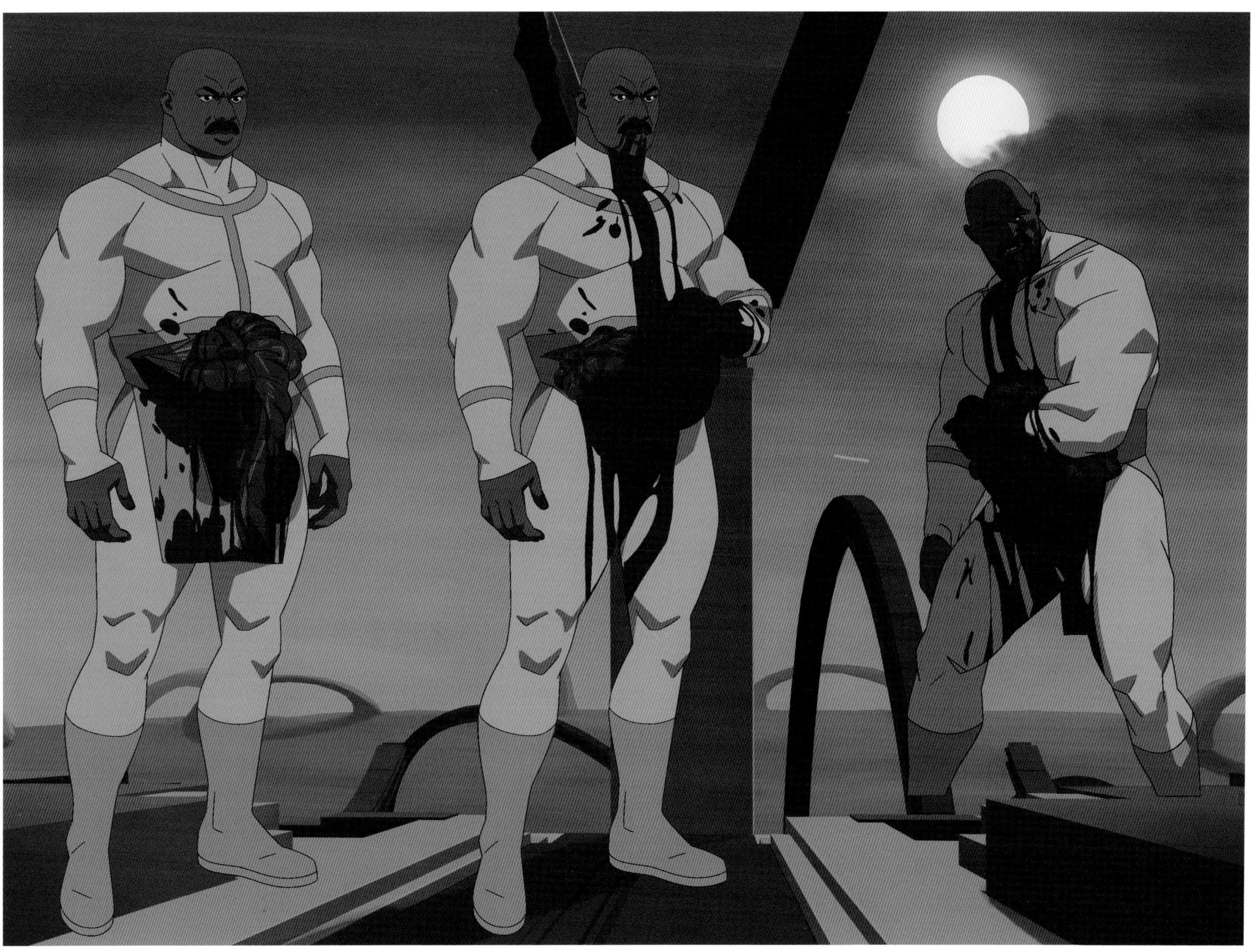

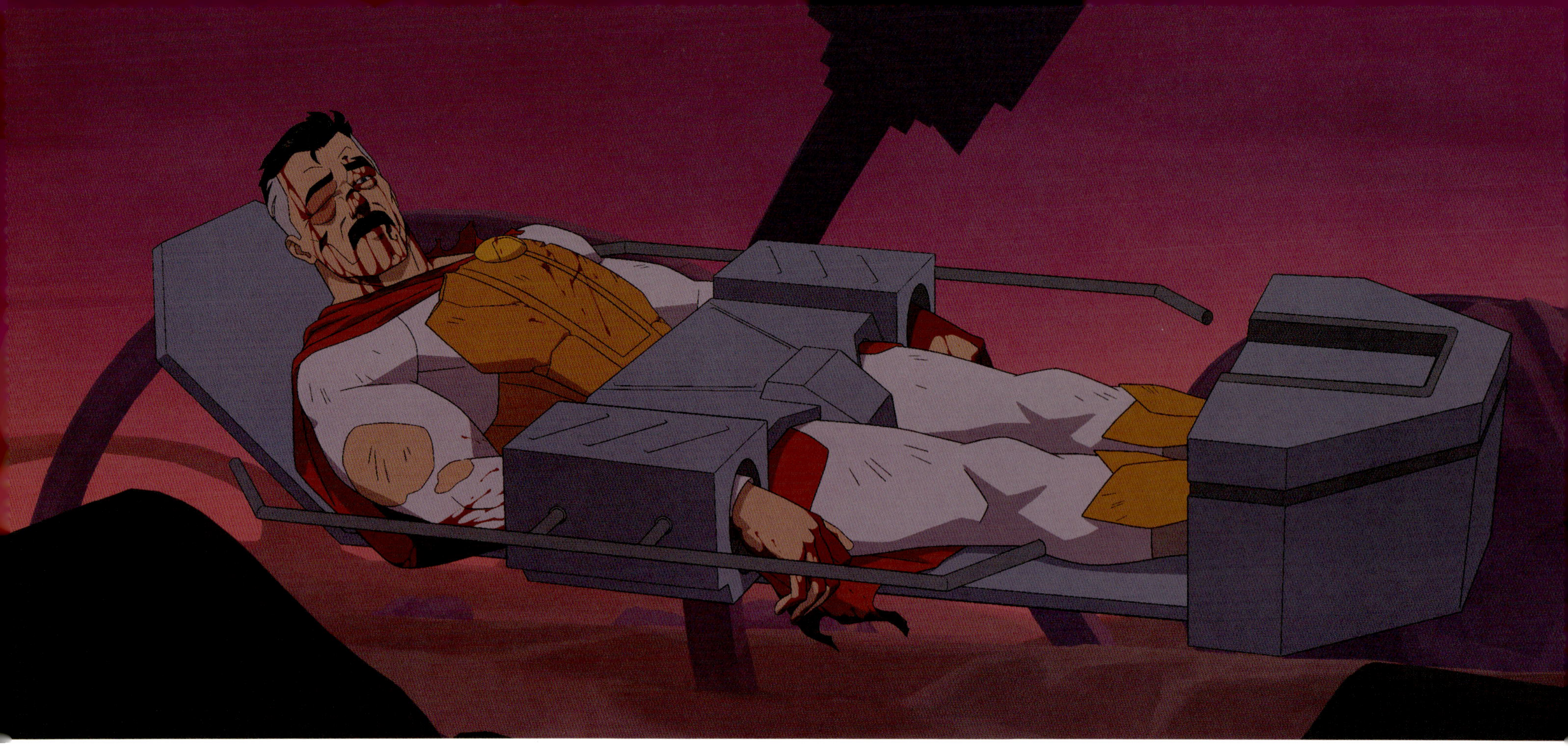

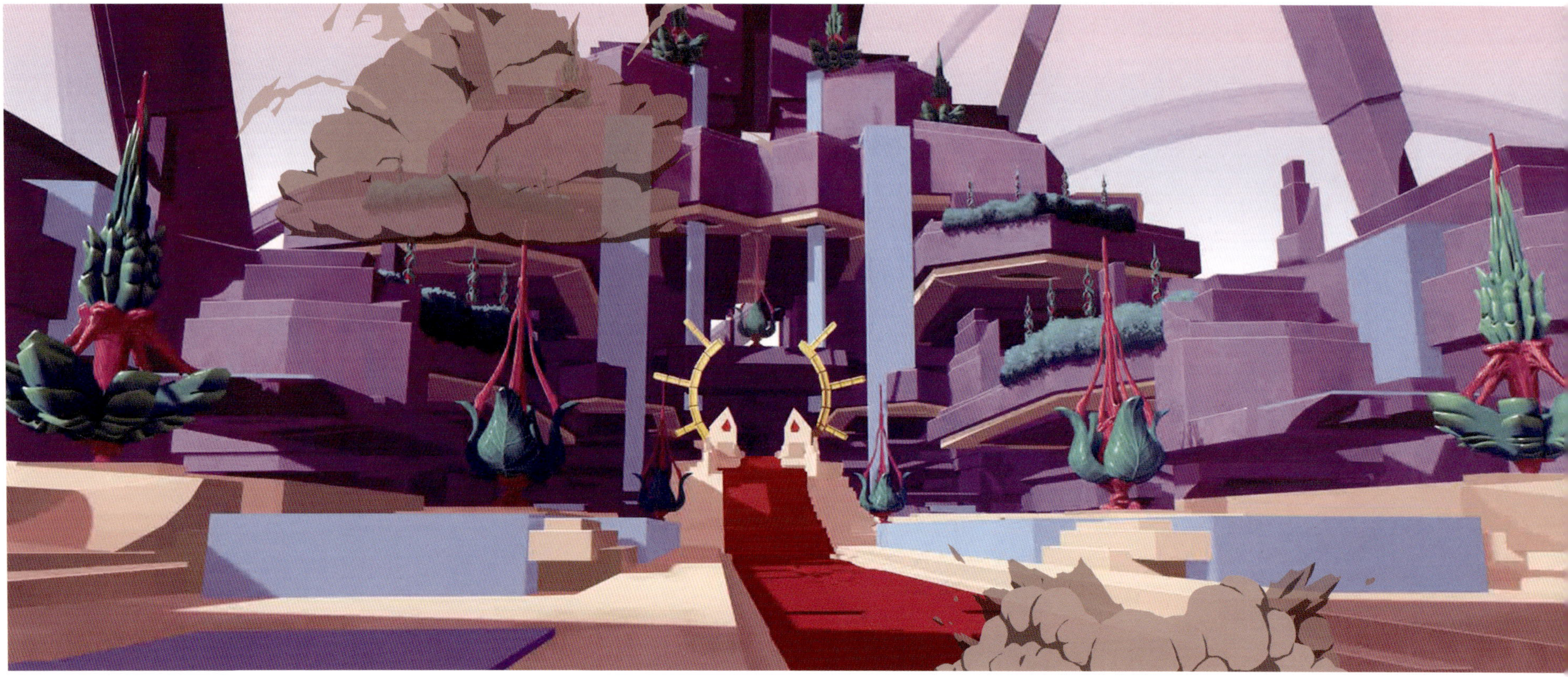

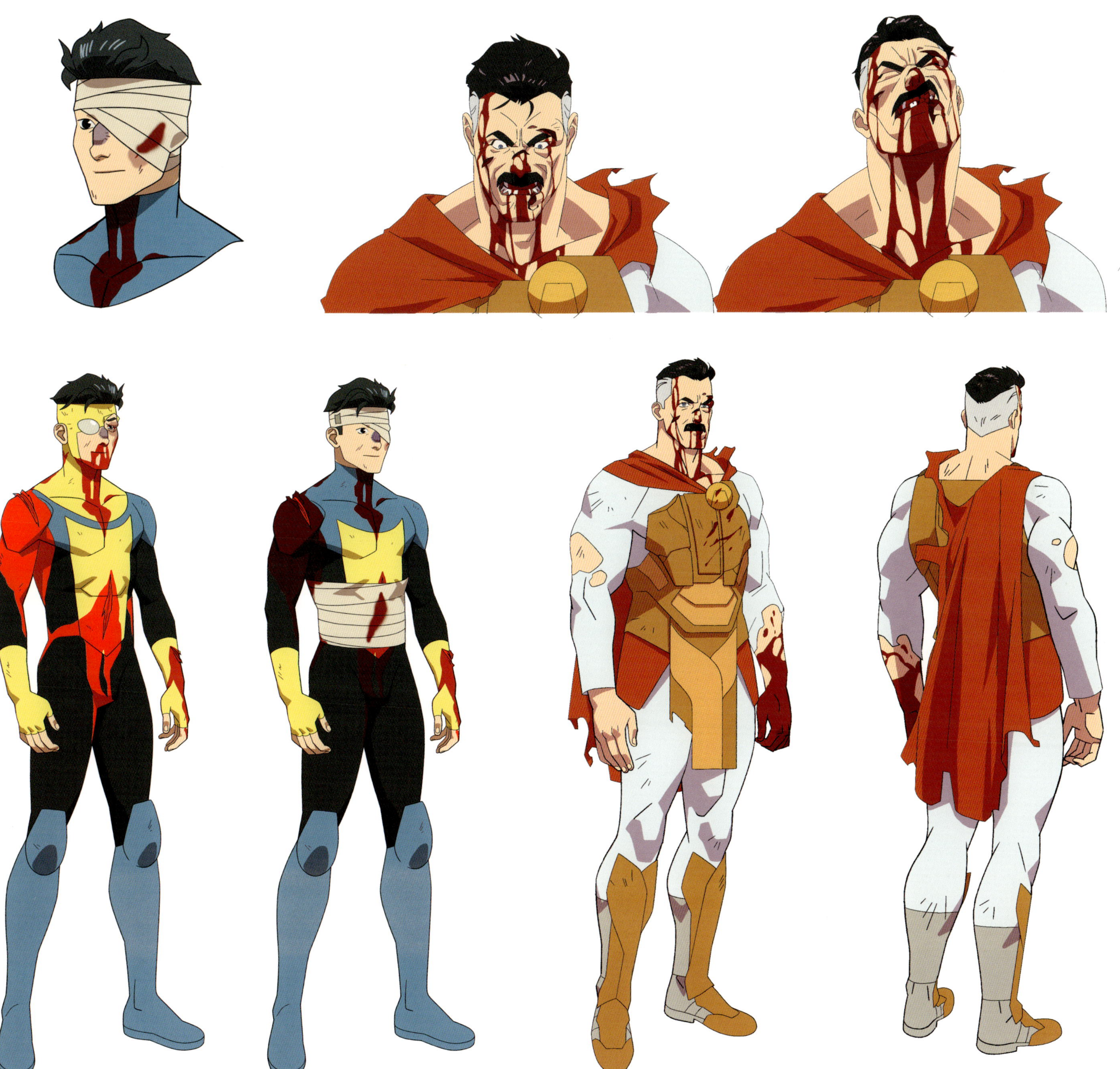

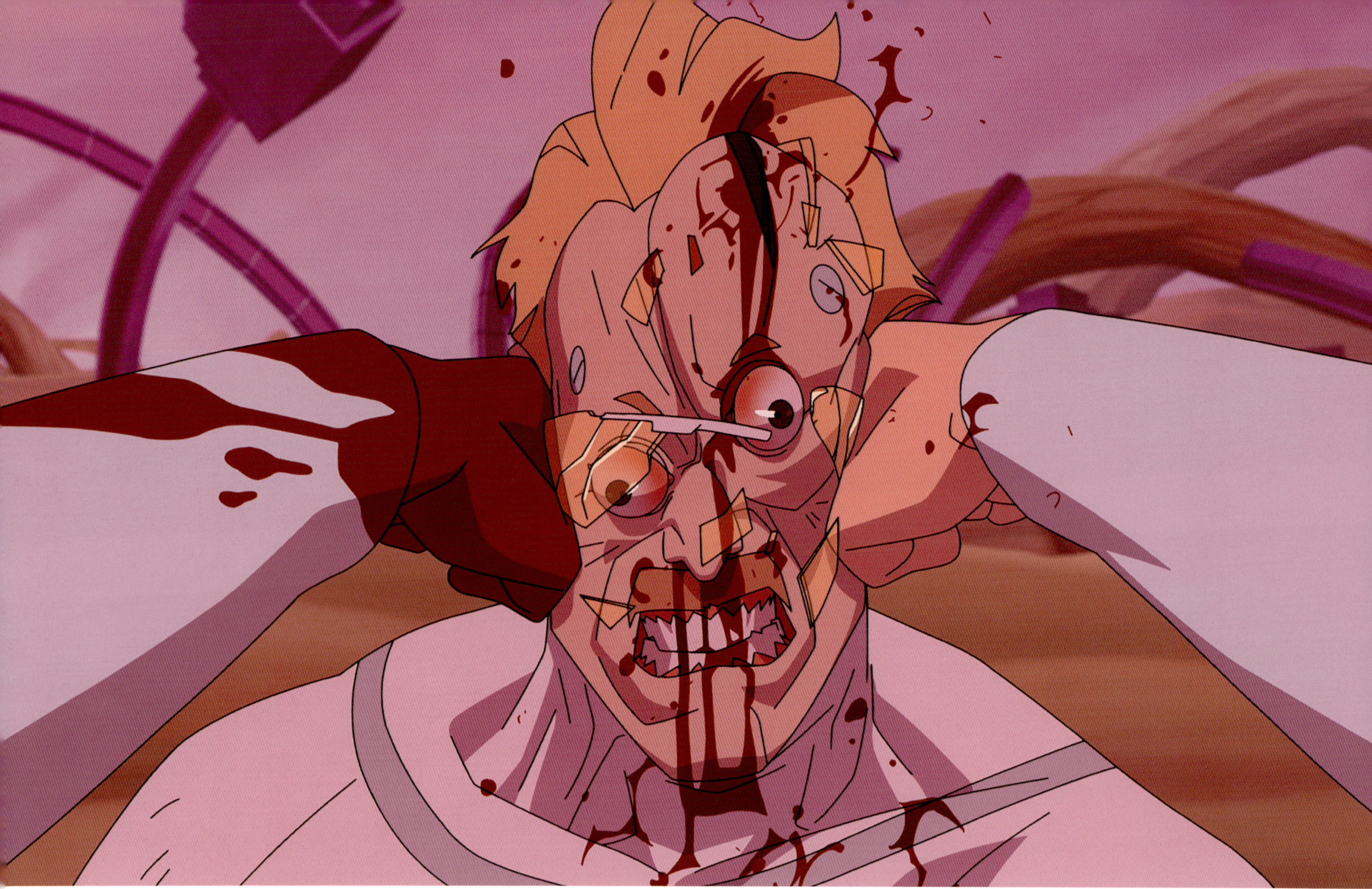

of the *Invincible* story team.

"Ross [Stracke] has been around forever," says Walker "I've known Ross for years. So it was funny to see an approximation of him get his head crushed. Yeah, the damage is pretty rough."

When Mark was deeply wounded in his fight against Thula, Omni-Man delivered a brutal blow that left her broken and bloodied jaw dangling from her face.

"Luke [Ashworth] wound up doing the bulk of the work for Thula's elbow to the jaw and a lot of the two poses associated with that," says O'Neil. "He took it like 90% of the way, and then we went back and forth the last 10% just on normal notes. But I like these things. I think it's a way to get away from normal anatomy."

"I feel bad that not everyone gets to watch the animatic," says Walker. "The animation is great, but there's just like a kinetic energy to rough drawings that you can't really capture in the finished clean line."

Though it seemed for a moment that Omni-Man had triumphed against his fellow Viltrumites, the wounded Lucan

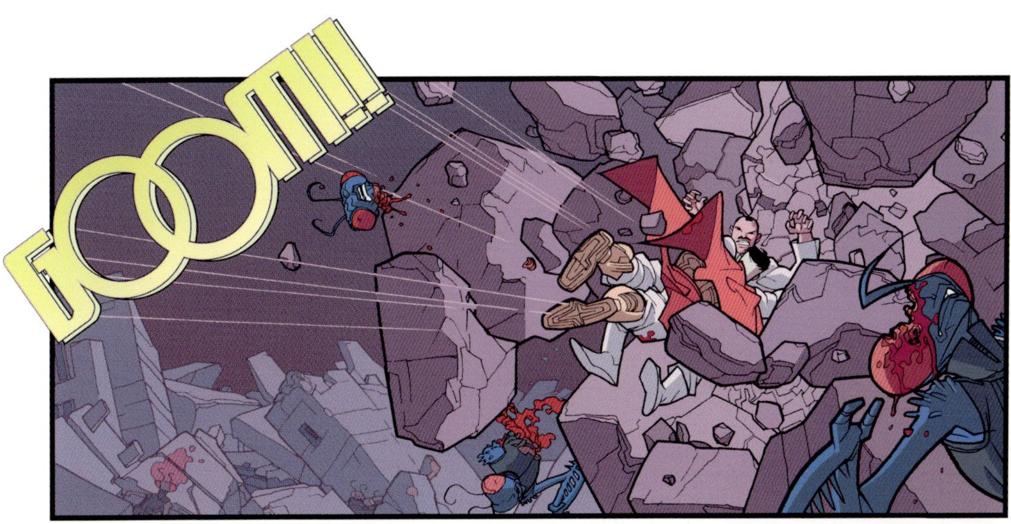

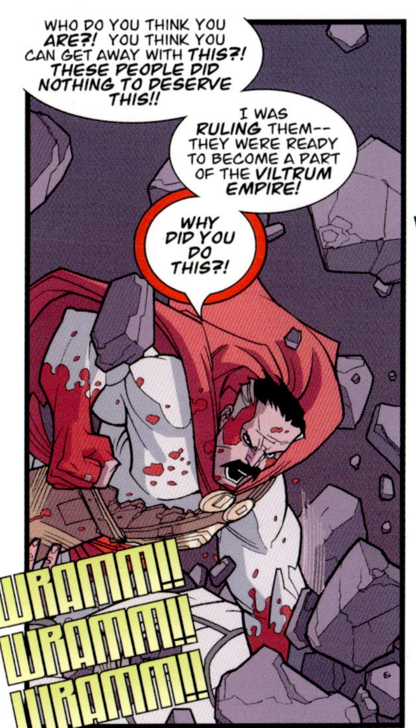

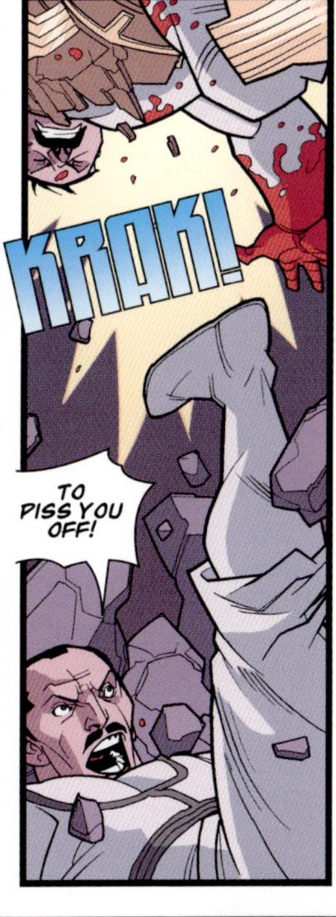

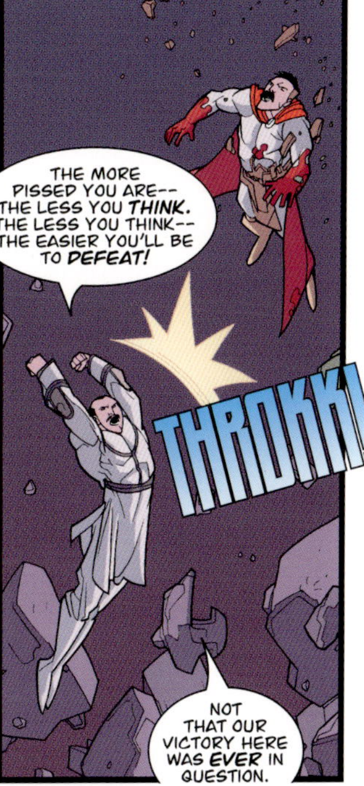

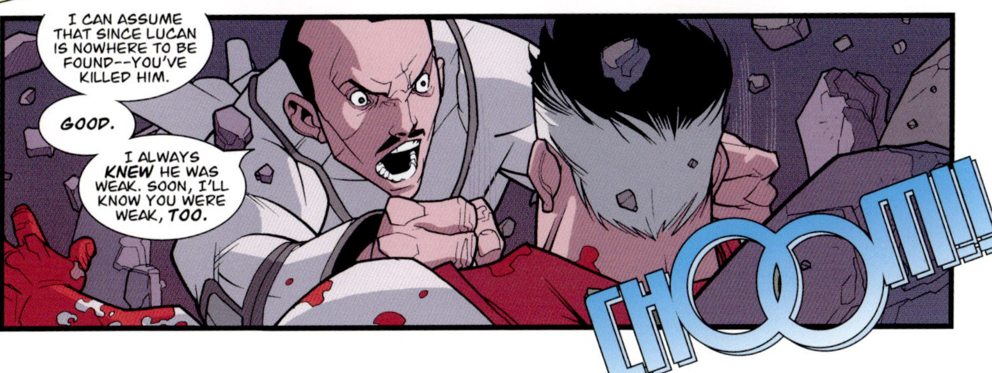

returned at the last moment and turned the tide.

"Ultimately, [Mark] and Nolan lose the fight even though they do some serious damage," says Racioppa. "We get a little hint of what Mark is capable of under the right circumstances, when he has no choice and he's defending the life of a baby and these people that he doesn't even know. It gives you a good look into Mark's heart. He's willing to do this, even for the father he hates at this point — or that he certainly has complicated feelings about — these people who tricked him to bring him here, that he's never met before, and his dad's new child. You know, I think we'd all do this for a baby, but to have Mark be like, 'Okay, fine. I will help you all and risk my life to do this,' gives us a good insight into who he is as a character. So that was super important there. And also, it's a great fight. We get to see some Viltrumites-on-Viltrumites, which we've never really seen before, and we're going to see more of in the show. So we just wanted to set that up."

"It was a big one," says Walker. "It ended up being a midseason finale, so I hope that fight was satisfying."

As Mark laid wounded on Thraxa's surface, viewers witnessed the arrival of another Viltrumite warrior who will have a lasting impact on the story to come — General Kregg. Eagle-eyed fans briefly glimpsed him alongside Thula during Nolan's flashback to Viltrum in the episode 108.

"I love the way that the sinister-ness of General Kregg's look comes through from Ryan [Ottley]'s design from the comics," says Kirkman. "There's just like a natural sneer to his face that is pretty neat."

Kregg's sinister appearance was enhanced by the work of voice actor Clancy Brown, who had previously played demon detective Damien Darkblood in *Invincible*'s first season.

"Clancy Brown pulled double duty playing General Kregg," says Kirkman. "I love that we have actors that are playing multiple characters on the show, and you can't really tell. I don't know that anybody is like, 'Oh, that sounds just like Damien Darkblood.' We didn't know how often Damien Darkblood was going to be showing up post-Season One, and we really wanted to keep Clancy Brown in the family. So we were trying to find some other role for him, and Kregg

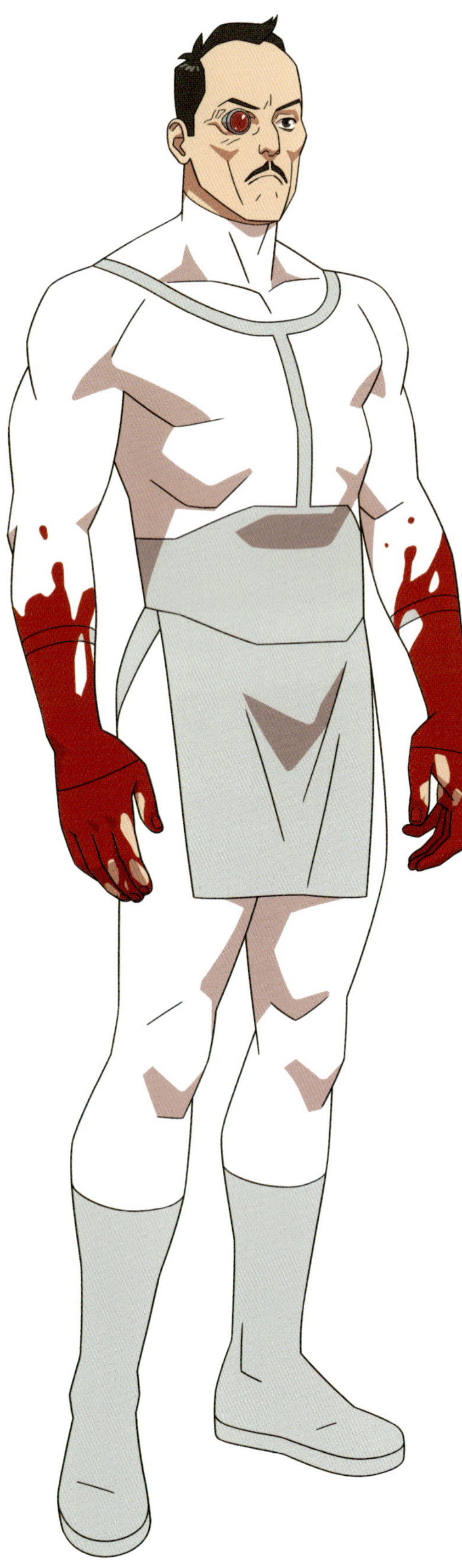

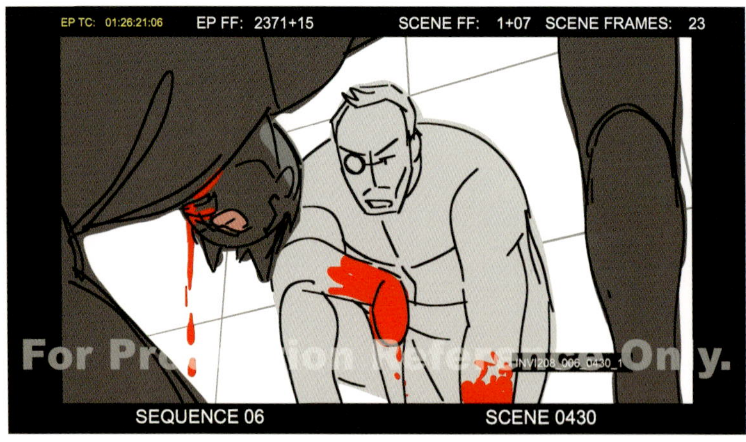

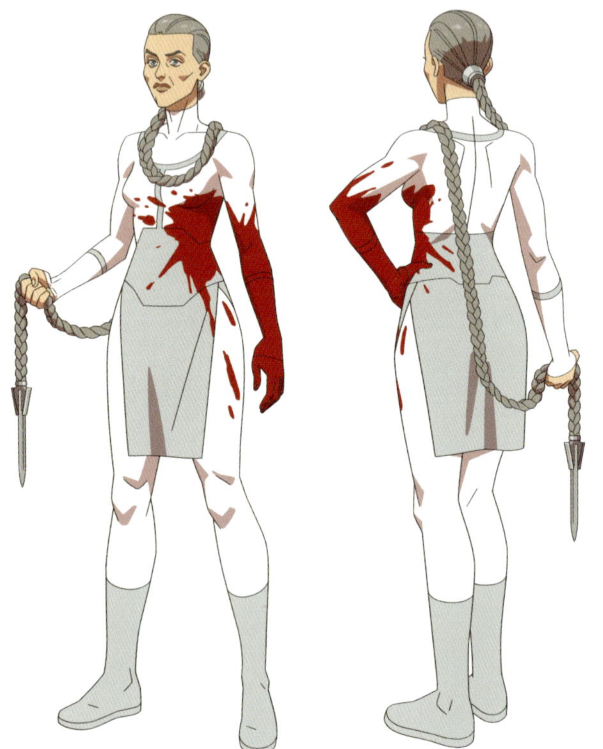

seemed like the perfect one."

As Kregg had Omni-Man hauled away to a Viltrumite prison for execution, he tasked Mark with completing the mission that his father had failed — preparing Earth for the Viltrumite invasion. Kregg threatened to kill millions if Mark refused to comply. It was yet another impossible choice that Mark was left with, and as the series entered its midseason hiatus, viewers would have to wait longer than usual to find out what the future would hold for the young hero and the planet he called home.

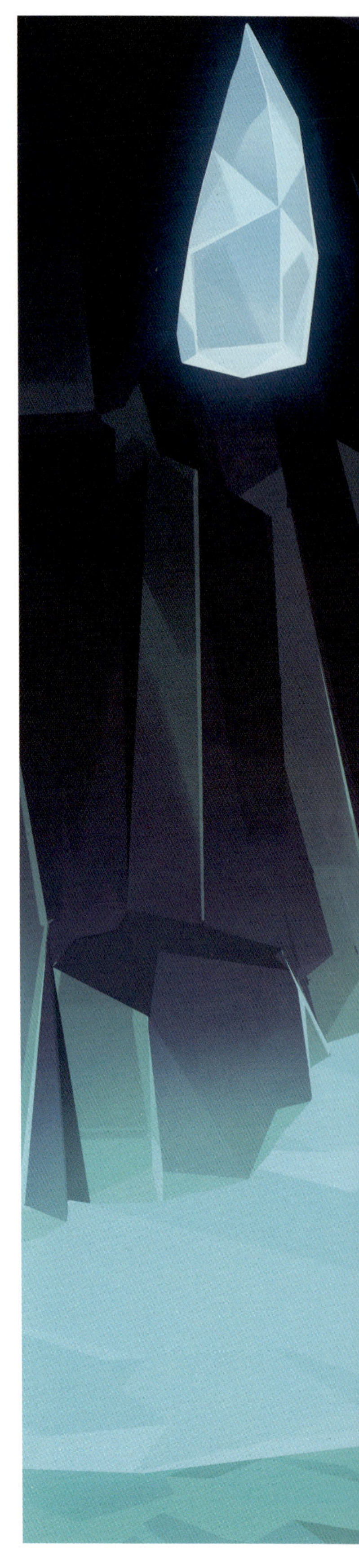

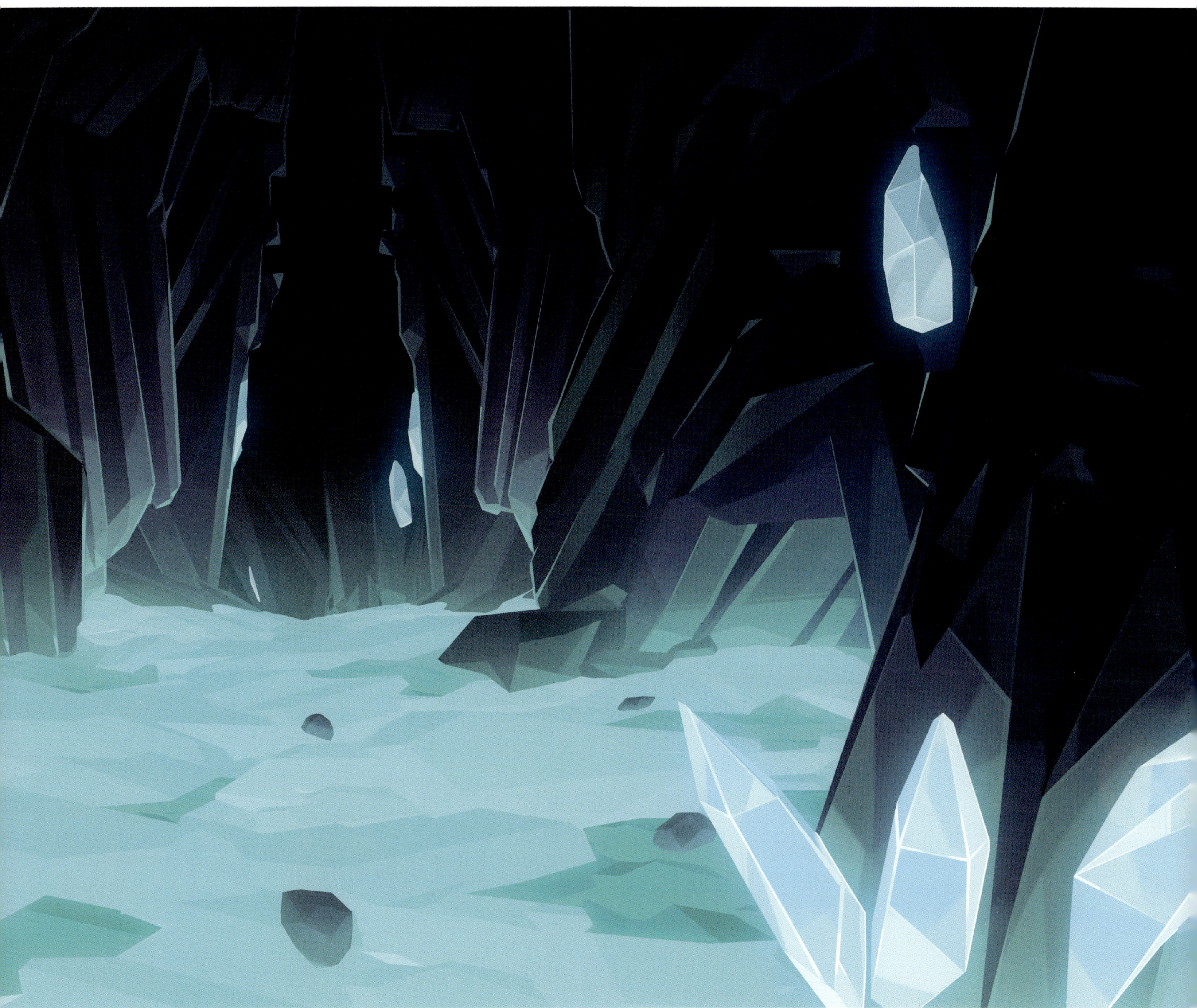

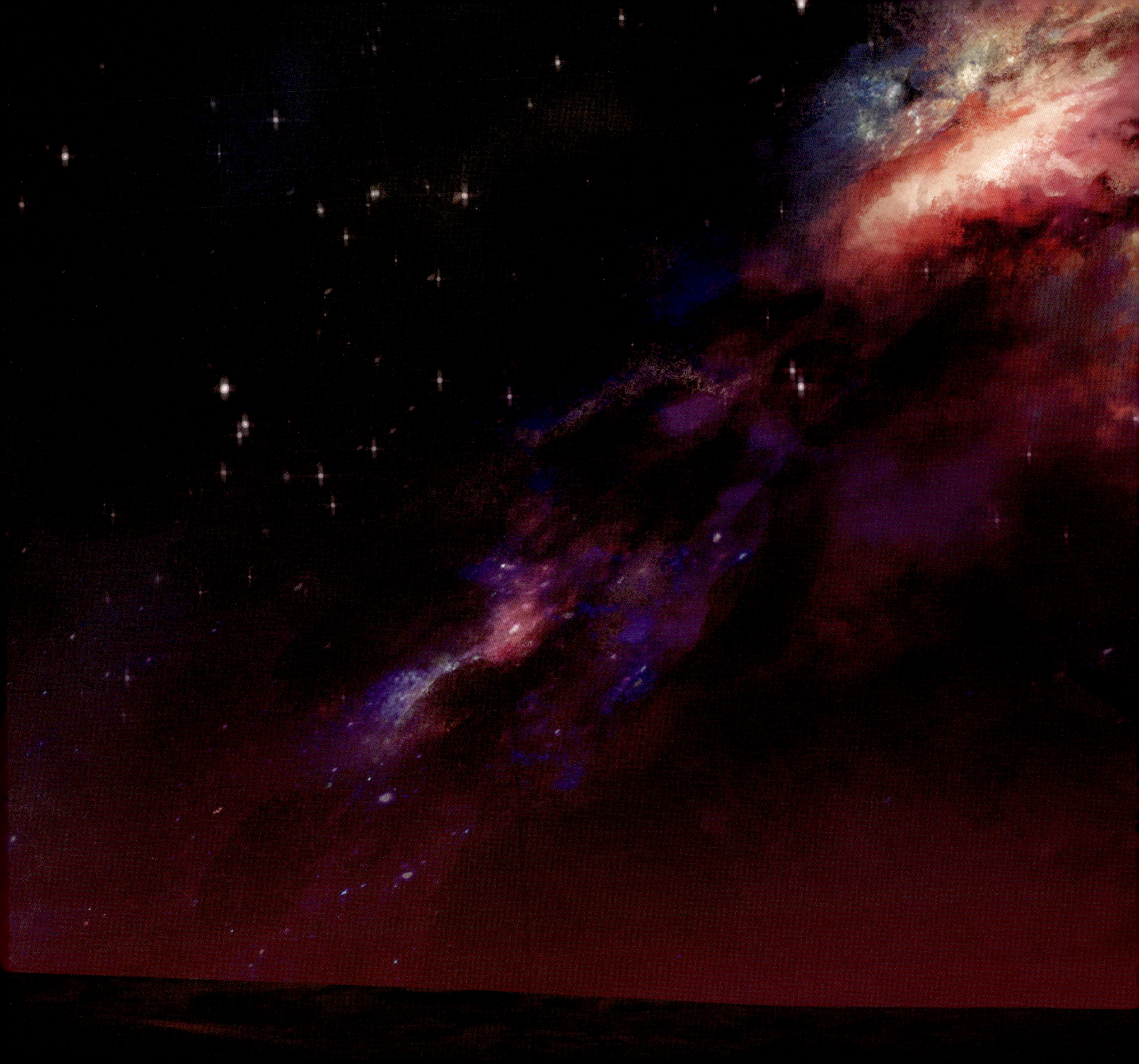

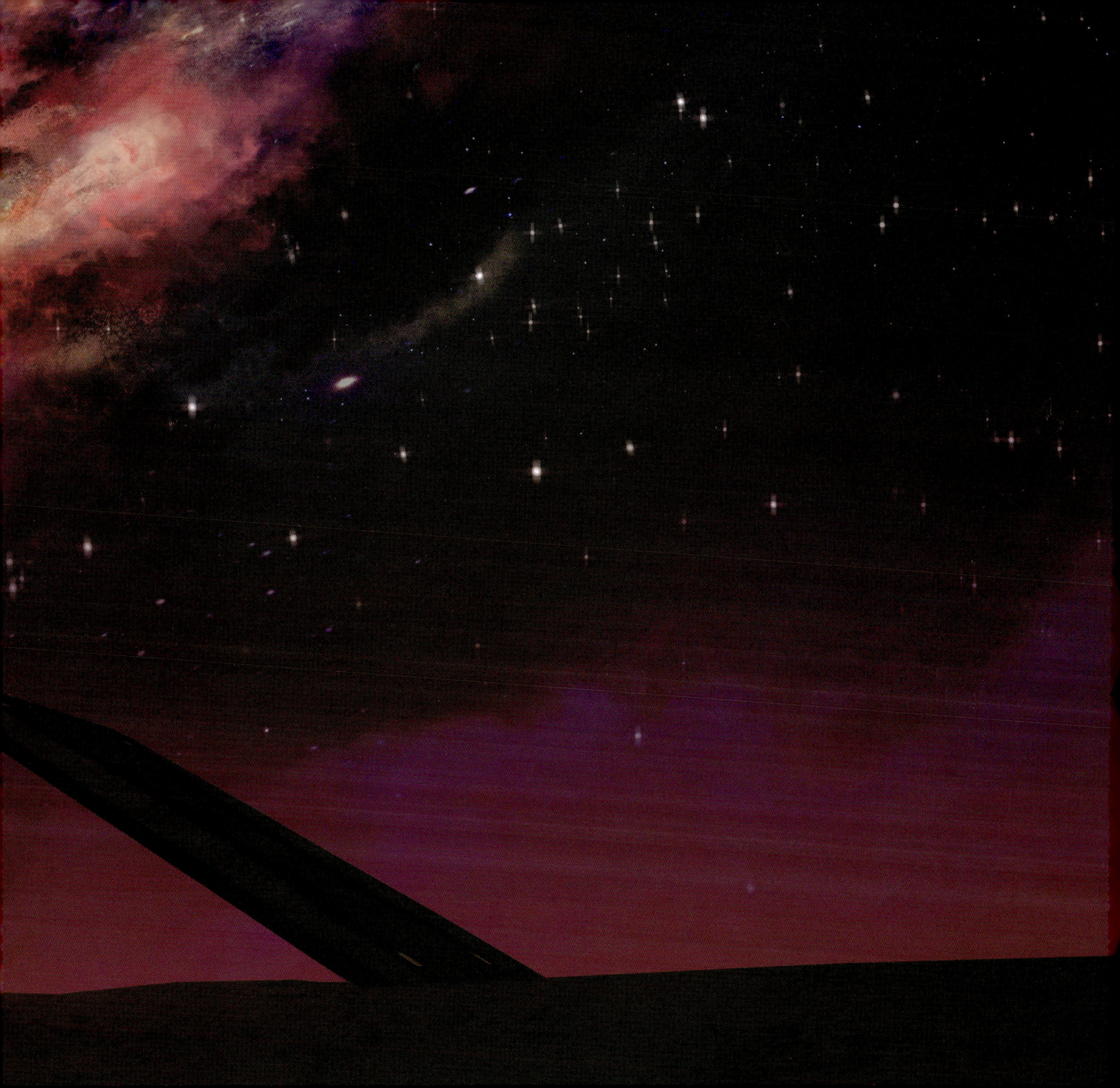

EPISODE 5:

THIS MUST COME AS A SHOCK

When *Invincible* returned for the second half of Season Two, Mark had been busy helping the citizens of Thraxa rebuild after the devastating events of Episode 204. Two months had gone by in his timeline, but slightly more time had passed between episodes in the real world.

"I think the gap was like three-and-a-half months or so," says Executive Producer and Co-Showrunner Simon Racioppa. "So it wasn't like we needed to remind you of everything. Obviously, the gap between [Episodes] 108 and 201 was like two-and-a-half years. So this wasn't quite as long. So we felt like, 'Let's just hit the ground. Let's just come in hard, remind everyone what we are, what the show is, and just get right back into it.' I think a lot of other shows have a big event and then, there's a lot of *denouement* after that. And sometimes we do that. I feel like Episode One [of Season Two] had a little bit of that coming off 108, but here, we just had this big event, this big fight on Thraxa, this big reveal. We see Nolan again, we see Nolan's child [Oliver]. And then you're expecting an episode that maybe has a little more breathing room. It slows down a little bit. It's a little more reflective on what you just saw. And, we were like, 'Well, why don't we just go bigger? What if we just keep the pressure on Mark again?'"

While Mark was still on Thraxa, Earth's heroes were keeping busy, as evidenced by a short battle scene that featured a veritable army of superheroes from the *Invincible* Universe, including the modern Guardians of the Globe and many ancillary heroes that hadn't been seen since Season One.

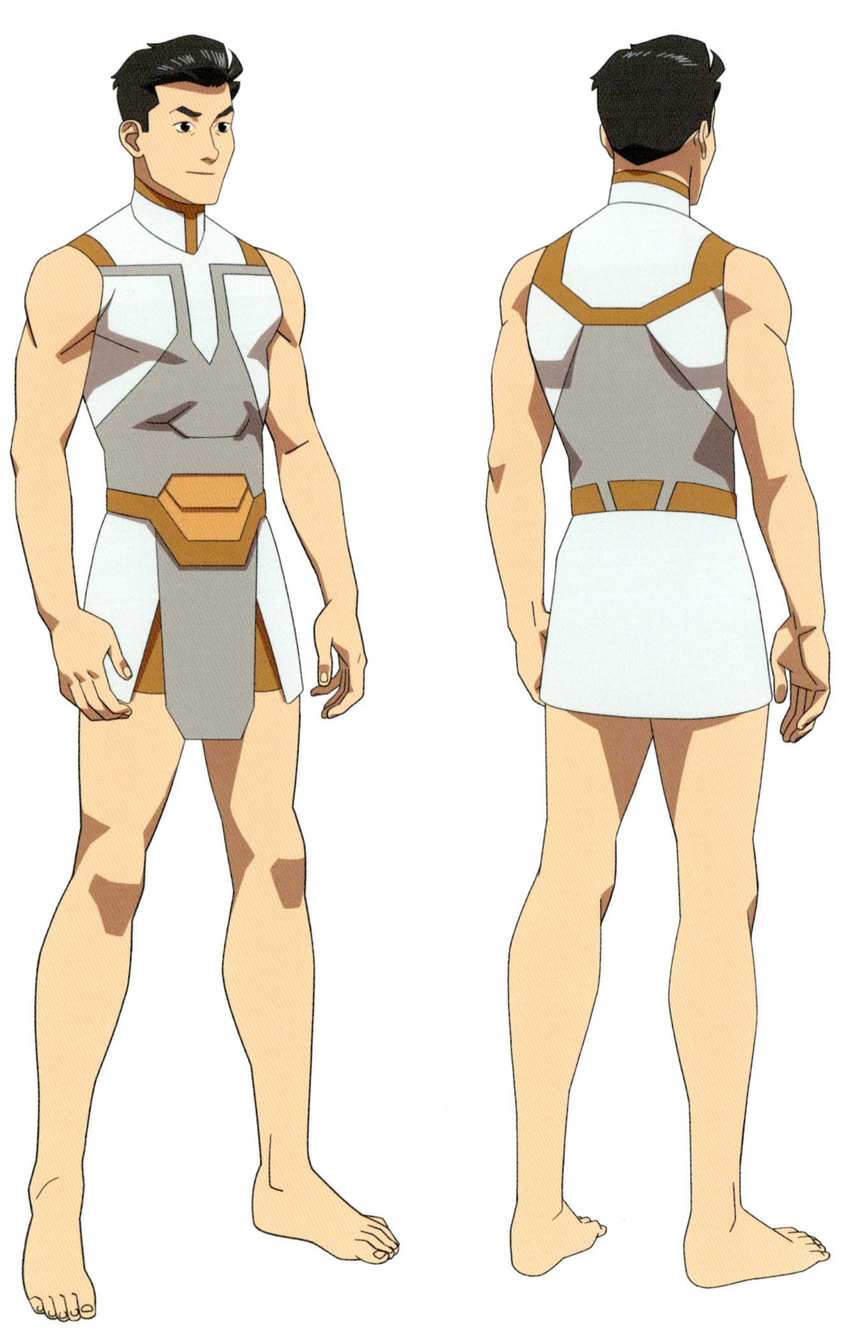

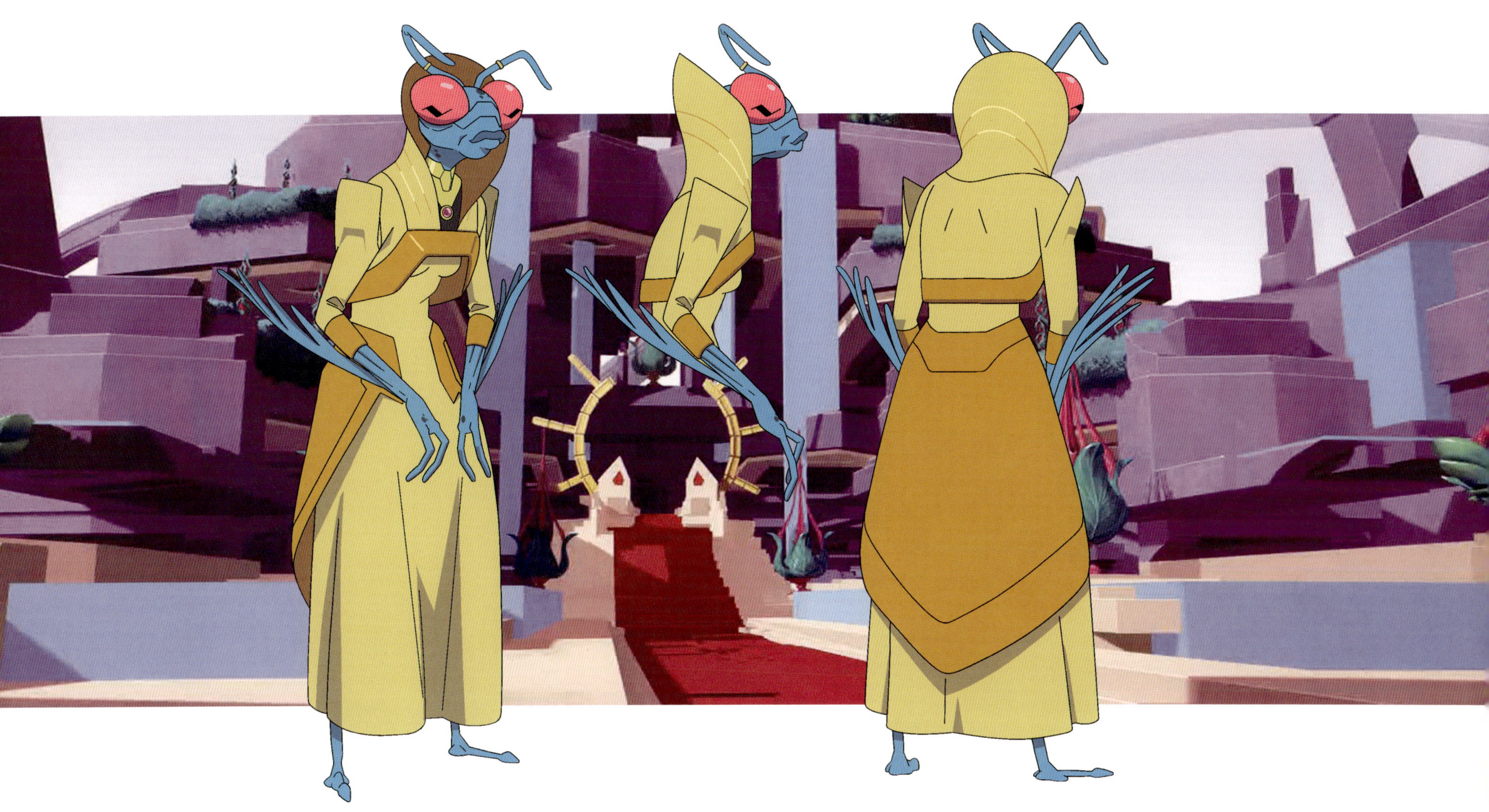

"Nothing gets forgotten," says Executive Producer, Co-Showrunner, and Co-Creator Robert Kirkman. "That's kind of the ethos of *Invincible*. You see a character in the background for three seconds, that guy is going to come back. There's going to be something with that person. You're going to see more of them. I love that we have this array of new characters that weren't present in the comics that show up. We'll get to have some fun with them as the series progresses."

"There's room in my heart for a bunch of them," says Art Director Shaun O'Neil, "because they were characters generated as a product of directing 103. We needed incidental superheroes for the [Guardians'] memorial at the beginning of the episode, and we had nothing. So I was just blocking in things, trying to get shape variations and interesting compositions. I was trying to design stuff on spec, but it was all on the rougher side because it's a storyboard. I work tight, but not that tight when it comes to boards. I think the silhouettes were all there, the core elements were all there. But then Cory took that stuff and tied it all down into these characters that are now staples in our story. Big Mildew. Business Baby. Two-Punch Man — always a favorite. I think Glass Hat came out of that. Red Fighting Hood. And Good Knight. I had been listening to a lot of GWAR. So it was just like, horns, shoulder pads, all that stuff. And he's just this very awesome, top-heavy design.

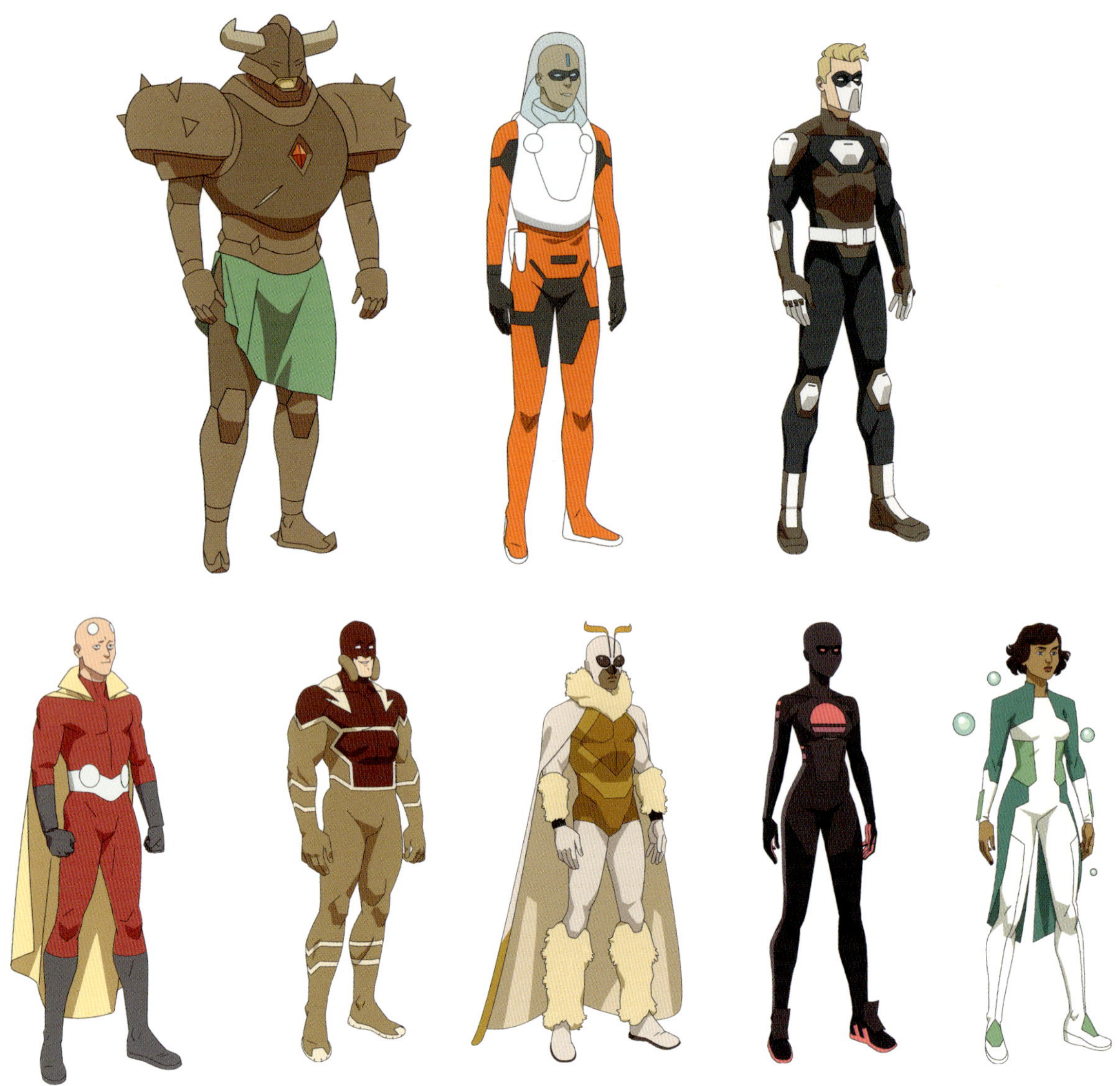

Cory fucking crushed. Just finalizing these into something that was on the mark for what I was going for, but is so different in final concept, it really feels like collaboration. Like true collaboration. And I fucking love it. A lot of those dudes are really cool."

"As brief as it was, it was cool to see all those characters assembled as they were," says Co-Executive Producer and Co-Creator Cory Walker. "And hopefully we'll get to see that again real soon."

"A bunch of them are just pure Cory," says O'Neil. "There are a lot of times where names and the premises for characters that he and Robert come up with are kind of dumb and you're just like, 'For real? This is what we're doing?' But over time, I couldn't see it any other way. They become so endearing that you're just like, 'I guess I kind of get it. It's funny. It's really good.'"

It would take a significant threat to bring together this many heavy-hitting heroes. That threat came in the form of Omnipotus, a character pulled straight from the *Invincible* comics.

"I like that character," says Kirkman. "He only has a brief appearance, but he's got a really cool design. Another design from the comics that Ryan Ottley did. I wanted to get a guy that kind of looked like a big, evil Skeletor. If you can think of a bigger, evil-er Skeletor. It was cool seeing that design translated into animation and the different tweaks

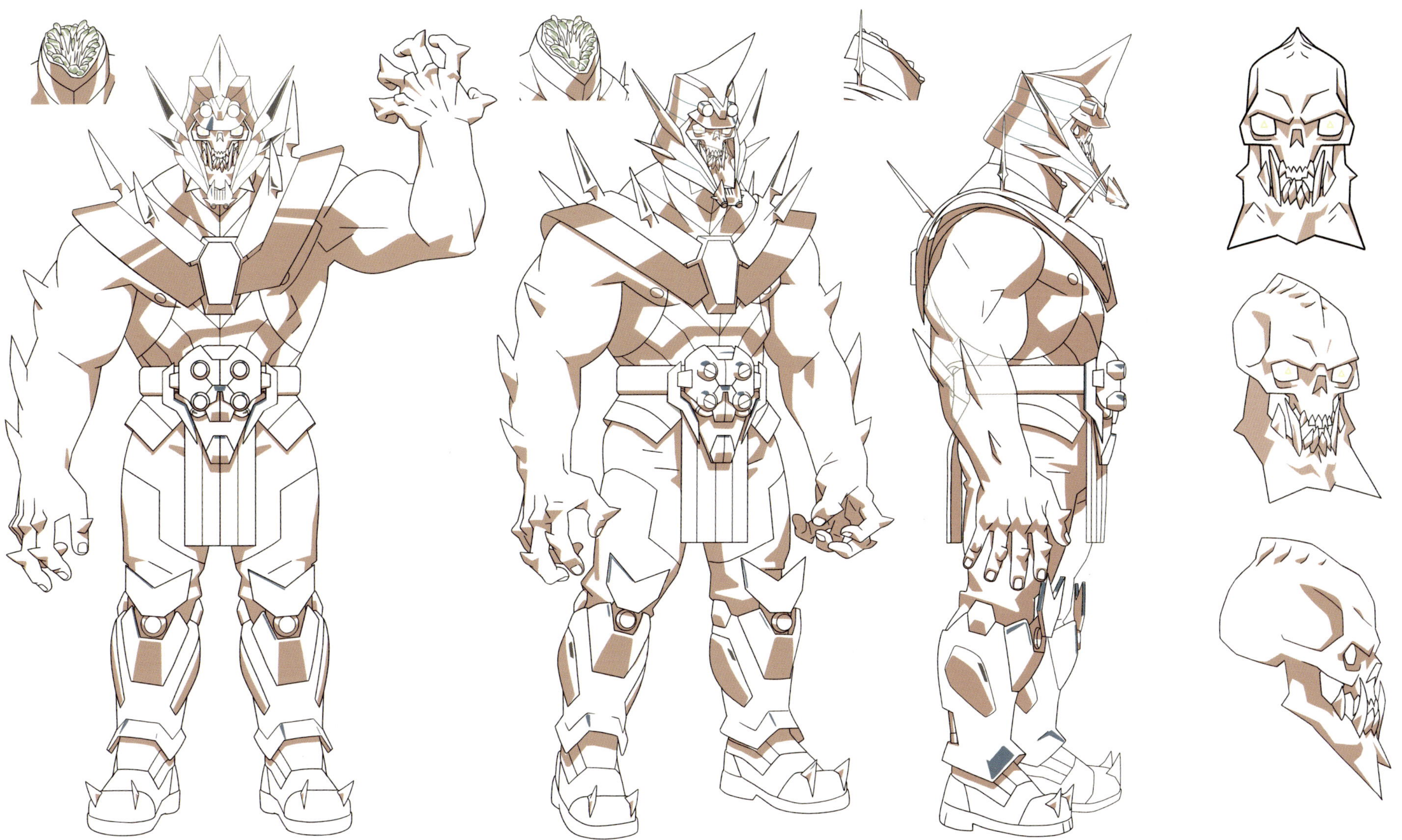

that were made and things that were streamlined."

"I loved the Omnipotus model," says Walker. "I don't know if it was exclusively Nate Bellegarde, but I know that he did a fair amount of work on that, and I really liked it. There was this pass where his head was floating on his body rather than being attached, because it's like a skull, and there was geode-like crystalline shit lining his neck. And I thought that was really cool, but it was a bit complex. The final model is still flippin' cool."

The legion of heroes managed to take down Omnipotus without the help of Invincible, but they'd need him to pitch in again soon after he returned to Earth due to a number of new threats that had materialized.

"He gets back, and then suddenly, there's these two big things," says Racioppa. "It's like, 'You remember the Sequids from Season One? Well, they're back and they're on their way, and we have to stop them'. And then, the Guardians who are left behind are ordering pizza, and then it's like, 'Oh, the Lizard League are doing something in the missile base.' And it's sort of like, 'Who cares about the Lizard League?' And we're like, 'No, these are the new Lizard League. They've got new leadership. They're much tougher than you think.' And we run these two traumatic events in parallel, because sometimes when it rains, it pours."

Before the Lizard League ever showed their scales, however, Mark was already on a shuttle with a small group

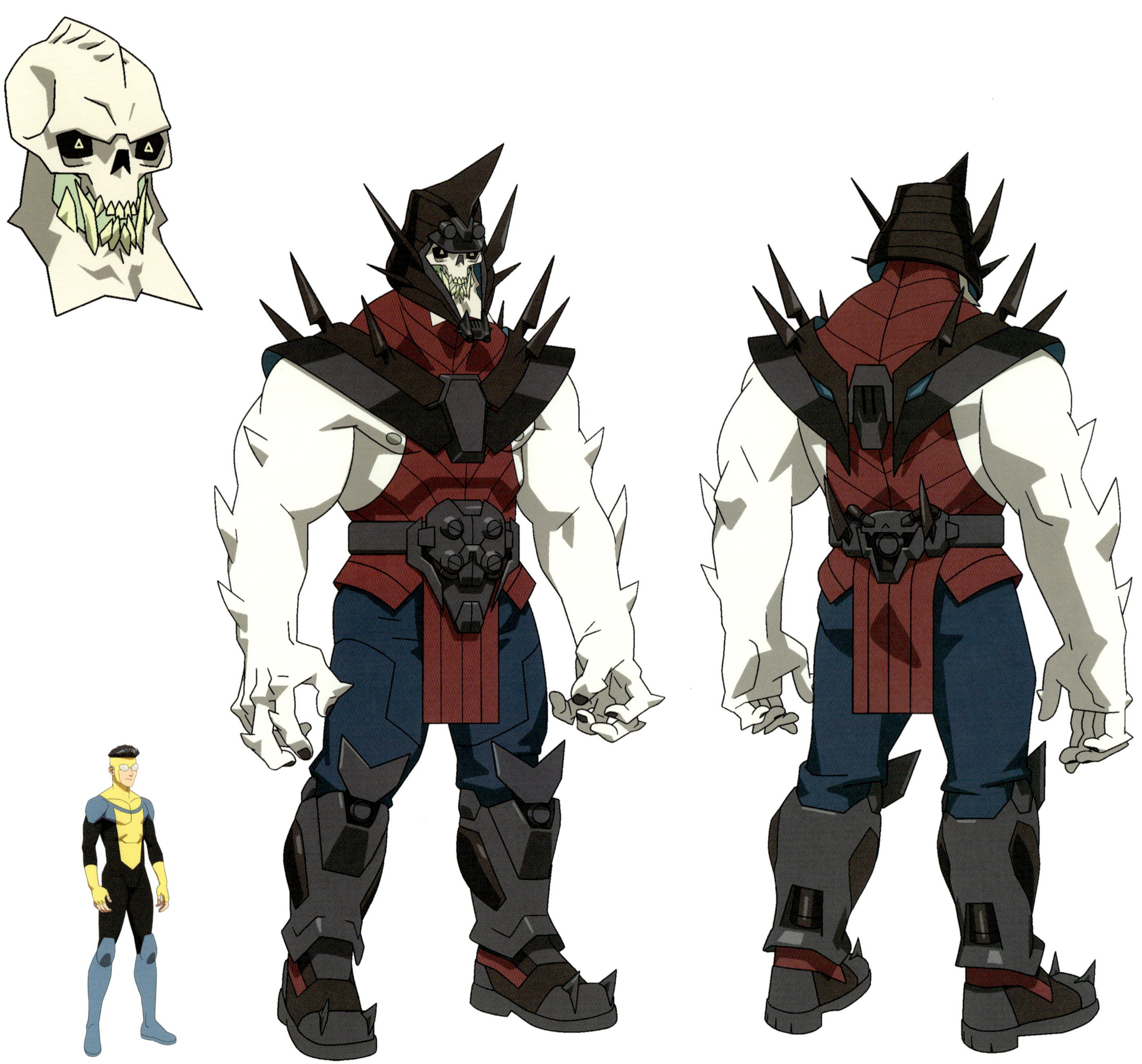

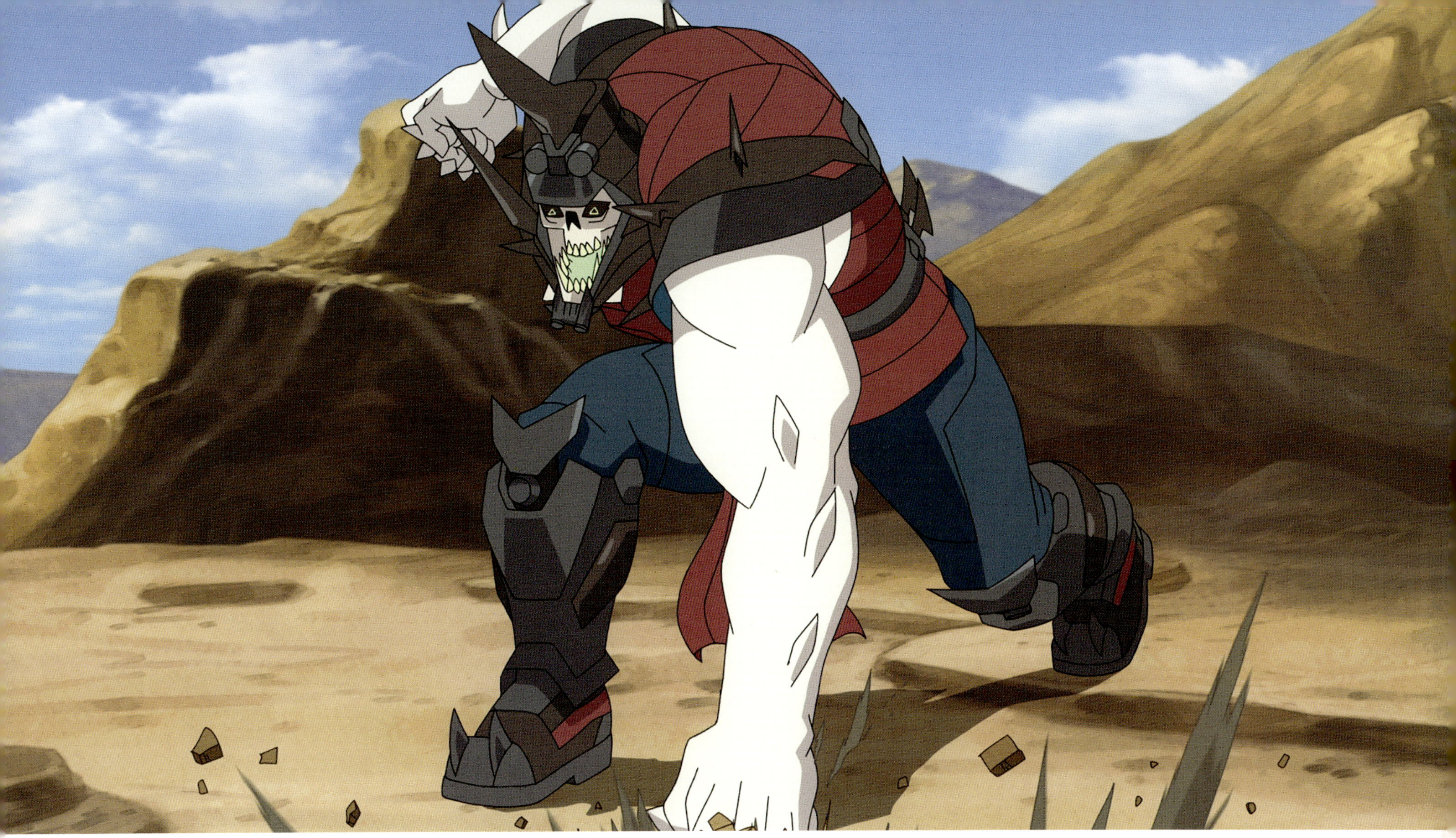

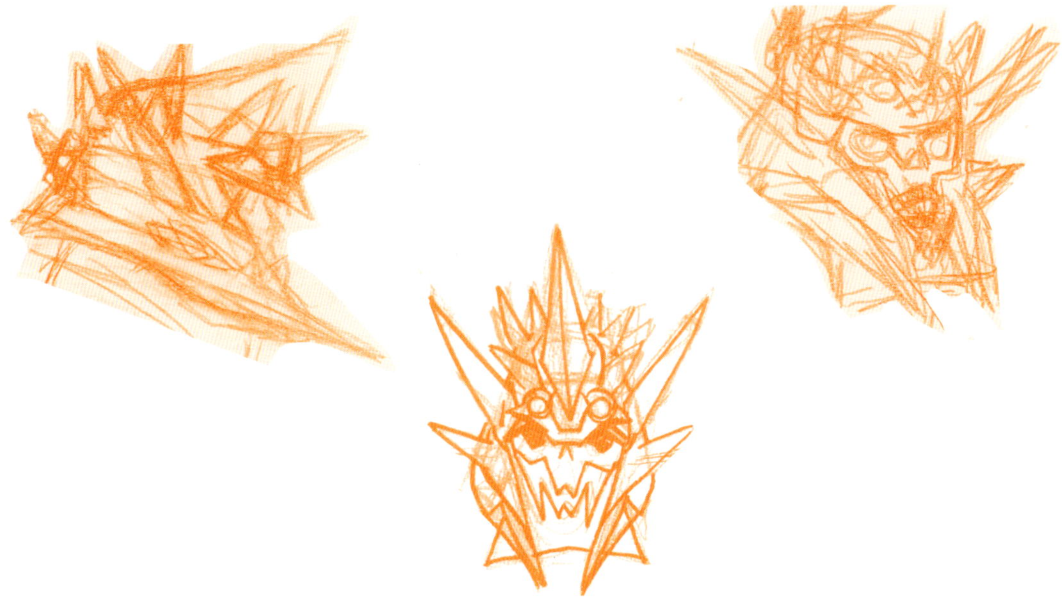

of Guardians, heading back into space to intercept a Martian ship full of Sequids. While Mark had visited Mars in Season One, this new sequence offered an opportunity to give the Martians and their general aesthetic a significant upgrade.

"Mostly, there were a few established decorative shapes in Season One that I think were the only real things that we we're beholden to," says Walker. "And so the team just put something together was unique and felt fully realized."

"Because we had gone to Mars previously, we got a mandate from Robert and Cory to reevaluate what that looked like," says O'Neil. "We did a lot of cool stuff rebuilding the Mars ship and concepting and putting together the hangar space it was in, riffing off some of the patterns and stuff from Season One. Those are some of

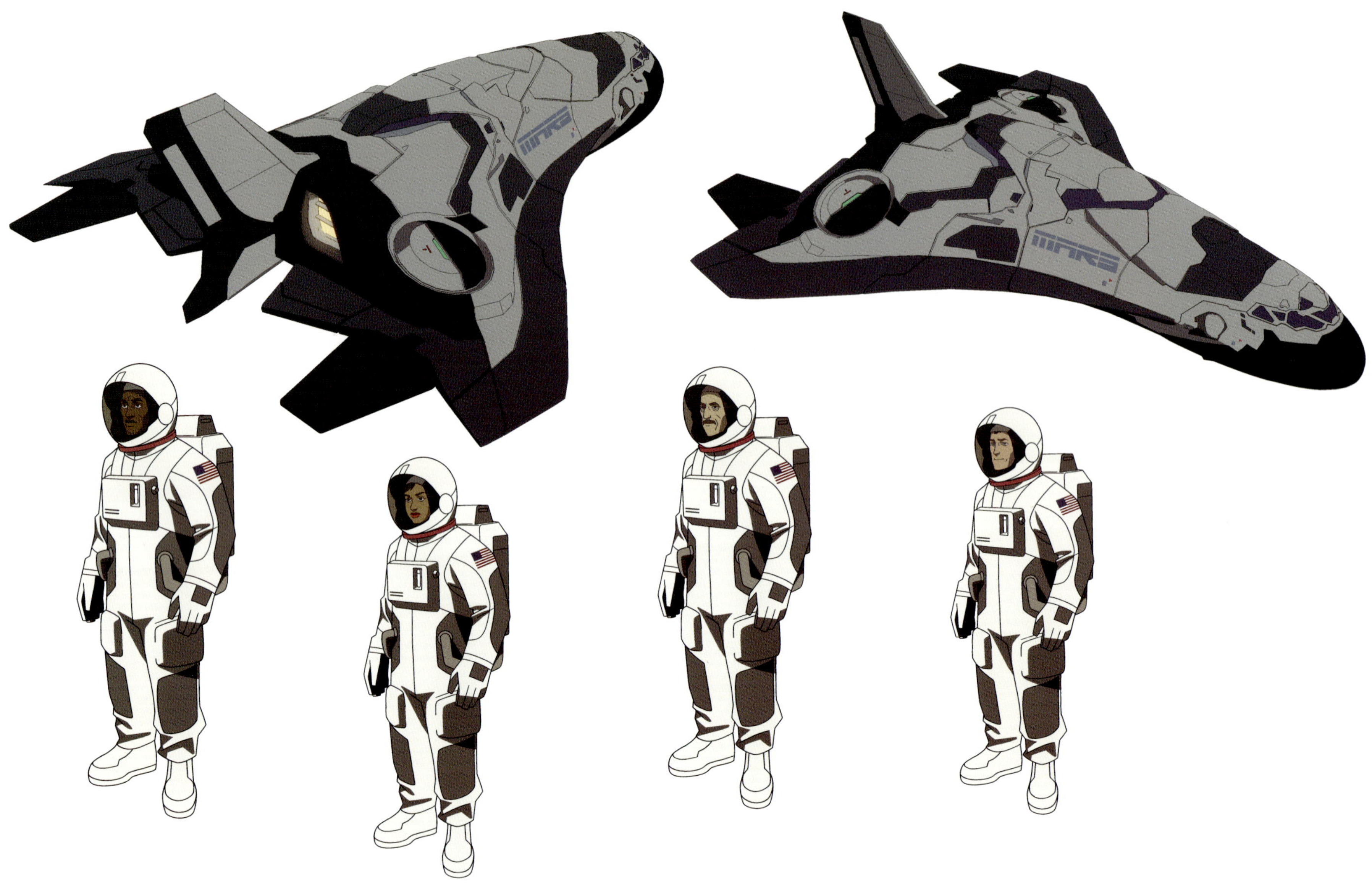

the earlier paintings that we did. Even before we got deep into 200 or 201, I think we were doing some exploratory stuff on Mars to try and make sure that we were pinning the mood more than anything else. We're going back to this space. Things have changed. It's overrun, maybe not well-lit. Trying to keep lighting for [Sequid-possessed astronaut Rus] Livingston kind of sickly and in this green hue, and trying to get down the lighting for the door reveal on the Martians, as they're all holding their fucking spears waiting for this dude. And then you get all the lights turning on in the big Mars ship. That was a very fun portion of this episode to work on. It went through lot of workshopping. I think Danielle Law, one of the painters, crushed. Just stayed with it and really made that space sing. It's one of the best looking spaces in the show to this day."

"Obviously there's also more Martians, the ship is bigger," says Racioppa. "We had the sequence of getting to the ship. So there's just way more design work. We also wanted to make sure the Martians were updated and weren't exactly the same ones. These are Martians on a ship coming to Earth. They're different than the ones in the tunnels, the guards around the Emperor from before. So the guys did an

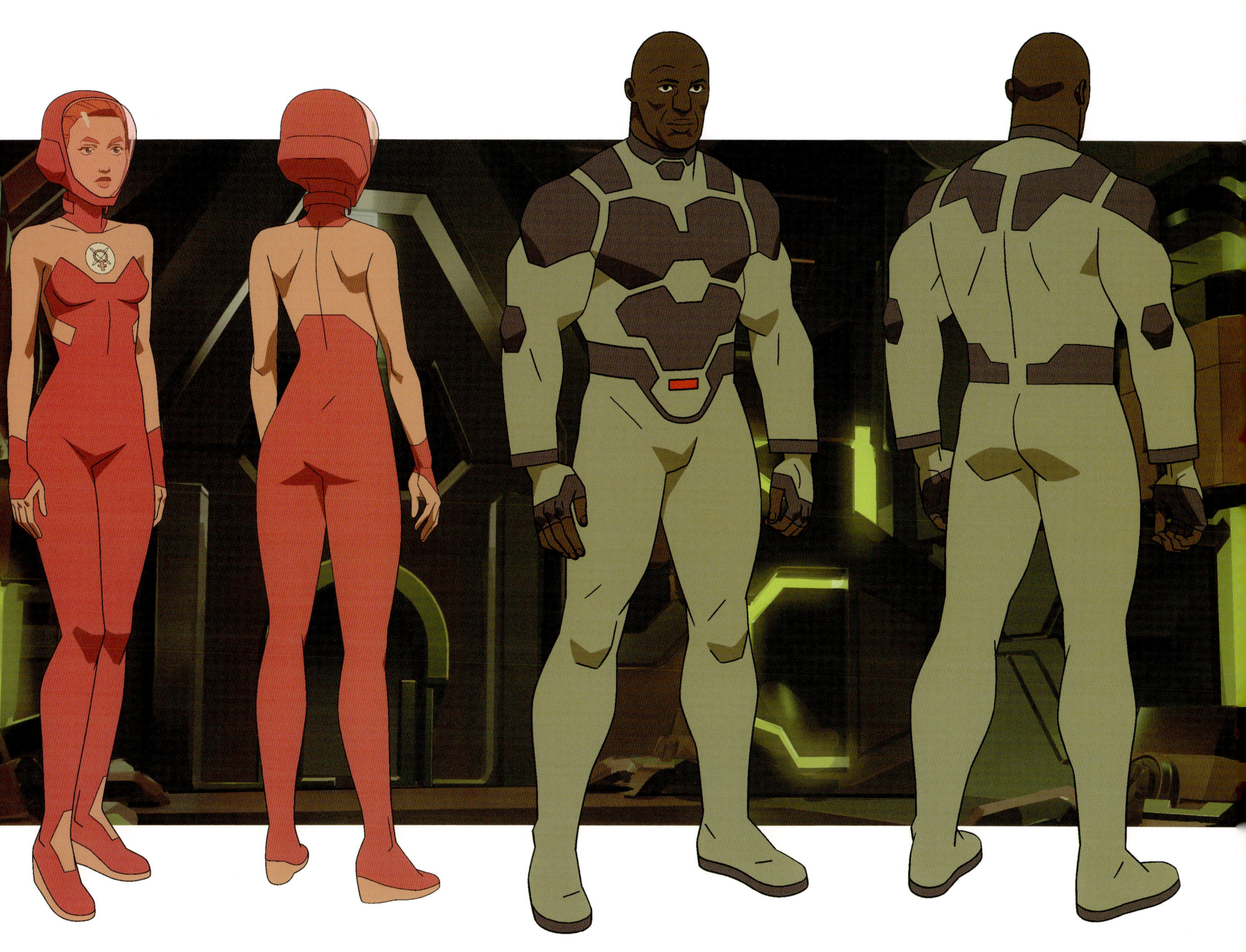

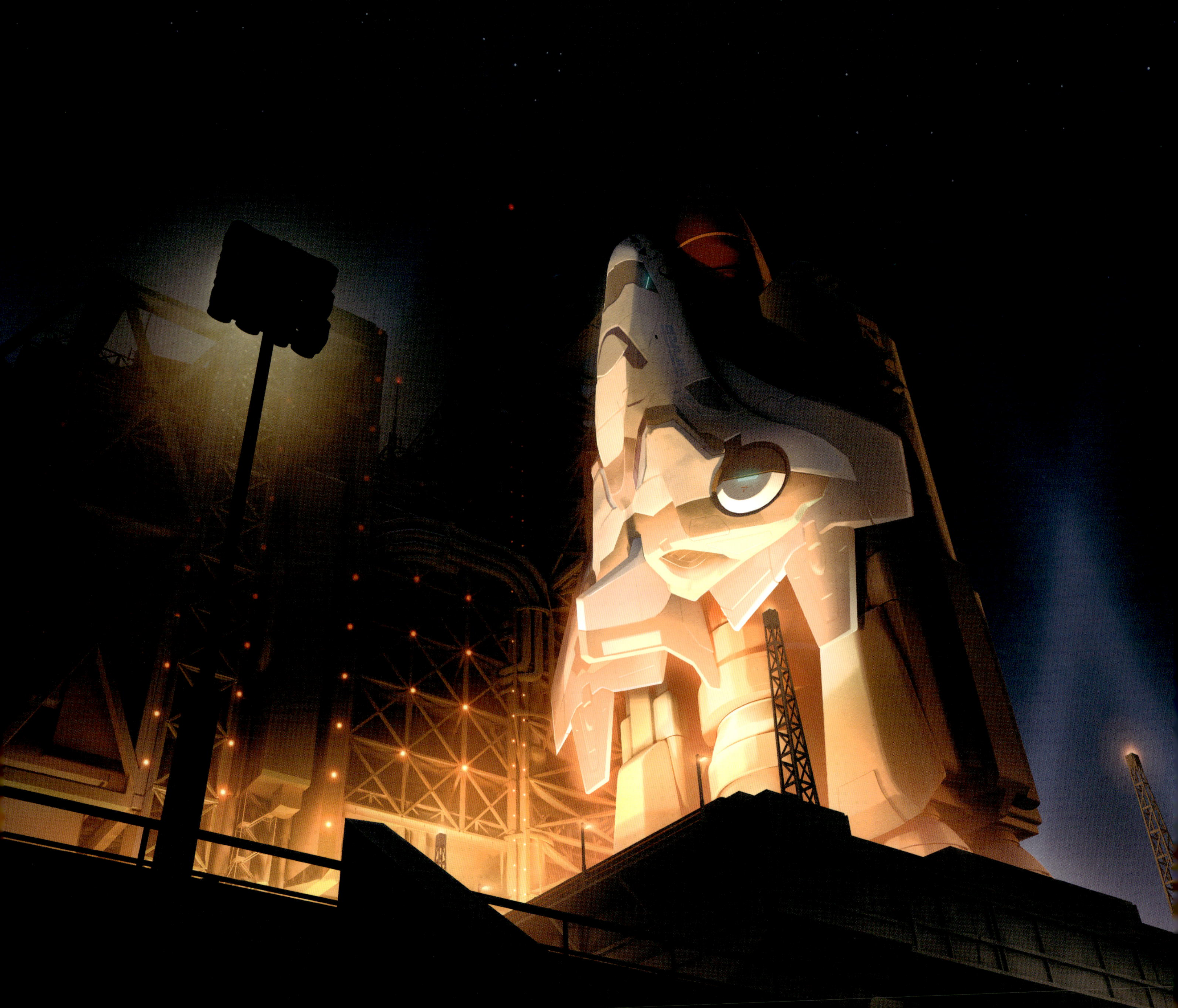

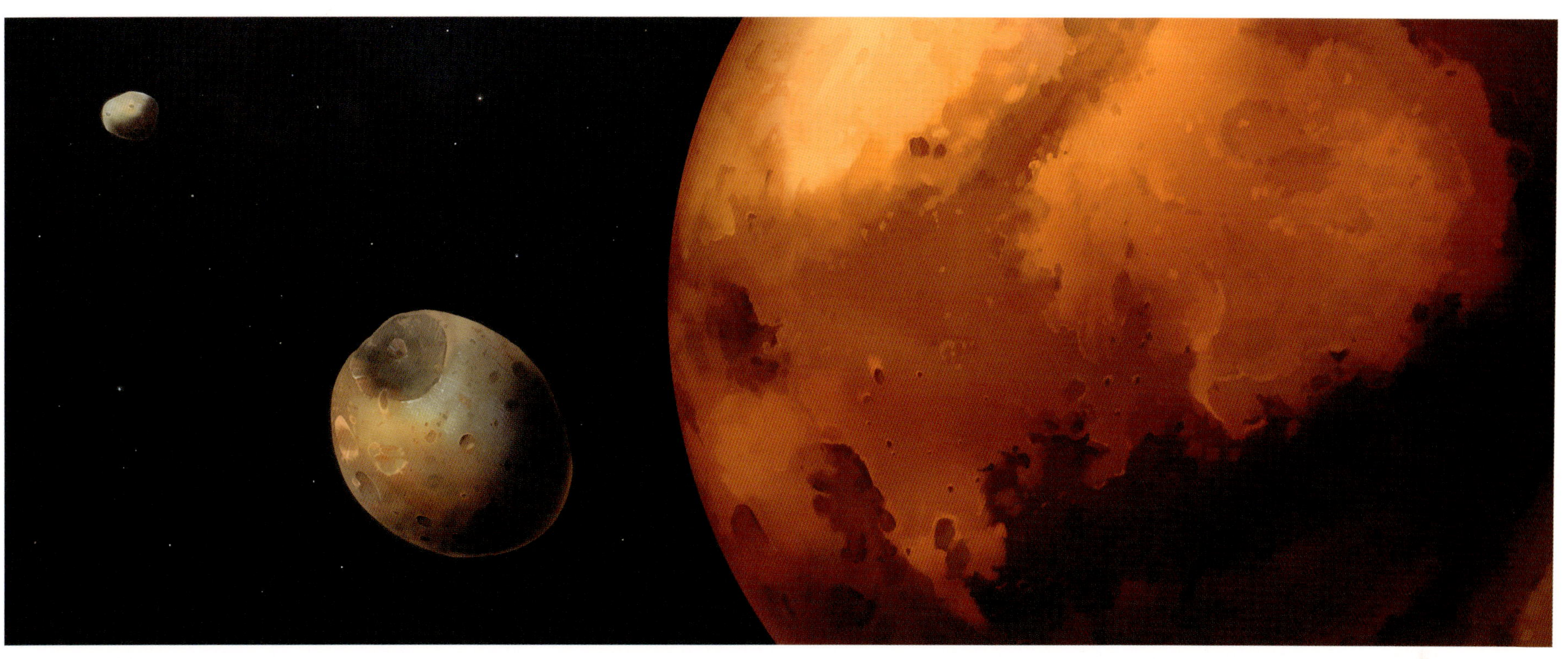

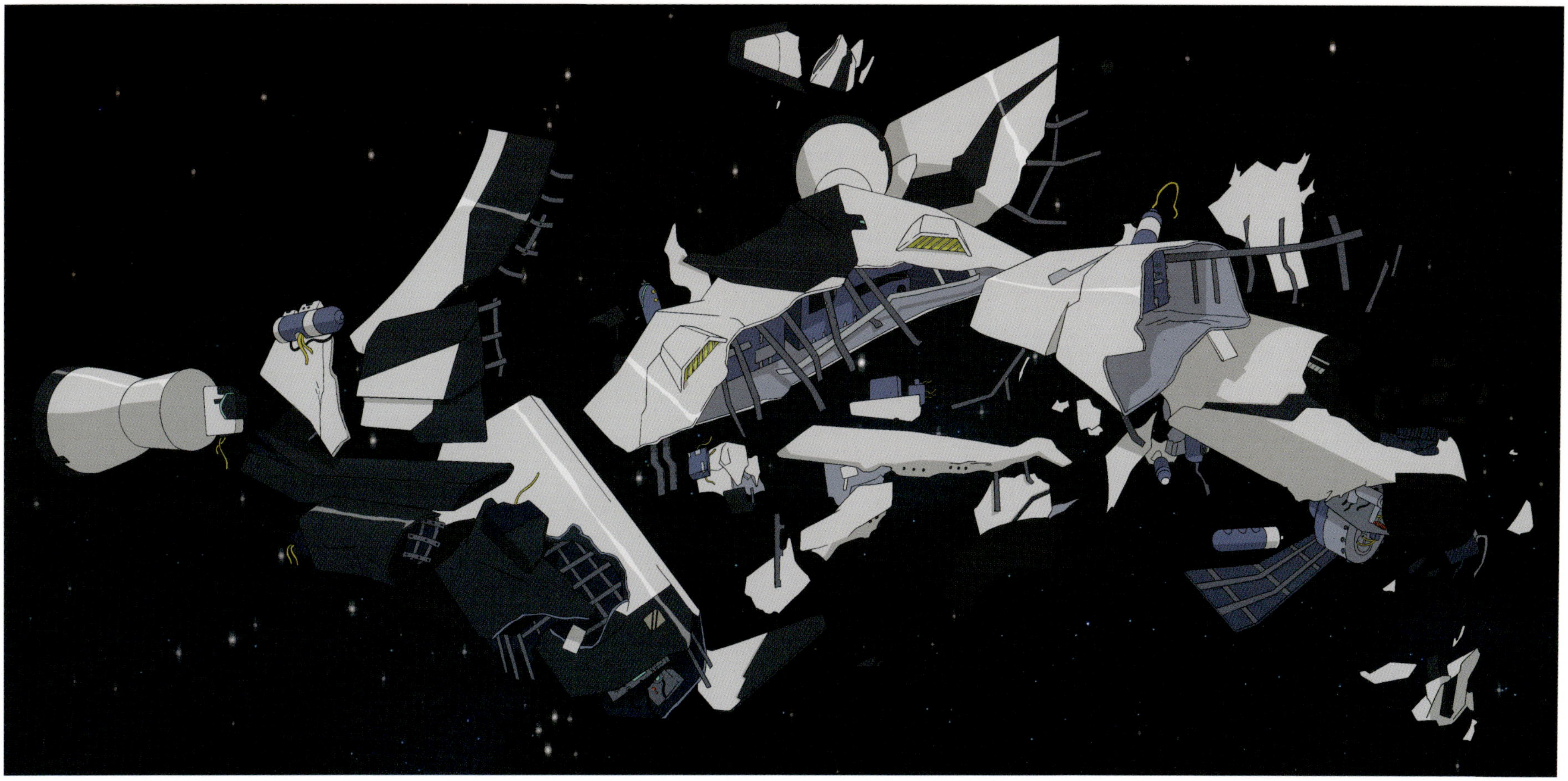

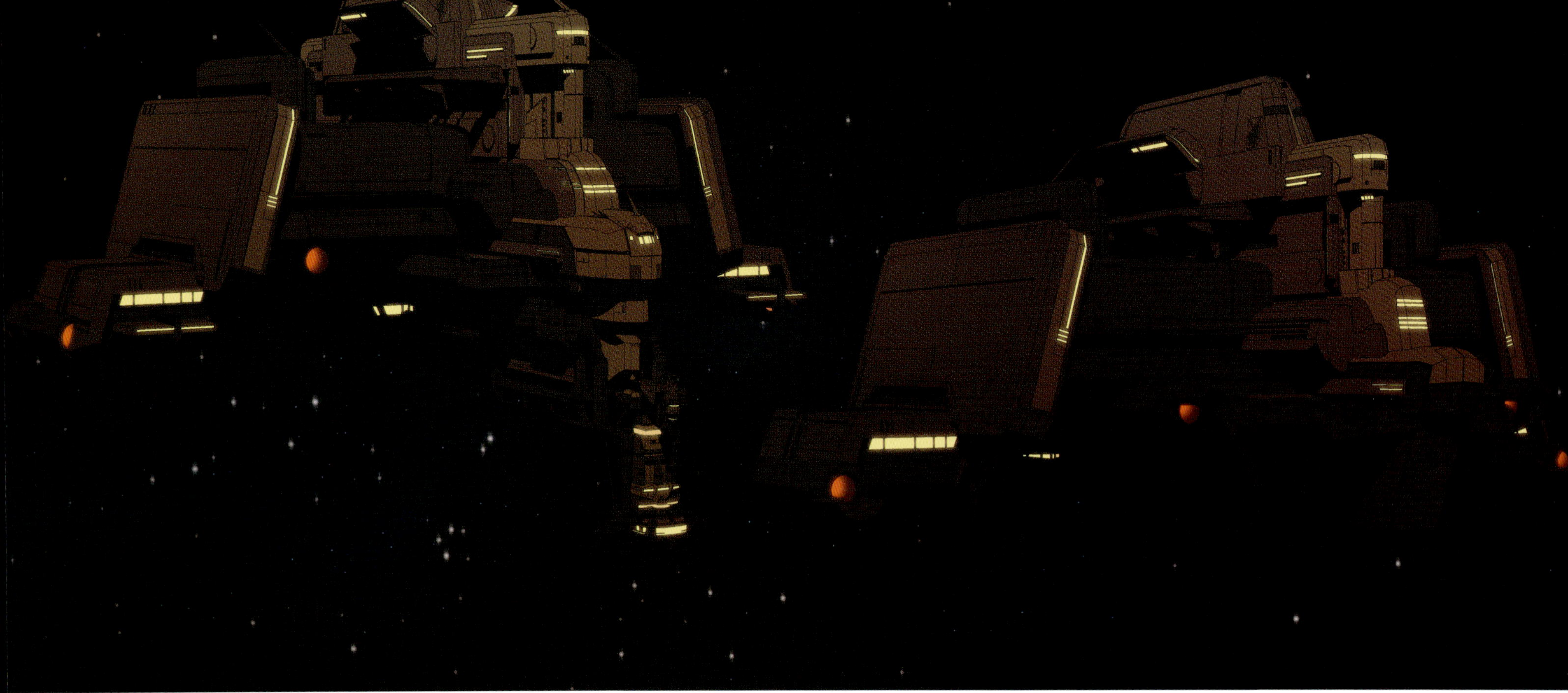

awesome job on that. So again, it's about the iteration. We're going to go back to the Martians, but we want to make sure that it's a step forwards in terms of design and visuals at the same time, even though they are familiar characters."

It was more than just the Martians themselves that needed serious design consideration. The mind-controlling, squid-like aliens known as Sequids were the true threat in this sequence, and there seemed to be a near infinite number of them that needed to be drawn.

"The Sequids are a massive undertaking," says Kirkman. "It took a few passes in the animation form to get it right. But luckily, [Supervising Director] Dan Duncan and Shaun O'Neil were able to work with the team overseas to try and make sure that it all worked."

Many shows would have relied on computer models to animate the Sequid horde, but the *Invincible* team had made

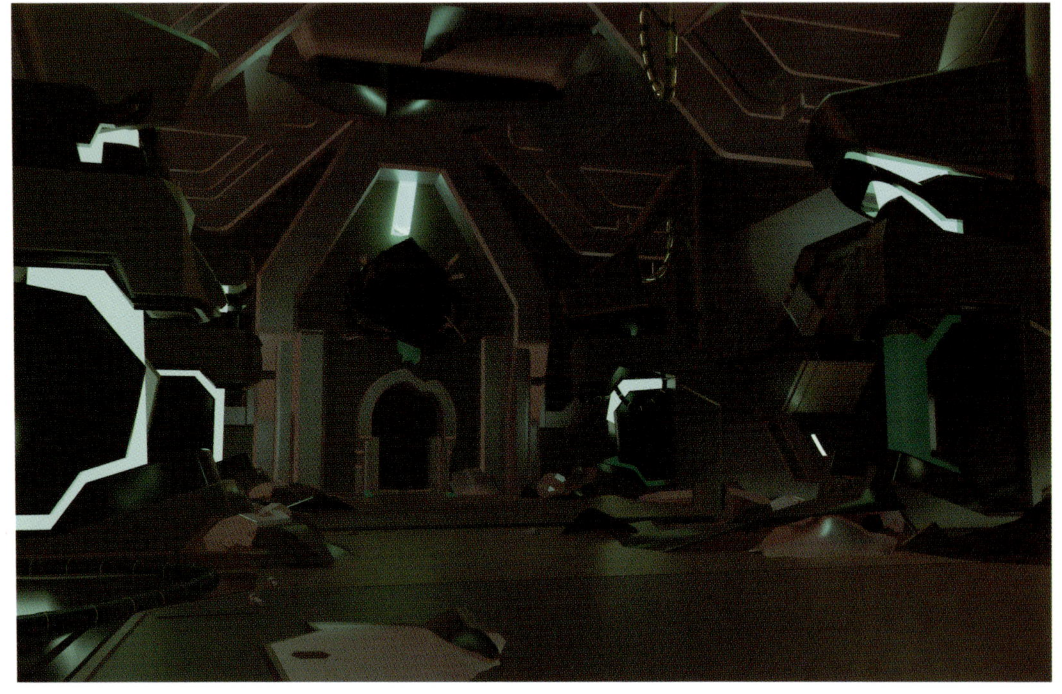

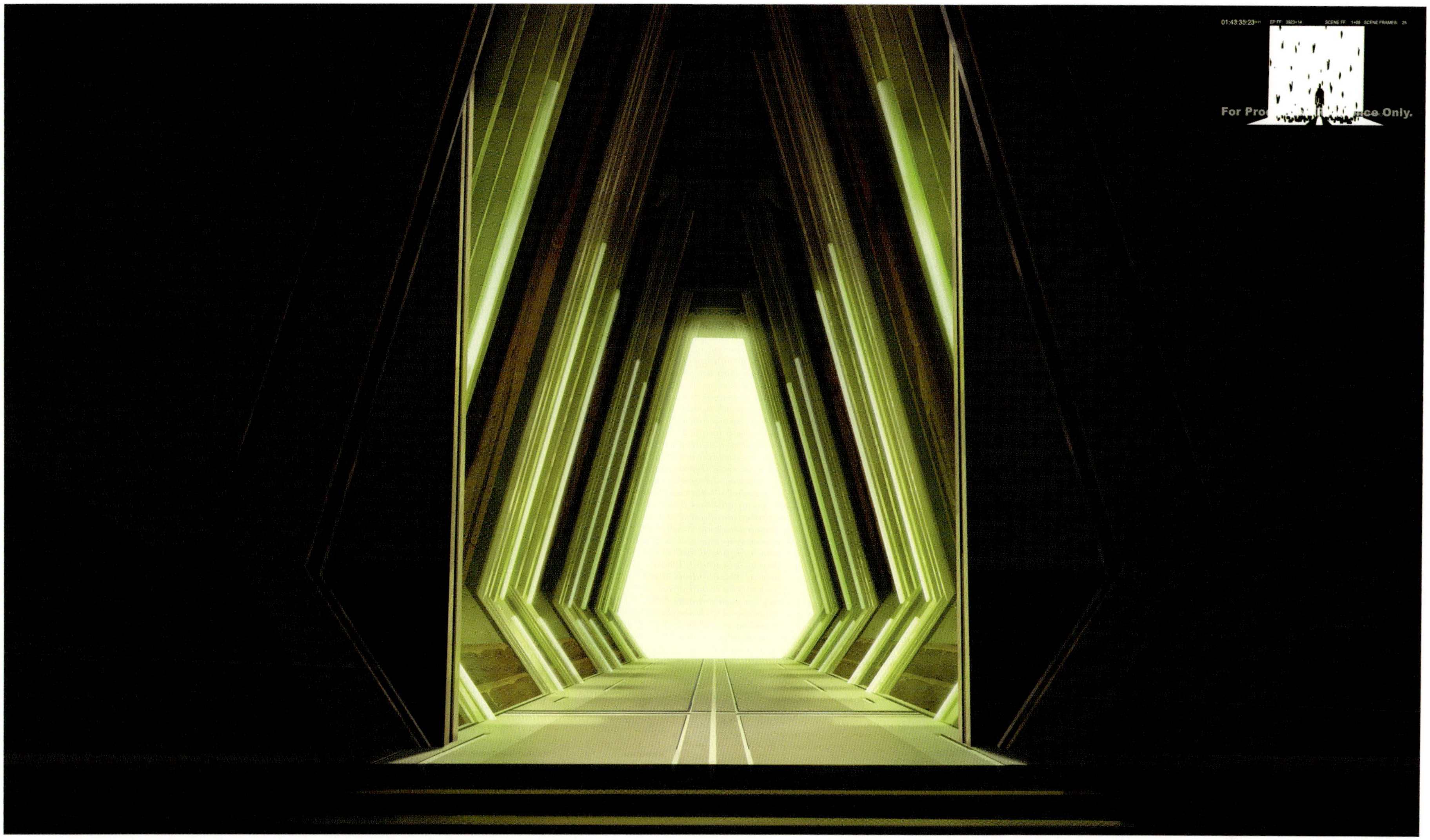

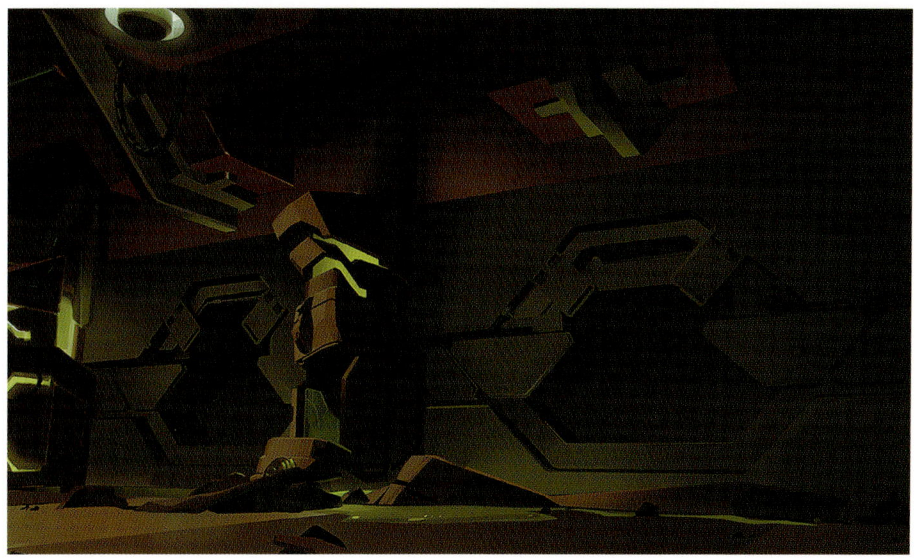

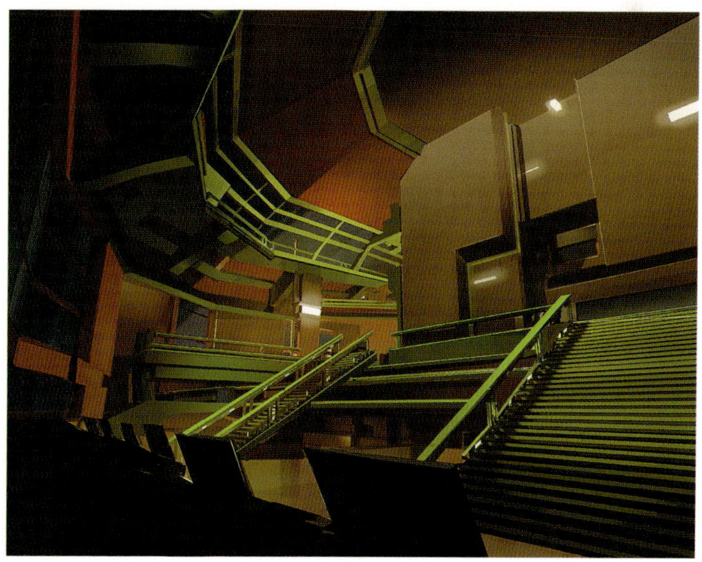

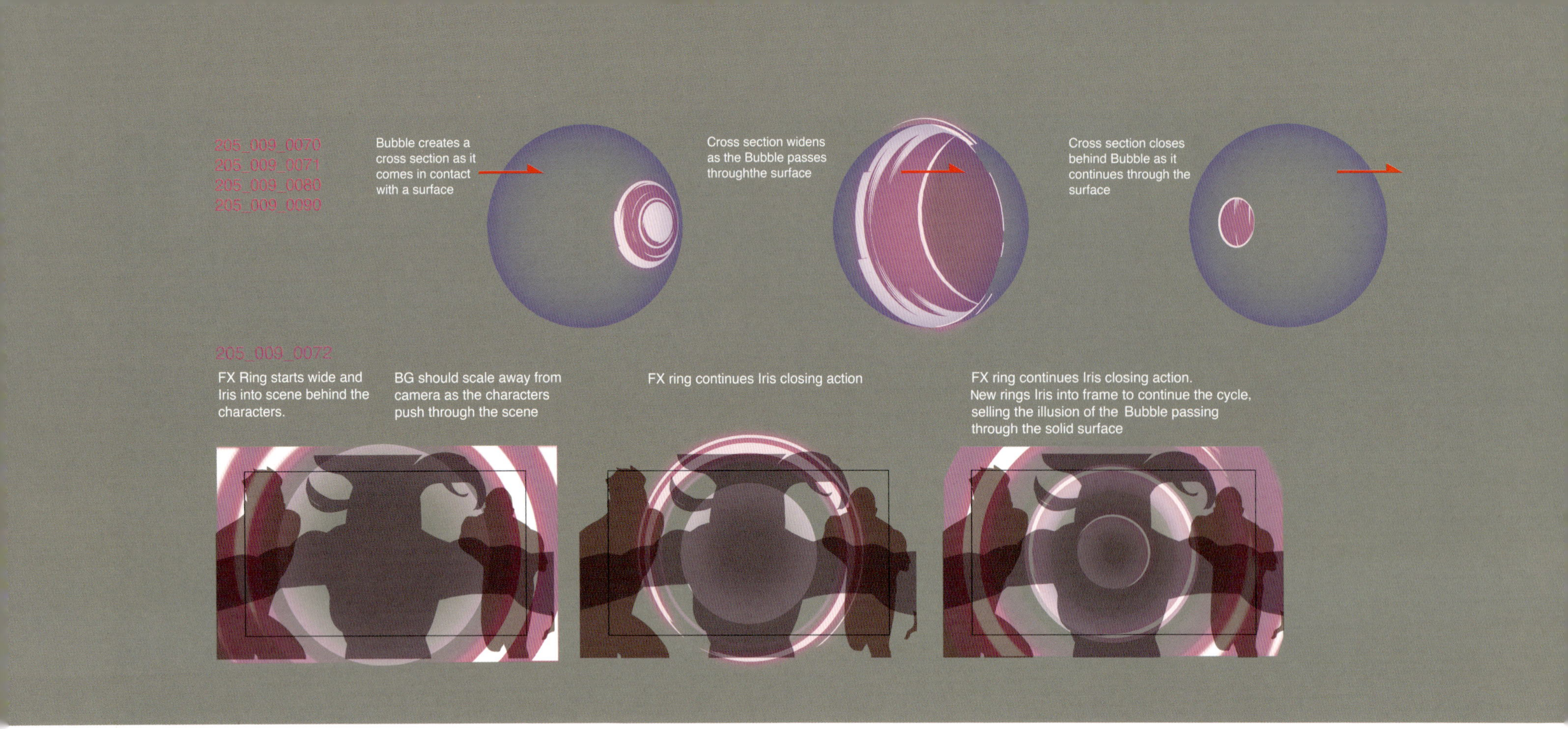

205_009_0070
205_009_0071
205_009_0080
205_009_0090

Bubble creates a cross section as it comes in contact with a surface

Cross section widens as the Bubble passes throughthe surface

Cross section closes behind Bubble as it continues through the surface

205_009_0072

FX Ring starts wide and Iris into scene behind the characters.

BG should scale away from camera as the characters push through the scene

FX ring continues Iris closing action

FX ring continues Iris closing action.
New rings Iris into frame to continue the cycle, selling the illusion of the Bubble passing through the solid surface

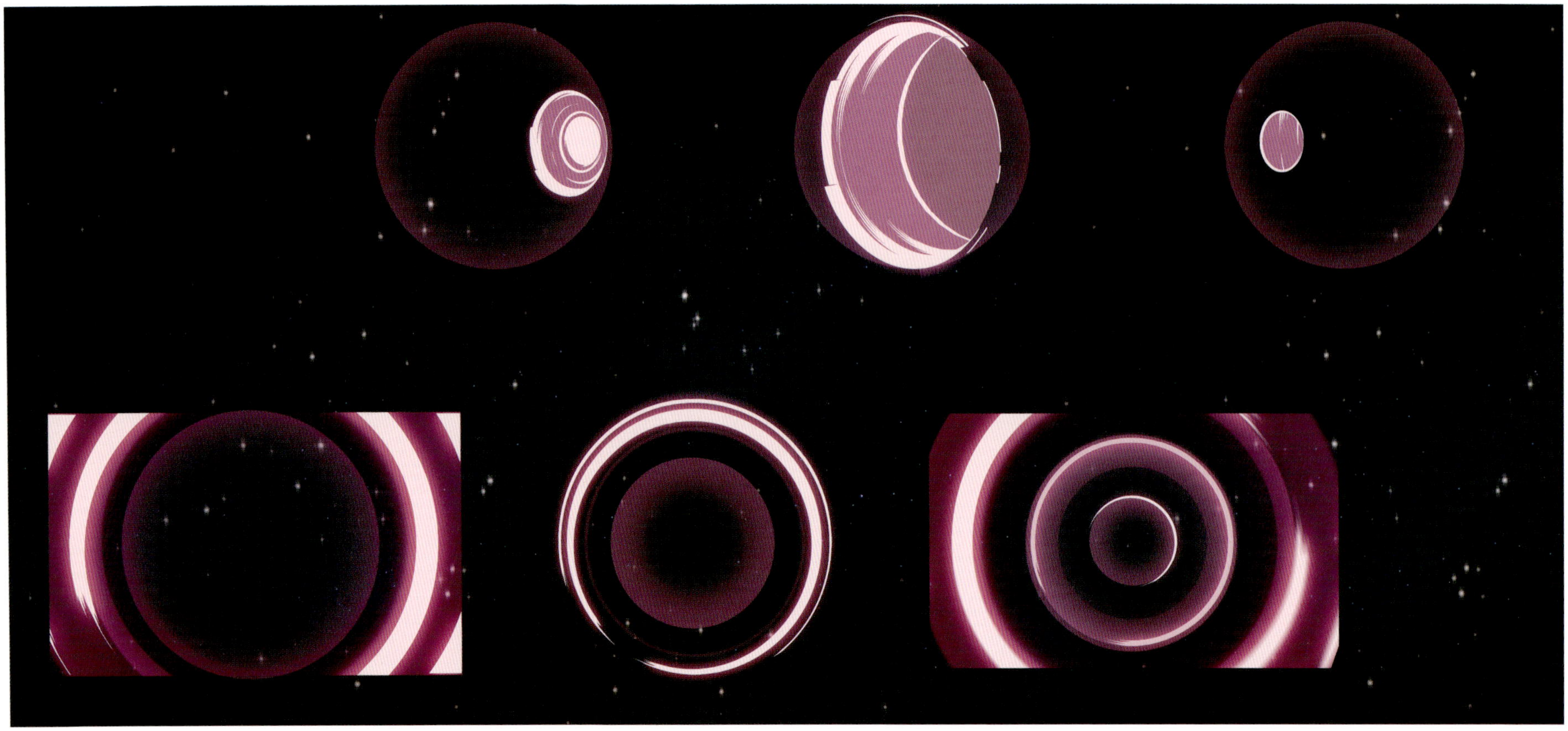

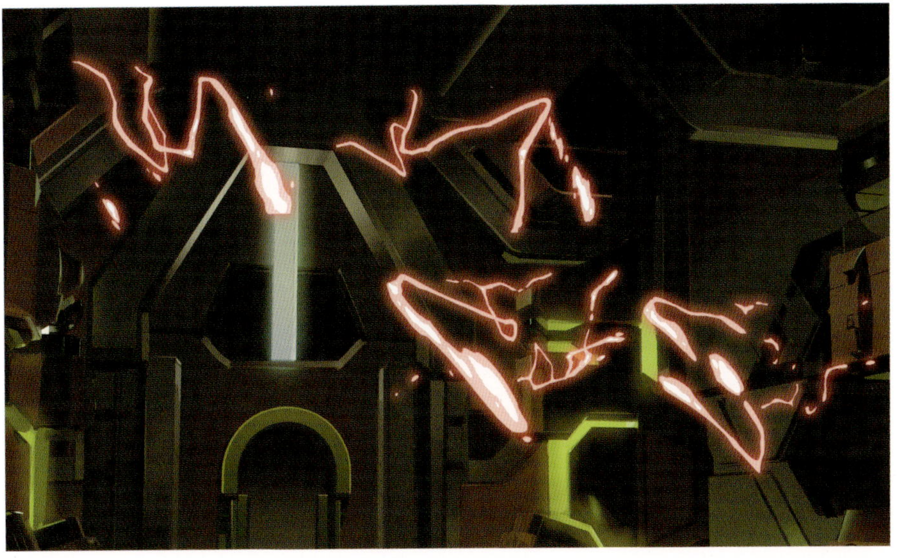

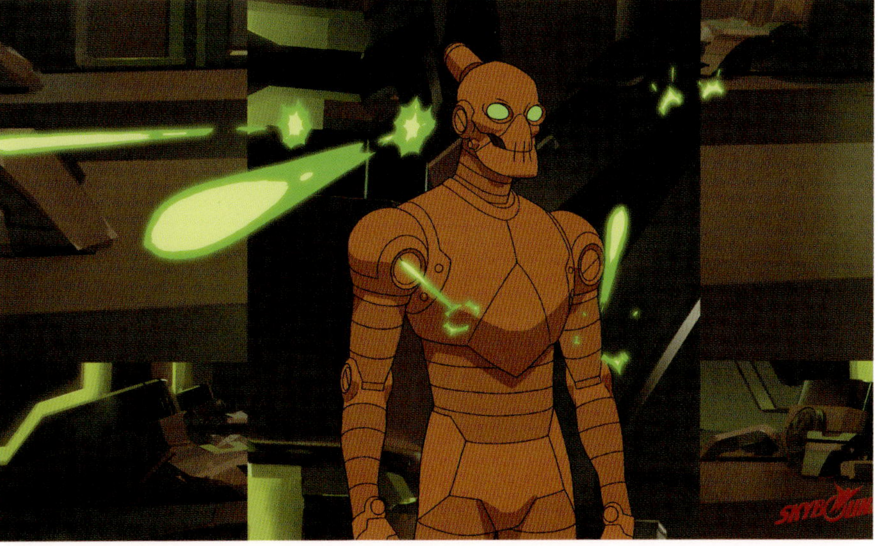

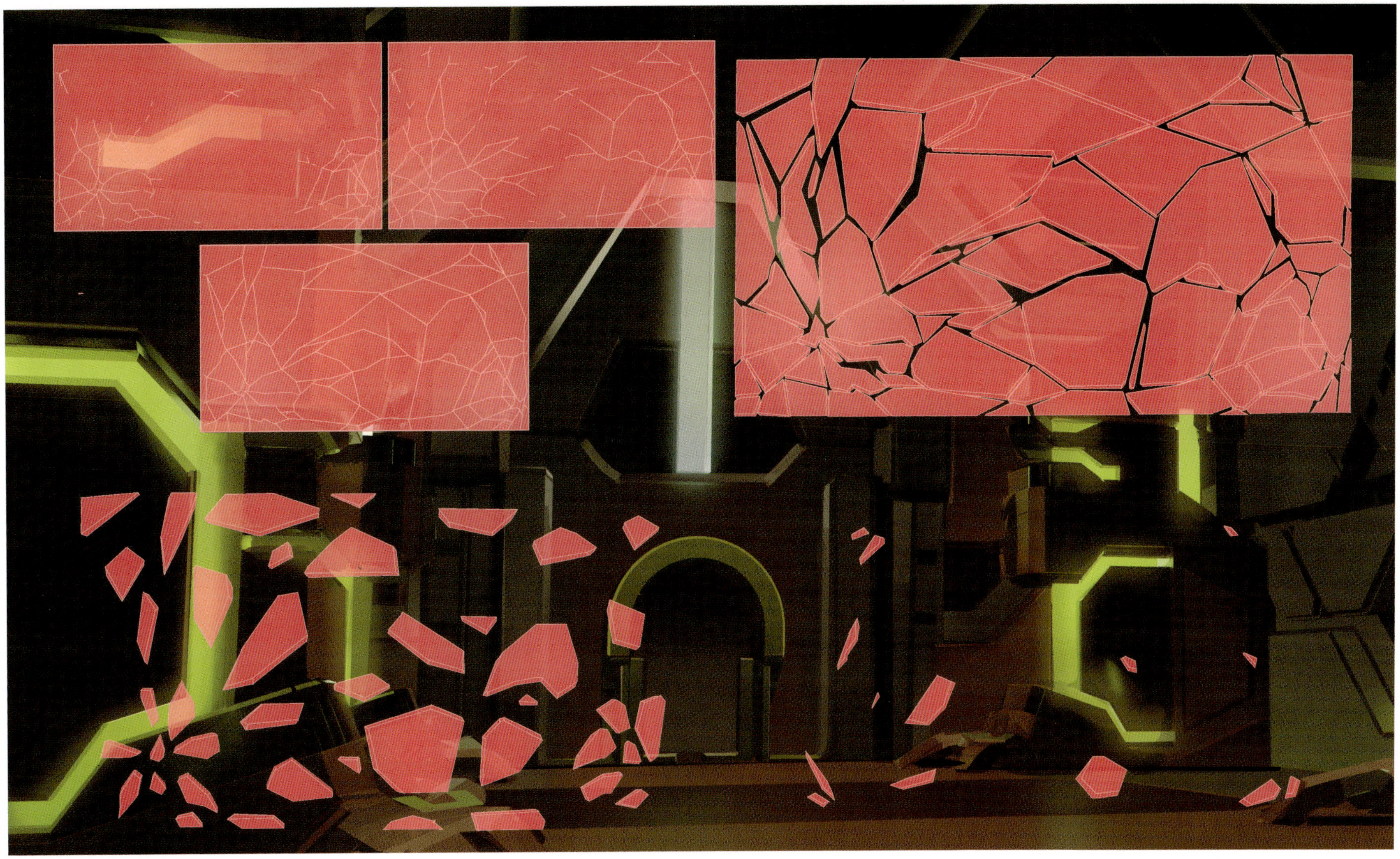

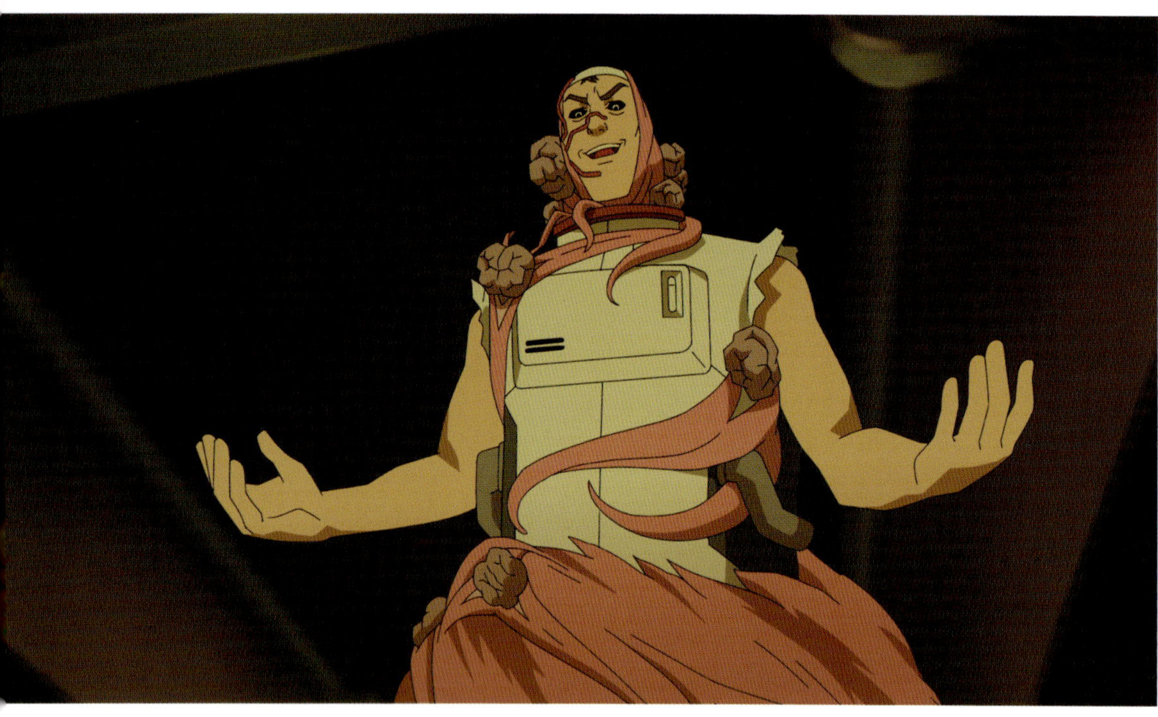

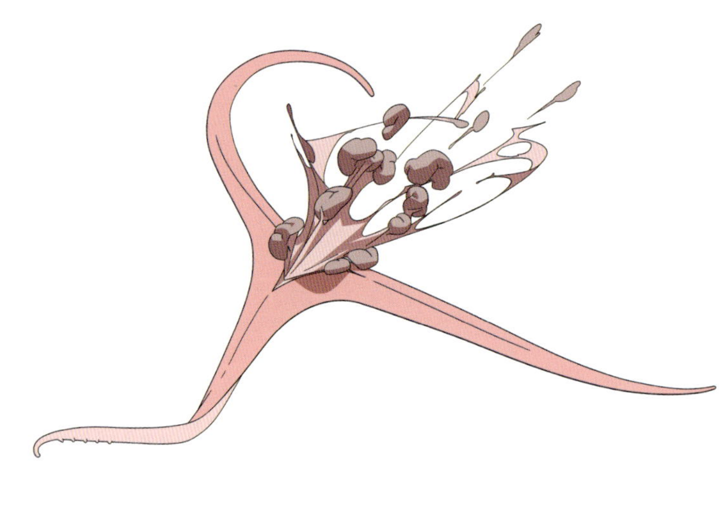

a conscious effort to move away from computer-generated assets after Season One.

"We made a decision not to use very many 3D models in Season Two and going forwards," says Racioppa. "That was something Dan felt strongly about, going back to hand-drawn. We do use some to plan out locations, and then do drawovers of those locations to make sure angles work, and sizing and scale and the layout are proper."

Unfortunately, not everyone got the memo.

"There was a miscommunication with one of the studios and we got CG Sequids," says Duncan. "So we had to go back and create new materials. A lot of in-house stuff that we recomped into the boards. Working with the studio to do retakes. For 206, it was every single Sequid shot we had to go back in and redo. So it was a beast."

The mix-up added an extra layer of difficulty on top of an already complicated episode.

"The Sequids were a giant pain," says O'Neil. "But I think they came out [right]. Super proud of how we pulled that one out in the end, as well. But I think we broke out the Swiss Army knife for 205. I feel like we stole a lot of elements

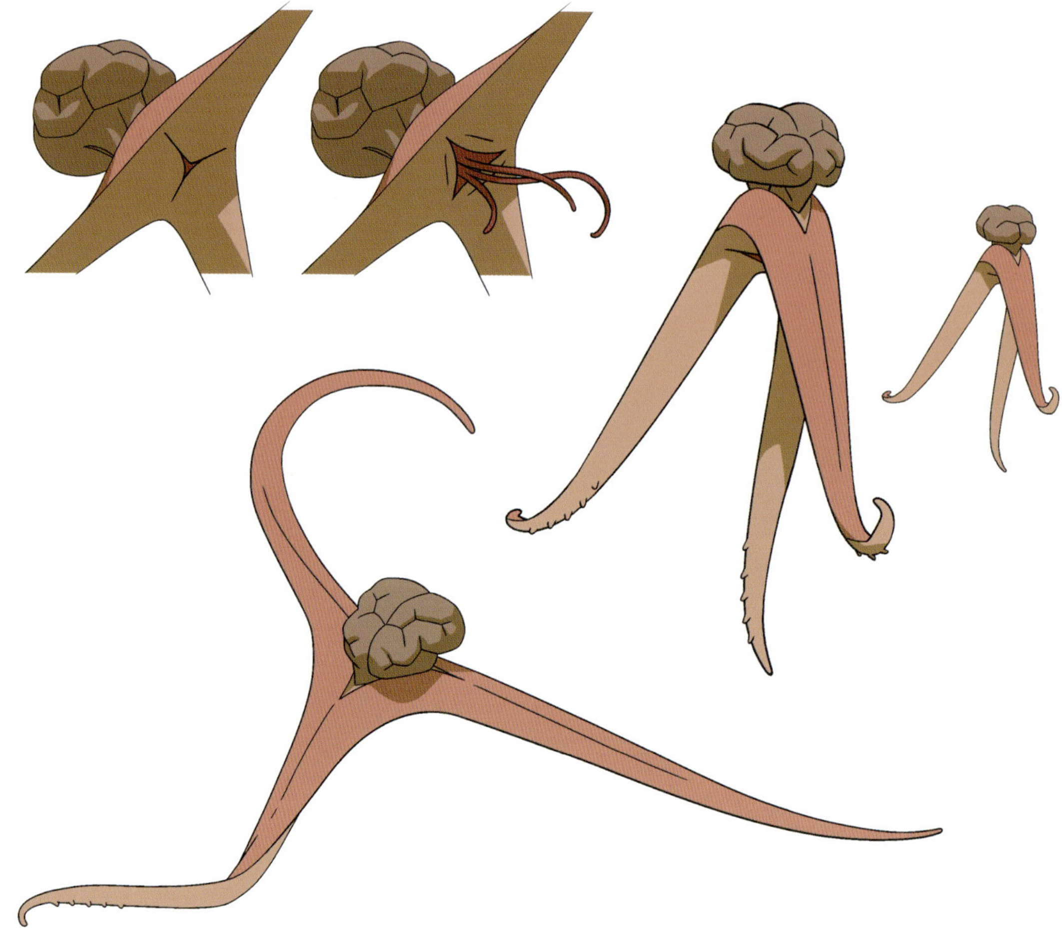

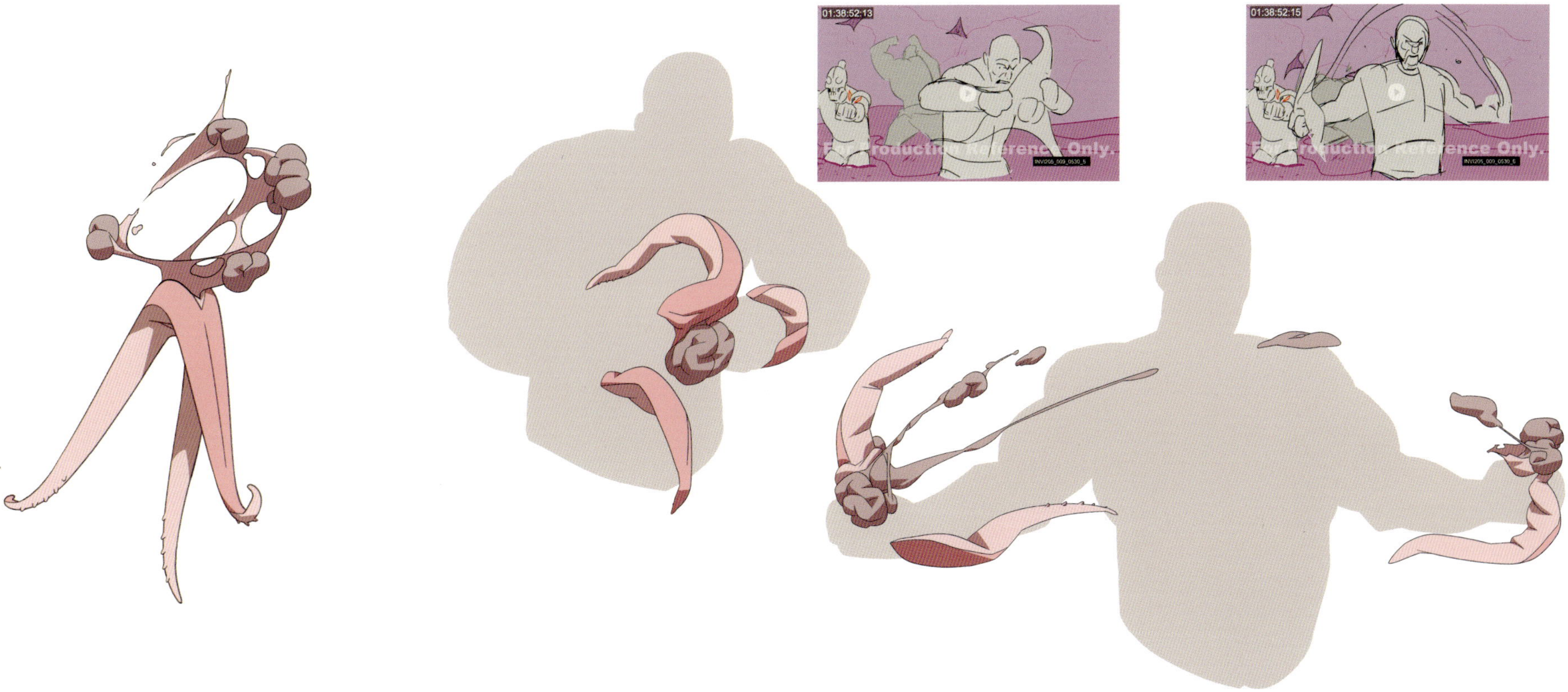

01:38:52:13

For Production Reference Only.

01:38:52:15

For Production Reference Only.

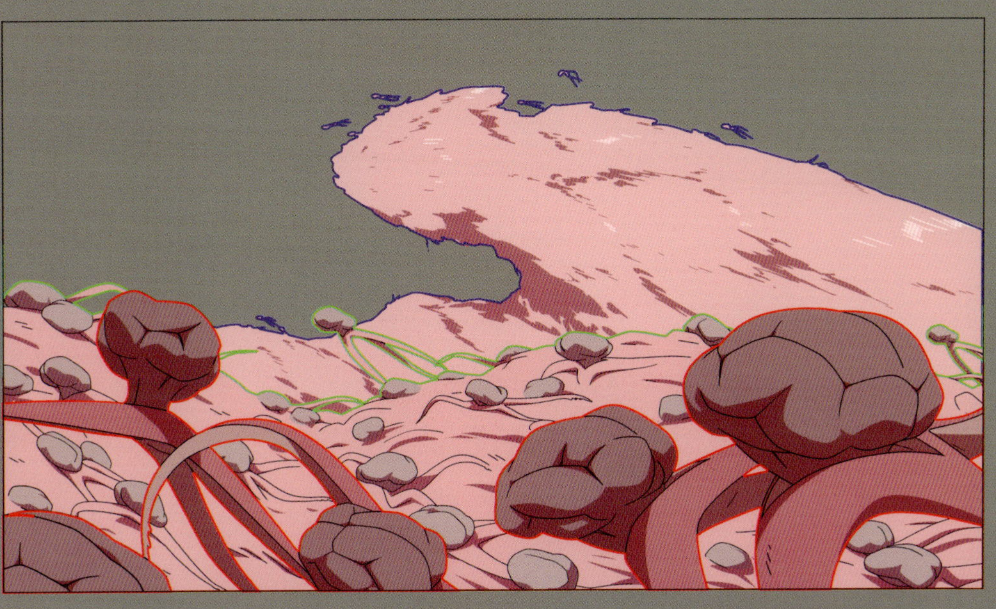

FG- Full detail

MG- Use scale variant from main model. Reduce line and color info. Individual Sequids travel within a larger mass

BG- Add Highlight layer. Sequids travel as single mass. Individual Sequid use should be minimal, Individual Sequids should be present toward the tops sides of the mass, used similarly to fish swimming upstream

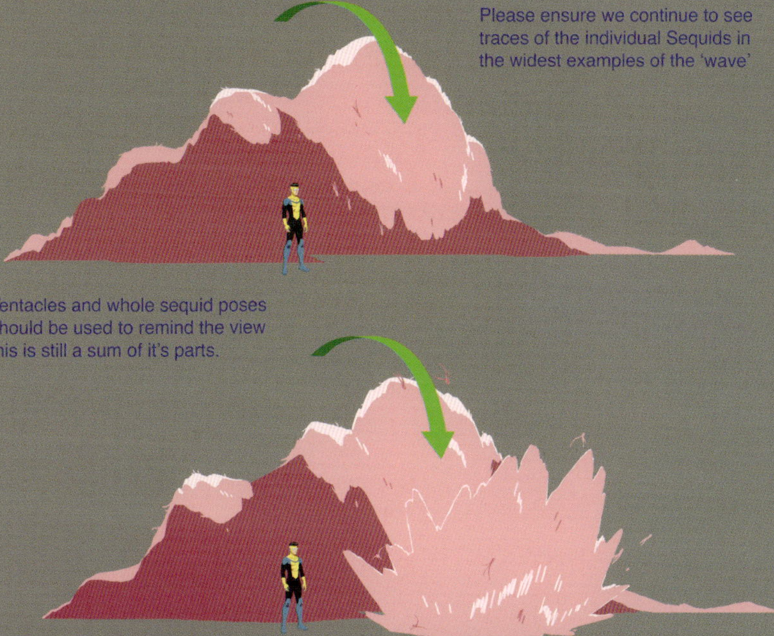

These elements can be oversimplified for ease of use, but ony in the widest examples

from scenes and used them to populate stuff just to get our hookups, just to get a lot of what was intended in the boards, just to try and handle as much of it here as we could, because there was so much that was going back to overseas for revision."

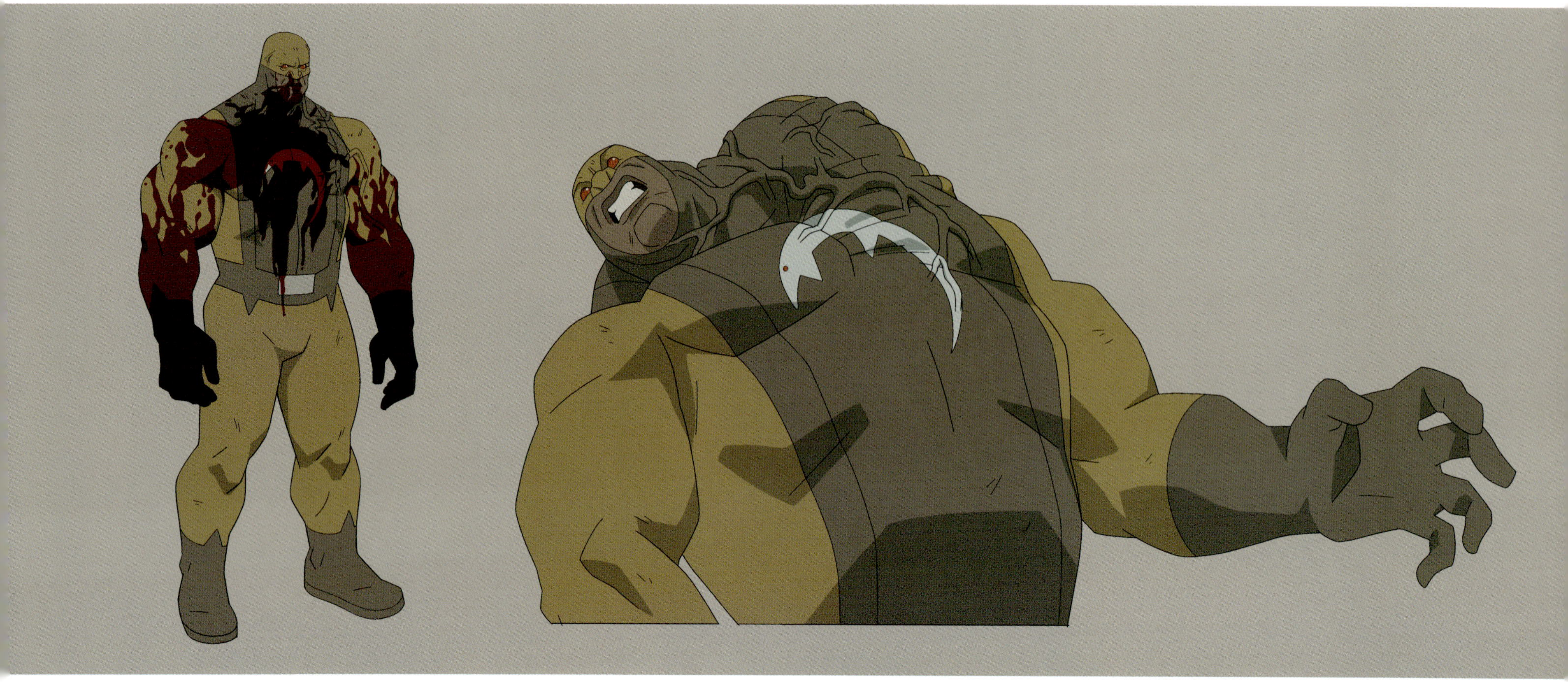

Despite the difficulties involved in animating the Sequid horde, the creative team was pleased with the final results.

"The Sequids, from a technical standpoint, were really great from our team," says Racioppa. "That's a hard ask of any animation company, especially when you're not doing CG. This is all hand-drawn. People had to actually animate the stuff by hand. So that was really fantastic."

While Mark and his fellow heroes dealt with the extraterrestrial invaders, a small handful of Guardians stayed behind on Earth, only to find themselves up against a much more straightforward threat. Or, at least, so it initially seemed.

"We wanted to make that sequence start and make you

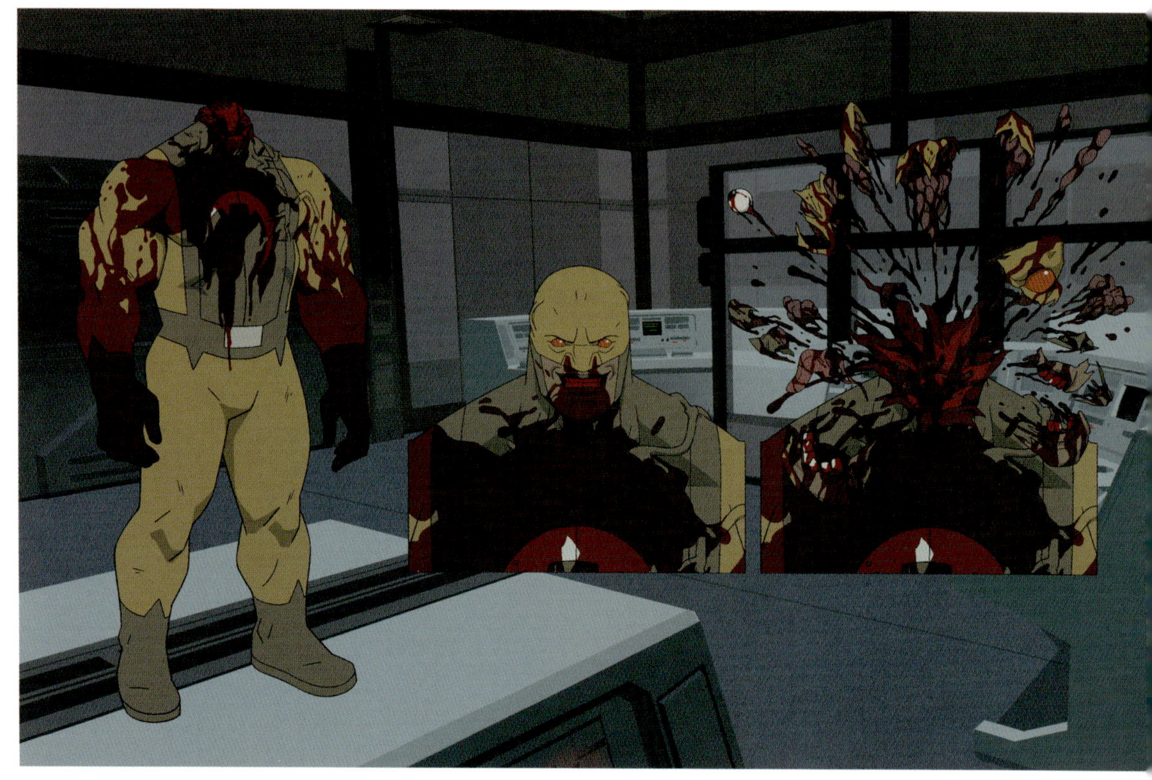

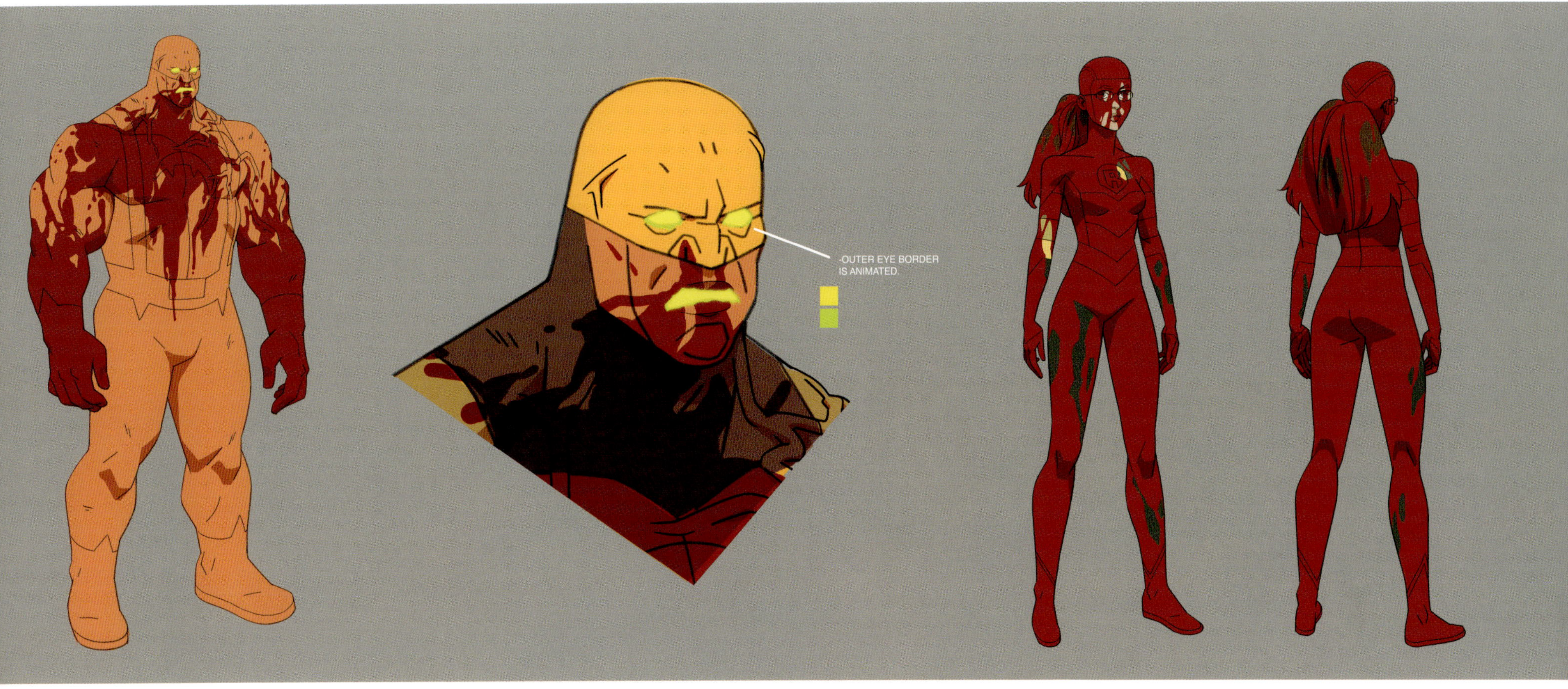

think, 'Oh, is this going to be an easy *G.I. Joe*-style sequence where they defeat the Lizard League,'" says Racioppa. "We've been playing the Lizard League up as a joke since early in Season One — the idea of, like, 'If you can't beat the Lizard League, you don't even deserve to be heroes.' But don't get complacent, right? New leadership, new plan. They're still villains to be worried about. And, obviously, even the Guardians come in feeling a little bit cocky about this. And then those tables quickly turn, as they can when you're dealing with combat. Somebody can get hurt."

Not only *can* they get hurt, they *do*. Very badly. The trio of Guardians — Rex Splode, Dupli-Kate, and Shrinking Rae — were caught off-guard by the Lizard League's savage attacks and suffered the consequences.

"They come in complacent, and they get taught a lesson," says Racioppa.

One lesson that Shrinking Rae learned the hard way is that super strong villains can be just as strong on the inside as they are on the outside.

"We do that great sequence where you expect Rae to be able to explode out of Komodo Dragon and just splatter everywhere," says Racioppa, "because she does that in Season One. There's a quick sequence of her in the penthouse fight when she's fighting Magmaniac when the Guardians come in. Magmaniac is obviously made out of magma. Robot puts her inside Magmaniac, she expands, BOOM, blows him up. So you're hoping as an audience member that she's just going to do this again. But it turns out that Komodo Dragon is super tough, the same as Nolan or Mark — we have these super invulnerable people — so wouldn't they also be super invulnerable on the inside? They're not wearing a coating on them. They're not wearing armor. All their cells are just so tight and strong. So he would be just as tough on the inside. So when he swallows Rae and then she tries to expand, he is able to crunch her back down by some great core strength, just crunching her and breaking her bones. And then she falls further down into his gullet, broken and bruised and probably dissolving slowly in his stomach acids, which would be unpleasant, obviously."

"Shrinking Rae inside of Komodo Dragon was something that was very important to me for this episode," says Kirkman. "Seeing his collarbone break, seeing the parts of Komodo Dragon expand, getting the sense that he was crushing her as she was trying to expand to break out of him. I think that, especially with shrinking people, somebody goes inside somebody else and blows them up… blows various body parts up. It's really the go-to thing in superhero stuff. You've got Drax the Destroyer in *Guardians of the Galaxy* busting out of big monsters. It's just something that you always expect. And so I wanted to do a thing where it doesn't work. The guy's too tough. You try to bust out and it breaks you up. So that was a sequence that we had to put a lot of work in. And I know Dan Duncan took that on and worked very heavily on getting that sequence right in the animatic form to make sure that, when it went overseas, we got it the right way. It was cool seeing him go the extra mile."

"All of the Lizard League stuff was crazy," says Duncan, "but Robert had such a specific idea for what he wanted for the Komodo Dragon stuff. We worked on that a handful of times. The design stuff, I know a bunch of different artists touched it. [Director] Haylee [Herrick] worked on it. Jon Lam worked on it. I worked on it. It took a team to get that one moment. And at the end of the day, it was [SFX studio] Boom Box that made that scene what it is. The sound design on that is what everybody reacts to when they watch that scene. And it was incredible."

"The sound design carried us," says O'Neil. "Full stop. The team always does a really good job bringing the visuals home. But Rae getting fucking eaten… There's some really gross stuff in there. There's just some really awful… Like you can hear Rae inside Komodo Dragon while they're fighting each other for space. And it's fucking awful. Just like bone

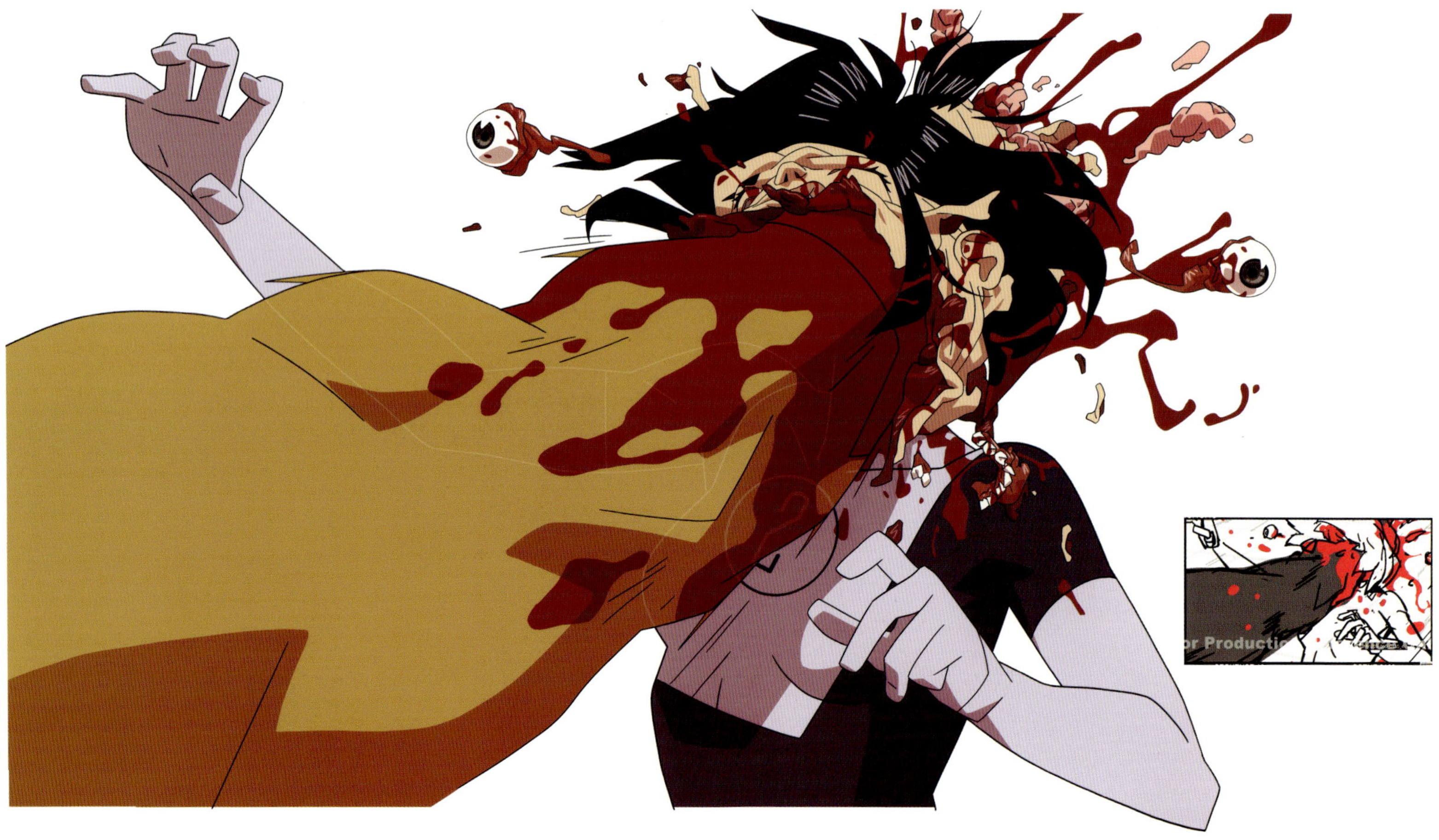

cracks and gross shit."

Another member of the Guardians is killed by the Lizard League not just once, but over a dozen times, each death more disturbing than the one before.

"Kate dies more than anybody else," says Racioppa. "Just over and over again... Obviously, Kate has died before that, too. You're like, 'Wait, is that the last Kate?' It's just like, 'Yeah, if you can catch her fast enough, this is what happens.'"

"Some of those dead Kates are just absolutely horrific looking," says Kirkman. "In some of the key designs for that stuff, their faces are all distorted and their eyes are bugging out, and it's just terrible looking in all the best ways."

Rex Splode was the last Guardian standing, but not for long. Even though he managed to split Iguana in half and blow the head off Komodo Dragon, he took some serious damage in the process.

"Rex gets his hand bitten off and then manages to explode Komodo Dragon's head," says Racioppa, "which is great because that'll free Rae later on, luckily."

Unluckily, an exhausted and near-hysterical Rex was too injured to continue the fight. That proved to be a major problem when King Lizard pointed a gun at the back of Rex's head. It was a moment that showed the grim reality of being a superhero.

"That's what I love about this show, from a story perspective," says Duncan. "Growing up, superhero stuff was always wish fulfillment. Just like, 'I want to be strong and punch bad guys and fly around.' And then a lot of people try and make it real, and they get into the politics of it or things like that. But this is just like superheroes via *Training Day*. Like, their job sucks. It's really hard. And you don't get to see that perspective a lot of the time. It's usually like, 'What does the world look like with superheroes?' And this is like, 'What does it look like for the superheroes?' I think it's really compelling and a really fun thing to explore."

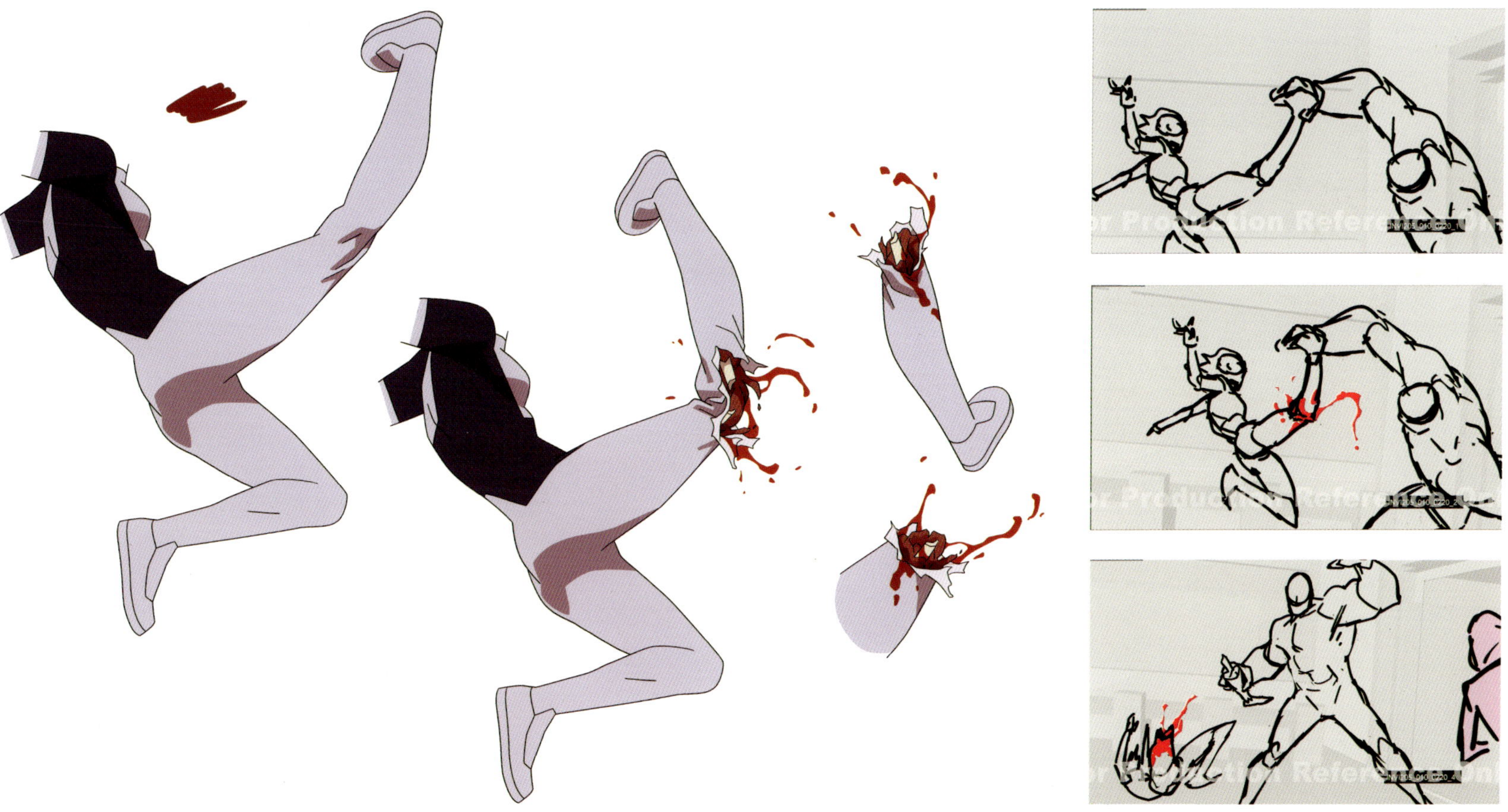

"It's neat, too, because it dovetails into some really great character moments later on," says O'Neil. "This is sort of a jump-off for some arcs that we see later that are just very cool."

As the fate of Rex Splode hung in the balance, another hero had finally recovered from the near-fatal wounds he had incurred in episode 203. Allen emerged from his life support pod, bigger and stronger than ever, thanks to the unorthodox efforts of Thaedus, the Coalition of Planets' leader.

"Allen is much bigger now," says Racioppa. "He's got a new design. Thaedus gambled with his life and was like, 'Maybe if I unplug your life support, you will actually heal stronger on your own.' Which was true. And Allen's now super ripped."

While Allen regained his bearings, Thaedus revealed an important secret about himself -- himself: he's a Viltrumite! But not just any Viltrumite. He was the only Viltrumite to ever rebel against the empire. Thaedus proved his identity to Allen by ripping out his beard with his bare hands, leaving only his people's signature mustache behind.

"It's a real beard," says Racioppa. "He pulls out his real beard. It's called a 'toolock pull'. It's a way for a Viltrumite in disguise to prove he's a real Viltrumite by removing his beard, but not his mustache. It would be immensely painful for anyone else, but for a Viltrumite it's okay. Which begs the question, is that how Nolan shaves? I don't know."

This unexpected moment capped off an episode full of shocking twists and turns, just as its title suggested.

"That's just how crazy this show is," says Kirkman, "that you can have the remnants of the Thraxa story and the Omnipotus bit and the Lizard League bit and the Mars bit with the Sequids all happening in one episode, with various different things happening at the same time. This is a really good example of the kind of ground that we cover in a random episode of the series and just what an undertaking this show is."

It was an episode that had its ups and downs during production, but that eventually came together in a memorable and satisfying way.

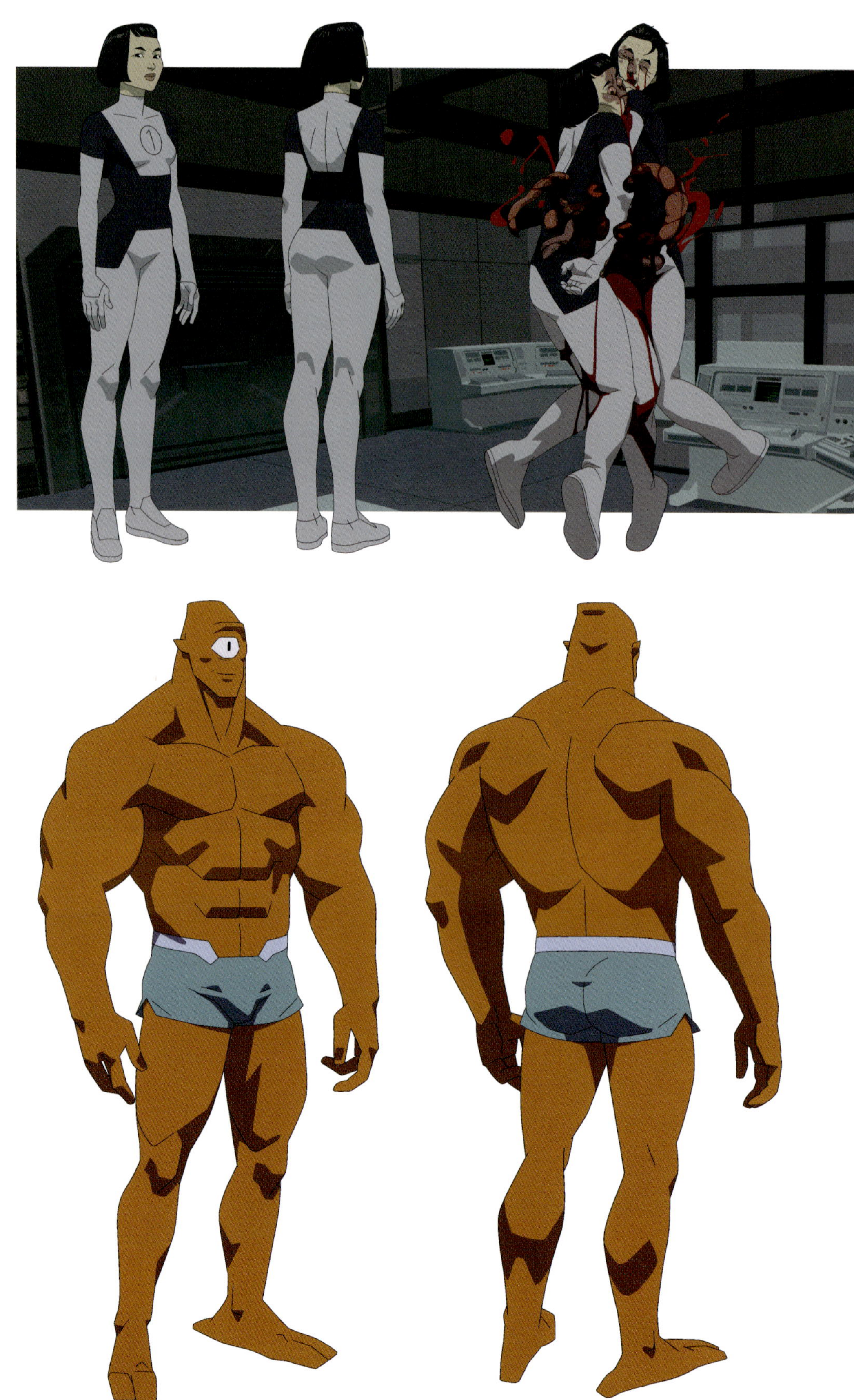

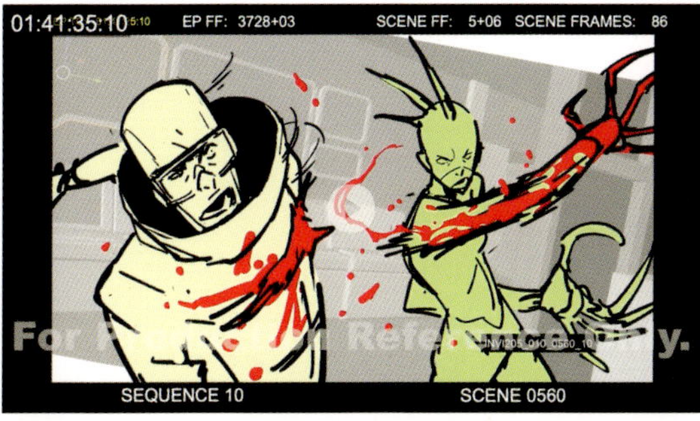

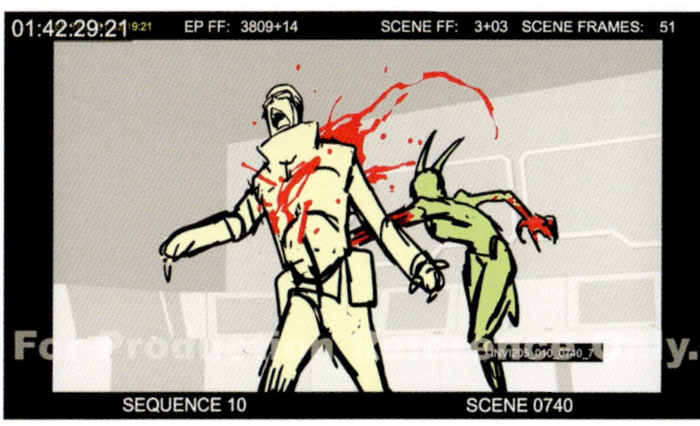

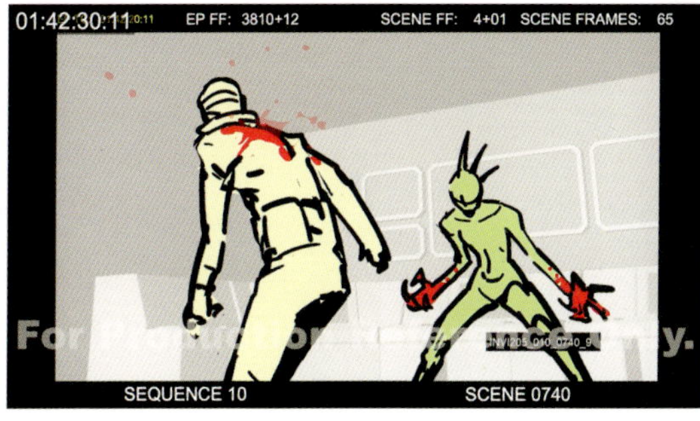

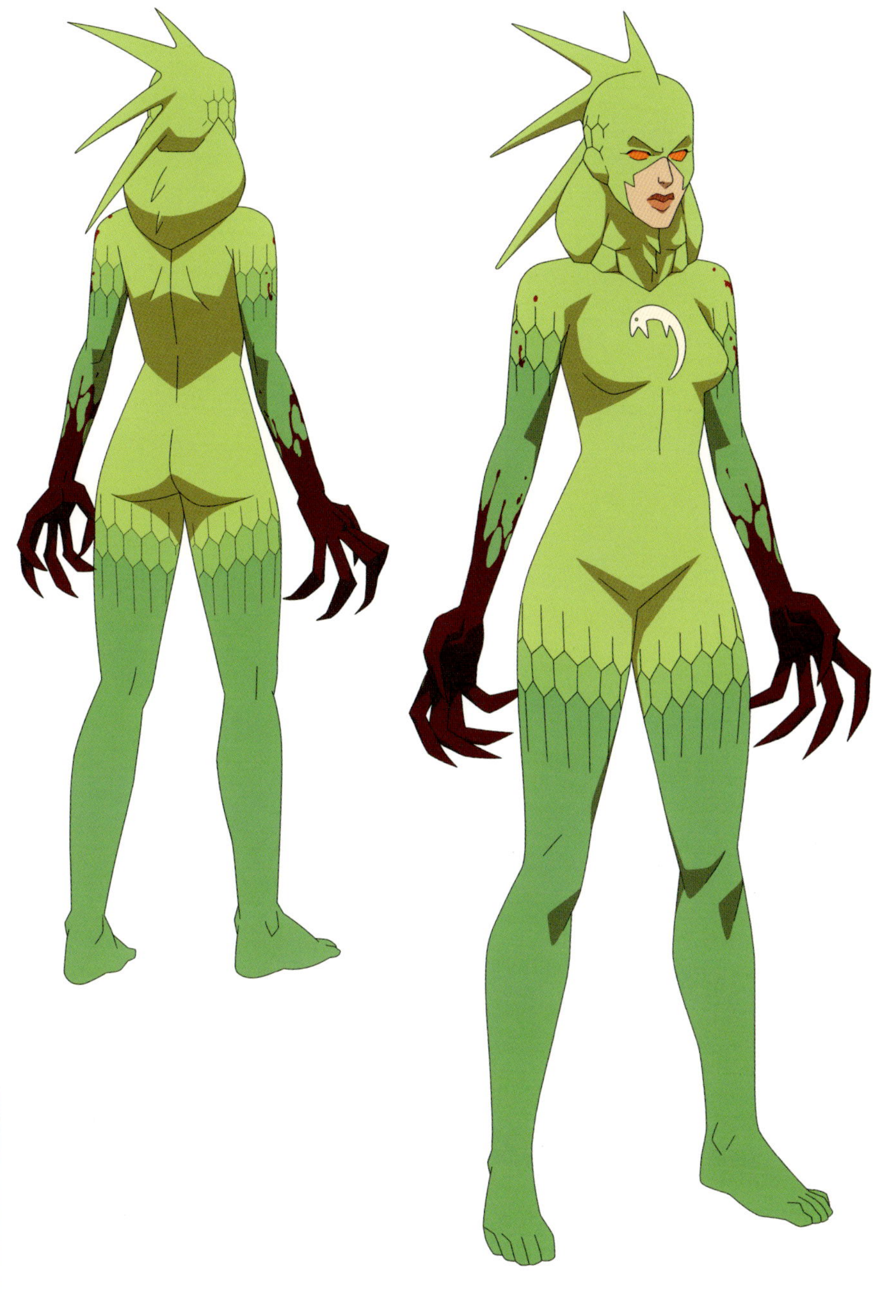

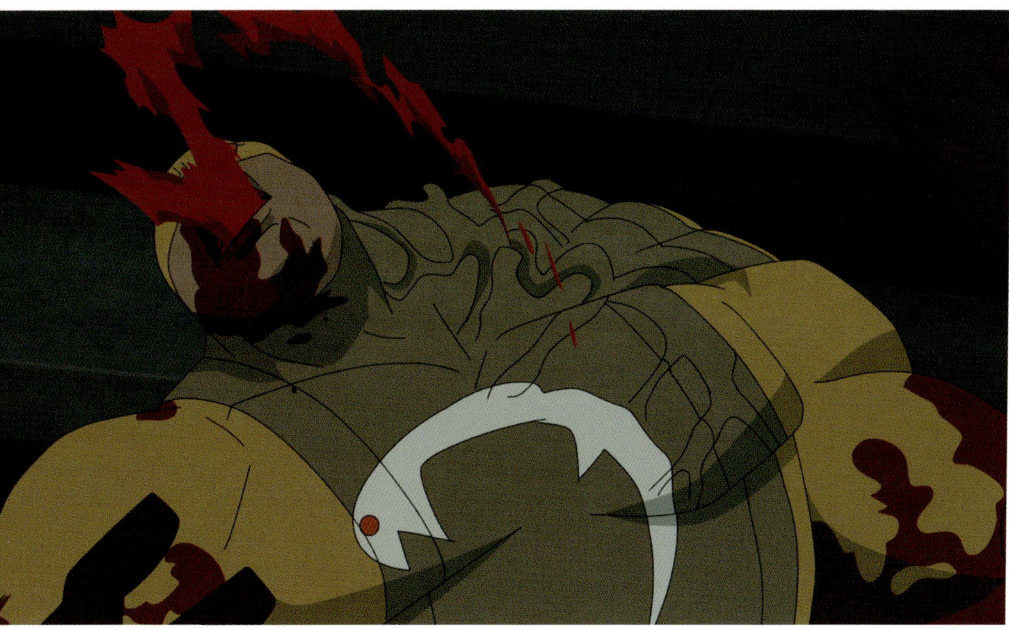

"The episode started with a lot of, 'We'll do in post' jokes," says O'Neil, "and by the end of it, those weren't funny anymore. It was just like, 'Okay, what can we do now?' But as far as episodes that came in weakest and ended strongest, I think 205 is a pretty heavy contender for that. We were done and in color correction and looking at it like, 'This is pretty good. This is not bad at all. Fucking high five. Let's celebrate and then move on to 206.'"

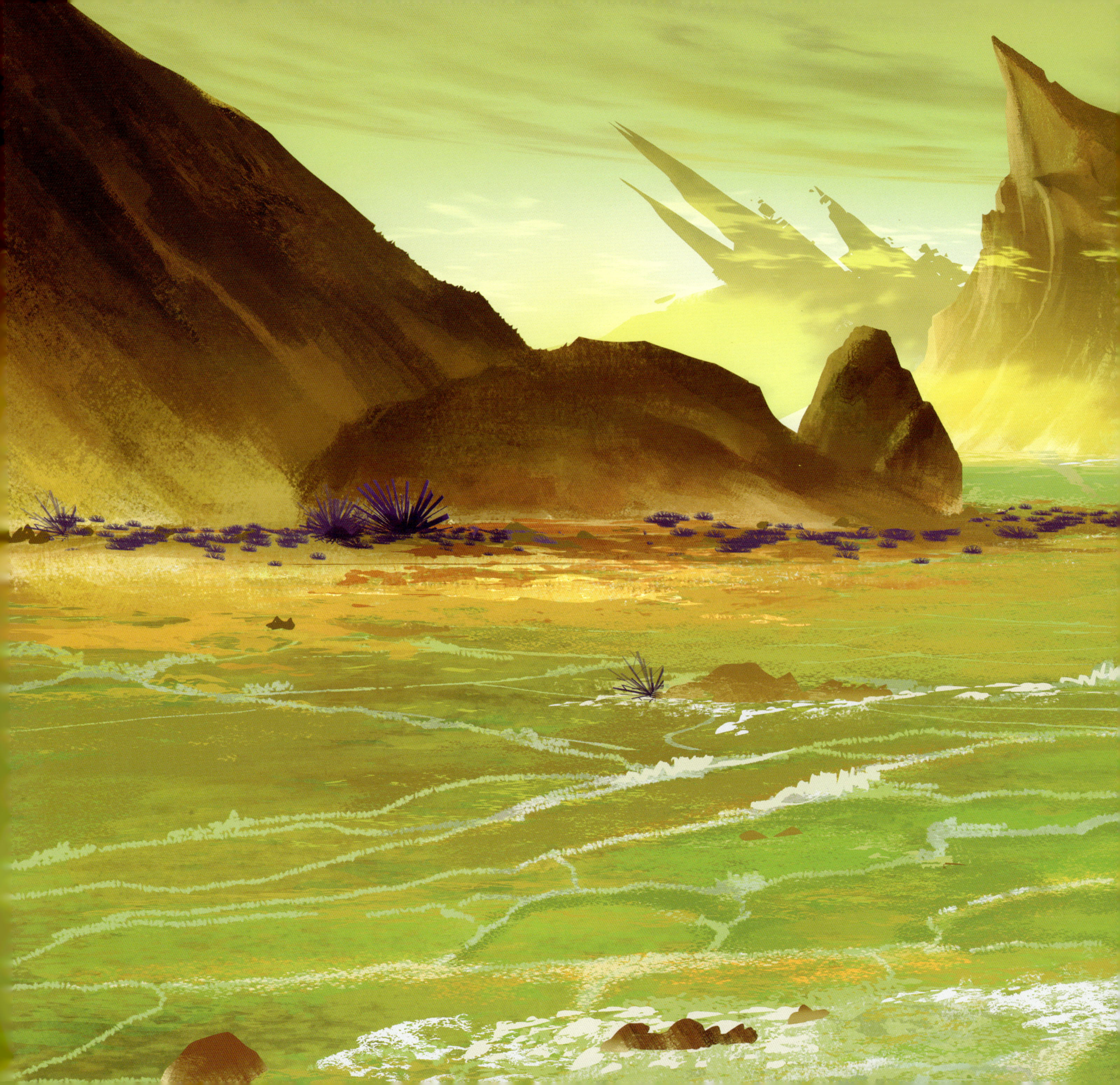

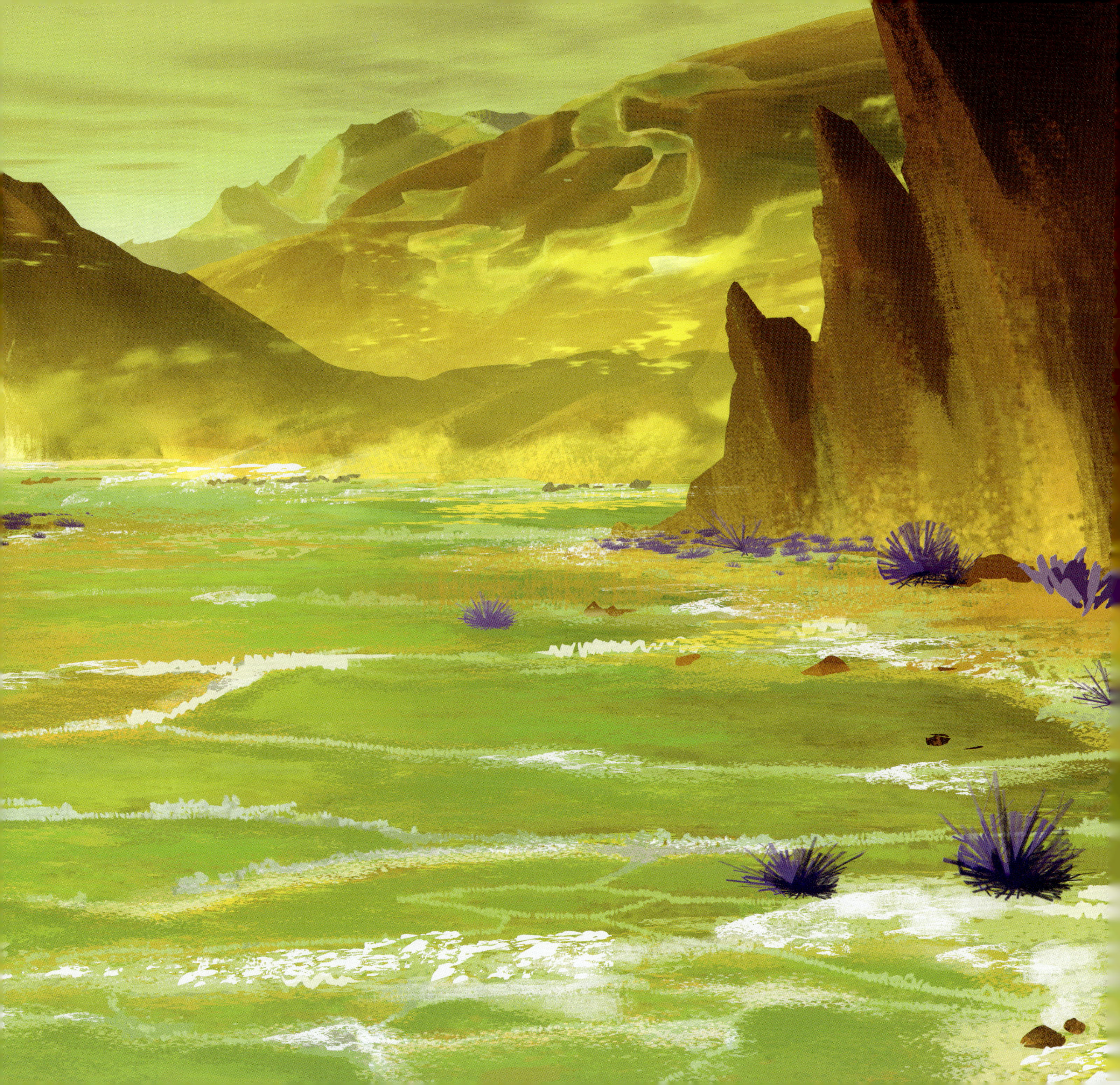

EPISODE 6:

IT'S NOT THAT SIMPLE

This episode of *Invincible* picked up almost exactly where the last one left off, with Rex Splode on his knees amongst the carnage caused by the Lizard League's attack. As King Lizard held his gun to the back of Rex's head, the hero dared the Lizard League's leader to pull the trigger. King Lizard quickly obliged.

The show's art team went above and beyond to make sure that Rex's severe injuries were as horrifying as possible, while still maintaining a level of authenticity.

"We have the designs for Rex getting shot in the head," says Executive Producer, Co-Showrunner, and Co-Creator Robert Kirkman. "Him missing the hand, and all the damage states that he's in. It's important that this stuff look realistic and horrific, as zany and comic book-y as it is. You want to have that grounding to make sure that those emotional punches land the way we want them to."

The impressive effort made by the designers to bring this gruesome moment to life were also reflected in the performance by Rex's voice actor, Jason Mantzoukas.

"That sequence with him getting shot in the head," says Executive Producer and Co-Showrunner Simon Racioppa, "we spent about two hours on that with Jason Mantzoukas just to get those emotions. [Rex] almost starts laughing after he comes back to life. We spent a long time on that. I think

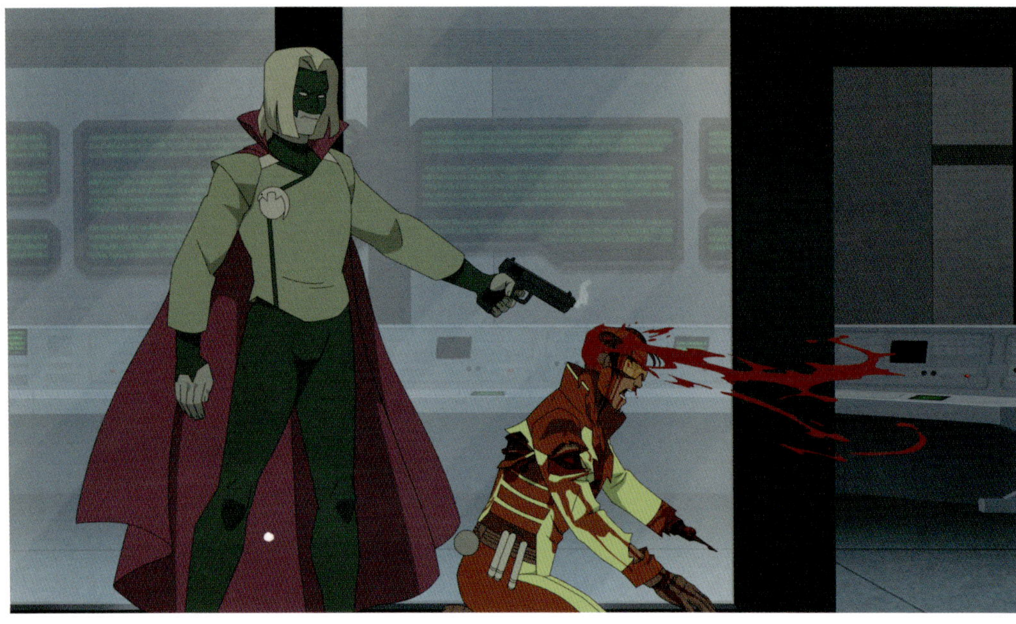

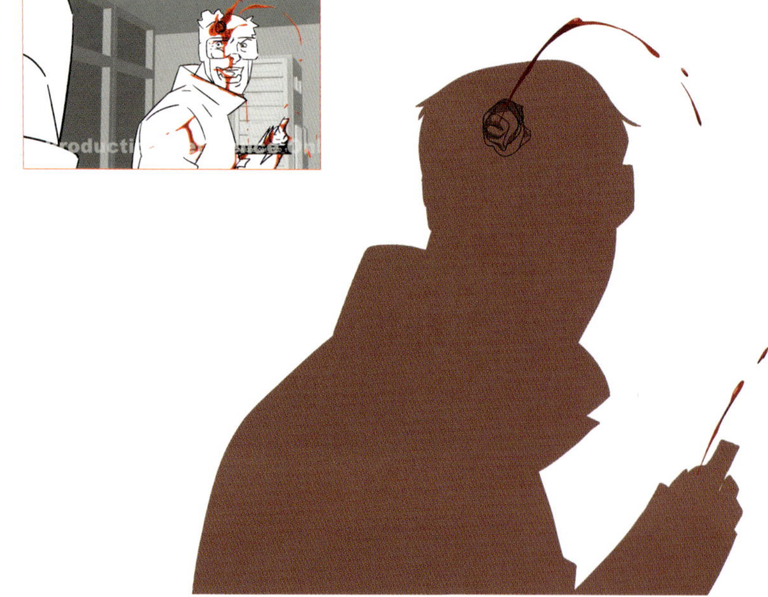

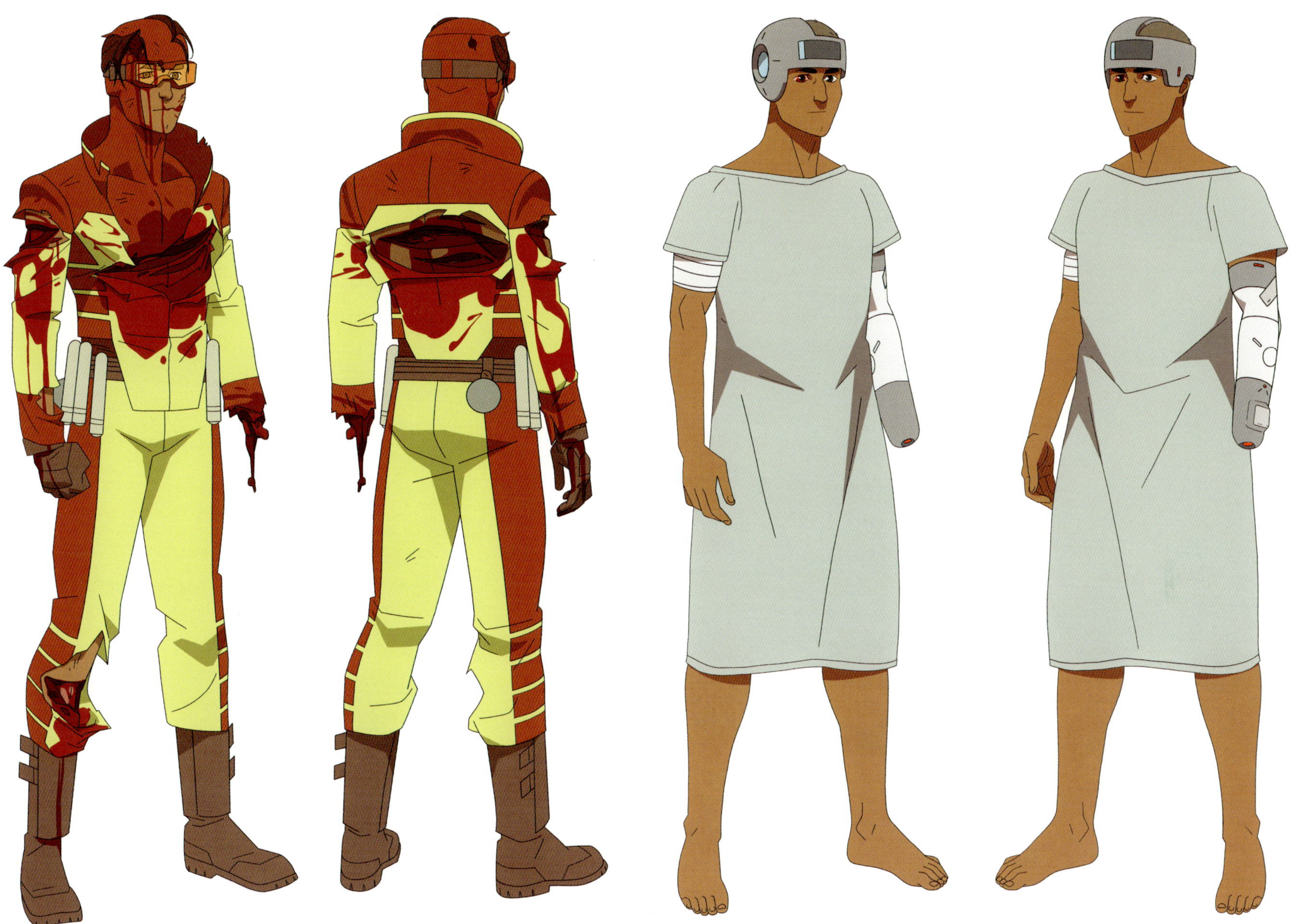

we probably did like twenty takes on that, not because he was doing anything wrong. We were just like, 'Oh, that's great. Let's go a little further. Let's try laughing.' He's like, 'Let me do it again.' We just kept on doing it until we finally landed in a place where we're like, 'Oh yeah, he's kind of manic,' because he's missing his hand, he's been shot in the head. It's a kind of crazy place to be for a character, or for anyone."

"He does a really great delivery," says Art Director Shaun O'Neil. "When he sits up and just gives that long winded 'Fuck,' that's one of the best. Soft focus in the foreground... he's just streaming blood out of his forehead, and you're just like, 'Okay, we've crossed the Rubicon, and now we're going someplace.' And that's that pivot. I'd be curious to know how many people were just like, 'Yeah, this is what I expected.' It's a nice aftermath to stuff. There's a part of me that feels good about watching all that shit happen in [episode] 205, and then watching Rex just beat the shit out of this dude in 206. It's just like, 'Yes, this feels earned. This feels justified. There's catharsis in this.'"

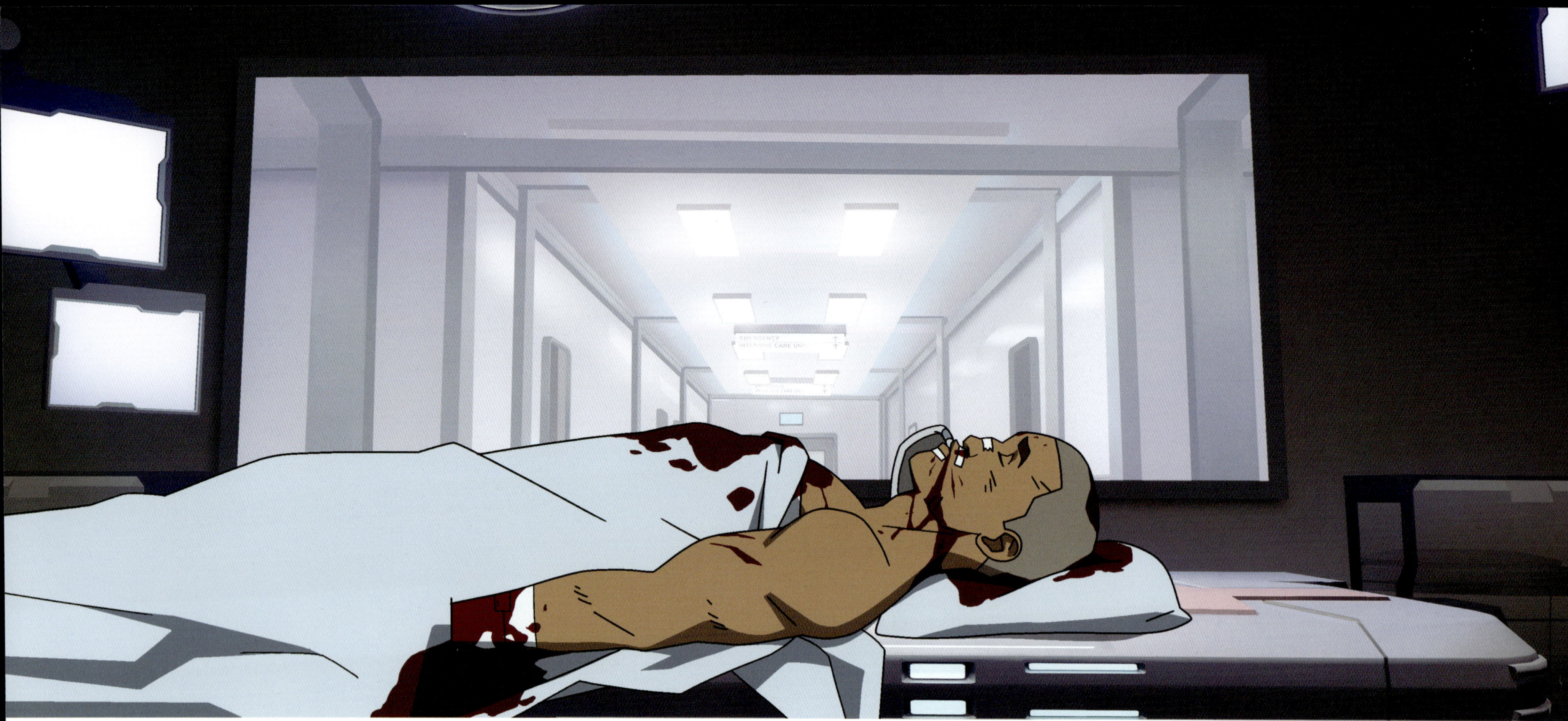

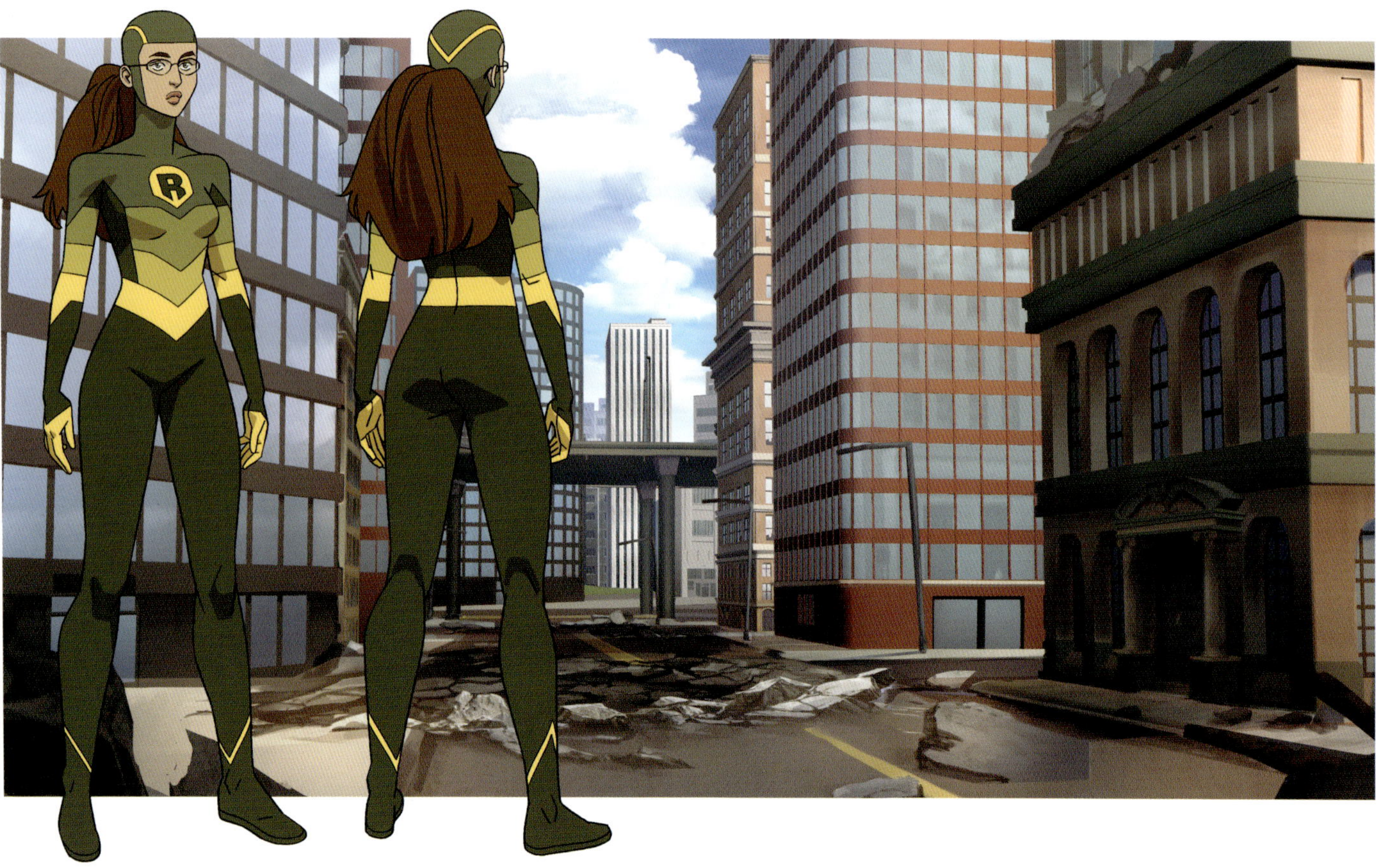

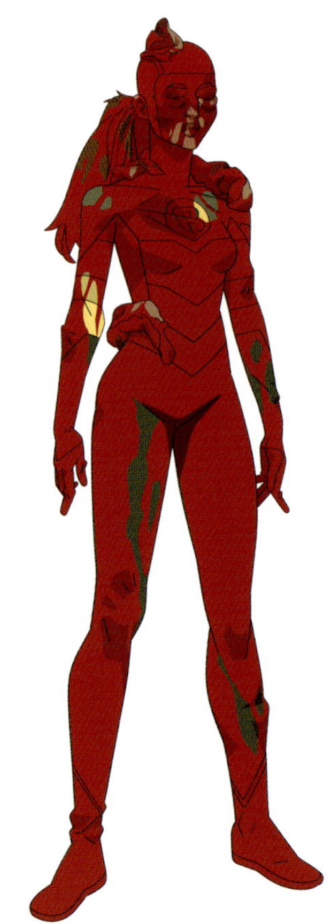

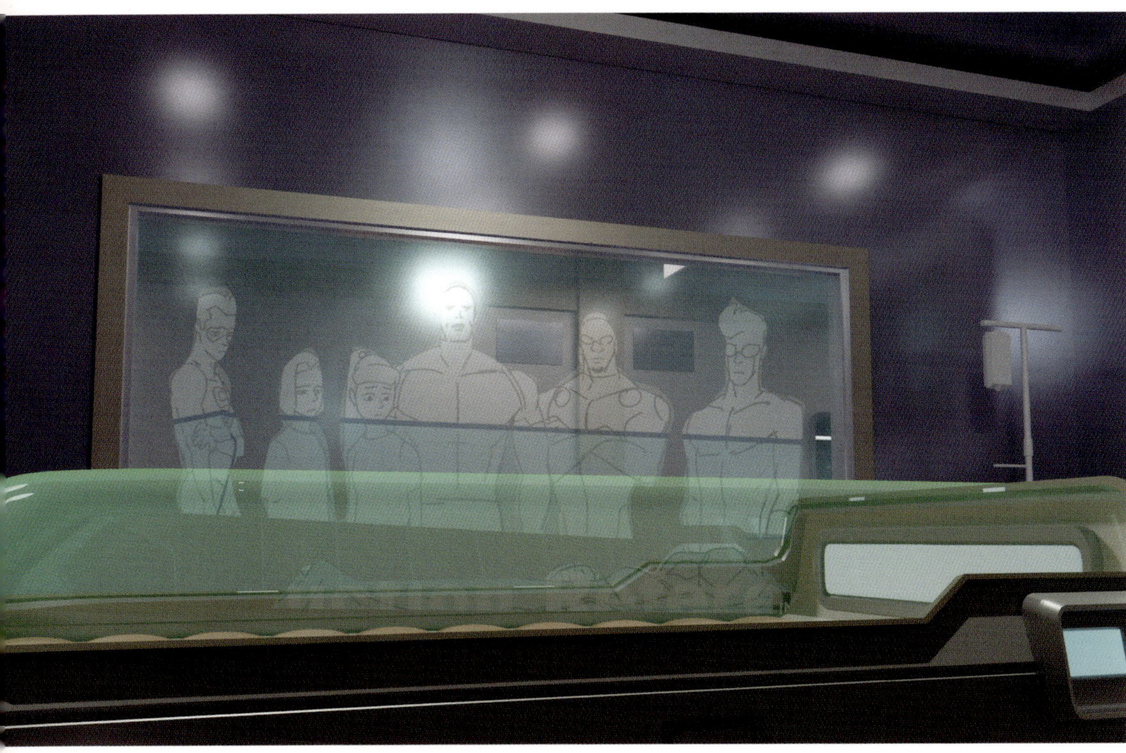

Rex somehow survived the shot to the head and went on to exact his revenge on King Lizard. Viewers soon learned that another member of the Guardians of the Globe also wasn't quite as dead as it originally appeared when Shrinking Rae emerged from the deceased Komodo Dragon's gaping neck hole.

"That was fun in the boards," says Supervising Director Dan Duncan. "It was fun to see the designs for that come in. It was fun to see animation for that... Rae and her *Ace Ventura 2* 'coming out of the rhino' moment. Just spectacular. It looked great. I think in post, Shaun got to do an extra Komodo Dragon neck because it wasn't anatomically correct enough."

"There were a couple of things that were gross, but they were not correct," says O'Neil. "And I was a big stickler for like, 'Gross for gross sake is no good.' You've got to look at it and see yourself in it. You've gotta look at it and be like, 'Nasty.' I'm thinking about what I'm like on the inside, and that is terrible. That's part of that shock value. If we're going to go there, we have to get that out of it."

However, even though Rex and Rae managed to survive

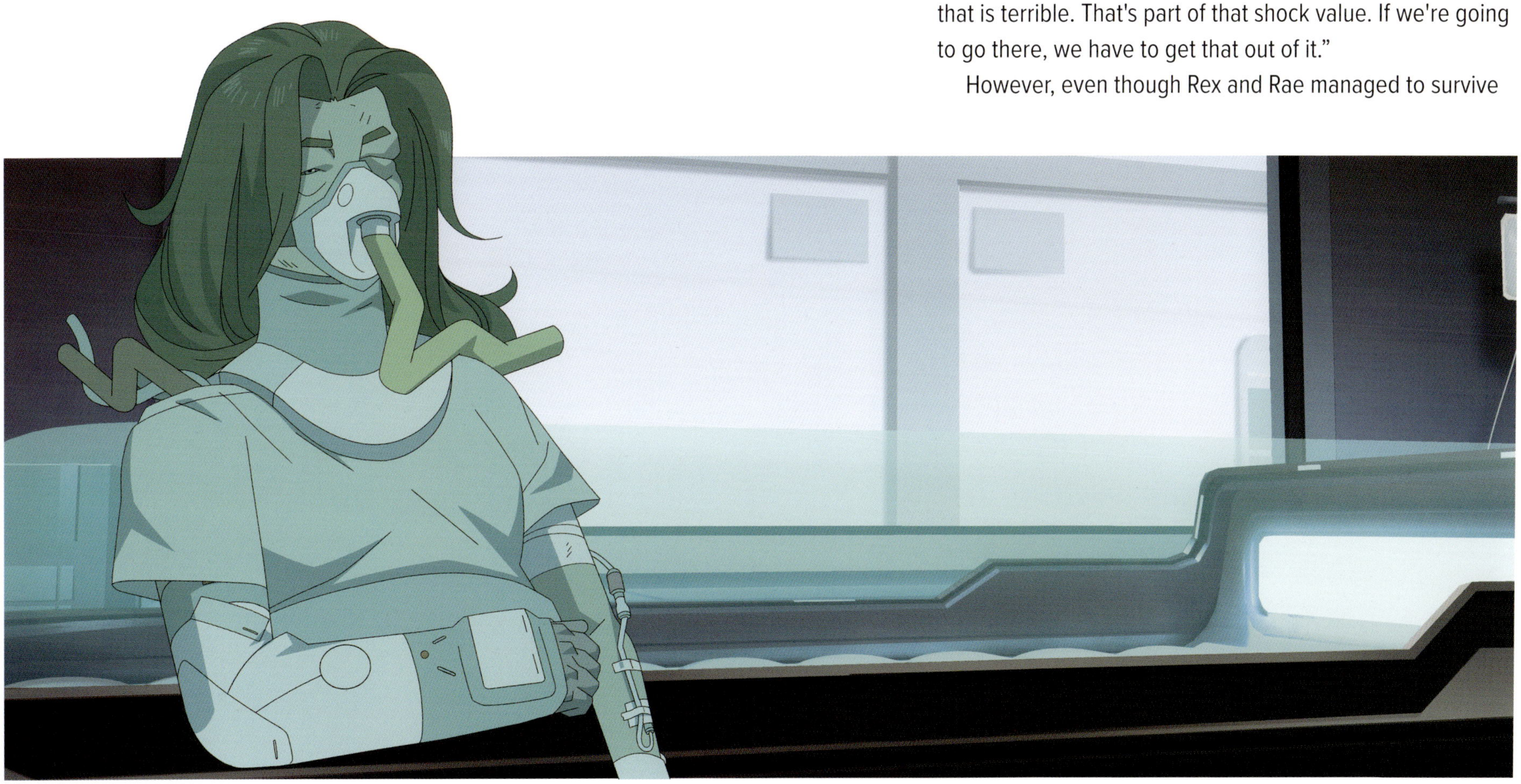

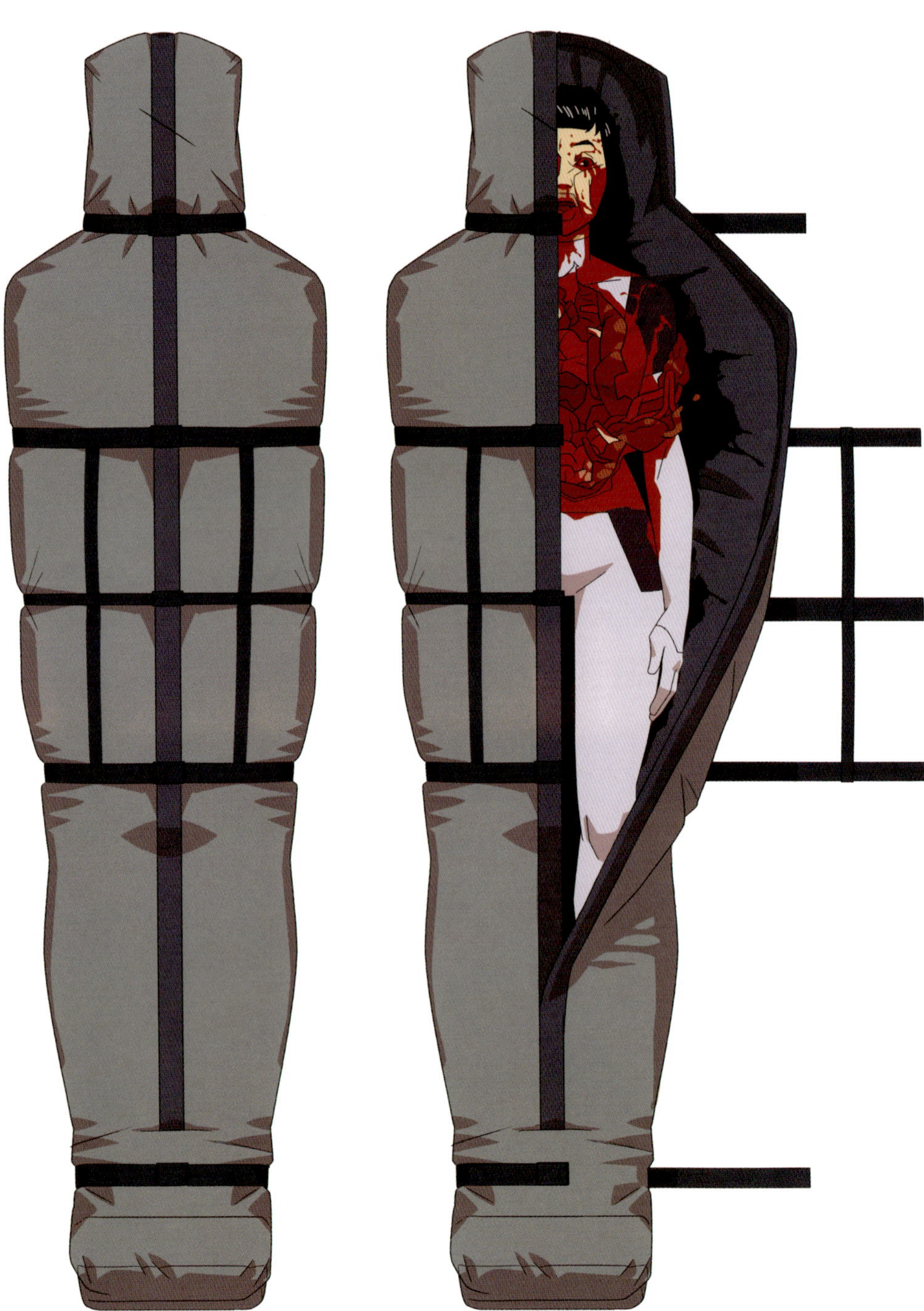

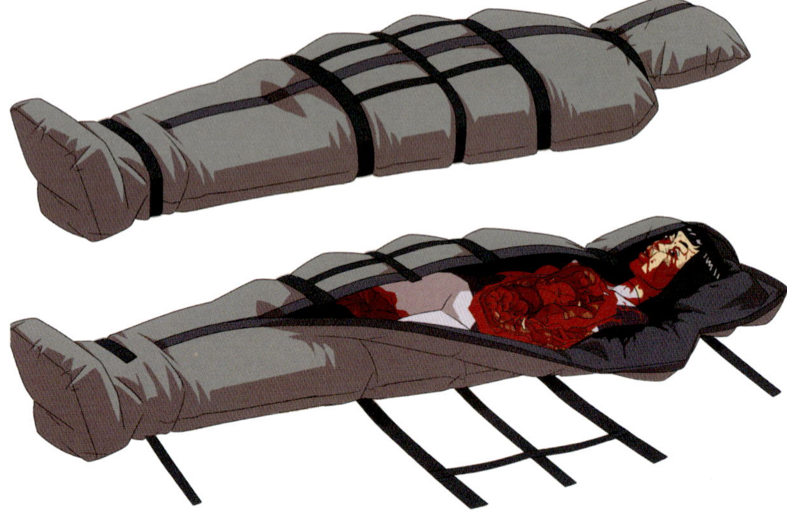

the Lizard League's assault, the final member of their team, Dupli-Kate, was seemingly not as lucky.

"I think there's a lot of Dupli-Kates in body bags that were done for this episode," says Kirkman. "Again, it's all about pulling the emotion out of the scene and making sure that you have that emotional punch."

Meanwhile, Mark and the other team of Guardians weren't faring all that well in their mission to stop the Sequids either. The sheer number of alien lifeforms nearly overwhelmed the heroes, not to mention the artists making the show.

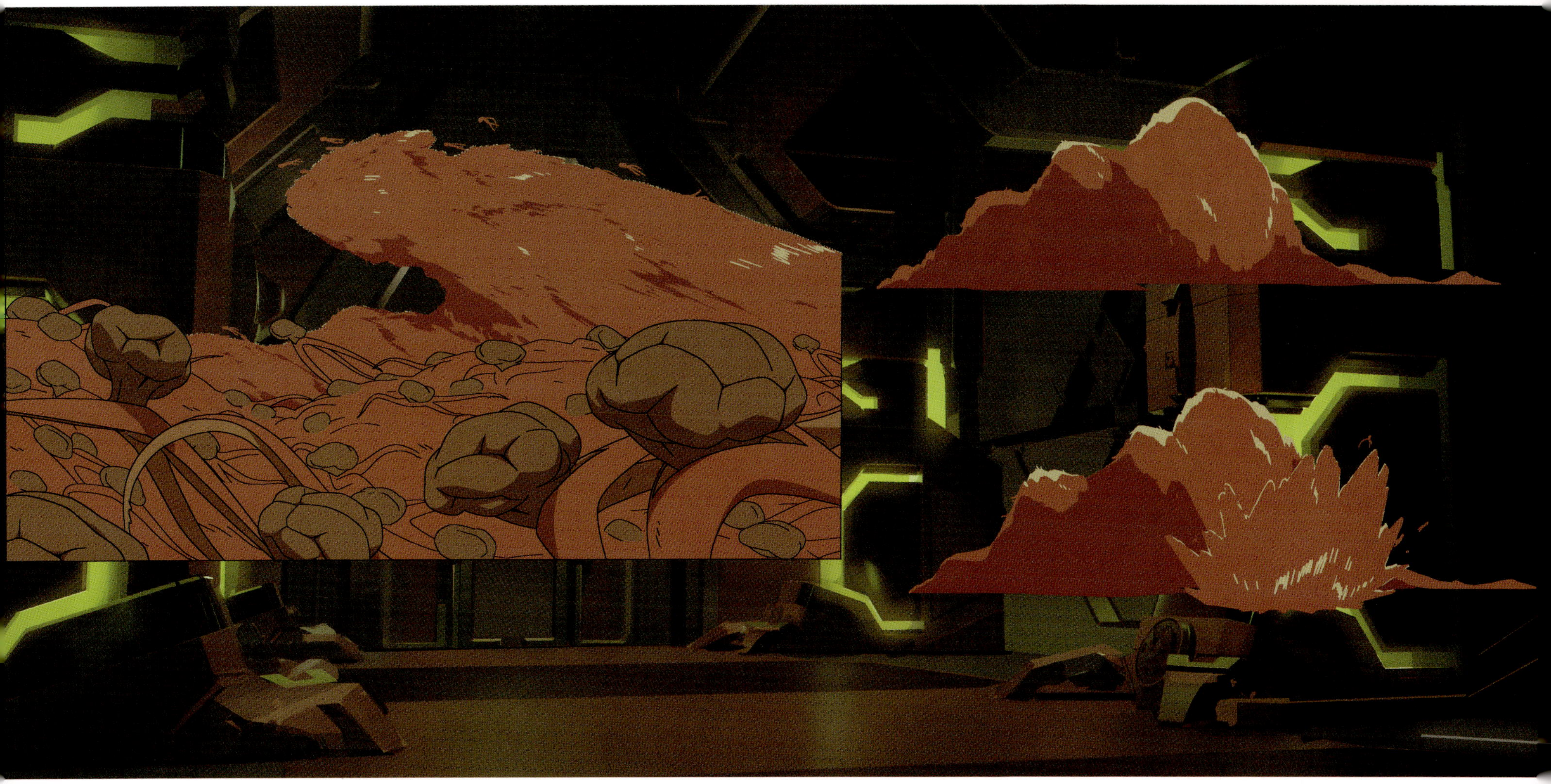

"I feel empathy for those guys," says Racioppa, "when they started looking at those scripts and being like, 'Wait, how many Sequids?' In Season One, when we see the Sequids and the Martians, it's a fairly contained sequence. We have the surface of Mars. A couple of tunnels, a couple guards, one emperor, and then the Sequids. And then at the end, I think there's a wave of them that you see coming up and over, but that's at a distance. It's not too hard to animate. Here, we were like, 'Oh no, they're going to be wading through a million of them? A couple hundred thousand?' It's a crazy high number and it's got to look cool and

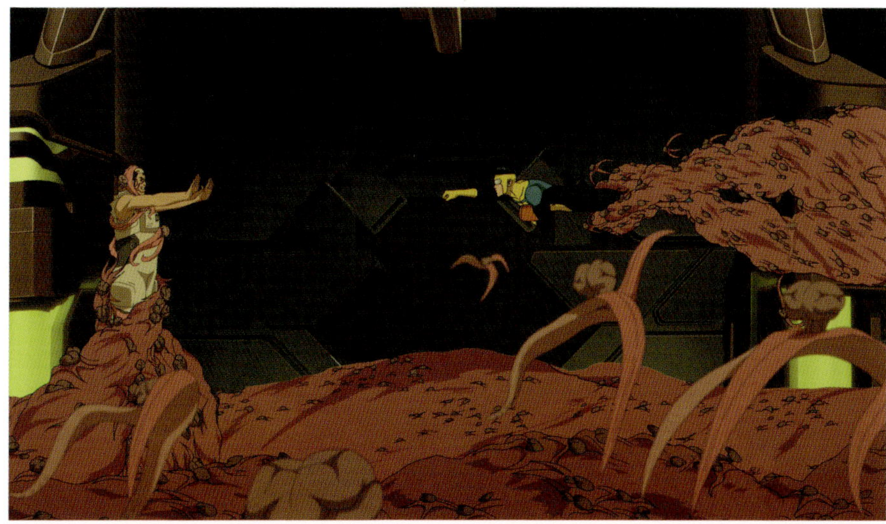

they've got to be moving, but still identifiable as Sequids. They don't become a liquid, even if they sometimes move like liquid. That was the analogy we had. Together they can kind of move like the ocean, move like liquid. But obviously, close up, they're still these individual facehugger things. So I know for Dan and Shaun, it was a huge challenge. And I think they knocked it out of the park, especially given a television schedule and a television budget."

The threat intensified further as Atom Eve and Rudy, Robot's human counterpart, briefly fell under the sway of the Sequids.

"That's a bit that's not in the comics at all," says Kirkman. "It's absolutely terrifying to think of those two characters being controlled by the Sequids. That was a really cool

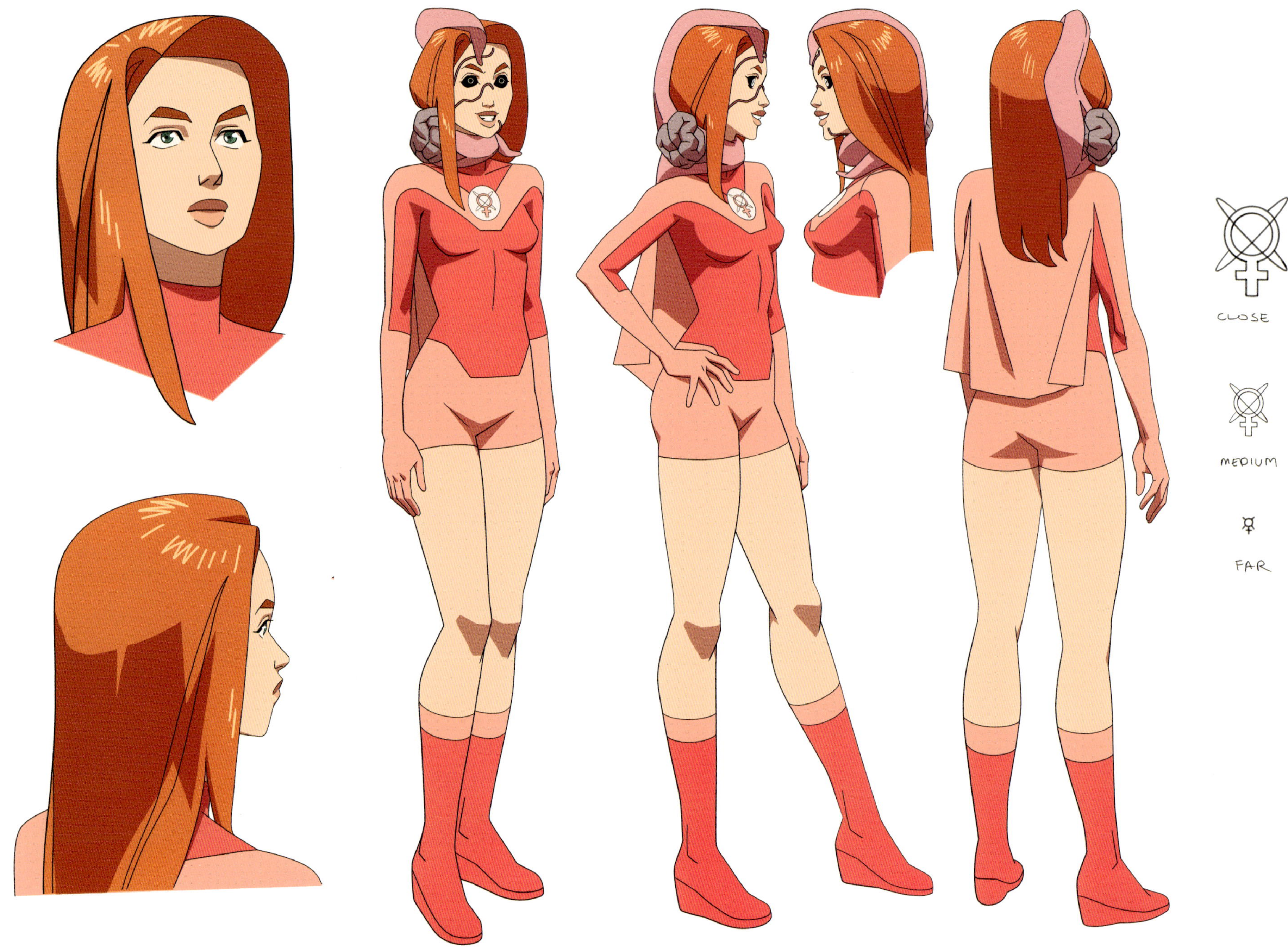

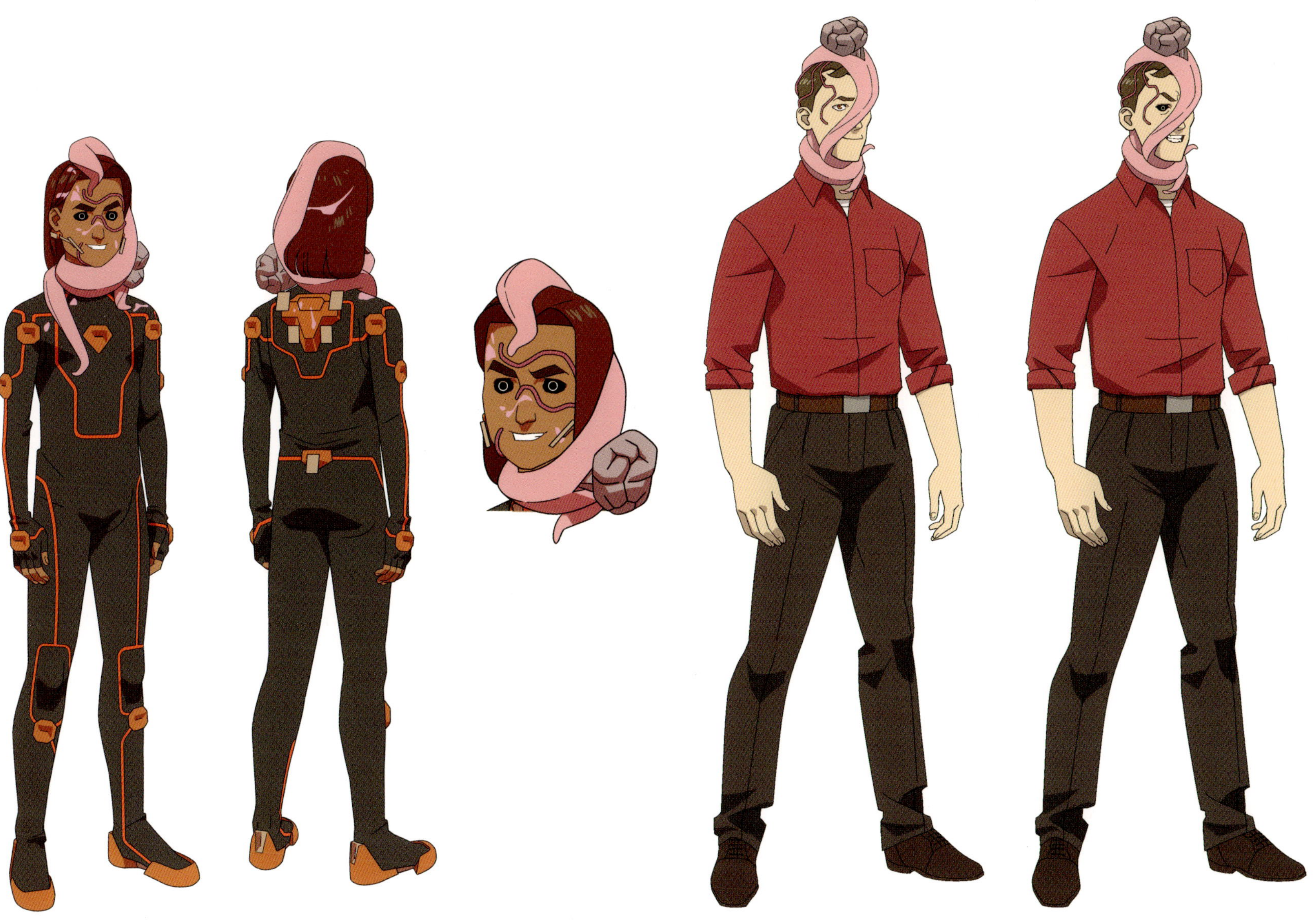

element that was unique to the show."

Despite all odds, Invincible and the Immortal found a way to break the Sequids' control of their fellow heroes and ended the alien threat… at least for the moment. But while Mark's team may have succeeded in their mission, they were about to learn about the horrors that their teammates had endured while they were away.

"If anything, the Guardians come out much worse from those two events," says Racioppa. "On the space side of things, Rudy and Eve get grabbed, but they're freed pretty quickly afterwards. The Sequids' plan doesn't work. They get stopped. At least it looks like that anyway. Everybody comes back alive. It's okay. The Martians get to turn the ship around, head back to Mars. But there's a great scene where [the heroes] come in, they land, and they see Donald's expression and they're like, 'Oh, something's gone wrong here on Earth.' And Kate's dead. Rex is in the hospital recovering. Rae is even worse. Again, this is the kind of thing the show does and promises to the audience, it's that they're not fine the next episode. Rae stays in the hospital the rest of the season. And what will happen next in Season Three? You have to watch and find out. But I can promise you, you don't get over being swallowed and crushed inside someone's gullet and left to die in their stomach in a month. That stuff will stay with you for a while. And the same for Rex. We see those characters in slightly different ways. Rex, he's had brain surgery. I mean, he gets access to the best doctors in the world, so that's great. He doesn't have to pay for health care, thank God. But his head is shaved. He's missing his hand. He's messed up after that. And we can see the effect that also has on Eve. Eve has obviously had her disagreements with Rex, but they're old friends. They've known each other since they were teenagers. So it's hard for her to see him like this. Same with Kate. We just try to make those things feel real on the show."

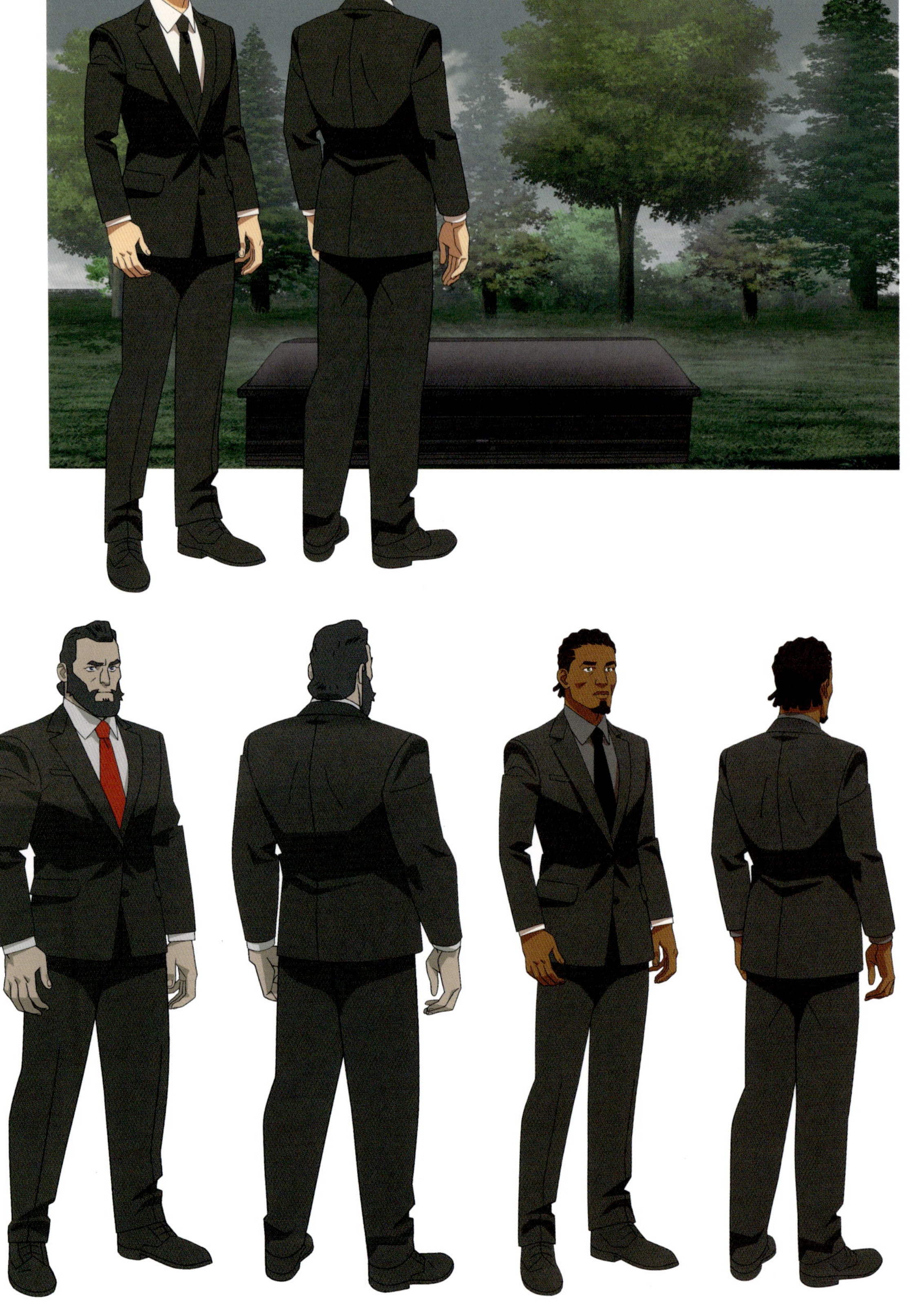

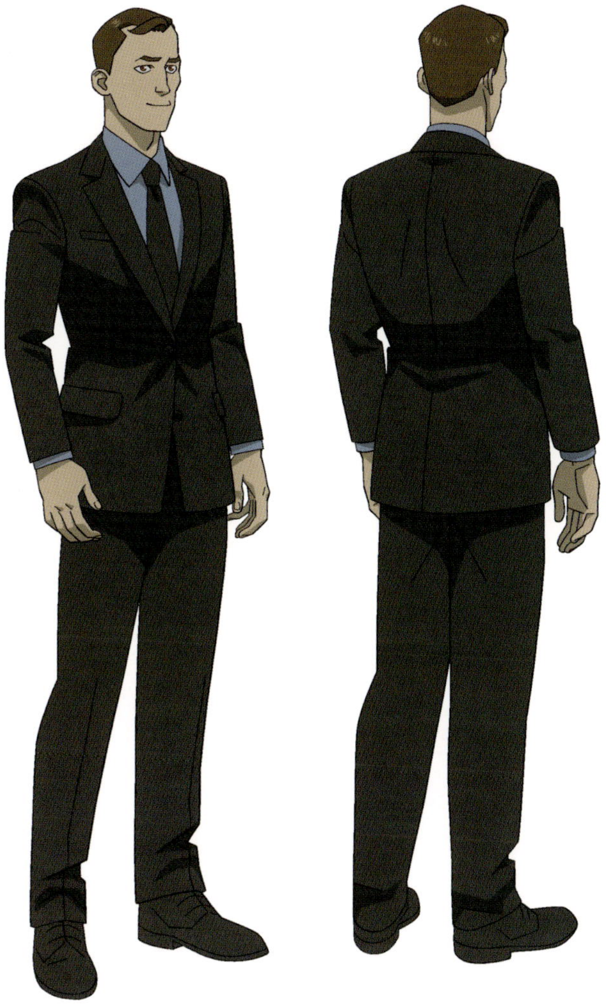

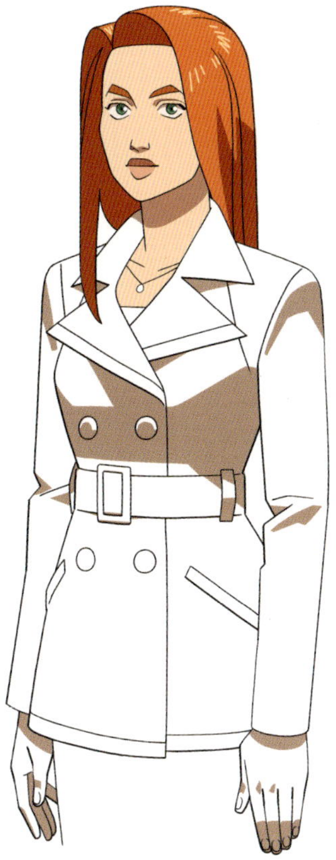

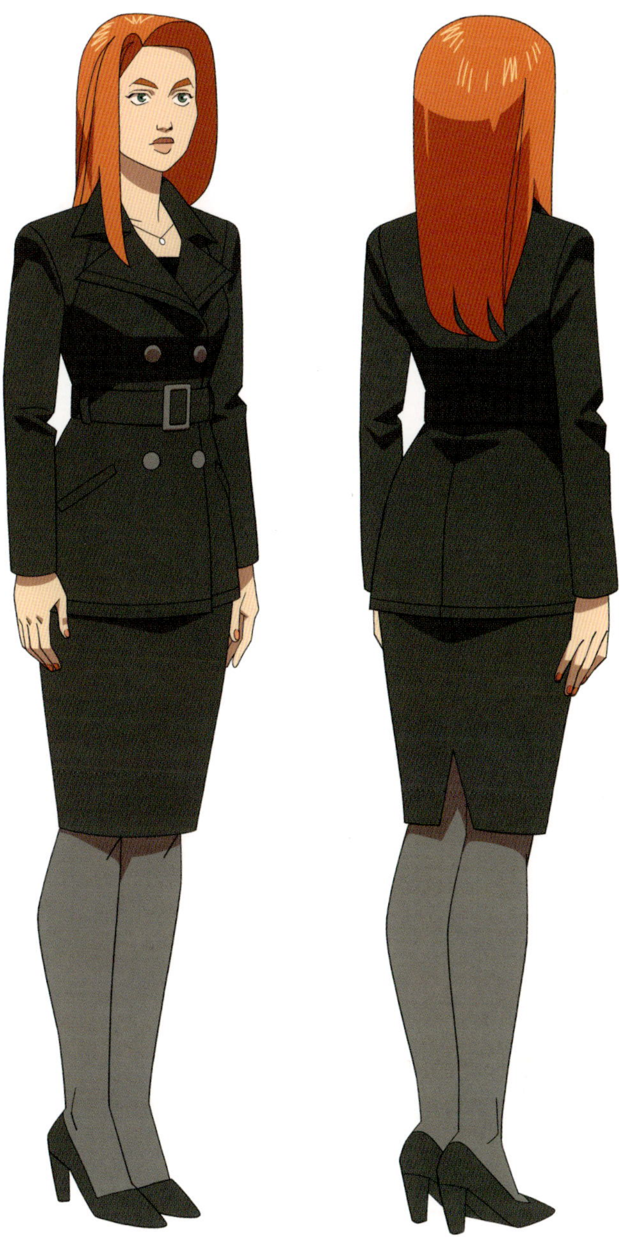

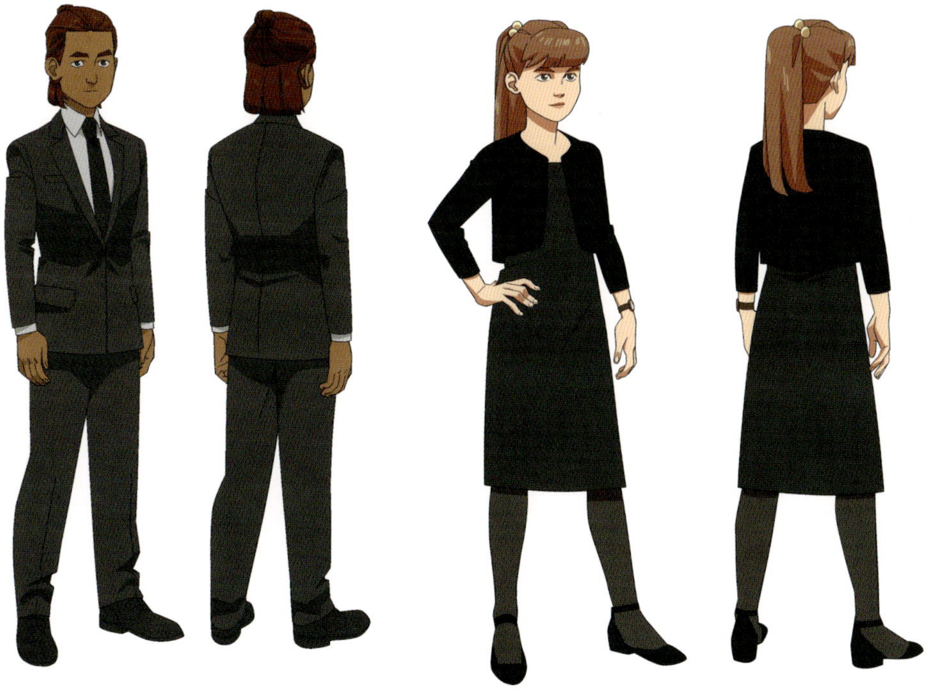

After the funeral for Dupli-Kate, Mark attempted to go back to his normal life for a bit. During that time, he managed to track down copies of several books written by his father, which Nolan had told Mark to find during their final moments together on Thraxa. At first, the books seemed like nothing more than cheesy science-fiction stories starring a character that was strangely similar to Nolan himself.

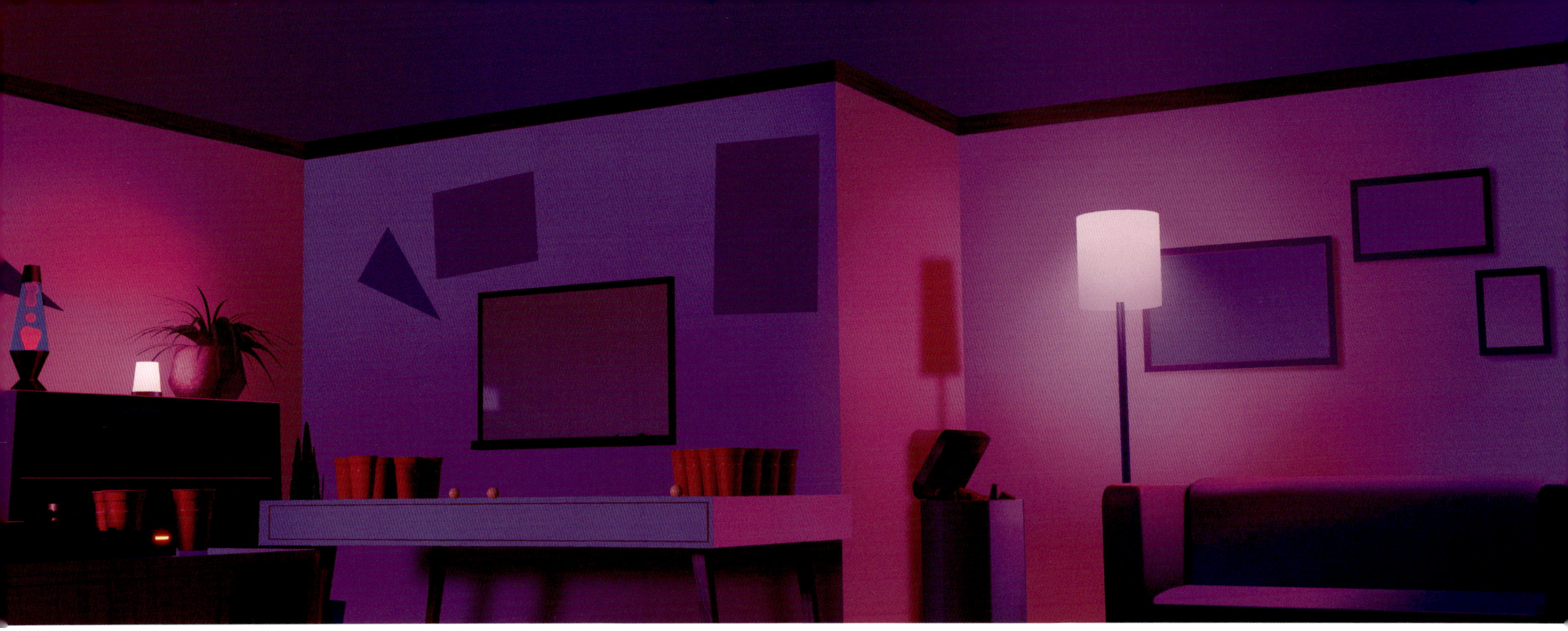

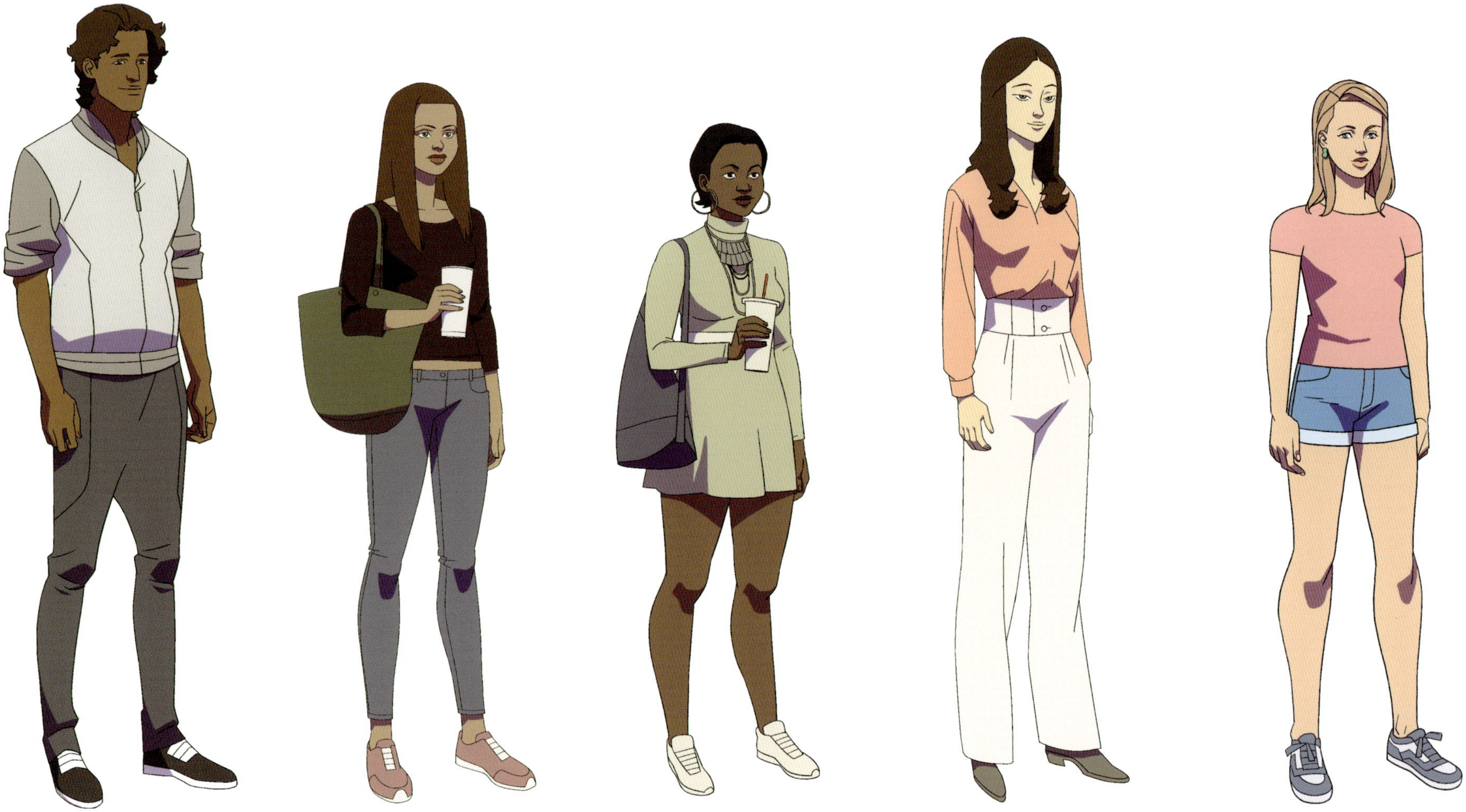

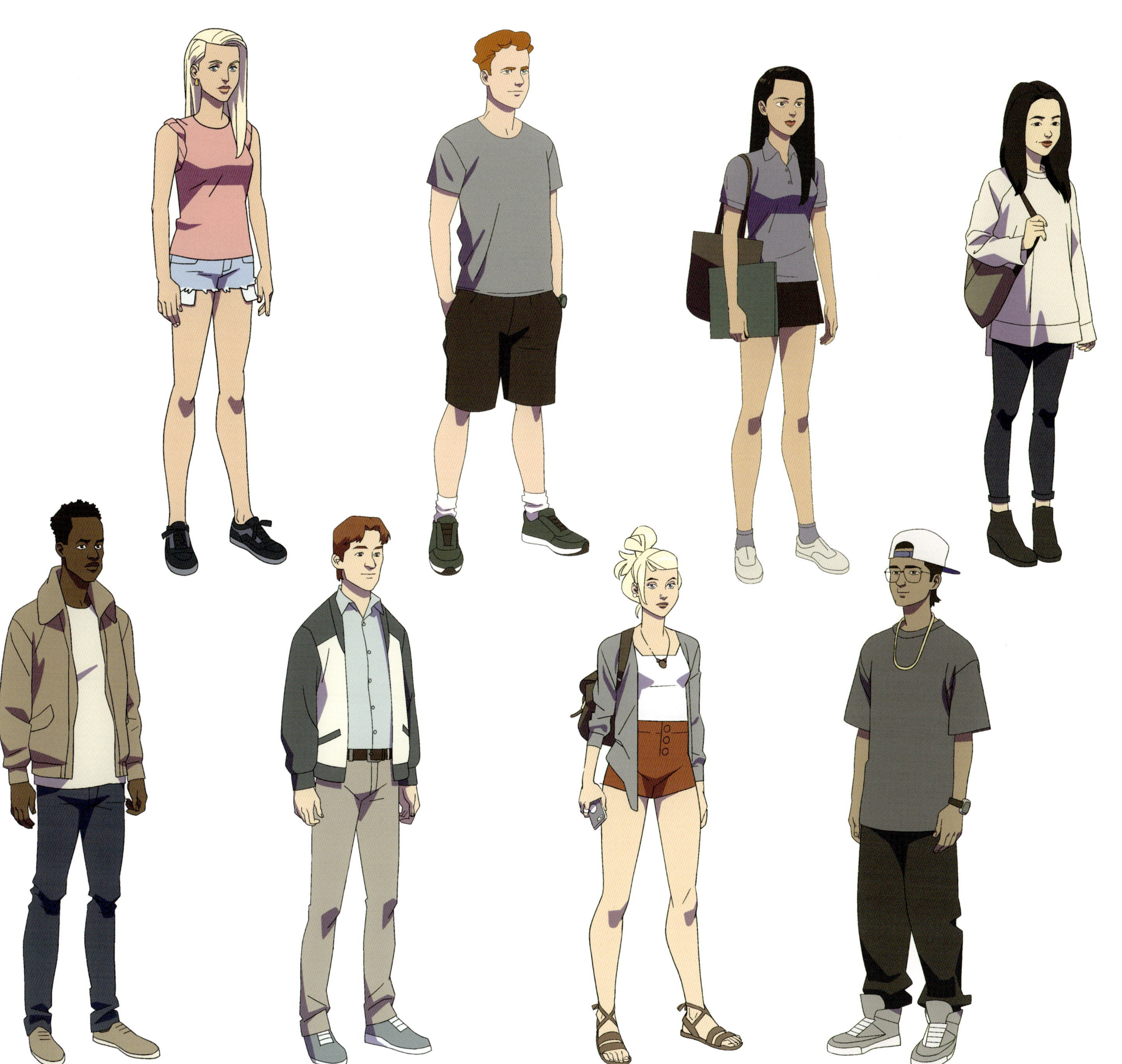

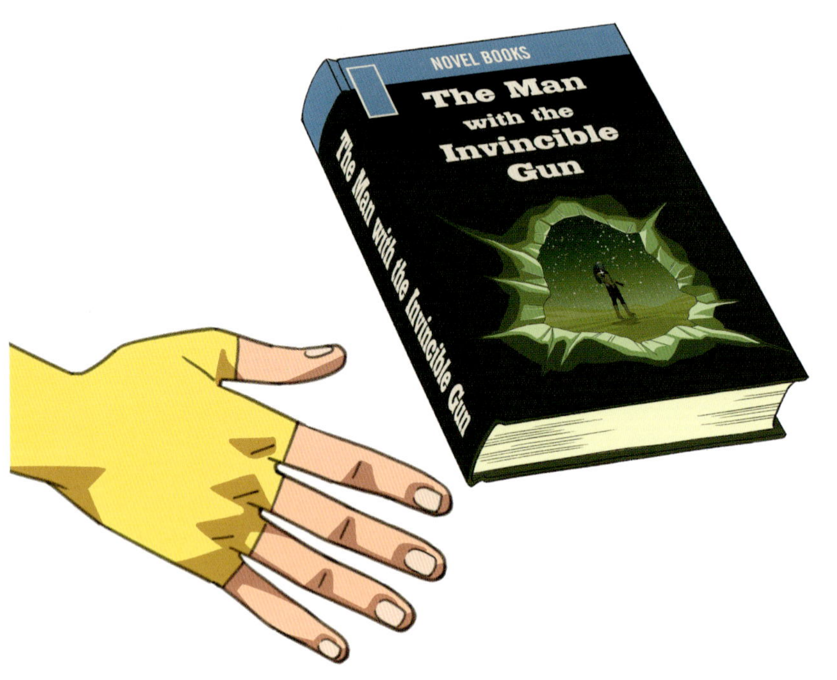

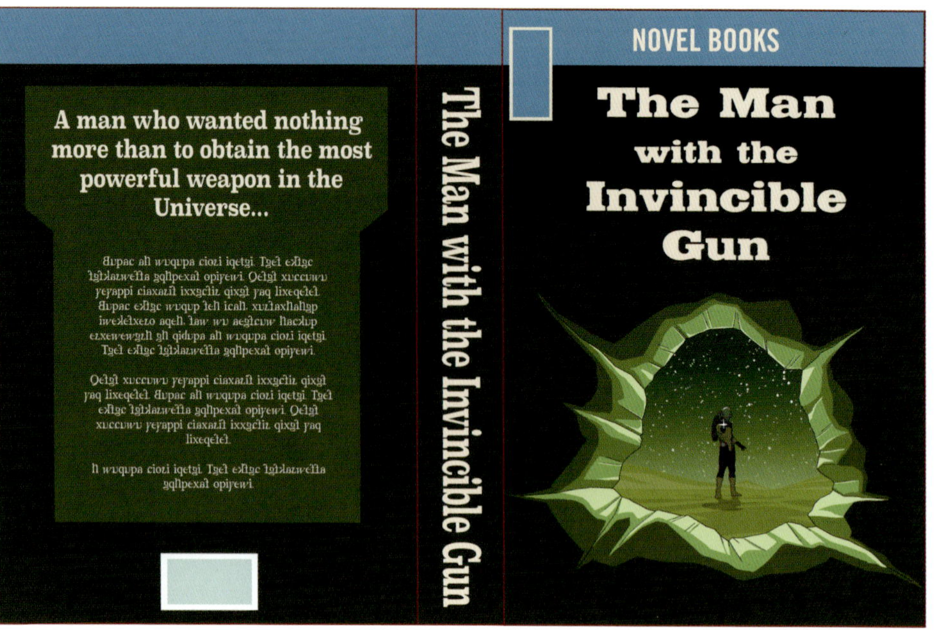

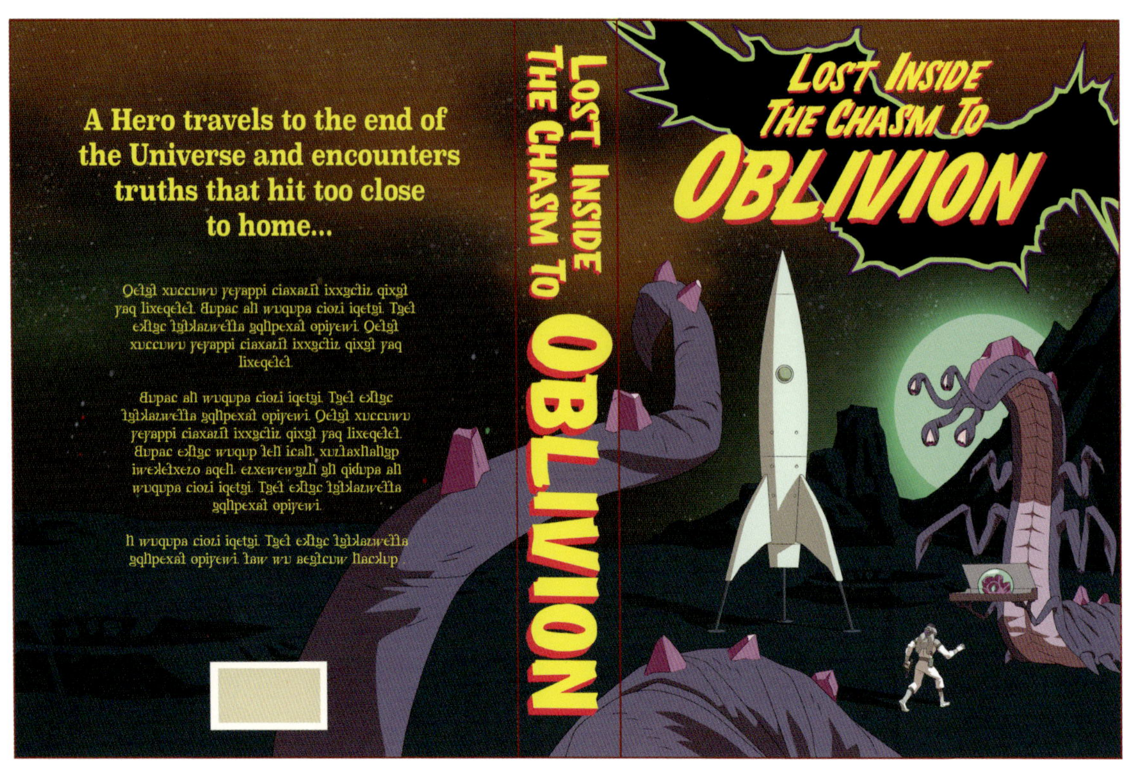

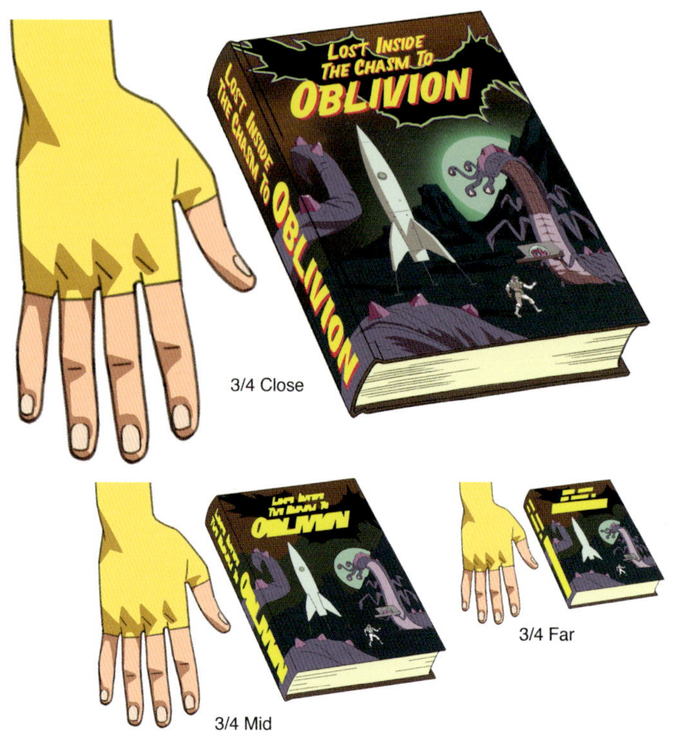

3/4 Close

3/4 Mid

3/4 Far

SCIENCE FICTION

HATE TRIBES ON the PLANET WREKK

Hate Tribes on the Planet Wrekk

To understand love, he must first understand hate...

“All the book covers are great,” says Racioppa. “I grew up reading pulp sci-fi, just endless paperback books you could buy for two dollars. Great stuff. So the fact that Nolan had these great pulpy books... Again, Dan and Shaun did a great job on the covers. The art team designed these great pulpy sci-fi covers for his books. And we go into those stories, which is fun because they're narrated by Nolan. But it's not quite Nolan, you know, because he's a space pioneer, kind of like a Buck Rogers character in the books who doesn't call himself a Viltrumite. So we wanted to carry that over when you see him fighting the Rognarrs on that planet.”

Since the scenes depicted were merely interpretations of the stories

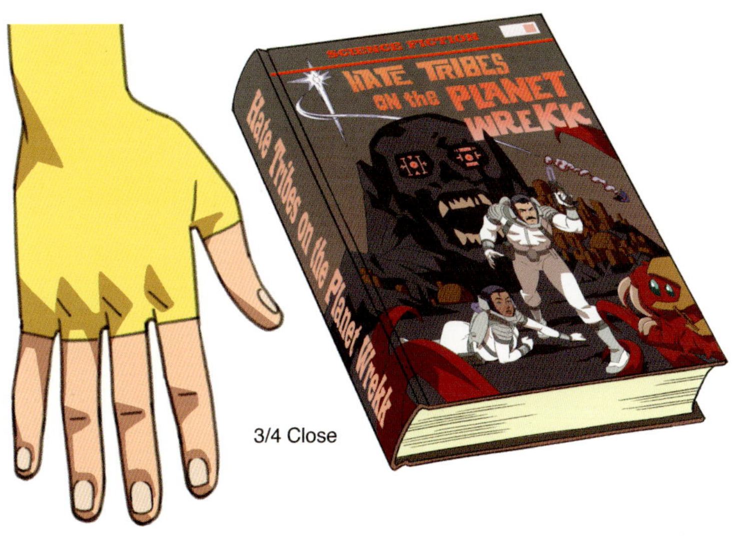

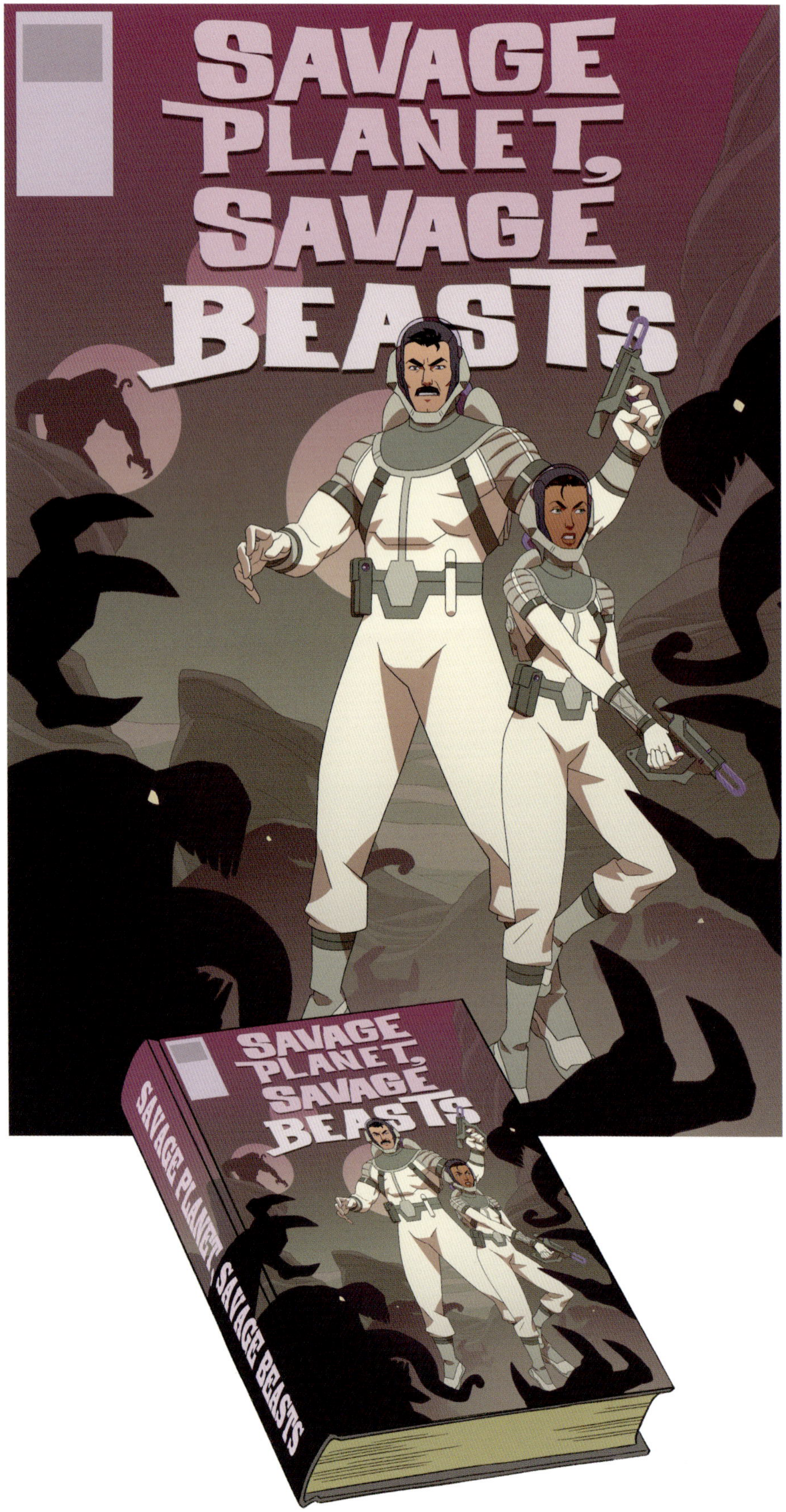

SAVAGE PLANET, SAVAGE BEASTS
NOVEL BOOKS
The Man with the Invincible Gun
SAVAGE PLANET, SAVAGE BEASTS
SAVAGE PLANET, SAVAGE BEASTS
NOVEL BOOKS 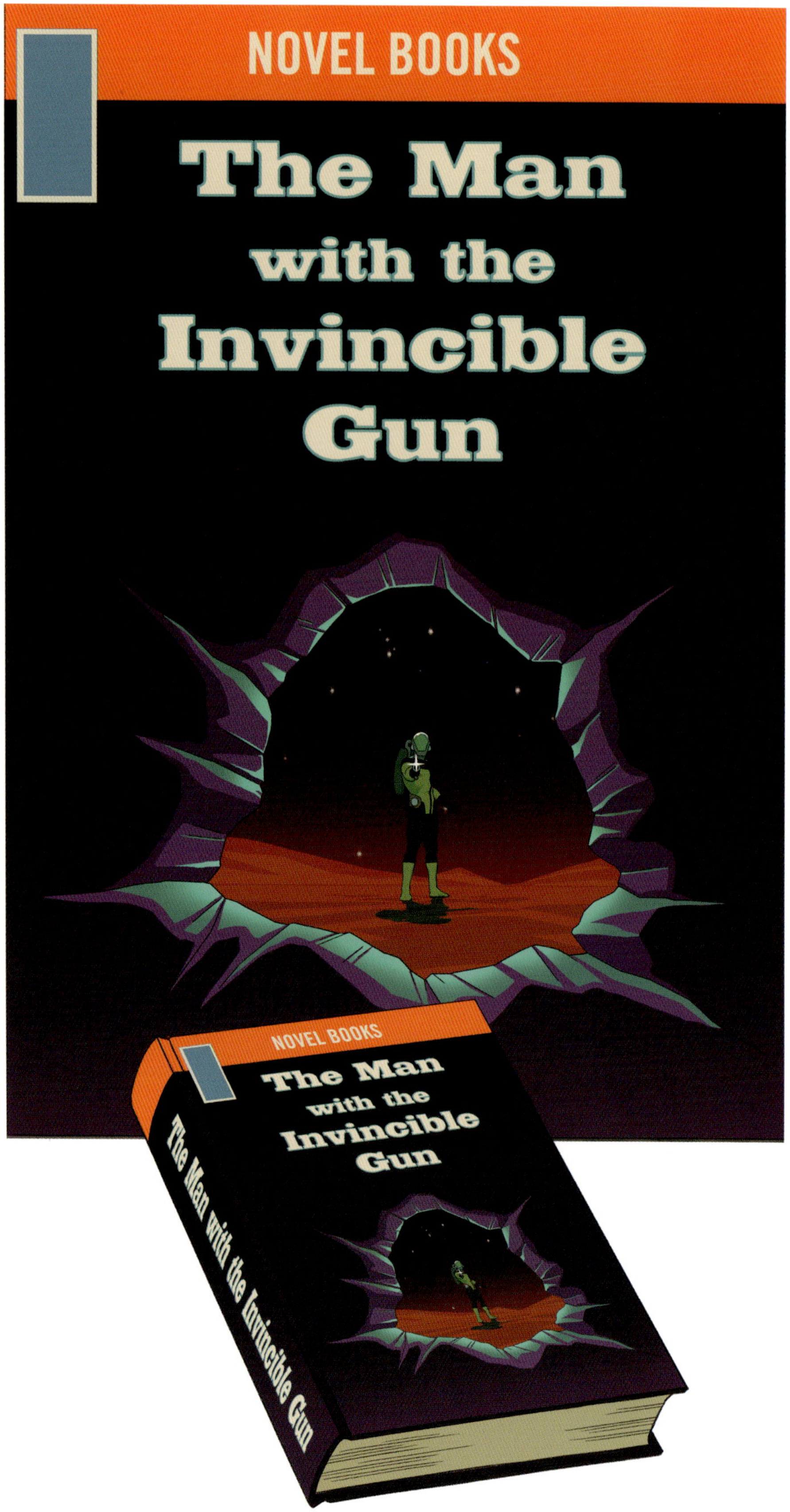
The Man with the Invincible Gun
The Man with the Invincible Gun

from Nolan's books, the art team considered pushing the character designs in a number of unexpected directions. Ultimately, they found it important to stay true to another book — the *Invincible* comic.

"I know there were tons of different options for Rognarrs that we came up with," says Kirkman. "And I think we ended up steering closer to the comics. Sometimes it just feels heartbreaking to get these crazy designs that are super awesome from people, and then it's like, 'I think the fanbase might want to see these looking like they are in the comics. Sorry.' That's kind of a bummer. Every now and then we'll take a wild swing. But some of these things we're just trying to make sure that you get a sense that these are the Rognarrs that the fanbase knows and loves."

Even though the designers tried to stay relatively true to the source material, they still found room to push the designs for the show further than how they first appeared.

"I think in the comic, when Mark is reading the Rognarr [book], it's just a picture of a Rognarr," says Co-Executive Producer and Co-Creator Cory Walker. "So coming up with the sort of Wally Wood-inspired costumes for the Viltrumites was a cool process to go through. Bringing all that stuff to

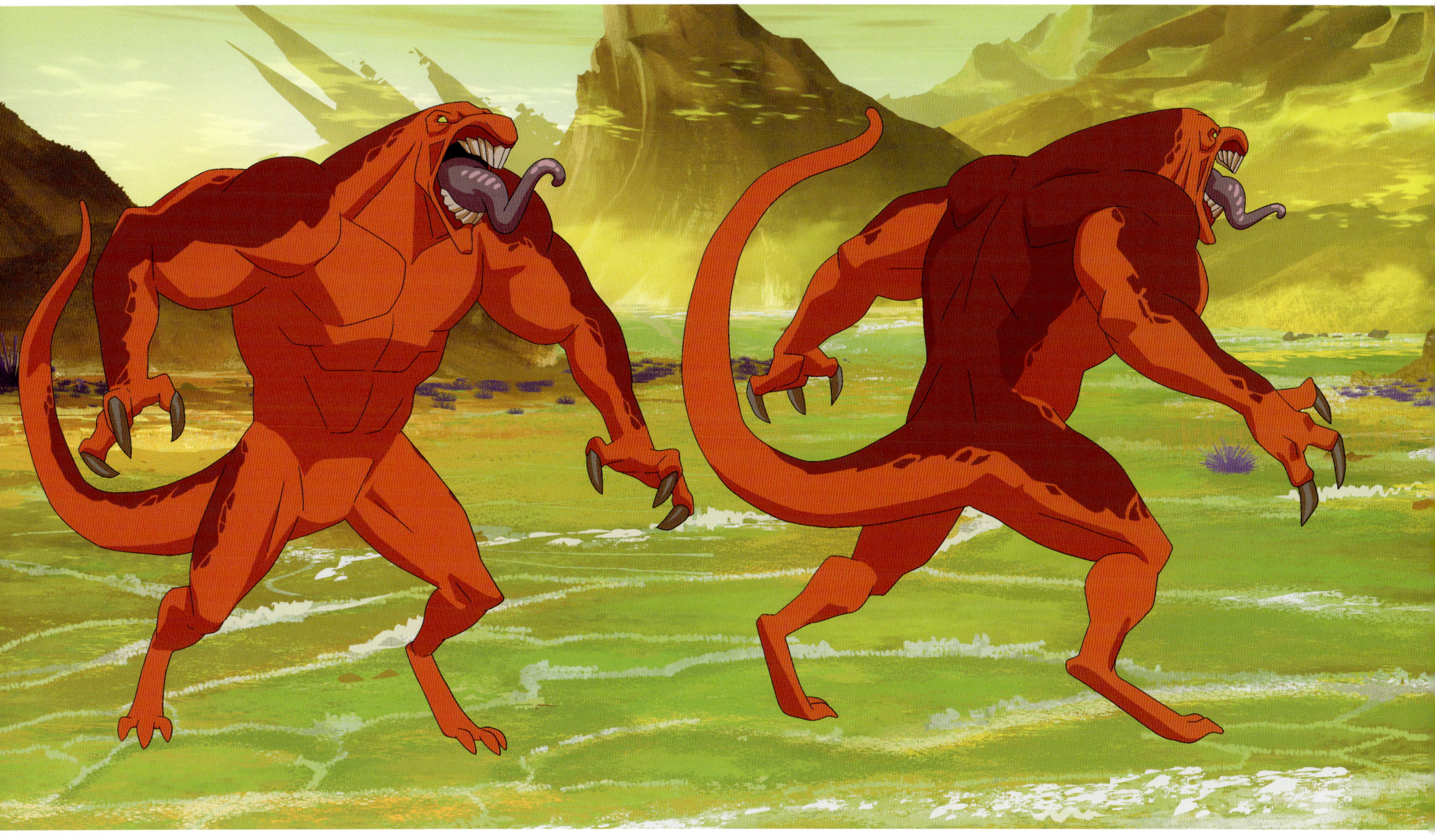

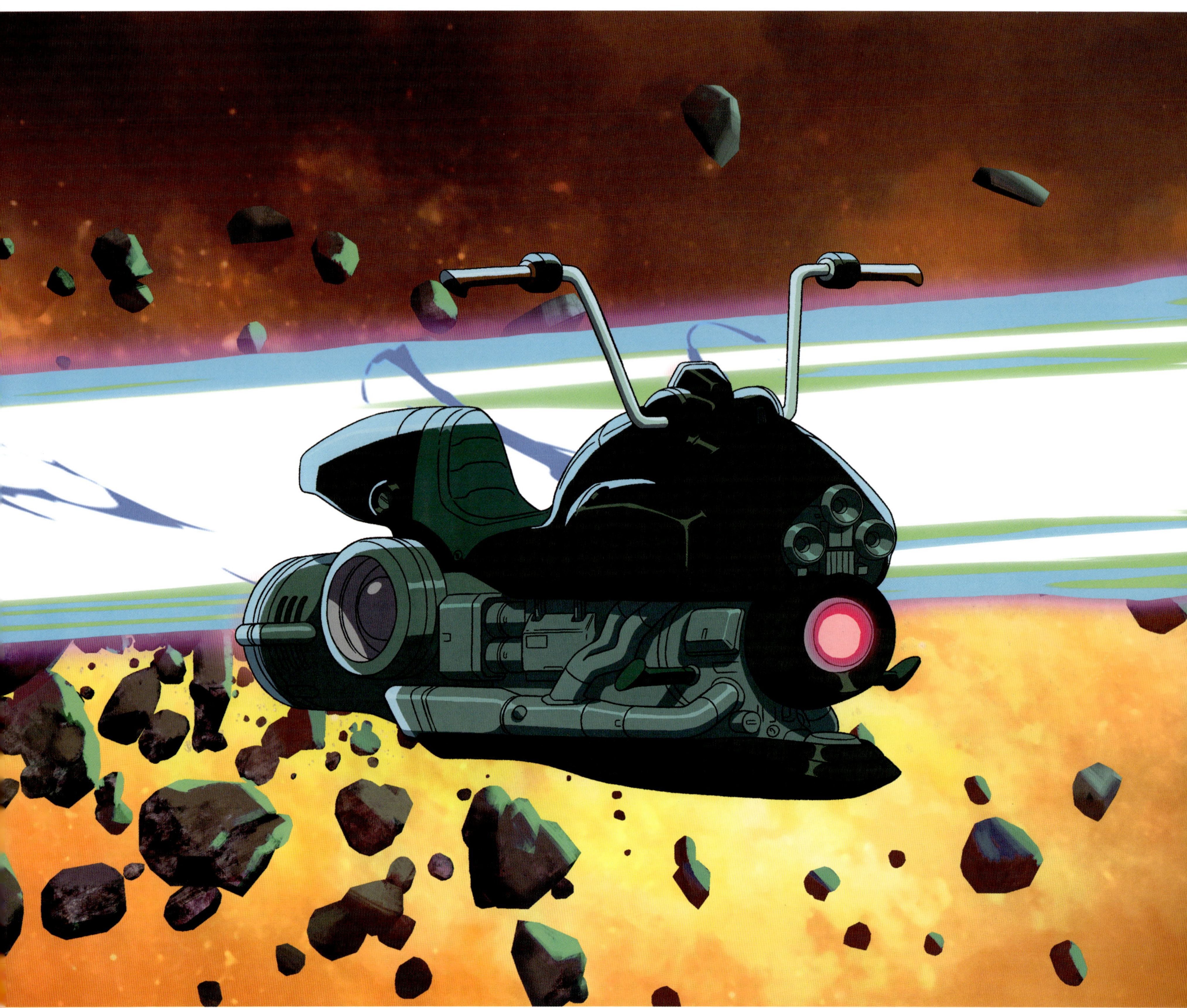

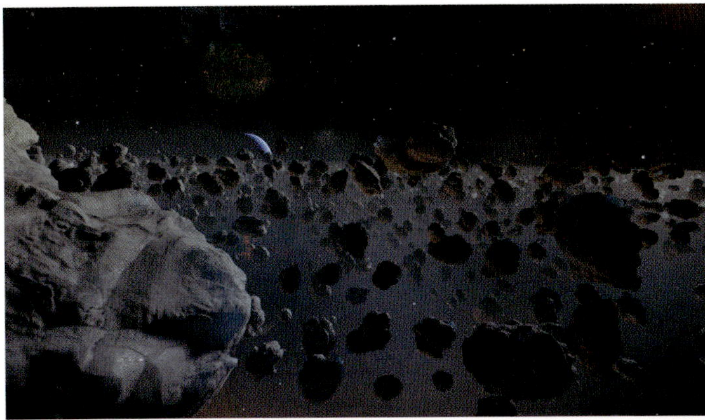

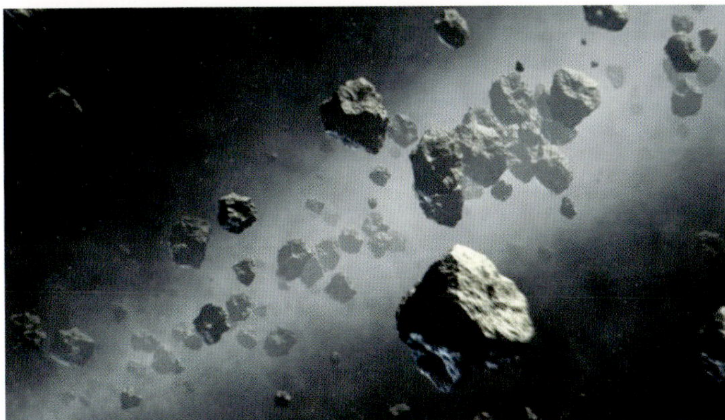

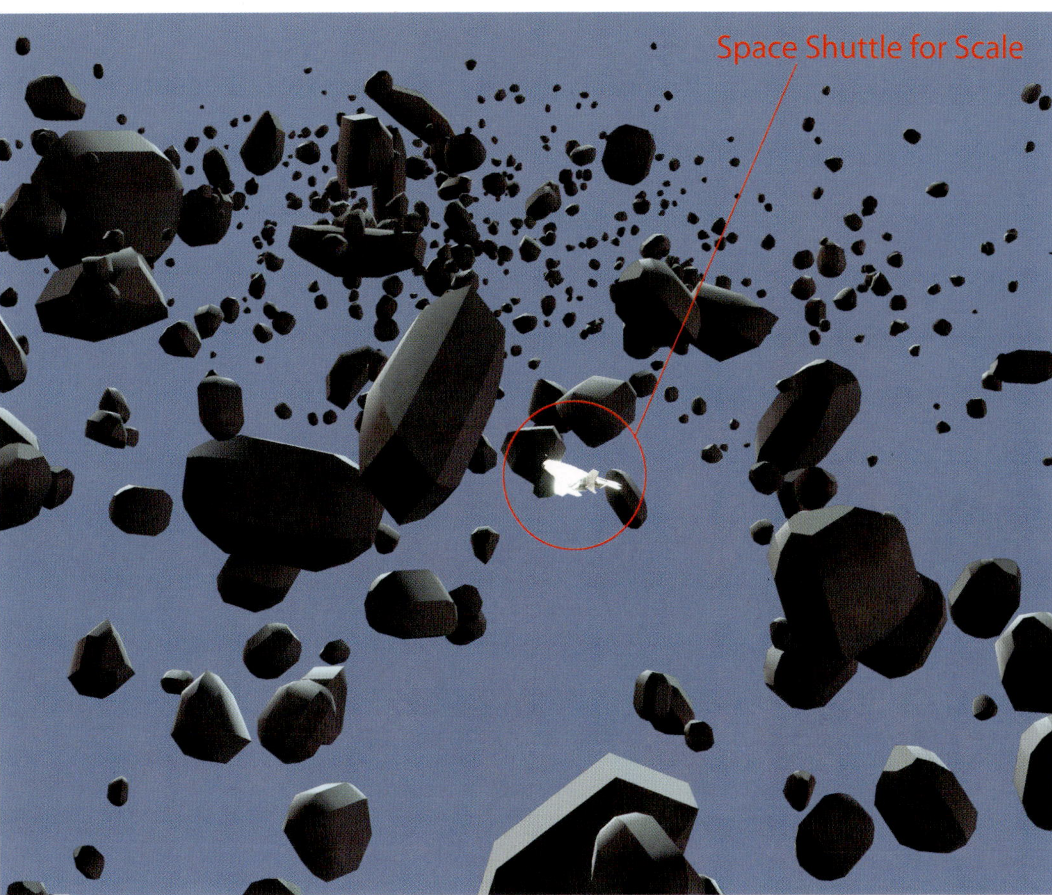
Space Shuttle for Scale

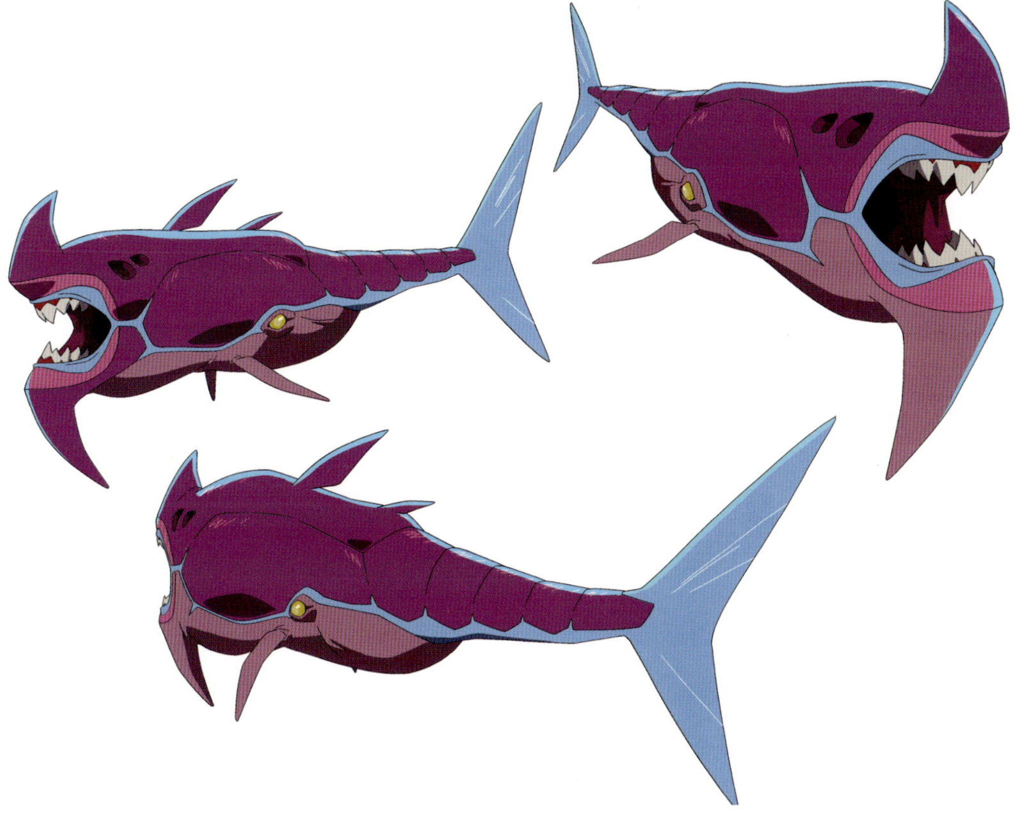

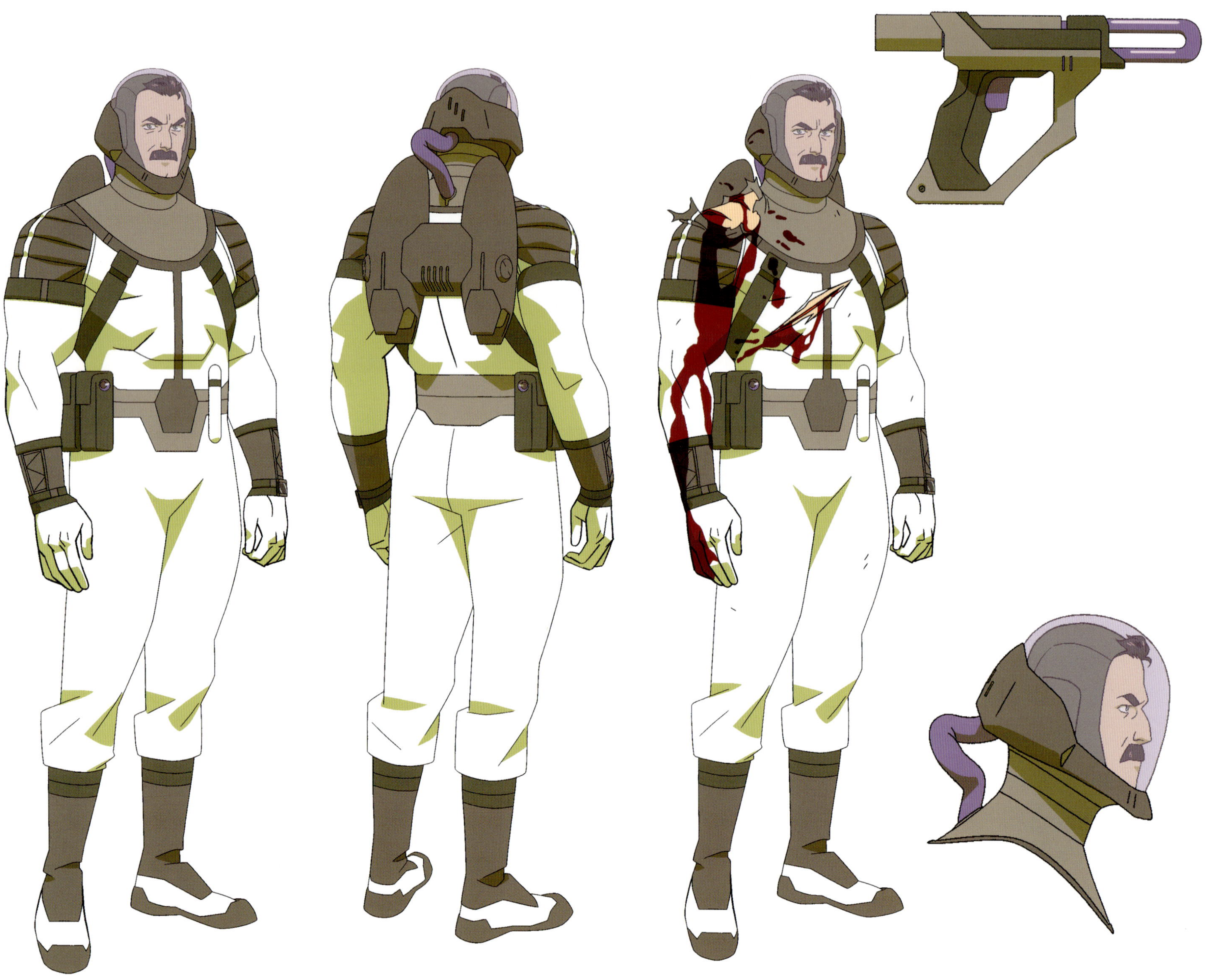

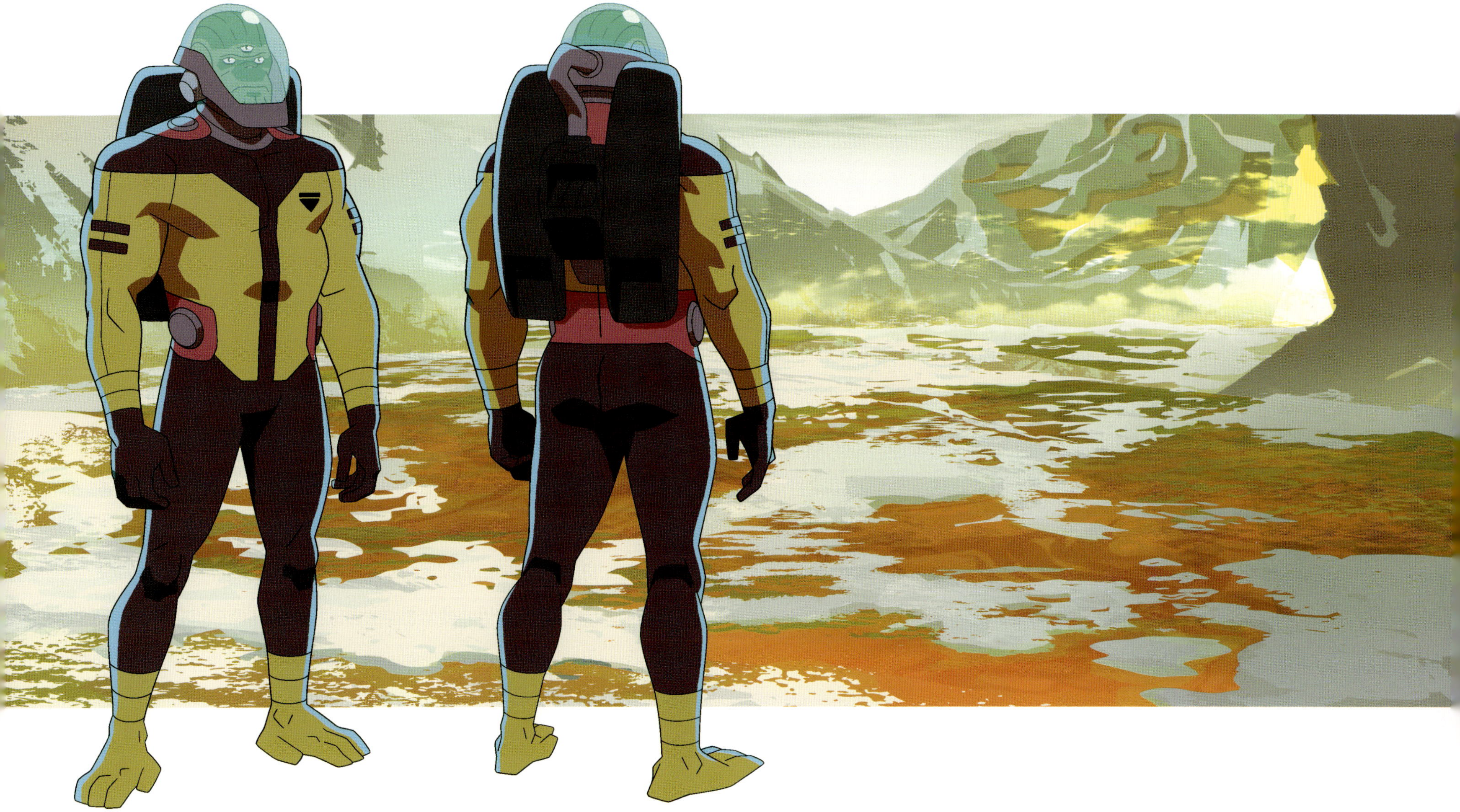

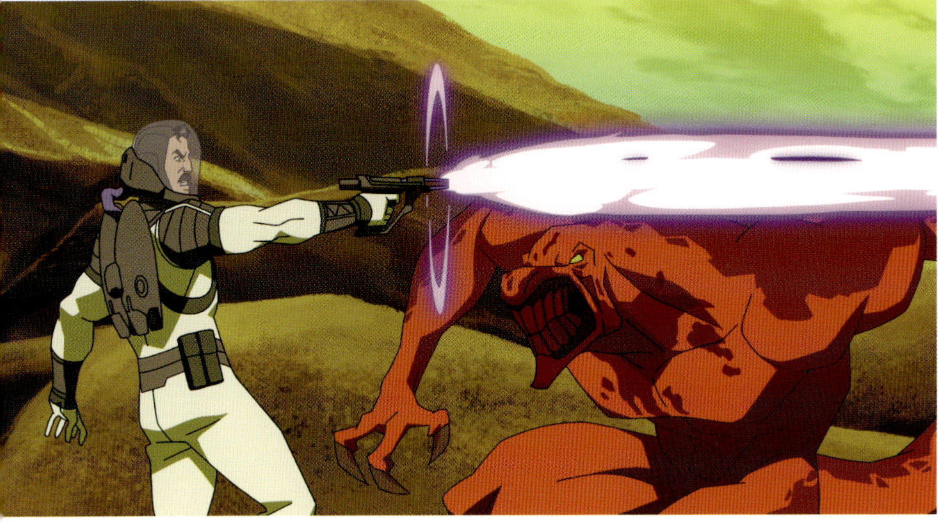

life was a real treat. The Space Racer stuff and space sharks. I always have a soft spot in my heart for the old Space Racer."

"Having hands for feet is a fairly unique element to that character," says Kirkman. "And that was something that we wanted to make sure we maintained."

"We had some really good direction from Cory and also from Robert," says O'Neil. "But big shout out to our Color Supervisor on these, because Ashley [Stoddard] really wanted to push color here. Because these are books. They're stories being told. We're going for something that's a slight fictional version of true events. I think Ashley and one of our painters, Amber Blade Jones, really crushed some of those spaces, really took them to spots

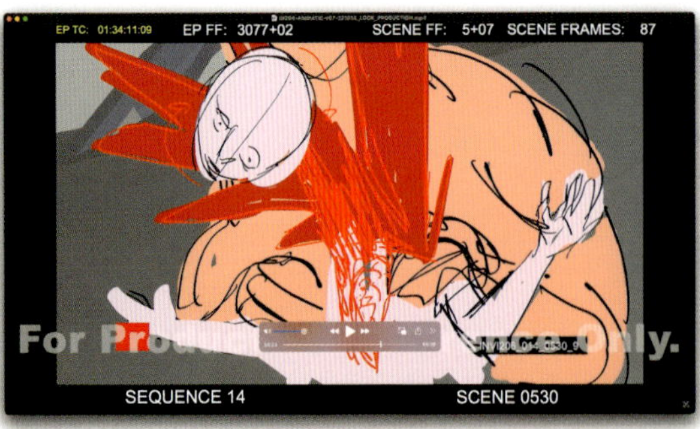

3077+02

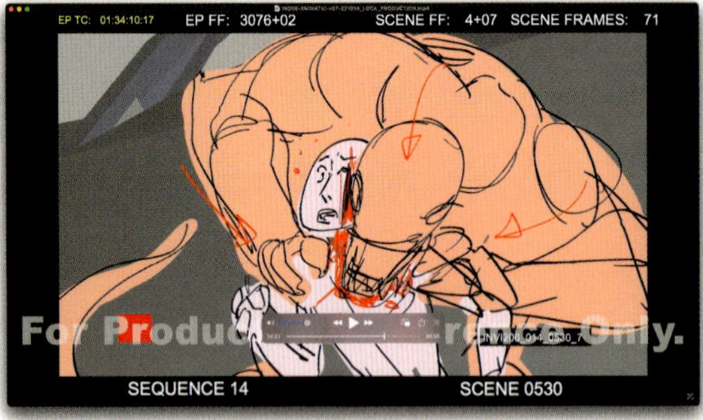

3076+02

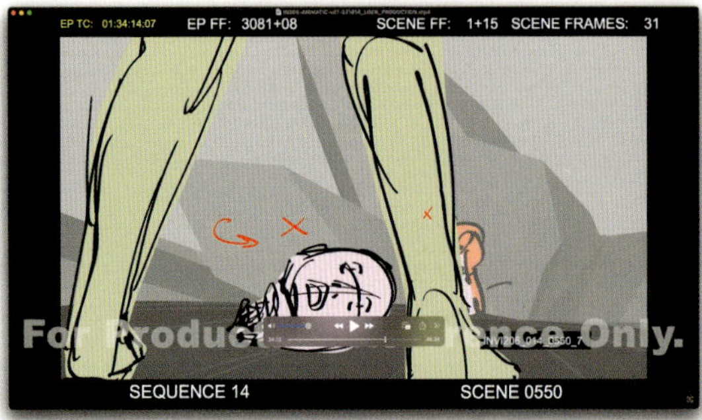

3081+08

close-up

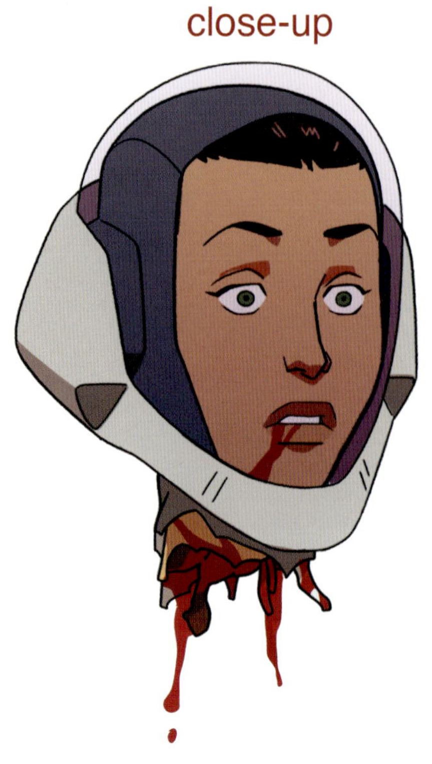

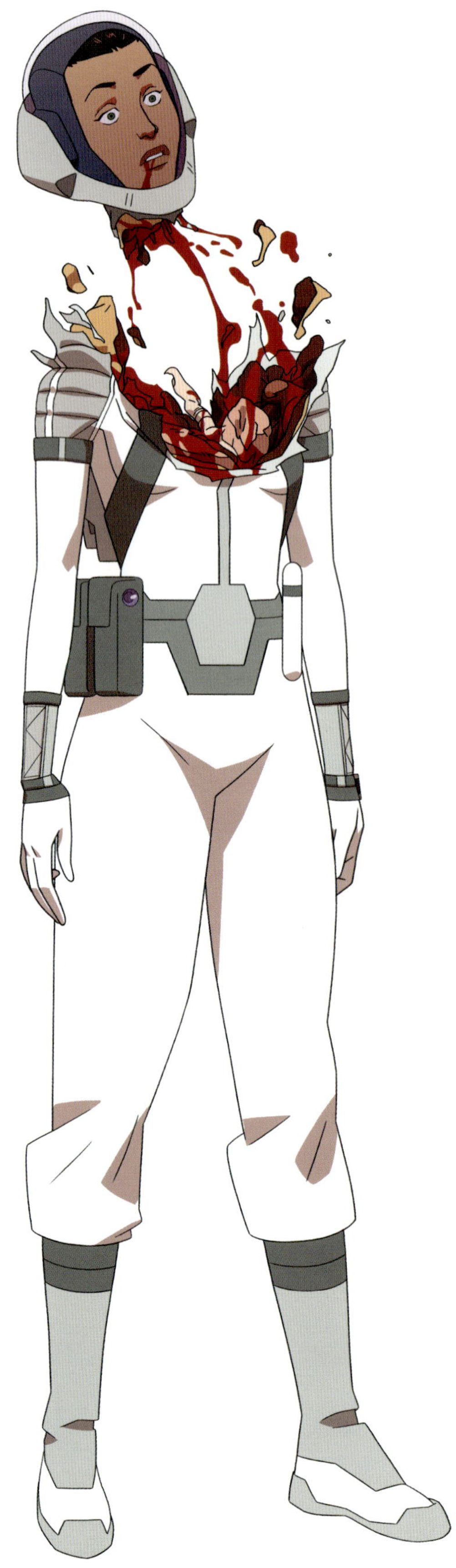

where you're just like, 'I don't know that I would have done it that way.' But as soon as they came in with the color scripts and they had their pitch and they were like, 'We kind of want to do it this way,' it was just like, 'This is great. This is kind of cool. It's different. It's wild. And we should run with it as hard as we can, because we've got some room to move, because these are depictions from a book. We don't necessarily have to hook up with them. We can have fun here and pick up the pieces later.' So that stuff was great. Those are super fun."

Allen the Alien paid a brief visit to Mark on Earth, sporting a brand new costume. He quickly realized that Nolan's books were based on true stories, and they might hold critical information about the Viltrumites' weaknesses.

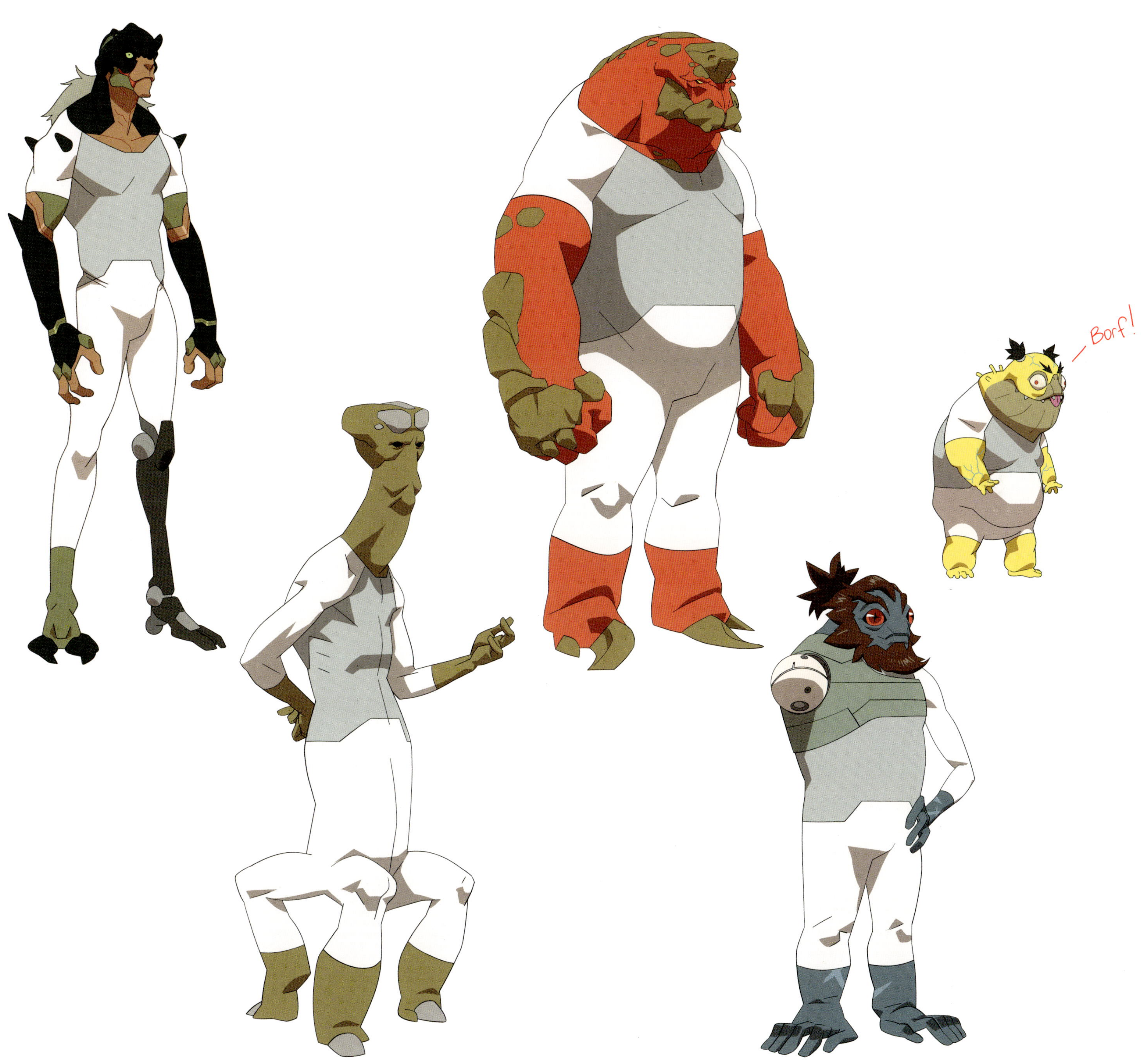
Borf!

"So he comes back, breaks Mark's bed by sitting on it, and then [scans] copies of the books and leaves," says Racioppa.

"It's nice having Allen come back in that green outfit," says O'Neil. "It's one of my favorites. Having him in the Coalition costume... I love it."

While Allen and Mark pondered what secrets might lie in the books, Nolan had more serious concerns. He was on the other side of the galaxy, being held in a Viltrumite prison, awaiting execution.

"The Viltrumite prison comes from a design in the books," says Racioppa. "If there was a design in the books, we generally start there. And so that design is a little more in-depth, a little more detailed, than it was in the comics."

Season One's biggest threat might have been locked away, but Season Two's main antagonist was finally about to reemerge. Angstrom Levy was busy putting the final touches on his plan to defeat Invincible, and he had a freshly tailored suit to go along with his scheme.

"Angstrom was a challenge," says Walker, "especially dressing him in a way that felt believable. Getting that drapery around that big, brainy neck of his. But as ever, I think it came out all right."

It wasn't just Levy's new look that came out all right. The episode as a whole was one that the show's creative team was proud to stand behind.

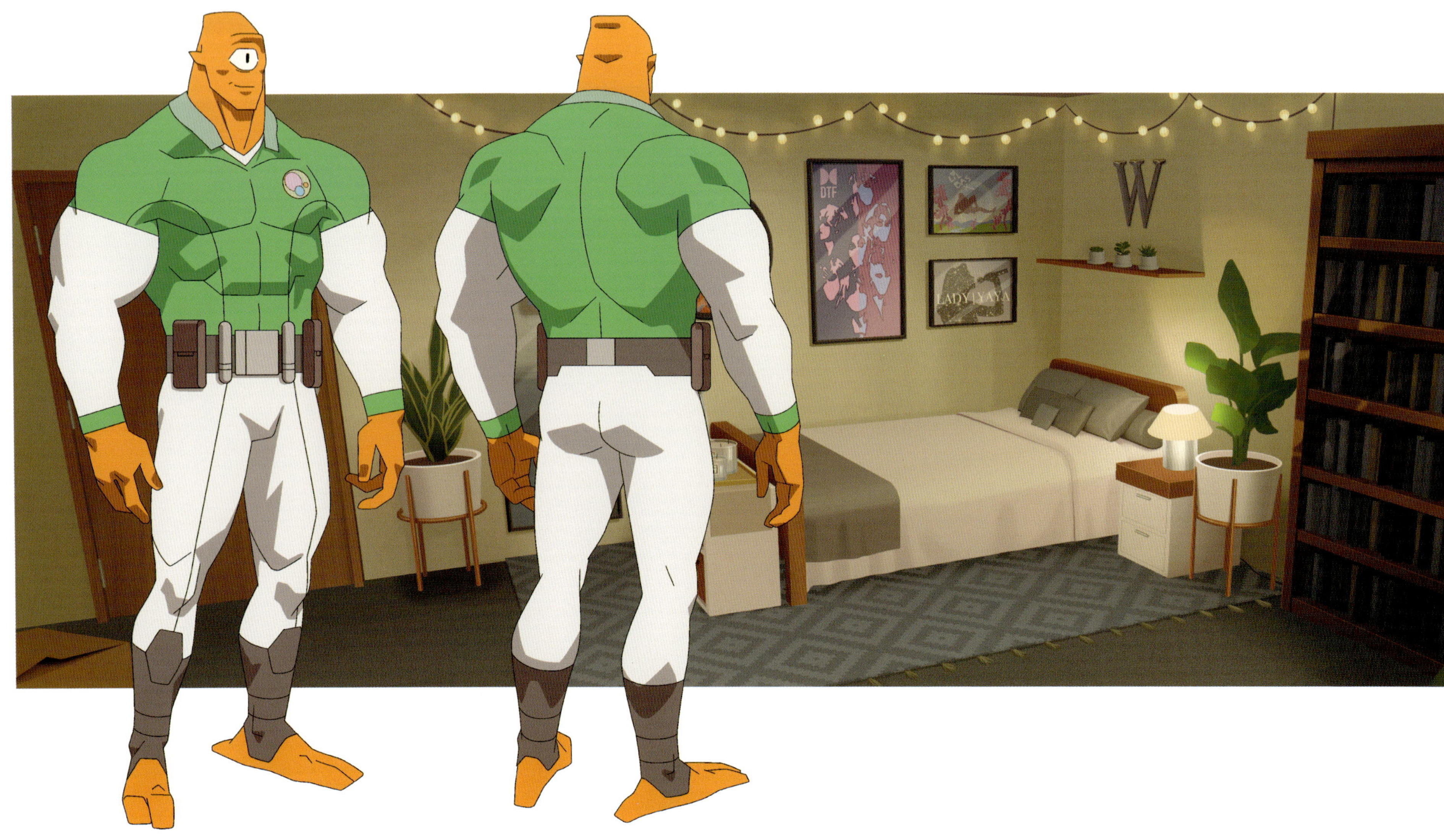

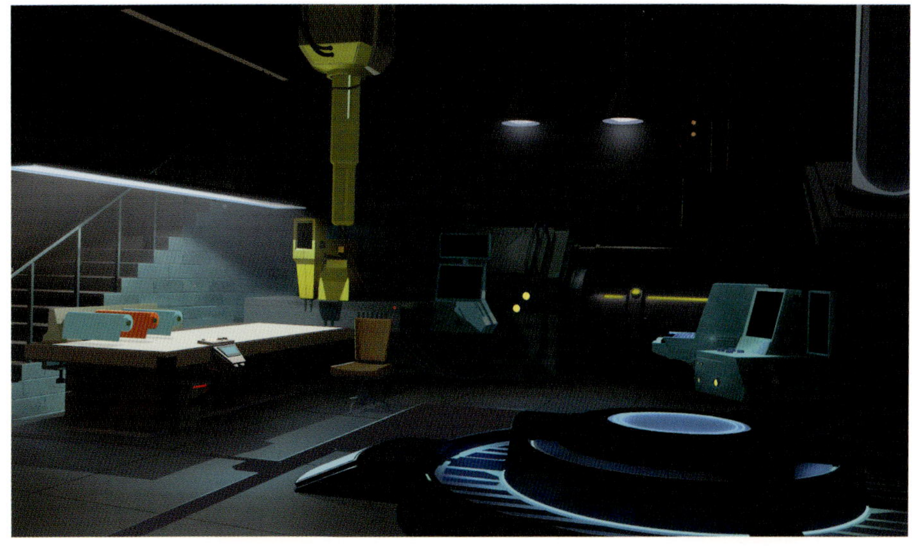

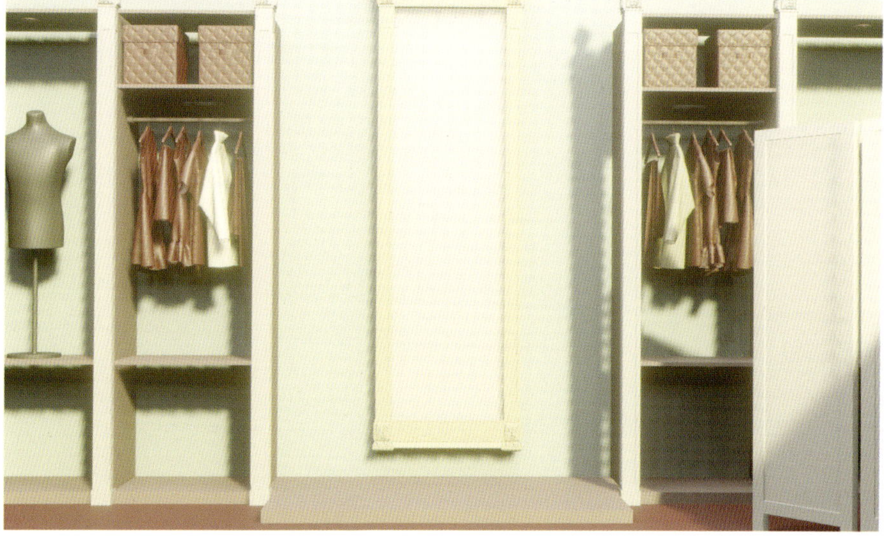

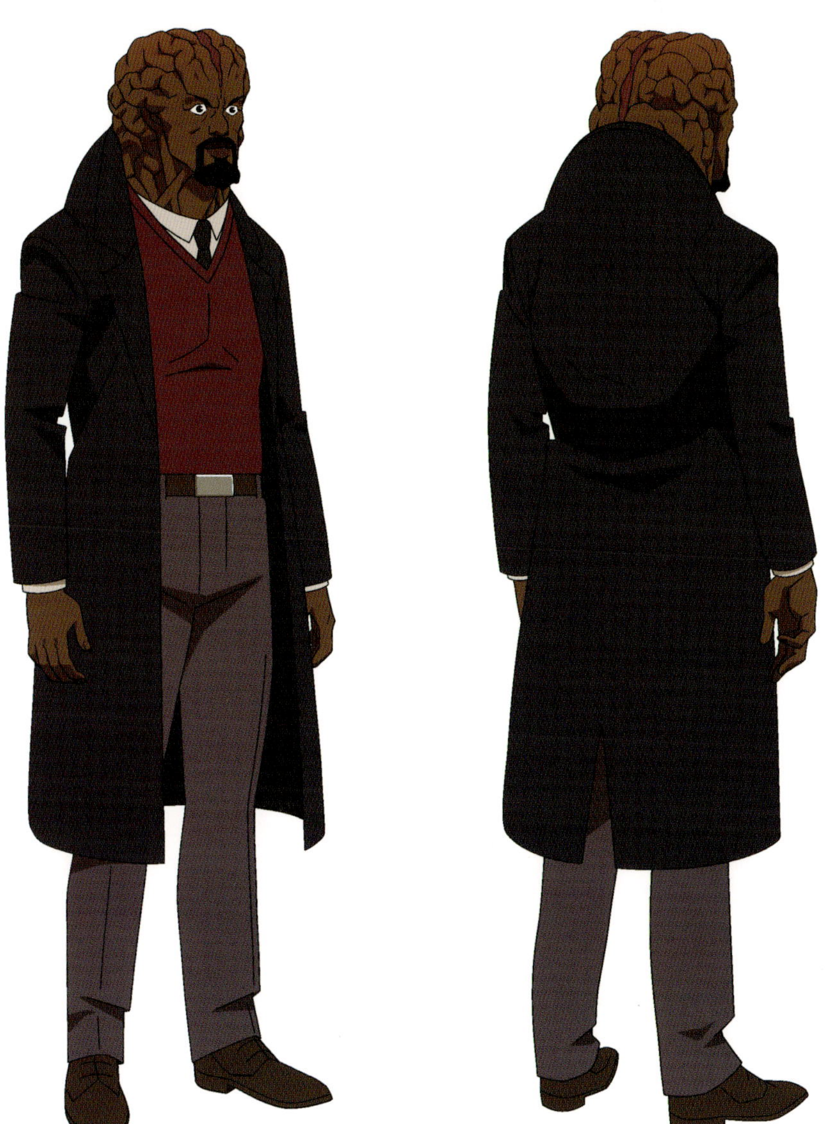

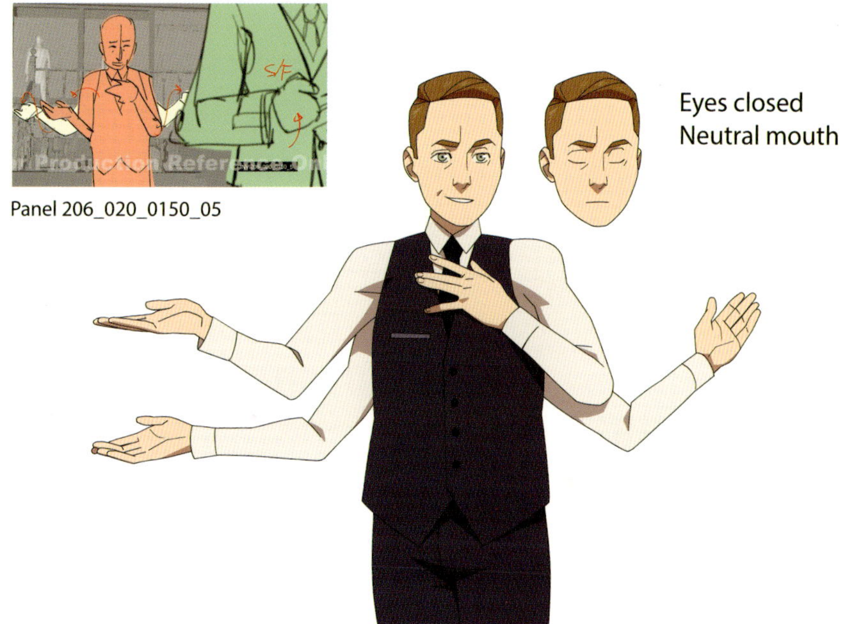

Panel 206_020_0150_05

"Subtlety is a good way to explain this episode," says Duncan. "The music was a little bit more subtle. The needle drops were more subtle. [Director] Sol [Choi] and his team did 201, and this was their second time at bat for this season, and it was a much different episode here. There is action in it. It's got its exciting moments, but it was really about the fallout of the last two episodes, and I think they handled it really well."

But the fallout of this season's events had only just begun, and Mark Grayson was about to be caught in the undertow.

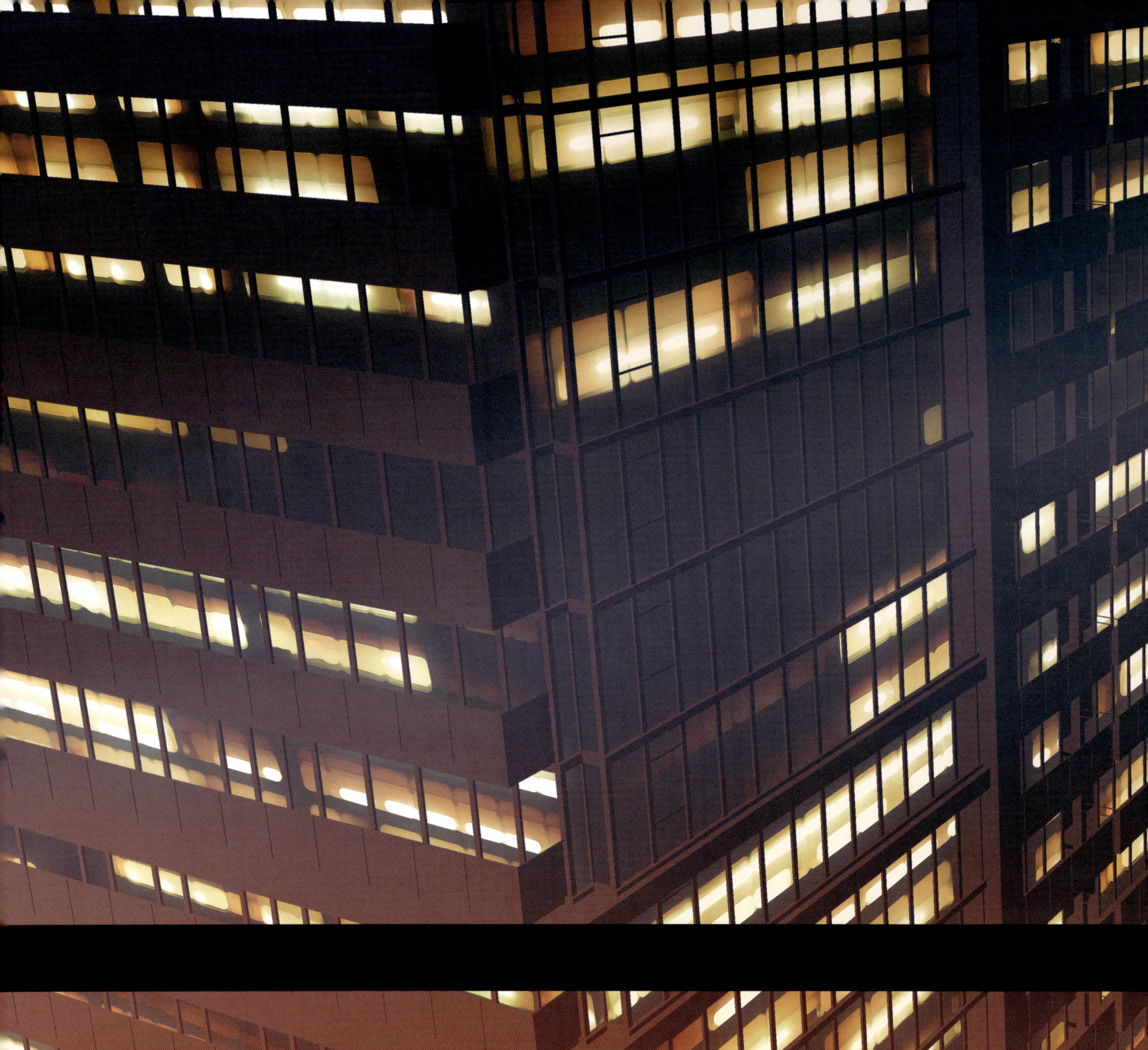

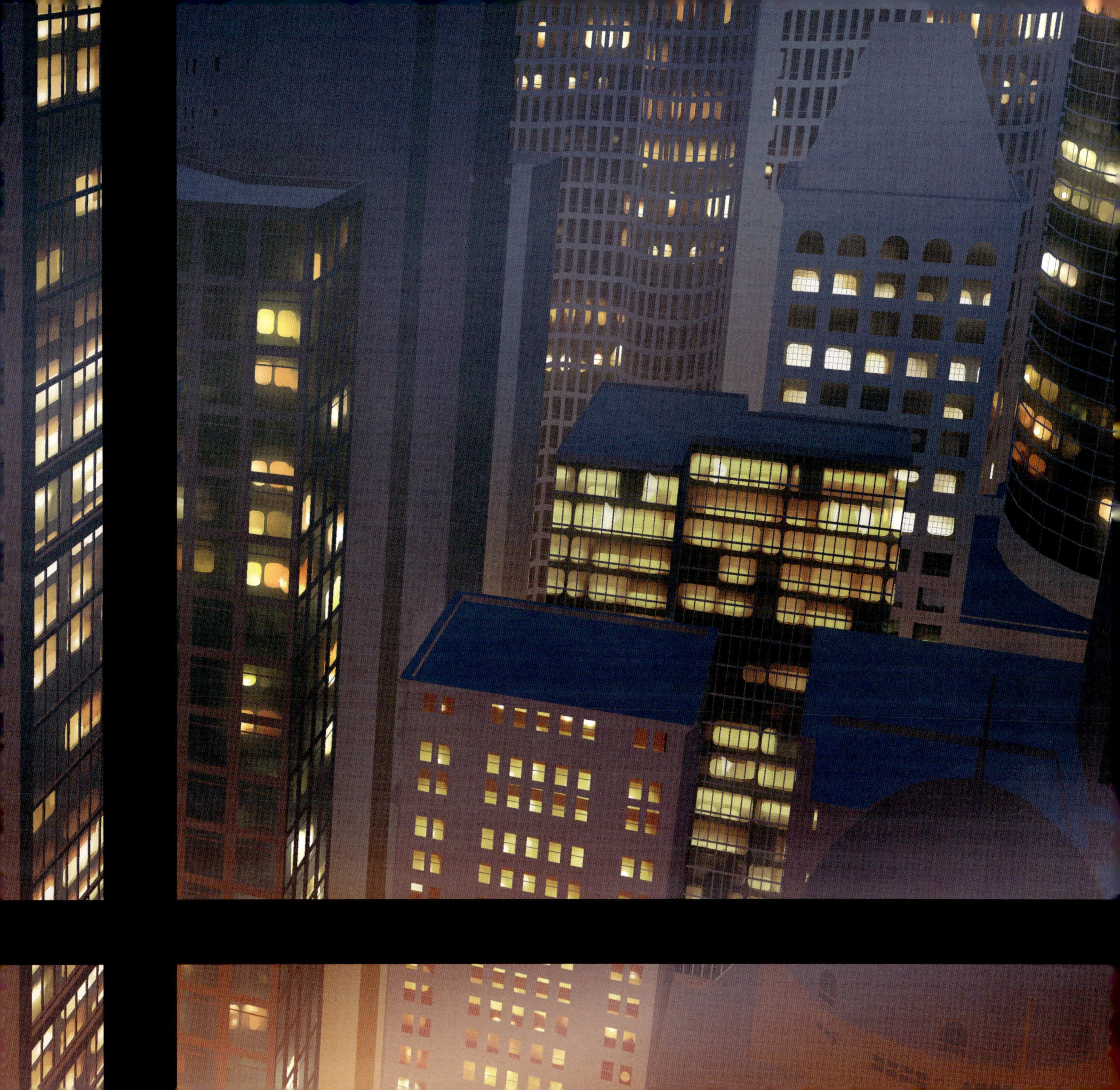

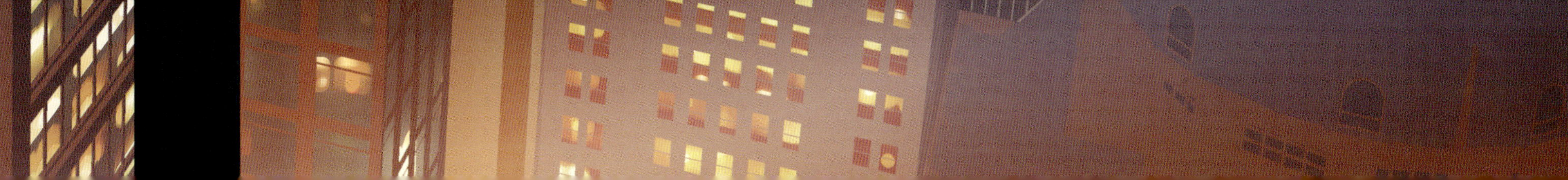

EPISODE 7:

I'M NOT GOING ANYWHERE

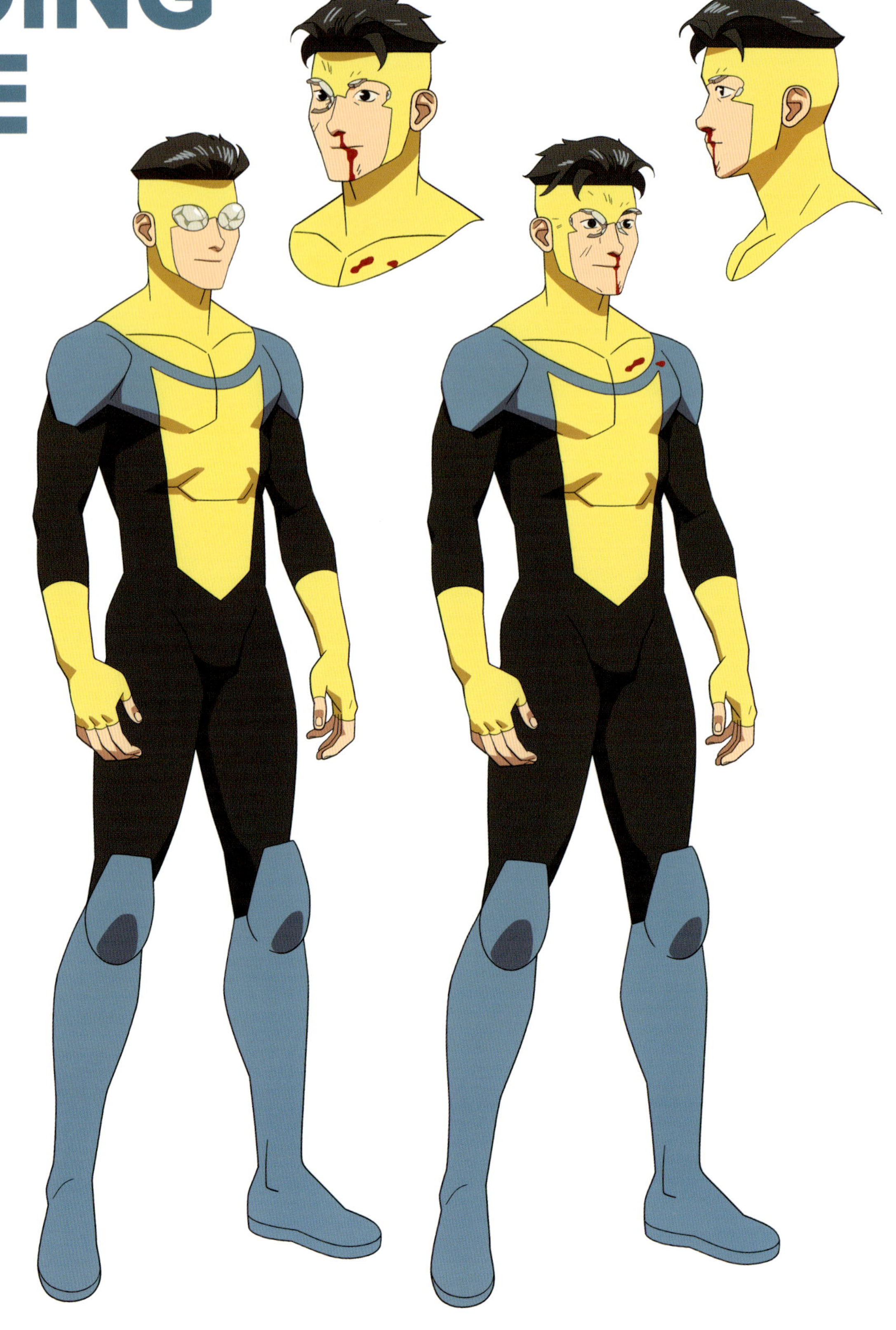

During the bulk of Season Two, Mark Grayson had to put his life as Invincible before his life as a normal teenager. As the season reached its penultimate episode, viewers got a deeper look at how Mark's responsibilities as a hero continued to impact him personally.

"This episode is really important in a way," says Executive Producer and Co-Showrunner Simon Racioppa, "because obviously we've been away. We've been to Thraxa, we've been to space, we've dealt with Sequids. All those things come at a cost to Mark's personal life. And this episode is where all that kind of comes due, for good and for bad. So he returns back. He's been away from Amber a lot of the season. That causes problems for the relationship. And I sort of wanted to make sure to try and portray it as realistically and as evenly from her perspective, as well. She's not saying Mark's a bad person. She's not getting angry or furious at him. She just saying, 'Hey, this isn't working. Of course, you going out and being a superhero and saving lives takes precedence. But also, I deserve to have a life, too. My life matters. It's not superhero-y and as big as yours, but it matters. And I want to have a good life.'"

At the start of the episode, Mark and Amber were still trying to make their relationship work, so they went on a date to a comic book convention. Unlike the alien worlds Mark visited in other episodes, this was a location that many of the show's fans were intimately familiar with.

"It's always a challenge doing a comic con scene," says Co-Executive Producer and Co-Creator Cory Walker. "If you're doing a comic con scene for *CSI: Miami*, who really cares? But if you're doing it for a crowd that presumably is

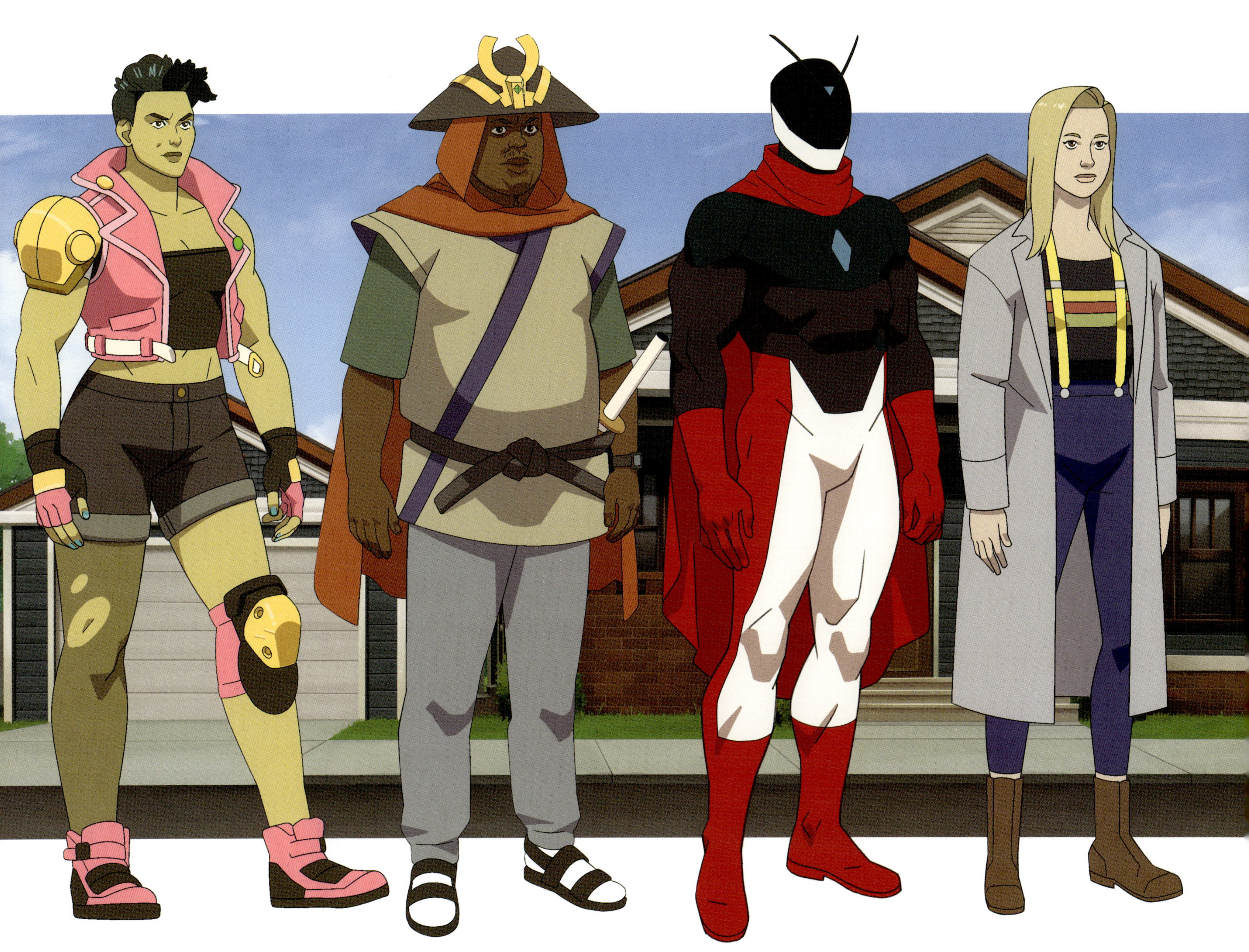

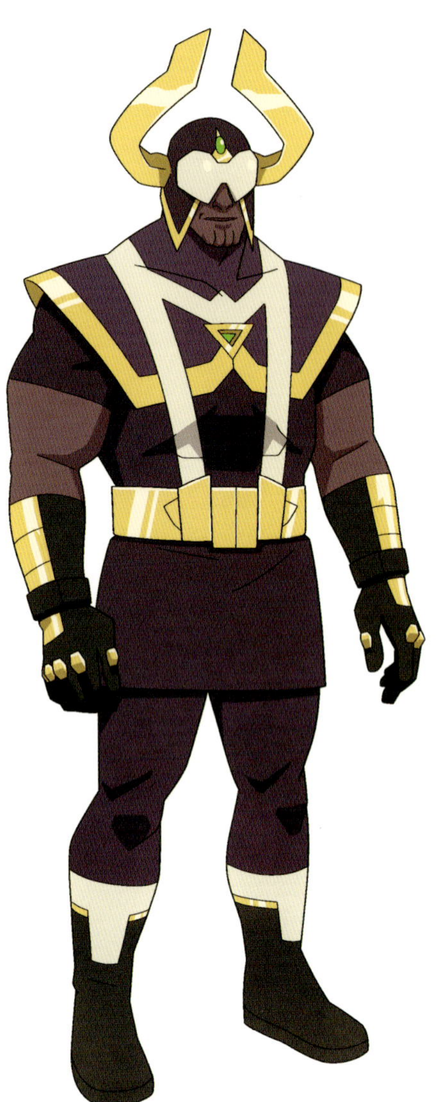

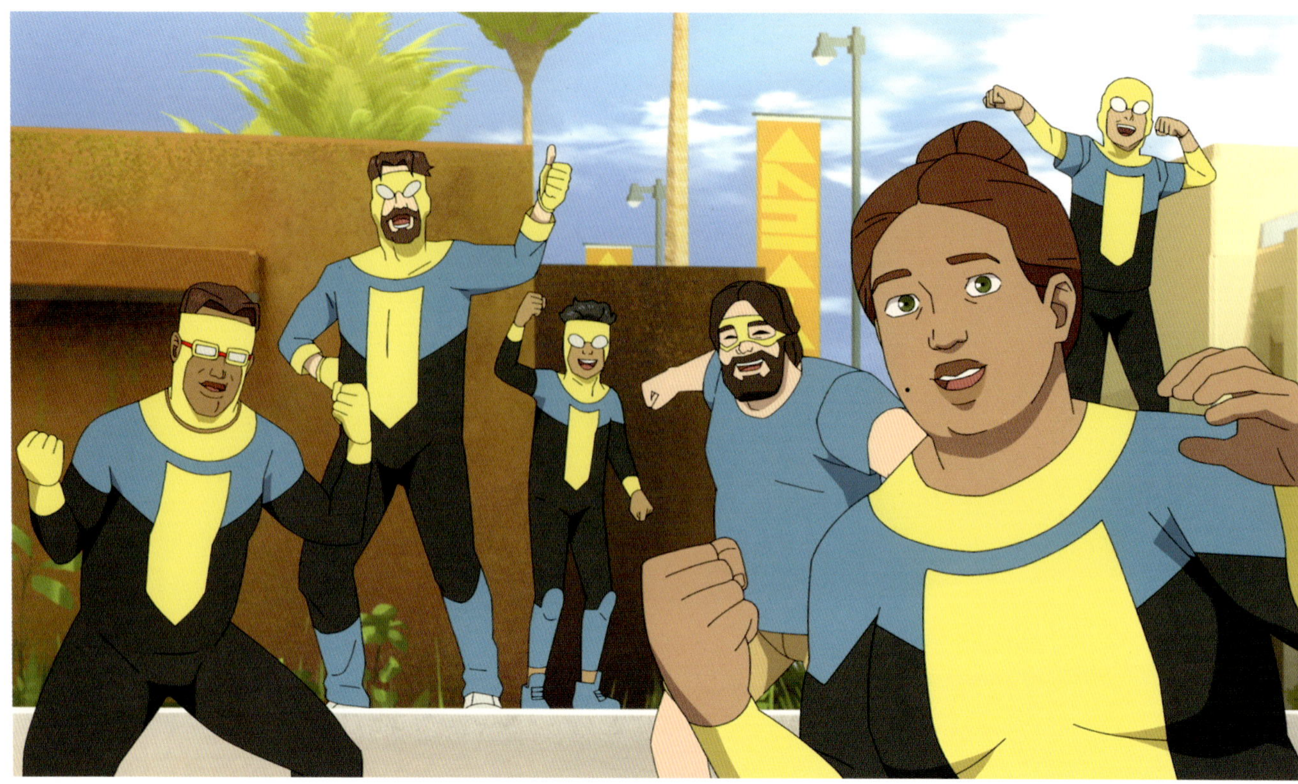

familiar with comic cons, it is hard, especially on the time budget that we're on, to be able to really flesh it out the way we wanted to. I think our hands were tied in some ways there, but it's a challenge. It's always a challenge. But it was fun to be able to do it at all."

"I'm happy with how that space turned out," says Art Director Shaun O'Neil. "In terms of asset count, in terms of how many things have to get attention on screen, that's kind of a nightmare scenario. It's always busy. You go to the floor at a comic con… and it's just swatches of color and detail all around you. So how do you break that down? It was trying to find intersections. Trying to cut off sight lines. Trying to really control how much of this space we saw and how we move through it. And I think the bummer was that we did design a ton more con incidentals than we got to see. I can't remember where the problem popped up, but in the footage we got back, it was just like the same five people on repeat. You're like, 'There's twenty dudes to use. Twenty people of varying costumes and colors.' And some of the stuff that we did were banners for fake things in the background, and then people on the floor dressed up as those things. And we never got to see any of it, because we got to the tail end of it all and we were super pressed for time, and there wasn't the ability to turn that stuff back around. So it was just color swaps and cutting people and moving things to the foreground. I think in the end it turned out well, but it was kind of sad. But it could have been worse. It could have been way worse."

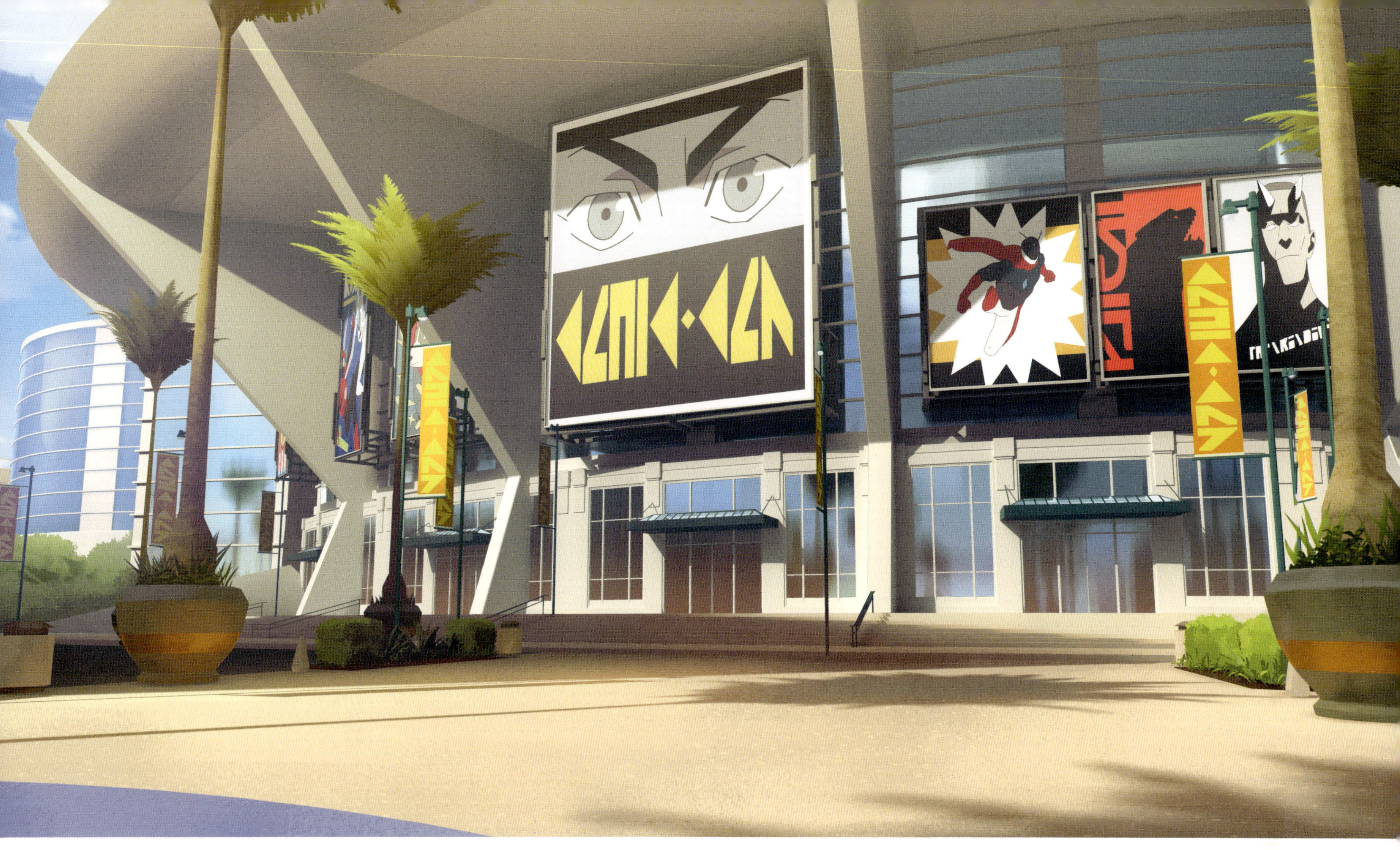

"I wish we could have done more," says Walker, "but we got to have a few incidentals in the background that were new, cool-looking characters, because they're obviously just people in cosplay. Maybe one or two nods to some of the designers' favorite properties."

Despite the effort required and the scrutiny that the scene was bound to receive from its fanbase, it was a setting that made sense for Mark's character on a number of levels.

"We've set up that Mark is a comic fan," says Racioppa, "and then we're like, 'Well, comic fans go to comic conventions.' That's a big comic thing. Also, we promote the show at [San Diego] Comic-Con. And then the idea popped up that people dress up at comic cons. There'd probably be a bunch of people there dressed up as [Invincible], even though he's not a comic book character, he's a superhero. Superheroes kind of fit in. So we were like, 'That would be a fun scene. Wouldn't that be weird seeing yourself, people dressed up as you, at a comic con?'"

"There was a lot of fun to be had with the different Invincible cosplayers," says Executive Producer, Co-Showrunner, and Co-Creator Robert Kirkman, "making them as unique and cool as possible. There's a lot of fun variety that we were able to play with there."

"I think the Invincible cosplayers was the only time where we had to rein some of the guys in a little bit," says Walker, "because they were going a little bit bonkers with what I assume were in-jokes. They had some crazy stuff they had done. It was like, ‘Dial it back a little bit. Just make them look like homemade, shitty Invincible costumes. Let's try to focus here.’”

Mark was less interested in the people dressed up like his super hero alter ego and more interested in the fact that one of his favorite comic book creators, Filip Schaff, creator of Séance Dog, was in attendance.

“In the books, there's a quick scene where Mark goes

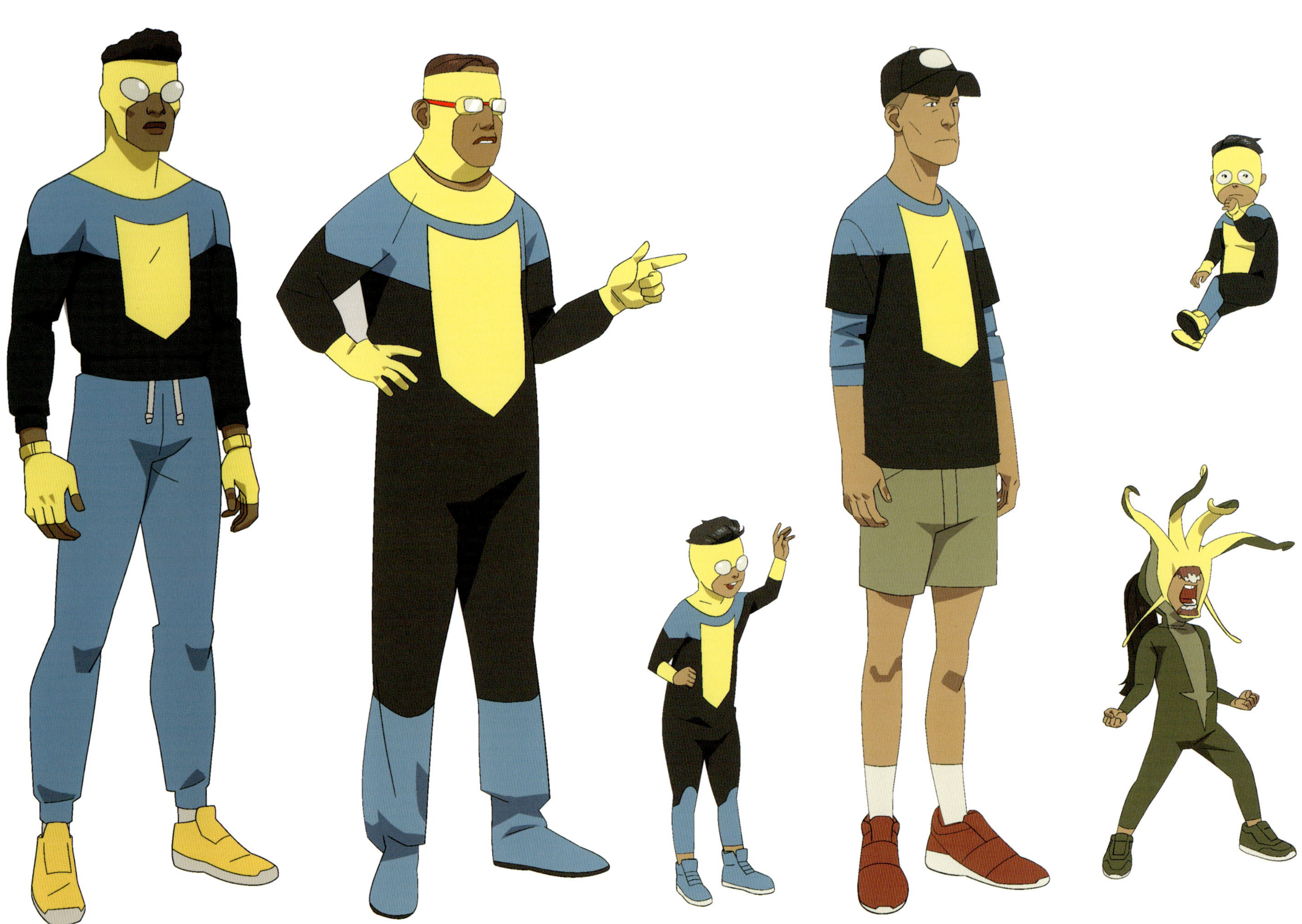

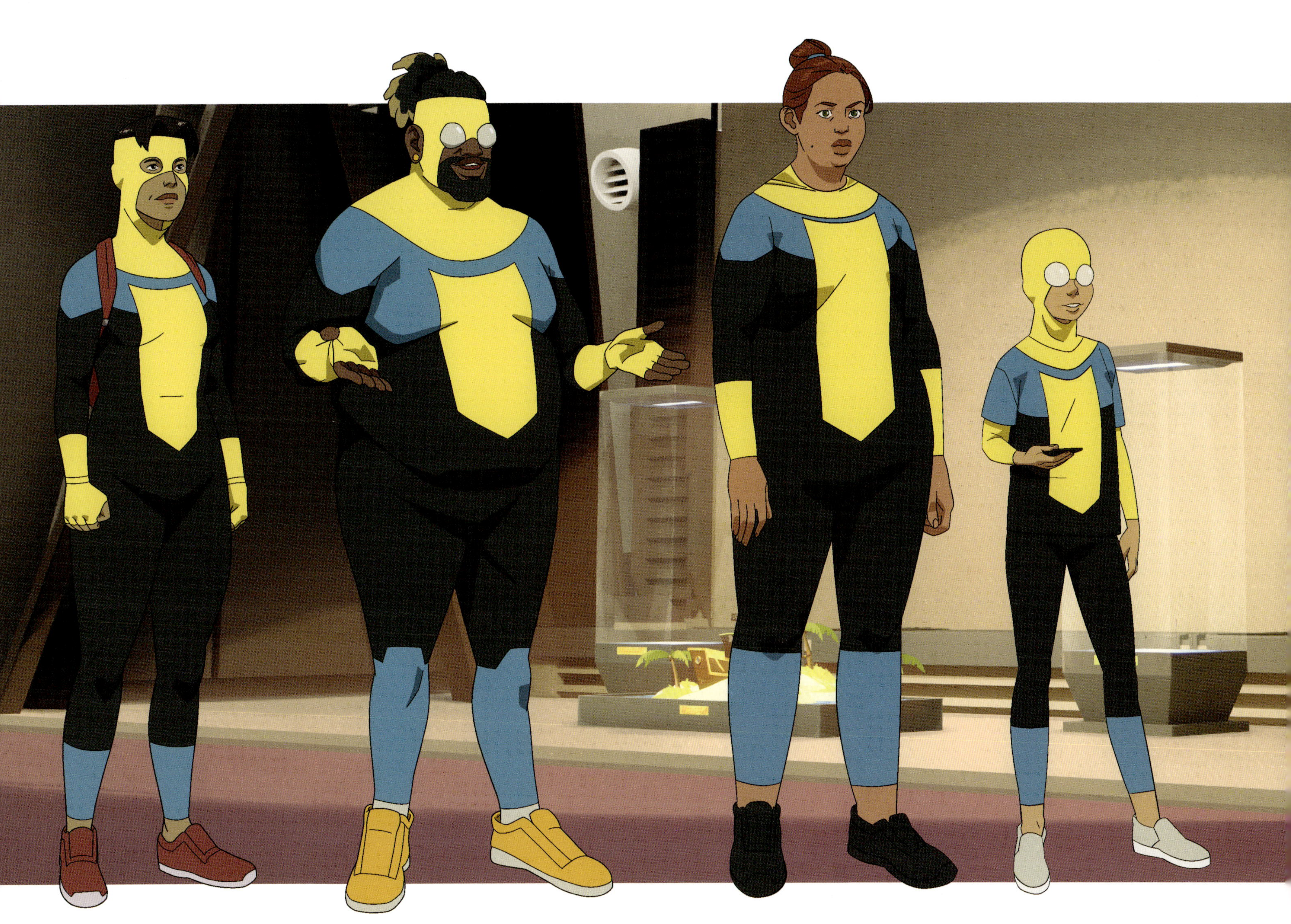

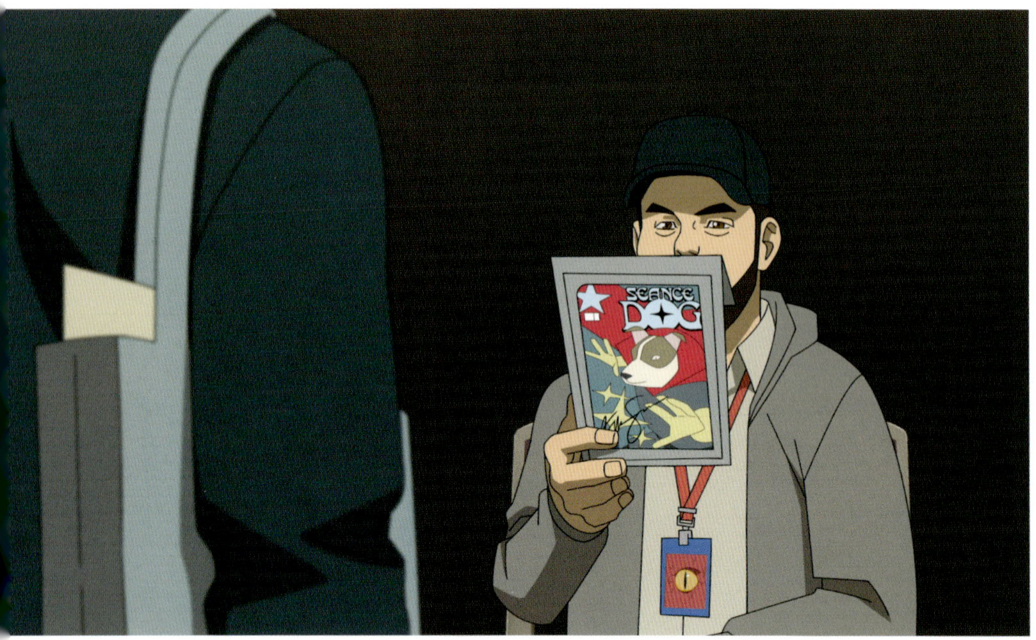

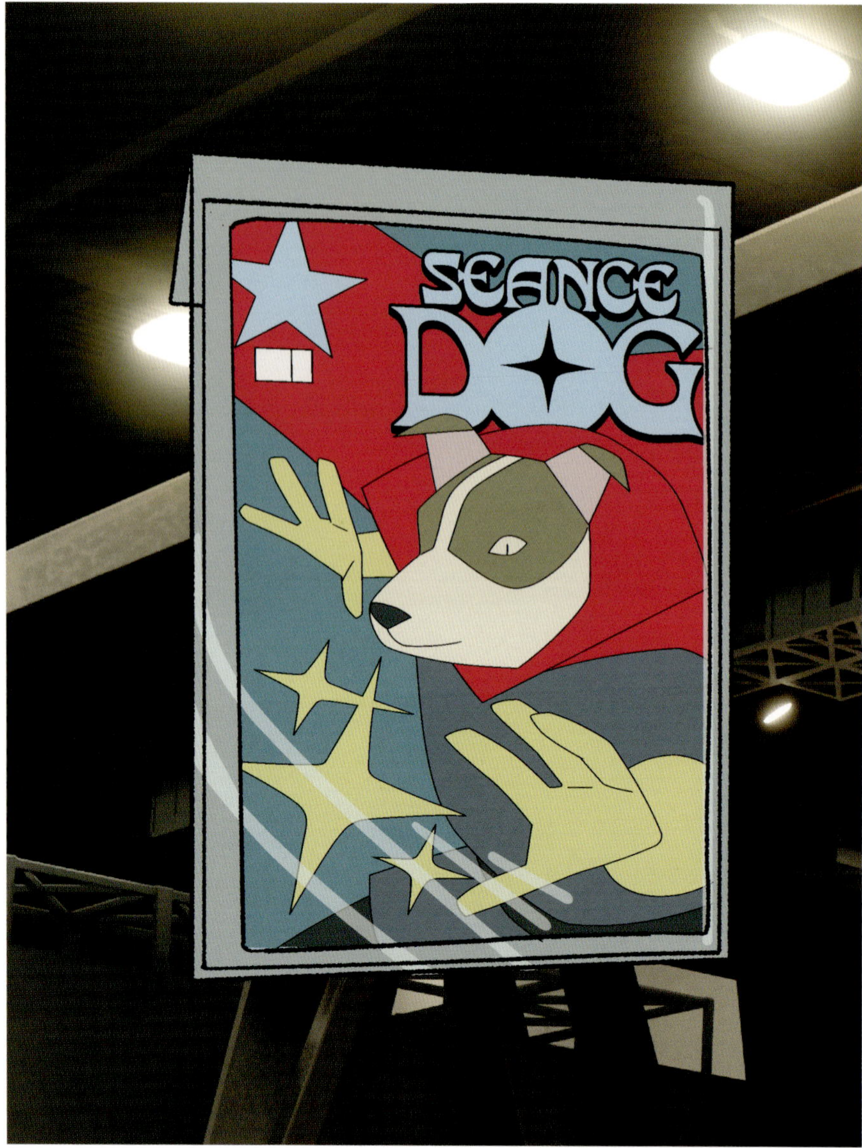

to see Filip Schaff," says Racioppa, "and they talk about how sometimes comic book artists hold the same panel for like six panels, and 'Isn't that lazy?' Filip Schaff is like, 'No, not really.' And they do that gag on the page and it's great. So we were like, 'What is the animation version of that?' So we came up with a couple cheats that we do in the show, like where you have a character talk [with their hand covering their mouth] or you frame them from behind or they're holding something in front of their face. It's stuff that you don't really recognize when you're watching the show until it's pointed out to you, and you're like, 'Oh yeah, of course this happens.' We use wide shots that you think are moving, but they're not moving. Sometimes with close-up drawings, we put more detail into them and they look a little bit too good for the show. All that stuff. So it was a fun sequence to do. And our animation team and our directors really got into it."

"That's all [Supervising Director] Dan [Duncan] and the board teams," says O'Neil. "That comic con stuff, that Filip Schaff conversation, interpreting that from the books turned out really great. Especially some of the quality changes in the picture as the conversation progresses. Really, really awesome. It's good writing to get us there. They started out with some pretty good bones, and then Dan just took it over the top. When we got to the animatic stage, and later in post, you're just finding those places to make some of the jokes really hit home visually. And they crushed it."

"Toniko [Pantoja] had originally boarded that scene along with [Director] Ian [Abando]," says Duncan. "They're a really good team with a great sense of humor, so I was glad they got that beat. It was another one that just

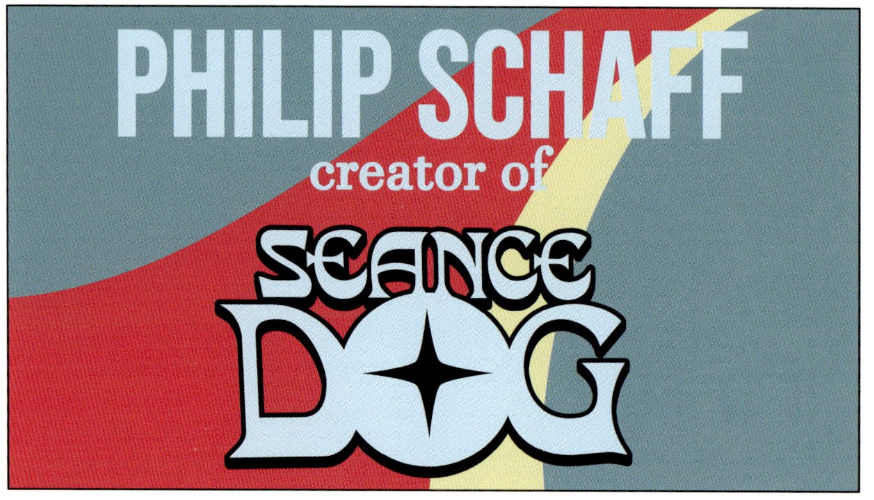

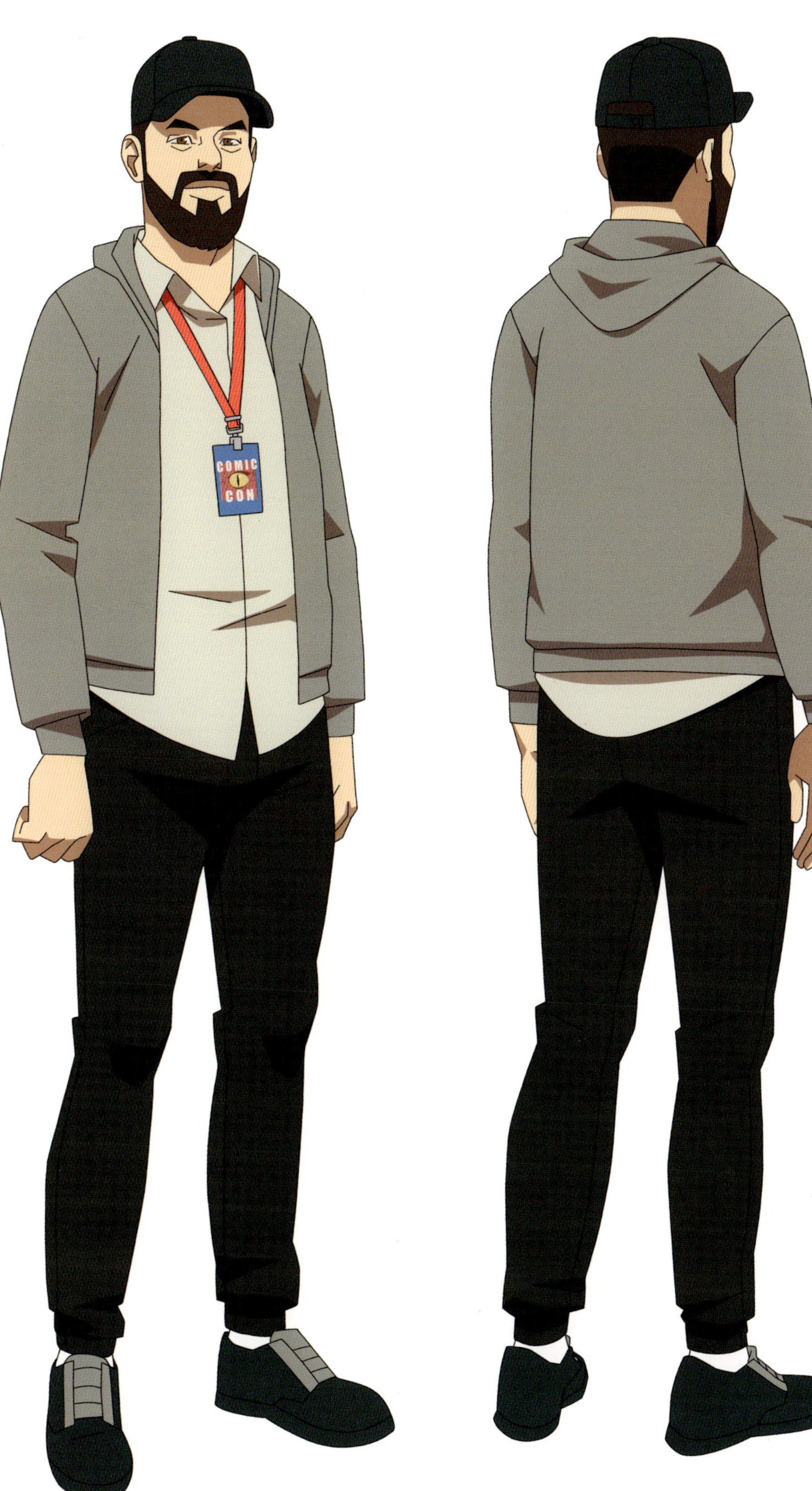

required a lot of nuance, so everybody got to hit it. And I got to jump in on that one, which was super duper fun, and carry it through to post. The benefits of my job sometimes… When we did get there and we had to do the glamor shot of Mark for that gag, I got to do that, work with Shaun to make sure it's all on model and looking good. I'm glad the audience reacted so well. We actually did this stuff in 203, for all of these reasons, when we went to Unopa. There's no animation in those scenes. And so, when you see the 207 script and Robert wrote a whole gag about all the stuff we did, it was fun."

"The Filip Schaff bit was something that Robert has been planning and dreaming about since the day we got greenlit for Season Two, if not before," says Walker. "It was very important that he translate the joke for comics into a joke for animation. So it's great. It was really nice to see the reaction to that. People seem to enjoy it. I wish we could have pushed it further."

The humorous look at the animation process was the clear focus of the fan and creator-favorite scene, so fans may have missed an interesting design choice for Filip Schaff himself.

"When it came to the actual Filip Schaff design," says Kirkman, "I did a thing where Cory had done this really unflattering drawing of himself — just an unflattering self-portrait. And I was like, 'This doesn't even look like you at all.' And so to mess with him, when Ryan [Ottley] signed on to the [*Invincible* comic] book and we did the very first Filip Schaff scene, I sent him Cory's unflattering self-portrait in the hopes that Ryan would draw it. And I basically didn't tell Ryan what it was. He had never met Cory. And so I was like, 'Hey, Cory did the design for that guy. So here's the design.' And so Ryan drew it based on this self-portrait that Cory did, not knowing that that's what Cory looked like. And then when the book came out, people were like, 'Oh, it looks like Cory.' Cory's that much of a great artist that his intent kind of shone through. So even though it's an unflattering portrayal of Cory, it still did kind of look a little bit like Cory in the same way that I look like every fat guy with a beard. So when it came to the show, Cory had the idea that, instead

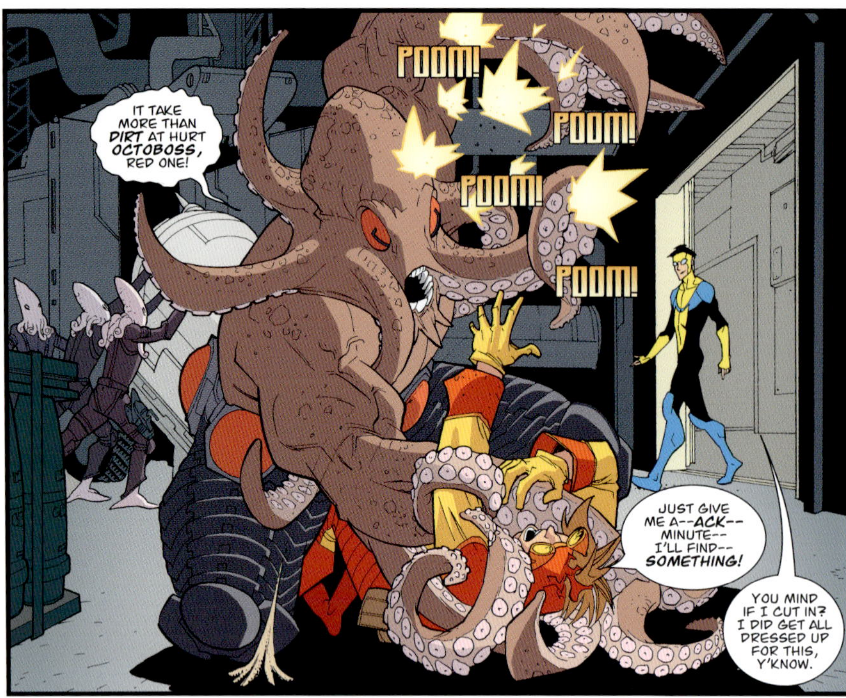

of making it an unflattering portrayal of himself, we would make it an overly flattering portrayal of Ryan Ottley. Because Ryan has, I'm going to say, gotten handsome in recent years as he has dropped a lot of weight. And so we thought it would be funny to just do an absolute dreamboat version of Ryan Ottley for Filip Schaff. And so that's what that design has ended up being. And again, it's unintentionally become a much more accurate portrayal of Ryan than we thought it was."

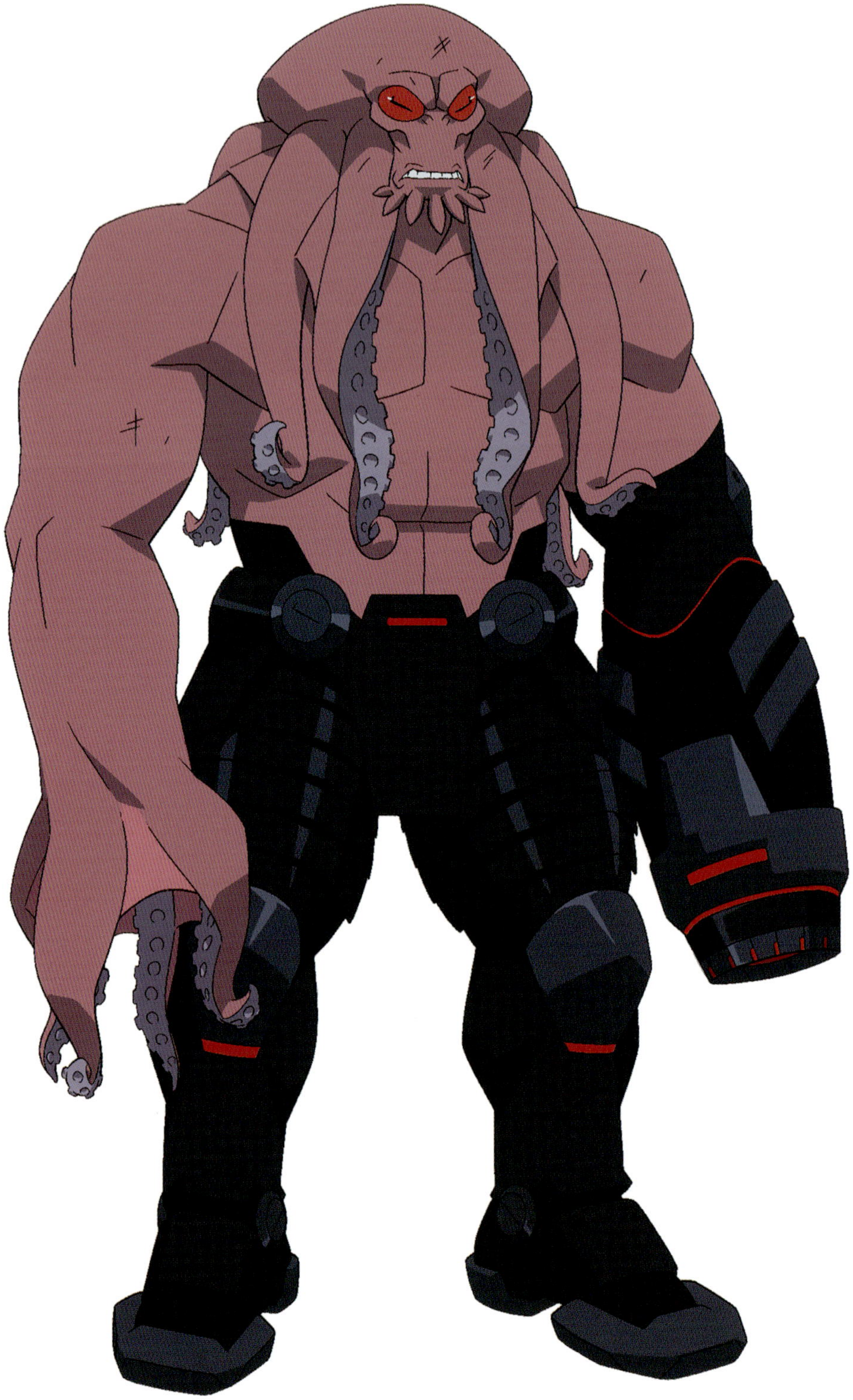

While Mark and Amber were enjoying comic books and inside jokes, Rex Splode was working through the trauma from his encounter with the Lizard League by getting back into action. His opponent was a villain making his first appearance in the animated series, the menacing mollusk known as Octoboss.

"Honestly, one of my favorite characters from the comics," says Kirkman. "I love writing Octoboss. I love his dialogue. It makes absolutely no sense. There are no rules as to what his dialogue does or how his dialogue works. So it's really hard to replicate. It's literally just like, 'This sounds interesting to me.' And so it's completely inconsistent, but I think it's fun. I guess Octoboss was an original design by

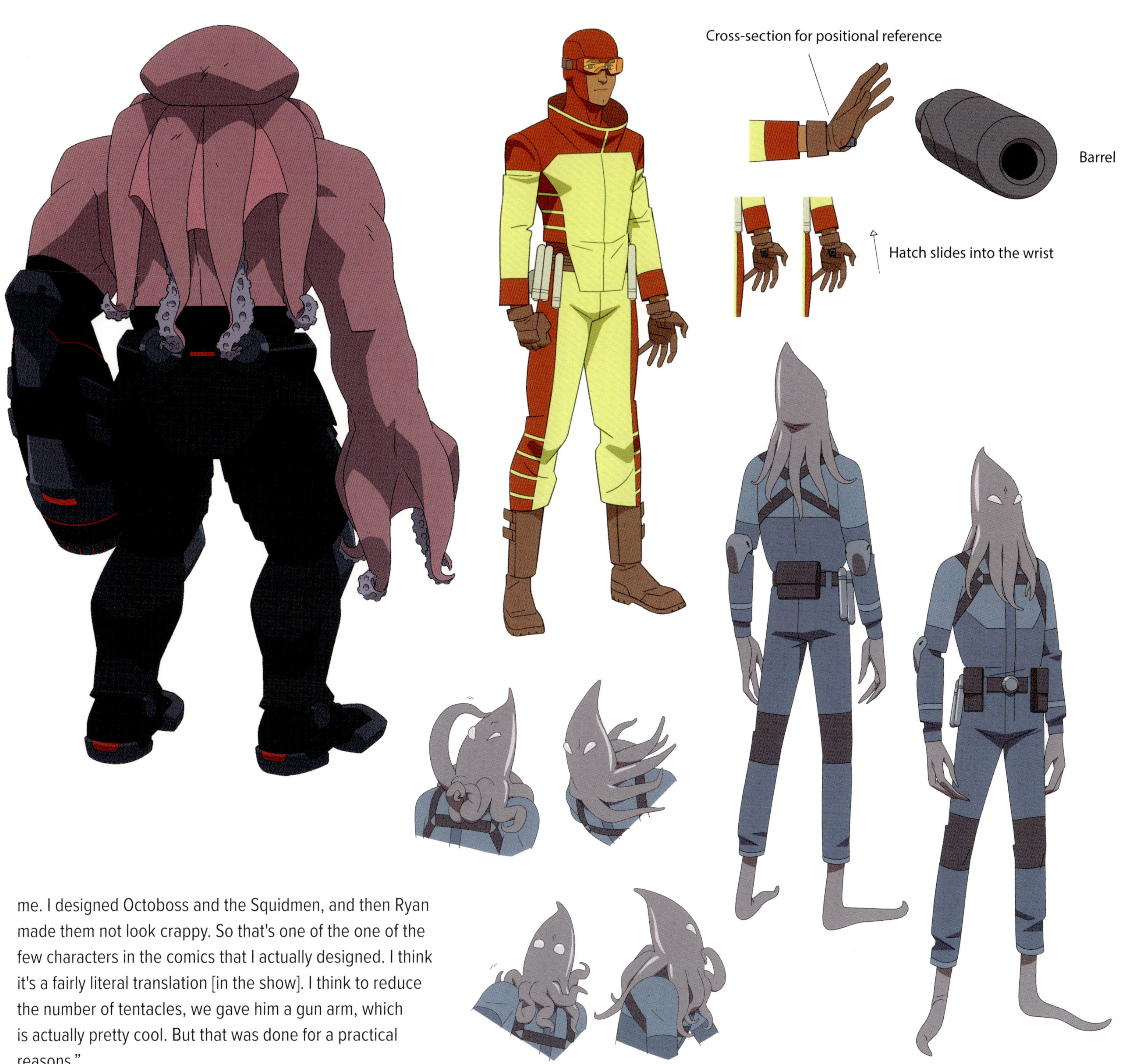

me. I designed Octoboss and the Squidmen, and then Ryan made them not look crappy. So that's one of the one of the few characters in the comics that I actually designed. I think it's a fairly literal translation [in the show]. I think to reduce the number of tentacles, we gave him a gun arm, which is actually pretty cool. But that was done for a practical reasons."

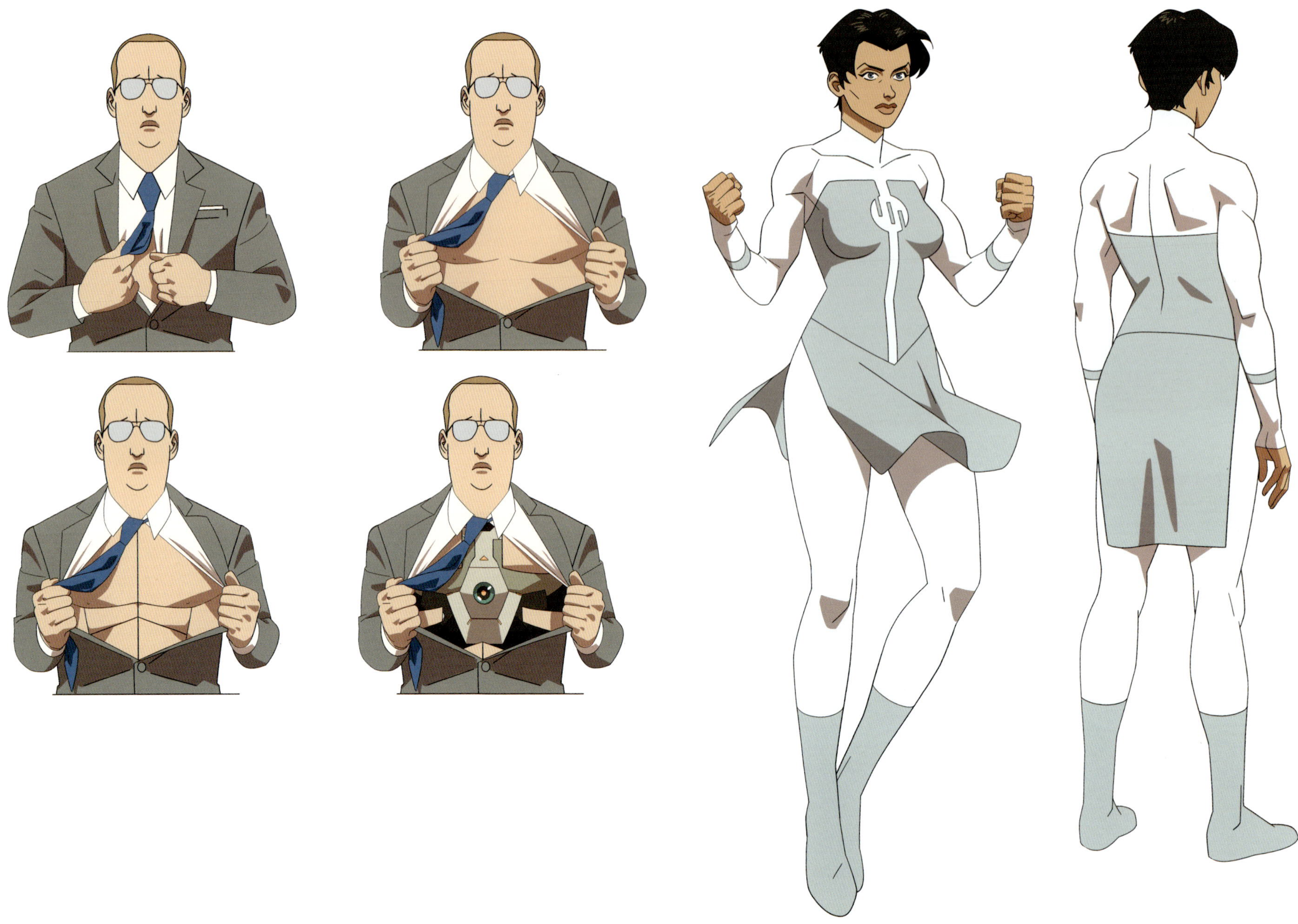

On the Upstate University campus, Mark's best friend and occasional roommate, William Clockwell, was trying to help his boyfriend Rick reacclimate to normal life after his transformation into one of mad scientist D.A. Sinclair's Reanimen in Season One.

"William and Rick, they're at university," says Racioppa. "I feel like they kind of help ground Mark a little bit, because they're like, 'Hey, we're normal people and we're friends and we just have to have lives, too.' And even though Rick's obviously gone through a fairly terrible experience, it helps to show Mark that these things have influences beyond just the superhero. These things that he's dealing with affect normal people — his friends, his family, his relationships. And even for the best heroes, there's a price to pay for being a hero, even when you're doing everything right."

The Global Defense Agency's Donald Ferguson paid the couple a visit, sharing his perspective with Rick. Donald himself had only recently learned that he had died 39 times,

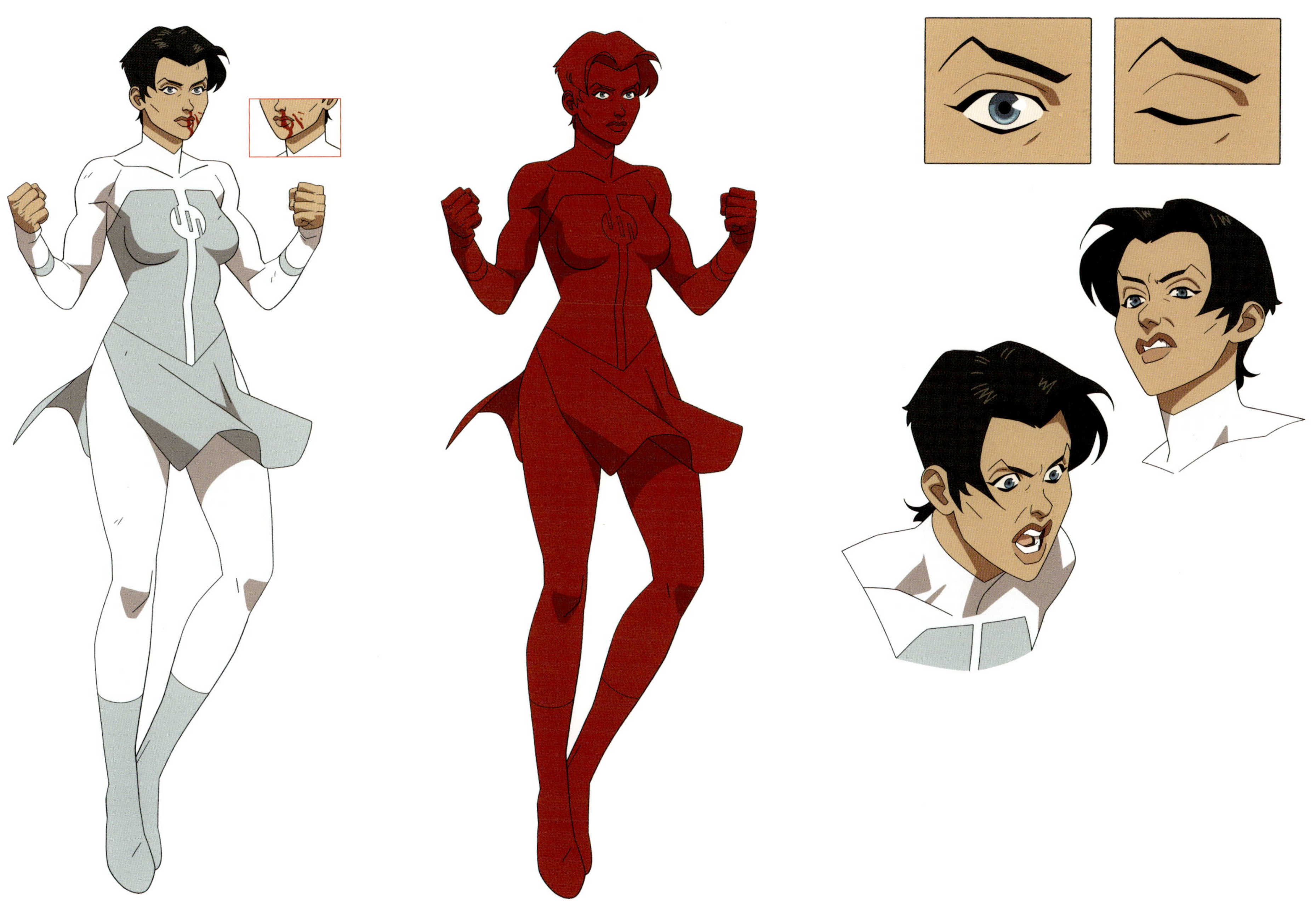

only to be brought back as a life-like android by the GDA every time.

"That scene exists in the books," says Racioppa. "We just took it a little bit further. Both Donald and Rick went through a similar trauma in a different way, and they're just sort of coming to terms with that. How do you move on with your life after something like that? You do it through the people you love. By taking care of those people and having them take care of you. I think it's a lesson Mark could take forwards in the series and hopefully it will help him. It helps you get through tough times, the other people in your life."

Meanwhile, Mark and Amber were sharing a romantic evening out that culminated at an outdoor café. Unfortunately, they were about to get far more than they ordered when a Viltrumite warrior named Anissa unexpectedly arrived.

"The Viltrumites promised, back when Mark was on Thraxa, that they would come and check on him," says

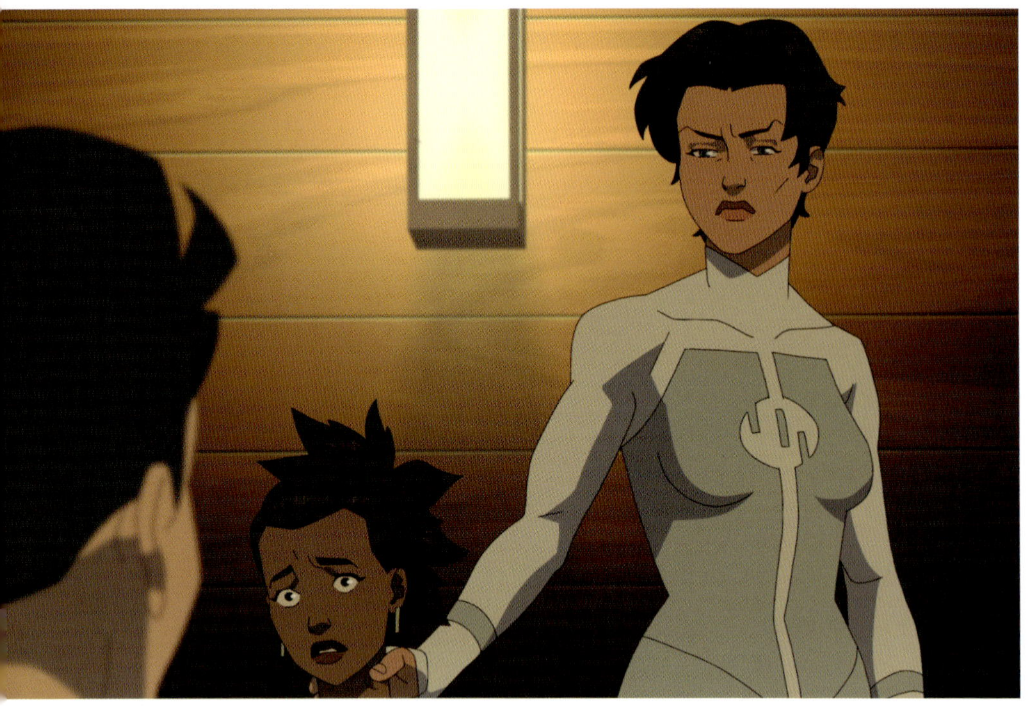

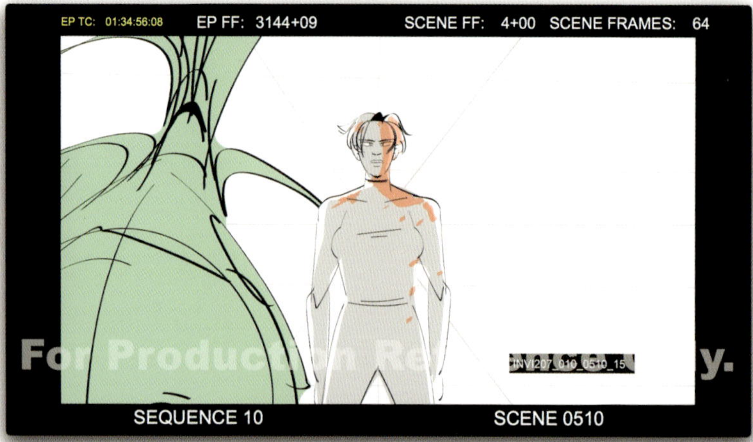

3144+09

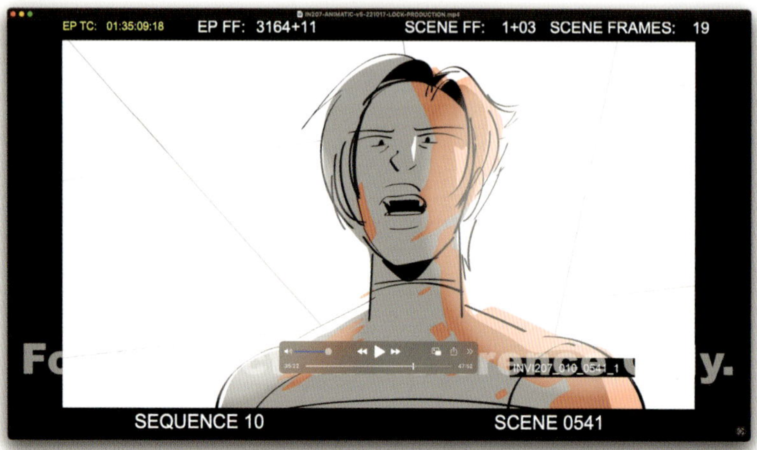

3164+11

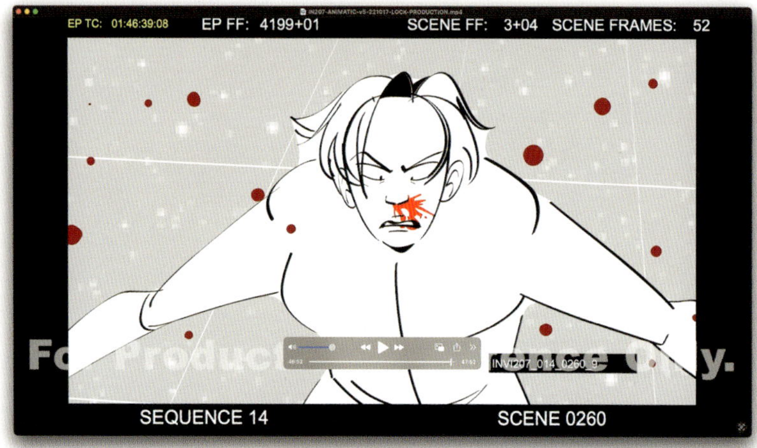

4199+01

Racioppa. "This is the first time they're coming to check on him to see how he's doing. And he's not doing what they wanted him to do, which is working towards taking over the planet."

Anissa immediately grabbed Amber by the back of the neck, threating to kill her and all of the other innocents at the café, if Mark didn't come with her to talk about his duty as a Viltrumite.

"The introduction of Anissa is chilling," says Walker. "She's great. I worked on that model, as well. I did my best at the time. I hope that I did the character justice. I just want her to come across the way she should. And I think she did."

"I wanted her to feel terrifying," says Racioppa. "We spent a lot of time on that scene where they're in the restaurant, and then she's there and she just puts her hand on Amber. I just wanted that to be the most terrifying scene ever. Even though it's in this restaurant, there's people all around, it's not usually where you experience something extremely scary and terrifying. But for Mark and Amber, that was just heart wrenching. We spent a lot of time making sure to get the realistic responses from Zazie Beetz, who plays Amber, who did a really great job there, and treated it a little more realistically than in the comics. If she was there, she could just tear Amber's head off in a second. She could kill everyone there and Mark could do nothing about that. So we wanted to make sure that that felt as real as possible."

Mark agreed to hear what Anissa had to say, as long as she didn't hurt Amber. When he met Anissa in the skies above the city, she informed Mark about the Viltrumites' plans for Earth. But the discussion was cut short when the GDA called Mark with an emergency. A cruise ship was being attacked by a giant monster. Mark told Anissa that if the Viltrumites truly cared about Earth so much, she should help him save its people.

"The sea monster is very similar to the way Ryan drew the sea monster in the comic," says Kirkman. "Anissa's

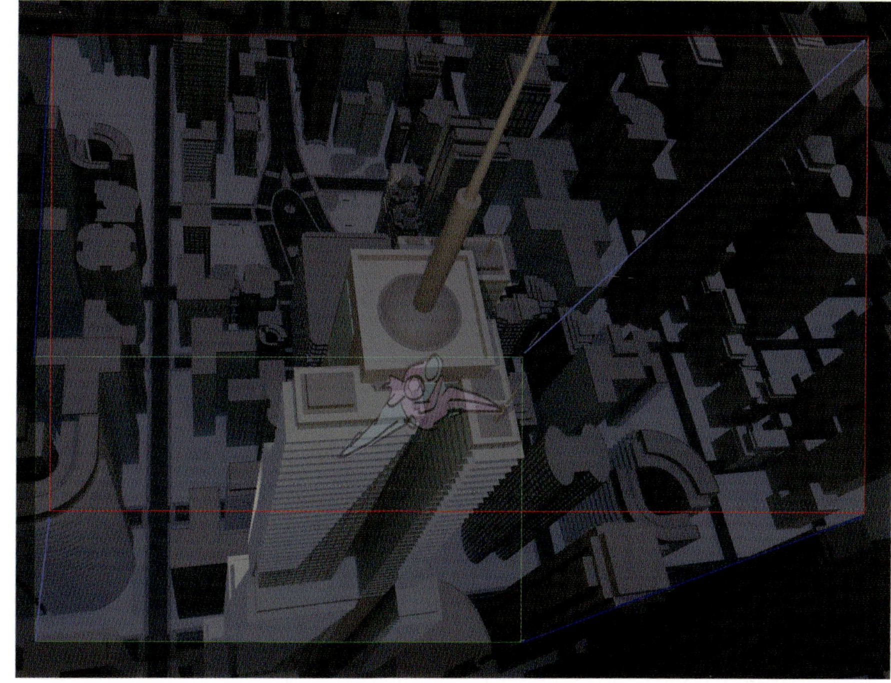

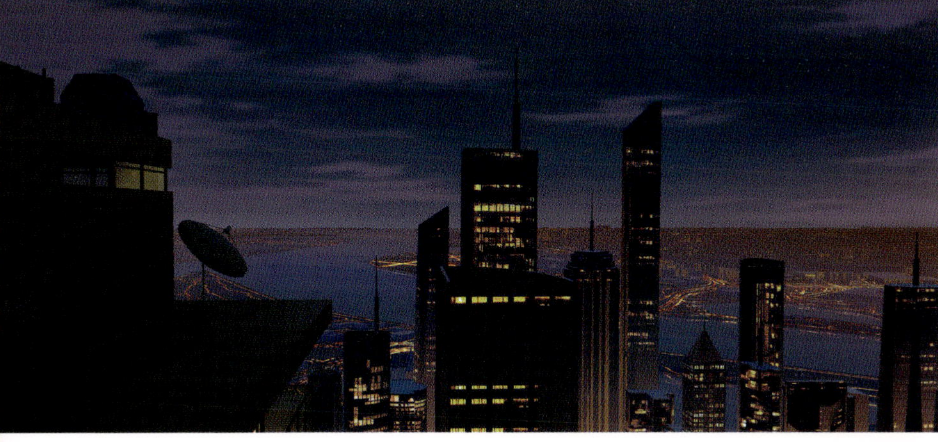

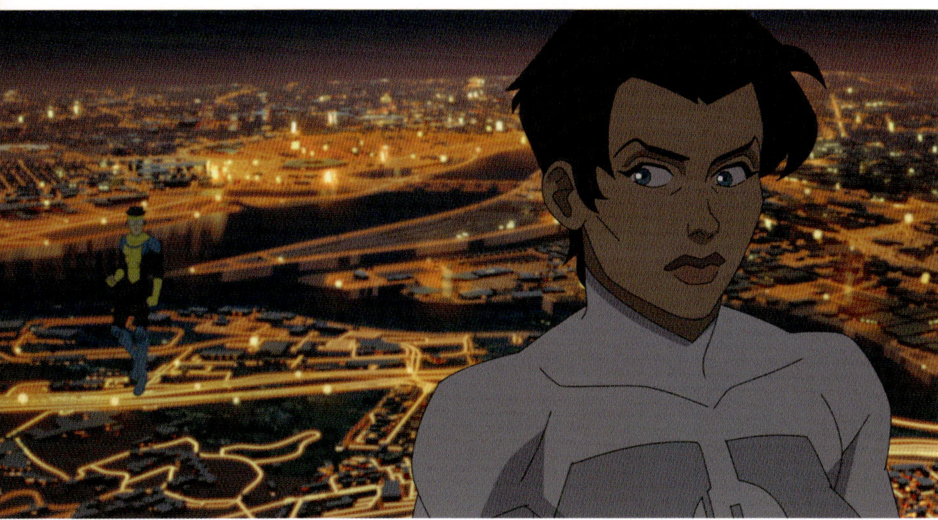

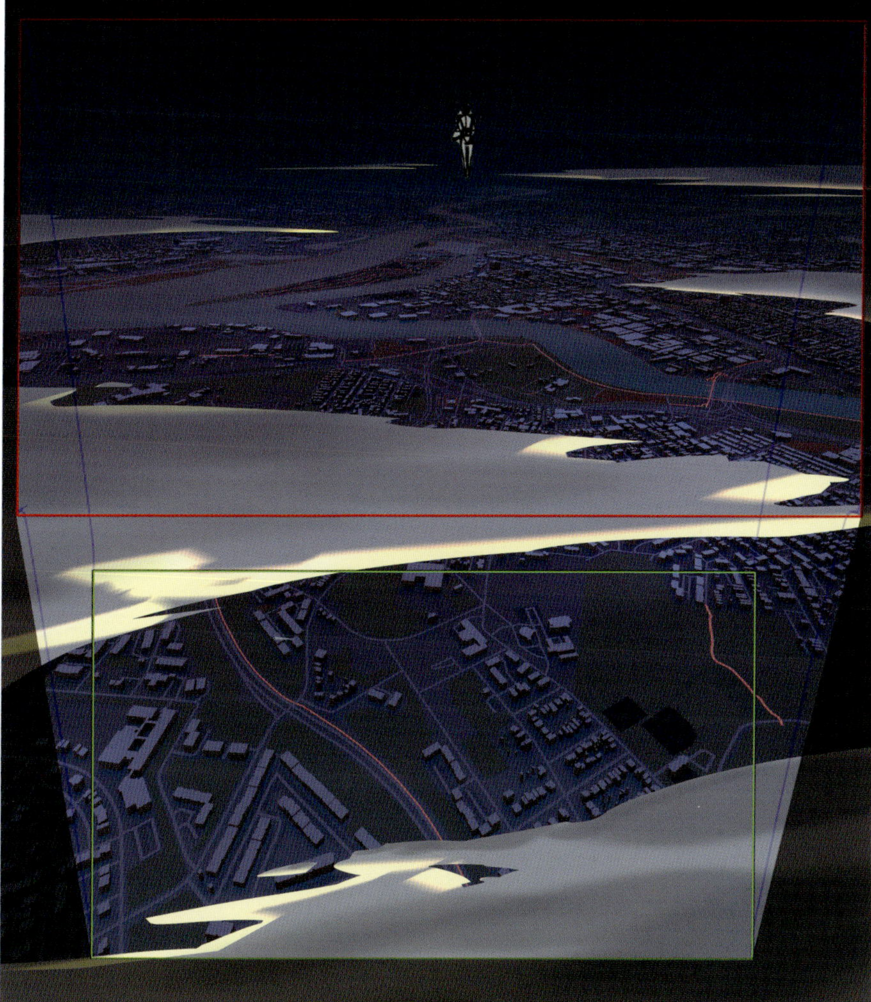

design is very similar to how Ryan drew Anissa in the comic. So not a lot of change there. A fairly pivotal scene. Kind of cool to see it come to life in animation. And Anissa is a very important character for the life of the series, so it's great to finally have her introduced. Somewhat of a controversial character, but you've got to break some eggs to make an omelet, I guess?"

Anissa watched as Mark took on the enormous kaiju by himself. A battle of that scale — especially one that took place in such a dynamic environment — would not be an easy task for the designers.

"I had concerns with that, because there are a lot of rules there," says O'Neil. "The monster is its own thing. The cruise ship is tough because they have to interact with each other. And we've got to sell that in water, which is always expensive. And then you have things like the cruise ship tilting and characters that are shifting their way through scenes, sliding down the deck or falling over the side or holding on for dear life. And I think all those things turned out really great."

Mark struggled to defeat the sea monster until Anissa finally decided to join the battle, killing the creature in a single blow. Once the ship's passengers were safe, Anissa turned her attention back to Mark.

"Anissa tries to convince him, through reason, to come over to their side," says Racioppa. "And when that doesn't work, she takes a more physical approach. And we see what even a single Viltrumite can do against Mark."

The battle between Anissa and Mark gave the creative team a chance to cut loose.

"Action beats are fun," says O'Neil. "I think after a career in action, you're just like, 'Yeah, I know what to do with that.' It's just drawing characters in poses that are cool. It's the stuff that you can kind of just slip into and do with an unparalleled confidence. I think when you start getting into the drama and the emotional things, that's where you really got to slow down and start paying attention. So this episode was kind of weighted with a lot of that at the start, and I think we did a really good job, collectively as a team. And then with that end sequence, it's just kind of like, 'Okay, time

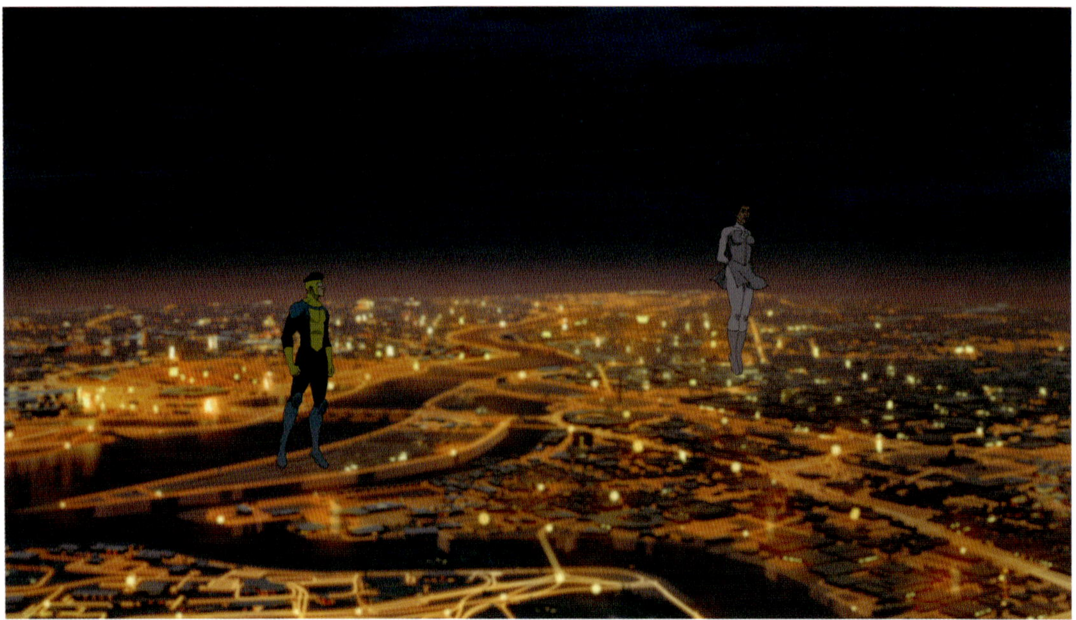

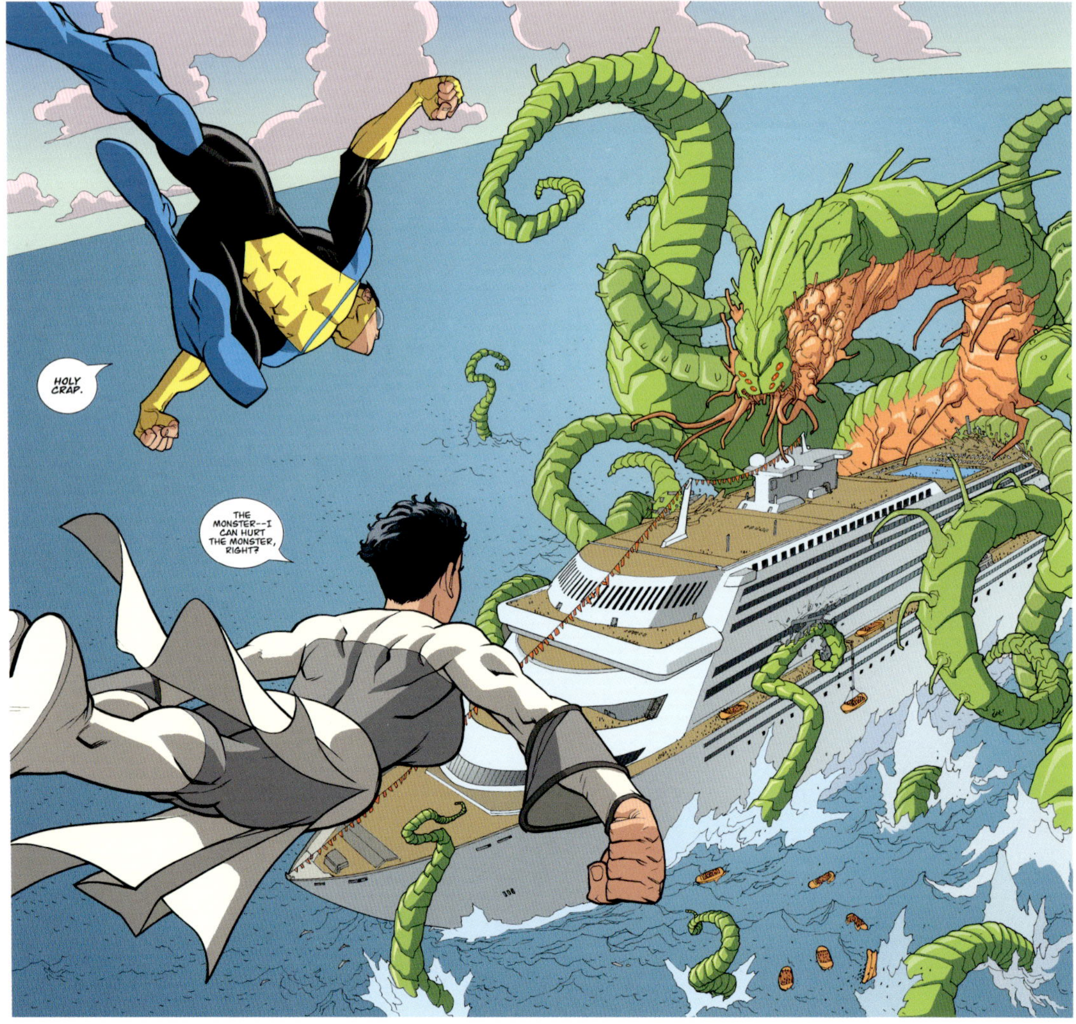

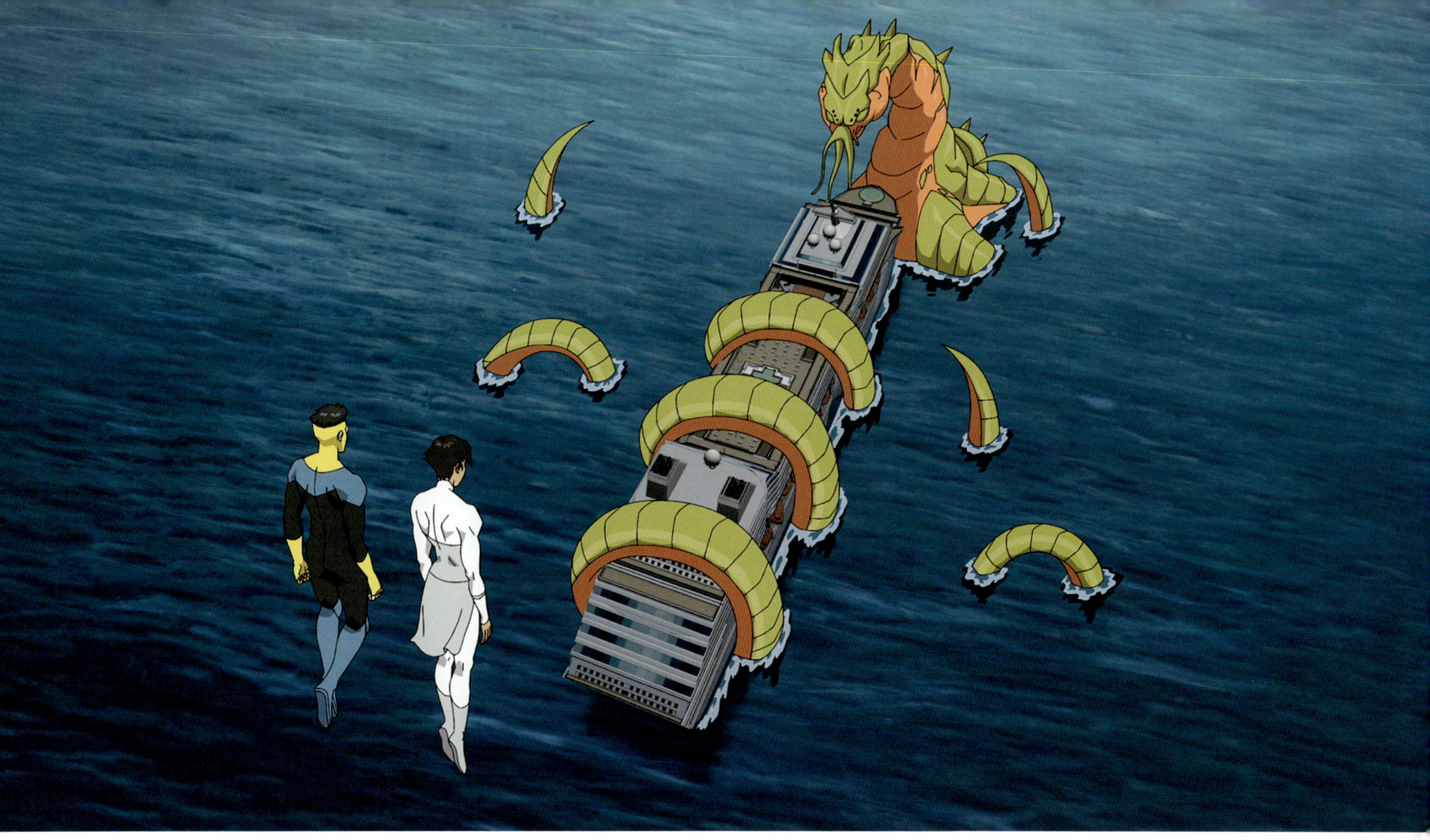

to pull out all the stops. Time to take what Dan and the story team put together and just take it as far as we can before the clock runs out."

"Warren [Fok] did the fight scene with Anissa," says Duncan, "and it's righteous. It was really good. The studio did a really good job bringing that to life. And I still can't decide if we called as many retakes as we did and did as much work on that as we did because it needed it, or because we just really wanted to work on those scenes and plus that stuff up."

"I think the action from the boards was dynamite," says O'Neil. "The whole anticipation of Anissa at her introduction, to the sort of passive resistance, to her taking action, all of that trying to make a case, albeit briefly, for 'join us', and then it goes south. A lot of that stuff turned out really well. I think, as an episode, it's structured really great. Just from the slower body of it, building up to that moment where she comes in and puts everything to a stop, and then you try to figure her out, and it inevitably climaxes where it does. Mark is just bested, and you're like, 'Fuck, where do we go from here?'"

Where we went was somewhat unexpected. Even though Anissa bludgeoned Mark to within inches of his life, she stopped short of taking him out permanently.

"She just shows up and beats the tar out of him, but doesn't kill him," says Racioppa. "And the interesting thing about that is there's a really good reason for that, which will become clearer to viewers in future seasons. Mark wasn't just protected by plot armor. There's actually a reason why she doesn't kill him. And she implies as much that she's not allowed to. And that someone even worse than her is coming."

"It was a great moment in the show," says Walker. "Especially the Cecil and Donald of it all. A little bit of pants-shitting over a Viltrumite being there. Mark's inability to just pretend to be a good boy, which ultimately works out for him. Great moments for the introduction of an important character."

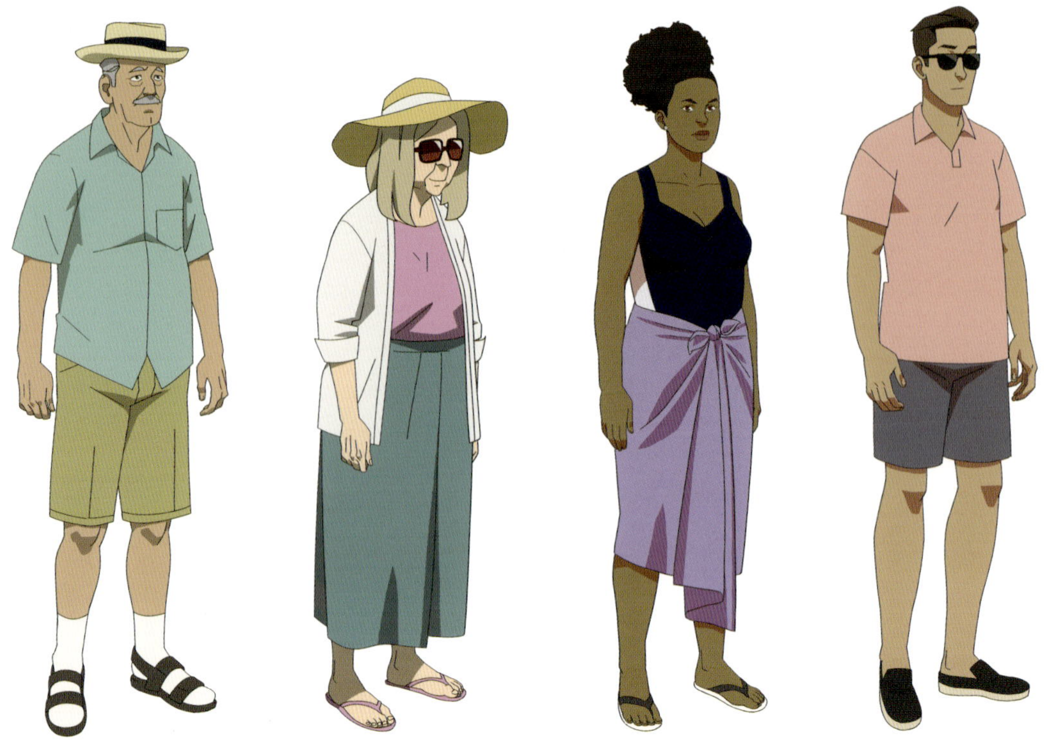

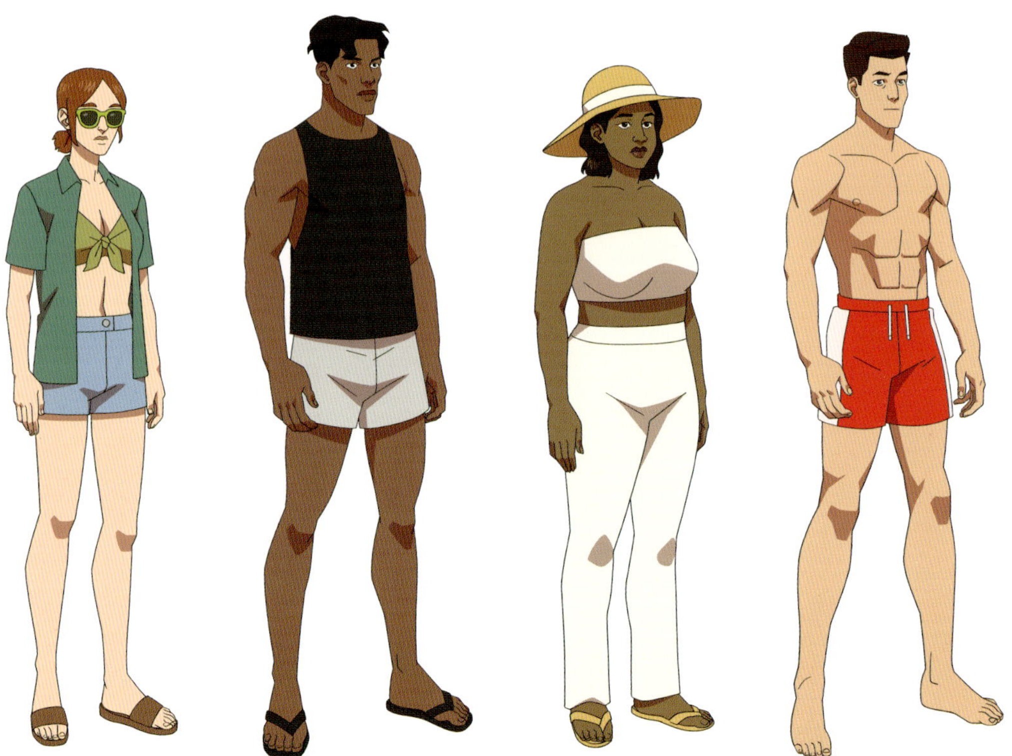

Anissa departed Earth, leaving the bloodied and broken Mark to consider his next steps. But he would soon realize that one decision was completely out of his hands.

"Afterwards, when Mark comes back in and they're talking about that experience, Amber is like, 'That was horrifying,'" says Racioppa. "People have terrible trauma from being mugged in the streets. This is much worse in a

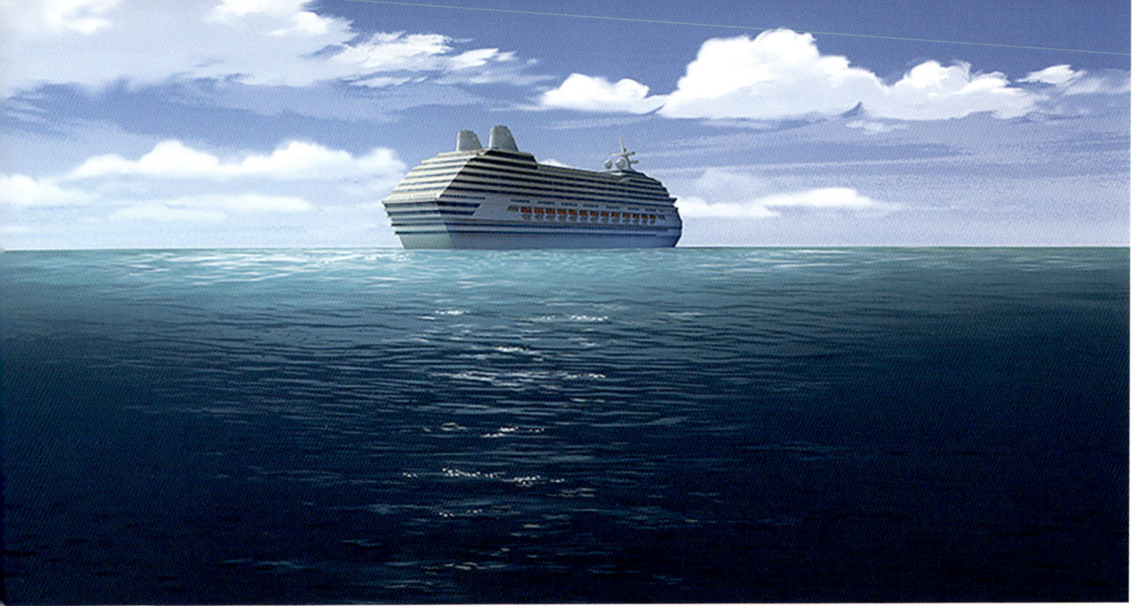

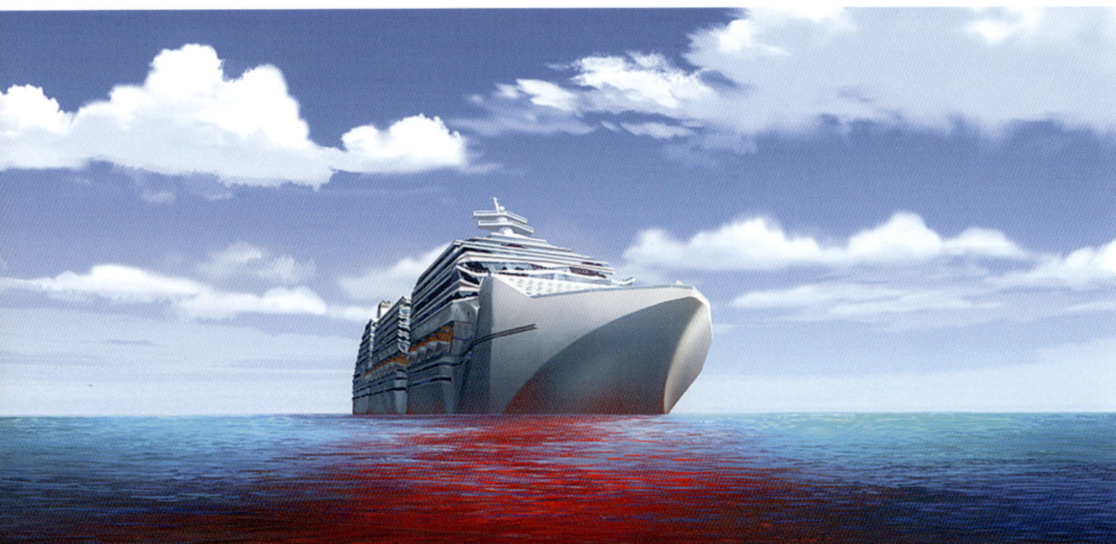

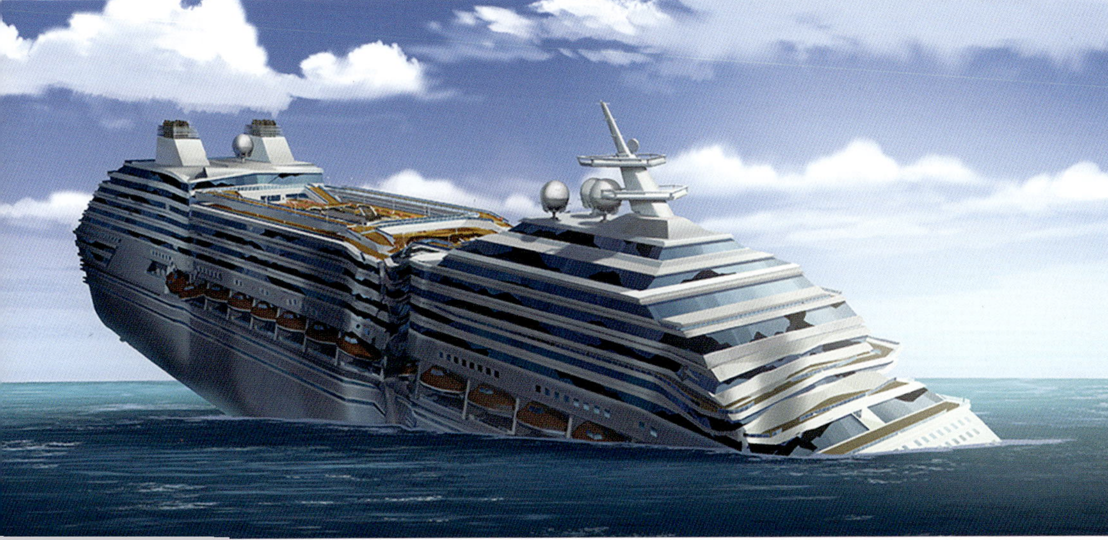

way. So we wanted to make sure that came through and that it was realistic. And again, that's what sort of like tips Amber into being like, 'This can't work like that. Our relationship can't work if this is what it is.'"

Mark was still reeling from Amber breaking up with him when he received a phone call from his mother. But it wasn't his mother on the other end of the line. It was Angstrom Levy, yet another villain threatening to harm someone who Mark loves. The moment served as an unsettling reminder of the dangers that come with being a superhero.

"Mark just gets home from space and then everything goes to shit, right?" says Racioppa. "And again, everything's coming home to roost. Mark hasn't seen [Levy] since Episode One — the audience has seen him a little bit through the season, but not a ton — but now he has to deal with this guy he doesn't even really remember at first. Obviously, he was there when Angstrom was created, in a way. I wouldn't say he was responsible for it, but he was definitely a player in those events. If Mark hadn't shown up, if the GDA hadn't sent Mark, what would have happened? Maybe Angstrom actually would have gotten all the memories, the plan would have worked out really well, he would have given the Maulers another dimension, and he would have made the world better. But that's obviously not how things happened. So, now he's back for revenge. And of course, Mark just lost his girlfriend in this terrible event with Anissa. And now it's his mom and his new baby brother at risk. So Mark does not get a break here, and he's coming in to this really tense, terrifying sequence of, 'Here's a guy who could, in a second, kill the people that you care about the most.' So, yeah... Mark does not get off easy at the end of the season."

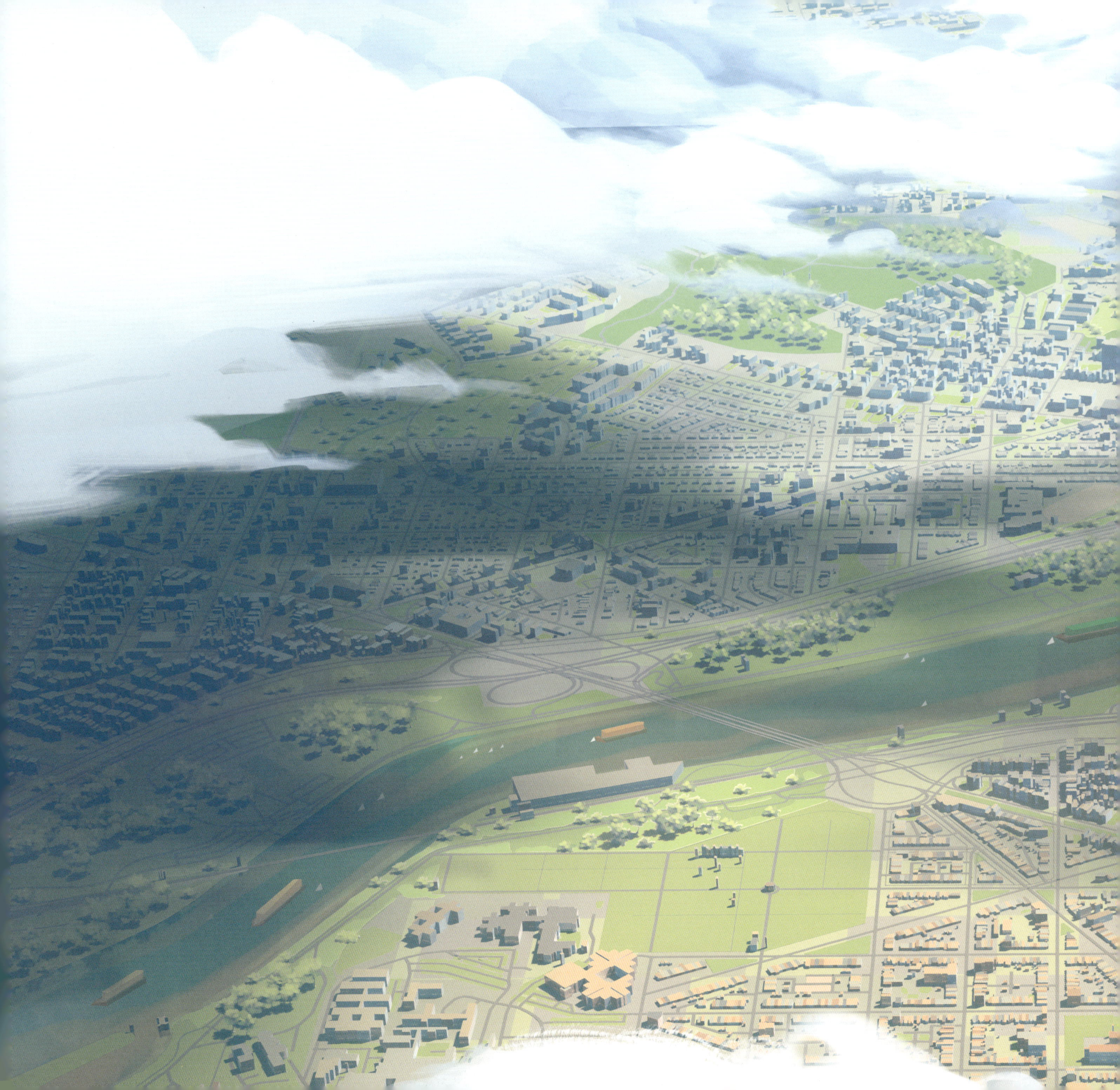

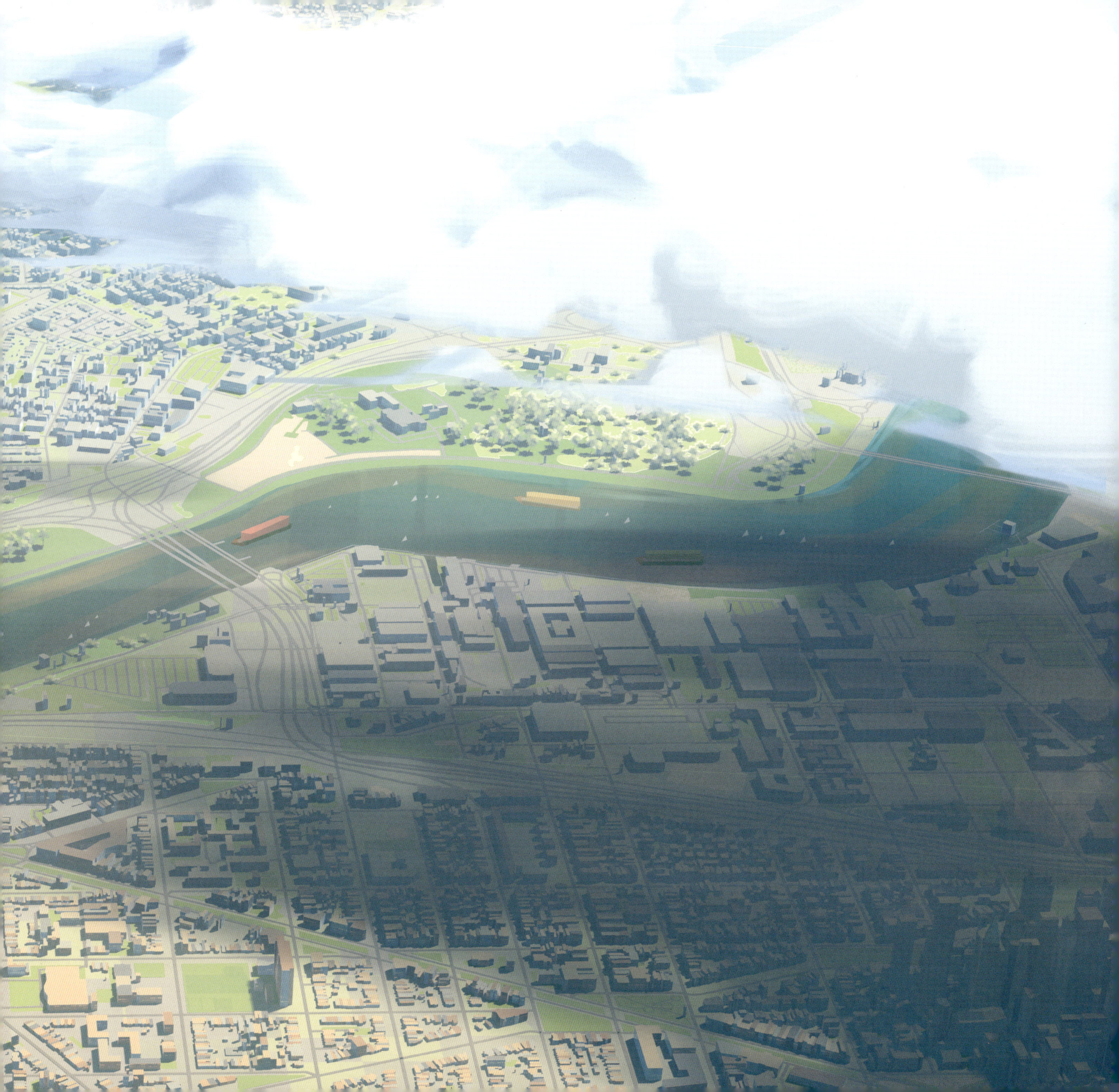

EPISODE 8:

I THOUGHT YOU WERE STRONGER

Invincible's Season Two finale began with Angstrom Levy in the Grayson household, using Mark's mother, Debbie, and his baby brother, Oliver — who Mark had brought back to Earth with him after the battle on Thraxa — as bait to lure Mark back home. This sinister version of Levy was a far cry from the man introduced in the season premiere, and his design reflected that.

"We have the final Angstrom form, in his coat and his jacket and everything," says Executive Producer, Co-Showrunner, and Co-Creator Robert Kirkman, "which technically appears in [Episode 206] for the first time. There was actually quite a bit of work put into that, because you had to figure out how the brain material fit under the clothes and how you'd show it in three dimensions, and how big that collar area was, with the brain and everything going down his back. Making that work is not quite as simple as it is in comics, where you can make everything inconsistent from different angles to make it work."

When Mark arrived home, he attempted to attack Levy, but the villain used his power to open interdimensional portals to send Mark to a variety of alternate realities.

"The fun thing is a lot of them came directly from the comic books," says Executive Producer and Co-Showrunner Simon Racioppa. "Our design team is great. That is a hard

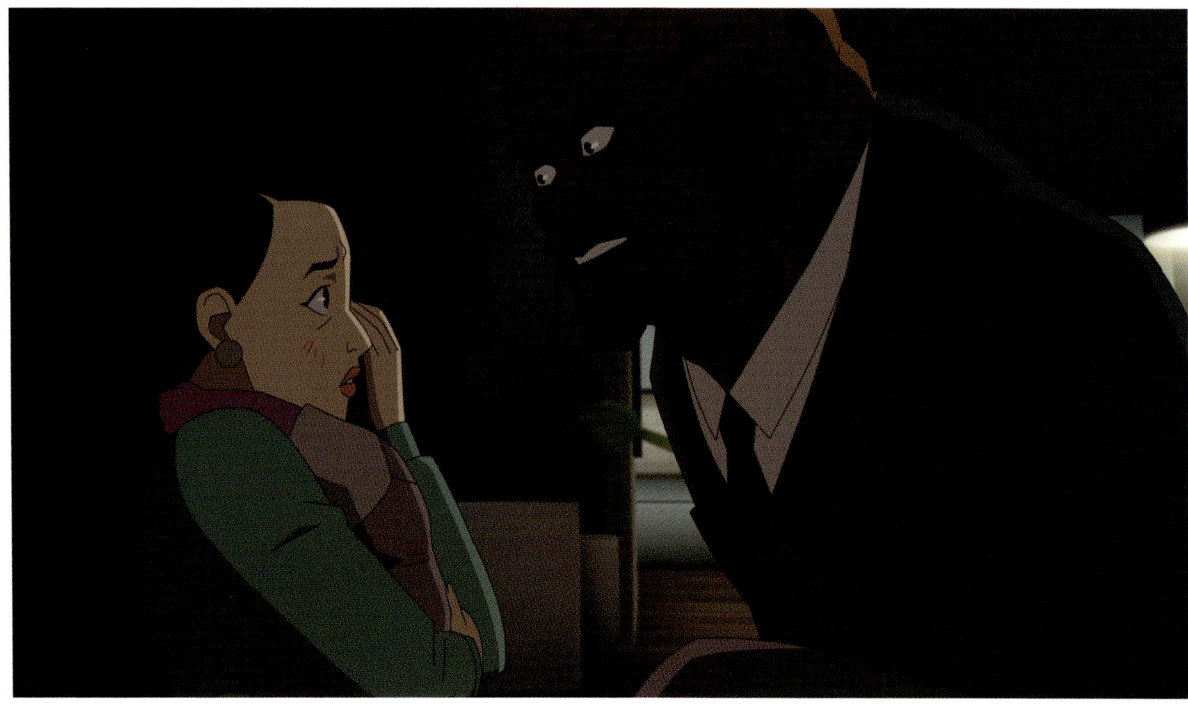

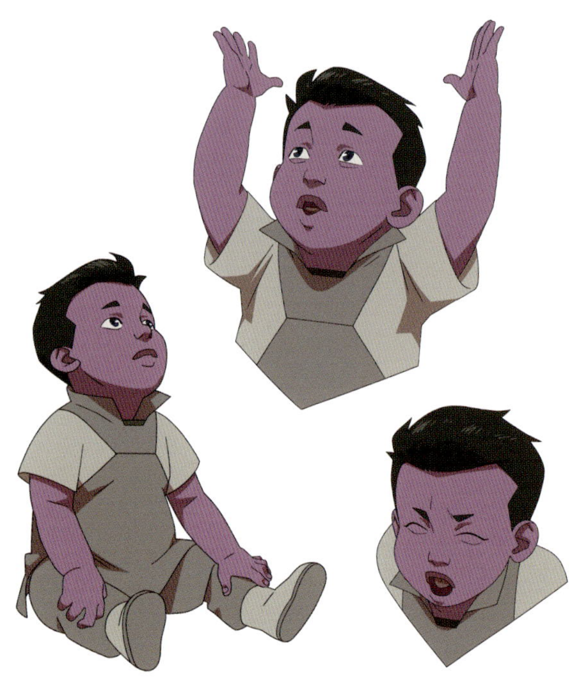

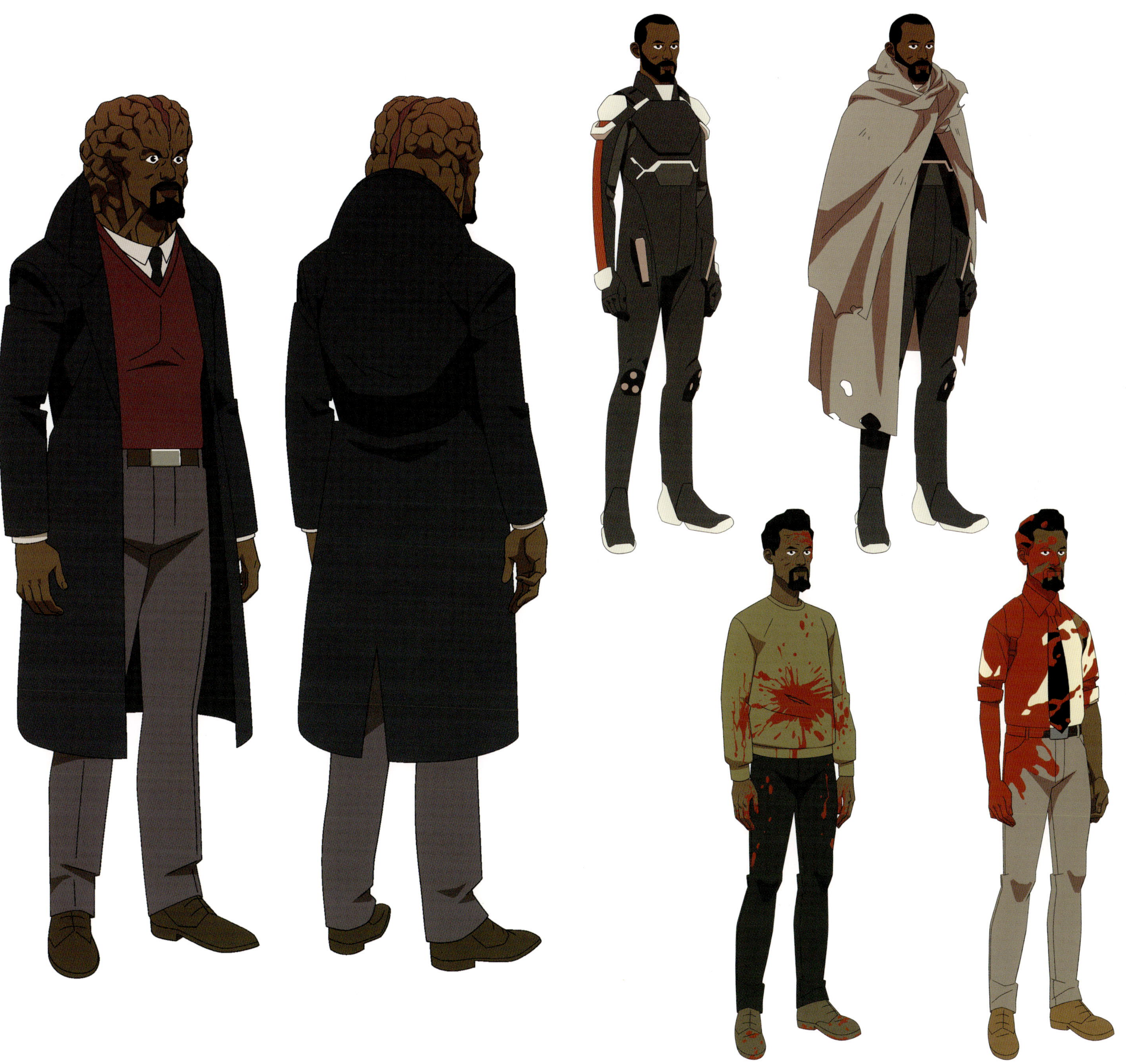

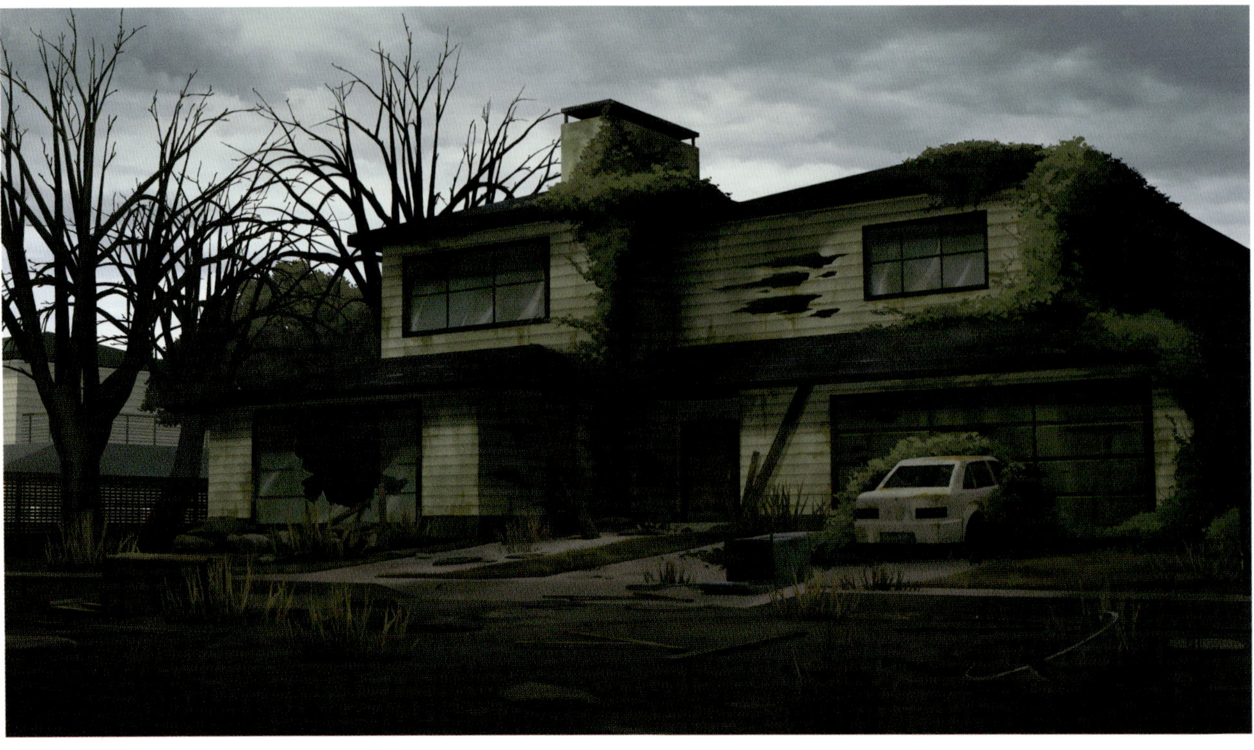

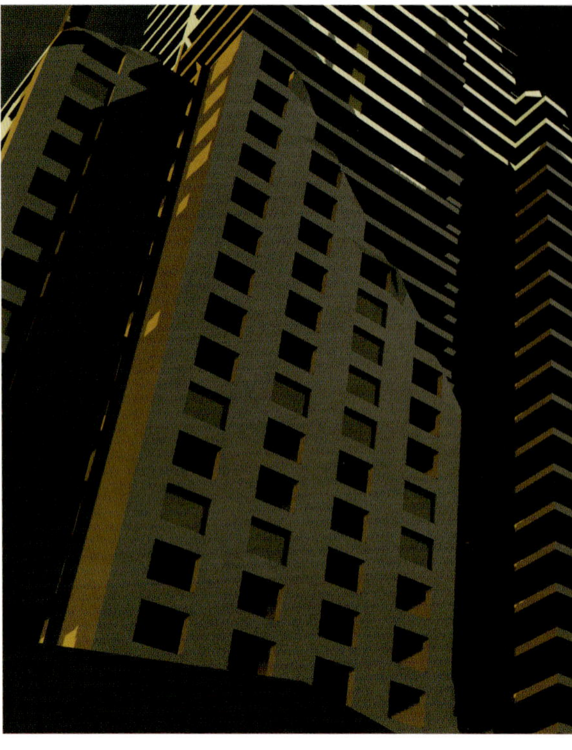

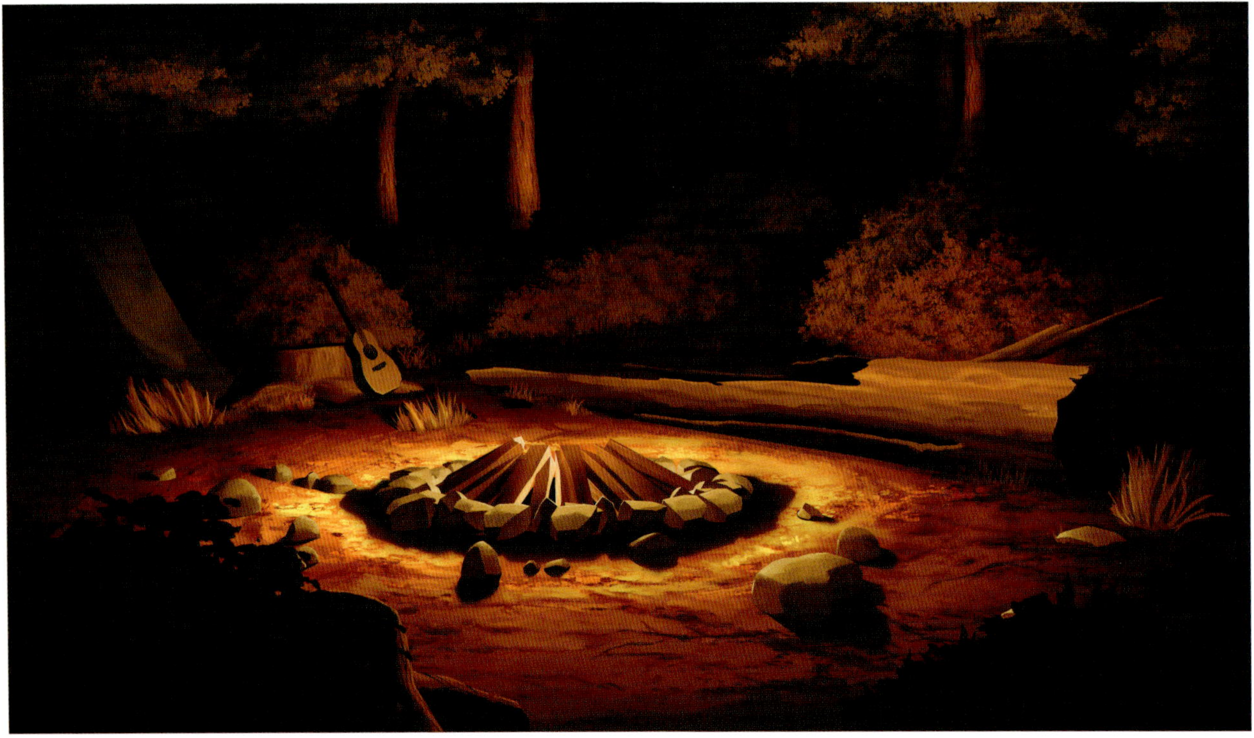

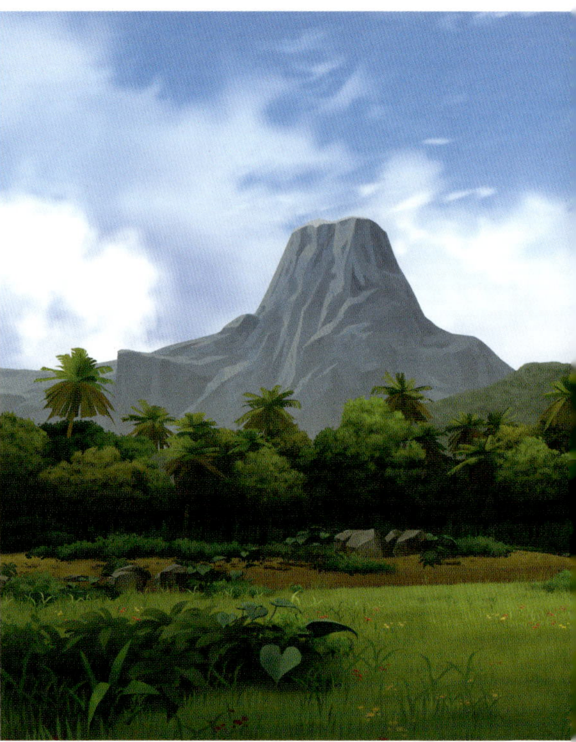

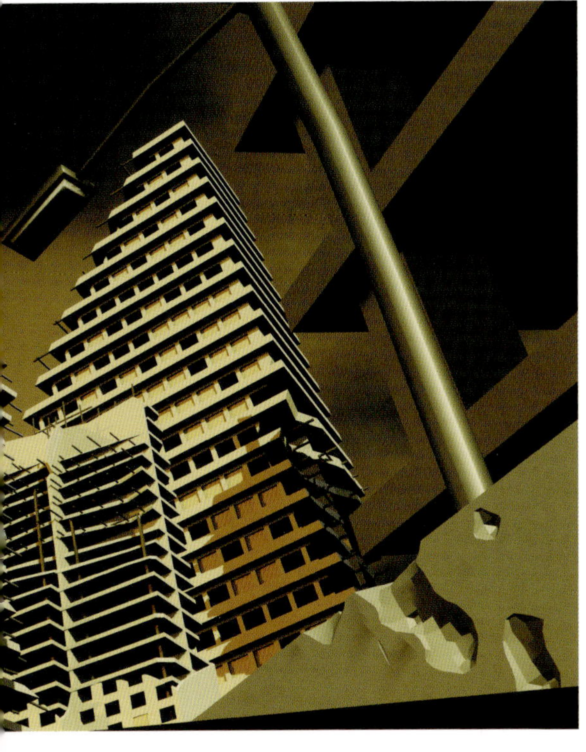
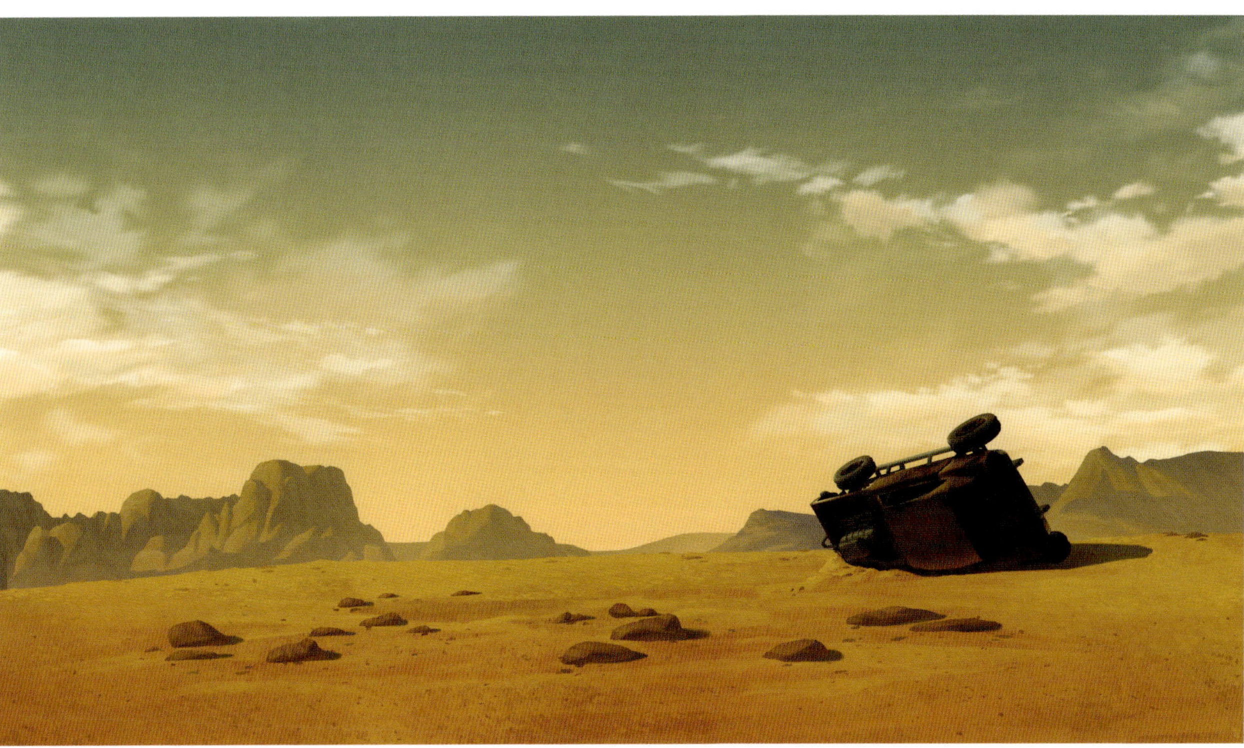
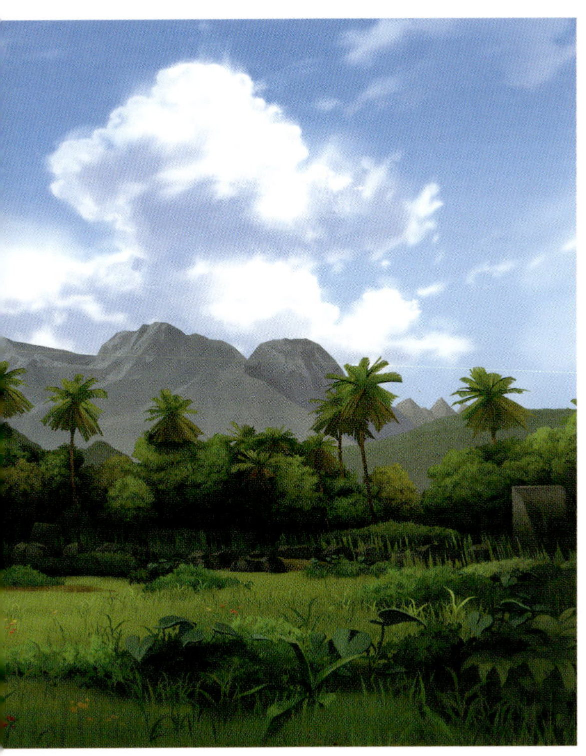
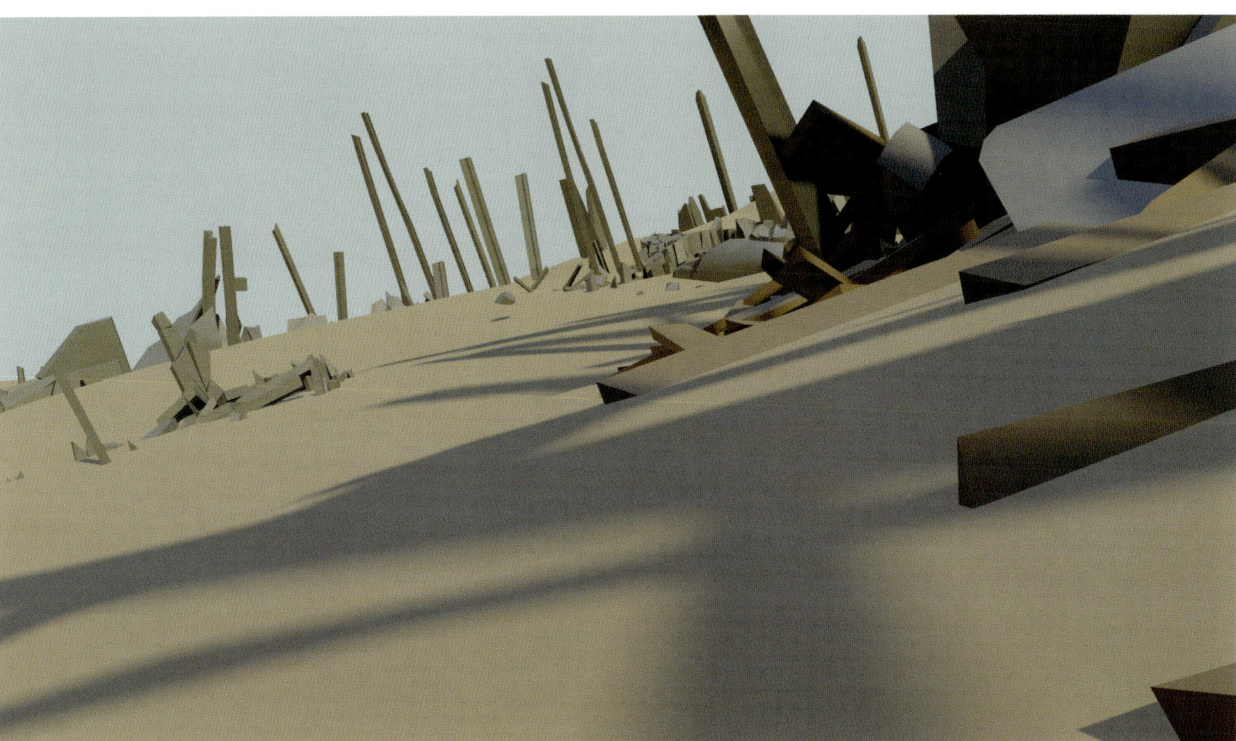

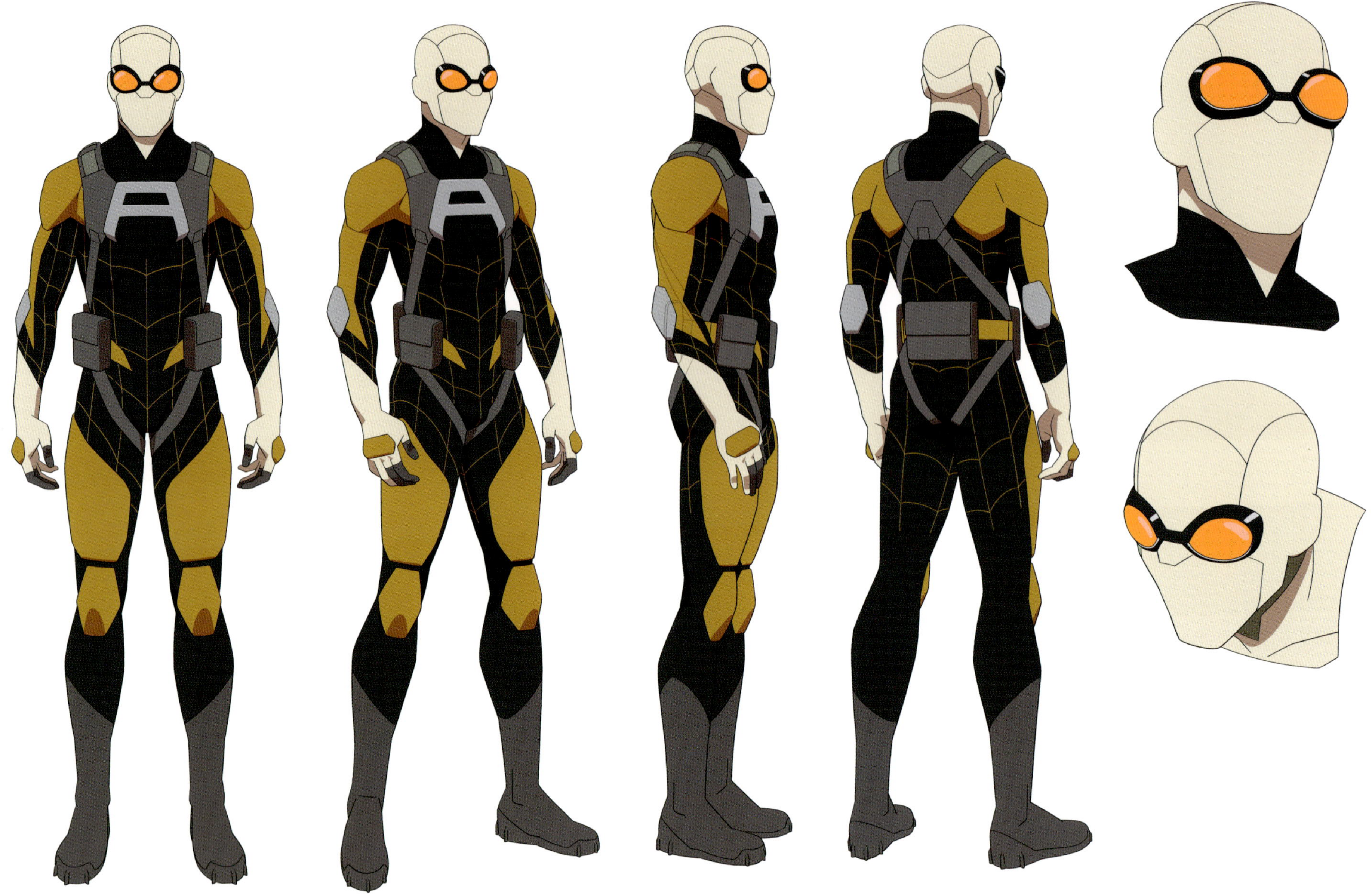

ask of them. We're like, 'Hey, create this background, this world. We're only going to use it for about two seconds, and then we're gonna pop to somewhere else.' But they're good sports about it. But that's a big ask of an animation team, to be like, 'We need all these realities, and we're only going to see them for a little bit and we're never going to go back to them.' So, kudos to our team for managing that and doing a great job with it."

One of the dimensions that Mark found himself in was home to a hero and villain who looked oddly familiar (but who, for legal reasons, most definitely were not).

"There was a sequence in the comics where we actually encountered Spider-Man," says Kirkman, "because I was able to have Invincible appear in an issue of *Marvel Team-Up* that I was writing. Some bizarre chain of events led to that happening. I wanted to kind of pay tribute to that, but also didn't want to get sued. And so we came up with the very original and completely unique Agent Spider and Professor Octopus, which I've got to say, the design team really knocked out of the park."

"I happened to draw the *Marvel Team-Up* issue where Mark teamed-up with an Agent Spider rip-off called 'Spider-Man'," says Co-Executive Producer and Co-Creator Cory Walker. "It's so cool to get Agent Spider in the show and see that iconic design translated for animation. I wish we got more of it."

And it wasn't just Kirkman and Walker who had fond memories of previously working on a similar spider-like hero.

"Me and [Art Director] Shaun [O'Neil] got our start on Spider-Man," says Supervising Director Dan Duncan. "He brought me into this business on *Ultimate Spider-Man*. And we also worked with Chris Palmer, who we got to board [the Agent Spider] sequence. The three of us being able to work on something Spider-Man-esque together on this show was a real highlight for that whole episode."

A lot of effort went into designing Agent Spider in a way that felt fresh, unique, and non-litigious.

"I wanted to have a character that felt like Spider-Man, and obviously gave you a sense of Spider-Man and made you think of Spider-Man," says Kirkman, "but I didn't want the design to be too derivative. I wanted him to look like a unique character that could stand on his own. And I think we accomplished that. Agent Spider, while obviously being a somewhat derivative character, does have enough unique elements to him that there's something cool there. And if we ever get the chance to tell more of Agent Spider's story, you'll see that he's very different than Spider-Man. It's a completely different set-up and a different origin. He's different in a lot of really cool ways that I hope to one day be able to reveal."

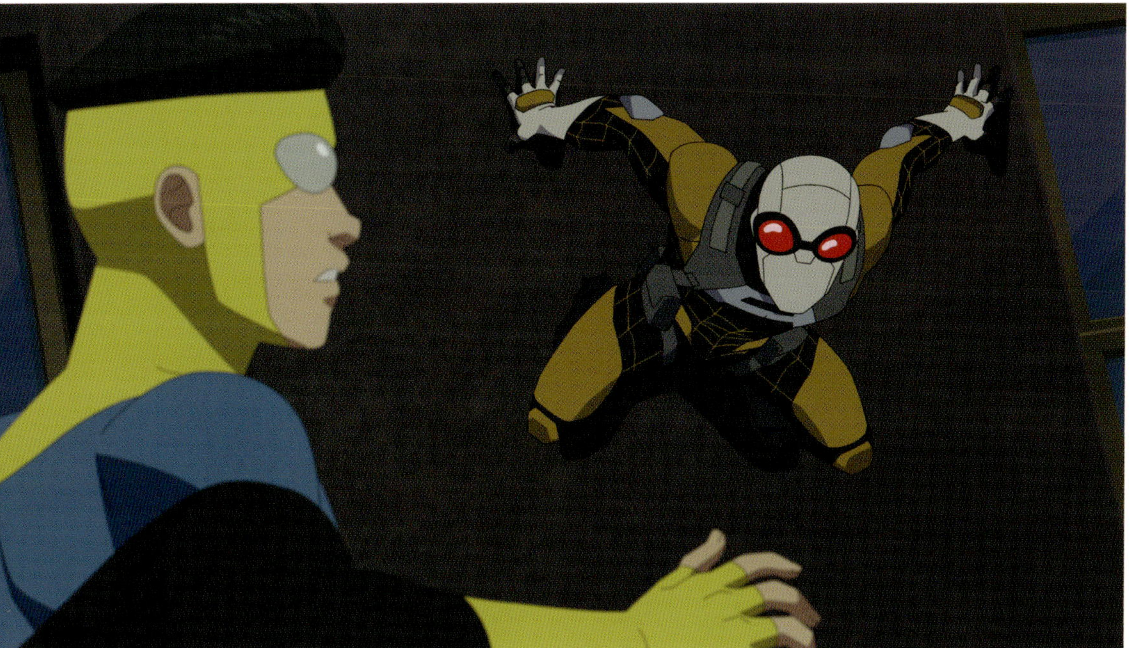

"The Agent Spider design was great," says O'Neil, "because how do you do Spider-Man, but not Spider-Man, and not have it just be something else? But I was super happy that people were receptive to it. I think Nick Lombardo did the majority of heavy lifting on that. We went back and forth on a couple of placement and detail reduction things."

One of the biggest challenges on Agent Spider was making sure that his costume's colors were just right.

"For Agent Spider, we went through some color options," says Kirkman. "I think originally I wanted him to be more purple than yellow or gold, but the final design ended up being really cool."

"[Character Designer] Tim Nicklas gave us a color pass on that," says O'Neil. "We started with this very green and purple design. And when we got back the shipment, I was just like, 'This is fucking awful. Why did we do this? Why did I think this was going to work?' And so I was like, 'Tim, can you give me a run of temp color fills on this guy so we can we can work some stuff out.' I try not to do obvious references, but he went through and he gave me a lineup of color fill choices that were all palettes of characters from *Metal Gear Solid* games, which are like some of my favorite shit on the face of the Earth. And we wound up landing on the Gray Fox cyborg ninja —white mask, orange and blue body suit."

For Agent Spider's nemesis, Professor Octopus, the design process was a bit easier.

"We went through a round of stuff on Agent Spider," says O'Neil. "But Professor Octopus, I think we did one design and it was like, 'That's it.' I think I think Nick came through with the big dome head and the tentacles coming off the helmet — as opposed to the rig on the chest — and the crazy fucking Sherlock Holmes outfit. It's just like, 'This is it. This is the whole thing.'"

It was a look that Kirkman wasn't convinced about at first, but one that he eventually warmed on.

"I know initially I hadn't wanted Professor Octopus to have that giant head with the tentacles coming out of it," says Kirkman, "because I thought it might be a little too silly. But it's a pretty cool design, and at the end it did turn out really great. So, I'm big enough to admit that I was wrong."

Agent Spider wasn't the only vaguely familiar hero that Mark came across as he traveled between alternate realities in this episode. But the creators insisted that these characters were definitely not who you thought they were.

"I'll say that was so not Batman that we actually had a glove visible at a certain point," says Kirkman, "and I was like, 'No, let's just do the cape. That's not Batman. Let's not give any kind of hints that it could be.'"

Even so, fans couldn't help but wonder if one of the dimensions Mark found himself in was connected to another of Kirkman's creations.

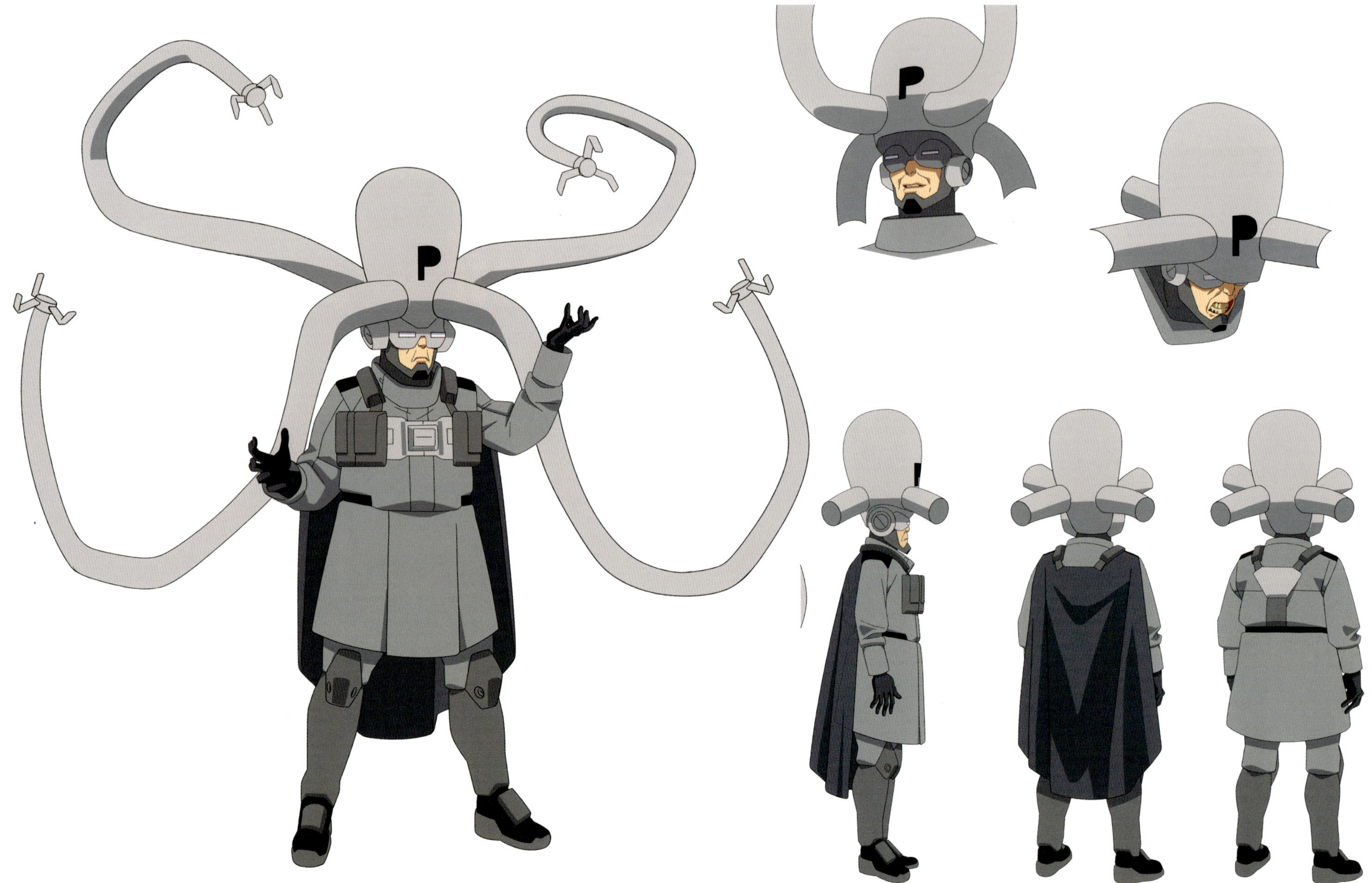

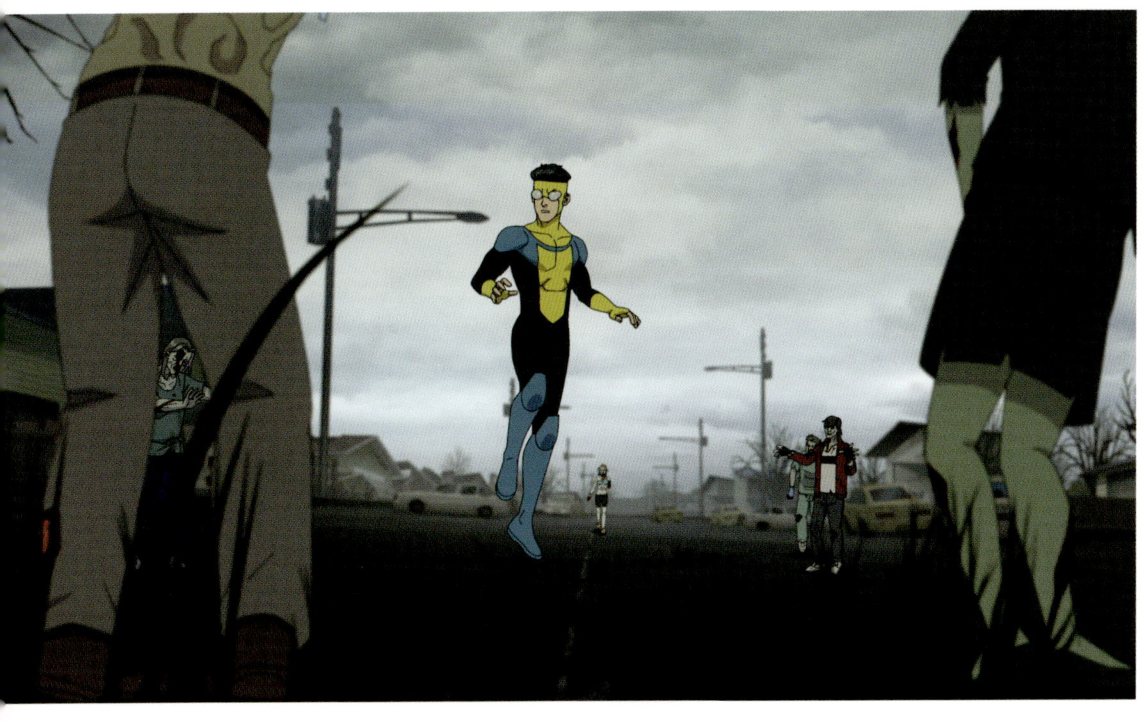

"Obviously, there's a zombie world," says Racioppa. "I don't know if that's something that people recognize from somewhere else in Robert's brain."

However, Kirkman made it clear that any ties to his popular comic book and television series *The Walking Dead* were purely coincidental.

"They're walking corpses," says Kirkman. "That's a fun, familiar trope to play with. I mean, anytime you're doing a multiverse thing, you're going to hit a dimension that's got zombies in. It doesn't necessarily mean it's connected to *The Walking Dead*. I mean, it very clearly isn't. The zombies in *The Walking Dead* do not speak. But you gotta throw a zombie universe in there or else, like, what are you doing? If you're doing a multiverse thing, if you don't have zombies, that's ridiculous."

One extradimensional Easter egg that was 100% official, however, was the appearance of a Dragon Fire Sniper Rifle

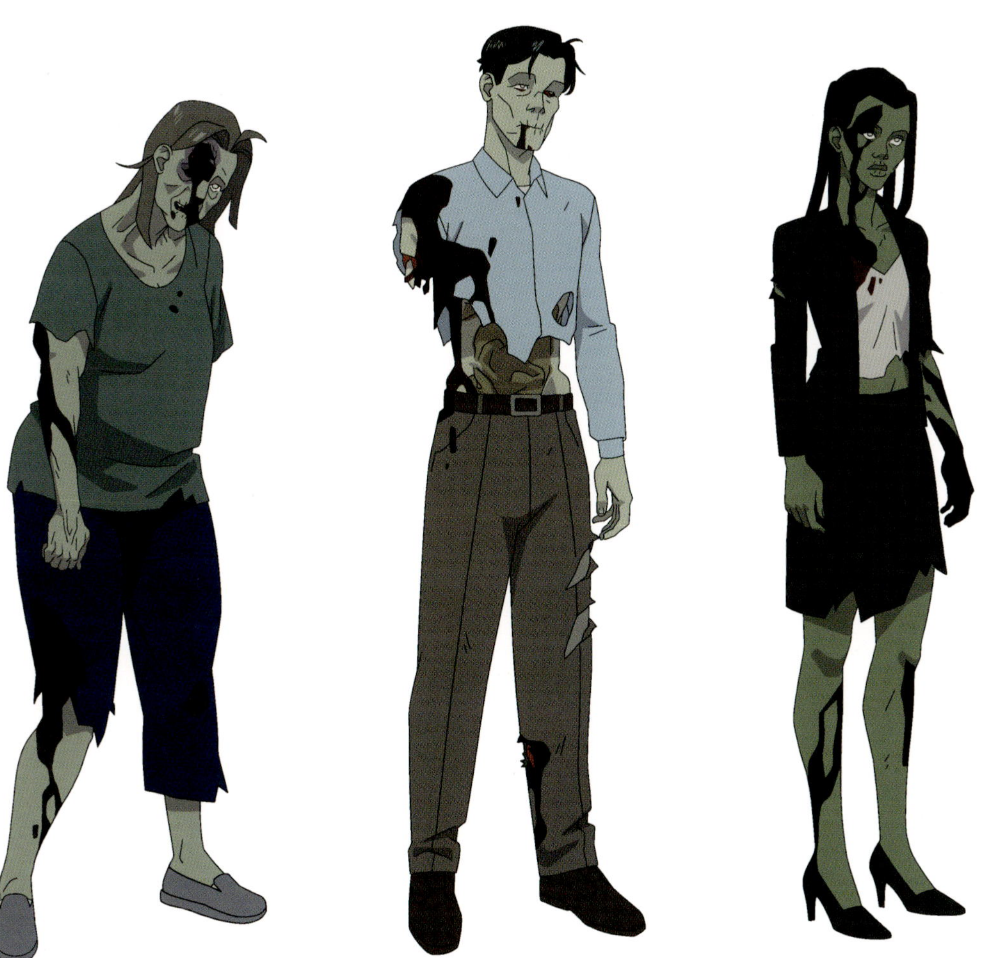

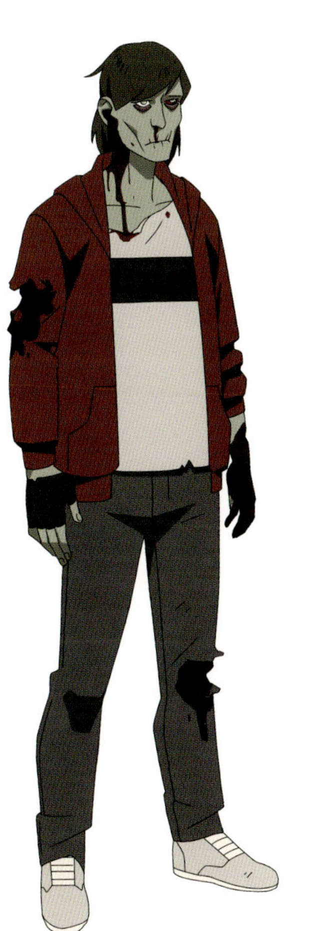

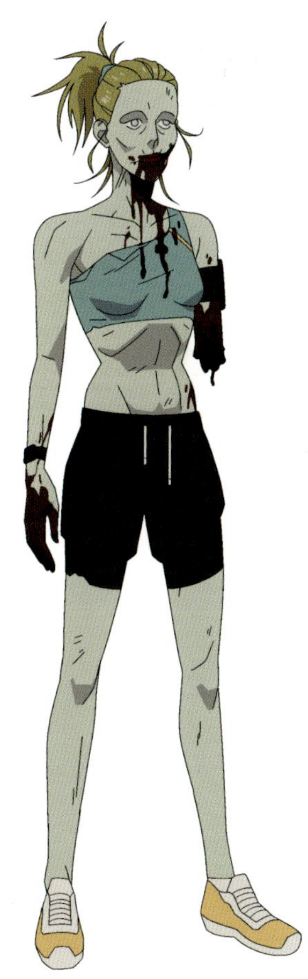

from the video game *Fortnite*. At the time, Kirkman was working with *Fortnite*'s dev team to add Invincible content into the game, so it made sense to see if some game content could be added into the show as well.

"I was working with good old Donald Mustard, who was the creative lead of *Fortnite*," says Kirkman. "I was like, 'Can we put an actual gun [from the game] in Invincible?' And he was like, 'We will totally do that.' And so he was very game to making the activation [of the Invincible content in *Fortnite*] as cool and embedded as possible. And so I like to think that it makes Mark doing all of those insane dances in *Fortnite* canon. Which, tonally, is a wreck. It's just like, 'Your mother's in danger, and you're running around *Fortnite* doing this? What is happening?' But whatever. It's fun."

It was more than just fun, though. It was also more evidence of just how adaptable the animated series could be in terms of tone.

"I think that the tonal flexibility that we're able to accomplish in Invincible is kind of insane," says Kirkman. "The fact that he comes out of that portal and smashes Angstrom with a *Fortnite* gun, and then sees that his

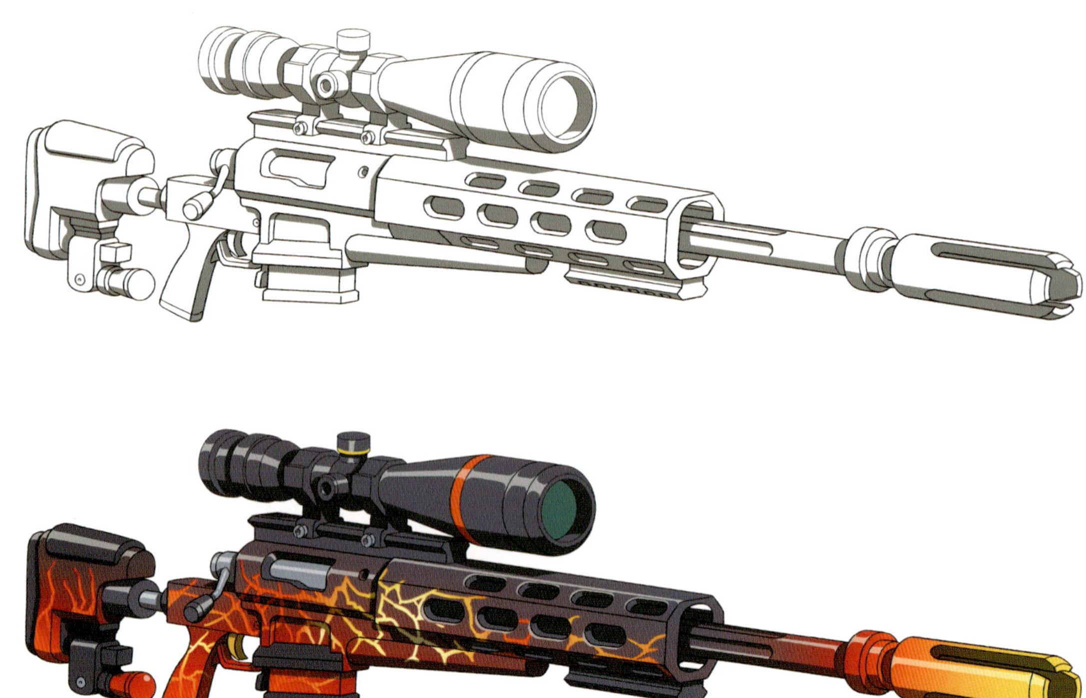

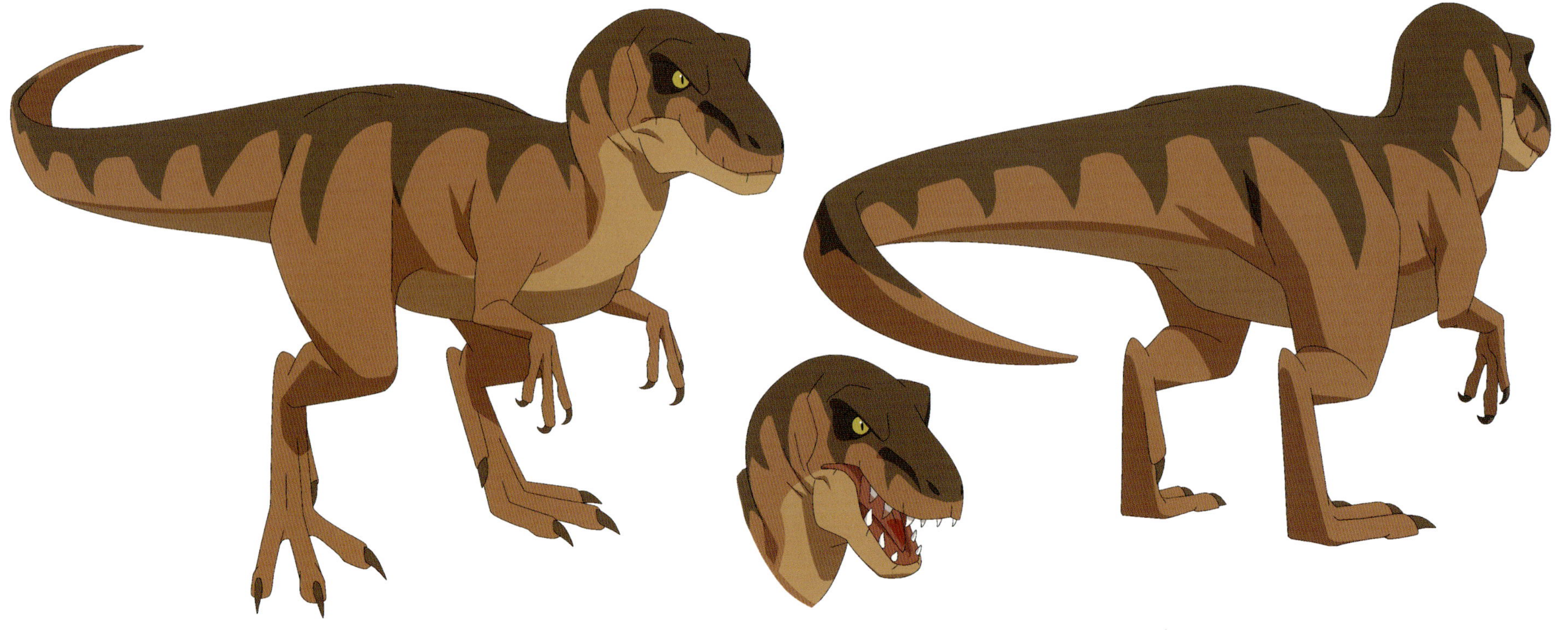

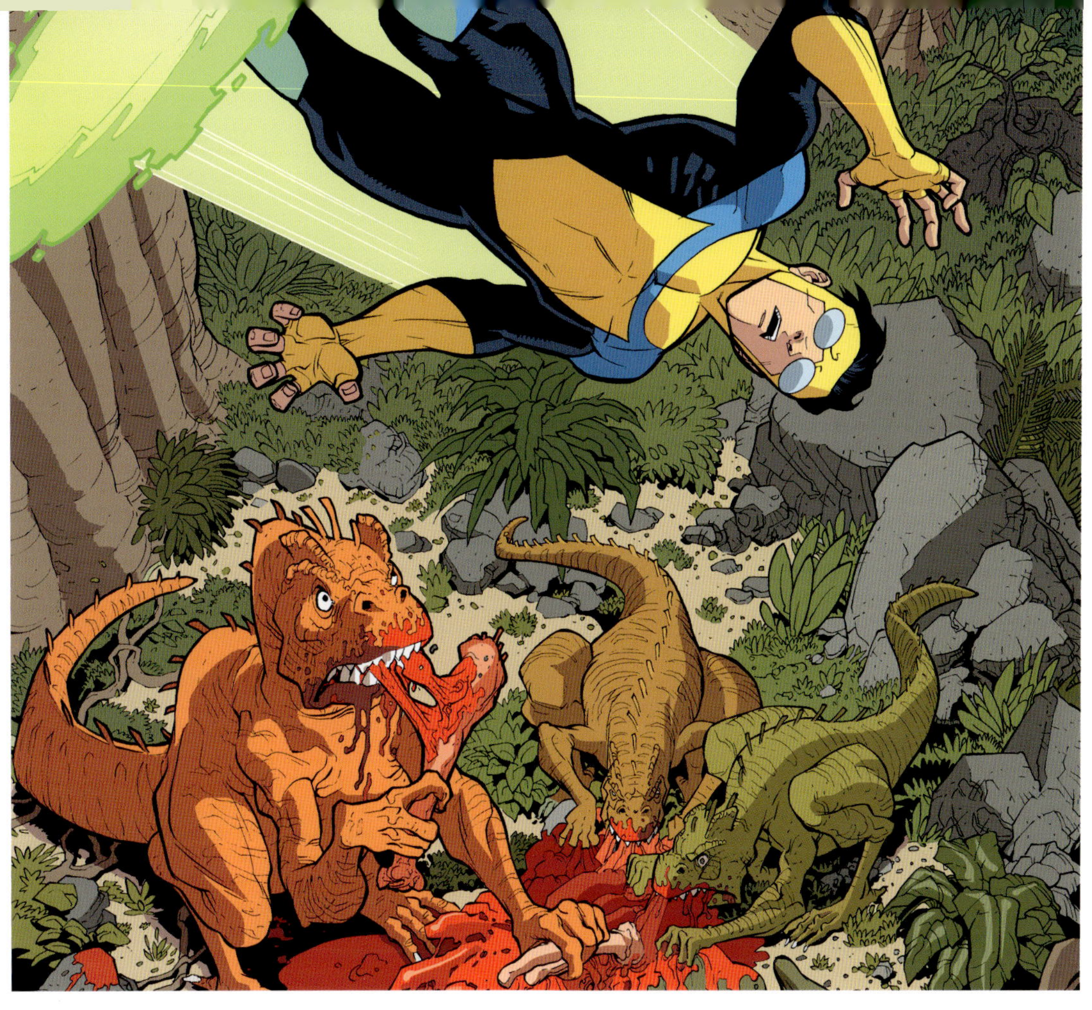

mother's arm is broken and freaks out over that. He's holding a video game gun two seconds ago, and now we're supposed to take it seriously? And I love that the audience has gotten savvy and advanced enough to be able to handle those kind of tonal shifts. It's the kind of thing most people wouldn't allow you to do because they would think it's stupid. But there's no rules on *Invincible*. We can do whatever dumb thing we want."

That included visiting dozens of other strange new worlds, like one populated by sophisticated, talking dinosaurs.

"I loved the dinosaurs," says Kirkman. "We got three dinosaur designs that were pretty awesome. I expanded that scene from what it was in the comics. I had a lot of fun playing with that and doing some different things. I loved the proper way of speaking that the dinosaurs had. Anytime you get to put intelligent dinosaurs in something, that's always fun."

While it was a treat for viewers to catch glimpses of so many different dimensions, each one of them required an immense amount of additional work from the show's design team.

"[Episode] 208 was just a beast for us in design," says O'Neil. "We go everywhere, we see everything. We do alternate versions of people and places. The tempo of that episode is incredible. It's always wild to me that most of

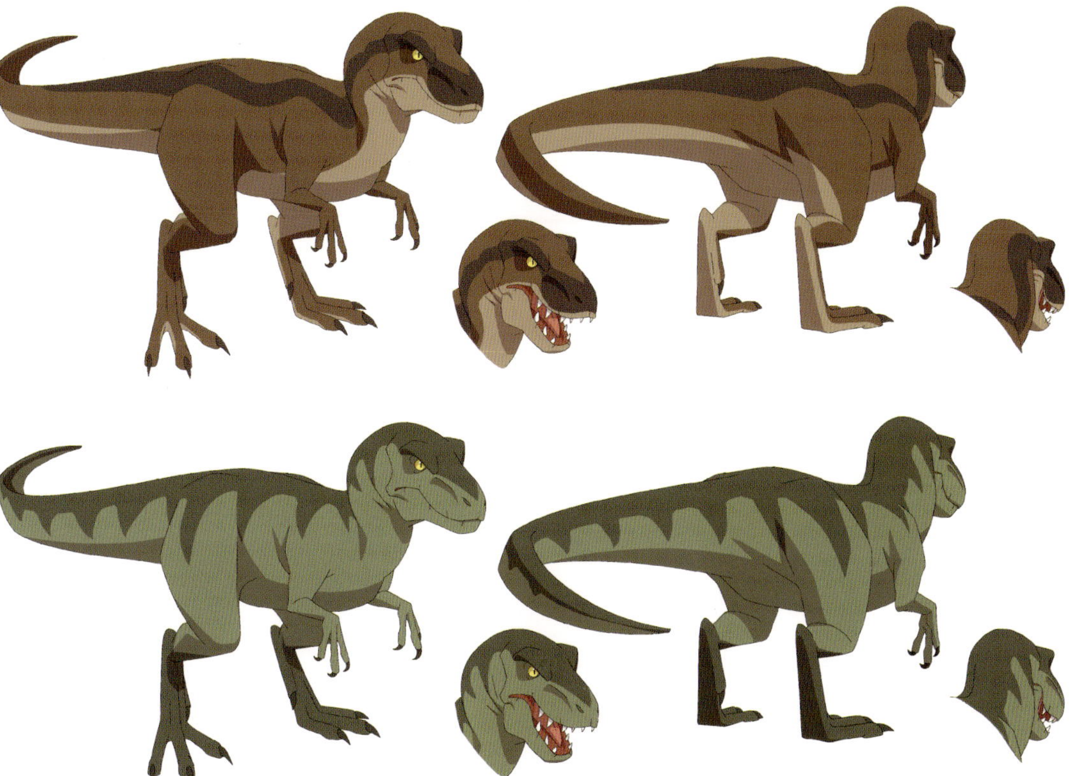

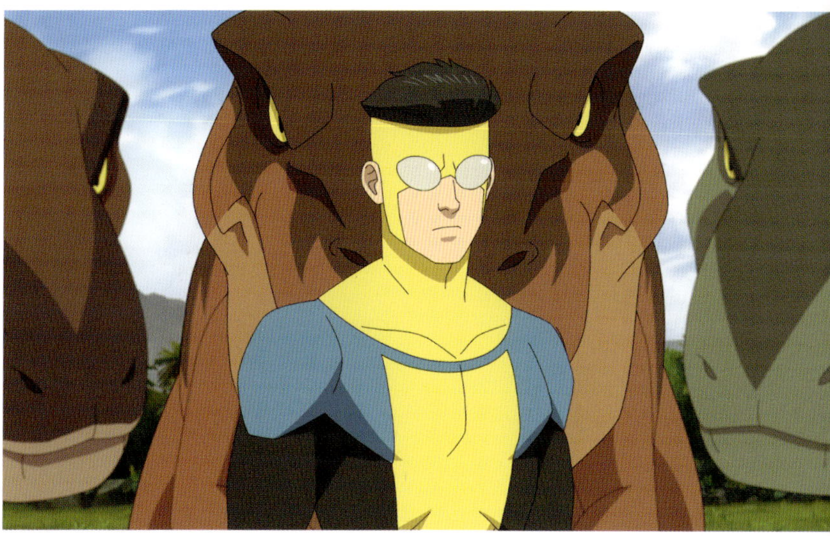

the action in 208 happens at the front end. It's the smallest percentage of the episode, but the amount of shit that's stuffed in there, the pace that was in the script, the pace that Dan and the board team managed to plus and get out of the script, you're just on this tour de force of trauma and visual rollercoasters."

With such a massive workload on the design front, the *Invincible* art team called in help from friends at other animation studios to make it all happen.

"We had a lot of help on the tail end of the season from some of our friends at Titmouse and Rooster Teeth," says O'Neil. "They brought a lot to the table because we were so pressed for time, and we had so much stuff to work through. Just looking at the breakdown for 208, there's like a hundred designs in this that we did in pre-design, just for characters. And that doesn't include the additional hundred designs of reused shit. Things that we had already kind of pinned down. It doesn't include another 10 to 15 things that we were just waiting to see where boards went so we could tie it down — damage states and shit like that. Same for everything. Props count was really high on this. The effects were crazy. The environment count was off the charts. So just trying to get through as much of this as we could with the help that we had was a mountain. But it was really cool. In this episode, we solved a lot of problems that I think carried us forward through future seasons. Just things where, in a pinch, we had to problem solve, we had to pivot. We had to do stuff differently, which revealed opportunities for process and for optimization. Lessons you learned of how not to do shit even. So it was a really crazy bullet-point 'period at the end of the season' sentence."

"It is a lot of work and sometimes you have to ask, 'Is it worth it?'" says Walker. "And the answer is 'Yes.' Because it's got to be done. And, hopefully, in some ways you can find opportunities to reuse things, so that it's not just for a tiny thing. Like I said about the Allen thing [in Episode 203], at the time we were basically starting a second show for half an episode, in terms of design. Luckily, a lot of that stuff gets reused, but that is the thing."

While Mark spent the early part of the episode cascading

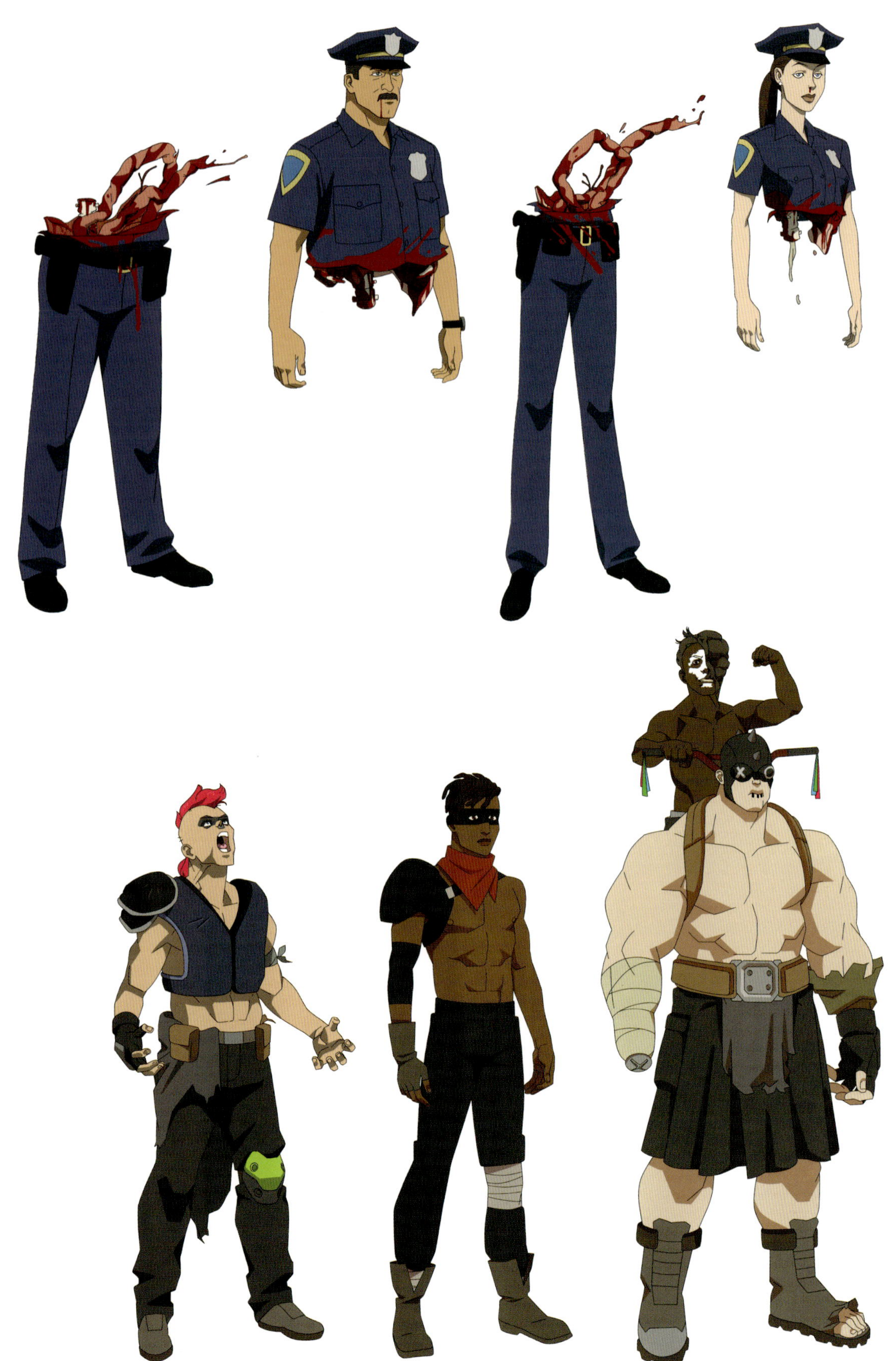

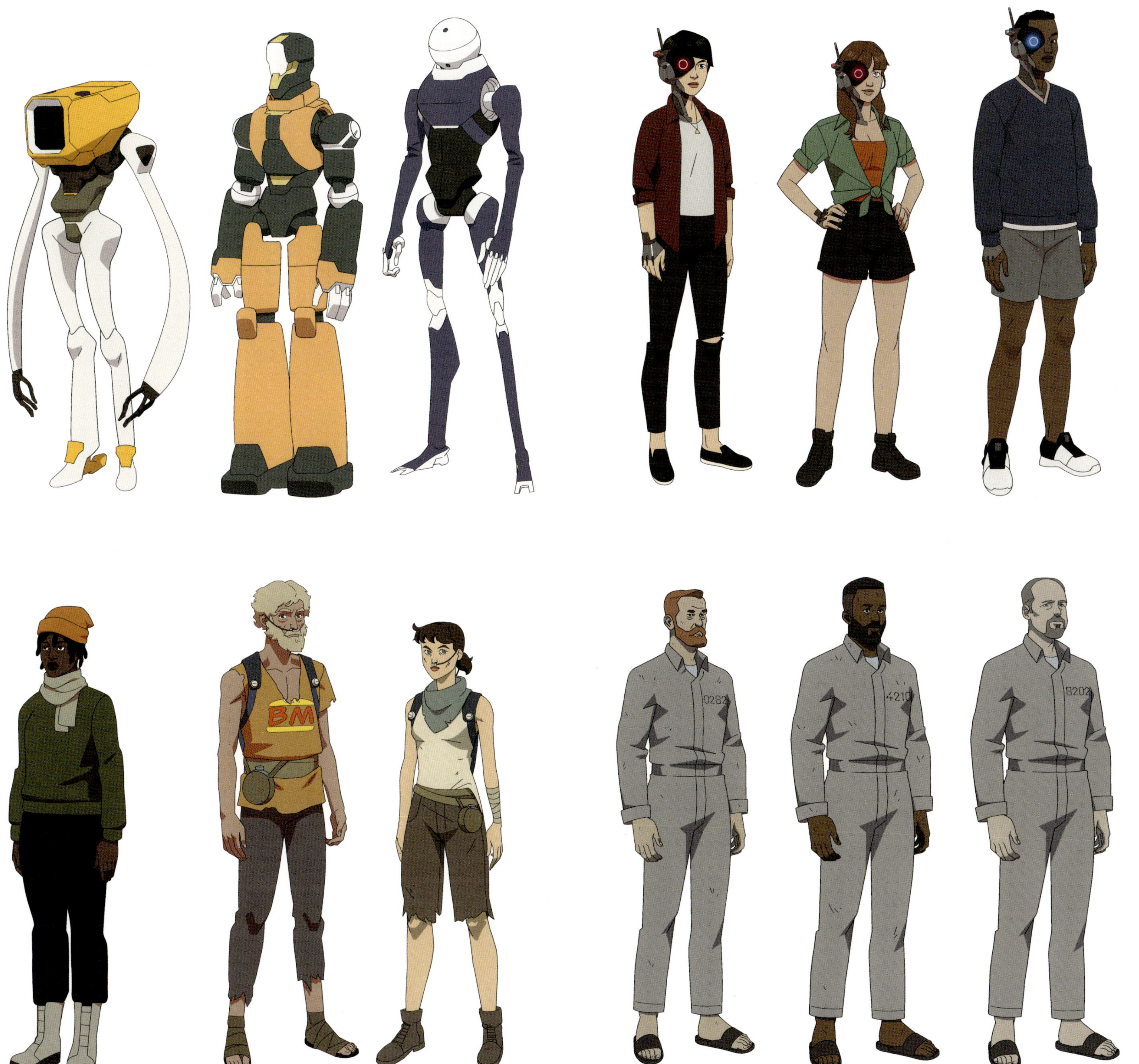
BM
0282
4210
8202

between alternate universes, he eventually returned back to his own reality long enough to see the pain that Levy had inflicted upon his mother.

"We wanted to make sure that you felt like Debbie could die in this episode," says Racioppa. "Like that was a thing that could happen. She doesn't, obviously, but she gets pretty badly hurt. We went over that sequence with Sandra [Oh], showed her the footage, and then we let her [record] live to the video. And we did that a couple times, just to try to get a realistic reaction, which actually ended up being a little smaller than you might think. It is not huge screams, but like gulping for air and trying to swallow the pain of just having your arm broken. So making that feel as real as possible and not this crazy cartoony thing where someone just gets her arm broken. We wanted to make sure this felt like someone really breaking their arm. The sound effects play for that, but mostly Sandra's performance."

"Sandra Oh is the best," says Kirkman. "Never a dry eye when she's doing her record sessions. The sounds that she came up with were unique, and not the canned pain sounds that you would think that somebody would come up with. She really put a lot of effort into like, 'Okay, I've actually seen people really get hurt before and they make sounds that are a little unusual.' And so she was able to bring that to the table, which was really great."

Beyond the masterful voice performance by Oh, the design work for Debbie's injuries had to get across the severe physical trauma that Levy had inflicted upon her.

"It's heartbreaking to see that kind of a damage state with the Debbie character," says Kirkman. "But this is the kind of show we're doing. We're pushing things."

"Again, it's his mom, who is obviously paying part of the price for something Mark was involved in months ago," says Racioppa.

Unwilling to let anyone else he loved suffer harm because of him, Mark took the fight directly to Levy. But Levy retaliated, sending the two of them spiraling through even more alternate dimensions together.

"For me, one of the best parts of the sequence is when Angstrom actually strikes back," says Racioppa, "and then

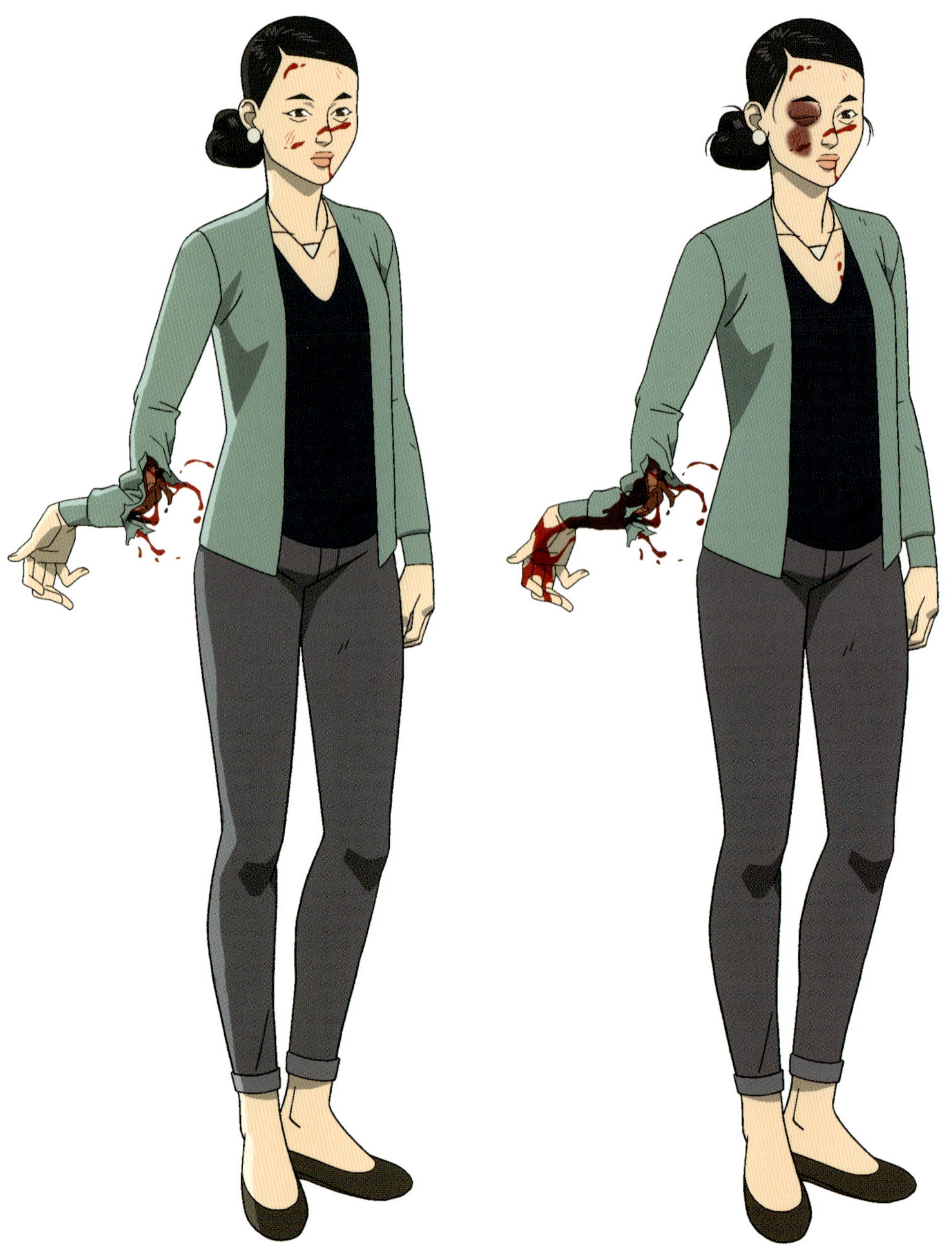

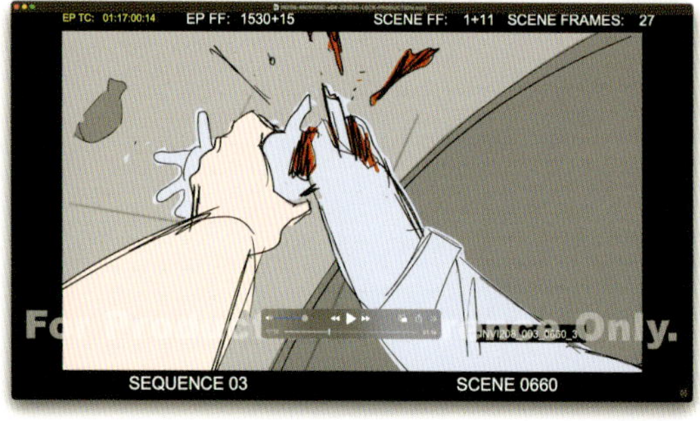

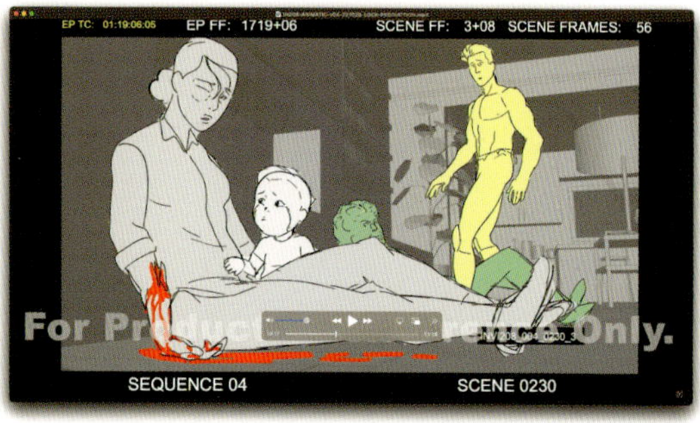

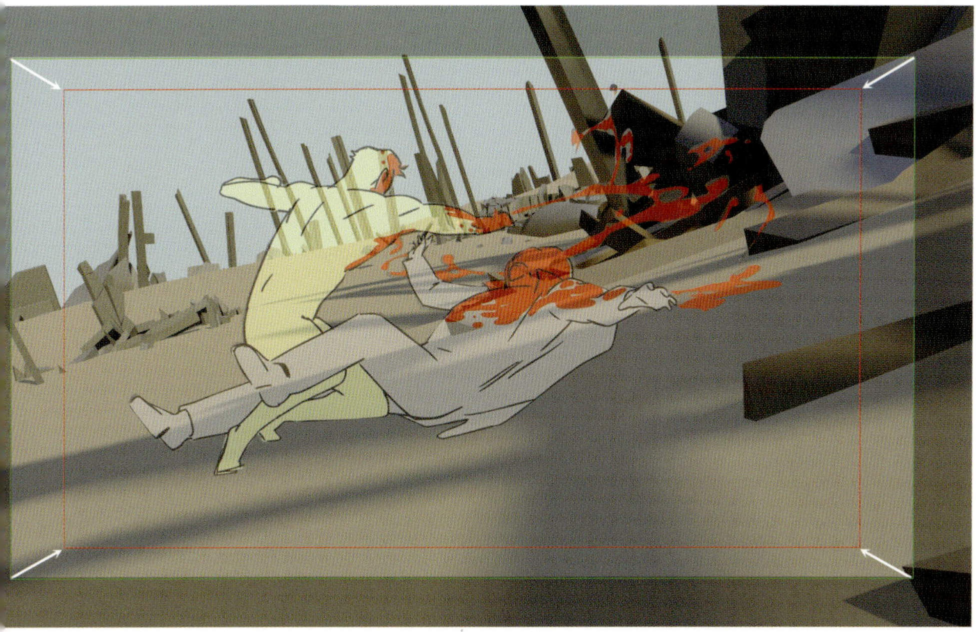

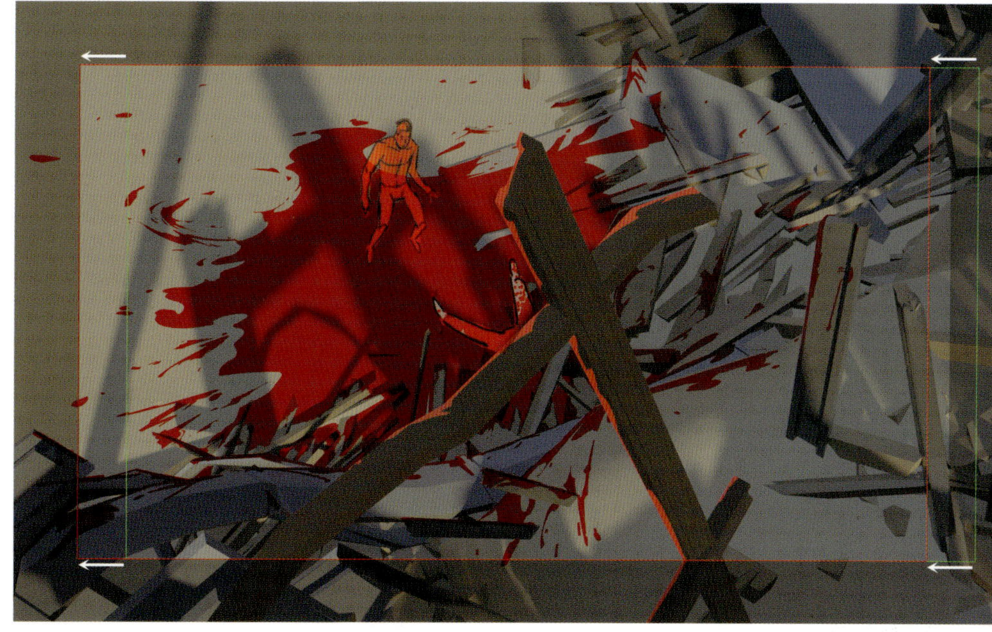

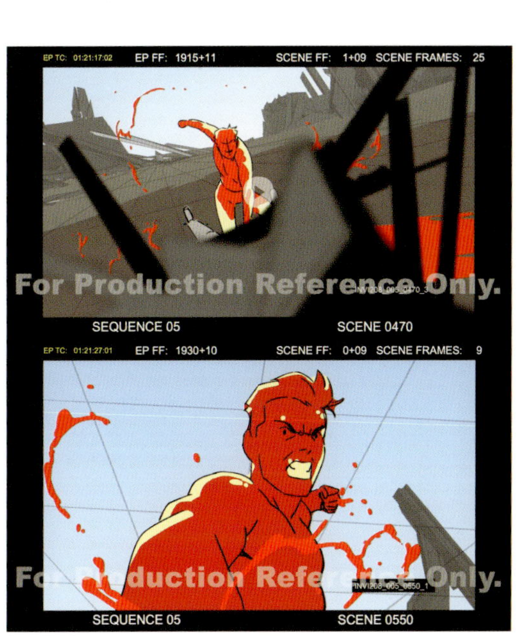
EP TC: 01:21:17:02
EP FF: 1915+11
SCENE FF: 1+09 SCENE FRAMES: 25
For Production Reference Only.
SEQUENCE 05
SCENE 0470
EP TC: 01:21:27:01
EP FF: 1930+10
SCENE FF: 0+09 SCENE FRAMES: 9
INVI208_005_0550_1
SEQUENCE 05
SCENE 0550

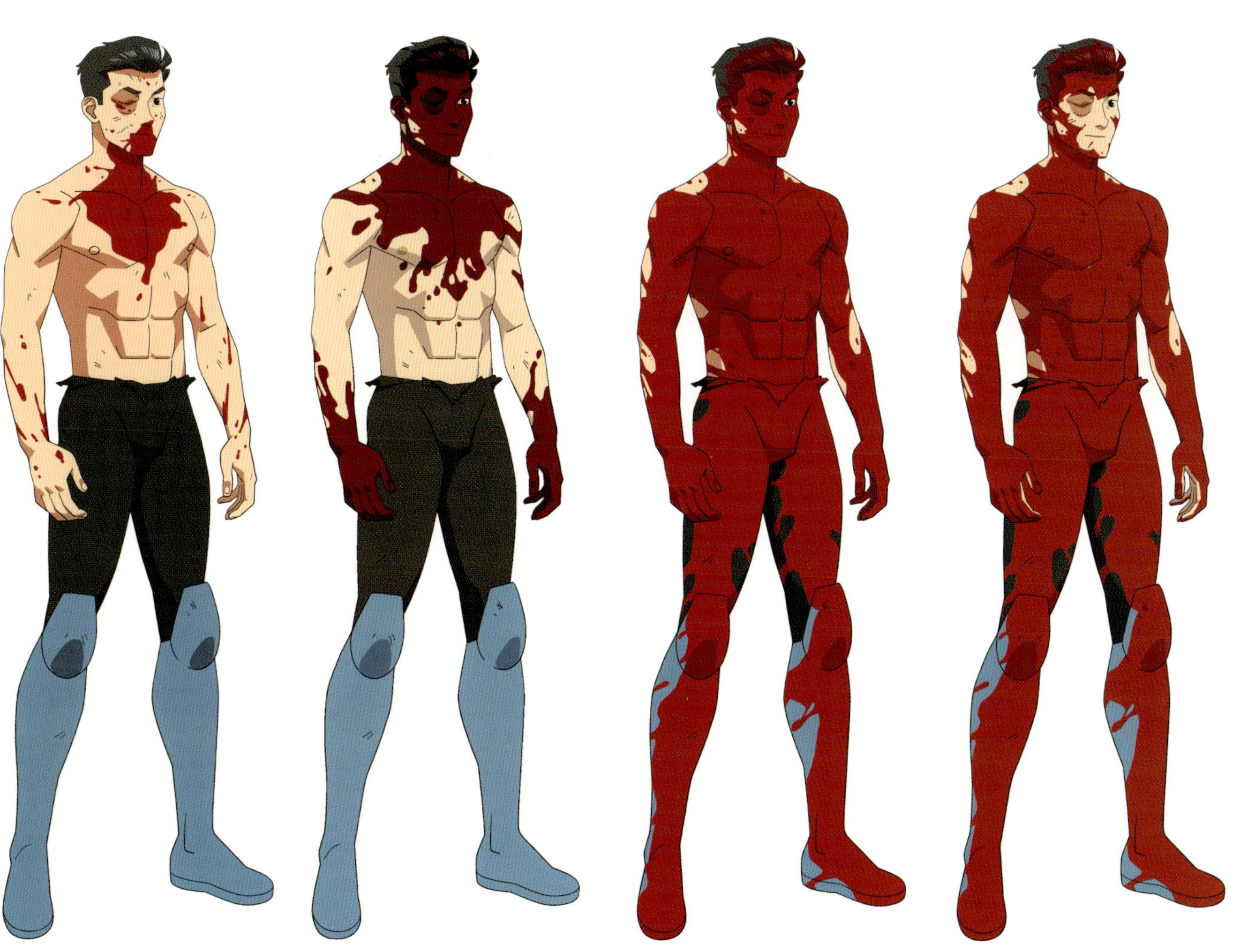

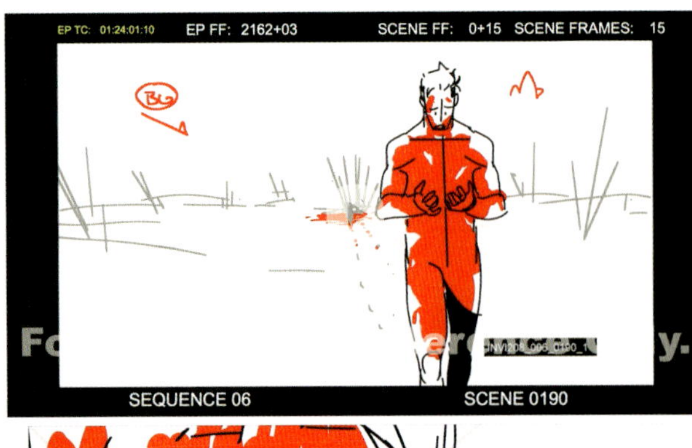
EP TC: 01:24:01:10
EP FF: 2162+03
SCENE FF: 0+15
SCENE FRAMES: 15
SEQUENCE 06
SCENE 0190

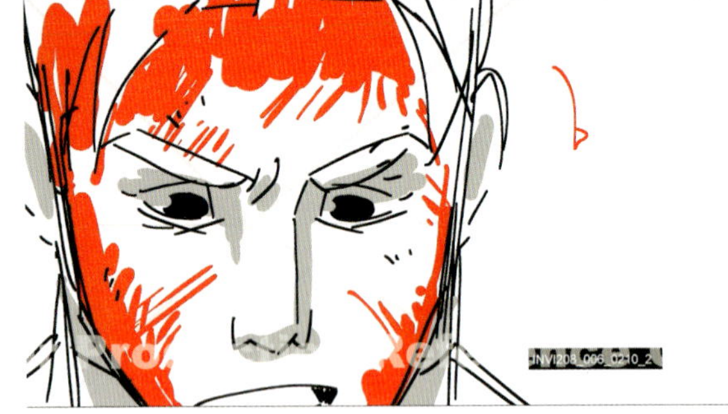

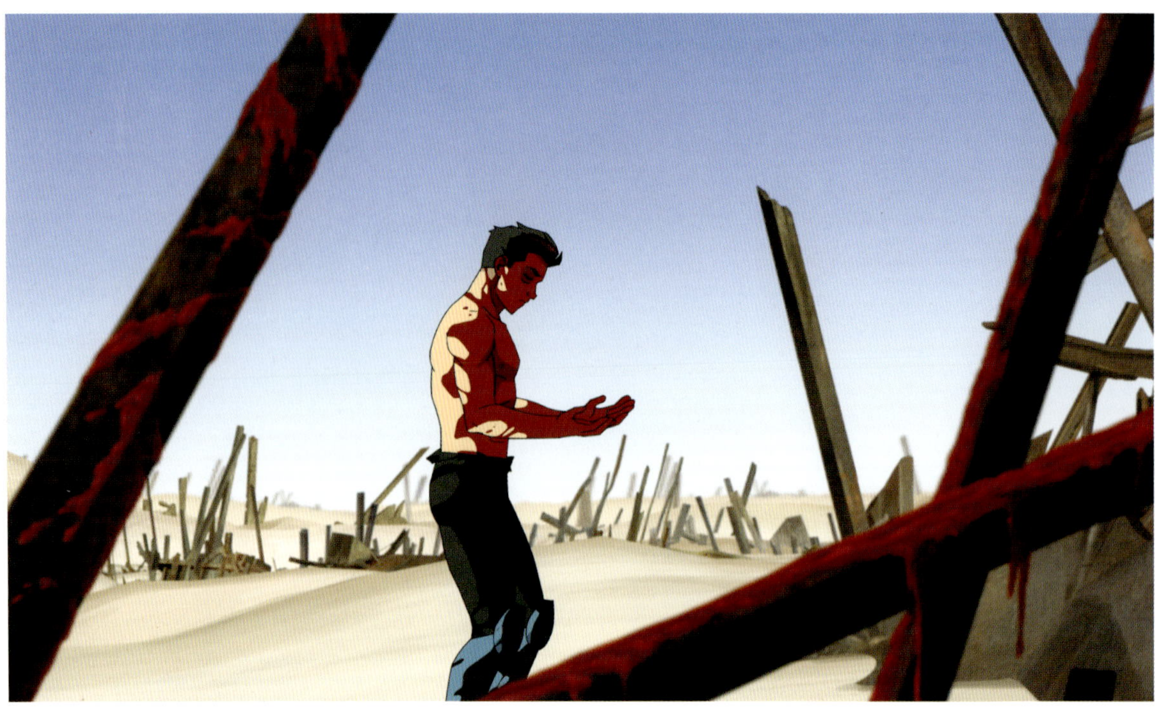

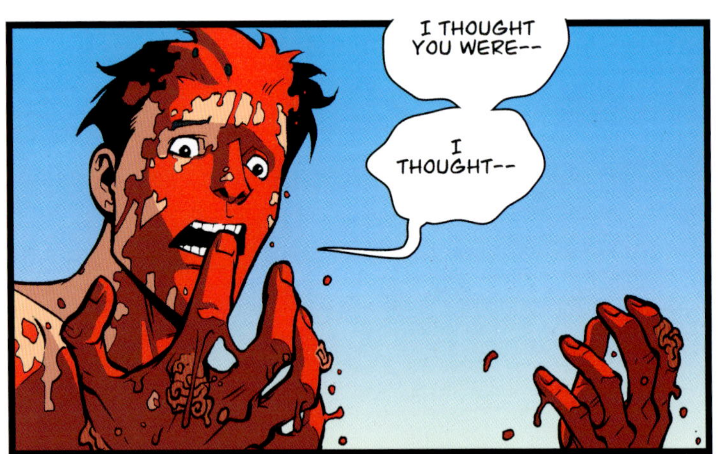
I THOUGHT YOU WERE--
I THOUGHT--

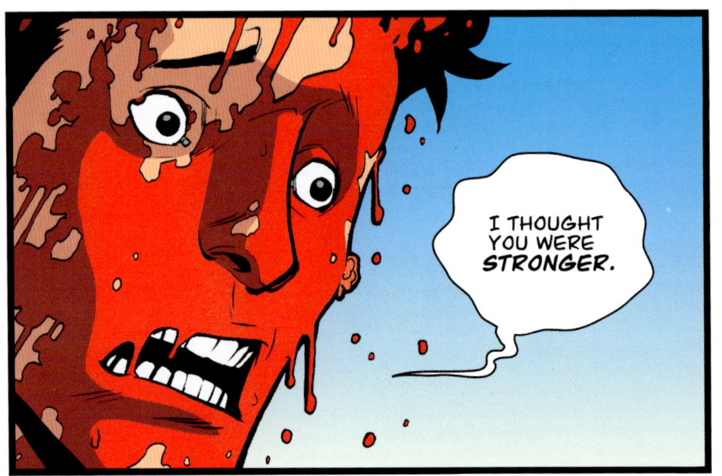
I THOUGHT YOU WERE STRONGER.

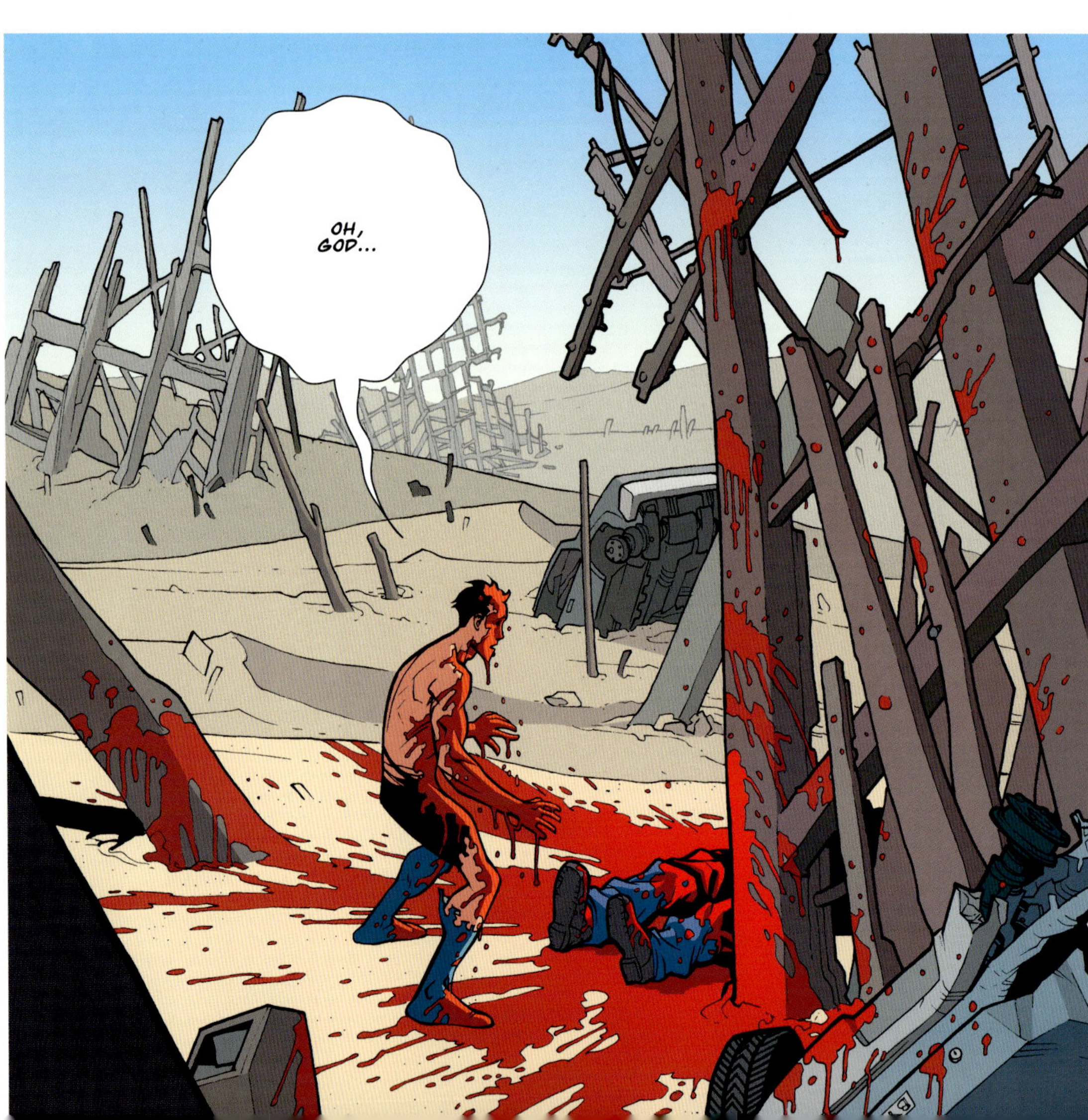
OH, GOD...

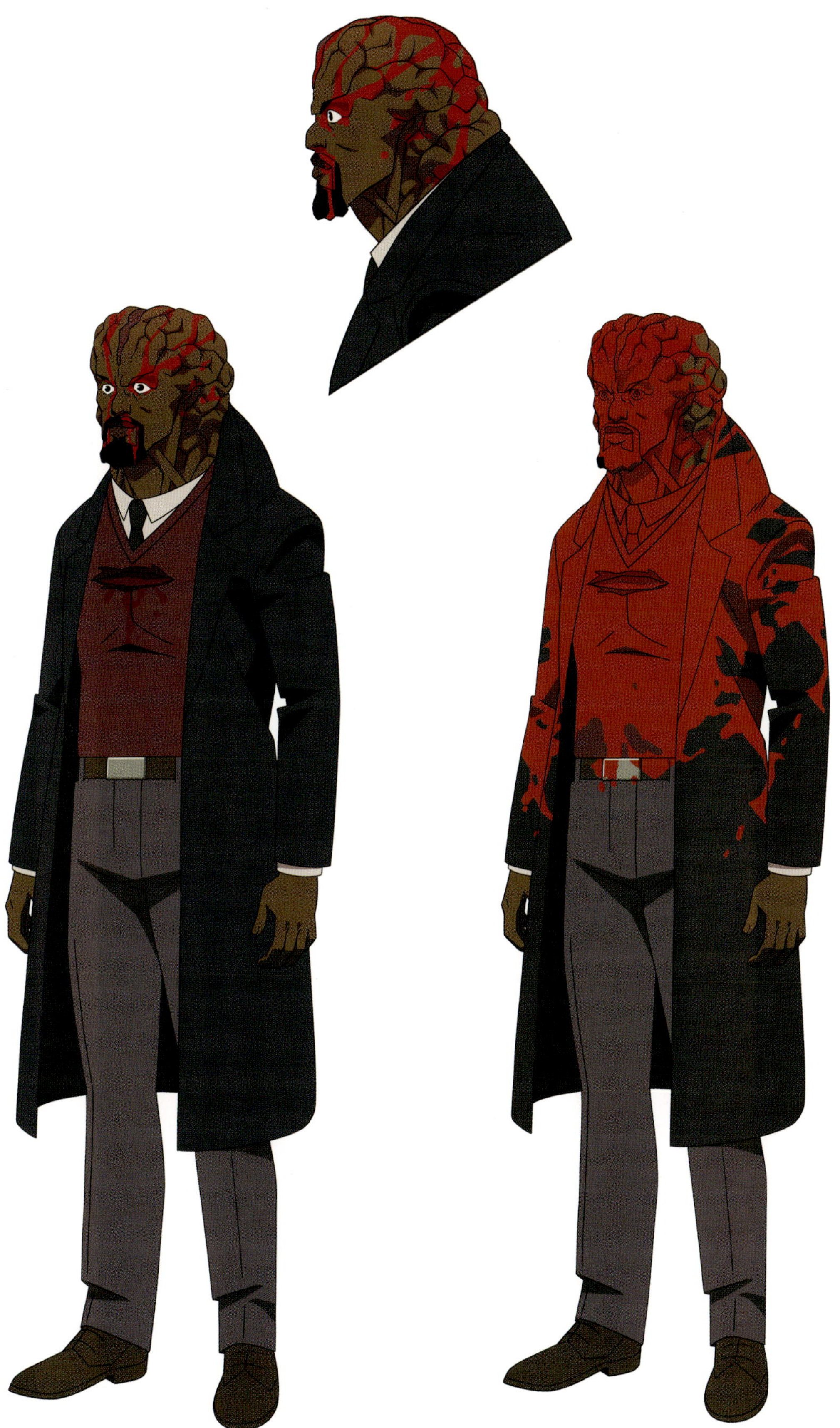

he and Mark are fighting and falling through portals, going through different worlds. I think that's great. There's a robot world. There's this desolate world where everyone has nose tubes, like from *Dune*. It's just this great sequence that ends on this kind of post-apocalyptic planet at the very, very end, where Mark tries to stop Angstrom, and maybe stops him a little too hard."

"We end in that nuclear wasteland," says O'Neil. "Again, I think a lot of the paints for that were done by Amber [Blade Jones]. It's hard to take barren spaces and make them feel textured and interesting. And Amber absolutely killed it. Absolutely crushed those spaces."

Once they finally landed in their final destination, Mark fought back with a ferocity that would have been unthinkable to him not long before. And he didn't stop fighting until Levy was dead.

"The whole season's working towards like, he's terrified of becoming his father," says Racioppa. "And then obviously, in that final sequence, there's shots of Nolan covered in blood at the end of Season One. So Mark, both visually and through his actions, in a way has become his father, has killed someone. I think there's an argument, obviously Mark is still Mark. He's not exactly like his father, but he's taken a step towards something his father's done, which is the death of — not an innocent person, but the death of someone on purpose. He's killed someone. Even if he thought he was stronger. Even if he didn't mean to do it. But for Mark, he's just had this terrible experience with Anissa. Amber almost got killed by Anissa, so that's put him on edge. And then to see his mom actually get hurt, I feel like his reaction is a very natural one. Most people would freak out and just be like, 'Stay away from my family.' He's been through a lot this season, and that rage just comes up and he takes it out on Angstrom. But it's not about being angry at Angstrom. It's about trying to make sure that Angstrom doesn't ever do this again. And then it just goes too far, obviously, and he loses a little bit of control and he kills Angstrom.

"Angstrom was not messing around," says Walker. "You know, as the old saying goes, 'Fuck around and find out,' am I right? That's what happened to the young man."

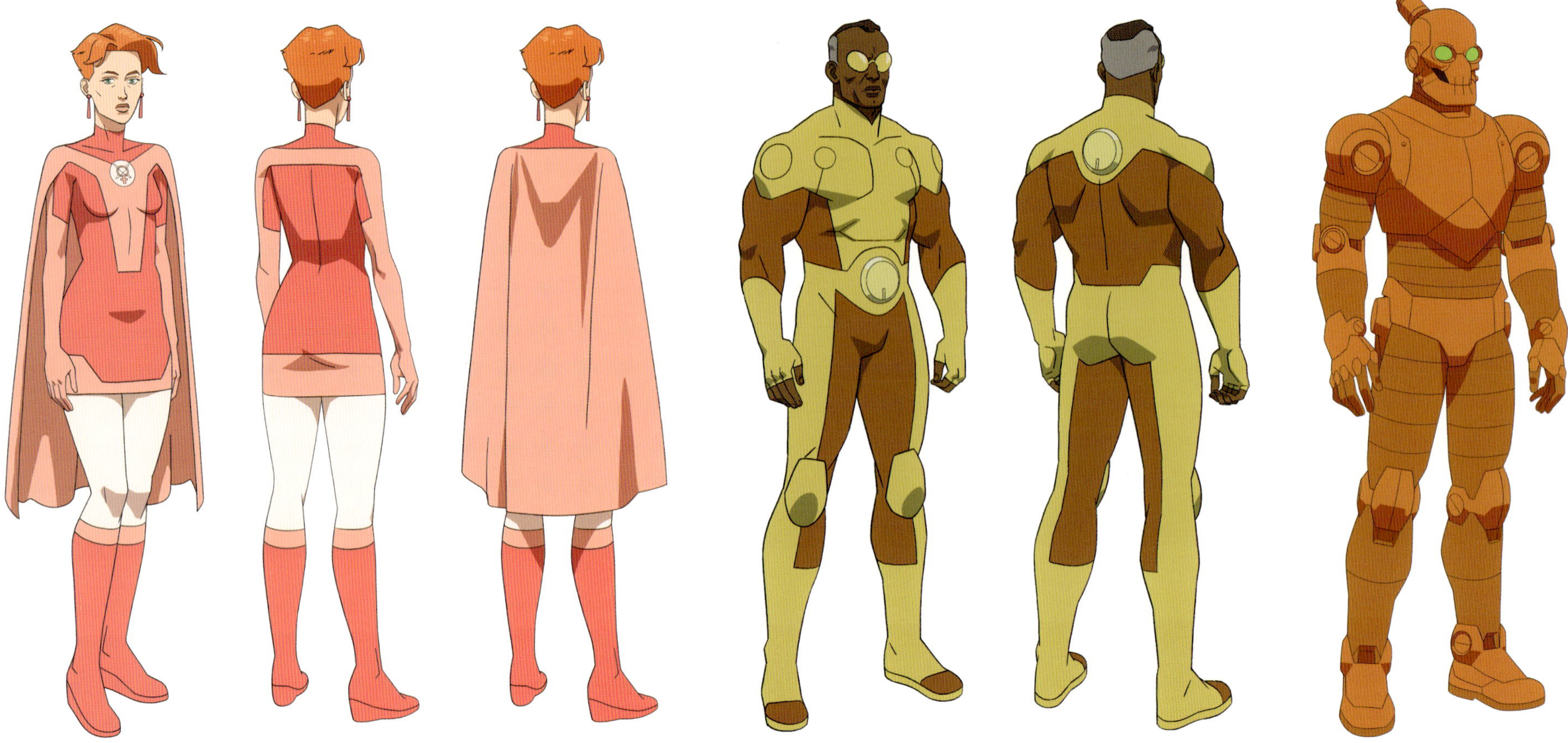

While the art and story teams pulled out all the stops for the final battle against Levy, the vocal performance by Steven Yeun helped capture Mark's emotional state brilliantly.

"Steven's performance when Mark was just losing it, kind of coming unraveled, was really great," says Walker.

Extra attention also was paid to the physical states of each character as the fight progressed, particularly in terms of how much blood — both Levy's and his own — that Mark would be drenched in by the time the battle reached its conclusion.

"To be able to see the difference in Mark as he's covered in various stages of blood," says Kirkman, "these are difficult things to accomplish that take a lot of man-hours and a lot of effort from a team. So they definitely should be recognized for going above and beyond on that front. A lot of cool stuff goes into that sequence."

"The final shot of Mark coming up just covered in blood is so nice," says Racioppa, "because it visually represents his journey across the entire season and sort of shows him looking like his father back from Season One."

With Levy dead, the villain's power to open portals between dimensions was no longer available. Thus, Mark found himself stranded in the wasteland world with no way home. Thankfully, it wasn't too long before a futuristic group of Guardians of the Globe arrived on the scene.

"Mark is rescued by a team of future Guardians from one timeline that is not maybe our current timeline," says Racioppa, "because it would split, depending on how you navigate your timeline physics in fictional universes. They show up because they've been looking for Mark for years. He disappeared. The world they're in, where Mark wasn't a part of it, is not a great one. We don't get into what happened there exactly, but you can kind of imagine. Maybe the Viltrumites came to Earth. Maybe things got really ugly. We kind of paint a picture of what happens when things go

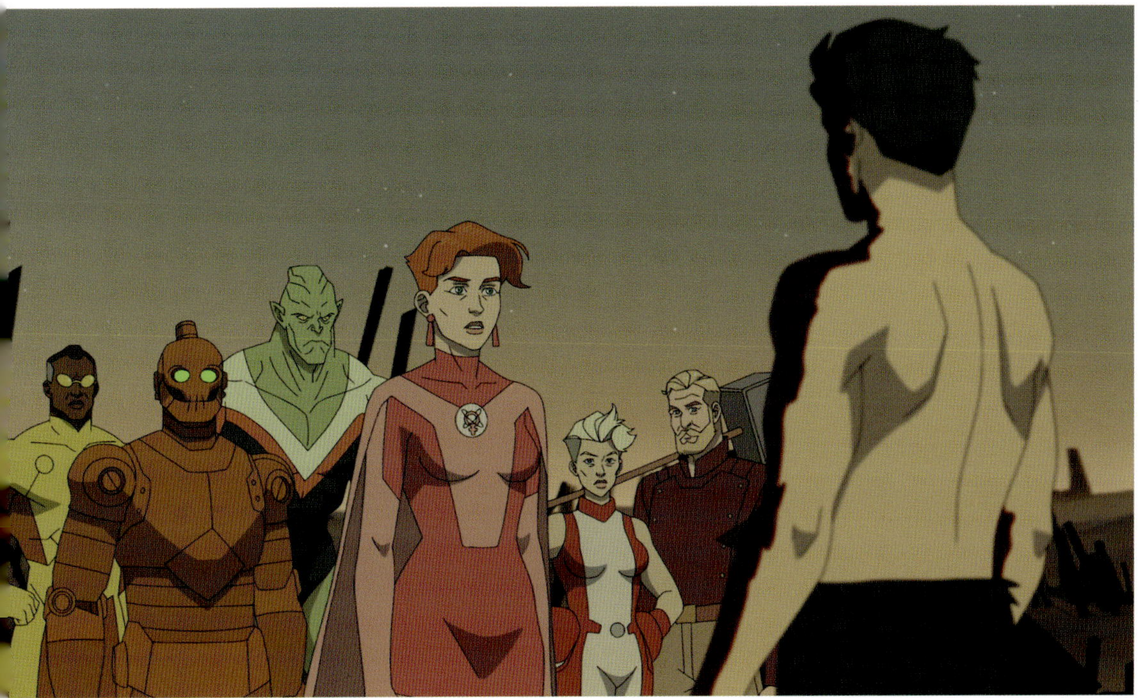

bad at the start of the season with Mark. And then we also get a hint of a different Robot — Rex in there — that may or may not be a hint of things to come in the future, even in our timeline. And then, of course, we get a little bit of drama from Eve approaching Mark. And even though this is an Eve from thirty years in the future, she's telling him how she felt back at the time when they were together in her past, and that maybe Mark should either say something or not say something. But either way, 'Let's do this or let's not do this, but don't leave me hanging.' And that's going to have some ramifications that you will see play out in future seasons. Maybe even the next season."

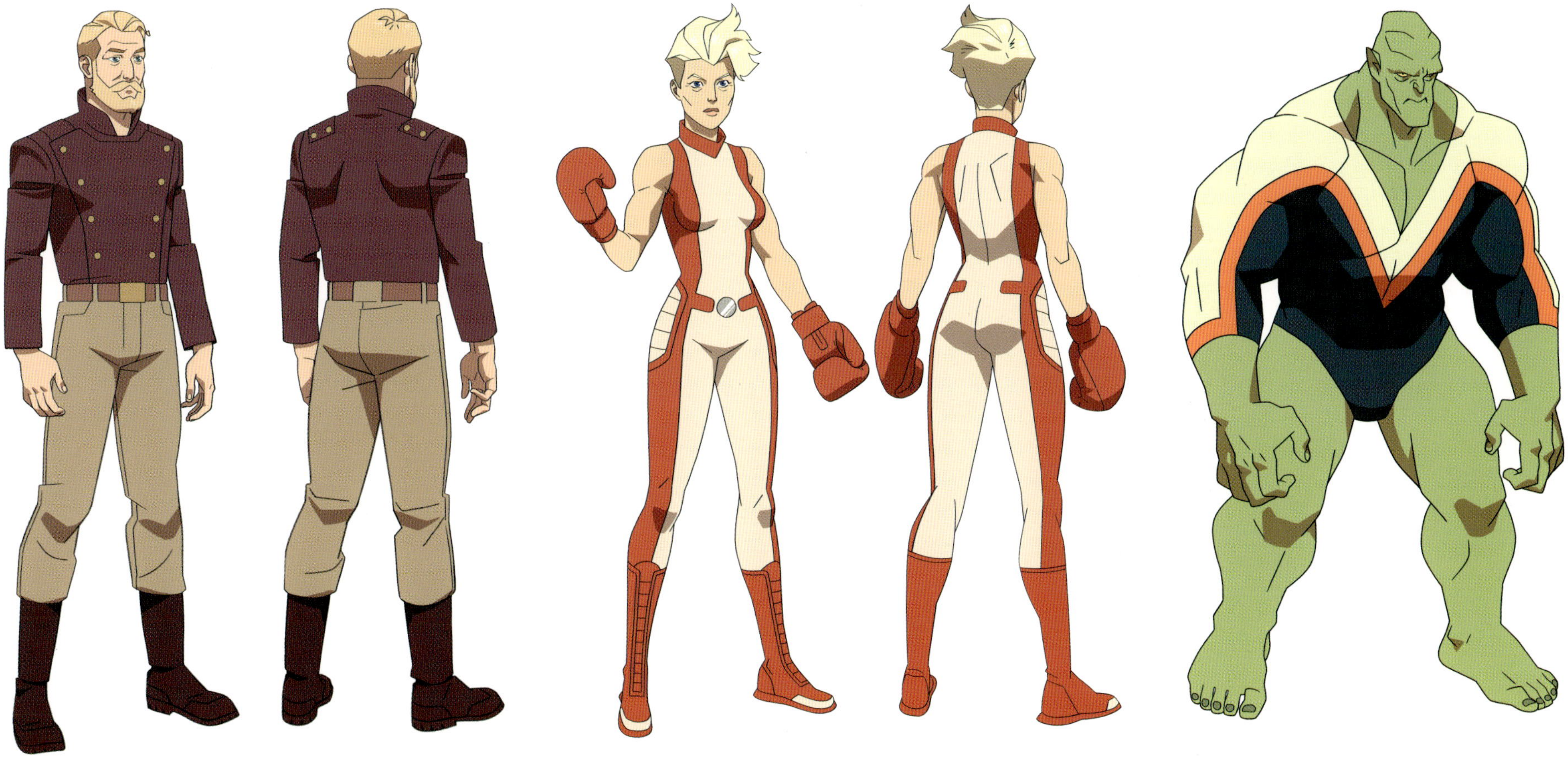

"With my love of alternate takes on existing characters, seeing the future Guardians come in to retrieve Mark was very cool," says Walker. "The take for the show on all of the characters was really good."

"We've got Monster Girl in a new costume, and we've got Eve in a new costume," says Kirkman. "Robot looks a little bit different, and Bulletproof looks older. We've got Kid Thor and Knockout, two characters from a completely different comic book series, CAPES, that are showing up kind of on loan from me to myself."

As Kirkman said before, nothing on *Invincible* gets forgotten, a sentiment that Racioppa was quick to reiterate regarding these future Guardians.

"If you got them in this season, maybe we're going to see them in future seasons of the show, as well," says Racioppa. "I mean, we spent all this time designing them..."

Though Mark's journey for the season was approaching its end, one character's life was about to get a fresh start.

"We discover that Dupli-Kate's not actually dead," says Racioppa. "We reveal that she's alive, because she always kept a copy for safekeeping. Which is great, because I feel like a lot of people were like, 'Wouldn't she just have one more copy hidden away somewhere?' Well, yeah, she would, and she did. But it doesn't work if everyone knows that copy exists, right? That kind of defeats the purpose of having your safe copy if everyone's like, 'Oh, she's got another one over here, so if we really want to kill her, we've got to kill that, too.' So Kate's not as dead as we thought she was."

Kate's return came as a welcome surprise to The Immortal, a fellow Guardian with whom she had developed a romantic relationship over the course of the second season.

"At the start of their relationship, which we built earlier in the season," says Racioppa, "they're the only two characters who have died as many times as each other. So that's something that they bond over. It's mostly off-screen, but we talk about it."

The scene also gave us a look at The Immortal's safehouse, where he kept many of the historically significant items that he acquired during his countless centuries alive.

"I like seeing The Immortal in his setting," says Walker, "his safe place with all of his shit he's accumulated throughout the years. I hope people get a real chance to look over that stuff in the book and spot some exciting, recognizable items."

The latter half of the episode also revisited a short sequence from Season One featuring the mysterious

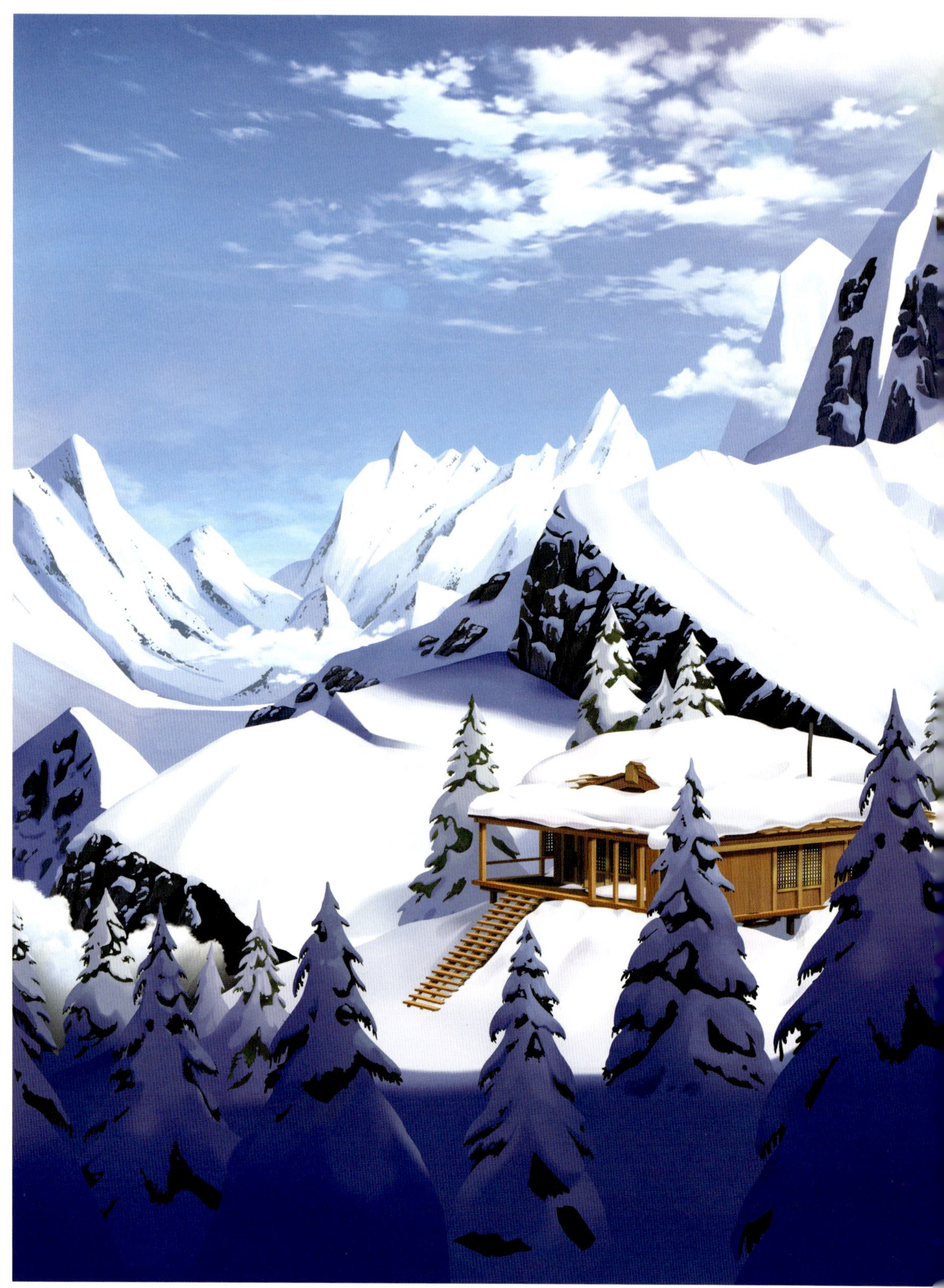

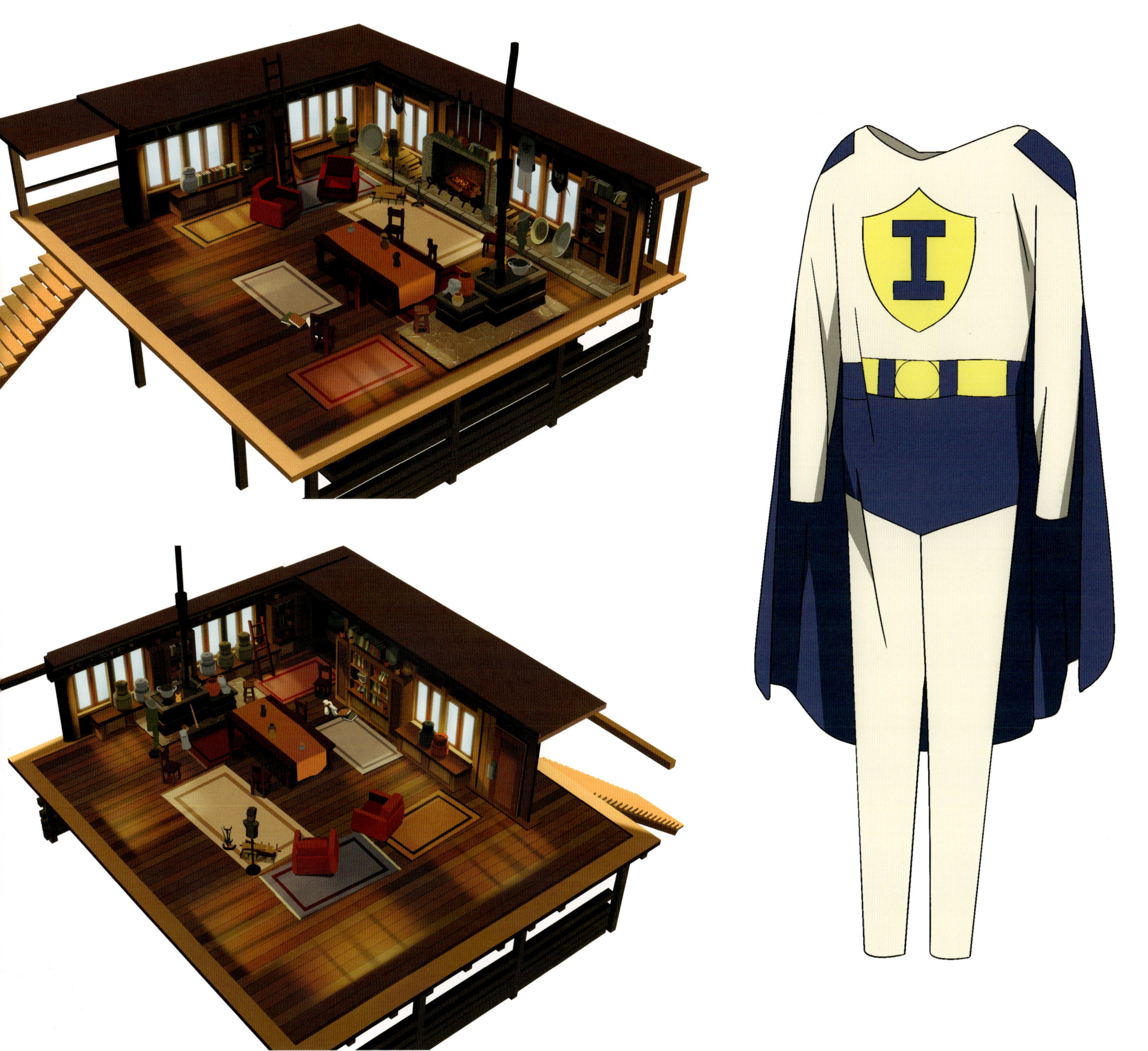

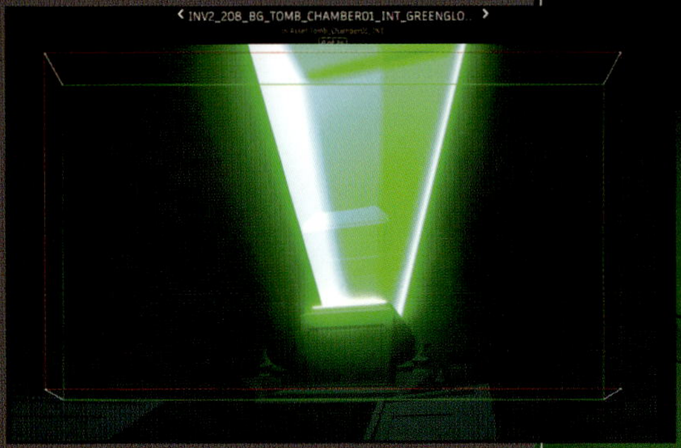
INV2_208_BG_TOMB_CHAMBER01_INT_GREENGLO..

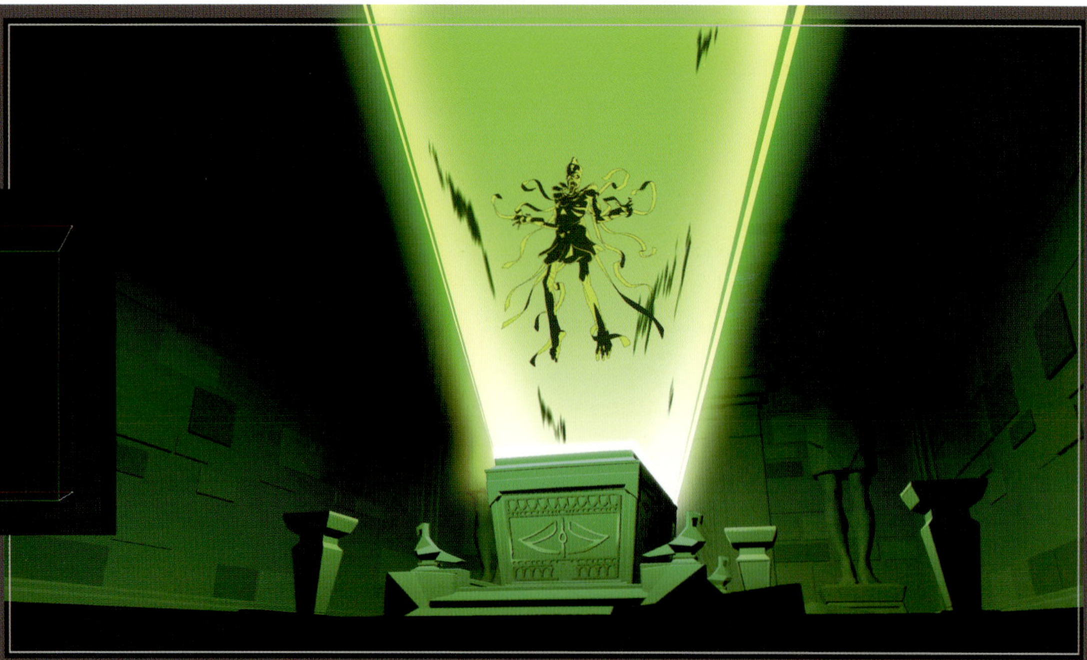

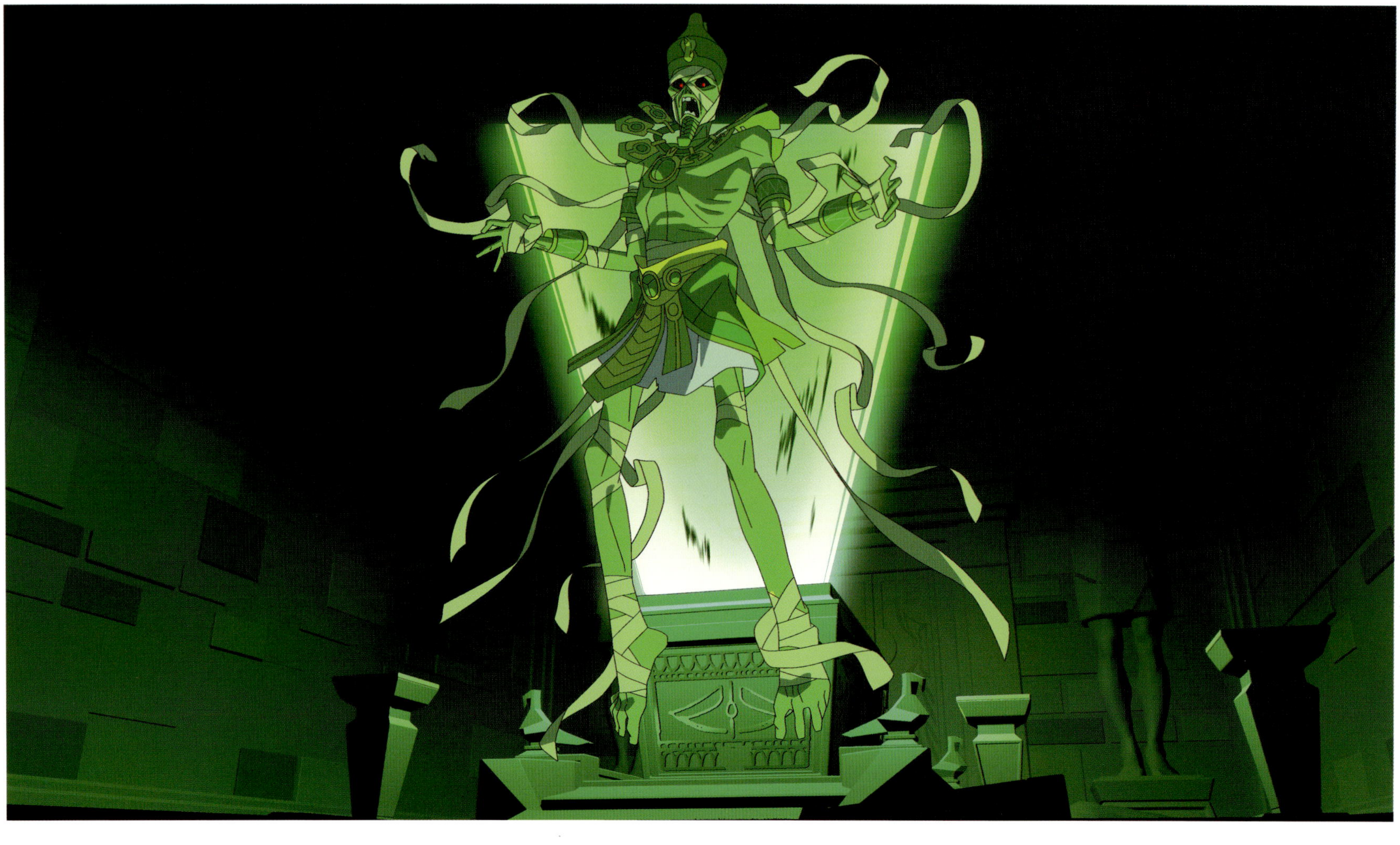

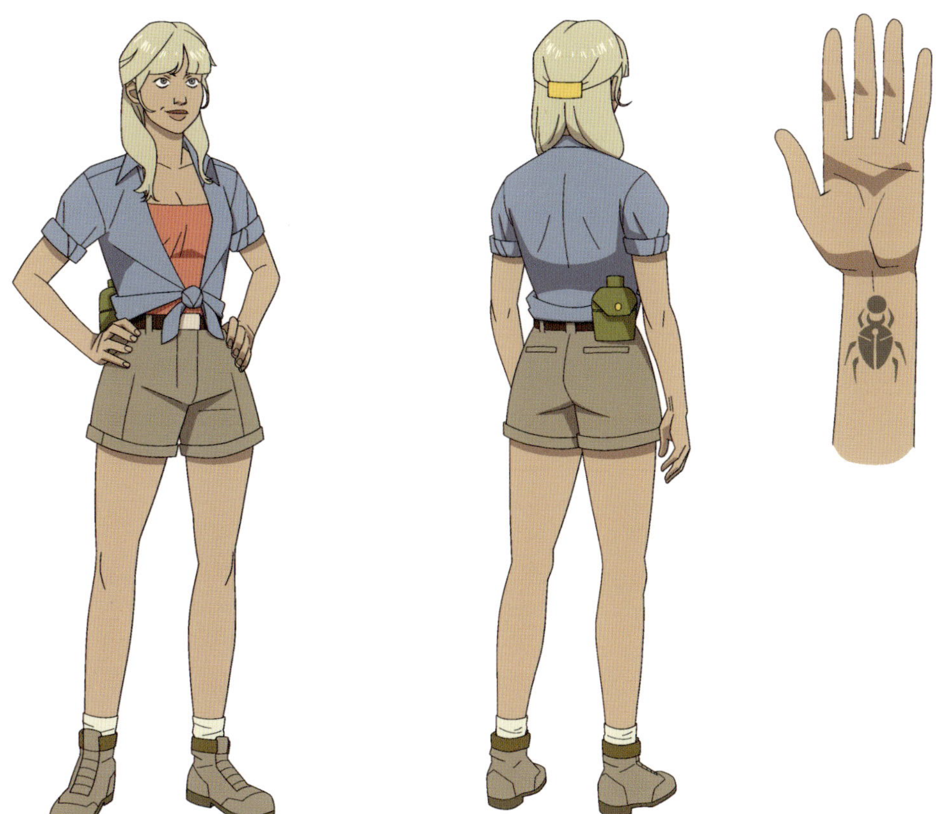

mummy called Ka-Hor, a character who started out as part of a random gag.

"My favorite gag ever—Ka-Hor," says Walker. "The funny thing about [the sequence in Season One] was that it was just so a bunch of guys could get covered in sand because Mark was flying too fast. And I guess I forgot who Robert is for a moment."

"Robert glommed onto it and loved this idea of this mummy who's a little misogynistic," says Racioppa. "And now he pops up in every season."

"I still don't know where it ultimately goes," says Kirkman. "But it's been something that I work into one of the episodes that I write for each season. I've become the Ka-Hor guy that puts him in episodes. I don't want to spoil it, but you'll see more Ka-Hor. Possibly just once a season, possibly more."

The sequence also introduced a duo of female characters named Jane and Riley, who may also be seen again in future seasons.

"Riley is a new character that actually has superpowers and is played by Chloe Bennet, and is somebody that is

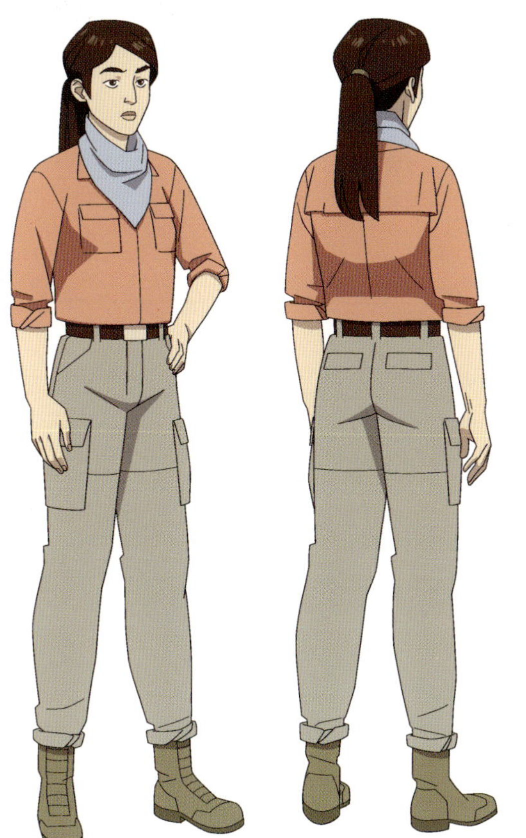

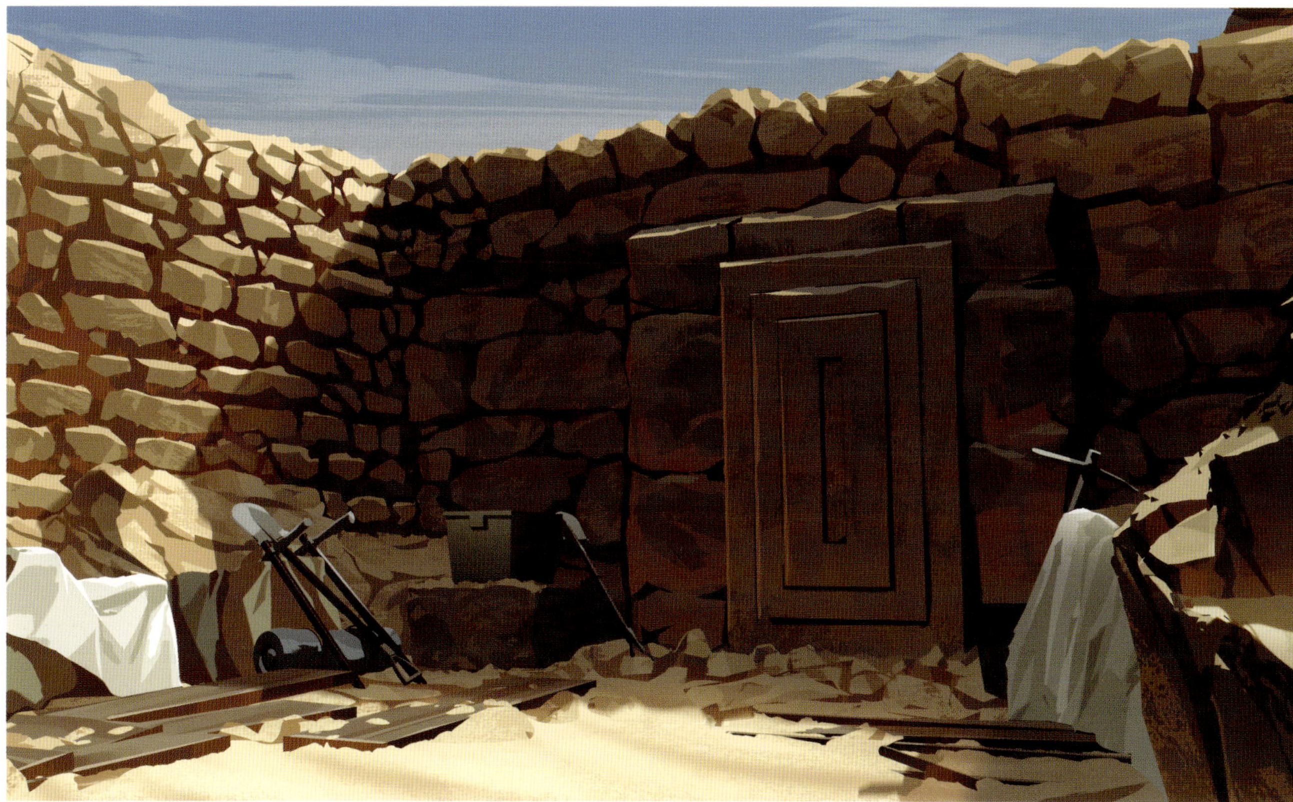

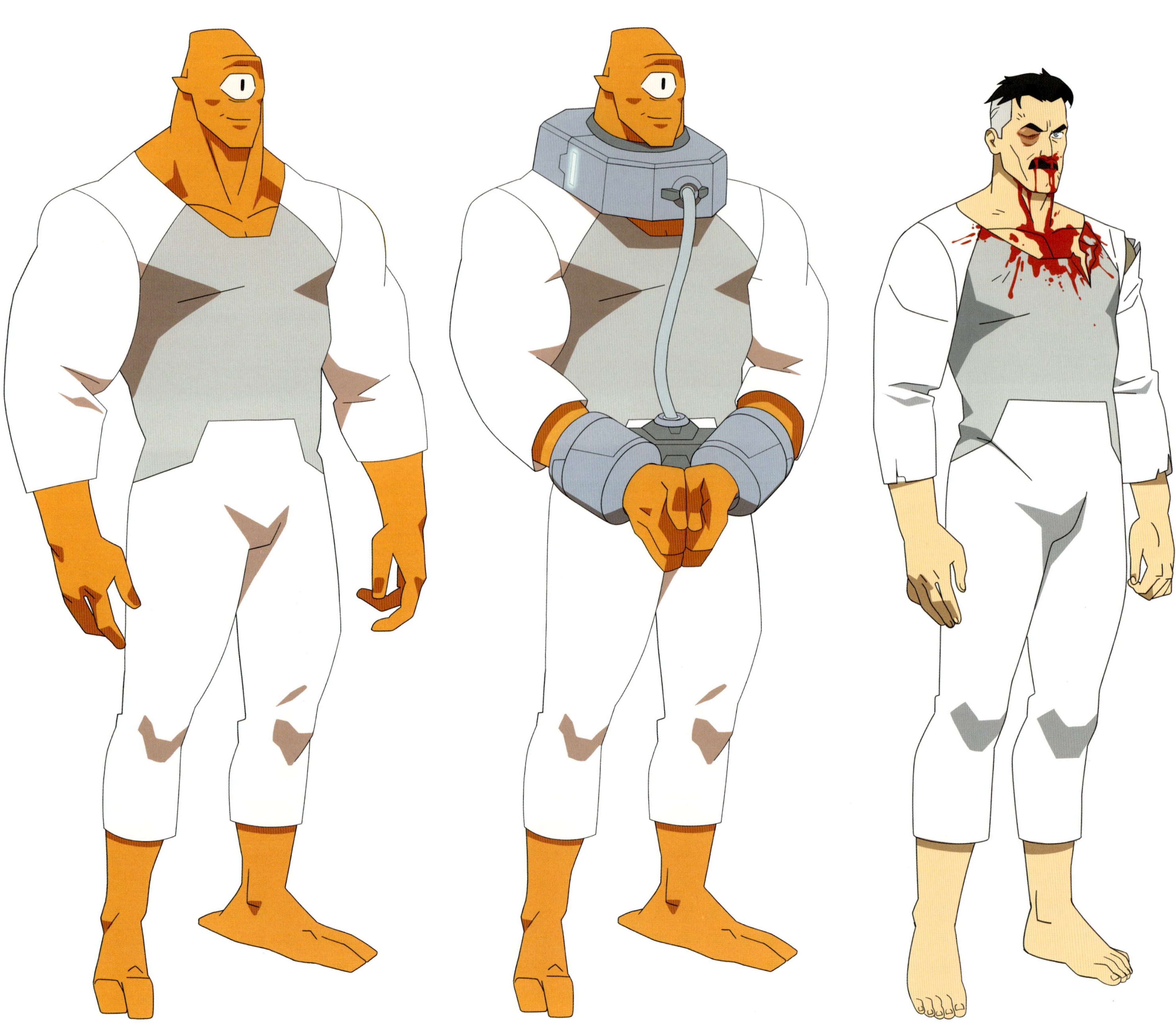

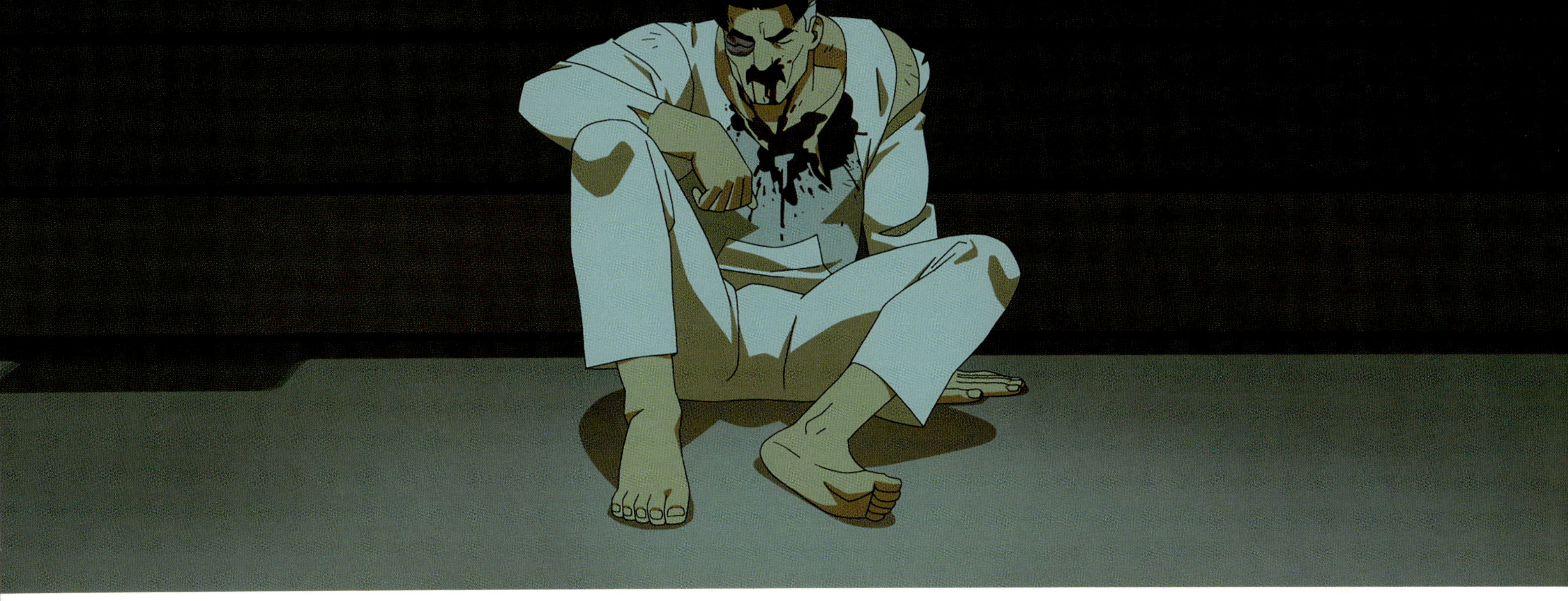

going to reoccur, which is pretty exciting. And then Jane is the daughter of the other Clancy Brown character [Bryant] that came in and discovered Ka-Hor. I think Clancy Brown also plays Ka-Hor. So that's a lot of Clancy Brown."

Speaking of Clancy Brown, the actor's other *Invincible* character, General Kregg, still had Mark's father on lockdown in a Viltrumite prison. But a new inmate arrived at the end of the episode and could very well offer Nolan a stay of execution.

"Allen's now in prison with Nolan to try and get him to join the Coalition," says Racioppa. "He's like, 'Hey, I could flip this guy. I could turn him over. His son's already kind of with us.' Nolan and Allen, at their power levels, could probably break out of that prison if they wanted to. But Nolan doesn't want to break out because he feels like he deserves what's coming for him. And Allen doesn't because he's trying to stay there and switch Nolan to his side."

The arrival of Allen at the Viltrumite prison offered an exciting glimpse of what might lie ahead in Season Three. But at one point, Kirkman considered offering an even larger look at what was to come.

"I will say, there was an earlier version of the script that had another sequence of teases at the end of this episode," says Kirkman. "I actually self-edited that and I deserve recognition for being responsible, because I was like, 'We're doing all this multiverse stuff. I can't hit them with five unique teases for future seasons.' But I really wanted to do that, because I thought it would be funny to do teases for future things at the end of this season when we hadn't even gotten to all the teases from the previous season finale. And I was like, 'I kind of want to do a couple that we're *never* going to follow up on, just to be like, who cares? It's fun.' But I cut that out of the script before I even turned it in. So most people haven't even seen those."

Kirkman may have chosen not to end the season with an extended look at what was on the horizon, but the events of the finale were more than enough to keep fans excited for more. Fortunately, by the time Season Two finished airing, the *Invincible* creative team was already hard at work on Season Three.

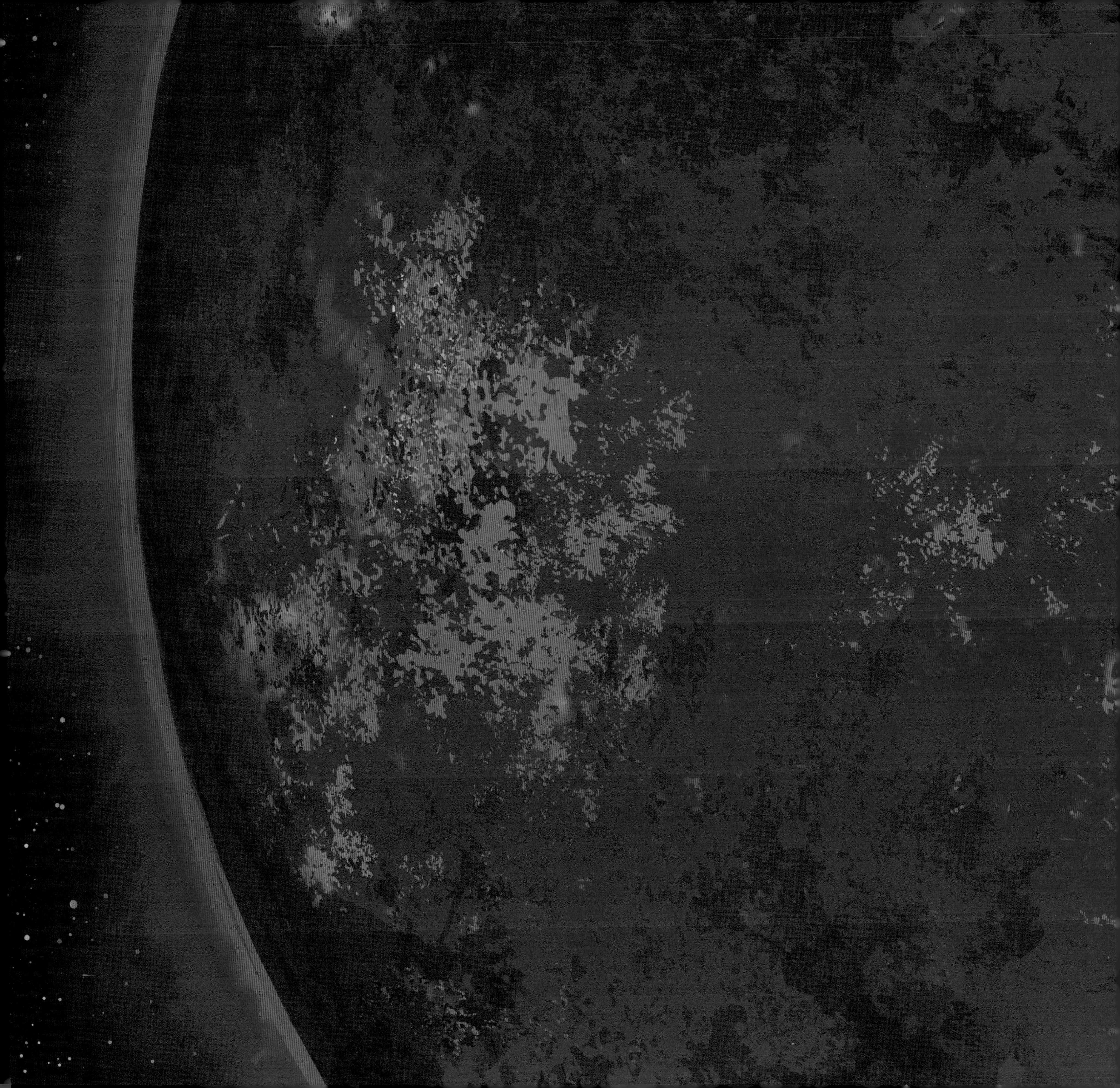

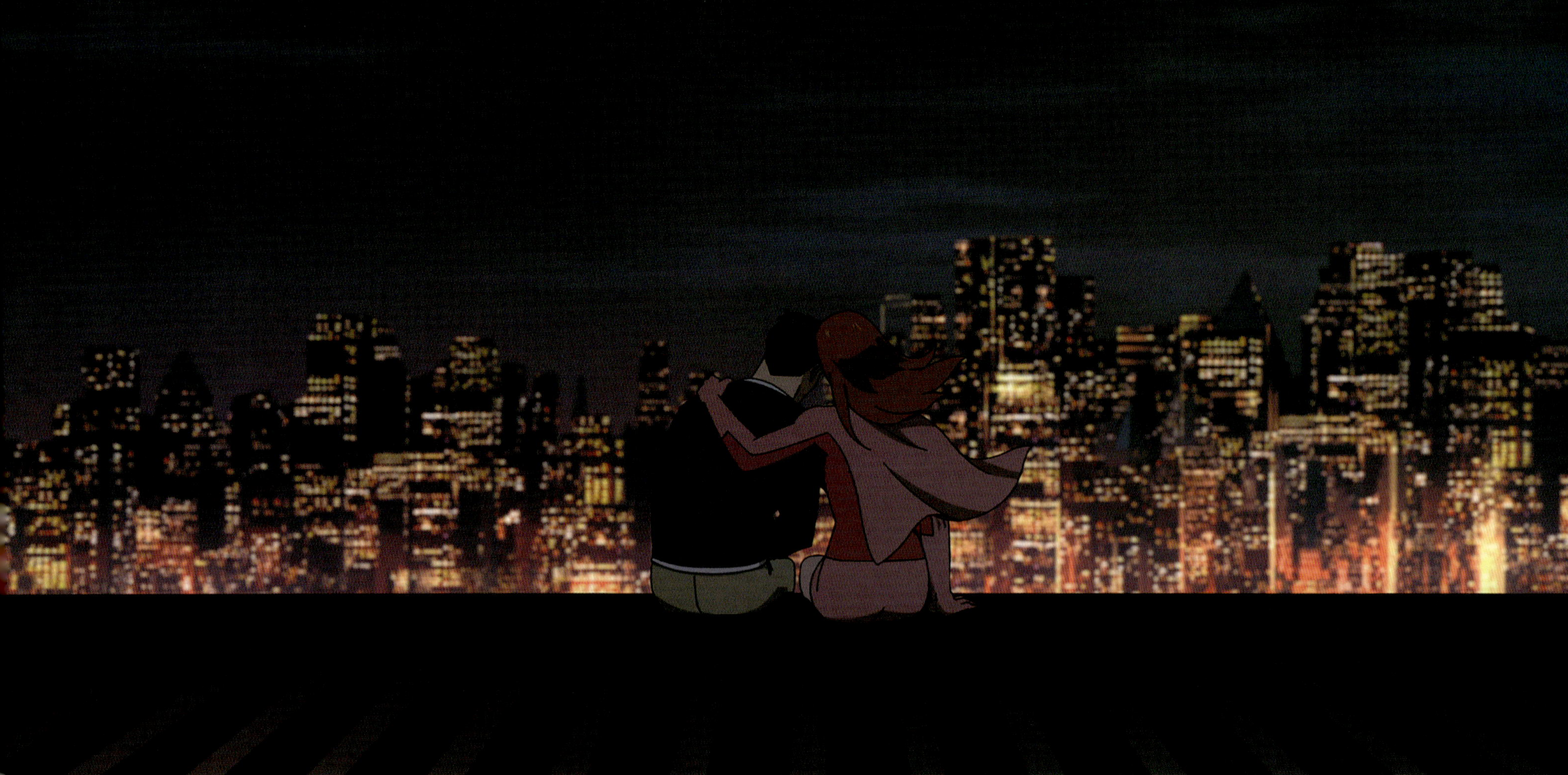

CONCLUSION

With *Invincible* Season Two completed, the talented creators behind the animated series were able to move forward with a clear purpose as they prepared to bring Mark's next round of adventures to the screen. What they learned from Season Two would help to inform what was yet to come.

"Sophomore seasons can be tough," says Executive Producer and Co-Showrunner Simon Racioppa. "You're always wondering if the success you had in Season One was a fluke, or just blind luck, or something else that's beyond your control. Plus there's that feeling of, 'How do we possibly do that again when it was so hard the first time?' For me, the answer is about focusing on how lucky I am that I get to do it again — and then working as hard as I can to make it bigger, badder, more emotional, and push our characters and the show further and further and further until the story's done."

"The team is constantly taking the temperature of the show and looking for ways to improve," says Art Director Shaun O'Neil. "We always say it's an evolution, not a revolution, and we've grown so much since Season Two. I'm very excited for our future."

"If Season One gave me confidence that there was an audience out there for our show," says Racioppa, "the response to Season Two proves that not only were our viewers still there waiting for us (sorry about the wait), but they're also game to follow us the rest of the way along Mark's journey — even to far-off planets populated by bug people who display affection in very strange ways — and beyond. Which is good, since Invincible has some crazy places to go yet..."

While the team was busy looking forward, they weren't about to lose sight on what had come before — not just from a story perspective, but in terms of the countless hours of hard work performed by the army of talented artists on the show's production staff.

"*Invincible* is lucky to have an incredibly dedicated and talented team of hundreds of people who care more about this show than you could imagine," says Racioppa. "If it was any other way, the sheer amount of work necessary for each season would drown us in a second..."

"I think my favorite part about an art book is it just shows the bar that we set," says O'Neil, "which I think is hard to see in the final picture, because there's so much stuff to do."

"I don't think a lot of people understand what goes into design and how much you have to spell out for a thing to be animated," says Co-Executive Producer and Co-Creator Cory Walker. "When the first season was coming out, there was an announcement that I was doing the character design, and someone was like, 'Yeah, he already designed the characters. They're in the comics.' They don't understand what that job is. You have to draw all this shit out from multiple angles so that animators know what to draw. And there's more work going into this stuff than you'll even see in this book. It's a massive undertaking. And I hope looking through these books, people see that and understand and appreciate all the hard work we do to bring them joy and suffering."

"This book will be a couple hundred pages," says O'Neil, "but it took a team of over a hundred creative and production team members two years to produce the content within. And that says nothing of multiple partner studios overseas and the vendors we work with for things like sound and final color. Any show is a mountain of tasks, but this show is Everest. Watch it, enjoy it, and remember the team behind it is moving mountains to make it better and better every time."

This book stands as a testament to those efforts, but the *Invincible* creative team isn't about to rest on their laurels.

"If you thought Season One and Season Two blew your mind," says Raciopps, "just wait..."

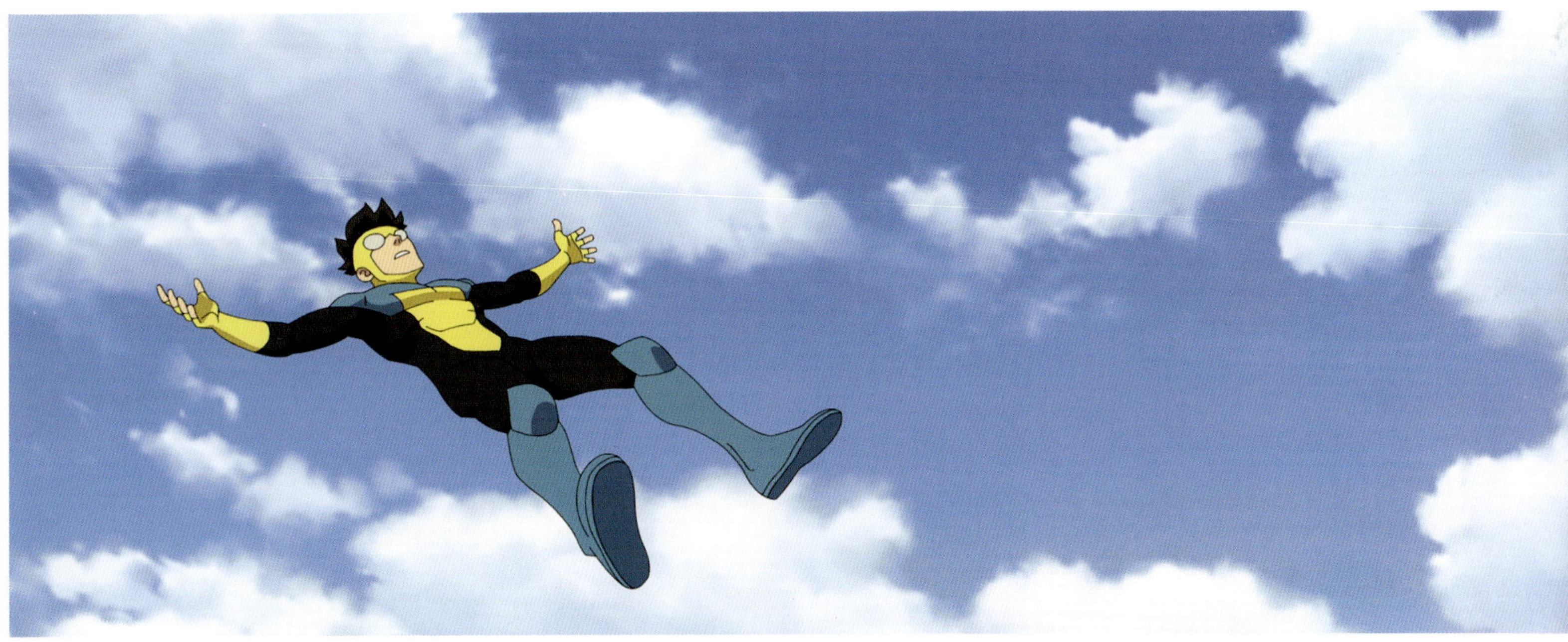

Creative Consultant
Ryan Ottley

Art Director
Shaun O'Neil

Character Designers
Luke Ashworth
Nate Bellegarde
Dou Hong
Nick Lombardo
Tim Nicklas
Johnathan N. Reyes
Charles Tan
Cory Walker
Alex Wilson

Environment Design Supervisor
Edwin Fong

Background Designers
Catherine Agor
Tsu-Wei Chen
Jon Christopher Finch
Kelly Mai
James T. Robb
Yoshi Vu
Pace Wilder

Colorist
Braden Boe

Color Supervisor
Ashley Stoddard

Color Designers
Maribel Pozos
Victoria Thornberry
Amelia Fins
Nick Nazzaro

Prop Designers
Damon Moran
Sinh Nguyen

Background Painters
Addison Bell
Patrick Charles Bryson
Thanh Dang
Sana Freeman
Danielle Law
Yichen Shen
Amber Blade Jones
Corwin Herse Woo
Deodato Pangandonyon

Effects Designer / Animator
Tony Unser

Visual Effects Artists
Sam Batterbury
Aaron Chavda
Elizabeth Jie
Burak N. Kurt

Supervising Director
Dan Duncan

Directors
Ian Abando
Sol Choi
Haylee Herrick
Tanner Johnson
Mari Yang
Jason Zurek

Animation Supervisor
Kofi Fiagome

Storyboard Artists
Adrian Barrios
Matthew Carbonella
Servan Castillo
Ben Choi
Jesse Cuffe
Warren Fok
Steven Go
Jalin Harden
Haylee Herrick
Lora Innes
Sinae Ellyse Jung
Florent Lagrange
Jon Lam
Kevin Molina-Ortiz
James Nguyen
Chris Palmer
Toniko Pantoja
Stephan Park
Wynton Redmond
Karl Savage
Sung Shin
Christopher Staggs
Tatiana Wen
Ae Ri Yoon

Storyboard Revisionists
Vickie Chau
Karon Clerk
Mark Galez
Yujin Lee
Omandi Moore-Washington
Chris Pimentel
Dan Quiles
Kaitrin Snodgrass
Chole W.
Suzi Whifler

Editor Nachie Marsham

Designers Jillian Crab and Richard Mercado

Special Thanks to Ryan Sands

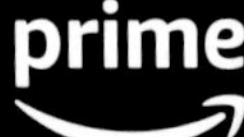

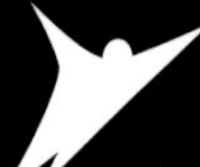

FOR SKYBOUND ENTERTAINMENT

ROBERT KIRKMAN CHAIRMAN
DAVID ALPERT CEO
SEAN MACKIEWICZ SVP, PUBLISHER
ANDRES JUAREZ CREATIVE DIRECTOR, EDITORIAL
ARUNE SINGH VP, BRAND, EDITORIAL
SHANNON MEEHAN SR. PUBLIC RELATIONS MANAGER
ALEX ANTONE EDITORIAL DIRECTOR
BEN ABERNATHY EXECUTIVE EDITOR
DIEGS LOPEZ SENIOR EDITOR
NACHIE MARSHAM SENIOR EDITOR
CAITLIN CHAPPELL ASSISTANT EDITOR
BLAKE KOBASHIGAWA SR. DIRECTOR, BUSINESS DEVELOPMENT, EDITORIAL

JILLIAN CRAB ASSOCIATE ART DIRECTOR, EDITORIAL
ASHBY FLORENCE PRODUCTION ARTIST
RICHARD MERCADO PRODUCTION ARTIST
ALEX HARGETT DIRECTOR OF BRAND, EDITORIAL
EV CLEMENTS BRAND SPECIALIST, EDITORIAL
ANNA GEORGE BRAND COORDINATOR, EDITORIAL
GREG FOREMAN SR. CROWDFUNDING MANAGER
DAN PETERSEN SENIOR DIRECTOR, PUBLISHING OPERATIONS
FOREIGN RIGHTS & LICENSING INQUIRIES:
FOREIGNLICENSING@SKYBOUND.COM

SKYBOUND.COM

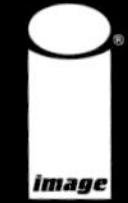

IMAGE COMICS, INC.

ROBERT KIRKMAN
CHIEF OPERATING OFFICER
ERIK LARSEN
CHIEF FINANCIAL OFFICER
TODD MCFARLANE
PRESIDENT
MARC SILVESTRI
CHIEF EXECUTIVE OFFICER
JIM VALENTINO
EXECUTIVE VICE PRESIDENT
ERIC STEPHENSON
PUBLISHER / CHIEF CREATIVE OFFICER

IMAGECOMICS.COM

THE ART OF INVINCIBLE SEASON TWO. FIRST PRINTING. ISBN: 978-1-5343-4833-2